Elspeth King

Presented on the Occasion
of your visit to Perth

Western Australia

from the Australian Labor Party
(WA Branch)

John Cowdell
A/ State Secretary.

THE
LIGHT ON
THE HILL

'I try to think of the Labour movement, not as putting an extra sixpence into somebody's pocket, or making somebody Prime Minister or Premier, but as a movement bringing something better to the people, better standards of living, greater happiness to the mass of the people. We have a great objective — the light on the hill — which we aim to reach by working for the betterment of mankind not only here but anywhere we may give a helping hand.'

Ben Chifley
Prime Minister of Australia
12 June 1949

THE
LIGHT ON THE HILL

The Australian Labor Party
1891 - 1991

Ross McMullin

OXFORD

OXFORD UNIVERSITY PRESS AUSTRALIA

Oxford   New York   Toronto
Delhi   Bombay   Calcutta   Madras   Karachi
Petaling Jaya   Singapore   Hong Kong   Tokyo
Nairobi   Dar es Salaam   Cape Town
Melbourne   Auckland

and associated companies in
Berlin   Ibadan

OXFORD is a trade mark of Oxford University Press

National Library of Australia
Cataloguing-in-Publication data:

McMullin, Ross, 1952–

    The light on the hill: the Australian Labor Party,
    1891–1991.
    Bibliography.
    Includes index.
    ISBN 0 19 554966 X.
    1. Australian Labor Party History. I. Title.

324.29407

Edited by Sarah Brenan
Designed by Sandra Nobes
Cover illustration by Kate Linton
Typeset by Abb-typesetting Pty Ltd, Victoria.
Printed by Impact Printing Pty Ltd, Victoria.
Published by Oxford University Press,
253 Normanby Road, South Melbourne, Australia

Contents

List of Illustrations

Preface

My aim in this book has been to write the rich, dense history of the Australian Labor Party (ALP) in one volume comprehensively and accurately while maximizing liveliness and readability. This is not a history of the labour movement as a whole, although it does of course refer frequently to the ALP's constituent unions. The story is told from the perspective of Labor's leading identities, local branch members and supporters, and covers their triumphs and failures in all states and federally during the party's first hundred years. A recurring theme is the tension between what the ALP's prominent politicians were doing or not doing, and what the rank-and-file activists wanted them to be doing. More implicit in this book, but an aspect of great significance when assessing the party's history, has been the influence of events originating outside Australia; wars, international economic fluctuations and other developments arising abroad have impinged heavily on the ALP's ability to improve the lot of its traditional supporters.

Telling the story through people has helped to illuminate the individuals who shaped the party's history. However, I am all too aware of the hazards and difficulties involved in purporting to re-create another person's life in a full-length biography, let alone in the brief character sketches which are all that is possible in a book of this scope. Nevertheless, while acutely conscious of the shortcomings of attempting to summarize someone in a paragraph – or in two sentences, or even in two adjectives! – I concluded that it was still worthwhile to do what was possible in the limited words at my disposal, even if my descriptions of some individuals may seem to some readers superficial or presumptuous.

The party has not always been known as the ALP. During its early years its formal title varied from colony to colony; in shortened form it was frequently referred to as both 'Labor' and 'Labour'. The title page of the report of federal conference, the party's supreme policy-making body, refers to 'Labor' in 1902, 'Labour' in 1905, 'Labour' in 1908 and 'Labor' from 1912 onwards. This book has adopted the convention of referring to 'Labor' as the political party, and 'the labour movement' as the more broadly based entity which includes the party.

While it is unfortunately not possible to mention everyone who assisted with the research and writing of this book, I would like to acknowledge some people specifically.

The months I spent based at the National Library as the holder of one of its fellowships greatly benefited my research. I remain very grateful for the assistance I received at the library, especially from the officers in the Manuscripts and Oral History collections. John Thompson and Mark Cranfield were particularly helpful. I would also like to record my gratitude to other libraries and institutions which assisted me in the course of research. A number of them provided the illustrations which appear in these pages; I have endeavoured to obtain the permission of all copyright holders of illustrations reproduced in this book.

The staff at the ALP National Secretariat were helpful and supportive while respecting my independence as a historian. I am particularly indebted to Lois Anderson and Gary Gray. Valuable practical assistance was cheerfully provided by Eleanor Lewis, Morag Williams and Deborah Walsh. In addition I thank Bob McMullan, Bob Hogg and Joan Tompsett.

Much appreciated assistance also came from Chris Cunneen, David Clune, Clyde Cameron, Sarah Brenan, Jan Bassett, Stuart Macintyre, Michael McKernan, Lyle Allan, Trevor Monti, Bruce McMullin, Betty Emms, Lesley McMullin, Gil Duthie, Bede Nairn, Peter Cook, Peter Love, the late Lloyd Robson, Brenda McAvoy, Norman Abjorensen and Helen McVay.

However, my greatest debts by far are to Joan Monti, and also to Kath Emms, who made an exceptional contribution, not only typing the manuscript but assisting in a number of other ways.

Ross McMullin

1 'The Ballot is the Thing', 1891

DURING THE FIRST days of 1891, the year when the Labor Party dramatically emerged in Australia, an explosive situation was developing in the colony of Queensland. These developments alarmed even the usually unflappable Albert Hinchcliffe, a diminutive Lancashire-born printer who had played a leading role in the formation of the Queensland province of the Australian Labour Federation (ALF) in 1889. On 13 January 1891 he sent an urgent warning by telegram to the local ALF secretary in Barcaldine:

> Private information. Federated pastoralists levying three hundred thousand pounds throughout Australia to fight Queensland. . .Employers plan to raise thousands black-legs to take district after district in rotation. Keep this strictly secret. Act cautiously. Big trouble ahead.

Big trouble was indeed ahead. The Queensland pastoralists were determined to smash the rural unions. The rapid recent growth of these bush unions was part of a general increase in the number and strength of Australian trade unions which had occurred during the 1880s, owing to a combination of economic conditions and the painstaking work undertaken by union leaders such as W.G. Spence. He had endured the dank, airless and hazardous underground life of a miner from the age of nine, and battled its legacy of silicosis for the rest of his days. Spence was awkward as a speechmaker and no theorist but, amiable and patient, he pursued his goal of a united trade union movement with tireless dedication. With the Queensland shearers and bush labourers organized into unions by 1889, Hinchcliffe and Spence had masterminded the ALF's first industrial victory in the Jondaryan dispute the following year, when Brisbane transport workers had refused to handle wool shorn by non-union labour. But this triumph had been immediately followed by one of the heaviest defeats ever suffered by Australian unions. The 1890 maritime strike which involved 50 000 miners, shearers and transport workers primarily in NSW, Victoria and SA (and even New Zealand) had been supported by Queensland workers, who shared in the bitterness of defeat caused by strikebreaking labour and exhaustion of strike funds. The Queensland pastoralists had by then decided to capitalize on the unions' weakness by proclaiming – like the employers in the maritime strike – 'freedom of contract', which by ignoring the unions effectively challenged their very

1

existence. Without consultation the pastoralists announced severe wage reductions, and refused to negotiate. They had made plans, as Hinchcliffe knew, to bring non-union labour to central Queensland when the bush unions there went on strike. The future looked ominous.

Hinchcliffe journeyed to Barcaldine, where he arranged that he and ALF president Charlie McDonald would meet the pastoralists. McDonald was a watchmaker in the mining town of Charters Towers. His small, trim figure and drooping moustache were a familiar sight as he cycled large distances in north Queensland on various missions for the labour movement. Secretary of the recently formed Charters Towers Republican Association, he was renowned as an argumentative bush lawyer, but he and Hinchcliffe made no headway with the pastoralists. As the strikebreaking labour began to arrive, the strikers assembled in a number of camps and prepared for a long struggle. The Queensland government arranged for special constables to be sworn in, dispatched a military force of artillery and mounted infantry to the area, and issued a proclamation ordering the strikers to disperse. Hinchcliffe protested vigorously. The acting Premier, a prominent pastoralist, responded, upholding freedom of contract. '[That] simply mean[s] freedom to victimize unionists', replied Hinchcliffe angrily; he again requested that the government hold an unconditional conference, instead of enforcing 'with ball cartridge and Gatling guns. . .the arbitrary and unreasonable claims of organized capitalism'. As tension escalated, newspaper editors sent correspondents to the combat zone. Queenslanders were gripped by fears of imminent bloodshed.

The main focus of anxiety and the site of the strikers' biggest camp was Barcaldine. It had come into existence only five years before with the arrival of the railway which had inched its way 358 miles westwards from the coast at Rockhampton. The railway made Barcaldine the hub of the surrounding pastoral region and a centre of strong union activity. When the shearers, shed hands, carriers and other itinerant labourers held their meetings, they tended to congregate under a spreading gum tree near the railway station. The Tree of Knowledge, as it came to be known, still retains its hallowed place in Labor folklore a century later.

With unionists, soldiers and strikebreaking labour pouring into Barcaldine and the surrounding area, the situation was critical. On 7 March there were ugly scenes when the pastoralists' strike executive arrived at Clermont and received a hostile welcome. Seven strikers were arrested, and more police and soldiers were hastily dispatched. By mid-March 4500 people were in Barcaldine or camped nearby, and a large part of central Queensland was on edge. There were some violent skirmishes, but overall the strikers remained impressively disciplined. They had their supporters. A dozen unionists rode to the strife-torn area from Bourke, 300 miles (480 km) away. They were led by a legendary shearer, Donald Macdonell, who was 6 feet 3 inches (191 cm) tall, immensely strong, and a gentle giant except when confronting scabs. His party had some lively encounters, and Macdonell narrowly escaped arrest. Not so fortunate were some Queensland railwaymen: merely for expressing sympathy with the strikers and promising to donate a day's pay each month to the cause, they were instantly dismissed.

Serious differences emerged among Labor leaders as the conflict developed. That steady man Hinchcliffe had been roused to fury by the forces ranged against the unionists, but if the strike was not winnable he preferred to withdraw, keep the unions' organization intact and live to fight another day. So did Charles Seymour, Mat Reid, David Bowman and Thomas Glassey. Seymour was a lanky,

2

dark-haired, sombre-faced seaman, earnest and cautious, not one for frivolous amusement. He had formed the Seamen's Union in Brisbane and helped establish the ALF, and his sturdy contribution to Queensland Labor matched Hinchcliffe's. Reid was a Scottish carpenter who had arrived in Brisbane in 1887, and had already made an impression as a forceful unionist and agitator. Bowman was a Bendigo-born bootmaker who moved to Queensland in 1888 because he thought his chronic throat infection would be less troublesome in the northern climate. When he immediately established a Brisbane bootmakers' union, employers blacklisted him. He had been responsible for organizing the shearers and bushworkers during the strike. Irish-born Glassey began work at the age of six in linen mills, earning a penny a day. From this unpromising start he became a miner and prominent unionist in northern England near Newcastle. Arriving in Brisbane in 1884, he became an auctioneer in Fortitude Valley. Other ex-Newcastle miners had travelled to Queensland, settling at Bundamba; Glassey helped them form a union and was its first secretary. In 1888 he was persuaded by his Bundamba friends to stand for parliament, and, declaring himself a Labor candidate supporting Premier Griffith, he became Labor's first member of the Queensland Legislative Assembly. (Four other Labor men contested this 1888 election, but were unsuccessful. One of them was Hinchcliffe, then a printer at the *Telegraph*; he was sacked for being a Labor candidate.) Glassey firmly supported the 1891 strikers in parliament, but he agreed with Hinchcliffe, Seymour, Reid and Bowman that the strike, which was essentially defensive, should be carefully contained.

Other Labor leaders, notably Gilbert Casey and William Lane, disagreed. Casey was an Irish-born firebrand who had been prominent since he helped form the Brisbane Wharf Labourers' Union in 1885. After being instrumental in founding the ALF, he had been elected chairman of the board of its new newspaper, the *Worker*. William Lane was the obvious choice as editor: his fame as an inspirational radical journalist had already made him the supreme Labor propagandist in Australia, and he was especially revered by the bushworkers. His writing in the *Worker* further extended his influence. He reported the events of 1891 with verve and passion – too much passion for Hinchcliffe and Reid – and fervently supported Casey's attempts to have a general strike declared. On this occasion the men of passion defeated the pragmatists: a general strike of all pastoral workers was declared on 24 March.

This action did not significantly affect the outcome, however, because the Queensland government, leaving nothing to chance, unleashed a daunting display of repressive machinery. It unearthed an obscure 1825 English conspiracy law which had been repealed in England but not in Queensland, and hurriedly told police and magistrates in central Queensland of this discovery. The Barcaldine magistrate, who had reported that the strikers' camp was law-abiding, was replaced, and about 200 strikers, including all the leaders, were systematically arrested on charges of conspiracy, intimidation and riot. Many were humiliated, and dragged around in chains. Most were convicted. Some of the trials were farcical. One judge abused the police for not opening fire on assembled unionists, bullied the jury for three days until it provided a guilty verdict, contemptuously ignored its recommendation for clemency, and sentenced twelve strike leaders to three years gaol for conspiracy. One of them, William Hamilton, received his three years for being present at the incident of 7 March although he had tried to restrain illegal acts by the strikers. The sentences stunned the labour movement and devastated the strikers, who were already

3

struggling to maintain morale in the face of declining funds and increasing hardships as heavy rain turned the Barcaldine camp into a swamp. Despite exhortations by Casey the firebrand, the strike was called off in mid-June.

This repression starkly highlighted the things Labor people were trying to change, and not just in Queensland. Labour movements in all the Australian colonies were striving to create a better, fairer life for working people. Progress was far from uniform, naturally, since each colony had its own constitutional and economic history; in Tasmania and WA convict origins had left an enduring legacy, unions had been slow to develop, and progress by 1891 was minimal. But in all colonies radicals had to contend with entrenched privilege in the Legislative Council and an electoral system which disadvantaged workers. Plural voting entitled a well-to-do man owning property in various areas to a number of votes, whereas an itinerant worker could not vote at all because of the onerous residency requirements. Elections were typically held on weekdays, which made it even more difficult for workers to vote, and were often spread over a number of days, so that wealthy men could exercise their voting rights in a number of electorates.

Many radicals declared themselves socialists while often disagreeing or being vague about what this meant. Australians were accustomed to a relatively high level of government activity. The penal settlements had been necessarily centralized, and with the advent of self-government in most of the colonies the pattern had continued: development in a harsh physical environment required government involvement in land administration, railways and education. Although this activity, authorized by conservative and middle-class legislators, was not at all derived from collectivist or socialist notions, the idea of the state intervening in daily life was accepted more readily in Australia than in Britain or America. When socialist doctrines began to circulate in Australia during the 1880s, one of the most discussed was the utopian brand outlined in Edward Bellamy's *Looking Backward*. The popularity in Australia of this American novel owed much to William Lane; he was so impressed with it that he formed a Bellamy Society in Brisbane, serialized *Looking Backward* in the *Worker* from its very first issue, and asserted that the book depicted his ideal form of social organization. Socialism in *Looking Backward* evolved as the culmination of a natural process without violence. According to Lane, this dovetailed neatly into his concept of a co-operative commonwealth along socialist lines, which would arrive inevitably and peacefully when everyone – even the capitalists – had grasped the logic and fairness of it. (When the maritime and shearers' strikes of 1890–91 showed the futility of expecting logic and fairness from everyone, Lane was quick to abandon peaceful inevitability and called for a general strike.) Lane's utopian socialism had much in common with the socialism espoused by the bush unions. They extolled the traditional virtues of the bushworker, preferred practical action to empty words, and knew what Lane meant when he wrote that 'Socialism is being mates'. Such notions were scorned by devotees of Karl Marx and other European theorists; in animated meetings they confidently agreed that the demise of such an unjust, immoral and inefficient system as capitalism was certain and earnestly debated what form of socialism would replace it.

Some people saw Henry George as the man with the answer. His solution had the virtue of simplicity. He blamed all the ills of the system on rent derived from the private ownership of land. George's cure was not the compulsory acquisition of land but the imposition of a graduated tax designed to make private ownership unprofitable unless the land was used to its full capacity. This sweeping remedy appealed particularly in Australia, where for decades 'the land question' had been a thorny political issue. Henry George and his single tax movement enjoyed widespread support, and large audiences flocked to his lectures during his three-month tour of Australia in 1890. Many Labor men and women were 'swept away by the magnetic personality of George, his earnestness and his burning sincerity', although his hostility to strikes, socialism and protection lost him some working-class admirers. His most enduring influence was the stimulus he gave to the issue of land reform.

During the 1880s there was a heightened awareness of the distinguishing features of Australia and its people. This nationalism was most frequently felt by the radical dreamers. Many of Labor's early leaders were born overseas, mostly in Britain, and they inevitably retained a measure of attachment to the land of their birth; however, nearly all were keenly aware that Britain had denied them hope, dignity and opportunity. In their adopted country they could help build a new society without having to overcome centuries of tradition and class rigidities. Further nationalist impetus came from a discernible restlessness with the British government's handling of Australian affairs. Some wanted to sever links with Britain altogether: there were a number of republican groups like McDonald's association in Charters Towers. Both a product and a propagandist of this developing nationalism was the *Bulletin*, a lively, independent, assertively Australian weekly which began in 1880 in Sydney and became extremely popular.

The *Bulletin*'s masthead trumpeted 'Australia for the Australians'. White Australians took for granted the superiority of their race, and the makers of the new society saw no place in it for coloured races. Having made significant advances in wages and conditions by 1890, Australian trade unionists were on guard against any erosion that might be caused by workers from other countries accustomed to lower living standards. Union vigilance was most pronounced in north Queensland, where sugar capitalists trimmed their wages bill by using Pacific Islanders known as kanakas. In addition there was a deep-seated antipathy to coloured peoples, especially the Chinese, on racial grounds. Those beacons of radical influence, the *Bulletin* and Lane's *Worker*, were both outspoken in their racism. Hardly anyone in the labour movement was concerned with the Australian Aborigines; survival of the fittest was regarded as an immutable law of nature, and the eventual disappearance of the Aborigines was seen as inevitable.

In 1888, one hundred years after the Aborigines were startled by the arrival of the first white settlers, the fifth Intercolonial Trade Union Congress (ITUC) was held in Brisbane. The delegates reiterated the desirability of direct Labor representation in parliament, and authorized the Queenslanders to draw up a scheme for a nationwide federation of trade unions. This was the genesis of the ALF. Hinchcliffe, Seymour and Reid set to work, and Seymour methodically presented their proposals to the 1889 ITUC in Hobart. Their federation would unite trade unions in a tight formal structure, with a governing council at the top of the pyramid and provincial and district councils underneath. Any union involved in a strike approved by the federation would be supported by a union movement more united than any in the world. The federation proposal aimed to improve working conditions, elevate Labor representatives into parliament, and stop 'Australians being degraded by competition to the level of Chinese and European labourers'. Although the constituent unions in the federation were allowed some autonomy, there was not enough to satisfy some of the congress delegates in Hobart, and to Seymour's dismay the proposal was rejected. Undaunted, confident that the scheme's opponents would see the light eventually, the Queenslanders inaugurated the Brisbane district council of the ALF in June 1889. Hinchcliffe, Glassey and Casey began an outstandingly successful tour of the colony, forming ALF district councils, generating interest in the *Worker*, and encouraging their large audiences to send Labor representatives into parliament to join Glassey. The response to their tour underlined Queensland's uniqueness among the Australian colonies in possessing a number of regional centres which were at least as progressive as the capital city.

The ALF's political programme reflected the buoyant optimism of Queensland Labor in August 1890. In that month John Hoolan won a by-election to become Labor's second Queensland parliamentarian. With the Jondaryan triumph behind them and the disastrous maritime and shearers' strikes yet to come, the ALF general council, which included Hinchcliffe, Seymour, McDonald and Casey, drew up a stirring manifesto. Lane's extravagant encouragement – he was describing the ALF as 'the most progressive body in Australasia, perhaps in the world' – influenced their reasoning that 'opposition. . .would be just as strong against a moderate programme as one declaring for a "whole-hog" policy'. Accordingly, all sources of wealth and all means of producing and exchanging it would be nationalized. This would provide funds for education and sanitation, as well as pensions for children, invalids and the aged. 'The Reorganization of Society upon the above lines [is] to be commenced at once and pursued uninterruptedly until social justice is fully secured to each and every citizen.' In 'The People's Parliamentary Platform' the ALF concurrently endorsed wide-ranging electoral reforms.

Seven months later, however, the ALF had bowed to the inevitable and watered down its programme. Even within the ALF there was strong opposition to the 'whole-hog' approach, despite the strenuous defence of it by McDonald, Lane and Hinchcliffe in the *Worker*: Charters Towers was the only district council to support it. The strikes also had a sobering effect. After extensive consultation the ALF released a brand-new platform in March 1891. In electoral reform it called for universal and equal suffrage, with votes for women (but not for coloured races), and the abolition of the Legislative Council. To improve working conditions it sought a statutory eight-hour day, a shops and factories act, a mines act, a wages act and the abolition of all conspiracy laws. Other measures included free compulsory education and lending libraries, pensions for orphans and the elderly, a state bank and state control of irrigation and water conservation.

Although 1891 had brought a legendary defeat for Queensland Labor, from the bitter legacy there emerged a determination to right the wrongs through committed parliamentary action. Lane, however, reacted differently. Profoundly affected by the strike, he was beginning to wonder whether it was possible to build a fairer society in Australia. He channelled his feelings into a sardonically titled novel, *The Workingman's Paradise*, which he wrote to raise money for the imprisoned strikers and to spread the Labor gospel. Two notable contributions to Lane's *Worker* during the strike were 'Freedom On The Wallaby' by little-known 23-year-old poet Henry Lawson, and 'The Ballot Is The Thing' by a Scottish-born Rockhampton bookseller, William Kidston. A public defender of the strikers, Kidston was dismissed from the local volunteers for refusing to be enrolled as a special constable. His verse counselled the strikers to seek retribution on election day:

Then keep your heads, I say, my boys; your comrades in the town
Will help you yet to win a vote and put your tyrants down.
Throw your old guns aside, my boys; the ballot is a thing
They did not have to reckon with when George the Fourth was king.*
The ballot is the thing, my boys, the ballot is the thing
Will show these men how long it is since George the Fourth was king.

This was precisely the moral of 1891 for the ALF leadership. Queensland Labor had been moving towards political representation, but the strike provided extra momentum. Even during it the ALF leaders were redoubling their efforts to maximize Labor's voting power: Glassey urged one strike leader to 'Leave no stone unturned to have every name placed on the Electorate Roll'. As one of the ALF delegates to the April 1891 ITUC, Bowman told fellow congress members that Queensland Labor 'has paid particular attention' to 'political action', and looked forward confidently to the next election.

POLITICS IN QUEENSLAND have been conducted with a coarseness more pronounced than elsewhere in Australia. In SA both the climate and the political temperature tend to be milder. Strong disagreements on the pace and priorities of change have been inevitable throughout the Labor Party's history, but by 1891 it was already noticeable that the radicals of Adelaide, the city of churches untainted by convict origins, handled such disputes relatively politely. Similarly, although the maritime strike produced drama and sharpened class antagonism in Adelaide, there was not the same atmosphere of searing conflict as in Sydney, Melbourne and Queensland. The daily press was more even-handed; despite employer requests, the SA government refused to follow the example of Victoria and NSW and enrol special constables; and whereas the Queensland government had used an obscure law to smash the strike, SA workers charged with assault and intimidation were defended in court by the previous (and future) Attorney-General, C.C. Kingston.

During the later 1880s SA Labor had pursued parliamentary representation halfheartedly. Although wheat dominated the basically rural SA economy, a number of urban trade unions combined in the United Trades and Labour Council (UTLC) in 1884. The ITUCs in the 1880s realized that workers could not enter parliament in significant numbers until union organization was improved, the working class was eligible and willing to vote, and parliamentarians were paid. At the 1888 Brisbane congress the SA delegates proudly claimed that seven of their nine UTLC-endorsed candidates had been elected to the SA House of Assembly in 1887, and payment of members had been introduced thanks to their efforts. However, these endorsed candidates tended to be men like Kingston, liberals with radical leanings who had no allegiance to the UTLC and were certain to be elected anyway. The only endorsed candidate closely connected to the UTLC, A.A. Kirkpatrick, was defeated. At the 1888 Upper House election the UTLC gave its blessing to G.W. Cotton, a retired carpenter and land agent; an MLC since 1882, he was re-elected and continued to strive for Labor goals until his death in 1892. For the 1890 Assembly election the UTLC endorsed Kirkpatrick, who lost again, and 19 liberals; 14 were elected, but afterwards 'none of them acknowledged the UTLC as their political guide or patron'.

As in Queensland, 1891 was a momentous year for Labor in SA. Although the

* A reference to the obscure 1825 conspiracy law used to gaol the strike leaders.

maritime strike was less acrimonious in SA than in other colonies, it nevertheless generated bitter hostility towards the employers, overturned widely expressed faith in the broad harmony of labour and capital in the colony, and galvanized the UTLC's lacklustre approach to parliamentary representation. The UTLC arranged a public meeting at the Selborne Hotel; at this meeting the United Labour Party (ULP) was formed. Important decisions were quickly taken. The new party would have its own candidates from its own class, and it was determined to control them: it would endorse only candidates who had pledged to work as a separate party in parliament and to refuse office in any non-Labor ministry. Elements of SA's flourishing German community provided socialist and single tax advocacy through their Allgemeiner Deutscher Verein, which was affiliated to the ULP. While the ULP platform reflected the single taxers' influence, it was in no sense a coherent socialist programme; it included electoral reform, industrial legislation, a state bank, and several measures designed to appeal to farmers.

At the 1891 Legislative Council election the ULP contested three vacancies. Andrew Kirkpatrick won preselection for Southern. A farm labourer at the age of nine, he was later apprenticed as a printer in Adelaide. By 1891 'Kirk' had his own printing firm and was a well-known Labor figure, upright, quick-witted and fluent in debate. The ULP chose David Charleston and Bob Guthrie for the two Central vacancies. Charleston was born in Cornwall and worked as an engineer in America before arriving in SA in 1884. A prominent craft unionist, single taxer and temperance advocate, he was an unsuccessful UTLC-endorsed candidate for the Council in 1890. Guthrie was another temperance stalwart. A squat Scot who went to sea, he was prone forever afterwards to unleash in a rich Scottish burr his obsessive anger at the appalling conditions of seamen. But he remained nostalgic about other aspects of the seafaring life, 'always wore a square pilot coat and billowy pants', regularly woke before dawn and maintained a heavy rolling gait. He had been an active unionist since settling in Adelaide in 1887.

The ULP campaigned with a zeal unprecedented in SA, and reaped the rewards. They jumped their opponents with circulars, eye-catching advertisements and extensive distribution of the platform. Charleston and Guthrie spoke nearly every night. Southern district, the large rural area south-east of Adelaide, was a stiff challenge for Kirkpatrick, and he spent £300 in covering it comprehensively. The solidarity which had brought SA unions into the maritime strike was again evident when the Queensland strike began capturing the headlines: after the UTLC formed a Queensland Labour Defence Committee, Spence traversed the SA countryside, and while using his formidable persuasive skills to secure sympathy and funds for the Queensland strikers, he stressed the importance of parliamentary representation. On 9 May, in a result the *Advertiser* described as 'positively a sensation', Charleston and Guthrie were both triumphant in Central; there were extraordinary scenes of Labor jubilation. Election day for Kirkpatrick was a week later, when he too was successful. The infant ULP had exceeded its wildest dreams. Charleston dared to hope that a new era was dawning. His excited supporters were sure of it.

VICTORIA'S POLITICAL HERITAGE was dominated by liberalism and protection. The breathtaking gold discoveries ushered in an era of confident prosperity and rapid growth, exemplified by 'Marvellous Melbourne'. Victorian trade unions were quick to benefit: in the 1850s stonemasons led the world in securing the eight-hour day and one of them entered parliament. During the three succeeding decades the Melbourne Trades Hall Council (THC) became the recognized instrument of responsible skilled artisans who were seeking their share of the colony's prosperity through negotiation rather than strikes. (However, when women exploited by a clothing manufacturer took direct action in 1882, the THC took over the strike, a tailoresses' union was formed and a parliamentary inquiry into sweating ensued. In 1882–83 women striking and forming a union were novelties in Australia, and perhaps in the world.) Victoria had much in common with SA. There was a similar faith in the partnership of labour and capital, a faith rudely jolted by the maritime strike (especially when a section of the Victorian Mounted Rifles, directed by the government to parade because of a mass meeting of 50 000 unionists, was given the notorious order by its commander to 'Fire low and lay them out'). The ULP's 1891 platform included a call for protection; in Victoria, which had a larger manufacturing sector than other colonies, protection was widely regarded as the foundation of the colony's prosperity. It was accepted by the unions and upheld vehemently by the parochial *Age* newspaper, which argued that high customs charges protected Victorian manufacturing industries, thereby providing jobs, higher wages, higher profits and economic growth. Liberals in government had presided over the successes of protection, and their spirited confrontations with the upper house reactionaries had enhanced their radical credentials. This governing tradition of protectionist liberalism retarded the development of a separate Labor party, despite the fact that Victoria had introduced payment of MPs in 1870, 16 years before any other colony.

However, Labor was represented in the Assembly. William Trenwith grew up in Tasmania, where he was a bootmaker as a seven-year-old and a fearsome boxer in his youth. Crossing to Victoria in 1857, he became a tough, aggressive bootmakers' union secretary, not averse to flattening his opponents. After a prolonged power struggle at the THC, Trenwith's group replaced an old guard who were resisting any concerted union involvement in politics. In 1889 Trenwith became MLA for Richmond, confirming his status as the colony's leading Labor figure. He was joined by Billy Maloney. A jaunty, warm-hearted, republican socialist, Maloney was born in Melbourne but studied medicine in London. He returned in 1887 as Dr Maloney, sporting a waxed moustache and goatee beard, and enthusiastically threw himself into a multitude of good causes. His humanitarianism and bohemian dress – cream silk suit, flaming red tie and large panama hat – contrasted with Trenwith's dourness and formal attire as they entered the Assembly together in 1889. Maloney promptly introduced reputedly the first bill in the British Empire for women's suffrage; there was no seconder.

Victorian Labor made significant strides towards further parliamentary representation in the autumn of 1891. In March the THC established local electorate committees to assist Labor candidates. In April the ITUC at Ballarat approved the proposed ALF (rejected at the 1889 Hobart congress), and unanimously resolved that 'every effort should be made to obtain direct representation of Labor in Parliament'. Also in April an Assembly by-election occurred in Collingwood, and the THC endorsed its ex-president, John Hancock, a London-born compositor. Easy-going, witty and a brilliant mimic, Hancock migrated to Australia in 1884. As THC president he had assured merchants at a Chamber of Commerce dinner that Australia needed 'not socialism but capital and civility'.

But the maritime strike, which he tried to prevent, radicalized him. He was reluctant to stand for Collingwood, sensing that primitive organization and no party platform were daunting handicaps. Despite these deficiencies and the fierce opposition of the *Age*, he won. There was great excitement at the THC, which maintained the momentum by organizing a political Labor convention. THC delegates, representatives of the miners' and shearers' unions and a Social Democratic Federation delegate combined in May to form the Progressive Political League (PPL) of Victoria. Its moderate programme revealed its aspirations to attract radical liberals beyond the working class (as did its name, by avoiding any mention of Labor). The maritime strike had been devastating but, buoyed by Hancock's victory and the creation of the PPL, the THC could survey the future with optimism.

THE POLITICAL HERITAGE of New South Wales, the oldest Australian colony, also was dominated by liberalism but not by protection: the converse doctrine of free trade had more adherents there. The fiscal issue was the great political question of the day, and the 1887 Assembly election accelerated the transformation of previously fluid parliamentary factions into tighter formations of Protectionists and Free Traders. In 1887 the Free Traders overcame the Protectionists' challenge, and did so again, more narrowly, in the 1889 election. But winds of change were blowing. British capital investment, which had underpinned the boom of the last two decades, had slackened. During the 1880s the Protectionists had gained in strength with the increased role of industry in the NSW economy, which had been traditionally governed by pastoral interests upholding free trade. The old Free Trade leaders were fading from the scene, and the labour movement was preparing to launch itself into parliament.

The NSW Trades and Labour Council (TLC) was formed in 1871. Its leaders were uncertain whether direct parliamentary representation was worthwhile; attitudes tended to vary with assessments of the effectiveness of industrial action outside parliament. In 1874 they embarked on a parliamentary experiment with carpenter Angus Cameron. While other labour movement sympathizers had sat in the Assembly, he was the first to be the TLC's specific representative; it paid him a wage, and he had to report regularly to the TLC and express its views on various issues. But he experienced exacting contradictions between TLC demands and the interests of his West Sydney constituents. With the cherished eight-hour day legislation no closer, some disenchanted unions stopped their contributions to Cameron's income. Sixteen months after its commencement, Cameron publicly revoked the arrangement. Not surprisingly, this episode reinforced TLC misgivings about parliamentary experiments. Although it maintained close links with some politicians, during the 1880s the TLC concentrated on industrial questions – extending the eight-hour day, creating more unions and exerting a mostly moderate influence in disputes. Towards the end of the decade some unionists, notably Peter Brennan, were arguing that parliamentary involvement might be useful after all; successive ITUCs had recommended it, and parliament had removed one obstacle by deciding in 1889 that MPs would be paid beyond the next election. Brennan, a Lancashire-born ship steward with considerable experience in NSW unions, stimulated a TLC debate on the question and spearheaded the compilation of a draft political platform. This was under consideration when the maritime strike intervened.

Labor leaders in all colonies collaborated in an extraordinary display of solidarity during the great London dock strike in 1889. The strike was saved from early collapse by spontaneous donations from Brisbane and Sydney unionists, and Australian contributions eventually exceeded £36 000; incredibly, this was three times the amount raised in Britain, and enabled the dockers to win. While much of the overall amount came from outside the unions, it was a remarkable performance by the Australian labour movement. Ironically, its very success deprived unions of funds which were desperately needed in their own great maritime strike shortly afterwards.

As in other colonies, the smashing of the maritime strike invigorated NSW Labor's moves towards political representation. Brennan, now TLC president, was chairman of the intercolonial strike committee, which included Queenslanders Hinchcliffe and Seymour, pugnacious Trenwith from Victoria and Guthrie the SA sea-dog. Spence, its secretary, and Brennan issued a joint manifesto on 8 October 1890 outlining the unions' predicament, and urging the labour movement to respond 'by sweeping monopolists and class representatives from the Parliament'. Later that month a by-election was held in West Sydney. The TLC chose Brennan as its candidate, but he withdrew after some unaffiliated maritime unions expressed their preference for A.G. Taylor, an eccentric journalist then editing *Truth* newspaper. Taylor won the by-election, claiming a victory for 'the holy and divine cause of labour as against capital', but he became more renowned for his parliamentary larrikinism than for his support for Labor objectives.

After lengthy debate the TLC finalized its amended political platform for the new party in April 1891. It was a carefully reformist list of specific measures which Labor members could press the parliament to implement. The first plank comprehensively sought the removal of distortions in the electoral process. The second called for universal 'free, compulsory and technical education'. Several planks dealt with basic union objectives. Others included 'stamping of Chinese-made furniture', a national bank and reform of local government. In only one plank did theoretical doctrines intrude, and it caused the most dissension within the TLC. This dealt with land taxation in Georgian jargon, which appalled sceptics of the single tax; they were persuaded to accept it because its wording did not preclude other forms of taxation. The platform was designed to appeal to all radicals, whatever their attitudes to socialism, single tax and the fiscal issue.

This new political party was named the Labor Electoral League (LEL), and the TLC authorized the creation of individual leagues or branches throughout the colony. The branches selected parliamentary candidates and maximized the Labor vote in their area. Branch autonomy in preselection was subject to all candidates accepting the LEL platform and signing a pledge. They had to promise to withdraw from the election if not preselected and support the endorsed Labor candidate(s) and, if elected to parliament, they undertook to sit on the cross-benches as an independent Labor party and resign if so directed by a two-thirds majority of electors. With an election not due for another year, organization began satisfactorily in Sydney, and also in the country where bush union leaders, especially J.M. Toomey, were conspicuous and effective. But there were alarming signs that the LEL's first test might occur before it was ready; indeed, in May the government only survived by the Speaker's vote, parliament was dissolved, and new elections were set for the period 17 June to 3 July 1891.

The next few weeks were hectic. There were difficulties in the four-member inner-city electorate of Redfern, where two candidates seeking endorsement

11

refused to promise to withdraw if not preselected; despite this, and the fact that they had already been endorsed by the Protectionists, a riotous meeting granted them preselection along with boilermaker Jim McGowen and printer William Sharp. McGowen's protest at the meeting had been overruled, but Sharp, the new TLC president, saw to it that he and McGowen were recognized as the only official LEL candidates for Redfern. In the contrasting electorate of Bourke in the vast north-west, the bush unions were right behind the Labor party idea, but felt the programme could be improved. They amended it when they formed their LEL branch, omitting the land tax plank and inserting 'Exclusion from the colonies of inferior races'. They also added a provision opposing the use of camels as beasts of burden, regarding this practice of Afghan carriers as jeopardizing their wages and conditions. Bourke LEL chose its jovial president, Hughie Langwell, as its anti-camel candidate. As in Redfern, however, the LEL central committee acted firmly, and refused to ratify the Bourke branch because of its amended platform.

There were problems in many other electorates besides Redfern and Bourke. In the furious rush some branches were erected on flimsy foundations, others gave support to unendorsed candidates and some contenders wrongly claimed LEL backing. There were often clashes within the branches between socialists, protectionists and single taxers. Funds for the election campaign were scarce. However, this ambitious undertaking prospered despite the difficulties, as a host of people fervently desired a new way and this new party promised to provide it. Contemptuous of this political embryo, both the Protectionists and Free Traders campaigned perfunctorily, distracted by leadership problems. On 17 June all metropolitan electorates and nine in the country were decided. Labor performed brilliantly. On that first election day, less than three months since its inception, the LEL captured 17 out of 53 seats. Euphoria at the TLC knew no bounds. 'We are at the dawn of a new era and a happier era for the workers of New South Wales', enthused Brennan. When the final results were known, Labor found itself holding the balance of power with 35 members in the new Assembly of 141. It was an astonishing achievement, one which transformed Australian politics.

The 35 elected were all men – no colony allowed women to vote, let alone stand for parliament. There were 16 metropolitan members. Twelve were unionists, and three others had close union connections; the exception was E.M. Clark, an enterprising brickworks manager. The 19 country members included only nine unionists, most of them miners. On the fiscal question, the new party contained almost equal numbers of protectionists and advocates of free trade. Only ten of the 35 were born in Australia, whereas about two-thirds of the NSW population in 1891 were native-born. Inexperience and youthfulness characterized this first LEL phalanx. Two of the 35 had parliamentary experience: both had been in the Assembly over a decade, were aged over fifty and had little influence in the new party. Only two of the others were over fifty, with ten in their forties, 15 in their thirties and six under thirty.

Five of the new members were English-born miners who had migrated to Australia during the previous dozen years; all but one were devout Methodists. John Cann had hoped to get work on the NSW railways, but had to return underground instead. During the maritime strike his leadership at Broken Hill guaranteed his election as its LEL representative. One of the new MLAs for Newcastle, John Fegan, was a man with a secret. In his new land he concealed for many years the fact that he had left a wife and two children in England. There was nothing secretive about rotund, rosy-cheeked Alf Edden, who did not let his

Methodism interfere with his hearty enjoyment of life; 'bubbling with energy and goodwill to all mankind', and notable for a broad Staffordshire accent and gargantuan thirst for beer, he entered the Assembly as member for Northumberland. Joe Cook shared Edden's Staffordshire mining background, but not his temperament. A man of limited ability but unlimited ambition, Cook knew that success for him depended on hard slog, and he never forgot it; he denied himself any indulgence in gambling, drinking or sport. In his spare time as a Lithgow coalminer, he pushed himself to learn accountancy and management skills in order to leave mining forever. After flirting with republicanism and the single tax, Cook won his unionist spurs during the maritime strike, when the Lithgow mines were worked by non-unionists protected by artillery; he became president of the Lithgow LEL and the earnest and humourless MLA for Hartley. John Nicholson had been secretary of the Illawarra Miners' Association for some years and was a natural choice to represent them; an Anglican, he had worked in Canada and America before settling in Australia, and was one of the oldest LEL men.

The LEL rural contingent were not all miners. For many years it was rare for a Labor politician to have attended university, and single taxer L.C. Hollis, a native-born Goulburn doctor, was an object of curiosity. So was 23-year-old carpenter Albert Gardiner, the youngest Labor member, who topped the poll at Forbes; an excellent cricketer, footballer and boxer, he was an Anglican and a strict temperance man. Tall and solidly built, Gardiner towered over Arthur Rae, the new MLA for Murrumbidgee. As organizer for the shearers' union, Rae had been fined for bringing the Riverina shearers out in support of the maritime strike; refusing to pay, he was sentenced to fourteen months gaol, and served a month before the government surrendered to a storm of protest and released him. Rae was a crucial figure in the hasty establishment of rural LELs. Humorous and resourceful, he was a redoubtable socialist and keen supporter of radical causes: when he heard that a Redfern Co-operative Laundry had been established to provide work for striking laundresses, he enthusiastically announced that he would encourage the venture by wearing several shirts simultaneously.

There were also some notable metropolitan LEL members. George Black was a tempestuous literary Scot whose passion was not confined to politics. During his voyage to Australia he ardently pursued a shipboard companion, Mrs Duggan, despite her husband's physical intervention; Black assured her that the only heaven he believed in was a woman's body. Their relationship blossomed ashore; by 1891 they had seven children (five others had died), and Black, after a multitude of jobs, was a *Bulletin* sub-editor in Sydney. Black was elected in West Sydney, and so was Jack Fitzgerald; both were republicans and members of the Australian Socialist League (ASL). A NSW-born compositor and journalist, Fitzgerald was elected to the TLC executive. In 1890 he went to England at his own expense to publicize the maritime strike, and to consolidate the comradeship shown by Australian support for the striking London dockers. Also successful in the waterfront electorate of West Sydney were Tom Davis, a seaman, and wharf labourer Andy Kelly. Balmain, where the first local league was formed early in April, was the other electorate to return four LEL members, including plasterer E. Darnley and boilermaker J. Johnston. Another, Methodist G.D. Clark, was obsessed with the drink problem, which concerned many Balmain residents. For some years Clark had edited a prohibitionist journal, claiming that 'Prohibition means prosperity'. Balmain's other representative, W.A. Murphy, was a prominent unionist during the maritime strike; he predicted that NSW would establish 'the first great Socialist Commonwealth'. As well as the Redfern pair, Sharp and McGowen, the 35 of 1891 also included two TLC identities important in the LEL's formation, printer T.J. Houghton, and Frank Cotton, an effusive single taxer with free trade connections who was regarded with suspicion in some Labor quarters despite his undeniable usefulness as an orator and propagandist.

'LABOUR HAS GONE into politics with a force and vigour that astonishes even its friends and partisans', wrote William Lane in mid-1891.

> South Australia has driven the Labour wedge into the very propertied chamber which for the first time in Australian history has heard its own members declare that privileged classes are iniquitous and that propertied chambers must go. Victoria has emerged flushed and victorious from a skirmish in which the Labour man put the representative of Capitalism on its back. And New South Wales! New South Wales has retrieved the maritime disaster. . .Queensland must follow in their footsteps. . .

In all the Australian colonies distinct labour movements had been gradually making progress towards direct representation in politics, but the first half of 1891 saw a tremendous breakthrough. Labor parties were formed in three colonies, and events in Queensland dramatized – in a manner that remained legendary for decades – the flagrant oppression and injustice which Labor sought to overcome through its own parliamentarians. In this 'stirring and romantic age', wrote the prominent Victorian liberal Alfred Deakin in 1891, the 'rise of the labour party in politics is more significant and more cosmic than the Crusades'.

2 Support in Return for Concessions, 1891–1904

AT THE FIRST LEL caucus meetings there was elation and wariness as the NSW pioneers of 1891 embarked on their novel undertaking. Only one MLA seeking admission to caucus was refused (Langwell). They preferred not to select a leader until the aspirants had shown parliamentary ability; instead caucus appointed a provisional managerial committee of Fitzgerald, Sharp, McGowen, Houghton and J.G. Gough, a rural ironmonger. Davis was made whip. The new pledge was moved by Black and seconded by McGowen: it omitted any reference to the platform, but bound all members to majority caucus decisions on important issues. Eight members, including Edden, Gough and Nicholson, immediately stressed their inability to sign any such pledge, since they had promised their constituents to support protection and caucus by majority vote might prefer free trade. Another committed protectionist, Houghton, came up with a skilful compromise whereby Labor would leave the colony's fiscal policy unaltered until a referendum was held on the issue. Even this was too much for one protectionist, who thereupon left the party. Clearly the fiscal issue was likely to cause trouble, and seasoned Protectionist and Free Trade strategists would ensure that it did.

The re-elected Free Trade government announced a programme sufficiently progressive to attract LEL support. However, a crafty Protectionist manoeuvre to test LEL solidarity on the fiscal question produced quick results for the opposition: eight LEL protectionists voted with the opposition, ignoring the Houghton referendum formula approved by caucus, and another three abstained. Much more creditable was Black's forthright speech announcing Labor's motto, 'Support in return for concessions'. If a government enacted LEL measures, support would continue; if it failed to perform, Labor would simply look elsewhere. 'We have not come into this House to support governments or oppositions. We have come into this House to make and unmake social conditions. . .'. Shortly afterwards the government resigned after Labor members included an eight-hour day provision in the Coal Mines Regulation Bill. The new Free Trade leader, G.H. Reid, put a cunning motion censuring the incoming Protectionist government for increasing protection when the proper way to settle the fiscal question was by a referendum under a reformed electoral system of one vote, one value. How was Labor to vote on this? There was bitter dissension inside and outside parliament as members sought in vain to reconcile several considerations: analysis of Reid's motion in the light of caucus policy (Houghton's formula), consistency with their own views and previous parliamentary vote on the fiscal issue, and maintenance of Labor solidarity. Reid's motion failed to unseat the government, but it succeeded in splitting the LEL: 16 protectionists voted against it, and the 17 who supported it were all free traders bar one. The exception was Labor's 36-year-old Jim McGowen, who clearly indicated in both his speech and his vote that adherence to Labor solidarity was more important to him than his personal views on the tariff issue. McGowen 'exuded a simple honesty':

> a benign, bluff, stolid man with a black cascading moustache and black hair, brushed back, he was heavily built and slow moving; far from brilliant, he was close to being wise. . .

McGowen's integrity and clear grasp of Labor's parliamentary role enabled him to escape the artful traps which had snared his comrades.

Throughout the Labor Party's history, exhibitions of parliamentary disunity have intensely annoyed members and supporters. This first instance was no exception, with stormy league meetings and disillusioned reflections in Labor publications. 'We marched forward like heroes at the last election and, by our unity, achieved wonders', recalled the *Australian Workman*; 'how sadly our hopes have been disappointed, and how the Labor party has failed'. Labor leaders in other colonies were dismayed. This 'Labor cohort stronger than ever seen before in History', wrote Lane, 'went to pieces without accomplishing anything'; 'we must conclude that the sea of politics abounds in such quicksands, rocks and currents as to threaten with shipwreck those who attempt to navigate it'. Trenwith was so appalled that he went to Sydney in a personal bid to restore harmony, but met with limited success. The Labor members remained split, but at least agreed to occasional joint meetings to discuss Labor issues. Trenwith had no joy at all concerning a separate dispute arising from the inaugural LEL conference in January 1892. After conference decided that TLC representation on the LEL central executive would be significantly reduced, the TLC for months refused to acquiesce. Eventually the TLC accepted a compromise, partly because the economic downturn was gathering momentum. As unemployment increased, some unions disaffiliated and others struggled to stay financially afloat. Harsh times were rapidly approaching. This only sharpened the labour movement's dissatisfaction with its parliamentarians, who were supposed to be ushering in a new era.

The compromise hammered out between the TLC and the LEL owed much to J.C. Watson. His parents were travelling from London to New Zealand when he was born at Valparaiso, Chile in 1867. Chris Watson grew up in New Zealand, began hard work at 13, and crossed to Sydney as a 19-year-old compositor. His intelligence and personal qualities guaranteed his rapid rise in the union movement. Humane, patient and reliable in his dealings with people, he had a calm wisdom unusual in one so young. He had just turned 24 when he was appointed secretary of one of the first LEL branches formed, West Sydney. His important role in the resolution of the struggle for LEL control was acknowledged in August 1892 when he became president of the TLC and chairman of the LEL.

He immediately had to contend with a bitter dispute at Broken Hill. In a repressive reminder of what Labor had entered parliament to prevent, strike leaders were arrested and gaoled. The labour movement was in uproar. Watson led on horseback a TLC deputation to parliament, to discuss Labor's attitude to Opposition Leader Reid's no-confidence motion. The TLC decided that a government treating strikers so outrageously had to be removed. However, Reid's motion failed narrowly, with 11 of Labor's original 35 voting against it; all were protectionists. Seven of them were no longer seen as real Labor men, but Fitzgerald, Sharp, Kelly and Johnston were prominent Sydney union leaders, two of them ex-presidents of the TLC. It was unthinkable that such men could support a government because of the fiscal question despite what it had done at Broken Hill, and an avalanche of fury descended upon them. Intense branch meetings reopened the fundamental question of what Labor's politicians were there for, and analysed the inadequate machinery of control over them. The Protectionists continued in office, and managed to overhaul the electoral process after lengthy negotiations with the Legislative Council: the next election would be held on one day, with 125 single-member seats and one man, one value.

With that next election drawing closer, a special conference was arranged to deal with unresolved problems likely to reduce the LEL vote. The impetus came from the indefatigable Toomey, who compiled a comprehensive scheme of electorate organization for the whole colony. The Labor members prepared themselves for this important 'unity conference' by at last electing their first leader. Their choice of Cook rather than McGowen reflected the strong free trade majority among the members still in caucus. About 200 delegates were present at the conference in November 1893. Nearly 70 were direct union delegates, in addition to the TLC's own group. The LEL central executive attended en masse, and LEL branches throughout the colony were represented. There had been no more representative gathering of the labour movement in the colony's history (although there were apparently no women delegates). Watson was chairman. The politicians present included Cook, Rae, Edden and also, as Bourke's delegate, Langwell, who had frequently aligned himself in parliament with the LEL. Frank Cotton and G.D. Clark were there, Cotton as zealous a watchdog for the single taxers as Clark was for the temperance believers.

Another conference delegate was 22-year-old William Holman. A London-born cabinetmaker, he had migrated to Australia in 1888 with his parents, both actors. From them he derived his wonderful gifts as a silver-tongued orator. 'Tall, wiry, graceful and handsome, with dark curly hair, Holman was conscious of his talents, but not his appearance.' An insatiable reader, he was already dazzling ASL audiences with erudite lectures on socialism and economics. At the conference he was allotted the task of presenting the executive's arguments for tighter controls over the politicians.

Socialists were well represented at the unity conference. Most retained their faith in the parliamentary road to socialism, although contemptuous of Fitzgerald and Kelly. Fitzgerald had been expelled from the ASL for his vote on the no-confidence motion, and Kelly had already left; both had mixed in decidedly anti-Labor circles, and Fitzgerald's stylishness had extended to kid gloves and overpowering perfume. Socialists were beginning to have doubts about Black too, although he had formed a flourishing Balmain ASL branch in 1892 with Holman and another energetic socialist, W.M. Hughes. Black had been disheartened by the difficulties of Labor members inside parliament and out – Labor men were under 'closer scrutiny' than even ministers, he said, and needed 'the wisdom of Solomon, the patience of Job, and, if possible, the hide of a hippopotamus'; he was also embarrassed politically by controversy in his private

17

life which, thanks to *Truth* newspaper, was not at all private. More acceptable to socialist purists perhaps were the two men at the unity conference representing the Active Service Brigade, a militant organization of the unemployed, formed in Sydney in 1893. One was flamboyant radical poet Arthur Desmond, a striking figure with red hair and beard who delighted in plastering 'GOING BUNG' stickers over banks about to collapse in the great crash. The other was excitable Tommy Dodd, a disciple of direct action who endured a chronic sore throat from continual public speaking.

It was a lively, often acrimonious and ultimately crucial conference. It confirmed that the TLC, which had established the new party, would not control it; that role would be performed by the rank and file of the political organization through its executive and annual conference. With the aim of burying the contentious fiscal issue, conference emphatically resolved that future Labor politicians must pledge themselves only to the platform and the majority vote of their caucus colleagues. Dodd emotionally spearheaded the expulsion of Fitzgerald, Kelly, Sharp and Johnston; his motion that these 'traitors to the sacred cause' should be 'treated with undying hostility' was carried overwhelmingly.

The politicians were disturbed by these notions of rank-and-file control and the harsh words accompanying the expulsions. Only McGowen, Davis and J. Kirkpatrick accepted the tightened pledge. Black suggested that the politicians knew what was 'possible in Parliament', and imposing 'impracticable regulations' upon them was not helpful. G.D. Clark refused to 'hand over to a caucus vote his religious convictions, his temperance principles, and his freedom of action on moral questions'. In April 1894 Cook released a statement signed by 19 Labor MPs attacking the pledge and the special conference resolutions, which he alleged were inspired by the activists' ambitions to secure the Labor members' seats. Some TLC leaders, notably Brennan, sought to mediate between the politicians and the executive, circulating alternative pledges and urging that proven men like Black and Houghton should not be refused endorsement. Spence, too, sided with the critics of conference. But Watson and the executive stood firm: the rank and file had made clear the type of party they wanted. If some branches endorsed candidates who would not sign the revised pledge, then new branches had to be formed to find 'solidarity' candidates who would sign it.

Labor's 'wretched squabbling', as one frustrated country branch described it, naturally affected the 1894 election result. Twenty-five of the original 35 of 1891 refused to accept the revised pledge, and stood with some three dozen others as independent Labor candidates; 13 (including 11 originals) were elected. Only four originals were re-elected as official LEL men – McGowen, Davis, Cann and Kirkpatrick. These 'solidarities' were joined by 10 newcomers, including Watson and two unionists gaoled for their leadership during the 1892 Broken Hill strike, engine-driver William Ferguson and shearer/miner Dick Sleath. There were two Methodist miners destined for long careers as Labor politicians, Josiah Thomas and David Watkins. Arthur Griffith was already Labor's best-known educated middle-class radical. Born in Ireland in 1861, he went to Scotch College in Melbourne, attended Arts lectures at Sydney University, and since 1884 had been a teacher at Sydney Grammar School. Author of *The Labor Platform: An Exposition*, published in 1893, he was also 'a dangerous heavy-weight boxer, a fair oar and a crack swimmer'. Caustic and vigorous, with bristling moustache, he was soon renowned as one of Labor's doughtiest members.

Another newcomer was W.M. Hughes. Born in London though his parents were Welsh, Hughes migrated in 1882 to Australia, where for many years he endured adversity and poverty. In 1890 he settled in Balmain, where he opened a small shop and was a resourceful odd-job man and umbrella mender. At this shop Hughes and Holman discussed socialism and hatched political plots. Unlike Holman, Hughes was short, deaf and raucous, and his stomach was always on strike. This chronic dyspepsia aggravated the mood swings of Hughes's mercurial personality, in which verve, imagination and charm oscillated with abrasiveness, tirades and tantrums. He was essentially a resilient fighter who pursued goals with flair and flexibility. In 1893 Hughes became one of Toomey's purposeful bush organizers, contributing to the success of Griffith, Watson and others in country electorates. Hughes's rural knowledge was crucial in the addition of 'where practicable' to the LEL eight-hour plank; Hughes, supported by Watson, persuasively asserted that without this change Labor's country vote would collapse. In 1894 he won a fiercely contested preselection for Sydney-Lang, and defeated several opponents, including Fitzgerald, at the election.

Reid's Free Traders formed the new government. Behind Reid's monocle and walrus moustache (and above his gross girth), there lurked a reformist streak and a nimble political mind, strikingly shown by the inclusion of Cook in his ministry. As the first working-class representative to be a minister, Cook was condemned as a blatant opportunist by the labour movement and remained a bitter enemy. The 'solidarities', with McGowen as leader and Griffith as secretary, supported Reid cohesively while Labor's organization was overhauled. After Spence had achieved the amalgamation of the bush unions in the Australian Workers' Union (AWU) in 1894, this powerful new force revived the ALF concept, previously shunned by the TLC. Now, however, weakened by union withdrawals, the TLC was looking for a saviour; the ALF absorbed it in 1895. Watson, Hughes, Griffith and the new LEL chairman, popular house painter Fred Flowers, were prominent in the ensuing negotiations which resulted in the ALF merging with the LEL to form the Political Labor League (PLL). Again the pledge was modified; Black and Edden declared this version acceptable, and were welcomed back into the party in time for the 1895 election. Reid had called an early election on the issue of upper house reform, after the Council had delayed or amended Labor-supported reforms including direct land and income tax legislation and the regulation of coal mines; one mediaeval MLC actually defended the 10-hour day for 14- to 18-year-old coalminers (the bill proposed an eight-hour day) because their labour was 'more play than work'. Reid's sudden manoeuvre caught Labor with its reorganization incomplete. In the circumstances, contesting fewer seats (47) than it would have liked, 18 members (11 rural, seven metropolitan) was a reasonable result. An important newcomer was Irish-born coachbuilding employer J.R. Dacey, one of Labor's first notable Catholics. A pleasing aspect was the sharp decline in the voting share of independent Labor candidates; clearly the PLL could consolidate without any concern for that quarter.

Tension between the politicians and the organization has been a characteristic throughout Labor's history and, with Reid returned to office, the policy of support in return for concessions was increasingly scrutinized. The 1896 PLL conference censured the politicians, and reminded them that a parliamentary seat was no 'reward for past services', but 'rather a widening of opportunity for further work'. Hughes angrily defended the politicians, as he did in reply to a frustrated outburst by Holman, an unsuccessful candidate in 1894 and 1895. 'If we potter along as we've been doing for the last two years *we're* done, *you're* done, the *cause* is done', Holman grumbled. Nonsense, replied Hughes: 'It seems to me when you sneer at Watson "putting in a clause here and amending a line there" you do him and us and yourself. . .a rank injustice'. Hughes also claimed that 'what we prevent is almost as important as what we do'. The parliamentarians influenced legislation covering shops and factories, electoral reform and exclusion of coloured races; legislation for land and income taxation and regulation of coal mines, previously rejected by the Council, was also enacted. The 1896 conference reshaped Labor's platform to include nationalization of mining, aged and invalid pensions, encouragement of state agriculture and womanhood suffrage (despite one delegate's allegation that 'not one per cent of females had identified themselves with the labour movement').

The next year, 1897, marked the zenith of socialist influence in early NSW Labor. The fiscal issue had been successfully buried and the single taxers were a waning influence, but the socialists were still a significant force within the party. They organized relentlessly to maximize their impact at the 1897 PLL conference, which ratified the Leichhardt league's proposed addition to the platform – nationalization of land and the means of production, distribution and exchange. The same conference selected Labor's candidates for the 1897 federation convention; all had at some stage associated themselves with socialism. Ten delegates from each colony were to discuss federation, and a vote of the whole colony would decide NSW's delegates. None of Labor's 10 was successful; McGowen did best, coming fifteenth. The decision of Cardinal Moran, a Labor sympathizer, to stand as a Catholic anti-socialist candidate was lamentable; it split the Labor vote, inflamed sectarianism, and played into the hands of the middle-class Protestants who comprised the vanguard of the federation movement. Holding the poll on a working day did not help Labor either. More fundamentally, however, the result showed that there was important conditioning Labor still had to overcome, so that voters would not assume that working-class representatives were out of place in constitution-making. Labor wariness about federation also contributed: many activists were uneasy about a federal constitution which shackled NSW to less progressive colonies, all the more when conservatives openly looked forward to this. This wariness, together with Labor's familiarity with the fossils in the NSW Legislative Council, led the socialist-controlled 1897 PLL conference to insist that Labor would only support federation if there were no federal upper house at all. This policy, however logical and sensible, was too advanced to be popular in 1897.

There was an emphatic backlash against the socialists. 'It is one thing to capture a conference, it's quite another to get electors to vote the ticket', wrote Donald Macdonell, a rising leader of the AWU. Labor went into politics to improve 'the people's material condition. . .and not to put some machinery in motion that after they had passed into dust would bring forth a millennium for some subsequent generation'. Importantly, even Holman joined the chorus. When a socialist suggested that the PLL should study economics, Holman retorted that it 'should study tactics instead of economics'. He thought the platform was advanced enough for twenty years, and Black described it as 'political striving for the unattainable', which had left 'the mass we hope to benefit. . .far in the rear'. Black denounced Labor's federation campaign, with its 'crude, ill-considered, bumptious manifesto', and criticized the damage inflicted by 'wire-pullers' at Labor conferences. Political experience had also chastened Ferguson, the Broken Hill strike leader gaoled in 1892: 'The man who comes forward to fight the workers' battle will find his bitterest opponents among the men he's fighting for'. Perhaps he had in mind the militant socialist who told the Labor MPs in 1896 that even though they had mostly voted properly in parliament, this was insufficient: 'You have utterly neglected the dissemination of Socialist truths. You have attended agricultural dinners, cricket matches, Governors' levees, regattas. . .'. The anti-socialist backlash was evident at the 1898 PLL conference. The country leagues, dominated by the AWU, combined with influential MPs to curb the socialists. Conference enlarged the executive to include all the MPs (although only five could vote) and the 'fighting platform' (measures to be emphasized in election campaigns) was purged of socialist overtones; the nationalization plank remained in a lowly position in the general platform and was excluded from the fighting platform. Many socialists resigned from the PLL, including its secretary. According to one of them, the Labor Party had 'degenerated into a mere vote-catching machine, doing no educational work, and generally following a policy of compromise and supineness'. An ASL conference later in 1898 confirmed the breach with the PLL.

The new PLL secretary was Hector Lamond, an important figure in NSW Labor's moderate path from 1898. He had 'reorganized' the branches before the 1898 conference to prevent socialist delegates controlling it. A boy from the bush, Lamond had spent 15 years on the Carcoar *Chronicle*, learning all aspects of journalism before being appointed to the Sydney staff of the *Worker*. This had originated in 1891 as the Wagga shearers' paper the *Hummer*, a rousing weekly inspired by Arthur Rae; it later became the subsidiary NSW edition of the Queensland *Worker*. By 1897, however, it was in poor shape; Macdonell's Bourke branch of the AWU took it over, and with Lamond revitalized it. This powerful AWU-*Worker* combination was cemented by Lamond's marriage to Spence's daughter. A *Worker* rival, the *Daily Post*, had a short and controversial life before its financially scandalous demise; one of its directors, Holman, although an innocent victim, endured a two-month gaol sentence which triggered a lasting nervous insomnia. Holman's association with the *Daily Post* did nothing for his already ragged reputation in the *Worker*. For years there had been a mutual antipathy between Spence, the architect of bush unionism, and Holman, the precocious, sophisticated urban socialist. Holman was still one of Labor's brightest stars; more resilient since his post-1893 tribulations, he had become less churlish and intolerant in debate. Ironically, he and Spence entered parliament together as Labor's illustrious acquisitions after the 1898 election (when the PLL campaigned as 'the watchdogs of the people'). Their wins in country seats countered losses in two metropolitan seats, one of them Black's.

Labor's misgivings about federation had persisted. Since 1891 its platform had supported federation on a national, not imperialistic, basis, but the draft constitution arising from the 1897 convention was insufficiently democratic. The concerted PLL campaign against this proposed constitution was significant in its rejection in NSW at the 1898 referendum. Further bargaining at a premiers' conference produced marginal amendments to the draft constitution. This revised version was put to a referendum in June 1899, and Labor spokesmen campaigned vigorously against it. Time was to vindicate their concerns about the constitution: they criticized the daunting difficulties in amending it, the excessive power of the Senate, and the shortcomings in democratic electoral safeguards. But they were not heeded, and federation on this unsatisfactory basis was approved. A more immediate problem for Labor was that Sleath and Ferguson defiantly campaigned in support of the constitution, which they saw as the best possible compromise. Outraged PLL branches called for their expulsion, but caucus reprieved them. Alienated by Reid's support of this defective constitution and his loss of reformist drive, 'the solid six' in caucus (Hughes, Holman, Edden, Dacey, Thomas and Newcastle miner J. Thomson) persuaded their colleagues to withdraw support from Reid and bring down his government.

Support in return for concessions continued under the new Premier, Lyne, and his successor, See. Lyne promised that the concessions from his government would be more frequent and so they were. Legislation was passed for aged pensions, shearers' accommodation and miners' accident relief. Early closing of shops was introduced. This had been Labor policy since the 1898 conference, when Hughes promoted it against spirited opposition. His opponents acknowledged the appalling working conditions of shop assistants, but emphasized their notorious anti-Labor sympathies; Hughes argued that this was the way to convert them. There was also an Arbitration Bill. Since 1890 employers had repeatedly refused to negotiate during industrial disputes; nearly all Labor people felt that a scheme of compulsory conciliation and arbitration, as introduced in New Zealand, would be most beneficial for workers. The NSW legislation, which bypassed conciliation and provided for compulsory arbitration, was rejected by the Council. After redoubled Labor pressure, compulsory arbitration – now heading Labor's fighting platform – was enacted in 1901.

Labor had its own 'peculiar aura, produced by an amalgam of comradeship, controlled bickering, and missionary fervour'. For a host of men and women who found life harsh, Labor represented 'the hope of something better'. The party gave people of humble origins the opportunity to participate in the process of creating a fairer society, but it was clear that money and persistent organization were crucial to that process. Labor stalwarts repeatedly complained that much more could be achieved with an organizer, but the party could not afford one. Campaigning costs were mainly borne by the branches, which raised their meagre funds from membership fees, fêtes, smoke concerts, dances and socials. As well as regular meetings for routine business, some branches arranged speech nights and debates; but between elections the branches were all too often inactive, neglecting the vital grinding work of education, canvassing and enrolment of voters. This neglect was being remedied, but very gradually.

With the distraction of federation settled, Labor entered a relatively united phase with the Boer War its only major hiccup. The Boers were determined bushmen resisting British encroachment on their independence, but the heroes of the croquet lawn were aroused, and in the wave of imperial hysteria it required courage to oppose Australian participation against the Boers. After Hughes led the way in parliament, describing British policy as 'ill-advised, ill-judged and immoral', Holman sparked a furore by declaring that he hoped England would lose. The fuss inhibited McGowen (and most of caucus) from supporting him, and McGowen's approval of Australian involvement was roundly condemned by Edden. Then Griffith, who was an articulate, energetic opponent of Australia's participation throughout the war, clashed heatedly with Sleath. Within the party the Boer War was the subject of vigorous debate, particularly at the 1902 PLL conference. For the labour movement it was disturbing that a minor war so far away could so easily threaten Labor's hard-won unity.

Labor's improving stocks were shown at the 1901 NSW election, when it enjoyed its best result since 1891 with 24 members (up five) and 18·7% of the overall vote (11·4% in 1898). Labor's representatives still tended to be younger

1. The strikers' library at their Barcaldine camp. (*Oxley Library*)

2. The gaoled unionists. Back (from left): H. Smith-Barry, W. Fothergill, A. Forrester, J. Stuart. Centre: G. Taylor, P. Griffin, E. Murphy, H. Blackwell. Front: A. Brown, R. Prince, W. Bennett, D. Murphy. Reclining: W. Hamilton. (*Oxley Library*)

3. William Lane. (*ANU Archives of Business and Labour*)

4. The main camp at Cosme, Paraguay. The tallest of the group of women on the left is Mary Gilmore, who later became a celebrated literary figure in Australia. On her left is Clara Laurence, who had been so inspired as a young nurse when Tommy Ryan won Barcoo in 1892 that she raised a red flag over Muttaburra hospital; when it was lowered she promptly hoisted it again. She stayed at Cosme until 1927, and when she died in 1964 aged 96 she was the last survivor of the first Paraguay contingent's adults. (*National Library*)

than other MPs, but this election increased the proportion of Labor's native-born from a quarter to a third and the number of Catholic Labor members from two to nine. Part of the Catholic influx was Andy Kelly: expelled in 1893 and unsuccessful as a Protectionist against Holman in 1898, he had been readmitted to the party and won Sydney-Denison in 1901. Catholics were increasingly voting Labor. In this era of rampant sectarianism the Catholic press was warming to the PLL, and Cardinal Moran was belatedly realizing that men like McGowen, Watson and Hughes were not socialists of the violent European variety he so abhorred. Again the efficient network of AWU branches was largely responsible for Labor's rural successes; bush solidarity inspired legendary deeds of selfless devotion to the cause. When Macdonell stood unsuccessfully for the Barwon, two men rode 70 miles (112 km) to vote for him. Even more dedicated was the aged bushman who staggered into an outback hut during one election; penniless, hungry, weak and ill, he was desperate to get to a polling booth and vote for Langwell. 'I want to give Hughie a vote', he said, 'I suppose it will be my last'. Sadly, his quest failed, as that night he died.

THE FLEETING EUPHORIA of the 1891 NSW triumph had soured well before Queensland Labor had an opportunity to emulate NSW at a general election. There were, however, successes in two by-elections to savour, and one of them, the first win by a formally endorsed Labor candidate in Queensland, was especially sweet. The member for Barcoo, an electorate embroiled in the 1891 strike upheaval, was the inaugural president of the Pastoral Employers' Association; he died in January 1892. A meeting under Barcaldine's Tree of Knowledge chose shearer and strike leader Tommy Ryan as Labor's candidate for the by-election. Ryan, who less than a year earlier had been arrested and put in irons before his acquittal of conspiracy, won Barcoo convincingly. At his campaign launch Ryan proudly associated himself with the origins of the Alice River co-operative settlement near Barcaldine. Conceived with a utopian flourish, this extension of the strikers' camp included Liberty Street, Freedom Street, Union Street and Nil Desperandum; another was named after Gilbert Casey. But this enthusiastic idealism did not last long, and the settlement became a government-endorsed co-operative providing employment and land settlement for hardy bushworkers. Co-operative settlements were established in the 1890s in the three other colonies where Labor had made its mark, but none prospered.

William Lane had in mind a more ambitious scheme altogether. His great dream was to start afresh with a band of kindred spirits in a new place, far away from the oppression and injustice so evident in the strike. The New Australia Co-operative Settlement Association was established in 1891. Lane was chairman, with Ryan and the NSW MLA, Arthur Rae, as vice-chairmen; treasurer was Walter Head, Rae's close bush union associate in the establishment of the *Hummer* and Labor branches in rural NSW. Earnest recruiting included a completely unsuccessful visit by Lane to Tasmania in search of single women. Having chosen 463 000 acres (187 000 ha) in distant Paraguay as the site of this grand vision, Lane planned to leave Sydney with the first contingent of 220 on 1 May 1893, which was not only May Day but the second anniversary of the beginning of the notorious Rockhampton conspiracy trials. But the NSW government deliberately delayed their departure with administrative hindrances. On 9 July there was a farewell meeting in the Domain chaired by Watson; one of the speakers was Holman, whose only brother was bound for Paraguay. A week later they set off with high hopes, escorted as far as the Heads by a steam launch containing Rae, Head and an emotional Spence.

Sadly, even before the second contingent of 190 left in December, Lane's great dream was in ruins. He was an unlikely leader. A 'delicate-looking man with drooping moustache and clear blue eyes behind gold-rimmed spectacles', he limped because of a deformed foot, and his eight years in Canada and America had given him 'a slight Yankee twang'. But he could talk as captivatingly as he wrote, and he was intensely committed to New Australia. However, this fanaticism made him autocratic, tactless and intolerant of human frailty. The pressures of a harsh environment in a strange land combined lethally with inadequate capital, distant markets and Lane's temperament. There was bitter strife. In mid-1894 a breakaway group of 63 led by Lane started a new settlement at Cosme, 45 miles (72 km) south of New Australia. Cosme's slower decline was sealed when Lane left Paraguay in August 1899; drained and depressed by the gruelling experience, he told Spence that 'this Labour movement. . .is a hopeless thing'. The AWU invited him to edit the Sydney *Worker*, but he lasted only a few months; his changed views had a happier home at the conservative *New Zealand Herald*, where he remained until his death in 1917.

Sceptics of the venture rejoiced in the outcome as proof that socialism was unworkable. Australian radicalism had contributed money and many of its leading idealists to the dream; the failure, and the gloating of conservatives, were depressing. Four of the gaoled Queensland strike leaders went, including Alec Forrester, who had been put on bread and water for reciting extracts from Lane's *The Workingman's Paradise* in prison; at Cosme his wife hanged herself. There was the irrepressible Casey, who had offered his Brisbane house as a raffle prize to raise funds for the New Australia Association. After the split in Paraguay, Casey journeyed to Sydney to take charge of the Association's affairs on behalf of the anti-Cosme group. But the Association had financial problems, and Casey found Head, who wanted to go to Cosme, obstructive and secretive; then the Association's financial records were 'lost' and Head disappeared. Nonetheless, Casey managed to return with funds and recruits to New Australia, where he continued to make his combative presence felt until he died in 1946. Other settlers stayed on in Paraguay, and their descendants live there still.

The saga of New Australia was still to unfold when, a few months after Ryan's success in Barcoo, the first Queensland Labor-in-Politics Convention was instigated by the four Labor MPs. The convention inaugurated an executive council of 12, including the four MPs, and ratified a platform broadly similar to the ALF's March 1891 version, with electoral reform again heading the list. The aspirations of some Labor people to pave the way for a legion of independent small farmers found expression in a new plank calling for a progressive tax on land values irrespective of improvements; land settlement was also the main focus when Seymour drafted the first manifesto. The views of teetotallers like Seymour, Hinchcliffe, Mat Reid and Bowman were reflected in a concluding recommendation that Labor candidates should be 'sober men'. Ryan was not in this category. Reid's emerging reputation as a tough enforcer grew apace with his insistence that Ryan should not be re-endorsed because of his drunkenness and indebtedness. But Reid's first victim did not complain: 'The friends were too warm, the whisky too strong, and the cushions too soft for Tommy Ryan', he said. 'His place is out amongst the shearers on the billabongs.'

In the 1893 election Labor endorsed 46 candidates for the 72 seats, and won 16 of them. Unlike their NSW counterparts in 1891, Labor's opponents in Queensland were not complacent: to deter Labor the government had halved parliamentary salaries, disenfranchised thousands of Labor voters by rigorous enforcement of the discriminatory electoral requirements, and used the strikes to link Labor with lawlessness and destruction of Queensland society. Glassey, Labor's leader in the campaign, was thrown onto the defensive and lost. Only Hoolan of Labor's previous quartet was successful, and caucus elected him as its new leader. Capable but unorthodox, Irish-born Hoolan was not called 'the Wild Man' for nothing. His radical newspapers in north Queensland mining centres pulled no punches, and when a Labor MP was suspended from parliament in 1894 Hoolan 'held him down by force and encouraged him to defy the Speaker'. Later that year Hoolan resigned his seat to enable Glassey to return to parliament and the leadership. The caucus he led included Reid and 'Fighting Charlie' McDonald, but not Hinchcliffe and Bowman, who were unsuccessful in Brisbane, where plural voting had most impact: the capital's 13 seats returned only two Labor members, Reid and socialist wharf labourer Harry Turley.

The northern mining areas elected seven of Labor's 16, including Hoolan and McDonald. From the thriving Charters Towers labour movement came two of the founders of its Republican Association, John Dunsford and Andy Dawson. Dunsford had a struggling store and newsagency which distributed the literature of Bellamy, Marx and Henry George. Dunsford was a thinker and a dreamer, but did not overlook the need for practical reforms: he maintained that one of the most urgently needed socialist measures was state-funded sheep dips. Dawson grew up in a Brisbane orphanage before becoming a miners' union leader at Charters Towers. Able, amiable and a good speaker, Dawson became the first editor of the Charters Towers *Eagle*, which he owned with Dunsford. London-born Billy Browne, formerly a seaman, had also been a miner at Charters Towers, and at many other Australian mining centres, before settling at Croydon near the Gulf of Carpentaria. There he helped form a miners' union and lost an eye in an accident. Quietly-spoken, with a small, frail appearance, Browne read widely and became a much admired caucus moderate. Ryan's successor in Barcoo, blacksmith George Kerr, was no strident socialist either. A Methodist and a Freemason, Kerr had an independent streak at odds with Labor's view of the parliamentarian as a delegate, and once convinced on any issue he was hard to shift. But his sincere, dedicated approach in parliament and in his electorate earned him the respect of his caucus colleagues and of Barcoo's bush unionists, two of whom once rode 200 miles (320 km) to vote for him.

Another newcomer was Andrew Fisher. His father was already fatally ill with miners' phthisis when Fisher followed him into the poorly ventilated Ayrshire coal mines as a youngster; before he had turned 20 he too knew the miners' cough and spat out the black phlegm. Already the local secretary of his union, he had seen it destroyed by a strike and found himself blacklisted. Close to his family and his Scottish heritage – he loved Robbie Burns's famous poetry about the area they had both grown up in – Fisher made the difficult decision to migrate to Queensland in 1885. Settling eventually in Gympie, he was quickly involved in the local labour movement, and formed a lifelong friendship with Maryborough printer Billy Demaine. After growing up in Yorkshire, Demaine had lived for a time in Uruguay and Argentina; his advice influenced his friend Lane to locate New Australia in Paraguay. At the 1892 Labor-in-Politics convention Demaine, as Maryborough's representative, was elected to the executive; Fisher was

Gympie's upright, sandy-haired, quietly assured delegate and, a year later, its first Labor MP.

Sixteen members seemed a healthy result, but Labor's support base in Brisbane and parts of south-east Queensland was thin. The strikes and severe depression had devastated the unions. In 1890 there were 54 unions with 21 379 registered members; in 1894 there were nine unions with 780 members, and the decline continued. Labor's executive dissolved in 1894. Hinchcliffe tried to organize a convention in 1895 – the first since 1892 – but had to give up owing to lack of funds. Donations for the 1896 campaign totalled less than £32 (£206 in 1893). The *Worker*, without Lane, was in trouble; Hinchcliffe kept it alive by the distasteful expedient of selling advertising space. It was only the *Worker*, Labor's numbers in the parliament, and the herculean endeavours of men like Hinchcliffe, Reid, Seymour, Bowman and Fisher that prevented the party from fragmenting.

In parliament Labor's effectiveness was limited by the combination of the two main non-Labor groups into the 'continuous ministry'. Rather than holding the balance of power as in NSW, Labor in Queensland was merely the major group in a small opposition. The Labor members did what they could. They worked diligently in the parliamentary library, and applied their knowledge effectively in the Assembly; they showed their disgust at the government's intransigence on electoral reform and the scandalous National Bank collapse; and they sensationally expressed their outrage at the government's response to another dispute involving the bush unions. As in 1891, the pastoralists imposed wage cuts on the weakened unions, and arrogantly ignored Hinchcliffe's mild overtures requesting a conference; when some unionists felt they had no option but to strike, the government helped the pastoralists with irregular police activity, arrests and remarkable legislation even by Queensland's standards. This Peace Preservation Bill imposing martial law was stoutly resisted by Labor members. Reid, Glassey, McDonald, Turley, Dawson, Browne and Kerr were all suspended from the Assembly during debate, and the remaining Labor men walked out in protest.

Despite this vigorous display of unity, which pleased Labor supporters, there was profound discord about parliamentary policy. Reid and Fisher in caucus, and Hinchcliffe, Seymour and Bowman outside, firmly believed that until Labor could govern in its own right it should remain an independent cross-bench party, unfettered by parliamentary coalitions which would obscure Labor's programme and retard its progress. Consistent with this policy, Hoolan led Labor's 16 of 1893 to the cross-benches and 'cheerfully' allowed a dissident liberal to become the formal Opposition Leader; this was despite the fact that the overwhelming government majority made any policy of support in return for concessions impossible. However, after concerted press campaigns and inadequate Labor funds unseated Reid and Fisher at the 1896 election, the leading lights in caucus – now Glassey, Dawson and Browne – all considered that worthwhile Labor objectives, especially the crucial electoral reforms, could be secured through closer links with liberal progressives in parliament. So did Labor's talented new MLA for Rockhampton, William Kidston, author of 'The Ballot Is The Thing'.

Other issues also produced tension between some parliamentarians and the organization. Glassey's lack of leadership qualities was becoming increasingly evident. Although honest and dogged, this slightly built Irishman was tactless, individualistic and lacked agility of mind. Also, like many Labor men elected to colonial parliaments before the machinery of pledge, executive and conference was refined, he was reluctant to acknowledge the organization's authority. So too was Hoolan, Glassey's close associate. He had returned to the Assembly at the 1896 election, despite his refusal to recognize Hinchcliffe's temporary pre-election executive. The Wild Man was now a small-scale grazier who found 'Socialism in our time' (the motto of the *Worker*) 'impracticable'; such wild ideas were 'a millstone around the neck of the Labor party'. When Labor's persistent probing of the National Bank affair brought to light further scandalous revel-ations, Glassey and Hoolan supported government assistance to the bank in order to prevent the depression from worsening, whereas McDonald led a caucus group opposed to further public funding of such a corrupt institution. Hoolan was involved in further controversy: despite the platform's unambiguous hos-tility to private railways, he and a Labor colleague broke solidarity with caucus to support a private line through their electorates.

ALF disquiet at its inadequate control over the politicians was aired at the June 1898 convention of 41 delegates. As ever, Hinchcliffe laid the convention foundations and, with Seymour and Bowman, was among the organization's leading representatives. The convention initiated a Central Political Executive (CPE) which was intended to be evenly balanced between the parliamentarians and the ALF; in practice, however, since CPE meetings were held in Brisbane, executive members from distant regions were often absent and the politicians tended to form a majority. The platform was given its first overhaul for six years. Comprehensive electoral reform remained the leading item. Various industrial reforms were listed, and there was an extensive array of state enterprises relating especially to farmers but also encompassing a bank and a coastal marine service. The revised platform confirmed the importance Labor attached to providing education, encouraging land settlement, discouraging coloured labour and abolishing the Legislative Council. The convention authorized Labor's MPs to discuss possible joint action with non-Labor parliamentarians; shortly after-wards, Glassey assumed the formal position of Opposition Leader. The con-vention also introduced a tougher pledge: whereas in 1893 and 1896 Labor candidates had only to promise to support any political reforms demanded by the party, candidates for preselection now had to promise to uphold the plat-form, and to withdraw from the election if not preselected. Glassey found the new pledge abhorrent, but reluctantly signed it; R.M. King, J.M. Cross (both MLAs since 1893) and Hoolan refused to sign. The remorseless Reid was sent north to 'cut the political throat[s]' of Hoolan and Cross. After his exhaustive tour of their mining electorates and his fiery speeches denouncing the moder-ation advocated by Labor's 'brainy democrats', Hoolan and Cross were so intimidated that neither contested preselection. In Maranoa, where King had a large personal following, the official Labor candidate polled poorly in the 1899 election but contributed to King's defeat. As a political enforcer Reid's repu-tation was now awesome, but he had made enemies; he lost again in 1899 when Hoolan and Cross helped his opponent.

Labor won 21 seats in 1899, confirming its strength in the north and north-west and its overall weakness elsewhere. Glassey concentrated only on retaining Bundaberg and gave no leadership during the campaign. After it he told caucus that he would not stand for leadership if opposed. When Dawson was nomi-nated, Glassey walked out of the meeting and the party. Unlike Reid, Fisher was back, but had lost ground as a prospective leader during his absence. The new leader, Dawson, who was friendly with a number of non-Labor members, an-nounced that he was prepared to co-operate with other parliamentary groups.

Before long Kidston's manoeuvring paid dividends. Enough disgruntled 'continuous ministry' supporters defected to induce the Premier to resign. Labor was still the next largest parliamentary group. Dawson and Kidston sought support from dissident conservatives, and received sufficient assurances from them to persuade caucus that it was a worthwhile opportunity to demonstrate Labor's willingness to govern. The first Labor government in the world, an unthinkable phenomenon in some quarters, was sworn in amid amazed gasps and shaking of heads on 1 December 1899. In their six days in office the new ministers uncovered evidence of incompetent administration and corruption by their predecessors. They were removed four hours after parliament reassembled on 7 December. This brief taste of government did not resolve Labor's internal dispute about its role. For Kidston, Dawson, Browne, Kerr and others it confirmed that judicious alliances could bring worthwhile results, whereas Hinchcliffe and Reid had their misgivings about premature assumption of office reinforced.

As in NSW, the Boer War and federation were troublesome issues for Queensland Labor. Majority Labor opinion initially opposed 'sending a mob of swashbucklers to South Africa to show off their uniforms', as Dawson put it. His stance, more outspoken than that of any other Australian politician, prompted the throwing of stones at his house and insults at his family; but British losses during Black Week in December 1899 moderated opposition in Queensland as elsewhere. In Queensland federation did not generate the same heat as in NSW – Queensland was completely unrepresented at the 1897–98 conventions – and Labor had no specific policy on the issue. Dawson, Dunsford, Browne, Fisher and Seymour were strongly in favour. Labor's anti-federationists had a variety of reasons. McDonald saw it as a middle-class diversion from Labor's priorities, and many leading Brisbane unionists agreed; Reid believed federation would increase the prevalence of black labour; Kidston thought it would damage Queensland's economy, but tried to establish full manhood suffrage for the federation referendum as a precedent for all Queensland elections. The pro-federation result in the colony's referendum owed much to the overwhelming 'Yes' vote in Labor's northern and north-western strongholds. Glassey, who supported federation and the Boer War, responded to frequent Labor attacks by suddenly resigning his seat and recontesting it as an independent; Labor, unprepared, endorsed Hinchcliffe for the acrimonious by-election, but Glassey won easily. Dawson stepped down from the leadership in August 1900; his worsening health, a legacy of his mining days, had already forced him to give up his legal studies. In his place caucus elected another ex-miner with health problems, Browne, whose recurrent acute asthma had provoked his resignation as caucus secretary in 1898.

Labor derived valuable support from the *Worker* and other loyal newspapers. In 1899 Fisher's friend Demaine started the Maryborough *Alert*, the steadfast radical weekly he was to edit for four decades. Other Labor papers included the Charters Towers *Eagle* (initiated by Dawson and Dunsford) and the Cairns *Advocate*, founded by Tom Givens, a tall, solidly built Irishman, who had been a miner and bush union organizer before his election as Labor's MLA for Cairns in 1899. Also making his mark, on several papers, was Labor's finest propagandist, Henry Boote. Born in Liverpool, he left school at 10 but he read voraciously and taught himself to paint. In 1899 he migrated to Australia, where his strong working-class affiliation drew him into the labour movement. His developing writing skills came under notice and when Labor's 1892 by-election success in one of Queensland's biggest sugar centres ('Bundaberg goes white' screeched the

Worker) was reversed at the 1893 election, Boote was dispatched there by the ALF to edit the *Bundaberg Guardian*, which vigorously opposed the employment of kanakas. Boote's journalism contributed to Glassey's recapture of the seat in 1896. Then he performed the same task for Fisher on the Gympie *Truth*, which they, with local stalwart George Ryland, founded and produced; it played a major role in Fisher's return to the Assembly in 1899. In Gympie Boote boarded with Fisher and they formed a close friendship. In 1902 Boote was back in Brisbane as the *Worker*'s editor. A cultured, sensitive idealist for whom socialism was always a moral crusade, he restored the *Worker* to its previous eminence under Lane.

Although the *Worker* had become a distinct commercial success, finance remained a desperate problem. No one was more aware of this than Hinchcliffe, ever busy as manager of the *Worker* (and one of its regular contributors), ALF secretary and CPE secretary. Funds were so scarce in January 1900 that the Queensland delegates at the Sydney conference to inaugurate a federal Labor party had to pay their own fares and expenses. At least the 1901 convention endorsed a proposal to provide some regular income for election campaigns and administration: henceforth branches and unions would be able to vote in preselections only if they paid an annual registration fee (minimum one pound) to the CPE.

The 1902 election represented a significant advance for Labor. With 58 endorsed candidates it won 25 seats (up four), including more than half the eastern seats. However, the results were again disappointing in Brisbane, where Labor's few metropolitan successes still tended to be based on a strong personal vote like Frank McDonnell's in Fortitude Valley. An extroverted drapery assistant from Ireland, McDonnell dominated the agitation for early closing of shops, and the 'clerks' hero' accomplished his goal with the 1900 Factories and Shops Act. Another McDonnell achievement was the extension of the grammar school scholarship system, which benefited Catholic schools and boosted Labor's Catholic support. The strong men of the ALF organization, Reid and Bowman, having both lost at the 1899 general election but won by-elections later that same year, lost again in 1902. Browne, the parliamentary leader, was a principled moderate but not a dominant personality and anyway his health was failing. The stage was set for Kidston. In January 1903 he publicly welcomed an alliance with other progressives to remove the 'continuous ministry', which he knew was racked with internal divisions, and confidently awaited developments.

IN SOUTH AUSTRALIA the ULP had to wait, like its Queensland counterpart, until 1893 for an Assembly election. It contested 12 of the 54 seats and won 10 of them, capturing nearly one-fifth of the overall vote. Two of these 10 were not parliamentary novices. Moonta miner Dicky Hooper had been the first Labor man elected to the Assembly. But he never joined the ULP, although he attended caucus meetings; in his decade as an Independent Labor man 'Dicky Hooper, the silent member' concentrated on local issues and made only one parliamentary speech. A far more magnetic figure was John McPherson, who as a 22-year-old printer had migrated from Scotland with his wife in 1882. Seven years later he was sacked from the Adelaide *Register*, which was then attempting – after a bitter dispute, unsuccessfully – to employ only non-union labour. The following year he became honorary secretary of the UTLC, and grappled with the dramatic issues of the maritime strike as well as the activities of the Working Women's Trade Union, the building and management of the Trades Hall, and the formation of the ULP. As the ULP's founding secretary, he became its first genuine member in the Assembly when he won a by-election in February 1892. Unlike Hooper, McPherson immediately made a fine impression in parliament, and he was a natural leader for the contingent joining him in the Assembly in 1893. Decent, honest and unostentatious, he combined the steel and sensitivity of a Labor standard-bearer who yearned for more leisure to indulge his love of poetry.

McPherson headed a strong team. London-born W.O. Archibald arrived in SA in his early thirties, and after a decade of varied employment was sufficiently known and admired to top the poll in Port Adelaide; 'rugged and strong with burly physique, bow legs and a bullet-like head, he was vehement, logical and analytical in approach'. Genial Fred Coneybeer, having learned the trade of horse-collar making, arrived in Adelaide in 1882 and rose within the union movement to become UTLC president in 1888. A Freemason and temperance man, Coneybeer was renowned as a negotiator in industrial disputes, a superb campaigner on the hustings, and a legendary master of ceremonies at umpteen Labor functions. Alex Poynton was born on the Victorian goldfields where his father participated in the Eureka revolt in 1854. He grew up to be a bushworker and bush union organizer, popular in the remote regions of Flinders, which he won in 1893. Like Hooper, Poynton attended caucus and aligned himself with the ULP in parliament, although he had not signed the Labor pledge.

Also entering the Assembly in 1893 were two distinguished Labor men, E.L. Batchelor and Tom Price. Batchelor was born and grew up in Adelaide. A promising pupil-teacher at 12, he developed a lifelong interest in education, but mechanics absorbed him and he became an engineer. Like McPherson, Batchelor rose to senior posts in his union, the UTLC and the ULP. When he topped the poll in the two-member electorate of West Adelaide in 1893, he relegated the formidable C.C. Kingston to second place. 'Batch' was a greatly admired moderate who remained calm when others did not; his 'unassuming manner masked a fund of quiet wisdom'. Tom Price's father was a Welsh stonemason whose addiction to the bottle cost him jobs and kept his family poor. When young Tom began cutting the stone, he was already a strict abstainer and Wesleyan Methodist. Two decades of stone-cutting damaged his lungs and, in 1883, aged 31, he decided to try the air of SA. There he worked on the building materials of the colony's Parliament House which he was to enter as a Labor MP. He was a likeable, astute, grizzly-bearded reformer with no frills, capable of fiery outbursts of oratory which made his lungs bleed.

In the Council the ULP was unable to make significant progress following its stunning success of 1891. That rude shock for the born-to-rule gentry had galvanized them to form the National Defence League, in order to safeguard the Council against further Labor inroads. The SA Council was one of Australia's most powerful conservative bulwarks. Although the ULP upper house trio (Kirkpatrick, Guthrie and Charleston) became a quartet in 1893 and increased to six the following year, this was not enough in the 24-member Council to achieve Labor's goal of weakening its powers. Labor derived what consolation it could from the arrival in the Council in 1894 of Gregor McGregor, a tough ex-wrestler who was just the man to take on the troglodytes. McGregor toiled as a labourer in Scotland and England before working his passage to SA in 1877. An accident while felling trees damaged his sight severely and permanently, but this beefy radical overcame his disability by utilizing his amazing memory: his forceful speeches were buttressed with streams of memorized statistics. Amiable outside political debate, McGregor preferred practical solutions to theoretical ones, and was one of Labor's most popular and trusted politicians.

SA politics in the 1890s were dominated by Kingston. A tempestuous, unconventional, dynamic liberal, Kingston was to remain Premier for six and a half years. For most of that period he enjoyed committed ULP backing, in a relationship superficially similar to NSW Labor's policy of support in return for concessions. However, the ULP's influence and bargaining power was in fact limited: the disorganization and/or hopeless conservatism of other parliamentary groups meant that there was no alternative for the ULP to threaten to support instead of Kingston, as he and Labor well knew. Nonetheless, Labor's solid support was an important element in Kingston's unprecedentedly stable government, which produced a fine reformist record from Labor's viewpoint: it included a state bank, regulation of factories, a conciliation and arbitration act, increased land and income taxation, more extensive workers' compensation, a protective tariff, a public works programme – and the most extensive women's suffrage reform anywhere in the world. From 1894 women could vote on the same terms as men, including postal voting, and were able to stand for parliament themselves. This was primarily due to the tireless lobbying of activists like Mary Lee, who organized a petition throughout the colony which ended up 400 feet (122 m) long, bearing 11 600 signatures; also SA's liberal traditions in the Assembly meant that such pressure was more likely to be rewarded than in, say, Queensland. Still, the ULP's consistent advocacy of this much-desired Labor objective since 1891 had undoubtedly played its part.

Any Labor ambitions to replace Kingston, in order to fully implement the ULP platform, depended on maintaining the electoral momentum. But this did not happen: Labor essentially marked time in the Assembly (10 seats in the 1893 election, 12 in 1896, 11 in 1899), and its numbers in the Council began to decline with Kirkpatrick's defeat in 1897. The ULP remained an Adelaide party, without a formal branch structure in country areas. Labor's rural representatives like Poynton, Hooper and the member for Gladstone from 1896, E.A. Roberts, continued to join caucus unaffected by the pledge binding Labor's metropolitan members. Even ULP branches in Labor's urban garrisons tended to be relatively inactive except at election times. Whereas Labor in NSW had its annual conference and the Queensland party had an occasional one, the ULP had no equivalent conference at all during the 1890s. The functions of a central executive were carried out by the low-key ULP council, which basically allowed the politicians to update the platform when required.

A gratifying development in 1894 was the establishment of the *Weekly Herald*, controlled by directors appointed by the ULP and the UTLC. Ever since the *Register* strike a Labor paper had been an objective close to McPherson's heart. Without breaking any circulation records, the *Herald* at least countered the constant anti-Labor influence of the *Advertiser* and the *Register*. Also significant was the attitude to Labor adopted by another newspaper, the *Southern Cross*, the organ of Adelaide's Roman Catholics. Its editor and co-founder, J.V. O'Loghlin MLC, was generally sympathetic to Labor, but resigned in 1896 to become Chief Secretary in Kingston's government. The new editor, W.J. Denny, had less freedom; by 1898 the paper was describing the ULP platform as 'hardly within the limits of practical politics', and seems to have turned some Catholic voters away from Labor.

Internal problems sapped Labor's cohesion. There was disagreement about whether non-unionists should be permitted as Labor candidates. Initially only unionists were eligible to stand, and when this was reversed in mid-1893 unionists were up in arms, concerned that this change threatened their influence in the party and even the ULP's very existence in view of SA's strong liberal traditions. Eighteen months later a plebiscite overwhelmingly restored the ban on non-unionist candidates, but the issue simmered divisively afterwards. In practice the rule seems to have been occasionally waived, as influential unionists gradually accepted – like most Labor people in other colonies – that reliable Labor representatives did not necessarily have union backgrounds. There was also intermittent grumbling about the ULP's insufficient progress towards its objectives. In 1895 Batchelor claimed that only a quarter of Labor's 1891 planks still remained on the platform unimplemented, and half the 1891 goals had been met. While Labor obviously could not claim all the credit, its 'persistent advocacy and solid votes' in parliament had been vital. Batchelor also pointed to the overall improved standard of parliamentary diligence caused by the Labor MPs' earnest approach. This applied in all colonies: most Labor MPs treated their duties much more seriously than the typical conservative politician of that era, who regarded parliament as a casual debating club to be attended when other activities permitted. Batchelor also claimed that the ULP members 'have held together doggedly. . .and are more firmly united to-day than ever'. This proud boast of 1895 soon had a hollow ring. Two years later Charleston, who had been annoying his colleagues by frequently breaching caucus solidarity in Council votes, resigned his seat and recontested it as an independent; in a heated by-election, he convincingly defeated his ULP opponent. He was accompanied out of the party by blacksmith R. Wood, MHA for North Adelaide since 1893, who took Charleston's side in the dispute. It was a most depressing episode for Labor.

Labor's 1897 woes also included the loss of its leader. By August McPherson was dying of cancer. Early in December he summoned Jim Hutchison to his bedside. Hutchison had worked with McPherson as a printer in Scotland before following him to Adelaide, where they had been sacked together in the *Register* dispute. McPherson uttered this farewell message to his mate: 'I never truckled to anyone. Tell the boys to stick together'. He died a few days later aged 37, leaving a wife and four children. A thousand mourners honored one of Labor's earliest heroes, following his coffin through Adelaide streets to the cemetery. Hutchison succeeded him as member for East Adelaide, and Batchelor became the new leader; both were worthy replacements, but McPherson's death was keenly felt.

Federation also proved troublesome for Labor in SA. The 1896 ULP platform called for 'federation on a democratic basis'. McPherson, Batchelor, McGregor and Charleston had stood for election as SA delegates to the federation convention, but were no more successful than their NSW counterparts. ULP misgivings about the draft constitution touched on the economic consequences for SA, but concentrated more on its democratic shortcomings. 'It was a declaration of war against the working classes', thundered Archibald. Guthrie typically sought a nautical metaphor to lash this proposed constitution 'framed amid the fragrant smoke of the finest Havana cigars and the smell of the most savoury turkeys and ducks, and launched on its maiden trip in a sea of champagne'. Price too denounced the draft as a 'mongrel Constitution. . .very unsatisfactory'; he was especially troubled by the Senate's powers. Conservatives and Kingston's liberals supported the draft, and in the 1898 referendum South Australians declared themselves to be clearly in favour of federation. While there were clusters of negative votes in some urban Labor citadels, the ULP's rural weakness was again evident. The revised version was put to the people in 1899. Labor's opposition to this defective constitution was to be vindicated after federation; however, since unscrupulous opponents had alleged that Labor opposed the generally popular cause of federation on any basis, the ULP decided in 1899 that further opposition would be pointless.

No one exemplified shifting attitudes to the Boer War more than Roberts. Born in London, he was educated on the island of Guernsey before becoming a merchant seaman like his father. After nearly five years at sea he migrated to Australia, and in 1888 settled at Port Pirie. There his radicalism and organizational flair were soon apparent, as he set up a co-operative bakery and a local workingmen's association. As that association's Labor candidate, Roberts narrowly lost Gladstone in 1893 but won in 1896. Being the youngest MHA did not inhibit him from aggressive parliamentary oratory and casting the first stone against Charleston. When Kingston committed SA to a contingent against the Boers, caucus by a majority vote decided to oppose this. In parliament Roberts went further than most ULP critics, scorning the 'feather-bed' soldiers who would involve themselves in such an unworthy enterprise. This provoked a predictable reaction from the 'my country right or wrong' brigade. In order to disarm the accusers of disloyalty, one Labor supporter advised Batchelor to sing 'God Save the Queen' at the outset of his speech opposing the SA contingent. As elsewhere, Labor's attitude in SA moderated, especially once it was clear that the British forces were floundering against the Boers. But Roberts's transformation was dazzling, culminating in his own enlistment. He became an officer, performed creditably in action, and even resigned Gladstone to return for a second stint of war service. Labor's difficulties concerning the war were heightened for. Roberts's rural ULP colleague Poynton by his son's enlistment and death in South Africa.

Before Roberts's departure he and Poynton threw the Kingston government and the ULP into turmoil. For most of Kingston's premiership the Council was unusually tolerant of reform, owing to the presence there of the ULP and certain liberals together with the frequent absence from the house of some reactionaries. But from 1897, with Labor's numbers dwindling, the flow of progressive legislation dried up. ULP dissatisfaction was publicly expressed in 1898 by Batchelor, Archibald and Price in the first no-confidence motion Kingston had faced. Eventually Labor voted against the motion, as the alternative was far worse, but Kingston was stung into action. Although the Council had sternly rebuffed nearly all efforts to make more South Australians eligible to vote for it, Kingston introduced legislation to drastically widen its franchise. When the Council again resisted, Kingston sought to bring it to heel with a double dissolution shortly after the 1899 election. Labor's programme now accorded top priority to reforming the Council; however, to avert the crisis, Roberts and Poynton crossed the floor with Wood and another government supporter to bring down the Kingston ministry. This sensational development shook the ULP. Roberts challenged Price to produce the caucus minute book, and was rebuked for speaking in parliament about 'sacredly private' matters. The incident was a consequence of the defectors' unpledged status; their justifications underlined their lack of commitment to the Adelaide-based ULP organization, which had no role in their electorates. A Kingston opponent hastily concocted a ministry which included Poynton, but this government lasted only a week before its lack of majority Assembly support was exposed. Roberts voted with caucus to remove it.

From this upheaval there was an unprecedented outcome for Labor. Kingston withdrew from the scene, travelling to London on federation business; one of his lieutenants, Holder, formed a government, including Batchelor as his Education and Agriculture minister. This was the first instance of a Labor member joining an anti-Labor ministry with the approval of caucus. Batchelor's colleagues presumably saw his elevation as a means of influencing government policy; also, with the Dawson government sworn in the previous week in Queensland, it was another prestigious opportunity to show that Labor politicians were able and willing to govern. However, with the ULP still smarting from the pain inflicted by Labor's unpledged rural members, special dispensations were no longer tolerated: Batchelor had to resign from caucus, which elected Price to succeed him as leader. Batchelor performed creditably as a minister; benefiting from his own experience as a youthful pupil-teacher, he introduced a new teacher training scheme incorporating university education. When Holder and Batchelor entered federal politics in 1901, the ULP was not asked to participate in the new government, which was liberal in name only. The new Premier, who supported a restricted franchise for the Council, was even less satisfactory than Holder had been, but Labor was unable to capitalize, and the 1902 SA election was a disaster. In a reduced Assembly (42 seats, formerly 54) the ULP could only muster five members – four metropolitan veterans of 1893 (Price, Coneybeer and the Port Adelaide duo of Archibald and wharf labourer Ivor McGillivray) plus Labor's new MLA for Wallaroo, another Moonta miner, John Verran. The hostile propaganda of the National Defence League and the *Southern Cross* had been effective; the improved economic conditions had cost Labor some voters drawn to it in earlier times; but Labor's own weaknesses in cohesion and rural organization had also been costly. The ULP appointed a committee to work out how to arrest the slump.

THE GREAT HOPES held for Victorian Labor in mid-1891 were comprehensively dashed. Protectionist liberalism and its mouthpiece, the *Age*, maintained such a tight grip on Victorian political orthodoxy that Labor found it hard to forge its own identity. Within 18 months of the creation of the PPL, it had flopped so disastrously that a union delegate asked a THC meeting whether it still existed. Some Labor people in Victoria doubted the wisdom of even attempting to build an independent Labor party; they were content to remain an advance wing of the liberals, and were pleased when the PPL was succeeded by the United Labour and Liberal Party of Victoria (ULLP) before the 1894 election. But the ULLP also foundered, and the THC had to create a United Labor Party (ULP) in 1896. The distinction between some liberals and Labor remained blurred; some endorsed Labor candidates, once elected, quickly disowned any Labor affiliation. In turn the ULP faltered, and had to be revived by the THC three years later. Then this version collapsed and gave way in 1901 to the Political Labor Council (PLC). These false starts were dispiriting for Labor enthusiasts.

They had been disheartened ever since the 1892 election. Labor won 11 of the 96 Assembly seats, all but one based in Melbourne's inner suburbs. Compared to the NSW triumph of 1891, this was regarded as a failure by friend and foe alike. Actually Victoria had nearly matched NSW in its proportion of Labor votes (over one-fifth), but they were clustered in the wrong places. Victoria did not have the same number of employed bushworkers as NSW and Queensland, and the rural bias in the Victorian electoral system worsened Labor's difficulties: country electorates contained considerably fewer voters than urban seats. The poor showing in the 1892 election (and again in 1894, 1897 and 1900) strengthened the views of those in the labour movement who felt that Labor should remain attached to the liberals.

This ordinary performance was even more disappointing since the non-Labor governments in this period hardly distinguished themselves. They had presided over the excesses of the land boom, which caused banks and building societies to crash and thousands to lose their investments. Many pillars of society, including politicians, were implicated in financial scandals which the Establishment did its best to conceal. Typical, but by no means the most flagrant, was the premier who appointed himself Agent-General in London and hastily departed to avoid his creditors. The depression that followed brought tough times to Labor supporters; there were no unemployment or sickness benefits, no aged or widows' pensions, no child endowment and no workers' compensation. Unemployment soared, and families were evicted onto the streets. Conservatives nonetheless maintained that it was not for governments to 'mitigate the lot of those forlorn ones who have fallen in the race of life'. One youngster growing up in this misery contracted diphtheria and was expected to die; he managed to survive, but his throat and voice were permanently damaged. His name was Arthur Calwell.

The calibre of Labor MPs was lower in Victoria than in other colonies during the 1890s. Their leader, Trenwith, exerted a strong influence in favour of staying attached to the liberals. The son of a convict, he dressed soberly and seemed to yearn for respectability. Former THC president Joe Winter, MLA for Melbourne South since 1892, was Trenwith's deputy from 1894. Two years later he died, but not before it became apparent that he was one of the politicians caught by the economic crash: he had accumulated £50 000 in debts and could pay only threepence in the pound. He had continued to sit in parliament despite the law preventing insolvents from doing so. His debts were petty cash compared with those of some upper-class villains, but his involvement hampered Labor's exploitation of the scandals. However, Hancock (MLA for Collingwood 1891–92 and Footscray 1894–99) had proved a mettlesome member. His maiden speech in 1891 had urged reform of the banking system, for which he was accused of damaging Victoria's credit in London. Hancock felt more keenly than most in caucus that Labor should cut itself adrift from the liberals.

In this he was strongly supported by Michael Prendergast, Labor's shining light in caucus during its initial struggles. The son of Irish immigrants, Prendergast worked as a printer in Victoria and NSW, before returning to Melbourne in 1888 and immersing himself in the labour movement. He was the PPL's first secretary, served a term as THC president, and won Melbourne North for Labor in 1894. Honest and tireless, he epitomized the fervent semi-religious faith in Labor's destiny which many of its champions felt during its early decades. 'Windy Mick' could speak furiously at great length, and often did. He also wrote prolifically for various Labor publications. Understandably irate at Labor's treatment in the major dailies, he was a founder of *Commonweal* (1891–93) and joint owner of *Boomerang*, which lasted for eight issues in 1894. Prendergast's outspoken insistence that Labor should go it alone made him a special target for *Age* attacks during the 1897 election, when he lost his seat (but he regained Melbourne North in 1900).

Like NSW and SA, Victoria had a record-breaking premier in the 1890s; no Victorian premier has had less charisma than G. Turner, a 'modest little man, who believed that the only statesmanship was economy'. It was the chastened reaction to the 1890s crash that allowed him to remain at the helm for over five years from 1894. Committed to protection, Labor could not countenance any conservative low-tariff alternative, so an absolute policy of support in return for concessions was not feasible in Victoria. Labor's moderately cohesive parliamentarians were pleased with the introduction of the minimum wage, which was included in 1896 legislation establishing the Victorian wages boards after an amendment moved by Prendergast. This legislation was the Turner government's finest achievement, a widely supported, creditable attempt to alleviate sweating and poverty as well as reform the hours and conditions of work in factories and shops.

The tradition of a strong left wing in Victorian Labor began in 1897 with the *Tocsin* socialists. This new Labor paper was Prendergast's brainchild, and he managed the co-operative society funding it. *Tocsin*'s main editor was Bernard O'Dowd, who had graduated in Law and Arts while working as a Supreme Court librarian; he was to become famous as a poet imbued with radical nationalism. *Tocsin*'s leading lights included Dr Maloney, Frank Anstey, Tom Tunnecliffe, J.P. Jones and Ted Findley. There has been no Labor orator more brilliant, inspirational and revered than Anstey. He arrived in Australia from England as an 11-year-old stowaway, and began a harsh decade working as a seaman. As he absorbed radical ideas – especially after he settled in Melbourne in his early twenties – he gradually developed the flair with words which became legendary. Tunnecliffe was a self-educated bootmaker and assiduous Labor publicist, 'a studious, witty and capable man with a taste for theory and history'. Jones emerged from a deprived Tasmanian boyhood to set up a prosperous tailoring business in Melbourne, and ploughed some of the profits into *Tocsin*. Findley was born and apprenticed as a compositor in Bendigo, and later was associated with Prendergast on the *Boomerang* in Melbourne. The year *Tocsin* first appeared he was president of his union and the THC. In 1900 he surprised by winning Melbourne for Labor, but was not in the Assembly for long. An Irish publication attacked King Edward VII, exaggerating the extent (but not the essence) of his extramarital adventures; it was reprinted in the Adelaide *Southern Cross* and then in *Tocsin*, unbeknown to Findley, who then happened to be designated *Tocsin*'s nominal publisher. The imperial grovellers and born-to-rulers had Findley expelled from parliament for seditious libel, but their real aim was to rectify the indignity of a Catholic socialist being parliamentary representative for the commercial hub of Marvellous Melbourne.

Tocsin ignited dissatisfaction with the Labor MPs' performance. It attacked Labor's 'policy of dilly-dally, drift and disaster':

> Plan of campaign it has none, democratic work it does none. It never meets as a party to decide on measures to be introduced. . .It is leaderless, functionless, out-classed: its existence is as a constitutional abortion, with neither the cohesion of a Party, nor the daring and initiative of a guerilla band or a company of free lances. . .

W.M. Hughes and his NSW colleagues also found Victorian Labor's slow progress exasperating: 'We don't recognize that there is a political labor party in Victoria', he said. Trenwith had reinforced misgivings about his leadership by his hostility to any form of pledge, and by his inclusion in the *Age*'s recommended 'Liberal Ten' candidates for election to the 1897 federation convention; all ten were duly elected, underlining the *Age*'s power, and Trenwith became the only Labor representative at the convention. *Tocsin* was appalled when that 'political traitor' gave his blessing to the draft constitution, which was opposed by a majority in caucus and the THC. When he compounded his sins by supporting Australian involvement in the Boer War, *Tocsin* called him 'a compromiser, a lickspittle to Liberalism and a recreant'. The lack of independence of Labor MPs was shown immediately after the 1900 election, when they met with Turner's liberals as a joint party and Turner promoted Trenwith into his ministry, with caucus approval. Trenwith was replaced as Labor leader by Fred Bromley (a tinsmith turned decorative painter, and member for Carlton since 1892), but continued to attend caucus meetings; as a minister he voted with the government in its outrageous manoeuvre to expel Findley.

After the turn of the century Victorian Labor was at last securely established with the creation of the PLC. In 1902 *Tocsin* jubilantly hailed its first proper conference, even though only eight branches sent representatives. The union movement was reviving after the harrowing 1890s, and 47 unions attended the 1902 conference. The THC was still characterized by limited horizons, parochialism and indifference to the plight of the unemployed. The ALF scheme for a national labour movement integrating the industrial and political wings was a casualty of the 1890s, having made little impact in NSW and none whatever in SA and Victoria; one of its major obstacles had been the hostility of the Melbourne THC. The refusal of certain Victorian unions such as the Amalgamated Miners' Association (AMA) to affiliate with Labor had also contributed to its rural weakness. The 1902 conference dealt with the rural question by authorizing the AWU to organize the country electorates; the PLC agreed to endorse candidates chosen by the AWU. Conference alleviated another chronic headache, finance, by levying an annual contribution from all branch and union members. Leadership remained a problem until Prendergast succeeded Bromley in 1904, but the 1902 election confirmed Labor's improvement in Victoria. For the first time it enforced an effective pledge on Labor members, now 12 in number; Frank Anstey was one of the newcomers.

Anstey's notorious association with John Wren may already have commenced. Wren was short, shrewd and unemotional; his most distinctive feature was his piercing gaze. A variety of shady activities, notably an illegal totalisator brazenly conducted in inner-urban Collingwood from 1893, had enabled him to rise from the slums to affluence. Wren thumbed his nose at the law and bribed the police supposedly enforcing it; his thugs protected his interests with bashings and intimidation. Outside the working class Wren was regarded as a grubby upstart. By 1898, as his activities began to impinge on Establishment racing and gambling revenues, it was clear that the government had him under hostile scrutiny. To safeguard his interests Wren turned to politics. Labor and Wren's enterprises were generally supported by the same people and opposed by the same institutions. Wren began to finance the electoral expenses of some Labor politicians; he organized boisterous support at meetings, and increased voting power by dubious means at certain preselection contests. Anstey was always short of money, and frequently received funds from Wren. Anstey never forgot the hardships and brutality of his youth; he was a remarkable crusader who gave himself unstintingly to Labor as orator, writer, organizer and, although he could not

afford it, as benefactor. He seems to have discounted the possibility that donations from Wren could compromise his political ideals. Certainly his acceptance of them was trifling compared to the rank conduct of Tommy Bent
and other non-Labor luminaries during the land boom. There were to be many
other Wren men. How far Wren's influence extended in the Labor Party is difficult to specify, but he remained a sinister figure behind the scenes for half a
century.

THE EARLY PROGRESS of Australian Labor in politics attracted the interest of the
rest of the world. Many curious visitors came to see Australia and New Zealand,
then 'certainly the most socially "advanced" countries on earth'. Since 1891 the
New Zealand radical liberal governments under Ballance (1891–93) and Seddon
(1893–1906) had initiated a range of progressive reforms which had aroused
overseas admiration and served as models for some Australian legislation. Albert
Métin spent half of 1901 observing Australasia before writing a book entitled *Le
Socialisme Sans Doctrines (Socialism Without Doctrine)*. Métin's title reflected
the contrast he and others found between Australasia and Europe. Socialists in
Europe tended to be pacifist, non-religious and internationalist in outlook, and
were preoccupied with theoretical debate. None of this was generally true of
Australasia, where the emphasis was on achievable practical measures. Métin
observed that the successful pursuit of limited goals – more than the European
socialists had achieved for the Continental toilers – had resulted in Australasia
'beginning to be known, not without some irony, as the workers' paradise'. He
was surprised by the number of respectable Labor partisans who said grace
before meals and toasted the monarchy. In Germany, the *Neue Zeit* and its
advocates of revolutionary socialism belittled Australian Labor as short-sighted
and pragmatic: typical was the commentator who mocked Queensland Labor for
regarding 'state purchases of pineapples and strawberries. . .as a big victory for
the cause of socialism'. On the other hand, Käthe Lux told readers of a prestigious German periodical that Australian wages were relatively high and working hours relatively low; she was 'very impressed with the extraordinary degree of
political success of the Australian Labor parties'. German socialists were intently
studying Australian developments as part of the debate within the German
Social-Democratic Party (SPD), the foremost socialist party in Europe. SPD
moderates hoped that Australian Labor's 'successes. . .will spur our German
comrades to match. . .the Australian achievements'. In its first decade Australian Labor had been instrumental in creating an exciting social laboratory,
which was leading the world in progressive legislation benefiting the working
class and attracting visitors from across the globe at a time when the infant
British Labour Party had made no impression whatever.

These visitors had little incentive to include Tasmania in their travels. The
labour movement there was fragmented, unassertive and conservative; unions
were few, and political Labor activity was minimal. The legacy of the convict era
was an enduring inferiority complex for Tasmania's working class. There was
even a restricted male suffrage for the lower house, and only a quarter of Tasmanian men could vote for the upper house, which tenaciously resisted reform.
There was, and is, no dominant urban capital – Launceston has always refused to
concede supremacy to Hobart. Mineral discoveries in the 1870s promised to
make the west coast fertile ground for Labor, but the AMA enrolled only a

minority of the miners; it remained deferential and inhibited in its dealings with the aggressive mining employers, until an influx from the mainland of miners with different attitudes began to take effect. Labor was further hampered by the isolation of the west coast – there is still no link with Hobart by rail, and in the 1890s even a road to the capital was decades away. Tasmania's general development was sluggish, and most adventurous souls emigrated to greener pastures in other colonies, New Zealand and Victoria especially. Those who stayed and tried to create a Labor party faced a daunting challenge: it was common for Labor Tasmanians to be sacked for their unionist and political activities.

A Trades and Labor Council (TLC) had been formed in Hobart in 1883. Hugh Kirk, 'an energetic man with a small goatee beard and hair perpetually on end', was its lively secretary, but its impact was limited. As the only Tasmanian representative at the 1886 and 1888 ITUCs, Kirk managed to secure Hobart as the venue for the 1889 ITUC. That conference exposed fundamental deficiencies in the local labour movement: 'The jealousy that existed between the north and south of Tasmania was greater than that between Victoria and New South Wales', complained the sole Launceston delegate. In the maritime strike the following year, Tasmanian unions quickly surrendered in the face of plentiful non-union labour. The ensuing depression brought further disasters. The Hobart TLC folded, and so did its Launceston equivalent. Kirk was sacked for his unionist activities, and was later given a three-year gaol sentence for forgery. Some ostensibly radical candidates were elected to the Assembly during the 1890s with the blessing of the labour movement, but except for Allan Macdonald (MHA 1893–97) they soon 'kicked away the ladder by which they mounted the pinnacle'.

Into this dire predicament came a man of mystery. He called himself Walter Woods, and was vague about his past. The quality of his assistance to the fledgling Labor journals in the 1890s revealed a rich experience in literature and radical politics. His big secret gradually leaked out. He was in fact Walter Head, bush union leader, co-founder of the *Hummer*, author of fine ballads about shearing and loyal secretary of Lane's New Australia Association. He had pursued the great dreams of the labour movement with unflagging commitment, and was keen to join his young son and the other visionaries in Paraguay. Personal tragedy (which inspired a short story by his friend Henry Lawson) intervened, and he did not go; his son never returned to Australia. The deteriorating financial situation of the Paraguayan venture was not Head's fault, but as secretary he was personally liable. After the split in Paraguay and Casey's break with Lane, Head refused to hand over to Casey the diminished assets that remained. Under increasing strain, and with his family life in disarray, Head suddenly disappeared. By 1895 he was in Tasmania where, as Woods, he was making a fresh start; still only in his mid-thirties, he looked much older. In view of Tasmanian Labor's problems, he concluded that its best hope lay in an extension of the AWU and its organizational skills to the Apple Isle. His flair and political idealism soon made him Labor's finest activist in his adopted colony. He became editor of Labor's best paper, the Hobart *Clipper*, and invigorated it with his radicalism and intellectual bite. Cultured and quick-witted, he was unafraid of controversy and looked beyond short-term solutions.

Despite Woods's endeavours, Tasmania was still without Labor parliamentarians at the turn of the century. However, two successful candidates at the first federal election, King O'Malley and David O'Keefe, were accepted by the federal Labor caucus, and so became Tasmania's first Labor MPs. This inspired George

Burns – formerly of NSW and Queensland but now a west coast miner – to convene a conference at the Zeehan AMA hall. It was chaired by John Earle, a determined Tasmanian-born self-improver and AMA leader: when the Mt Lyell Company manager compiled a secret list of 28 'disloyal and treacherous men', Earle's union work and vehement opposition to the Boer War ensured that he headed the list. The Zeehan conference confirmed the depressingly small degree of unionism in the west; there was much to do, although the Labor platform drafted by the conference was a useful starting-point. The federal Labor Party had a vested interest in a strong Labor presence in all states, and was ready to assist in Tasmania. The 1903 state election underlined Tasmanian Labor's reliance on this aid: when the federal members were delayed and prevented from providing the expected campaign support in Hobart, Labor's activists there withdrew their candidate. Labor's three successes in the election all won west-coast seats, and Earle missed a fourth by only four votes. The new MPs were Burns, miner 'Big Jim' Long and a mine manager who soon defected from Labor. The Mt Lyell Company had blacklisted Long and Earle, and sacked some of their supporters; many miners were too intimidated to back Labor publicly. The Hobart withdrawal had appalled the labour movement on the west coast. Its relations with Hobart Labor had often been frosty, and each had its own moderate, non-socialist platform. Getting some Labor members into the Tasmanian parliament was something, but there was still no permanent state-wide organization: 'we are slow and unsatisfactory in Tasmania', admitted a *Tocsin* correspondent.

WHEN LABOR SENSATIONALLY won 35 NSW seats in 1891, aghast right-thinking Western Australians consoled themselves with the realization that such a dreadful affliction was impossible in their colony. This was quickly proved when John Marshall, an unsuccessful Labor candidate in that election, arrived in Perth in October full of enthusiasm about Labor's great mission; his attempts to establish Labor branches met with no interest. The handful of parochial unions in WA preferred to engage in 'inter-village feuds between Perth and Fremantle', which threatened the fragile unity of the just-formed Trades and Labour Council (TLC). WA's history had stunted the development of its labour movement. Self-government had been granted only the previous year, much later than the other Australian colonies; as in Tasmania, only property owners with a 'stake in the country' could vote (WA had manhood suffrage from 1893, but Tasmania was without it until 1900). Transportation of convicts to WA had not ceased until 1868. Undeveloped, with a meagre, distant, rural population, WA was dominated by the interlocking commercial interests of the 'Six Families' until it was transformed by the fabulous gold discoveries at Coolgardie and Kalgoorlie. Adventurers flocked westwards from all colonies, especially Victoria, draining its labour movement of much-needed vitality. For WA Labor this mass migration was a tremendous fillip.

George Pearce helped form the first WA Labor party in 1893. He had arrived in Perth two years before as a 21-year-old carpenter from South Australia. Tall, with wavy dark hair and moustache, Pearce was a serious, honest and quietly efficient tradesman. He did not sparkle as a thinker or orator; it was his thorough, orderly, solid reliability that brought him under notice. He spent much of his leisure at the State Library educating himself in politics and economics, and amused his co-tenants at home by practising speechmaking alone or to them. He and G.C. Baker, an English printer, were instrumental in establishing the Progressive Political League (PPL), but it fared no better than the Victorian party of the same name. The WA PPL was torn by internal dissension, and struggled to survive the disruptive gold fever. Even Pearce dropped his earnest pursuits for a brief interlude while he tried his luck.

The goldfields were a maelstrom of radical influences from the rest of Australia and beyond. There were vibrant eccentrics like Fred Vosper, the mercurial, impetuous, hard-drinking dreamer who had edited the *Australian Republican* at Charters Towers. Frequently in strife for his inflammatory journalism, he was so outraged when his head was shaved during a stint in prison that he resolved never to cut his hair again. His 'streaming mane' and fiery prose, unleashed from a soapbox or in his *Coolgardie Miner*, made him a celebrated goldfields personality. Julian Stuart and George 'Mulga' Taylor also came from Queensland; both had served long prison sentences for their leadership in the 1891 strike. They provided a continuing link between WA radicals and the Queensland-based ALF. J.B. Holman and Jabez Dodd came from Broken Hill; both had been prominent in the bitter strikes there. Hugh de Largie, like Andrew Fisher, was active in his local miners' union in Scotland after following his father into the coal mines as a youngster. Bearded, dour and not easily ruffled, de Largie married a fellow Catholic, migrated to Queensland, helped Glassey into parliament, then moved to NSW. His prominence in the Newcastle ASL and LEL resulted in his unemployment, and he joined the throng of Westralian goldseekers in 1895. In January 1897 a conference of six unions at Coolgardie established the Amalgamated Workers' Association (AWA) with a political platform, an ALF-like hierarchical structure, and de Largie as its president. Its founders saw the AWA as a large-scale organization embracing all workers – the skilled, the unskilled and even the self-employed. The coastal craft unions, on the other hand, tended to be inward-looking and suspicious of outsiders.

In Perth the movement tried again. The Political Labour Party came into existence, and sought candidates for the 1897 election who were prepared to pledge their solidarity. Candidates were hard to find, as MPs were not yet paid in WA; Premier Forrest delayed payment of members until 1900, well after all other colonies had introduced it. Vosper sought endorsement for North-East Coolgardie, was rejected because he refused to sign the pledge, but stood anyway and won in a blazing personal triumph. Builder and ex-TLC president Charles Oldham won Perth North, and two Labor-endorsed liberals were successful; however, even allowing for the unfairness of the outdated electoral system, Labor had not distinguished itself.

The goldfields labour movement was furious about Forrest's apparent inclination to keep WA out of federation. He was wary because many of his supporters opposed it; when Western Australians were belatedly allowed a vote on federation, they approved it overwhelmingly. There was emphatic support for it on the goldfields, where a Separation for Federation League sought independent federation for the goldfields if the rest of WA stayed out; the League executive included de Largie and future Labor MPs John Reside, Hugh Mahon and Dr H.A. Ellis.

With disagreements about the merits of political or union action as well as significant regional variation, WA Labor's biggest early problem was how to unite and control its divergent strands without impinging unduly on regional autonomy. This was the aim of the first Trades Union and Labor Congress of WA at Coolgardie in April 1899. The formula it came up with was to make WA a division of the ALF with separate district councils on the goldfields and the coast; a joint parliamentary committee was to co-ordinate political activity. But in practice the desired unity was a long time coming. There was a split in the powerful AWA. A group headed by Dodd and ex-New Zealand carpenter W.D. Johnson broke away and called itself the Amalgamated Miners' Association (AMA). It alleged that the AWA leadership was too political, incompetent and swayed by Catholics close to de Largie; there were also complaints that de Largie's preselection for the Senate was conducted improperly, as indeed it was. With both federal and state elections in 1901, further preselection irregularities and wrangles harmed Labor's cause. In the circumstances the success at the first federal election of four of its candidates (there were 11 WA seats) was a pleasant surprise, which reflected adversely on the cohesion of Labor's opponents: 'Happy-go-lucky individualism will have to be abandoned', frowned the anti-Labor *West Australian*. The state election was again conducted on a flagrantly distorted electoral system: electorates varied from 108 to 5805 voters. Contesting 22 of the 50 seats, Labor won six in another reasonably satisfying result, which underlined the debt WA Labor owed to 't'othersiders'. All its new MPs had arrived in WA during the 1890s, and five won goldfields seats; the exception was Subiaco councillor Henry Daglish, a tall, lean ex-Victorian public servant. The goldfields contingent comprised Scots Robert Hastie (ex-New Zealand and Victoria) and Fergie Reid (ex-Newcastle), engine driver John Reside who hailed from Bendigo, W.D. Johnson and 'Mulga' Taylor.

Johnson, in addition to his AMA activities, was the first business manager of the *Westralian Worker*, which had been launched at Kalgoorlie the previous September. 'Tell the Boys to Pull Together' was its motto, a tribute to gallant John McPherson's final message. The paper was fortunate in its early editors. The first was Shakespeare fanatic Thomas Bath, a 25-year-old NSW miner with no journalistic training but plenty of flair; when Reside died late in 1901, Bath won the Hannans by-election. He had already been succeeded as editor by Wallace Nelson, a tiny (4 ft 8 in/142 cm) bundle of energy who had edited Kidston's *People's Newspaper* in Rockhampton. Trenchantly attacking Australia's participation in the Boer War and the employment of kanakas, Nelson had nearly won a federal seat for Labor in Queensland the previous March. He was to follow Bath into the WA Assembly in 1904, but resigned from the editorial chair well before then, after finding employment by trade unionists uncongenial. Julian Stuart edited the *Worker* in lively style from 1903 to 1906, when he too went into parliament. The paper overcame early financial problems and gradually consolidated its position as Labor's mouthpiece in the West.

Forrest had transferred to federal politics, and without him the non-Labor members were a disorganized rabble. Sadly, Labor was not much better. With minority governments and a fluid parliamentary situation, there was scope for support in return for concessions, so a caucus majority decided to back the liberal governments headed by Leake and James. This was condemned by angry Labor radicals who, in a repetition of Queensland Labor's internal debate, insisted that Labor must adhere to a policy of inflexible independence. It was an ex-Queenslander within caucus, 'Mulga' Taylor, who led the hostility to parliamentary policy; he defiantly sat on the cross-benches and exchanged insults with his Labor colleagues. Caucus divisions were aggravated by the escalating conflict between the AWA and AMA. Taylor and J.B. Holman, who won a December

1901 by-election, were both members of the AWA general council which opposed the parliamentary policy; Johnson was secretary of the AMA. Most Labor MPs became ensnared in the factionalism. Under the editorship of Stuart, who had been gaoled with Taylor in 1891, the *Westralian Worker* was an uncompromising AWA supporter; it described Johnson (its initial manager) as a 'capitalistic tout' and a 'jackal' 'with an intense hatred of the AWA'. Taylor alleged that Hastie, Labor's reluctant and mediocre leader, had been corrupted by the promise of a government job. When the 1902 congress began discussing MPs' performance, Daglish led the politicians in a spirited assertion of their independence from congress; it thereupon exonerated all the Labor members, even Taylor, and decreed that caucus solidarity was only required on platform issues.

WA Labor differed little in its aims from Labor in the east. Its platform included such standard items as electoral reform, land taxation and regulation of factories. Labor's animosity to non-white labour was intense; racial hatreds on the goldfields, where Afghan camel drivers were a special target, were whipped up by Vosper (who died of appendicitis in 1901). It also sought, predictably, reform of the ramshackle mining laws prevailing on the goldfields. Compulsory arbitration was a cherished objective, which Forrest had resisted until the severe Fremantle lumpers' strike was settled by arbitration in 1899. As part of a political deal which enabled him to survive a no-confidence motion, Forrest introduced a Conciliation and Arbitration Bill in 1900. That measure was far from perfect, and Labor successfully pressed important amendments on the Leake government in 1902. But Forrest's legislation brought unions into the recognized social fabric of WA, which became the first colony to legislate for compulsory arbitration. Legislation extending workers' compensation was another pleasing achievement for WA Labor. Although socialism was commended as a Labor goal by the first congress, its absence in the platform, together with the Labor parliamentarians' indifferent display, turned many radicals towards the Social Democratic Federation, a shortlived socialist organization formed by the remarkable veteran socialist Monty Miller. Labor's fundamental problems remained unresolved:

> political organization was still quite haphazard. . .In principle, there was little opposition to the idea of a co-ordinated organization but in practice it always broke down because the small unions distrusted the big ones, the coast distrusted the goldfields, unions distrusted leagues, and nobody was prepared to delegate an atom of real power to a central body.

THROUGHOUT ITS EXISTENCE the Labor Party has been a coalition of competing, sometimes overlapping, interest groups or factions. In Labor's early years in NSW, protectionists, free traders, single taxers and socialists jostled for control of the party, and the same kind of process occurred, with significant variations, in each colony. These variations – although clearly outweighed by what Labor in each colony had in common – made the preparation of a united Labor policy for the first federal election no easy task. This was tackled in January 1900 at a conference called by NSW Labor at the *Worker*'s Sydney office, 'a longish, barn-like hall, low ceiled and not too well lighted; with bare floor and wooden benches and nothing of ornamentation'. Twenty-seven delegates attended from NSW,

Queensland, SA and Victoria. After much discussion they sensibly restricted the federal policy to items which received unanimous support. This ruled out such measures as a protectionist tariff (despite the Victorians' protest) and a citizen army. Old age pensions and electoral reform providing one adult, one vote were two of the meagre four planks. The Queenslanders' proposal for the 'total exclusion of coloured and other undesirable races' found a receptive audience. The remaining plank reflected Labor's justified unease about the constitution even before it came into operation. Labor already had plenty of experience of the frustrations inflicted on reformers by powerful upper houses, and instead of the double dissolution mechanism to resolve deadlocks between the federal houses Labor simply proposed a national referendum; this constitutional reform also adopted the Swiss procedure, whereby a proportion of the electorate could compel a national referendum on a proposed constitutional amendment.

From the outset federal politics attracted the heavyweights. This was literally true of the first federal cabinet, which included the titans Forrest, Kingston and Lyne (another, Reid, was Opposition Leader). Also in the ministry were prominent federationists Deakin and 'Toby Toss-pot' Barton, Australia's first prime minister; Turner was his miserly Treasurer. Labor, too, had many leading lights as candidates. Its six NSW successes, all former MLAs, included Watson, Watkins and Thomas. Spence won Darling, and Macdonell succeeded him in state parliament as the AWU member for those vast western plains. W.A. Holman expressed interest in Canobolas, won for Labor by Thomas Brown, but withdrew from the preselection and remained in state parliament; so did McGowen, who was defeated in South Sydney after being Labor's acting leader during the campaign. Hughes, like Queensland's highly strung 'Fighting Charlie' McDonald, vigorously opposed the final constitutional shape federation took, but once it was settled he had no doubt that the national arena was for him; he comfortably defeated a teetotaller named Beer in West Sydney. With McDonald from Queensland came Fisher and Dawson. Labor's two victors in SA (where Price was among the vanquished) were Batchelor and McGregor, and its WA Senators were Pearce and de Largie. Familiar names in Cook, Glassey, Charleston and Poynton were elected, but they were renegades.

Other talented Labor men had been elected. WA contributed two prickly loners, including a devoted friend of Ireland, Hugh Mahon. In 1881 he was gaoled in Dublin with Irish nationalists including Parnell, and as their paid agent journeyed to Australia under a false name the following year. Employed as a journalist on various newspapers, he went to the Westralian goldfields in 1895. There he displayed his flair for making enemies with a series of libel actions and spectacular feuds; the *Westralian Worker* described him as 'professedly. . .a democrat whose snobbish coldness of demeanour would make a snake shudder'. The Coolgardie MHR's caucus colleagues found his aloofness off-putting, but they were glad to have his vindictive satire in their arsenal. Labor's MHR for Perth, James Fowler, was another who lacked personal warmth; well versed in financial questions, he was often heard in parliament criticizing and complaining in a high-pitched Scottish accent. A complete contrast was amiable Fred Bamford, who strenuously upheld the north Queensland concerns of White Australia and protection for the sugar industry: 'Everyone likes Fred', said the Queensland *Worker*. Senator W.G. Higgs was a tall, solidly-built native-born socialist who had assured Sydney unionists in 1889 that parliamentary action was 'your far superior method of warfare'. He chaired the first LEL conference in

January 1892 and edited the *Australian Workman*. In 1893 he moved to Brisbane as editor of the Queensland *Worker*, which he published under the motto 'Socialism In Our Time' (discontinued by his successor) until 1899, when he entered the Queensland parliament. Victoria provided two protectionist MHRs, Scottish-born Presbyterian clergyman J.B. Ronald and felt hatter Frank Tudor, a kind-hearted pillar of the Congregational Church who, as TLC president in 1901, was a strong advocate of Labor distancing itself from the Victorian liberals. He became an indefatigable local member, always turning up to political, sporting and other community functions in his beloved Richmond.

As Labor's members gathered in Melbourne for the opening of federal parliament, they found a bizarre sight awaiting them: a tall, garishly dressed man with thick reddish-brown hair and beard, sporting a dazzling tiepin of precious stones and 'a gigantic felt hat'; with his Yankee twang, he 'suggested a three-fold compromise between a wild west romantic hero from the cattle ranches, a spruiker from Barnum's Circus, and a Western American statesman'. His name was King O'Malley. His origins are obscure, partly owing to his fundamental insecurity which led him to distort the truth and exaggerate his role in events. He apparently left America in 1888, and sold insurance in Victoria, Tasmania and probably WA, before arriving in Adelaide in 1893. He served a term in the SA Assembly, where he did not join Labor and crusaded for the abolition of barmaids and 'stagger juice' (alcohol). Defeated in 1899, he crossed to Tasmania. His showmanship went down well with Tasmania's west coast miners. But those who dismissed him as an eccentric buffoon missed the complex radical underneath, who now wanted to implement his quirky reform agenda through the Labor Party. Also hoping to join caucus although not elected as Labor candidates were miner and journalist David O'Keefe, another Tasmanian, and Queensland free trader Jim Page, easy-going yet forceful in political debate. Page had enlisted in the British army as a young artilleryman and served in South Africa; since arriving in Queensland in 1883 he had been a bricklayer, a railwayman and a publican at Barcaldine. With the acquisition of O'Malley, O'Keefe and Page, Labor had a caucus of 24. This surprised even its own supporters after its poor showing in elections for the federal conventions.

All but Mahon and Hughes were present at the inaugural meeting of the Federal Parliamentary Labor Party (FPLP) on 8 May 1901 in a stuffy room in the basement of Victorian Parliament House, the national parliament's home until 1927. McDonald, whose bush-lawyer attributes were very evident in the FPLP's early years, moved the formation of a federal party. Caucus chose Watson over Fisher for leader, acknowledging his personal qualities and his splendid work in NSW, the most advanced Labor state. Hughes was then tremendously busy with the affairs of two unions he had established, the Wharf Labourers and the Trolley, Draymen and Carters, together with the law course he – like Holman and D.R. Hall, MLA for Gunnedah from 1901 and Holman's ambitious associate – had commenced. Surprised that the leadership had been settled in his absence, Hughes swallowed his disappointment and proved a loyal and resourceful colleague for Watson. McGregor was chosen as the Senate leader. The question of the FPLP's constitution and rules was delegated to a committee, comprising McDonald, Watson, Batchelor, de Largie, Ronald and O'Keefe. The scrupulous representation of each state foreshadowed the tenacious hold which state rights were to exert on federal Labor.

This committee's recommendations were accepted by caucus. The platform was amended to include a citizen army and compulsory arbitration; the constitutional plank utilizing the referendum, which was disliked by some members from the smaller states, was omitted. In parliament Labor would clearly assert its independence and sit on the cross-benches. Caucus would meet weekly (usually on Wednesday) when parliament was sitting, and more often if required. Members had a free hand on the hot-potato question of the tariff, but on all matters relating to the platform members would be bound by the majority vote of caucus.

Support in return for concessions seemed a natural policy for the FPLP. There were (and remained until 1949) 75 House of Representatives seats and 36 Senate seats. In the lower house the Protectionists won 32, the Free Traders 27 and Labor 16 (having contested only 26), and the Senate outcome was 11 Protectionists, 17 Free Traders and 8 Labor; so the Protectionist government needed Labor's support in both houses. Support in return for concessions suited Watson's temperament, and he was experienced in implementing it. But it was not that simple. In sensibly avoiding an internal brawl over the tariff, Labor reduced its bargaining power with the other parties since, on the issue that mattered most to them, Labor could not deliver support. Furthermore, the platform-related questions, where a caucus majority could enforce a united FPLP parliamentary vote, were few. McDonald wanted the FPLP bound by majority vote of caucus on *all* questions except the tariff, but his colleagues rejected this; so the Labor members could assess much parliamentary business flexibly and independently of their caucus comrades. (The non-Labor parties too were very fluid by later standards.) The FPLP's votes were split on issues such as the Boer War and the Judiciary Bill establishing the High Court, as well as the tariff; parliament eventually authorized a compromise level of protection which satisfied none of the faithful of either fiscal persuasion. With Labor's informal support the Protectionists managed to survive until the December 1903 election.

The newly elected federal members who assembled in Melbourne, a strange city for most of them, came from different (or barely existing) state Labor parties; many had previously had no contact with Labor members beyond their own state. While there were inevitably some tensions – those flamboyant showmen Hughes and O'Malley quickly developed a mutual dislike – in general their common devotion to the cause drew them together. So did their isolation. Tudor and Ronald could go home to their families each night, but the others were without family and friends. Some moved into a boarding house together. (With long sittings and the forbidding travelling time separating WA from Melbourne, Pearce soon settled his family in Melbourne; Mahon, Hughes and Fisher later did likewise.) They relied on each other in preparing speeches on subjects new to them; staff assistance for backbench MPs was decades away. Their presence in Melbourne significantly helped Labor in Victoria, where they were big drawcards as speakers at branch meetings. Occasionally some of them travelled to Tasmania, where their assistance to the labour movement was invaluable.

Heading the list of the FPLP's revised platform was White Australia. Labor's relentless stance on this question contributed to its surprising success in Queensland – which produced seven federal members, more than any other state – and influenced the government's prompt introduction of legislation. The Immigration Restriction Act and the separate Pacific Islands Labourers Act (dealing with the gradual removal of kanakas from the Queensland sugar fields) were the first major policy acts of the federal parliament. The Immigration Restriction Bill incorporated the device of a dictation test instead of outright exclusion which, according to the British government, would jeopardize British strategic interests. Labor preferred straight-out prohibition, and Watson's amendment sought the exclusion of 'any person who is an aboriginal native of Asia, Africa or of the islands thereof'; but when the amendment failed, Labor supported the bill. During this era Labor justified White Australia by a combination of racist notions of white superiority and a desire to protect hard-won wages and working conditions. Which factor was given greater weight varied from speaker to speaker, and often – and this of course is true of politicians generally – the speakers varied their emphases on different occasions or before different audiences. 'The chief objection is entirely racial', said Pearce in this first major debate in the federal parliament. Watson's opinion was 'to a large extent tinged with considerations of an industrial nature', but even that decent, enlightened and usually tolerant man added that 'The question is whether we would desire that our sisters or our brothers should be married into any of these races to which we object'. The labour movement remained ever alert on this issue. Alleged breaches of the legislation were repeatedly discussed in caucus and frequently raised in parliament. In those days almost everyone believed in white superiority (apart from a tiny number of admirable idealists; the capitalists resisting White Australia were racist too, but cared more about increasing their profits by using cheap labour). Not all the FPLP wore racist blinkers continually. When extensions of the federal franchise were debated, Mahon and Ronald spoke up for Aboriginal rights.

Labor held its second federal conference in December 1902. The Senate-like formula for representation, six delegates from each state, remained an incongruous method for many years while Labor was fulminating against the undemocratic restrictions of the Senate and threatening to abolish it. In 1902 Tasmanian Labor, short of funds, had to include proxies from other states in its delegation; at subsequent federal conferences Tasmania was not the only state to resort to this practice. Conference resolved that all federal Labor candidates would have to pledge to withdraw if not preselected, do their utmost to implement the platform, and vote with the caucus majority on all platform questions. This closely followed the version favoured by NSW Labor, which in 1901 had enforced such a pledge on its federal candidates. In revising the platform, conference retained White Australia as the leading plank but rephrased it vigilantly as 'Maintenance of White Australia'. With adult suffrage achieved, the rest of the fighting platform comprised compulsory arbitration, old age pensions and a citizen defence force, together with some new inclusions – nationalization of monopolies, restriction of public borrowing and navigation laws.

The FPLP's commitment to the second item on its new fighting platform, compulsory arbitration, was redoubled by the dramatic Victorian railway strike in May 1903. The key figure was the Premier, the implacable conservative 'Iceberg' Irvine. He slashed the wages and downgraded the working conditions of railway workers; aggravated their discontent (already simmering, owing to earlier cutbacks and deteriorating rolling stock) with his domineering attitude; announced that railwaymen would henceforth have separate political representation; ordered rail unions to disaffiliate from the THC; and treated the week-long strike (in response to his provocation) of 1300 engine drivers, firemen and cleaners as a grave threat to the very fabric of society. Irvine and his supporters, aided and abetted by the *Age* and *Argus*, claimed that this first-ever strike by Victorian government employees was no mere industrial dispute but a mutiny against constituted authority. Recalling parliament, he introduced a savage

Strike Suppression Bill. All the small parliamentary Labor contingent could do was stonewall; by taking it in turns to speak as long as they could before succumbing to exhaustion, they prolonged debate for two days, and were still going when the strike leaders (against the strikers' wishes) called off the strike. Maloney, for example, spoke for five hours: 'Your day will come, my smooth beauty!' he yelled at Irvine.

This episode made the FPLP determined to curb the excesses of men like Irvine. Memories of the strike were still fresh when Deakin, soon to become Prime Minister with Barton's departure to the High Court, introduced the long-awaited Conciliation and Arbitration Bill. Kingston had resigned when cabinet prevented him from honouring assurances he had given to Guthrie and other unionists that the bill would improve the working conditions of seamen. An amendment by Fisher extending the bill to cover public servants was narrowly defeated, but McDonald's amendment bringing railway workers within its ambit was carried. The government reacted by hastily dropping the bill. The FPLP was stunned, and Labor opinion throughout the country was exemplified by the Kalgoorlie branch's resolution protesting against the government's 'treachery' in abandoning the bill. This resolution was forwarded by Kalgoorlie's candidate for the imminent election, 23-year-old engine driver Charlie Frazer, another 't'othersider' from Victoria. Armed with an electioneering pamphlet drafted by Mahon, the FPLP threw itself into the fray.

The results were most heartening. In the Representatives Labor so improved its position at the expense of the Protectionists that the 75 seats were divided almost equally between the three parties. In the Senate Labor also shone, winning all three seats in Queensland, SA and WA; the new Senate contained 14 Labor, 13 Free Traders and nine Protectionists. From New Zealand the Wellington TLC sent its congratulations: 'Your splendid achievement has surprised the world and ought to encourage the Workers of all countries to strenuously endeavour to accomplish like results'. Labor's Senate acquisitions included Guthrie, Queenslanders Givens and Turley, and Findley, who bounced back with a fine campaign after his expulsion from the Victorian parliament. In the Representatives Labor gained two SA members, with Poynton's return to the fold and Hutchison's arrival (greatly smoothed by Batchelor, who left a safe seat to him and defeated an ex-premier in a riskier contest). William Webster, an industrious English-born quarryman with experience in local government and state parliament, captured Gwydir (NSW). Also successful was young Frazer in Kalgoorlie; tall, handsome and confident, fond of a drink and a bet, he was a popular goldfields figure with his radicalism and firm advocacy of White Australia. His opponent, a well-known newspaperman, attributed the result to an organization so effective that Labor there 'could return a lamp post if they liked against any non-Labor man in the Commonwealth'. The contest for Melbourne, which Maloney narrowly lost, was declared void and a stormy by-election held. The victory of 'the little doctor' over a shipping magnate was greeted with great excitement in Labor ranks and anguish among the diehards ('What will they say in England!' wailed the *Argus*). Maloney was to remain MHR for Melbourne for 36 years.

'Affable Alfred' Deakin was appalled by the results. With three equal parties each resisting a coalition, government was unworkable. Deakin sympathized with some of Labor's aims but found its apparatus of caucus, pledge and conference coercive and alienating. Articulate, sensitive and cultured, he shared a friendship of mutual regard with the equally affable Watson; Pearce idolized him. After customary introspection Deakin decided to force the issue immediately, hoping to produce an environment more conducive to parliamentary alliances. He fatalistically reintroduced the Conciliation and Arbitration Bill, indicating that he would resign if an amendment was carried extending its coverage to state public servants (which he argued was unconstitutional). Fisher moved that amendment, which was carried; Deakin cheerfully resigned, and advised the Governor-General to send for Watson. At 3 pm on 23 April 1904 caucus excitedly assembled and heard their leader announce that he had accepted a commission to form a government. Watson, the compositor who during a period of low employment in his chosen trade had earned a crust shovelling manure at Government House, would be leading the first national Labor government in the world.

3 'To Lose Our Distinctness Would Mean Failure': Flirting with Alliances, 1904–1910

'TO SAY WE were astonished at finding ourselves in office', wrote Hughes, 'describes our feelings very mildly'. The FPLP was also uncertain about how to proceed as a minority government. When Watson told caucus he was Prime Minister, Higgs suggested that Watson approach Deakin about the composition of a coalition ministry containing 'at least four paid Labour Ministers'. This proposal was rejected, and an alternative motion granting Watson a free hand was carried unanimously.

That evening, a Saturday, Watson retired to his parliamentary room to select his cabinet. He asked two automatic inclusions, Hughes and the ex-SA minister Batchelor, to join in the deliberations. All too aware of their ministerial inexperience, they regretted the unavailability of Kingston, then stricken with an incapacitating and ultimately fatal illness. The FPLP's only lawyer, Hughes, was a most unlikely shrinking violet, but he had qualified for the Bar so recently that he declined the portfolio of Attorney-General. For a well-credentialled lawyer Watson turned to H.B. Higgins, a Deakinite Victorian liberal; this fearless opponent of the Boer War frequently infuriated conservatives with his radicalism and individualism. He was the only person ever to serve in a national Labor ministry without being a party member. McGregor and Fisher were unsurprising inclusions. Another Senator was required and, although Pearce had made a fine impression, Watson reluctantly opted for experience in the form of Dawson, the former Queensland leader and fleeting premier. Dawson's parliamentary absences had caused concern; his health problems had worsened in the Melbourne climate, and so had his heavy drinking. Watson gave him Defence, an ironic sequel to his strident criticism of Australian involvement against the Boers. For the final place Watson wanted a West Australian and, although Fowler pressed his claims personally, Watson preferred the undoubted, if chilly, ability of Mahon. McGregor, almost blind, was unsuited to the detailed administration of a department, but the roles of Vice-President of the Executive Council and government spokesman in the Senate neatly complemented his unique talents. At the swearing-in the following Wednesday, having memorized what his colleagues had just read aloud, McGregor stunned onlookers by reciting it perfectly. That night, elated but exhausted, External Affairs minister Hughes returned to his lodgings and fell asleep on the couch, only to be rudely awakened by a posse of pressmen wanting to know what he proposed to do about a New Guinea 'massacre'.

Some Australians regarded a national Labor government as unthinkable. Fancy a nation's affairs being in the hands of a compositor, whose ministry included miners, a labourer and, horror of horrors, an Irish fanatic! 'It will exist entirely on sufferance', sniffed the *Argus*, and 'has no claim to an extended life'. The sight of the new ministers occupying the Treasury benches reduced Forrest to apoplexy: 'Mr Speaker, what are these men doing in our places? Those are our seats', expostulated the Westralian dinosaur. He and others outraged by a Labor government lost no time in plotting to remove it, despite Deakin's assurances of 'the utmost fair play'. The government looked very vulnerable. Watson reopened in caucus the question of an alliance with the more radical Protectionists and, after prolonged debate at several caucus meetings, on 26 May the FPLP voted 24 to 8 in favour of a coalition. Watson wrote to Deakin proposing an alliance. But the Protectionists themselves were split on the issue, and Deakin replied that a coalition was impossible in 'present circumstances'.

So the Labor government battled on alone. As it continued to administer the affairs of state, Australians became accustomed to the idea of a national Labor government; this was an important achievement, but as he fruitlessly laboured day and night to find a way to enshrine Labor objectives in legislation, even Watson became exasperated: 'I despair of seeing any good come out of this Parliament', he told Higgins. The Conciliation and Arbitration Bill lurched along, with Watson making unwilling concessions rather than abandoning the measure altogether; but when an amendment was carried against the government on the question of preference to unionists, Watson gratefully and honourably relinquished his burden by resigning on 17 August, having discussed the situation with caucus beforehand. Unionists expressed their satisfaction with this principled action. While O'Malley was relieved, having felt 'muzzled' as a government backbencher, some Labor members were angered by the technical parliamentary ruse adopted to narrowly defeat the government on an issue vital to it. In the ensuing histrionics Hughes led the way; his performance, according to Deakin, resembled 'the ill-bred urchin whom one sees dragged from a tart-shop, kicking and screaming as he goes'.

Labor's internal debate about the wisdom of alliances resumed in earnest. The Protectionists continued to be split, with their conservatives sinking the fiscal issue and embracing Reid's Free Traders; four were rewarded with portfolios in the new Reid ministry. The radical Protectionists, however, were closer to Labor and had four meetings with caucus in September and October 1904 to discuss an alliance. Articles of Alliance were drawn up and published. The platform was similar to Labor's own, but the labour movement found the conditions of alliance, involving reciprocal organizational support and electoral immunity, disturbing. The frustrations of Labor MPs charged with the task of securing Labor objectives in unworkable parliamentary circumstances cannot be denied, but the party organizations and rank and file tended to take the longer view. In their eyes Labor was clearly on the march, 'the coming party', and Labor parliamentary majorities were just around the corner. They saw pacts of electoral immunity as shortsighted stupidity, especially as the seats held by the (mostly Victorian) radical Protectionists were precisely the ones Labor could most easily capture. The state Labor organizations controlled federal preselections, and the FPLP coalitionists derived no comfort from the Victorian executive's prompt announcement that it 'in no way' endorsed the alliance and refused to consider electoral immunity. As in May, hostility to the alliance came from a tenacious caucus minority. Fowler aired his opposition defiantly in parliament, and Frazer unsuccessfully moved that coalitionists sign the alliance individually rather than Watson sign on behalf of the whole caucus.

During the Watson government's struggles the labour movement was uplifted by a sudden thunderbolt from across the Nullarbor. At the WA state election Labor confounded all expectations by winning 22 of the 50 seats. Labor's campaign had managed to disguise its organizational weaknesses and was reasonably cohesive – that stormy petrel 'Mulga' Taylor, 'having issued one tremendous blast against the parliamentary leaders, then fell silent' – but more crucial to Labor's success was the James government's removal of the worst electoral distortions. To remain premier, James needed support from most of the 10 independents, but this was denied him and Labor took office on 10 August. The euphoria overlooked the difficulties. Labor had no guaranteed parliamentary majority, Premier Daglish had little experience of leadership, and none of his team were seasoned MPs. Furthermore, the constitution required a minister from the Council, where Labor was unrepresented; Daglish chose J.M. Drew, the Catholic editor of the well-known *Geraldton Express*, the 'scourge of injustice, the scourge of inhumanity, the scourge of the oppressors of the poor'. Drew accepted the Lands ministry, but appalled Labor supporters by announcing that he would not join the party or support Labor policy in significant areas, including the abolition of the Council and aspects of his portfolio. Also in the cabinet were Johnson, Hastie, J.B. Holman, Taylor and the new MLA for East Fremantle (where he had settled in 1892), Cornish carpenter W.C. Angwin, a diligent terrier.

Daglish's shortcomings as a Labor leader were soon apparent. He did not possess the political acumen, personal warmth or integral commitment to Labor principles which would have compensated for his lack of a solid grounding in the union movement. A coastal public servant, he presided over a cabinet containing leaders of both the feuding goldfields unions. Some of the independents deserted Labor, deliberately denying the government the necessary majority to implement its policy in the Assembly; any reforms reaching the Council suffered further rough treatment. Daglish seemed too easily intimidated by these testing circumstances. Alarmed by his first impressions of the government's financial position, without consulting anybody he delivered a keynote speech which referred to the necessity for a 'mark time policy'. Labor enthusiasts were devastated.

The situation deteriorated when a delegation of union secretaries was simply refused a hearing by Holman, and unionists were further outraged when the government reappointed an Arbitration Court judge who was no friend of the workers. A joint committee set up in Fremantle to enable MPs and union leaders to maintain regular contact collapsed: the MPs dismissed it as an impertinence, and the goldfields unions saw it as attempted coastal control of the party. The government limped into 1905. In March three backbenchers announced that if the government failed to improve they would consider crossing the floor to remove it. One of them, Nelson, was now editing a new coastal Labor paper, the *Democrat*; its pages echoed the *Westralian Worker*'s condemnation of the ineffectual ministry. Daglish resorted to a heavyhanded ministerial reshuffle, dropping Taylor and Holman and promoting Bath and an Irishman, Paddy Lynch, who seemed intimidating with his strong build, fierce black beard and aggressive florid oratory but in fact was 'artless and friendly', 'the gentlest man imaginable'.

WA Labor's chaotic organization was embarrassingly revealed at the 1905 inter-state conference when seven WA delegates were endorsed instead of six and Mahon had to withdraw. When parliament resumed in July the opposition moved a no-confidence motion. Daglish contemplated a coalition, initially with some independents and then, incredibly, with the opposition, but no alliance proved possible. On 17 August Daglish notified the Assembly that the government intended to purchase a railway company for £1 500 000. This amount was so excessive that there were howls of rage from Daglish's audience, Labor back-benchers included; a vote on the issue was humiliatingly lost by the government on the voices without a division. Daglish announced his ministry's resignation on 22 August and stepped down as Labor leader, admitting that he had never approved of the party pledge. The October election, which saw Labor's MPs decline to 14 with Johnson and Angwin among the defeated, completed 'an inglorious episode' for the party.

Reconstruction took two years. A recession produced a decline in union membership figures, which facilitated a number of union mergers during 1906–7; even the AWA and AMA buried the hatchet. The longstanding friction between the goldfields and coastal Labor also eased. The time the goldfields MPs spent in Perth helped them to break down the barriers of mutual suspicion; as well, miners began drifting to the coast and elsewhere as the extraordinary mining boom at last slackened. Pearce was approached to lead the party out of its slump, but preferred to stay in federal politics. Instead caucus turned to Bath. Widely admired, trusted, and with 'an impeccable union background', he served the party well and his capable leadership enhanced the healing process. He had become a farmer, which helped Labor's cause in the country. Significant structural changes were ratified at the 1907 congress, which unified the movement in WA under an amended version of the ALF scheme. A triennial general council became the supreme body. The central executive comprised officials appointed by the general council and representatives from the district councils. Each of these councils consisted of unions and political branches, and selected, endorsed and financed election candidates in its district. In no other state did Labor integrate its political and industrial wings so completely, and the WA division of the ALF functioned so effectively that its structure was hardly altered for over half a century.

Between 1902 and 1909 the celebrated English socialist Tom Mann visited all Australian states and New Zealand, and the various labour movements benefited significantly from his enthusiasm, famous oratory and organizational expertise. This applied especially to Victoria, where Mann was tremendously influential as the PLC's organizer, 'helping to expand it from a small, beleaguered Melbourne-based party to a state-wide organization with significant parliamentary representation'. (Although electoral anomalies limited Labor's gains in state seats, federally the PLC's improvement became clearly evident.) Mann's colleagues in the revitalization of the PLC included the remarkable Harry Scott Bennett, another marvellous socialist orator and one of the finest crusaders for enlightenment and the underprivileged Australia has known. He served a term in the Victorian Assembly as a hard-working Labor MP, using his railway pass to travel throughout the state educating Victorians about socialism, before deciding that he could no longer stomach the compromises involved in parliamentary politics.

Other forces were at work in the Victorian PLC. John Wren's horse Murmur won the 1904 Caulfield Cup in a race that was rumoured to have been rigged by the winning owner. When some 500 members and friends gathered at Wren's

Tattersall's Club to celebrate the win, Labor politicians were conspicuous; Dawson proposed Wren's health and Findley responded on Wren's behalf. Also that year a Melbourne security guard, C. Crowe, discovered that corrupt policemen involved in burglary had escaped prosecution because of Wren's powerful connections. Crowe tried to have the matter investigated without success, and in printed circulars attributed his failure to Wren's influence with Labor politicians and control of party branches near his tote. In December 1904, two months after Murmur's win, Crowe was bashed senseless by assailants wielding iron bars. He had no doubt who had sent them.

Developments in Queensland had proceeded just as Kidston had planned. The 'continuous ministry' had fallen, and its replacement was a coalition in which Labor was represented by Browne and himself. The previous Speaker, Morgan, was Premier, and his government included other moderate liberals and disgruntled 'continuous ministry' supporters whom Kidston had persuaded to defect. Caucus was reluctant to sanction any entanglement in a formal coalition, and influential individuals outside caucus such as Hinchcliffe, Reid and Boote were even more wary. But they were placated by Browne's declaration that Labor would maintain its autonomy and freedom to detach itself from the coalition once the desperately desired electoral reforms were attained. Browne's portfolios, Mines and Public Works, complemented his background and interests. Kidston quickly showed that he was a more capable Treasurer than any of his predecessors; after the exodus of Queensland MPs to federal politics, he was 'a giant among pygmies' in the state parliament. Labor's two ministers resigned from caucus, which continued to meet separately although Labor MPs also attended coalition meetings. The new Labor leader was Lancashire-born schoolteacher Peter Airey. His prominence in teacher union campaigns for higher wages had reputedly been punished by a departmental posting to Hughenden in 1901. Airey had a secret career as a writer, contributing frequently to the *Bulletin* and other periodicals under such pseudonyms as 'Philander Flam'. A fine speaker, he was promoted into the ministry after Browne's death in April 1904. Kidston had wanted McDonnell as the new minister, hoping to boost Labor's popularity among Catholics, but not even Kidston could get his way all the time. McDonnell also had his supporters for the vacated party leadership, but Kerr, a Methodist Freemason, resented the sectarian overtones involved. 'I have never dragged my religion into the party', he told Fisher, 'and I am not going to stand them doing it', so he contested the leadership himself, and won it.

Despite Kidston's endeavours the coalition had a shaky majority in the Assembly until the 1904 election, when Labor won 34 of the 72 seats. Kidston was not tempted to proceed alone; he insisted that Labor's electoral base remained weak, and it was imperative to remain in coalition until the electoral reforms were carried. He did not even claim increased ministerial representation as a result of the changed parliamentary numbers of the coalition partners, or the premiership for himself. Airey pushed through the electoral reforms immediately, but the Council rejected them on a technicality. On the second attempt the government threatened the non-elected Council that it would be swamped with reformist appointees if it continued to resist. The Council gave way, and at last Queensland emerged from the Dark Ages in electoral arrangements. No longer would women be prevented from voting in state elections; postal voting was allowed and plural voting abolished.

The party resumed its debate about the wisdom of coalitions. Kidston argued that coalition with Morgan had produced a public works programme to boost

5. Tommy Dodd, a disciple of direct action. His perpetual sore throat from too much public speaking was so well-known that wherever he went comrades would ask him 'How's the throat, Tommy?' (*Mitchell Library*)

6. The Dawson ministry, 1899, the first Labor government in the world, leaving Government House after the swearing-in. (*Oxley Library*)

Religion in Politics!

A WESLEYAN MINISTER'S WARNING.

Speaking at the **Wesleyan Church, Coolgardie**, on Sunday evening, 24th March, 1901, the Rev. MR. POOLE, Wesleyan clergyman, reminded all his hearers of their duty at the Federal Election on Friday, and exhorted them to

Vote For Protestant Candidates

only. It was a noticeable fact that Catholic countries had retrograded, whereas those countries ruled by Protestant statesmen were the most progressive and prosperous in the world. If Australia was to go ahead, it was necessary that

Catholics Should Be Excluded

rigidly from Parliament, and from all positions where they could influence the government of the country.

7. Some of the delegates at the 1900 intercolonial Labor conference. Queenslanders J. Lesina, A. Hinchcliffe, W. G. Higgs, C. McDonald and J. C. Stewart are standing at the back; South Australians W. H. Carpenter and T. Price and Victorians J. Barrett and J. Hyman are seated, with NSW MLC J. Hepher standing beside them; squatting at the front are NSW delegates J. Thomas, J. McGowen, W. M. Hughes and J. C. Watson. (*National Library*)

8. A brochure used in the unsuccessful attempt to prevent Hugh Mahon from winning Coolgardie at the inaugural federal election in 1901. (*National Library*)

9. The FPLP, 1901. Back (from left): C. McDonald, G. Pearce, J. Thomas, J. Page, J. Fowler, J. Barrett, D. O'Keefe. Centre: D. Watkins, T. Brown, K. O'Malley, H. Mahon, W. G. Higgs, A. Fisher, H. de Largie, F. Bamford. Front (seated): W. G. Spence, A. Dawson, G. McGregor, J. C. Watson, J. C. Stewart, E. L. Batchelor, J. B. Ronald. Front (on floor): F. Tudor, W. M. Hughes. (*National Library*)

10. The Watson ministry, 1904, Australia's first national Labor government. Standing (from left): E. L. Batchelor, A. Dawson, A. Fisher, H. Mahon, W. M. Hughes. Seated: G. McGregor, J. C. Watson, H. B. Higgins. (*National Library*)

11. Frank Anstey (left) and Charlie McGrath promoting Labor's cause in rural Victoria. (*National Library*)

12. Tom Price. (*Old Parliament House*)

employment, fairer taxation and electoral systems, and further reforms were possible. Why jeopardize this with a leap into the unknown? Because Labor had to be true to its fundamental beliefs, replied the voluble Clermont MLA Joe Lesina, a 'nervy, restless dark little man of passing good looks' who was a self-appointed guardian of Labor principles. Bowman shared Lesina's views about the coalition if not his erratic individualism; back in parliament as McDonnell's fellow member for Fortitude Valley, Bowman acted both as a link between caucus and the organization's anti-coalitionists and, within caucus, as a focus for the anti-coalitionist MPs. Whereas the friendly, likeable Bowman had found a seat he held until his death, his close colleague Reid, the feared enforcer, lost in Toowong again in 1904 and was then defeated at a 1905 by-election; these setbacks hardened his resolve as Labor's zealous watchdog, merciless when he detected any straying from 'straight Labor' ideals. Hinchcliffe, meanwhile, wanted to give up one of his jobs after finding the management of Queensland's 1903 federal election campaign too exhausting even for him. He resigned as CPE secretary but was persuaded to continue, only to find himself with yet another job when Kidston arranged for him to become one of the first Labor MLCs. The ALF was delighted, but if Kidston thought this might moderate Hinchcliffe's grave misgivings about the coalition, he was mistaken. Boote, too, eyed Kidston warily: 'Intellectually he is worth a busload of some of the men who represent us and as a politician he is probably animated by the best intentions in the world'. However, Boote felt that the 'enervating' coalition had distracted Labor from its socialist 'essence'.

Boote foreshadowed the mood of the 1905 Labor-in-Politics convention:

> The movement must become consciously socialistic. . .It must drop all pretensions to be statesmanlike and continue to be agitative. Discontent is still the divine gospel; we are all damned as soon as we congratulate ourselves.

Reid and Hinchcliffe had organized the convention numbers well. The convention authorized a number of changes, including a tighter pledge, and acted to curb the tendency of politicians to get on to executives which were initially intended to control them. The most controversial innovation came after a 12-hour debate on the collective ownership of monopolies as a proposed long-term objective when Reid moved an amendment replacing 'monopolies' by 'the means of production, distribution and exchange'. Kidston and Airey spoke against the amendment but, not being credentialled delegates, could not vote. When the amendment was carried 28 to 10, Queensland Labor had a socialist objective. Kerr was aghast. He refused nomination as CPE president, a post traditionally held by the parliamentary leader; Reid filled the presidential vacancy. Kerr and Kidston drafted a statement criticizing the objective and calling for another more representative convention; it was released, as intended, to the press on behalf of all Labor MPs, but only after caucus divided 24 to 10 on the wisdom of this step. The objective 'will infallibly drive away' loyal Labor supporters, claimed the statement; it will also put at risk Labor's benefits from 'prudent alliances'. The call for another convention fell on deaf ears, and the effect of the statement was to distance Kidston, Kerr and their caucus supporters from the CPE and anti-coalitionists in the branches. The statement spoke of 'avoiding a fatal division in our own ranks', but only made such an eventuality more likely. The situation was 'very unsatisfactory', observed Fisher's Gympie friend Tom Dunstan. 'If care is not taken, there may be a bad split.'

NSW Labor also debated the question of an objective at its 1905 conference. Cann proposed a socialist objective, but a sub-committee comprising Cann, Watson, Holman, Griffith, Welsh-born barman J.J. Morrish, Rae and Gardiner recommended a two-part non-socialist objective, which conference accepted:

1 The cultivation of an Australian sentiment based upon the maintenance of racial purity, and the development in Australia of an enlightened and self-reliant community.
2 The securing of the full results of their industry to all producers by the collective ownership of monopolies, and the extension of the industrial and economic functions of the State and Municipality.

This formulation reflected the continued dominance of moderates in the PLL. The 1904 state election had confirmed Labor's electoral progress – it now had 25 members (up one in an Assembly reduced from 125 to 90) and 23% of the overall vote (18·7% in 1901). At the conference a succession of delegates attributed this improvement to Labor's 'practical work' and downgrading of 'theories'. With NSW's non-Labor government tainted by corruption in land dealings – which Gardiner in particular pursued vigorously in parliament – Labor was confident of making further electoral inroads. Holman calculated that his party could realistically aim at an Assembly majority at the election after next, but only after a thorough organizational campaign, especially in country electorates. He was already applying his abundant gifts to this onerous task.

The 1905 PLL conference discussed Catholic concerns about socialism. In view of the continued growth in Catholic support for Labor, placating Catholic sensibilities was increasingly important to the party. Some devout Catholics were troubled when papal encyclicals expressed attitudes hostile to socialism. At the conference Watson soothingly explained that the papal remarks referred not to Labor's brand of socialism but to the altogether different 'demolishers of society' in Europe. The Catholic *Freeman's Journal* agreed, as did Cardinal Moran.

Prime Minister Reid had been searching for an issue, as free trade seemed a lost cause in federal politics. He seized on this episode as an opportunity to take the initiative with a cynical campaign against the evils of socialism. Reid was no reader – he had never heard of Henry Lawson or 'Banjo' Paterson – and instructed his secretary to extract material for the campaign from all the books on socialism he could find; the secretary found the arguments so compelling that he was converted to socialism. In the hallowed tradition of conservative scare campaigns, Reid depicted Labor as a socialist tiger about to burst from its cage and wreak havoc, threatening religion, marriage and the family home. (McGowen, Labor's leader in NSW for over a decade, was happily married with eight children and had been Sunday school superintendent at his Redfern church for 32 years.) Reid was untroubled when reminded that as NSW Premier he had enjoyed the support of these terrible socialists and introduced legislation to please them. He was, however, miffed when Cardinal Moran attacked Reid's campaign, claiming that Australia's great enemy was 'not socialism. . .but imperial jingoism'. Despite a friendly press and large financial backing, Reid was countered effectively by rejoinders like Watson's:

The very people who objected to socialism were immersed in it. They rode in socialistic railways, sent their children to socialistic schools, received their letters through a

socialistic post-office, read them by a socialistic light, rang up their friends on a socialistic telephone, washed in socialistic baths, read in socialistic libraries, and if through
studying the advantages of individualism they became insane, they retired to a socialistic lunatic asylum.

In July 1905 the third interstate Labor conference adopted a federal objective.
Watson proposed the NSW version, which he said was consistent with Labor's
history of not 'crying for the moon' but accepting 'what was practical and immediate'. Queensland's Turley criticized the NSW objective as a 'hybrid' aimed
at 'catching votes'; Scott Bennett objected to its emphasis on Australian sentiment and racial purity, and felt Labor should acknowledge it was 'part and parcel
of the world-wide Socialist movement'. No other delegate mentioned this aspect.
Queensland and Victoria proposed socialist objectives. Macdonell of the AWU
was reluctant to endorse any objective at all. The NSW objective won the day; its
only opponents were Queenslanders and Victorians.

Two delegates abstained from voting. One was the conference chairman, Prendergast; the other was the first female representative at an interstate conference,
Lilian Locke. A clergyman's daughter who wrote poetry, she had organized in SA
and Tasmania as well as Victoria, where she had worked with Tom Mann (who
was an honoured guest at the conference), and briefly succeeded him as PLC
organizer after his resignation; she was to marry the Tasmanian MHA George
Burns. As a Tasmanian delegate at the 1905 conference she was supposed to
support the NSW objective, but this 'would be untrue to her Socialistic propaganda work' so she abstained. Her other contributions at the conference included
a motion upholding the principle of 'civil equality of women and men', and an
appropriate rocket blasting the Victorian parliament for being the only Australian legislature still denying women the vote.

The conference debate on the vexed question of alliances had a dramatic
immediacy. On 22 June Watson had confidentially encouraged Deakin to remove G.H. Reid:

> You can rely on our active support, and I think our people would prefer that to joining
> in a coalition. We, and especially myself, don't want office, but I have the utmost
> anxiety to stop the retrogressive movement which Reid is heading. . .

On the 28th Watson and Deakin had discussed how to commit Labor to supporting a new Deakin government without getting Watson into trouble with
Labor's anti-coalitionists at the imminent conference. Reid wanted a dissolution
of parliament; instead, Deakin was granted a commission on his assurance that
whereas during the previous Deakin government he had learned Labor's intentions 'only from day to day', now Watson had promised him 'a cordial and
generous support for this Parliament' and 'a pledge of cooperation in both
Houses'. On 5 July a caucus majority carried Watson's motion that the FPLP
give the Deakin government 'general support during this Parliament'. Six days
later at the conference Victorian PLC secretary Patrick Heagney moved that the
FPLP pledge be amended to prevent caucus from forming any alliance not ratified beforehand by a special interstate conference. Those intransigent anti-
coalitionists Fowler and Frazer supported the motion. Watson replied that the
alliance with the Protectionists 'had more than justified itself'; while the organizations had undisputed charge of policy, platform and preselections, they had
no business dictating parliamentary tactics to the politicians. Spence, O'Malley

and O'Keefe supported their leader. Tense Queensland divisions on the issue were exposed. Kerr declared that 'the idea of the inside party having to refer to an outside organization was absurd'; Turley, Fisher, Hinchcliffe and Mat Reid, however, considered that alliances were certainly unjustifiable when they extended 'beyond the then existing Parliament', and an amendment to this effect, coupled with Pearce's addition disallowing electoral immunity to coalition partners, was carried.

Frazer was involved in another conference motion which disturbed Watson. The young West Australian's main preoccupation in parliament had been poring over legal textbooks; undaunted by his inexperience, he had occasionally risen to vilify Labor's opponents. The goldfields labour movement wanted the selection of Labor ministers subject to the fundamental Labor principles of equality and decision-making by the majority – a radical departure from the conventional practice of the government leader choosing the cabinet – and Frazer (as the goldfields representative) had proposed this to caucus and again at the conference. His motion was eventually carried, but only after Lilian Locke suggested, as a compromise, that the ministers be recommended (instead of selected) by caucus.

Later in July Watson staggered the FPLP by asking to be relieved of the leadership. If 'given no greater voice' in selecting ministers 'than the rawest recruit in the Party', he wrote, tilting clearly at Frazer, 'I most decidedly could not continue to lead'. That conference resolution was 'a censure upon myself. . . and it was particularly hard to find it supported by several' FPLP members. The pressures of leadership in the unwieldy parliamentary situation were telling, he had health problems and there was minimal administrative assistance to lighten his load. After his caucus colleagues inundated him with generous assurances of support and admiration and urged him to continue, he withdrew his resignation. Maloney proposed that there should be a deputy leader to assist Watson, and suggested Fisher, who was duly appointed.

The same caucus meeting which persuaded Watson not to resign discussed the pleasing developments in SA. The ULP's poor showing in 1902 had caused a painful review of its ineffective organization and selection of candidates, its indulgence in allowing MPs to determine the platform themselves, and its almost non-existent rural base. The party was transformed in 1904. That year saw its first annual conference, held deliberately during the Adelaide Show to encourage country delegates to attend. With conference made the supreme decision-making body and the party placed in control over its MPs, the ULP's structure was now on more traditional Labor lines. The commitment to attract rural support was confirmed: three of the seven planks in the fighting platform covered country concerns. As leader, Price was all in favour of the rural drive, and ULP radicals wary of any weakening of Labor's working-class purity were further upset by Price's co-operative approach to employers. In his 1905 policy speech Price told the electorate that the ULP 'would not be frightened by the nonsense' of Reid's socialist tiger, but would pursue its 'policy of. . .development and progress. . . prosperity and honest government'. At the election Labor trebled its 1902 Assembly representation with 15 members (11 of the 12 metropolitan seats, and four in the country). 'Dismal Dick' Butler's conservative government now had 18 supporters, and there was a group of eight liberals under A.H. Peake. Price and Peake commenced negotiations, and found they had sufficient common ground to form a government. On 26 July Price was sworn in as Premier.

The ULP gave its esteemed leader a free hand in his arrangements with Peake, and the two leaders agreed that Labor and Peake's group would each provide two ministers. Price – not caucus – chose Kirkpatrick as the other ULP minister; both resigned from caucus, which elected Archibald as its new leader. Price made it clear that the ULP was not bound as a party to the coalition. 'The Labor Party accepts no responsibility for ministerial actions', explained the *Weekly Herald*.

SA politics were soon dominated once again by the Legislative Council. Labor's platform now sought abolition of the Council or, 'failing that, Adult Suffrage for both Houses'. Peake could not be enticed to go further than a moderate reduction in the property qualification required of voters. A bill to reduce this qualification to £15 annual rental was treated as contemptuously by the Council as other Price government reforms. Price refused to accept this situation, resigned and obtained a dissolution. The election in November 1906, which was fought on the issue of Council reform, saw Labor improve further with a clean sweep in metropolitan seats and 19 members in all. Peake's liberals won 10 seats. Despite its success at the polls the government found itself as hamstrung as before by the Council. A compromise unfolded, granting a Council vote to certain occupational groups (including postmasters, stationmasters and ministers of religion) and to other adults paying £17 rent. This compromise satisfied Peake, but it was well short of Labor's policy; caucus was disgruntled when Price accepted it as an 'instalment of the great reform they were looking for'.

Price was an able and popular Premier, but criticism was inevitable in view of the sabotage of the Council and the constraints imposed by his less reformist coalition partner. Price was active in education, controversially appointing a zealous reformer as director of education and backing him to the hilt. His 1906 Factories Act introduced wages boards, which were welcomed by the unions. He decisively reversed the Butler government's plan to surrender Adelaide's transport system to private enterprise, and successfully modernized its trams with an electrified system; even here he was hampered by the Council, which disallowed aspects of his scheme affecting the financial interests of wealthy MLCs. Price sensibly ceded administration of the Northern Territory, which had long been an economic burden on SA, to the federal government. Price's upbringing was evident in his reforms regarding the supply of alcohol and the control and care of drunkards. He also provoked predictable howls by persistently advocating that a South Australian should be the next state Governor; the British government refused to co-operate.

Prime Minister Reid was still busy flogging his socialist tiger throughout the country. Challenged to debate the question of socialism in the Labor Party, Reid refused unless NSW Labor nominated an accredited speaker. Holman was their unsurprising choice. The debate was held in Sydney's Centenary Hall on two successive evenings in April 1906. Reid, 'portlier than ever, was past his best but still formidable and a favourite of Sydney'. His campaign had received much press attention; the debate attracted capacity crowds and huge nationwide interest. Holman was aware that his performance would affect Labor's prospects, and 'prepared for the event like a prize-fighter'. There was no vote or formal winner, but Holman's superb display brought congratulations from all over Australia. Labor reaped the rewards at the federal election in December. After a stirring campaign by Hughes, whose 'verbal pyrotechnics. . .tore Reid's exaggerations to shreds', Labor captured four seats from Reid's party in NSW alone.

The election left the overall situation unchanged. Labor entered the new parliament with 26 seats (up one) in the Representatives. In the Senate Labor had five new members, making 15 Senators in all. Deakin's Protectionists lost some support to become the weakest of the three major parties, but Deakin continued in office after encouragement to do so from Watson. The FPLP had publicly announced the names of 11 Protectionists who deserved electoral immunity, but not all of them received it.

Deakin, the MHR for Ballarat, was not included in this list of 11 Protectionists, but Watson considered that Labor would be making 'a great mistake' if it opposed him. Labor Party feeling in Ballarat, however, was strongly against electoral immunity – the East Ballarat branch had already sent the FPLP a protest against the alliance – and they were determined to run a candidate against Deakin. They chose a local grocer, Jim Scullin, who had made a name for himself as a debater; born in Victoria of Irish farming stock, Scullin was an avid reader, especially of Irish writers, and was active in the Catholic Young Men's Society. During the campaign he had good support from Anstey, their friend Charles 'Bull' McGrath (a local MLA), the local campaign organizer Arch Stewart of the AWU, and from an unlikely quarter – the newly elected British Labour MP Ramsay MacDonald, then on an Australian tour – but he lost convincingly.

Poor results in Queensland prevented Labor from progressing further in 1906, and Dawson was at the centre of its Senate campaign shambles. He was uncertain whether or not to stand again, and the Queensland CPE had misgivings about re-endorsing him. In the end he stood as an independent and finished last, but split the Labor vote; the preselected trio (including the talented Higgs) all lost. It was an inglorious exit, but worse was to follow; the ex-miner whose name was taught to generations of Queensland schoolchildren as 'the first Labor premier in the world' died in July 1910 of alcoholism.

But Dawson's waywardness was not the main reason why Labor lost three Queensland MHRs as well as missing out in the Senate. While 'Dawson cut into our vote considerably', Watson observed, the 'real trouble. . .lay in the dissensions among the members of the local Labor party'. Kidston had become an increasingly divisive figure. Now Premier (since Morgan's resignation in January 1906), Kidston delivered a pre-election speech at Rockhampton in February 1907 confirming his commitment to Labor's reforms but insisting that the MPs pledge themselves to him alone and not the party. Such delusions of grandeur were intolerable to Mat Reid. With his henchmen Hinchcliffe and Bowman he made swift and thorough preparations for the Labor-in-Politics convention the following month. Fisher attended the convention and supported the anti-Kidston majority, which by 36 to six carried the crucial amendment binding all Labor candidates to the platform and disallowing any other obligation. 'To lose our distinctness would mean failure', Reid told the delegates in a blistering presidential address which remains a classical exhortation by a principled militant contemptuous of opportunist politicians.

'The parting of the ways has been reached', thundered Reid, 'and each will have to decide for himself'. Many Labor Queenslanders and most of the MPs (including Kerr and Airey) sided with Kidston, as the severe split that had long threatened became a painful reality. At the May election the Kidstonites and the endorsed Labor candidates hurled abuse at each other. Not surprisingly, Labor's vote plummeted; in the 72-member Assembly only 18 Labor MPs were elected (34 in 1904). Labor under Bowman sat resolutely on the cross-benches, supporting a minority Kidston government reluctantly and only as a lesser evil than the conservatives. Parliamentary hostilities deepened the schism. When even Kidston's imperturbable reformism was blunted by Council obstruction, and his approaches for an alliance with Labor were firmly rejected, he felt driven into the arms of the conservatives. This union inflicted its own pressures on a restless reformer and, in 1911, still Premier, he retired from politics. Labor gradually regained ground, winning 27 seats at the 1909 state election, but this was not fast enough for some Labor people, especially those who blamed Reid for the split; in their eyes he was an inflexible 'ogre. . .who stood between Labor and success'. In 1909 Reid objected to Lesina's re-endorsement and, when overruled by a majority of the CPE, suddenly resigned all his positions in the party.

> For him, twenty years of service. . . had produced little. He had been the hardest working and most effective organizer, bringing shufflers and trimmers to heel, codifying the rules and constitution, and maintaining the pristine purity of Labor principles. . .yet he remained one of the least popular men in the party. His resignation was accepted with barely a ripple of comment.

'No man rendered greater service to the infant Labour Party' was Boote's later verdict.

The popular and influential Victorian Socialist Party (VSP) originated as a social questions committee formed in May 1905 by Tom Mann, J.P. Jones and others to investigate unemployment in Melbourne. By March 1906, when it changed its name and began publishing the *Socialist* edited by Mann, it already boasted 758 members. Mann was no longer the PLC's organizer, but his faith in the Labor Party as a vehicle for socialism remained intact. The VSP was not aiming to oppose the PLC, but to act 'as a ginger-group for socialism'. Accordingly, it was not unusual for socialists like Frank Hyett and John Curtin to be active in both parties simultaneously. Born in Ballarat and brought up in Melbourne's inner suburbs, Hyett had only a rudimentary schooling and became a clerk. Curtin's path was similar. Son of an Irish Catholic policeman, he grew up close to Ballarat in another goldfields centre, Creswick, home of Spence and the artistic Lindsay family. His father's chronic rheumatism necessitated premature retirement and young Jack, after a basic and undistinguished education, supported his family (now in Melbourne) in a succession of menial jobs, including stints as an *Age* copy-boy and messenger for the Lindsays' Bohemian rag the *Rambler*. Curtin and Hyett were voracious readers and passionate sporting enthusiasts; both played first-grade football for Brunswick. After they met at a Brunswick PLC function, they became the closest of friends. Like thousands of others, they had been inspired by Mann's socialist oratory; their particular hero and friend was Anstey. Under his guidance they refined their ideas and developed into outstanding crusaders, adept at oratory and pamphleteering. Curtin was sensitive, complex, and prone to wildly fluctuating mood swings; 'Hell-fire Hyett', three years older, was physically and emotionally tougher. Hyett married Ethel Gunn, sister of their friend and VSP colleague Jack Gunn, and Curtin poured out his hopes and dreams in a protracted correspondence with another sister, Jessie.

By 1907 the VSP was the most important socialist organization in Australia with a membership approaching 2000. Family involvement was actively encouraged with socials, dances, picnics and camps; it even had its own band, football team and Sunday school. There were regular lectures, debates, pamphlets, educational courses and spruiking sessions at the Yarra Bank. When a VSP trio including Hyett and Curtin debated socialism against a group of anti-socialists, the VSP speakers 'wiped the floor with us', as one of the losers, Alf Foster, recalled; he was so convinced by their arguments that he joined the VSP and regarded the debate as a turning point in his life. The Prahran Council banned the VSP from public speaking. So began the Prahran Free Speech Fight, which saw a group including Mann, Hyett and four women convicted and gaoled. The VSP's readiness to stand up for a principle reinforced its standing and popularity, which benefited the labour movement in suburban Melbourne and the larger regional centres.

Elsewhere in Victoria, however, Labor was struggling to maintain the rural momentum created by Mann's organizing skills and augmented by Scott Bennett, who had now resigned from parliament. There were no funds to employ an organizer. Those trying to fill the vacuum had a difficult time: one Labor man told the PLC executive that after receiving its consignment of leaflets he had been sacked the next day. In the 1908 state election PLC candidates contested only 28 of the 65 seats, winning 21. The AWU came to the rescue. It had been slow to take up the leading role in the country assigned to it by the 1902 PLC conference. The way may have been smoothed by the PLC's 1907 decision to accept facsimile slips in the *Worker* as valid votes in preselection ballots. The following year the AWU appointed Scullin its political organizer to work the rural areas on the PLC's behalf; he did well, reviving flagging branches and creating new ones. Furthermore, when Heagney resigned as the PLC's lowly paid secretary, the AWU had the vacancy filled by Arch Stewart.

In October 1907, when Watson – who was then only 40 – announced that he was definitely resigning, he was gratified by the desperate attempts from all levels of the party to change his mind. He said the strain had frayed his nerves; caucus offered to arrange a fund to finance an extended voyage for him and his wife. He complained about the grinding burden of routine correspondence which he had to carry unaided; caucus belatedly offered to pay for secretarial assistance. From the Blue Mountains came a heartfelt plea: 'From your most influential supporter to the humblest navvy such as myself in the great and growing army of Labor, but one sentiment proceeds: don't leave us on the verge of your and our triumph'. With the same purpose a Labor women's delegation visited Mrs Watson, but was disarmed by her response that 'I only want what you women all want – my husband at home with me'. There lay a telling factor in Watson's resignation, thought Pearce (who saw it as a tragedy) and other shrewd onlookers. The only sour note concerned a Brunswick branch meeting, where one speaker said he was pleased that Watson was going and hoped a more uncompromising leader would succeed him; an exaggerated version was reported in the *Age* and elsewhere. The Brunswick branch gathered again a week later, when there was a 'Record attendance of Members and great interest taken'. It indignantly repudiated the press versions, recorded its appreciation of Watson's 'sterling qualities', and expressed its regret at his retirement. Chairing the meeting which displayed such sensitivity to the pressures of federal Labor leadership was the branch president, John Curtin.

However, this time Watson had made up his mind. He was prepared to continue until the next election in a senior advisory role, but not as leader. The workload, the 1905 interstate conference resolutions, the travel between Sydney and Melbourne and his wife's impatience with his absences all weighed heavily; moreover, his health was suffering. He had 'never been the same man since' the trying time as Prime Minister 'knocked his nerves to tatters'. His friend Deakin had overstretched himself and suffered a breakdown; Watson had no desire to emulate him. His dread of leading another minority administration influenced his attitude to the Deakin government, then piloting a raised tariff through the parliament. In view of its divisions on the tariff question, argued Watson, Labor's better course, despite its greater parliamentary numbers than the Protectionists, was to avoid office and encourage the government to enact progressive legislation. This argument had an obvious flaw: if the government was well aware that Labor dreaded office and saw Reid's party as an impossible alternative government, the FPLP's bargaining power was slight. A growing number in caucus wanted to press the government hard on issues like aged pensions, but Watson refused. Although Watson's detractors in the party sometimes wished he had more fire, no Labor leader was more skilled at relating harmoniously with all sections of the party and with other parties. His qualities of amiability and sweet reasonableness were most suited to Labor's early years, when the FPLP opted to pursue its goals in concert with other politicians and was keen to assure the electors that it was not, as its enemies alleged, a bunch of wild-eyed extremists.

Fisher, Hughes, Batchelor and Spence were nominated for the leadership. Batchelor declined the nomination; Spence, who 'never seemed quite at home' in politics, had little support. Fisher and Hughes had a game of billiards while caucus deliberated over its choice of opposites. In Hughes it had a mercurial snatcher of expedients, a pocket dynamo with a singularly incongruous appearance for an aspiring leader; while he compensated for this with eloquence and imaginativeness, his abrasiveness had made enemies and there were doubts about his reliability. He had just commenced a regular series, 'The Case For Labor', published in the Sydney *Daily Telegraph* each Saturday for four years. 'Dashed off at top speed and at odd moments' (often during parliamentary debates), these articles were excellent Labor propaganda: with wit, irony and verve Hughes entertained the *Telegraph*'s middle-class readers and undermined their prejudices. Fisher was a complete contrast in physique and temperament. His height, silver-grey hair and imposing moustache gave him a distinguished presence, but with his ponderous platform style and baffling Scottish burr he was not a rousing speaker. Uncomplicated, cautious and sincere, he had a sound grasp of the nuances of his party; absolutely incorruptible, he was enraged more by impropriety or skulduggery than anything else; a slow thinker, he was inclined to inflexibility. The one characteristic he and Hughes shared was a great faith in their own ability. (Each had also married his landlady's daughter.) Caucus members discontented with Watson's attitude to the Deakin government voted for Fisher: he shared the generally more radical approach of his fellow Queenslanders, whereas Hughes was more closely linked to Watson. Caucus sensibly decided that the party would be best served by placing Fisher at the helm, where he could utilize Hughes's brilliance and check his more extravagant excesses. Hughes accepted the verdict and was a loyal, energetic colleague, rarely allowing his frustrations to surface.

In his presidential address at the 1908 interstate conference Fisher specifically praised the 'invaluable' contribution of women in the party, and looked forward to their endorsement as Labor candidates. He was 'pleased to see women delegates present at the conference'. One of them, the legendary Emma Miller, was in her seventieth year and had been politically active for over half a century. After arriving in Brisbane in 1879, 'Mother Miller' had helped form a women workers' union and a women's suffrage association, and served as president of an organization of Queensland Labor women; she was the first woman to travel west organizing for the AWU, and always championed equal pay and equal opportunity. The other female delegate was Kate Dwyer. After growing up in Tambaroora, she and her sisters Annie and Belle Golding, all devout Catholics, moved to Sydney, where they served the twin causes of Labor and women's rights with dedication and zeal for many years. Fisher's attitude to Labor women was not typical of his party. That Miller, Dwyer and Lilian Locke rose to positions of some influence in the party spoke volumes about their own qualities; it did not indicate that women were generally encouraged to contribute beyond 'bringing a plate' and making endless cups of tea for their menfolk. However, since women could now vote, there was a spreading awareness in the party that it made sense to form Labor women's organizations or branches so that specific concerns affecting women voters would not be overlooked. Shortly after women first voted in a NSW state election in 1904, the PLL Women's Organizing Committee was set up with direct representation at conference and on the executive; Dwyer was its inaugural president and in 1905 sat on the executive. The equivalent Victorian organization, the PLC Women's Organizing Committee, had a stop-start existence. Initially Locke was its mainstay, but now others like Jean Daley and Patrick Heagney's daughter Muriel were becoming active. In WA Jean Beadle was outstanding, forming a Labor women's organization in Fremantle in 1905 and the Eastern Goldfields Women's Labor League the following year.

The 1908 conference ratified a change in the platform which was the culmination of an agitation by Hughes. In 1901 he first outlined his scheme for compulsory military training so that Australia would possess 'an efficiently drilled, adequately paid, and sufficiently numerous' defensive citizen army at its disposal to deter and repel invaders. The physical and moral side-effects would also be beneficial, he argued, but few were convinced. By 1903 he had persuaded Watson and Spence, but few others: Fisher tersely dismissed the proposals as conscription and scorned any notion that 'barrack life' would improve Australians' 'moral backbone'. Hughes was undeterred. With Darwinian fervour he colourfully described the sorry plight of the weak. To nationalists and democrats he proclaimed the virtues of national self-reliance and the democratic fairness of compulsion for all; to sceptical Labor colleagues concerned about militarism, he contended that his proposal would take the armed forces out of the hands of militarists and conservative leaders who had used soldiers to smash strikes. In England in 1907, Hughes clashed with British Labour leaders critical of his scheme: 'for the Socialist to complain about compulsion is like the devil complaining about sin', he told them. The turning point in Hughes's campaign was Japan's defeat of Russia in 1905. This revelation of Japan's naval and military capacity aggravated Australian nervousness about Asian expansion, and caused many – including Pearce, who had been an outspoken critic of militarism and Australia's role in the Boer War – to agree with Hughes that Australia's defence preparedness had been lacking.

At the 1908 conference Watson paid tribute to Hughes, who was not a delegate, in moving that compulsory military training be inserted in the platform. Hutchison, Holman, de Largie, Spence, Givens and Batchelor spoke in support. Fisher was silent. Kate Dwyer 'bitterly regretted that anything legalising murder should emanate from a Labour man at all'. Victorians Anstey, Tudor and Findley all opposed the motion. O'Malley 'wondered if the Labour party had gone mad on militarism'; it was 'foolish', he claimed, 'to adopt the most diabolical methods of Europe, and give the gilt-spurred roosters power'. A majority of 24 to seven voted Hughes's idea into the platform.

At the 1908 conference there was indignation at a recent High Court verdict invalidating New Protection. Even free traders in the FPLP supported New Protection, which purported to make tariff protection to Australian employers conditional on 'fair and reasonable' wages for their workers. Mr Justice Higgins in his celebrated Harvester judgement in the Arbitration Court had extended the concept to incorporate the 'basic wage', which was a pleasing development (although criticized by a later generation on feminist grounds), but Higgins and Isaacs were in the minority when the High Court ruled that New Protection exceeded the national government's constitutional powers. This not only threatened New Protection, but had disturbing implications for the arbitration system. At the conference Givens advocated a constitutional amendment enabling the national government to enact 'uniform industrial legislation'. Supporting speakers included Watson, Spence, de Largie, Fisher, and several Tasmanians who referred to the futility of getting industrial reforms through their 'hopelessly Conservative Upper House'. However, NSW delegates Holman, McGowen and Dwyer fiercely resisted what they saw as a sweeping encroachment on a sphere of state activity. An acceptable compromise emerged: 'Amendment of the Constitution to ensure effective Federal legislation for New Protection and Arbitration'. Conference unanimously approved this addition to the platform, but it was clear that attempts to extend the powers of the national government could cause trouble.

The Labor politicians' attachment to arbitration was not shared by some workers. There was now a new generation of toilers with neither knowledge nor interest in how arbitration and other Labor reforms had modified the industrial jungle; they focused on the deficiencies of the arbitration system, whereas older workers were more likely to see arbitration as sound in principle but ineptly administered. Disgruntled workers were susceptible to ideas of direct action propagated by militant socialists including Tom Mann, who had given up his attempts through the VSP to make Labor a more socialist party. Division had arisen in the VSP concerning its relationship to Labor; the debate raged for years, draining the VSP of members, cohesion and influence. Curtin and Hyett wished to maintain the close connection; others, influenced by socialist organizations in other states and by the doctrines of the Industrial Workers of the World (IWW), wanted to sever all links with Labor. The IWW originated in America and unambiguously promoted the class war. Its influence was most pronounced in NSW, the most populated and industrialized state, where workers felt especially let down by arbitration. In 1908, a year which saw a sharp rise in the cost of living, there was a wave of strikes, especially in NSW. The savagery of the class struggle experienced in mining communities was demonstrated during 1908–9 in protracted bitter disputes at Broken Hill and Newcastle. In Newcastle Hughes scurried around frantically, trying to restrain the militant leaders, isolate the employers and generate public support for the men. Hughes's conviction that strikes were generally counterproductive for workers had been heeded in the past, but the mood was different this time. The NSW government's ham-fisted intervention in the dispute did it much harm and increased Labor's confidence about the state and federal elections due in 1910.

There was a discernible restlessness in a section of the FPLP about its attitude to the Deakin government. Spearheading this dissatisfaction was Frazer. He had regretfully abandoned his legal studies, and now devoted himself to persuading his colleagues that Labor should support Deakin no longer. His 'caustic, bitter tongue' was inflicting 'rhetorical assault and battery' on the government at every opportunity. In April 1908 Webster, who had a well-developed sense of self-importance and a passion for the minutiae of postal administration, moved in parliament for the establishment of a royal commission into the Post Office.

Sufficient Labor members supported Webster to carry the motion against the government. Fisher and Watson discussed the government's instability with Deakin, who proposed a coalition with Labor. By 20 to 13 caucus warily agreed to a coalition, provided that Labor had most ministers and action was guaranteed on old age pensions, New Protection and land taxation. With Fisher's blessing Watson handled the detailed bargaining with Deakin. Ultimately it was arranged that the government should stay until the almost-completed tariff legislation passed through the parliament. This was quickly achieved. So too, in response to renewed FPLP pressure, was legislation for pensions; at last the strenuous efforts of O'Malley, Frazer, Pearce and others on this issue had been rewarded. During a parliamentary adjournment 18 caucus members, who comprised half the delegates at the Brisbane interstate conference, travelled north to attend it. Conference carried a strong motion by Findley opposing any alliance or electoral immunity. The Queenslanders' outspoken support reflected their bitterness at the Kidstonites' betrayal; Watson conceded that 'the feeling of Conference was against alliances, and that must be respected'. When parliament resumed the FPLP keenly awaited Deakin's plan to revive New Protection after the High Court judgement, but were disappointed by his wishy-washy proposal. Frazer seized his chance, and moved in caucus that the FPLP withdraw support from the government. On 4 November his motion was carried with a majority of 12, and later that month Fisher became Labor's second prime minister.

Watson fought a strong rearguard action on the issue of ministerial selection. In his view a leader should have the cabinet of his choice. Frazer was not a delegate at the 1908 interstate conference, but in his absence both his pet concerns were looked after by Findley, who followed the motion on alliances with another, also carried overwhelmingly, that caucus should choose Labor ministers. However, Watson moved in caucus on 12 November 1908 that the FPLP, 'having every confidence in its Leader, leaves the selection of his colleagues in his hands'. The predictable amendment came from Findley, with Frazer seconding, that caucus implement the conference resolution: it was carried 24 to 17. Watson then tried to have the selection conducted by open ballot for nominated candidates, but was again unsuccessful. Still he persisted. With Fisher and Senate leader McGregor exempted from the ballot, Fisher (after consulting Pearce) produced a list of the men he wanted; Watson played a crucial lobbying role in caucus to ensure he was given them. Fisher's ticket of Pearce, Hughes, Tudor, Batchelor, Thomas and Mahon was elected in full. All the 1904 ministry still available for inclusion thus obtained a place, and Watson managed to keep Frazer, O'Malley, Page and Findley out of the ministry. The last position went to Hutchison. 'A firebrand who lived on his nerves', Hutchison had been bankrupted in 1902 by the costs he incurred fighting a libel suit; this had arisen from his forceful opposition to the proposed handing over of Adelaide's tramways to private enterprise (which Price later prevented). Hughes was now willing to become Attorney-General. Pearce became the ninth Defence minister within eight years and had a startling initiation to ministerial administration. The outgoing minister breezily showed him a locked cache of dangerous 'lost' files which could 'wreck a government'. 'Pearce, old boy', he said, 'take my advice, leave them there. The country will go on just as well without them'. Pearce did no such thing.

Fisher's steadfastness was soon displayed to advantage. When it was suddenly alleged in London that British authorities had underestimated the burgeoning power of the German navy, which might soon have more modern battleships (known as dreadnoughts) than the British navy, alarm spread quickly. In Australia the hysteria and insecurity were, if anything, even more pronounced. There were emotional demands, orchestrated by the *Age* and *Argus* in particular, that Australia must help restore Britain's superiority in dreadnoughts by donating one (as the New Zealand government did immediately). There were subscription lists of donors, animated meetings and emphatic resolutions; the conservative governments of Victoria and NSW offered to provide a dreadnought between them if the national government refused to do its 'duty'; the Governor-General added some private lobbying of his own. Fisher refused to be hustled: Labor's policy was to create an Australian navy, not send money to England to strengthen theirs. Some years earlier Labor had been mocked when it first advocated an Australian navy; now Pearce set this in motion by authorizing the construction of three destroyers. Labor people were very satisfied with Fisher's conduct, and not only in Australia: the British Labour Party wrote to 'congratulate' him for not succumbing to 'a panic which has been engineered here for political purposes'.

Fisher returned to his home town of Gympie to deliver a major policy speech on 30 March 1909. He promised a land tax, increased expenditure on pensions and on defence (munitions factories, compulsory military training for young males and a three-year plan to build a fleet of coastal destroyers), a transcontinental railway, development of the national capital, acquisition of the Northern Territory, protection for the sugar industry, and provision for the changing financial relationship between the states and the national government. There would be a referendum to reinstate New Protection and another, if required, to nationalize the iron industry. The one significant omission from Labor's platform was tactical, and strongly urged by Hughes:

> Above all things we must be practical and avoid flights into idealism...About the Commonwealth Bank we must be dumb...If we do so we can carry the rest – staggering under it – but still we can do it.

So Fisher foreshadowed the introduction of national banknotes but, to avoid a frenzied outcry, stopped short of committing Labor to a Commonwealth Bank. Still, his speech was 'the boldest and most National Australian policy ever enunciated', according to Spence. 'Anti-Labor was struck dumb, and failed to find a flaw in it.'

Ever since Labor took office in November its opponents had been plotting to somehow bring the various non-Labor elements under one banner. A distinct obstacle to any such arrangement was removed 'with indecent haste' when Reid was coerced into resigning within a week. The new leader of his party was Joe Cook, one of the 35 of 1891 but for many years an avowed enemy of Labor. Ultimately, in May, the fusion was achieved with the ailing Deakin's reluctant acquiescence. In parliament the dagger was hastily wielded by the FPLP's most loathed opponent, an Eton-educated socialite who wished to prevent Pearce's imminent departure for London to represent Australia at an important naval conference. Although the fusion was common knowledge, Fisher was nonetheless bewildered and angry when his government was defeated. In the most rowdy, bitter scenes the federal parliament had experienced, Hughes was in his element; caucus distributed 50 000 copies of his speeches lambasting the insincerity, duplicity and unprincipled hunger for office displayed by Deakin and his new followers. One vitriolic all-night sitting turned to tragedy when the respected

Speaker, Holder, who was upset by the angry exchanges, muttered 'Dreadful! Dreadful!', collapsed and died.

Labor sought a dissolution of parliament, and Fisher asked Governor-General Dudley for time to prepare a written argument. This task naturally fell to Hughes, 'who spent the week-end with wet towels round his head working at high pressure, and was far from pleased when Fisher, spick and span after a week-end's rest', turned up to collect the 50-page memorandum. Fisher had no time to go through it before he was due to present it to Dudley, who did not read it either. Relying on advice from the Chief Justice, Dudley refused a dissolution and the Labor government had to resign. While this was regrettable some Labor people were delighted that the political situation had at last been simplified:

> On the one side there are the land monopolists, syndicators, money-grabbers, rings, trusts, combines, and the whole body of exploiters of society...On the other side stands the people's party – those who work for the uplifting of the masses and the setting up of social justice.

While Hughes was furiously compiling his memorandum for Dudley, Fisher received an enthusiastic message of support from Tasmania's youthful MHA, Ben Watkins.

> Monster meeting yesterday declared confidence Labor Ministry and demanded dissolution. Another crowded meeting Town Hall tonight enthusiastically reaffirmed resolutions. Tassie is awake.

It was indeed something of a turning point for Labor in Tasmania. A conference in Hobart in June 1903 attended by Watson had formally established the first Tasmania-wide Labor organization, but its secretary, Woods, laboured under daunting difficulties. Funds were scarce, regional hostilities continued unabated, the unions were generally weak and the stronger ones unco-operative. For the 1906 state election Watson, Spence, Anstey and O'Malley crossed the Tasman to assist the campaign, and Labor's parliamentary strength increased to seven. 'This is the beginning, where the end will be, no one can say', moaned the conservative *Mercury*. This seemed rather exaggerated at a time when a Labor conference was attended by only nine delegates who were unable to elect a president because three members tied for the position. As in Victoria, the mighty AWU became Labor's organizational saviour, as Woods had long hoped it would. It was very successful in forming new Labor branches in country areas, especially after the state election in April 1909 which saw Labor's parliamentary representation rise to 12. Only then did unions begin organizing and affiliating in earnest, with the Hobart TLC belatedly re-established. In other states the Labor Party emerged from the unions, observed Woods, but the reverse more correctly described events in Tasmania. The new MPs included blacksmith Jim Guy, schoolteacher Joe Lyons and timber merchant and farmer Jim Belton. The men they joined in parliament included their leader Earle, Long, former miner and AMA president Joe Ogden, wealthy publican Jens Jensen, Watkins, who was 22 when elected in 1906, and Woods, whose new life in Tasmania was about to be further cemented by marriage to Watkins's sister.

Labor's encouraging success in 1909 masked its organizational weaknesses and was ironically caused by its opponents. In an attempt to avoid a repetition of

Labor's mainland progress, the Tasmanian government introduced the Hare-Clark proportional representation electoral system; but it backfired on them, working to Labor's advantage in the short term. Furthermore, division among the conservatives enabled Labor in October 1909 to form a minority government headed by Earle, the former blacksmith and engine driver who had been blacklisted at Mt Lyell for being a dangerous agitator. Caucus elected Jensen, Ogden and Long as his ministers. They barely had time to open the ministerial files before the reality of a Labor government predictably caused their opponents to hastily settle their differences. Tasmania's first Labor government lasted only a week.

Earlier that year the death of Price, Labor's popular Premier of SA, had led to a political controversy in that state. Peake, the acting Premier, had already requested electoral immunity from Labor for his party at the next election, but the ULP refused. Caucus elected Verran to succeed Price, and were surprised and angered when Peake refused to step down as Premier. Labor insisted on its right to the position, as the stronger parliamentary force. Neither party budged, and the coalition ceased. Like Deakin, Peake came to an agreement with his conservative opponents which enabled him to form a government. Like their federal colleagues, ULP members attacked the way the new administration had secured office, but were pleased to be able to campaign in the next election unfettered by links or obligations to any other party.

At both elections, in SA on 2 April 1910 and in the federal contest 11 days later, Labor was victorious. The ULP won 22 of the 42 SA Assembly seats to achieve narrowly the unprecedented feat of a majority in its own right in the lower house. No Labor party anywhere had managed this, and the Peake government's unwillingness to surrender office immediately did not inhibit the understandable jubilation at 'the triumph of *progress* and freedom and *right* and *truth*. . .'. Even that success was eclipsed by the federal landslide, which remains one of the biggest highlights in the entire history of Australian Labor. The battle was keenly contested, with a striking increase in voter participation: Victorians and Queenslanders voted in greater numbers than at their state elections. (From 1910 nearly all voters in all states but NSW regarded the national government as more important than their state government.) Not since federation had any party had a majority in either house but Labor now had 41 MHRs out of 75, 22 Senators out of 36: 'the people do not deserve self-government', growled Forrest. Into the national parliament came Anstey, Scullin and burly printer Jim Fenton from Victoria, Long and Jensen from Tasmania, and the NSW veterans of 1891 Rae and Gardiner. O'Keefe and Higgs, both defeated in 1906, returned. J.M. Chanter, a Deakinite Protectionist appalled by the fusion, retained Riverina as a Labor candidate. Hunter was captured by the tall, likeable and dedicated Matt Charlton, a prominent mining unionist and NSW MLA. Also transferring from state politics was Archibald, who filled the vacancy in Hindmarsh created by the 'sudden and shocking' death of Hutchison, who left a widow and six children.

Labor's period of flirtation with other parties was over. Under Kidston and Price some important – but, overall, perhaps limited – benefits had accrued via alliances in two states. In the national sphere Labor had taken the Protectionists as far in the direction of progressive legislation as possible. Some Labor activists wished their party had ended the relationship and forged ahead alone much earlier. Yet even the most fanatical enthusiast with an unshakeable faith in the inevitability of Labor's destiny had private moments of disbelief at the magnitude of the achievement. Labor had travelled far in less than two decades. As a novel political entity it had developed procedures based on ideals of democracy and solidarity so that theoretically all party members had an equal voice in its direction. Under Fisher, who epitomized the virtues of that structure, Labor exuded trustworthiness, competence and stability. It had developed policies which were attuned to widespread national aspirations, and established mechanisms to refine those policies when necessary. There was another precious ingredient,

> a mystical element quite unknown to members of other political bodies. . .there was a crusading quality in the Labor Party that produced, at least in people of imagination, a sense of knight-errantry, of riding forth on a charger to right the wrongs of the world.

Across the nation the marvellous victory was saluted by cheering members and supporters who believed that Labor was poised to become Australia's natural governing party.

4 'Our Unequalled Progress': Planks Made Law, 1910–1914

FISHER SALUTED THE great victory as a culmination of 'twenty years of arduous work'. When the excited FPLP assembled on 26 April, Fisher announced that he had declined a commission until his leadership was confirmed; caucus re-affirmed it immediately. The ballots for ministerial positions occurred three days later. Some Queenslanders and West Australians had difficulty in getting to Melbourne by then. Page, a narrowly defeated ministerial aspirant in 1908, was unable to attend the vital meeting; Frazer, also just pipped in 1908, managed to arrive from the West in time to press his claims only by chartering a special boat to whisk him from the steamer to the wharf.

There was one major ministerial surprise. Caucus decided that the ministry must contain three Senators, and McGregor, Pearce and Findley were the pre-ferred trio. The election for the six MHRs other than Fisher was not so straight-forward. At the first ballot Hughes, Batchelor and Tudor were the choice of over half the caucus and were deemed elected. With 29 votes Mahon was one vote short of joining them, but he received only 21 in the following ballot for the remaining three positions, which went to Thomas, O'Malley and Frazer (who became the youngest ever federal minister). Mahon's omission caused a stir, especially in Catholic circles where the cry of sectarianism was heard; yet even the *Catholic Press* acknowledged that sectarianism was not behind the demise of such a prominent Catholic of undoubted ability. As Labor's earnest MHR for Cook, Jimmy Catts, publicly observed, it was Mahon's aloofness and unwilling-ness to shoulder his share of propaganda work that told against him. On the backbench Mahon was a sulky, brooding figure; he especially resented Frazer's elevation into the ministry, and they were not on speaking terms. Like McGregor (again Vice-President of the Executive Council), Frazer and Findley were min-isters without portfolio. The other new minister, O'Malley, was given Home Affairs. Over the past decade he had displayed – in typically exuberant style – an interest and capacity in financial matters. (Indeed, his election as minister was probably attributable in part to the fact that several caucus colleagues owed him money.) During the recent election campaign he had dismissed Deakin as 'a lovable man' but 'as destitute of financial knowledge as a frog was of feathers', and had rashly predicted that he would be Treasurer in a Labor government. As in 1908, however, Fisher kept the Treasury for himself.

Hughes was back in the saddle as Labor's dynamic Attorney-General. He was remarkably busy, still prominent in the union movement as president of the Waterside Workers' Federation and the Trolley, Draymen and Carters' Union; then forming the Transport Workers' Federation, he also became its president. Again the only lawyer in cabinet, he was instrumental in drafting much of Labor's wide-ranging legislation and vigorously piloted it through parliament. When Hughes was absent, Fisher often asked that technical questions about the government's legislation be placed on notice (so that Hughes could answer them when he returned). After Fisher departed late in 1910 on an official visit to South Africa, leaving Hughes with an additional, but welcome, burden as acting Prime Minister, Hughes's peremptory style provoked a serious incident. When Labor members voiced objections in the Representatives to Hughes's legislation for the establishment of Duntroon military college, he became frustrated and rude, and adjourned the debate. At a fiery emergency caucus meeting Hughes eventually agreed to postpone any legislation if Labor members felt strongly that the party should reconsider it, but the episode was a chastening taste of Hughes's defects as a prospective leader.

In October 1910 the flowing tide to Labor produced another triumph with the election of the party's first government in NSW. With 46 MLAs in the 90-member Assembly, Labor had a narrow majority in its own right. In leadership NSW Labor resembled the FPLP: 'Honest Jim' McGowen, the new Premier, was in the Fisher mould with his 'rock-like lack of brilliance', while his adjutant Holman was as scintillating, wily and nimble-witted as Hughes. But Holman had no monopoly on ability in the McGowen government. Griffith was an enterprising Public Works minister, authorizing new construction worth £4 million in his first 18 months; railways were duplicated and state-owned industries established in brickworks, limeworks and quarries. Lawyer George Beeby, a leading member of the party since its inception, had two important portfolios. As Public Instruction minister Beeby approved important educational reforms, and as Labour and Industry minister he began the major task of remodelling the arbitration system. Niels Nielsen had an Irish mother and a Danish father who emigrated to Australia to avoid conscription. He grew up in Young, where he became an early stalwart of the emerging bush unions. Elected to parliament in 1899, he developed a particular expertise in the quagmire of NSW's land laws. Lands was his obvious portfolio. With A.C. Carmichael, rural newspaperman J.L. Trefle and Labor veterans Edden, Macdonell and Flowers, it was a talented ministry. Dacey was a surprising omission, but sectarianism was an unlikely factor, since 17 of his caucus colleagues were fellow Catholics, as were three of the ministers – Macdonell, Trefle and Nielsen.

The NSW government was soon on a collision course with the Fisher government over constitutional reform. The NSW delegates' objections at the 1908 federal conference had been followed by a disagreement concerning an unsuccessful referendum held concurrently with the 1910 federal election. The referendum proposed the insertion into the Constitution of a fixed per capita entitlement payable by the national government to the states; the FPLP broadly approved the scheme – the Fisher government later introduced it – but opposed entrenching it into the Constitution in perpetuity. Holman and McGowen had rocked the boat by supporting that referendum, and they again disagreed with the FPLP when Hughes set in train referenda proposals to extend the national government's powers over trade and commerce, labour and employment, corporations and monopolies. McGowen, Holman and Beeby made a special trip to

Melbourne in a fruitless bid to persuade Hughes to alter his proposals, contending that they clearly contravened the compromise arranged at the 1908 conference. Hughes argued that the national government should have such powers, and Labor's platform authorized the FPLP to seek them.

The issue erupted at the PLL's 1911 conference. Despite Holman's forceful opposition, conference strongly endorsed the referenda. Holman assured conference that he and his colleagues would abide by its decision; later, taking advantage of a lull in proceedings, he tried to whip through three resolutions inconsistent with that assurance. Two of them were narrowly carried, but were quickly reversed when conference rowdily reassembled. Lamond led the counter-attack. The hostility towards Holman always evident in Lamond's editorship of the *Worker* had been revived in earnest: the *Worker* referred to referenda opponents, especially Holman, as 'State Insects' frustrating the visionary 'Big Australians'. At the conference Lamond labelled the referenda opponents 'traitors' and invited Holman to leave the party. A concurrent AWU conference angrily expressed similar anti-Holman sentiments.

After launching the referenda campaign, Fisher took little further part in it. Confident of a positive outcome, he sailed with Batchelor and Pearce to England for the Imperial Conference and the Coronation of King George V. The campaign, with much else, was left to Hughes. While nominally silent, Holman indirectly undermined and infuriated Hughes. Anti-Labor, of course, opposed the referenda: Premier Kidston claimed that the proposals 'if carried will ringbark the Federal system of government'. The result was a setback for the FPLP. In only one state, WA, did 'Yes' finish ahead, and the overall 'No' majority was overwhelming. The voters who gave the FPLP such a resounding electoral victory had within a year refused to grant the powers the FPLP had claimed were essential to implement Labor's policies. Hughes's decision to group all but one of the proposals together was retrospectively judged unwise, as voters who disliked one item probably rejected the whole package; he resolved to resubmit them individually, perhaps in conjunction with an election. NSW Labor's sabotage was certainly damaging; Holman could not resist pointing out that the NSW 'Yes' vote was less than half the Labor votes at the 1910 state election. The AWU sought a special conference to discipline Holman and other politicians who had 'betrayed the Conference decision'.

Before this conference could be held a crisis concerning land reform gripped the NSW government. McGowen was abroad, visiting London for the Coronation; some Labor people like Senator Rae disapproved of the elaborate arrangements made 'in order that some people may go and act the goat in the Old Country'. Nielsen, who was devoted to the merits of leasehold, correctly argued that proper implementation of the second plank of Labor's fighting platform ('immediate cessation of Crown Land sales') necessitated repeal of the 1908 Conversion Act enabling homestead selectors on leasehold to convert to freehold tenure. This disturbed many rural Labor members, and a bitter fight developed. Nielsen was not amenable to compromise solutions: strong-willed and opinionated, he had spent years coming to grips with NSW's land laws and wanted to fix them up his way without delay. On 26 July Holman was fending off an opposition censure motion with his one-vote Assembly majority when he 'was utterly dumbfounded' to learn that two rural Labor backbenchers had resigned over the land question. Caucus then resolved not to proceed with the Conversion Repeal Bill, which caused Nielsen's resignation as minister. The government seemed to be tottering.

In the ensuing political and constitutional drama Holman completely out-witted his opponents. Cann had resigned the speakership to provide another vote in the critical parliamentary divisions, and Holman accepted Griffith's sugges-tion to approach an opposition MLA, H. Willis, who incensed his anti-Labor colleagues by agreeing to act as a temporary Speaker. Outrageous parliamentary scenes followed; Labor members had to physically install Willis in the Speaker's chair. After the parliamentary turmoil subsided and sundry by-elections were resolved, Labor emerged with an increased Assembly majority and improved standing in the electorate generally. The August 1911 special conference debated a censure from Randwick PLL and a call from the Bourke branch of the AWU to expel politicians, including Holman and Beeby, for not supporting the referenda, but both motions were defeated. Hughes tried to have the interpretation of fed-eral platform planks between federal conferences made the sole preserve of the FPLP, but his motion was doomed to failure once Holman opposed it.

Fisher, Pearce and Batchelor had time to reflect during their voyage to England that their government, apart from the referenda reverse, had made a satisfactory start. After it acquired the Northern Territory from SA, Batchelor as External Affairs minister (and a South Australian) had taken over its adminis-tration. Australia's 'treatment of the natives formed the blackest page in its history', he asserted, and he wanted to 'ameliorate the present conditions' and to assist 'the preservation of the native tribes'. Pearce had pushed himself so hard at Defence that his health gave way and he had to take a prolonged rest. After his return he reduced his working hours but remained a methodical, indefatigable administrator. On the ship he read copiously, devouring reports and other of-ficial literature like chocolates; Batchelor also made sure he kept on top of his ministerial responsibilities; Fisher played chess and dreamed of Scotland. On arrival in London Fisher immediately travelled north to visit his birthplace, accompanied by his friend Keir Hardie who had slaved down the Ayrshire mines with Fisher as a youngster and had risen to lead the British Labour Party. After this sentimental journey Fisher tackled the serious business in London. He wanted Britain to consult its dominions more before making decisions affecting their interests, but made little headway. What Australia's ministerial trio was given was an unprecedented private briefing about Britain's foreign policy. Even this was selective and included some brazen lying, but the three Australians emerged convinced of the strong likelihood of imminent European war. The Australian delegation was intensely relieved to learn that Britain's treaty with Japan, the country Australians feared most, would be renewed until 1921: 'Now we're safe for another ten years', remarked Fisher. Nevertheless, the Australian ministers resolved to further invigorate Australia's defence so that their nation would be prepared for any crisis arising in unsettled Europe.

Batchelor's contribution, however, was curtailed. In October 1911, shortly after his return, 'Batch' was enjoying a bushwalking trek at Mt Donna Buang, Victoria, when he suffered a heart attack and died immediately. His death at 46 was a tragic loss to Labor. At the recent international forum in London his 'sound commonsense and cool judgement' had been warmly praised. Watson described him as 'one of the sanest and most gracious colleagues one ever had'. On 14 October Fisher announced a minor cabinet reshuffle, with Frazer promoted to Postmaster-General and Thomas switched from that portfolio to succeed Batchelor. At the next caucus meeting a motion from Gardiner and Rae regret-ting 'that the Government did not take the party into its confidence before rearranging portfolios' was lost, and the FPLP's choice to fill the cabinet vacancy was none other than the ULP's pre-federation young man in a hurry, E.A. Roberts. After returning from the Boer War, Roberts edited Labor's *Herald* and re-entered state parliament in 1905. When Kingston died in May 1908, Roberts won the by-election for Labor. In federal parliament his sharp, assertive, flamboyant parliamentary style was quickly evident: it was his amendment which had prompted the November 1910 emergency caucus meeting about Hughes's conduct as acting Prime Minister. Less than four years after entering federal parliament the ambitious Roberts was a minister and being mentioned as a possible future leader. Frazer also coveted that position eventually. He had filled in capably at the Treasury during Fisher's overseas trips, and proved a better Postmaster-General than Thomas. That department had been unduly starved of funds by non-Labor governments since federation, causing inefficiency and low morale. Labor turned this around, initially under Thomas and more dramatically under Frazer, and reduced postal charges, introducing a uniform penny postage with new national stamps.

Pearce presided over a vigorous defence programme. The government pressed on with construction of an Australian navy. It founded a naval college at Jervis Bay and even a flying school at Point Cook as well as Duntroon military college. It overhauled and modernized the production and supply of munitions and other defence equipment. More controversial was the sort of compulsory training scheme which Hughes had been advocating for years. O'Malley, Higgs and other FPLP members had doubts about the scheme. Rae's personal experience of the great strikes of 1890–91, when governments used the military against strikers, induced him to move an amendment in the Senate guaranteeing that this citizen defence force would never be used that way; only three Labor Senators supported him, but a similar resolution was carried shortly afterwards at Labor's 1912 federal conference. Reaction to the scheme in the community ranged from enthusiasm to apathy, with perhaps the predominant response being grudging acquiescence. There was also, however, some significant opposition from pacifists (who included many socialists) and unwilling cadets who had better things to do than drill, like the young East Sydney tearaway from a battling family, Eddie Ward, who had already organized his classmates in an abortive strike against school conditions; he had similar ill-luck with his rebellion against military training, being sent to a disciplinary camp for a week. As prosecutions for non-compliance mounted, there was considerable uneasiness within the labour movement. Fenton spoke out in the Representatives, Rae and Gardiner in the Senate, and from SA Verran expressed his concern privately to Fisher. Some local Labor branches were also animated. Pearce's generally sensible and flexible administration deflected some of the disquiet.

The Fisher government enacted far more legislation than any previous national ministry. Its graduated tax on unimproved land values was intended to break up the big estates and provide increased scope for small-scale farming. The arbitration system was extended to cover federal public servants, domestics and agricultural workers. Expenditure on welfare was increased: invalid pensions were introduced, and women became eligible for the old-age pension at 60 instead of 65. A popular measure was the baby bonus, an allowance of five pounds payable at the birth of each white Australian child. By enabling more births to be attended by doctors, this innovation helped to reduce infant mortality: by 1926 white Australians (and New Zealanders) had the lowest rates in the world. The government authorized preliminary surveys for a railway northwards from SA through its newly acquired Northern Territory, and involved itself purposefully

75

in lighthouses, quarantine, copyright and uniform railway gauges. Another novelty was Fisher's acquisition of a motor vehicle for his government's use. Fisher was a plain man with no frills – nothing would induce him to wear lace at the Coronation, for example – but at the same time he was extremely sensitive to any perceived affront to Labor when its leader was treated differently from any other prime minister. Labor did flaunt its different values in parliament where McDonald as Speaker in the Representatives and Turley as Senate President dispensed with the traditional regalia of office, the wig, gown and Speaker's mace.

Caucus pushed the government into doing something about an increase in newspaper animosity towards Labor. The changes provided that all electoral comment in a newspaper had to be signed by the author, and any political article which the proprietor was paid to publish had to be clearly headed 'advertisement'; predictably, these reforms angered the press. The FPLP's hostility to the press did not preclude close friendships with individual journalists, particularly the *Age*'s ambitious parliamentary reporter, Keith Murdoch, who capitalized on the friendship his father (a Presbyterian minister) had with Fisher, and became close to Pearce, Hughes, Fisher and other Labor MPs, entertaining some of them at his aunt's guest-house at Sassafras. Also significant was the relationship between *Argus* journalist Lloyd Dumas and WA Senator 'Paddy' Lynch. Although the leader was the only FPLP member authorized to inform the press about caucus proceedings, leaks to the press were common; in order to correct what Lynch claimed were mischievous distortions, he often gave his version of events to the *Argus* through Dumas.

At Home Affairs O'Malley's departmental head was a disciplinarian proud of his war service and fond of his military title of colonel. O'Malley was all for efficiency, but abhorred any militaristic overtones: he customarily addressed other staff members, especially the young lad who was his messenger, as 'colonel'. The freewheeling individualism of the 'jagged thorn in the buttocks of fossildom' was bound to unsettle more orthodox cabinet colleagues. There was a storm over preference to unionists, both within cabinet and in parliament, when O'Malley implemented this principle in his department without cabinet's imprimatur. Hughes complained to Fisher that 'we never know what he'll do next'. Hughes had long been an O'Malley antagonist, but even the more equable Fisher came to regard his Home Affairs minister with undisguised irritation. While O'Malley's showmanship appealed to politically unsophisticated electors, it invited ridicule from conservative organs of public opinion. This intensely annoyed Fisher, who was at pains to show that a Labor government could administer the nation's affairs at least as capably as its opponents. In parliament Fisher was noticeably edgy when O'Malley spoke, and sometimes intervened to answer questions directed to 'the King'. In cabinet the dignified, humourless Prime Minister did not enjoy O'Malley's taunts and frivolity: 'This is not a damned circus', he snorted during one meeting. For one brief period Fisher was so exasperated that he uncharacteristically resorted to informal cabinet meetings with O'Malley the only uninvited minister.

O'Malley was often controversial as minister responsible for the new Federal Capital Territory. Formerly unenthusiastic about moving to such a 'wilderness', he became an impassioned convert overnight when he was made responsible for its development. For the design of this bush capital – nicknamed 'Thirstyville' after O'Malley banned hotels (or 'stagger-juiceries' as he called them) from the

Territory – he launched a worldwide competition: 'If an Australian can produce a design, it will be accepted; but we require the best we can get, whether it comes from Swede or Dane, from Quaker, Shaker or Holy Roller'. The composition of the judging panel drew intense criticism, and when the winner was announced sceptics ignored his superb design and highlighted his American nationality, suspecting Australia's Yankee-twanged minister of influencing the judges. Another great Home Affairs development, the east-west transcontinental railway across the barren Nullarbor desert, was overseen by O'Malley and received its share of his 'spreadeagle' rhetoric: 'This line. . .will open up millions of acres of soil unsurpassed in richness, possessing a fascinating, undulating beauty of surface with a health-producing climate. . .and worthy of being either the central pivot or a mighty outpost of Australian civilization'. However, he ignored technical advice and appointed Henry Chinn, a shady go-getter, as supervising engineer on the railway. Chinn's dubious qualifications and unsavoury past became the subject of a royal commission, which did not reflect well on O'Malley or the government. There was also a fuss about the choice of timber used for the railway's sleepers, which provoked even Labor backbenchers, not for the first time, to criticize O'Malley's administration.

Also controversial was O'Malley's role in one of the Fisher government's best-known reforms, the Commonwealth Bank. He promoted the cause of banking reform in and out of parliament for years, although the insertion of a state bank in Labor platforms during the 1890s preceded his involvement in the party. It was first included in a lowly position in Labor's federal platform at the 1902 federal conference (which O'Malley did not attend). At the 1908 conference, which devoted much attention to intergovernmental financial relations, O'Malley moved that essential to that relationship was a national postal bank of deposit, issue, exchange and reserve. Conference loosely endorsed his general scheme, and 'Commonwealth Bank' became plank six of the fighting platform. In 1910 the Labor government quickly introduced uniform Australian banknotes, but divorced from any projected national bank. Despite criticism of 'Fisher's Flimsies' the note issue was an overdue innovation and a handy source of revenue, but it was not – as O'Malley knew and Anstey regretfully pointed out in the 'torrent of words' that was his rousing maiden speech in federal parliament – part of an integrated scheme giving the government control of the Australian monetary system. O'Malley and others have claimed that the cabinet – principally Fisher and Hughes – was reluctant to proceed with a national bank, and its introduction only occurred because O'Malley organized a caucus 'torpedo brigade' which coerced the cabinet in a dramatic caucus showdown several weeks after the 1911 parliamentary sittings commenced. O'Malley provided several versions, with himself the vital figure in each one. In fact, when Fisher announced the government's sessional programme at the FPLP's very first 1911 meeting, a 'National Bank' headed the list which caucus approved in its entirety. The FPLP minutes contain no sign of the alleged caucus showdown. When the Commonwealth Bank Bill was presented to parliament, it was Fisher who introduced it; he and other speakers referred to O'Malley's sustained advocacy, but 'the King' himself was silent during the debate. This silence probably reflected his disappointment that the bank was not initially given the thoroughgoing powers of a true central bank. Instead, it was modestly inaugurated as a trading and savings bank, unconventional only in its exclusive handling of the government's financial business and the fact that the government owned it. Fisher and

Hughes were determined that the bank as originally unveiled would be 'a plain business-like and practical measure' with 'no hint of a millennium'. Only later did the bank assume a grander role more to O'Malley's liking.

In SA, after Peake's party had been defeated as soon as parliament met following the 1910 election, the Labor government took office in June. Four of the six-member cabinet had trade union backgrounds. Premier Verran was a colourful Cornishman and Methodist lay preacher, 'folksy, flamboyant and nearly illiterate'. Before his election to the Assembly in 1901 he had been president of the Moonta Miners' Association for 18 years. Coneybeer, the Education minister, was the only member of the talented SA Labor influx of 1893 still in the Assembly. The Attorney-General was the same W.J. Denny who had edited the Catholic *Southern Cross* during its late 1890s anti-Labor phase: as the sitting MHA for Adelaide he had applied to join the ULP before the 1905 election and had been accepted. He began legal studies aged 31 and qualified in 1908. Women were not allowed to practise law in SA until his 1911 Women Lawyers Act enabled them to do so. The Treasurer, Crawford Vaughan, had attended stately Prince Alfred College and, like Denny, first contested parliament as an independent liberal. Formerly a prominent single taxer, Vaughan worked as a clerk and journalist before entering the Assembly in 1905, the year he also became party secretary.

The Verran government was tormented by industrial unrest. Declining real wages made SA toilers more ready to listen to militants like Frank Lundie, who preferred direct action to arbitration. Lundie began hard work as an 11-year-old farm labourer and grew up a confirmed teetotaller. In 1910 he was completing his first decade as the AWU's SA secretary, having served previously as its president and full-time organizer; like many other AWU officials, he pedalled a bicycle far and wide on union business. Lundie, the 'industrial King of Adelaide', was also president of an aggressive organization of unskilled workers formed in 1907, the United Labourers' Union (ULU). He inspired workers with his 'uncompromising socialist rectitude and humanity', and 'provoked conservatives with his fiery temper and militancy'. A tall, angular figure, he had a neck too long and thin for his shirt collars. His philosophy was out of step with that of SA Labor moderates as well as AWU leaders such as Spence and Macdonell. When railway navvies from the ULU went on strike in September 1910, Verran declared that 'The labor party of today cannot be dictated to by the revolutionary socialists of this state'. There were other disputes involving ULU workers, including a strike by tarpavers in Adelaide's Rundle Street which became violent when strikebreaking labour was brought in from Melbourne. In ugly skirmishes policemen wielded their batons freely to protect the strikebreakers, and Verran endorsed their conduct: 'the police will do their duty in regard to the protection of persons and property'. Lundie and other militants began to refer to 'the so called Labor government'. Eventually Denny managed to arrange a settlement, but it was a damaging episode for the government.

Even more serious was the drivers' strike in December 1910. Tired of waiting for a wages board to amend their low pay and long working hours, the Drivers' Union directly confronted the arbitration system with a protracted strike which brought Adelaide's commercial traffic to a standstill. It was skilfully managed by the union's secretary, 26-year-old John Gunn; formerly a close VSP colleague of Hyett and Curtin, he had moved to Adelaide two years previously and found work as a horse-lorry driver. Lundie told the cheering strikers that they would obtain more in three days by direct action than they would in three years through the 'damned Wages Board system'. It took longer than three days, but after more 'violence, police action, a series of pained statements from the government' and alarming rumours of famine, the dispute was settled on terms favourable to the strikers. Union militants found themselves at loggerheads with the government in further strikes, and they were also riled by its lack of support for the Fisher government's 1911 referenda proposals.

The government tried to reduce the incidence of strikes with a reform package incorporating an expanded wages board system, union preference, an industrial court and the banning of strikes, but the Council (with only four ULP members out of 18) amended it so savagely that the proposal had to be dropped. This was typical: nearly half the bills passed by the Assembly during the Verran government's period in office were rejected. The government managed to ease the plight of Aborigines and acted to make home ownership more possible for the needy, but even its modest forays into state enterprises were sabotaged by the Council. Verran's government drew up legislation to introduce adult suffrage for the Council and to limit its powers, but the Council refused to tolerate such democratic intrusions despite the recent precedent in London, where the House of Lords had been forced to accept significantly diminished powers. (If Australian federation had occurred after this development at Westminster instead of preceding it, conservative diehards would have found it more difficult to impede reform in Australia through the creation of a powerful Senate. Also, if federation had taken place when Labor had fully developed as a political force, less would have been heard of the nonsense of the Senate purporting to be a states' house rather than one divided on party lines.) The Verran government made a second attempt based on the House of Lords precedent, but again the Council was unmoved. Verran then tried a direct approach to the British government, asking it to amend the SA constitution. Meanwhile a crisis had arisen when the Verran government 'tacked' onto a supply bill a proposal to establish a state brickworks, and the Council rejected the bill. The British government responded that it would not interfere unless all SA constitutional measures had been used and the electorate clearly endorsed such intervention. The Verran government went to the people on 10 February 1912 and was defeated. After this unhappy experience of government the ULP derived some consolation when Peake, back in office, soon had severe problems of his own.

The SA parliamentary crisis prevented four of SA's delegates from travelling to Hobart to attend Labor's fifth federal conference in January 1912. Conference proudly introduced a new platform category, Planks Made Law, citing White Australia, pensions, land taxation, 'Citizen defence force with compulsory military training and Australian-owned and controlled navy', Commonwealth Bank and electoral reform. Heading the amended fighting platform was maintenance of both White Australia and land taxation. Next in line was resubmission of the 1911 referenda proposals. Hughes was not a delegate but told Fisher, who was, that conference should not restrict the government's flexibility in wording the proposals when they were again put before the people. Conference met his wishes in this respect, and carried a motion from Toowong branch directing the government to resubmit the referenda at the next federal election. Hughes also hoped that conference would affirm that the interpretation of the federal platform between federal conferences was solely a matter for the FPLP, but – as at the 1911 NSW conference – no such motion was carried. The High Court decisions and the failure of the 1911 referenda had led some Labor people to contemplate wistfully the virtues of unification: this concept involved complete legislative sovereignty for the national parliament with or without abolition of state legislatures. Fisher was among the minority supporting unification. It was common knowledge that the Constitution was not a workable one, he observed; 'It might be necessary to re-distribute the powers, and give the whole of the political power to the Commonwealth in a larger and more general way'. As in 1908, conference discussed but shelved the Queensland proposal for a national executive. State righters had another victory when conference rejected by one vote a plan by Givens to amend federal conference representation so that the bigger states had additional delegates in proportion to their population above the basic six for each state. The existing Senate-like system was, according to Watson, 'not democratic and it's no use saying that it is', but it remained unaltered for another 70 years.

Later that month Brisbane was paralysed by a general strike. With real wages generally falling in Queensland, particular trouble had long been brewing in the privately owned Brisbane Tramway Company, which was controlled from London and managed by J.S. Badger, an arrogant American who hated unions. Badger had ruthlessly suppressed attempts by Bowman and others to establish a union of tramway workers. When a union was eventually created, Badger refused to recognize it and badgered unionists with threats of dismissal if they wore their union badge. This edict from an obnoxious foreigner was offensive on nationalistic grounds, as well as denying the tramwaymen's right to organize. On 19 January 1912 the tramway unionists ceremonially pinned on their badges, and were immediately sacked. Other unions sensed a widespread onslaught against unionism, and when the tramwaymen went on strike a meeting called by the ALF's Brisbane district council decided to call a general strike. Queensland's anti-Labor government revived its flagging stocks by posturing as an upholder of law and order. Special constables were sworn in and, on 2 February, the infamous 'Black Friday' or 'Baton Friday', the specials combined with police to brutally disperse a strikers' procession. The day's only highlight for radicals concerned a deputation of women marching to Parliament House: when the deputation was caught up in the mêlée its leader, 72-year-old Emma Miller, tangled with Police Commissioner Cahill and wielded her hatpin on his unfortunate horse so effectively that Cahill was thrown. The Queensland government asked the Prime Minister to furnish military assistance to maintain law and order, and the strikers wanted him to provide protection against the authorities' excesses: Fisher refused both requests, but sent a donation to the strike funds. The one-sided reporting of these events in the daily press was countered by the publication each evening of a *Strike Bulletin* edited by J. Silver Collings, a 'florid, melodramatic orator' and regular Labor candidate in unwinnable seats. 'It is a bigger sin to starve than to steal in a land of plenty', he told the 1912 strikers. The Queensland government and its law enforcement agencies were determined to smash the strike completely and eventually did so.

The strike had important consequences. It contributed to Labor's defeat at the SA election on 10 February. Then Queensland's conservative government extended its law-and-order campaign into an early election which it also won comfortably. Labor lost ground in its traditionally strong rural electorates, which were influenced by reports of revolution in the capital city. On the other hand, voters in Brisbane knew what had occurred and were familiar with Badger's reputation; Labor did better there than ever before, winning six seats and coming close in three others. One of its successes was Mick Kirwan, an amiable train-caller who was sacked from the railways for his involvement in the strike and adapted his renowned vocal power to the apparently hopeless task of capturing Brisbane from its longstanding sitting member. The dream of a daily Labor paper, rekindled by the publication and popularity of the *Strike Bulletin*, came to reality later in 1912 with the launch of the *Daily Standard*. The strike also underlined Bowman's shortcomings as party leader, and his deteriorating health. During the strike he was simply too unwell to attend many of the numerous meetings and rallies, and he was noticeably overshadowed by some of Labor's newer, younger parliamentarians. He stayed on as leader after the election, blasting the government's Industrial Peace Act as 'the worst, the most tyrannical, and most coercive Bill that has ever existed' in Australia, before stepping down after suffering a stroke in parliament later in 1912.

His successor was T.J. Ryan. The son of an illiterate Irish farm labourer who migrated to Victoria, Tom Ryan won a scholarship to Xavier College in Melbourne, and went on to graduate in Arts and Law. He taught classics at various schools before being admitted as a barrister in 1901. In Melbourne he was influenced by Deakinite protectionism; after moving to Queensland his initial political candidature was as a radical liberal, but in 1904 he joined the Labor Party. He admired Kidston, but did not follow him out of the party. Kerr, who did, was still MLA for Barcoo when Ryan won preselection for that seat in 1909 with the assistance of Jackie Howe, the legendary bushworker and Labor activist renowned for his record-breaking shearing feats. Kerr had succeeded Tommy Ryan (also T.J.) as member for Barcoo in 1893, but was defeated by this other T.J. Ryan 16 years later. In the Assembly Ryan quickly impressed colleagues suspicious of 'intellectuals'. He had charm, presence, analytical ability, detailed knowledge of Queensland's laws, and the useful knack of expressing complex problems in plain language. During the general strike he emerged as Labor's outstanding figure in Queensland, acting as the unions' legal adviser and delivering incisive speeches from the platform.

Meanwhile a new force was transforming the Queensland labour movement. It was formed in 1907 as the Amalgamated Workers' Association (AWA) by Ted Theodore and Bill McCormack, two tough, vibrant, Australian-born miners. Theodore was only 21 and McCormack six years older when they forged their close friendship in 1906. At WA and Broken Hill 'Red Ted' Theodore had experienced the benefits for toilers of the sort of industrial organization that was lacking in north Queensland (except for pastoral workers covered by the AWU). He and McCormack had the ability, drive and strength of character to organize the nomadic miners, railway navvies, smelter hands and general labourers when all previous attempts had failed. Their familiarity with socialist literature gave them an intellectual edge over their comrades, but if rational argument was insufficient they were not fussy about their methods: physical intimidation was occasionally used to persuade workers to join their union. The AWA's objectives were strictly pragmatic, with working conditions paramount and utopian visions shunned. Its structure was highly centralized, with control exercised by an all-powerful executive. The AWA notched up a series of victories and extended its influence to sugar workers. When a local Labor MLA aligned himself with Kidston in the split, Theodore and McCormack apparently tossed a coin to decide which of them would contest the seat; the coin favoured Theodore, and he won the election. The AWA's biggest test was the prolonged 1911 sugar strike. Thorough preparation (lacking in the general strike not long afterwards) paid dividends in a tremendous victory for the union and McCormack, its commanding chief.

The general strike's failure was instrumental in the demise of the ALF as Queensland's dominant political-industrial entity. Aware that the defeat had left the ALF's constituent craft unions in impoverished disarray, McCormack sensed a power vacuum which the AWA could aspire to fill. He and Theodore renewed their message that the best approach was amalgamation of unions into an even larger organization with powerful central control; the idea embodied in the ALF, they argued, with the unions in the federation retaining their autonomy, was shown by the general strike to be outdated and ineffective. With Bowman ailing, Reid retired and Boote writing for the *Australian Worker* in Sydney, the ALF leadership was not what it had been, and Hinchcliffe was tied up with his secretaryship of the Fisher government's royal commission into the sugar industry. Afterwards, with rank-and-file unionists preferring amalgamation to federation, Hinchcliffe found himself outmanoeuvred. Theodore and McCormack organized the amalgamation of the AWA with the old pastorally-based AWU and several smaller southern unions into a new Australian Workers' Union (AWU), with the ALF virtually absorbed in the process. The Queensland branch of this mighty creation was established with AWA-type centralized control, and began its enduring reign over Queensland Labor. Its two leaders were quickly successful in the Labor Party. McCormack won Cairns in 1912 and was soon party whip. Theodore's force and far-sightedness were eye-catching attributes, and his rough edges were partly refined through wider social contacts, marriage and lessons in public speaking. When Ryan became leader in 1912, caucus created one of Labor's finest leadership partnerships by electing Theodore as his deputy.

So Hinchcliffe's long Queensland career drew to a close. In 1910 he had at last managed to shed one of his jobs when he stood down as CPE secretary, but only after a levy on branches, unions and MPs provided the funds to enable his successor to become Queensland Labor's first paid full-time party secretary. This successor was his protégé Lewis McDonald, a cheery printer who 'inherited Hinchcliffe's mantle but lacked his innovatory skills and political feel'. Hinchcliffe eventually settled in Sydney as business manager of the *Australian Worker*, teaming up again with his friend Boote who had also moved south for a combination of work and family reasons. From 1914 Boote edited the *Australian Worker* with verve, stylishness and commitment for nearly three decades.

In October 1911 Labor enjoyed its biggest ever WA election victory, winning 34 of the Assembly's 50 seats after a brilliant campaign orchestrated by Mahon and J.B. Holman. Bath was no longer Labor's leader; worn out by his workload, which included the co-production of the *Westralian Worker* with another busy parliamentarian (Stuart), he resigned in July 1910. Jack Scaddan was aged 35 when he became the first Labor premier to govern with a substantial majority; he was also the youngest ever WA premier. Born at Moonta (SA) of Cornish parents, he worked in the Bendigo mines before joining the goldseekers flocking to the West. There, like his friend Charlie Frazer, he worked as an engine driver and was an active unionist. A popular optimist known as 'Happy Jack', he was elected in 1904 and continued his intellectual development under Bath's tutelage. Bath was included in the Scaddan ministry elected by caucus; so were Johnson and Angwin, who had both returned to the Assembly in 1906. The Council was represented in cabinet by Drew, who this time agreed to become a loyal party member, and Jabez Dodd, who with Johnson had founded the breakaway AMA a decade earlier when the WA labour movement lacked the cohesion which the ALF structure now provided. Apart from Drew, only one caucus member was born in WA. One of the ex-Victorians was Phillip Collier, the new Mines and Railways minister; as the founding secretary of the Northcote PLC, he had been Anstey's campaign director before moving to Boulder on the Westralian gold-fields, which he was to represent in the Assembly for 42 years. The remaining minister, the oldest at 53, was Thomas Walker. After his extraordinarily adventurous and diverse experiences as spiritualist, populist, poet, dramatist, NSW MLA, temperance lecturer, journalist and farmer, he was sworn in as Scaddan's Attorney-General the very day he was admitted as a barrister and solicitor.

The Scaddan government lost no time in launching an extensive array of state enterprises. Government activity to help the capitalist system function better in a big harsh country had been part of the Australian experience, especially in WA's underdeveloped community, and Labor propagandists pointed this out with understandable frequency to counter their opponents' attempts to alarm voters about socialism. Yet these reforms did represent a radical, comprehensive commitment to government involvement in activities for the workers' benefit. The government's sense of purpose was shown by the way it bypassed the re-actionaries in control of the Legislative Council; aware that they would disallow reformist legislation, the government used its executive powers to good effect. It acted quickly to establish state enterprises in shipping, dairy produce, sawmills, metropolitan tramways and every aspect of the meat industry. Others were to follow in river ferries, electric power supply, brickworks, agricultural machinery, fish and hotels. When the Council was able to obstruct, it did so with a will; considering the damage inflicted by the Council wreckers, the government's achievements were all the more creditable.

The government was commendably active in other areas. The rate of railway construction was the highest ever in WA. The farmers settling in the eastern wheat belt, frequently former miners displaced as goldmining slackened, were assisted by technical expertise, liberalized lending arrangements and new railways to transport the greatly increased production that resulted. In an initiative closely related to the state enterprises in building supplies, the government established a Workers' Homes Board to increase home ownership among battling families. Workers were also assisted by extensions to the arbitration system and workers' compensation. There were significant reforms in education, irrigation, criminal law and divorce. Although land taxation was increased and a graduated income tax was introduced, the government's free-spending approach produced hefty deficits; when the deficit exceeded £1 million Scaddan was dubbed 'Gone-a-Million Jack'. There were inevitably some disagreements between the ministry and the labour movement, notably disputes involving Collier who found the railway workers difficult to satisfy. Heated parliamentary clashes occurred between Scaddan and that inveterate stirrer, 'Mulga' Taylor. Backbenchers enjoyed a surprisingly high degree of freedom to cross the floor on particular issues, but with such a large majority Scaddan could afford to be relaxed. He knew that this government was held in high regard by both the electorate generally and its own supporters. With wheat harvests rising in response to the government's initiatives, there was little to cloud Scaddan's optimism as his government ended its second year in office.

The situation was altogether different in NSW, where the labour movement had become increasingly critical of its Labor government. The McGowen government made good early progress with state enterprises, housing for workers and important reforms in arbitration, income tax and electoral law. But the PLL executive expressed its regret that no action had been taken against the Council –

its abolition was a plank on the fighting platform – especially as it had delayed and pruned the arbitration reforms. The government responded halfheartedly by appointing 11 men to the Council, only six of whom were clearly Labor supporters. The party was unimpressed, especially when some of these nominees contributed to the rejection of government legislation. In August 1912 a PLL vice-president formed a Labor Principles Defence Committee to keep the government honest about Council abolition. Another major bone of contention was a deal the government made with BHP to help the company set up a steelworks at Newcastle. This controversial decision resulted in the government being censured at the 1913 PLL conference for assisting a private monopoly instead of establishing the industry as a state enterprise.

The McGowen government's instability made its task no easier. Whereas the Scaddan ministry remained unchanged until it faced the electors in 1914 and the Fisher cabinet was altered once, slightly, when Batchelor died, the NSW cabinet was repeatedly reshuffled. Nielsen's resignation over land policy followed the departure of Macdonell, who had been battling declining health for many years but broke down completely in January 1911. He moved to a Melbourne hospital where he died the following October of cancer, aged 49. He was greatly admired: Henry Lawson described him as 'the tallest, straightest and perhaps the best of the Bourke-side bush-leaders', and the AWU named its Sydney headquarters after him. Dacey's surprise omission in 1910 was rectified when he filled the first ministerial vacancy and, after Carmichael resigned following a petty dispute with Holman which brought credit to neither, Dacey found himself Treasurer. He was starting to fulfil his undoubted promise when he died of kidney failure in April 1912, too soon for him to see the fruits of his plans for low-cost workers' housing. Flowers, initially a minister without portfolio, was promoted to administer a department. Although the Opposition Leader sneeringly queried whether this would be beyond a mere house painter, Flowers proved him spectacularly wrong, particularly with his humane, effective and wide-ranging reforms in Public Health. Carmichael returned after a short absence and was 'energetic, innovative and successful' in the realm of education. Cann came into the ministry as Treasurer. D.R. Hall was one of the Legislative Council appointments, accepting Holman's invitation to return from federal parliament and lighten Holman's burden by taking over the Justice ministry.

The ministerial instability went right to the top. Holman was becoming frustrated with McGowen's unwillingness after 18 years as NSW Labor leader to make way for him. 'Old Jim' McGowen's limitations had been exposed as Premier. Most of the direction came from Holman; it was his masterly manoeuvring which enabled the government to survive in 1911 while McGowen was away. But late in 1912 Holman was feeling ragged and wanted a change: 'I was out of sorts with myself, the party and the world', he recalled. Rumours began to circulate that he and Beeby, who was equally restless and increasingly irked by the constraints Labor imposed on its MPs, would form a new centre party. Holman hoped for the Labor leadership or, failing that, a break from mainstream politics as Agent-General in London; in either event he felt that Beeby would be the best choice as deputy leader and told him so. All their negotiations suddenly fell apart when Beeby, without telling Holman, sensationally resigned. Holman was livid. 'I feel utterly broken up', he told his wife. 'A mob like that are not worth being associated with.' Then Nielsen, who had been overseas on an official trade mission for the government, resigned as an MLA. 'The double catastrophe has driven our men crazy', Holman noted. In this mood Holman instantly accepted when his friend Hugh McIntosh, a hustling entrepreneur, offered to finance a holiday trip to England. While he was away there was a major strike by Sydney gasworkers, who refused to negotiate. The dispute put other toilers out of work, and as it dragged on there was mounting pressure on the government to find a solution. Ultimately, an exasperated McGowen threatened to break the strike with volunteer labour if the gasworkers maintained their stand. There was a hostile reaction from an appalled labour movement, including MPs nervous about the difficult election the government would face later in 1913. McGowen became convinced that it was time to quit. Holman returned, reinvigorated after his sojourn, early in June. Later that month, despite the opposition of influential party figures including Watson, Holman was delighted to take over as Premier.

While NSW Labor was contemplating who should lead it, Hughes was contemplating who should sit on the High Court. The failure of the 1911 referenda coupled with the High Court majority's continued restrictive interpretation of the national government's powers made the Fisher government's choices all the more important. The traditional source for judicial appointments has been eminent barristers, precisely the sort of lawyers whose clients and everyday social contacts have for decades comprised the powerful, the wealthy and the conservative. The NSW and Victorian Bars, in particular, managed to endow this 'natural' process with an aura of sacredness backed by all the pomp, majesty and mystique of 'The Law'. Any deviation from it risked a furious outcry from these Bars and the conservative press which could influence some voters. While all national Labor governments making High Court appointments have had to confront this dilemma, it was at its most acute when Hughes tackled it in 1912–13; in those days there were hardly any 'Labor lawyers', let alone societies of them.

Hughes had three vacancies to fill. One judge had died, and two extra judges were to be appointed owing to the increasing volume of work, including cases in the Arbitration Court. Hughes wanted, if possible, to make the court more amenable to Labor's view of the Constitution without provoking controversy. He was embarrassed when Fisher and McGregor straightforwardly declared that Labor should be 'represented' on the bench. With a small range to choose from, Hughes opted for liberally inclined men who he hoped were not too enamoured of state rights. While his first appointment was reasonably conventional, his second was 'a mediocrity' who received sustained criticism but resiliently weathered the storm. The third appointment, A.B. Piddington, was a humane, enlightened liberal with advanced views and an outstanding academic record; he had served a term in the NSW Assembly as a radical Free Trader in the 1890s, when he strongly opposed the basis for federation which became ratified as the Constitution. Knowing Piddington too slightly to be certain of his views on constitutional questions, Hughes asked Piddington's brother-in-law, poet and NSW Labor MLA (and father of novelist Eleanor Dark) Dowell O'Reilly to check. O'Reilly cabled Piddington, then returning from a visit to England; 'In sympathy with supremacy of Commonwealth powers' was the reply. Piddington's appointment was greeted by a 'blizzard of scandalized protest'. The NSW and Victorian Bars formally resolved not to congratulate him. Sensitive, distressed by the frenzied uproar and concurrent family worries, Piddington wilted, and announced his resignation, citing unspecified private reasons. To replace him Hughes chose a 'constitutionally colourless' NSW Supreme Court judge.

Fortunately for Labor, the nature of Hughes's unsubtle preliminary approach to Piddington was not public knowledge during the federal election campaign

85

shortly afterwards. It would have been a bonanza for the anti-Labor press, which attacked the Fisher government at every opportunity during the campaign but struggled to find compelling ammunition. The government had been energetically reformist without making any major blunders, and was more cohesive and better led than its opponents. The economy under Labor had been buoyant; Fisher was a competent Treasurer and, as Mahon pointed out, gross savings bank deposits in Australia during 1910-13 soared by 138%. O'Malley, however, gave the press an opening. With Labor's opponents alleging extravagance in the Postmaster-General's department, Frazer was infuriated by O'Malley's casual observation that although Frazer had done everything possible the postal administration, unlike O'Malley's own splendidly organized department, 'was still kicking like a mule and going backwards'. Frazer cabled Fisher urging him to restrain O'Malley: 'in my opinion he is an irresponsible incompetent unquestionable blatherskite'. Anti-Labor newspapers in Victoria made a telling contribution by dramatizing a log of claims made by the Rural Workers' Union. The timing of the claims placed Labor's country members like Scullin and J.K. McDougall in an invidious position. Pestered to declare their attitude, they alienated some farmers by supporting the unionists' aspirations for improved working conditions. The newspapers' distortions on this issue and others led to redoubled calls after the campaign for a daily Labor paper in all states.

It was an extremely close election and the results were not clear for some time. The voters rejected all six referenda: each was approved in three states (Queensland, WA and SA) instead of the required four, and by over 49% of the total vote without quite attaining the necessary majority, so Labor missed obtaining the powers a national government should have by a whisker. So near and yet so far also summed up the election result: Labor lost by one seat in the Representatives (the FPLP had so many non-retiring Senators in 1913 that it easily retained its Senate majority). Labor may have suffered from Fisher's understandable emphasis on his government's proud record in office; electoral strategists many years later acknowledged that 'there are no votes in yesterday's reforms'. Also, a redistribution had changed the character of some seats, most importantly from Labor's viewpoint in WA where Mahon was defeated after his seat was renamed Dampier and lost its mining component to the adjoining seat of Kalgoorlie held by his Labor rival Frazer. But the election was fundamentally determined by a rural swing away from the government. Labor lost five NSW country seats (and narrowly won one), while in Victoria the loss of four rural members including Scullin and McDougall was only partly compensated for by the capture of a metropolitan seat together with Bendigo (won by talented miner's son Jack Arthur) and the seat vacated by Deakin, Ballarat (won by McGrath). With Labor consolidating in a number of urban seats, its future federal success would increasingly depend on its ability to win country electorates. Linking the referenda with the election was risky: if voters reluctant to approve referenda could be induced by obfuscation or scare tactics to vote 'No', they would be most unlikely to vote Labor. The Fisher government tried to counter this strategy by having printed arguments for and against the referenda proposals distributed to the voters. This time Labor was ostensibly united on the referenda, although there were still defiant rumblings from some elements of the party in NSW. Holman's absence abroad facilitated Labor's more united referenda front, but his brilliant campaigning, evident in 1910, was sorely missed, especially in the crucial rural NSW seats.

Holman's importance was emphasized when he led Labor to victory at the

13. AWU hall, Chillagoe. (*Oxley Library*)

14. Labor's setback at the 1911 referenda. (by Norman Lindsay; *National Library*)

15. King O'Malley. (by Will Dyson; *National Library*)

16. Labor Senators 'Big Jim' Long and Arthur Rae pretend to resolve their disagreement about the capital territory site. (*National Library*)

17. The Verran ministry, 1910–1912. Standing (from left): F. Coneybeer, W. J. Denny, C. Vaughan. Seated: J. P. Wilson, J. Verran, F. S. Wallis. (*Old Parliament House*)

18. Part of the force of police and mounted 'specials' awaiting the strikers' procession in Brisbane on 'Black Friday', 2 February 1912. (*Oxley Library*)

19. Emma Miller. (*Pam Young*)

20. Henry Boote (left) and Albert Hinchcliffe. (*Oxley Library*)

NSW election in December. Beeby's National Progressive Party was brushed aside; its 13 candidates, including Beeby, all lost. During the campaign Holman had asked for a mandate to take on the Council, which had butchered much of Labor's legislation. The electorate had provided him with a comfortable majority, and the party was looking for prompt action. Yet Holman hesitated. The reason was his private pledge to appoint to the Council his friend and benefactor Hugh McIntosh, who was not a Labor Party member. Holman knew that such an appointment would provoke a major row with the PLL, which at its annual conference in January 1914 laid down strict guidelines for the government's nominations to the Council, including a pledge that they work for its abolition. Like the PLL executive, caucus asserted its right to approve Council nominations. Holman dismissed both claims, saying it was solely a matter for cabinet. His prodigious ego – previously restrained, but out of control since the election triumph – was leading him into dangerous waters. An anti-Holman group emerged in caucus, electing R.D. Meagher, a controversial ex-lawyer, as Labor's nomination for the speakership instead of Holman's choice, McGowen. Lamond supported the caucus anti-Holmanites in the *Australian Worker* and elsewhere. In April Holman clashed publicly with Meagher, now PLL president, over caucus approval of Council nominees. Still no appointments were made, and the Council was soon knocking back legislation as before. Clearly, lively times for Holman and his party lay ahead.

December 1913 was also the month when Victoria became the sixth state to experience a Labor government. Like Labor's first taste of office as a minority government in Queensland and Tasmania, it was short and not very sweet. As in Queensland and Tasmania, the unwelcome sight of Labor in office quickly galvanized its opponents to settle their differences sufficiently to remove the intruder. After nearly a decade as Victorian party leader, Prendergast had stepped down earlier in 1913 because of ill-health; in the 13-day ministry he was Chief Secretary. Victoria's first Labor premier was George Elmslie, a decent, determined stonemason of modest ability who was well aware that he was unable to control the fate of his government.

John Wren had closed his Collingwood tote and was extending his operations interstate. His 'business activities' were becoming no less 'respectable' than those of many other entrepreneurs who were closely linked to Labor's political opponents. Although his control of inner-suburban branches like Fitzroy was sewn up, his efforts to ensure a preselection win for talented lawyer Frank Brennan by manipulating the ballot resulted in a state executive inquiry which confirmed that party rules had been broken. This underlined the limits to Wren's influence in the party. As he later realized, donations to non-Labor politicians could produce simpler results without such troublesome complications as preselection battles, fierce internal policy debates and strong executives prepared to intervene. Brennan himself was cleared of any wrongdoing. A kind-hearted, volatile individualist known for his biting wit, he was always indifferent to Labor's internal politics, and as MHR for the safe seat of Batman (from 1911) could afford to be.

In state politics Victorian Labor had not matched its fine contribution in federal elections. Even if it had, the Victorian electoral system was so scandalously unfair to Labor that it was certain to struggle in the state sphere. The voters came to see state Labor, which was powerless to alter the iniquitous electoral system, as a failure. A perpetuating factor was the gravitation of talented candidates towards federal parliament, which they could attend without having to travel interstate. Labor's dispirited state remnant tended to settle for a subordinate role with a 'lowering of intellectual, ideological and perhaps moral expectations'. Anti-Labor could afford to indulge in factional fights over the spoils of victory in the seedy atmosphere which characterized Victorian state politics for many years.

Tasmania's conservatives continued their feverish resistance to Labor's advance. During the 1912 election campaign 'almost every conceivable kind of falsehood was stated about the party'. For his advocacy of breaking up the big estates Lyons was assaulted on a platform by an enraged landowner brandishing a whip, and there were other unseemly incidents. In this election Labor won 14 seats (up two) in the 30-member Assembly. The proportional representation system tended to entrench similar strengths in the Assembly for the two major parties; slender government majorities, or independents holding the balance of power, were common in Tasmania with its five six-member electorates. Another product of the voting system was a degree of infighting by candidates as concerned about party colleagues beating them to a seat as they were about the common enemy. Anti-Labor instability (abetted by Earle, who gnawed with judicious intrigue at the government's narrow majority) resulted in a snap election in January 1913. As usual, Labor's island campaigners were reinforced by 'gladiators from across the Straits', this time including Curtin, whose union work often brought him to Tasmania. (Curtin and Hyett, like their former VSP colleague Gunn, had become effective union secretaries, Hyett at the Victorian Railways Union and Curtin at the Timber Workers.) The result was the same: Labor 14, anti-Labor 16. A year later Labor drew level when it captured a seat in a by-election. Labor's opportunity to take office came when an eccentric Irish MHA, J.T.H. Whitsitt, defected from the government because it would not override mainland refusals to receive decayed potatoes from Tasmania. After the government was defeated in the Assembly, Earle was commissioned by the Governor subject to onerous conditions. Earle accepted the conditions and took office in April 1914, but breached his undertaking by refusing to hold the immediate election he had promised. Instead, Labor used its Assembly majority to refer the question to the Colonial Office, which repudiated the Governor's conduct.

Labor faced daunting obstacles, including continued reliance on the capricious Whitsitt for its parliamentary majority, its lack of representation in the Council and the pressure-group activities of the Catholic Federation. There was also an economic crisis triggered by a sudden mining slump in the Labor stronghold of Zeehan. The government took prompt action to keep the mines open; Ogden, the first ex-miner to become Tasmanian Mines minister, especially distinguished himself. Earle was an effective Attorney-General despite his lack of legal training. Belton had two portfolios, Agriculture together with Land and Works, and Lyons had three – Treasury, Education and Railways. Lyons had risen rapidly through the party to become Earle's deputy. Imbued with his parents' Irish Catholicism and radicalism, he started work as a nine-year-old to support his impoverished family before being rescued by two aunts who enabled him to become a schoolteacher. No intellectual, Lyons 'was influenced by people, not books'. A fine speaker and a genuine radical who insisted that the entire Labor platform was 'inviolate', he had political shrewdness and an engaging, uncontrived warmth which attracted admirers. In 1907, when he first moved to Hobart, he had joined a Labor discussion group where he befriended L.F. Giblin, a Hobart-born Cambridge graduate who was to become one of Australia's leading economists. As Treasurer in 1914, Lyons relied heavily on advice from Giblin, a recently elected MHA for Denison; together they began to renovate the state's financial system. A portent of the future was the swift takeover of an ailing company involved in a hydro-electric scheme at the Great Lake.

The FPLP was playing it hard in opposition. When parliament resumed Fisher was not the only nomination for leader. A group of caucus radicals led by Catts marshalled support for Higgs, but Fisher won convincingly: caucus minutes record the voting figures as Fisher 42, Higgs 18, Hughes 1. Caucus also elected an executive, which met frequently during the following year to discuss tactics as events unfolded in a parliament where their commanding Senate majority could make life very difficult for the anti-Labor government with its one-seat Representatives majority. The FPLP showed it no mercy. It soon became clear that the government had its eye on a double dissolution. Caucus decided that an early election was in the best interests of the party and the nation, but its ideal was another Representatives election only; it was understandably less keen on an unprecedented double dissolution which would put its Senate supremacy at risk. A militant FPLP fragment, including Rae, perhaps Gardiner and others, was keen to use Labor's Senate power to the full, but caucus scotched a proposal from Rae that Labor's Senators refuse to deal with any government business (presumably including Supply bills). The FPLP hotly disputed the correctness of Governor-General Munro Ferguson's decision to grant the double dissolution: Labor advocates argued that it was nonsense to claim – as the government did – that he was bound to follow his ministers' advice. Hughes described the decision as 'constitutional butchery'. Despite this grievance Labor entered the election positively. This time Labor would be without its self-imposed burden of concurrent referenda. Fisher's policy speech was more forward-looking, and emphasized policies which would appeal to voters in the marginal rural seats.

Labor's campaign was hampered when yet another of its prominent figures suddenly died in harness. When Labor's 'rough-hewn' veteran Gregor McGregor succumbed to a heart ailment, the FPLP had not only lost one of its most experienced and admired leaders; campaign schedules had to be hastily rearranged, and the timing of his death after nominations closed virtually handed his seat to the enemy. But at least the 65-year-old McGregor's best days were behind him, which could not at all be said of the two federal members, both possible future leaders, tragically lost to Labor since the May election. In November Charlie Frazer spent an enjoyable Saturday at Wren's Epsom racecourse, awoke next morning with pneumonia and died two days later. His colleagues were devastated. Still only 33, he had achieved plenty but had much more to offer. A week after Frazer's death, E.A. Roberts was involved in one of the sharp clashes typical of this parliament; he strode out of the chamber and across Queen's Hall before collapsing with a fatal heart attack alongside Queen Victoria's statue. He was 44. Capable, voluble and opinionated, Roberts had also felt he was destined for higher office. There was an ironical twist to these Labor tragedies when Frazer's enemy Mahon, seemingly dead and buried politically, managed an unexpected comeback by winning preselection to succeed Frazer in Kalgoorlie. He returned to parliament a new man, restored to health and intent on dispelling his image as Labor's 'contemptuously cold, bitingly sarcastic...emotionless and superior' iceberg.

Labor people commonly criticized their MPs for not being icy enough. They saw parliament as a comfortable club which seduced Labor members with facilities way beyond the reach of a typical toiler – higher wages, comfortable leather chairs, billiard tables, dining room, well-stocked library, free rail travel and invitations to lavish functions. Close contact with Labor's adversaries could be disarming too. After lashing union bashers on the hustings, it was a different matter altogether to confront them in relaxing surroundings and find that they were not bad blokes to share a drink or game of cards with. Many Labor men 'were obliged to adjust, and often did so without being aware of the process'. Another ever-present hazard was absorption in the trivia of parliamentary life – the grandstanding, point-scoring, intrigue and gossip – to the detriment of their perception of events in the world outside. Elevation to the ministry only accentuated these tendencies. Whereas party supporters wanted quick results, Labor ministers faced financial limitations, constitutional constraints, obstructive departmental procedure and an overwhelming array of conflicting demands. Party militants had other grievances. They grumbled about the number of MPs elected to senior positions in the party organization, and they were disillusioned by Labor's orientation in office towards the whole community rather than the working class exclusively. In the perennial contest between principle and expediency, radicals were peeved by the concessions Labor had to make in connection with such sacred cows as British loyalty, religious (especially Catholic) sensibilities and farmers' interests, in order to get enough votes to properly implement its platform. Labor's performance was also criticized in mid-1913 by a distant observer, V.I. Lenin: 'What a peculiar capitalist country is this in which Labor predominates in the *upper* house and recently predominated in the lower, and yet the capitalist system has not been exposed to any danger?' Lenin scorned any idea that Labor was a truly socialist party, but socialism has different meanings for different people. To Lenin, socialism meant the violent overthrow of the capitalist system including the institution of parliament, whereas most ALP socialists subscribed to an altogether milder variant involving gradual progress through parliamentary reform towards more fairness and equality in Australia. 'We are all Socialists now', said Fisher in 1908, 'and indeed the only qualification you hear from anybody is probably that he is "not an extreme Socialist"'. Although anti-Labor would inevitably be dredging up the socialist bogey at future elections, Labor leaders were confident that these alarmist shrieks had lost their potency, especially since Reid's 'socialist tiger' campaign had been discredited and the voters had experienced Labor governments.

Labor was justifiably proud of its achievements. Its 1912 federal conference report claimed that 'the eyes of all reformers throughout the civilised world are upon us, watching with sympathy and interest our unequalled progress', and indeed British Labour identities like Keir Hardie and Ramsay MacDonald came to inspect it for themselves. Hardie later wrote to Fisher asking him to arrange a resolution by the Australian parliament in favour of women's suffrage, then universal in Australia but still denied to British women. Maloney moved the appropriate resolution, which Hardie felt would assist the suffragettes in England – he clearly thought international notice was taken of Australian reforms. Apart from occasional contact with British Labour figures, Australian Labor's affinity with its overseas equivalents was slight. Federal conference in 1912, not for the first time, recommended that the party should be represented at the International Socialist Conference, but Europe was too far away and the costs involved too prohibitive for a party always starved of funds. Conference contented itself with dispatching a paper to be read at the international gathering and conveying fraternal greetings to the German SPD. Compared to other countries Australia was relatively advanced in living standards and social reform, and Labor could take much of the credit. While Deakin and other non-Labor figures were instrumental in some progressive innovations in this era of social optimism, the main driving force was the Labor Party. Its dynamic presence was the dominant factor in turning yesterday's heresies into contemporary orthodoxies, whether or not it was Labor governments that eventually introduced them. Its visionaries felt that Labor was poised to fulfil the dream of the party's founders and fashion a distinctively Australian response to the fundamental problem of creating a fairer society. Others, less sanguine, wondered how much more was possible while Australia was chained to the dictates of international economic fluctuations and the yoke of British imperialism. As Europe slid into catastrophe in July 1914, the implications for Australia and its Labor Party meant that the hopes of the visionaries would be cruelly crushed.

5 'Blowing the Labor Party to Shreds': The Great War and the Great Split, 1914–1919

INITIALLY AUSTRALIANS WERE extraordinarily enthusiastic about the great madness in Europe that was to engulf a generation. Socialists and radicals were among the tiny minority of Australians who queried their country's automatic entry alongside Britain, the other dominions, France and Russia against Germany and its allies. Nearly all Australians possessed a strong pride in Britain's heritage; family links, educational influences and social conditioning combined to make this inevitable. Australian nationalists saw the war also as an opportunity for their newly federated nation to make its mark internationally and create its own proud traditions. The song 'Australia Will Be There' became an instant popular success. There was apprehension in the air as well. Germany was a powerful nation intent on increasing its empire; fears were held that if it conquered Britain Australia would be very vulnerable. In the rush to enlist, some men were inspired by strong patriotic feelings; some in tedious jobs were prompted by a sense of adventure and the once-in-a-lifetime prospect of travel overseas; some felt the need to impress or escape from particular women; others made a spontaneous decision to be in it with their mates. Many were influenced by the prevailing wisdom that the war would not last long and might be over by Christmas. Another factor may have statistically inflated working-class support for the war: the rupture of trade with Germany and other sudden economic adjustments threw many unionists out of work and made them far more likely to enlist.

Labor attitudes to the European crisis were ominously varied from the outset. To the *Labor Call* it was 'unthinkable to believe that because an archduke and his missus were slain by a fanatic the whole of Europe should become a seething battlefield, and deplorable misery brought upon the people'. In the *Australian Worker* Henry Boote was, as throughout the war, forthright and insightful. There was 'no great principle' at stake to justify bloodshed, he contended, and 'Australia will suffer much' with unemployment and price rises. Nevertheless,

> We must protect our country. We must keep sacred from the mailed fist this splendid heritage. For that our Army of Defence was formed, and our Navy built. But we hope no wave of jingo madness will sweep over the land, unbalancing the judgment of its leaders, and inciting its population to wild measures, spurred on by the vile press.

Fisher, on the hustings at Colac during the federal election campaign, borrowed a catchcry from the Boer War when he asserted that if necessary Australia would assist Britain 'to our last man and our last shilling'. For 'Happy Jack' Scaddan 1914 had been anything but happy, owing to a disastrous wheat crop in WA, a sharp increase in unemployment and growing criticism of the financial losses incurred by his government's state enterprises; on his birthday (and W.A. Holman's), 4 August, the die was cast when Britain declared war on Germany. Even before this news reached Australia Hughes was feverishly trying to persuade all and sundry that the election should be cancelled; he already saw the looming war as Armageddon, an almighty struggle that had to be won at all costs. Desperate to press his views on Fisher, who was campaigning in the Riverina, Hughes utilized an unlikely messenger in Senator Rae, the FPLP's most hostile critic of lavish defence expenditure by Labor governments. Fisher was unmoved: 'I am absolutely in disagreement with your views', he advised Hughes. Yet he had no illusions about the difficulties ahead if Labor won the election. 'Should the war prevent success we may not miss much', he told his wife in an understatement of acute retrospective poignancy, but 'I am ready for any responsibility the country may impose on me'.

He soon had responsibility aplenty. Labor's convincing election win was attributed by some observers to its clearly superior record on defence. The FPLP captured five Representatives seats, all in Victoria and NSW; only one was not rural. In this double dissolution all 36 Senate seats were contested, and Labor won 31; Rae, however, was rejected by the voters because of his lack of enthusiasm about the war. Some caucus members felt that all states should be represented in Fisher's ministry, and this was in fact the outcome. The Senate's ministerial trio comprised Pearce, Gardiner and fluent debater and VSP stalwart Ted Russell. In the Representatives Hughes was first elected, followed by Arthur, Archibald, Spence, Jensen, Tudor and Mahon. The crucial figures would again be Treasurer Fisher, Attorney-General Hughes and Pearce at Defence. Having suffered a breakdown as Defence minister in peacetime, Pearce had understandable misgivings about the huge burden of that portfolio in wartime, but there was hardly a politician in the country better equipped to shoulder it. The new External Affairs minister, Jack Arthur, had risen from humble origins to achieve dazzling academic results at Melbourne University and become a leading barrister. Little more than a year after wresting Bendigo from its incumbent since federation, he had been elevated by his colleagues into the ministry, but at 39 he was already afflicted with the kidney illness that was to prove fatal within three months – yet another Labor career of outstanding promise cut short. Mahon's remarkable resurrection continued when he became Arthur's successor at External Affairs.

So Australian Labor settled to the task which faced no other labour or socialist party. Its equivalents in other belligerent nations merely had to react to their respective governments' administration of the war. Only in Australia did Labor have the onerous undertaking of directing their country's involvement in a conflagration far beyond anyone's expectation or experience. As the colossal armies clashed in France and Belgium the result was not sweeping victory for one of them but deadlock, and the struggle bogged down into prolonged trench warfare. For some time only a hazy appreciation of these developments penetrated Australia. Information from Britain or the battle front was rigorously censored before publication in the newspapers, and private British enlightenment to the

Fisher government's senior ministers was meagre. The war dominated the government's activities. To finance Australia's participation Fisher negotiated a loan from Britain, extended land taxation and introduced an inheritance tax. Hughes busied himself with such wartime legislation as the Enemy Contracts Annulment Act, the Trading With The Enemy Act and, in particular, the all-powerful War Precautions Act (WPA). Under Pearce's supervision the new Australian Imperial Force (AIF) was provided with officers, uniforms, equipment, munitions, shipping, rations, animals and several weeks' training prior to embarkation. The knowledge that German cruisers were on the loose made Fisher very worried about allowing the convoy of Australian troopships to leave. Overruling assurances from the British Admiralty and the AIF commander, Fisher delayed the convoy's departure until he was satisfied it was safe. Ironically, one of its escorts was a powerful Japanese cruiser. With the war by no means over by Christmas and beginning to be referred to as the War, Fisher was already so drained by the pressures of leadership that he slipped across to New Zealand for a rest.

Diverging attitudes to the war within the Labor Party contributed to Fisher's worries. Some Labor people agreed with Hughes that Australia had to do its utmost to assist the British to victory by whatever means possible, in order to protect Labor's achievements. Many in the party felt that a commitment to the British cause might require some abnormal authoritarian arrangements during wartime, but need not preclude further progress towards Labor's objectives. Others were suspicious of the war as the justification for both the downgrading of Labor's platform goals and the introduction of government measures inconsistent with Labor ideals; they emphasized that Australia had nothing to do with the war's origins, and doubted the wisdom of such a heavy emotional, human and financial commitment to a war so far away.

Within the FPLP Anstey was the most prominent sceptic. He was

a fiery and eloquent speaker, an actor who threw himself with abandon into every speech. Passionately sincere, he was a master of sarcasm, his favourite form a crescendo of rhetorical questions mounting to a deadly climax.

When the government announced a grant of £100 000 to Belgium because of the devastation it had suffered since being invaded by Germany, Anstey launched into one of his tirades. He recalled Australia's different reaction several years earlier when Belgian strikers were shot by their government: 'For them we had no expression of sympathy, no recognition of their great struggle, not a penny of help'.

The scalping knife and the tomahawk of the savage were humane weapons compared with those which modern science has forged for this conflict. . .What a mockery to call this curse of war the upholding of civilization! We, the Labor party, should take the opportunity to point out to the masses of the people that this war is the product and the outcome of the domination of trade and commerce, and the greed of wealth.

The only MHRs to join Anstey in opposing the grant to Belgium were four Labor men (Catts, McGrath, George Burns and G.E. Yates) who all considered that the money should be used to alleviate unemployment and distress in Australia. When caucus evaluated Fisher's budget in November 1914 Anstey's disaffection with the government's financial priorities was again eloquently displayed. Words and perspiration poured from him as he insisted that Fisher's proposals were insufficiently radical. When Fisher remained impassive Anstey stormed out, scattering a pile of books as he went.

Anstey and other backbenchers became increasingly critical of the War Precautions Act. In its initial form it had been passed by the parliament in October 1914 with little debate. Since then, however, various grievances about the administration of the WPA had made some caucus members uneasy about its sweeping powers. When Hughes brusquely proposed amendments to the WPA in April 1915, introducing them to parliament without the normal caucus scrutiny beforehand, several FPLP members protested angrily. Anstey led the chorus:

If anyone can show me that dangers menace us, I am prepared to give up the right of free speech, and of a free press – to give up every individual right – in order to maintain the existence of the country. . .We are simply being swept away by one vast tide that is overwhelming our ideas of human rights and liberty. . .

O'Malley asserted that the legislation's 'godfather is Labour, but. . .its real father is a military, gilt-spurred rooster'. Hughes replied that Anstey had 'drowned his judgement in the sea of his emotions'; this legislation was necessary 'to deal with unique circumstances which threaten our very existence'. Hughes became especially animated when countering O'Malley's thrust that the measures were exaggerated for a conflict so far away.

The war is 12 000 miles away because every day we live thousands of men die horrible deaths and endure untold sufferings to keep it away. . .But no-one is to say when these tremendous pent-up forces of destruction may burst the barrier which now hedges them about and then the war will not be 12 000 miles away, but at our very doors.

There was already an abyss between Labor members with different perceptions of this calamity on the other side of the world. When Anstey's fellow Victorian Brennan, another passionate idealist, reproached Labor ministers for 'making themselves the mouthpieces of military power', Fisher, flustered but conciliatory, intervened to soothe his disgruntled backbenchers. Anstey remained unappeased. As the legislation was passed on 29 April, he truculently declared that he owed 'no allegiance after to-night to this government, or to the men I find associated with them'.

That Anstey outburst occurred four days after the AIF made its spectacular debut at Gallipoli, but the Australian government and people still knew less about the operation than its military opponents did even before it began. When British strategists sought to overcome the Western Front deadlock by forcing the Dardanelles (controlled by Germany's ally Turkey) in order to open an alternative supply route to Russia, they unwisely opted for a purely naval attack. This failed attempt only advertised Britain's intentions; when its army and navy then made arrogantly undisguised plans for a joint operation in the vicinity, the enemy prepared well for this next assault. The men of the AIF put ashore at Gallipoli did remarkably well, and when a detailed account of the landing belatedly reached Australia there was intense jubilation and relief that they had so distinguished themselves: the news 'has simply sent Australia wild with joy', wrote Pearce, normally a most unexuberant, measured correspondent. But the continuous casualty lists began to show that Australia had paid a heavy price. Killed in action on that first Anzac Day was Labor's popular NSW MLA for Willoughby, Ted Larkin, a former rugby champion who had represented

Australia and later, as an administrator, made Rugby League Sydney's dominant winter sport.

Labor's state governments in office since the outbreak of war were disappointing their supporters, notably in WA where the Scaddan government had scraped home in the October 1914 election. Mounting unemployment and inefficiency in some of the state enterprises contributed to the swing against the government; another factor was the advent of a new political force, the Country Party. Chastened by the result and weakened by Bath's retirement from politics, the government resisted pressure from party activists to expand the state enterprises. Prices began to rise rapidly. In April Scaddan and Johnson embroiled the government in controversy when they decided – overruling departmental advice and without consulting cabinet – to place the construction of a meatworks at Wyndham in the hands of a financier, S.V. Nevanas; they then changed their minds, and 'granted Nevanas an extraordinarily generous inducement to abandon the contract'. This transaction disturbed Labor backbenchers and supporters alike.

In Tasmania the Earle government had infuriated many Labor devotees with its response to the war. Earle spoke of the need for a 'party truce' and refused to introduce preference to unionists (then heading the Labor platform) since this would unfairly benefit one section of the community. With the government's few progressive measures cheerfully savaged by the Council, some Labor enthusiasts began reflecting on the pointlessness of pursuing reform through parliament.

NSW Labor people were similarly annoyed when Holman suggested that a parliamentary truce with anti-Labor was appropriate. They were horrified when he announced that cabinet was considering the suspension of industrial awards. The Holman government evaded Fisher's strict wartime controls on state borrowing when it proceeded with the controversial Norton-Griffiths agreement to finance public works worth £10 million. The January 1915 AWU conference flayed the government's performance, but stopped short of the drastic step urged by some delegates of withdrawing financial support from NSW Labor. The annual PLL conference three months later was also stormy. Its agenda contained 14 separate motions of censure on the government: they induced 'a nice homely feeling', Holman assured delegates, but he had the numbers and could afford to be sarcastic. At the conference he had yet another sharp clash with Hughes over extensions to the national government's powers. There was also criticism of the Norton-Griffiths agreement, which Holman conceded was 'a departure from the Labor platform', and denunciation of the government's inactivity against the Council.

In March 1915 the ULP returned to office in SA. Its electoral success owed much to the Peake government's economic difficulties arising from a severe Australia-wide drought and the loss of Broken Hill's German markets. Winning all 15 metropolitan seats and making inroads in the country, Labor won 26 of the 46 seats in the enlarged and redistributed Assembly. An ugly undercurrent in the campaign was the harassment of the long-established German-Australian community in SA. Hughes and Pearce were convinced that proven instances of treacherous activity by a few justified the authoritarian rigour inflicted upon all German-Australians, but this was another aspect of war administration which generated disquiet in Labor ranks: O'Malley accused Hughes of behaving like 'an Egyptian emperor' and being 'saturated with feeling against Germany and the Germans'. The SA election showed that some voters were becoming similarly saturated, and the aching loss of thousands of Australians on a distant shore inevitably aggravated such tensions. Hermann Homburg, son of a former Chief Justice of SA, had been working in his office as Peake's Attorney-General when it was raided by soldiers with fixed bayonets; he lost his seat at the 1915 election, and all other candidates with a German background were defeated. Premier Peake, an outspoken supporter of SA's German-Australians, also lost his seat. Verran had retired as ULP leader after the 1912 defeat and his successor, Crawford Vaughan, became the new Premier. Caucus elected two of the Premier's relatives into the ministry, his brother J.H. Vaughan and brother-in-law, farmer Clarence Goode, together with A.W. Styles, an accountant MLC; the only ministers with orthodox Labor backgrounds were wharf labourer Harry Jackson and Reg Blundell of the Tobacco Twisters' Union. Later there were unionist complaints that this ministry contained too much of the 'black-coated brigade', but it began work with impressive energy and purpose.

The ULP's success was followed by Queensland Labor's sensational election victory in May. Labor ran a fine campaign with innovative ideas from Theodore and McCormack, effective organization from Collings, and exhilarating optimism from Labor supporters: 'Probably at no other time in Queensland history was such idealism so openly encountered'. Never before had Labor held a majority of seats in the Queensland Assembly, but it broke through with a vengeance in 1915 to win 45 of the 72 seats.

The Ryan government showed itself to be genuinely radical. It was undeterred by the exigencies of war or conservative bleats that Labor's reform programme should be postponed until peacetime. It was resolute in tackling the Council. It overhauled the sugar industry, breaking the stranglehold enjoyed by the CSR corporation for so long; cane price boards were established, ensuring fair wages for sugar workers and fair returns for growers. Its electoral reforms included giving women the right to stand for parliament. Its industrial reforms gave workers a new deal. Its state enterprises aimed to make capitalism function for the people rather than a privileged few. In difficult times Labor devotees had a government of reformist zeal and splendid leadership to match their highest expectations.

Ryan took the portfolios of Attorney-General and Chief Secretary and Theodore Treasury and Public Works. Bowman's popularity ensured his election to cabinet despite his ill-health; Ryan appointed him Home Secretary. Ryan's legal and political talents and Theodore's drive and familiarity with the union movement were neatly complemented by the business acumen of two senior ministers who entered parliament in 1907, J.M. Hunter (Lands) and W. Lennon (Agriculture and Stock). Hunter's parents were Scottish, Lennon's Irish; both were successful businessmen and noted community leaders, Hunter at Roma and Lennon at Townsville. They were crucial figures in the government's wide-ranging involvement in state enterprises, which was pursued despite the obstruction of the Council and wartime curbs on borrowing for purposes not directly related to the war. The Ryan government established a state-owned fishery, coal mine, insurance office and even a hotel, as well as sawmills and the most successful enterprise of all, a chain of butchers' shops which sold meat more cheaply than elsewhere and were very popular. The Railways minister, John Adamson, was a Presbyterian minister and an idealistic dreamer whose political speeches 'were monuments to his self-education' and sounded like sermons. H.F. Hardacre, as befitted a Labor veteran of that name, had been preoccupied with land reform since his election to the Assembly in 1893, but Ryan placed him in charge of education. Ryan's allocation of portfolios was consistent with his party's priorities – Labor did not rank education highly – but a dynamic and imaginative minister could have achieved a great deal in education.

Filling the last ministerial position proved awkward for Ryan. He correctly insisted that under the law it had to be filled by a member of the Council, but that institution was so detested by many Labor members that only after he had applied all his considerable powers of persuasion, tact and diplomacy did caucus grudgingly concede. The man they chose as the eighth minister was a Labor legend in Queensland, Bill Hamilton. One of the martyred strike leaders of 1891, he was sentenced to three years gaol for his role in a disturbance when he had in fact restrained illegal acts by strikers. Offered a reduced sentence, he retorted 'I will see you in Hell before I'll scab on my mates', and served his full term at notorious St Helena prison. After marrying the daughter of a Eureka rebel, he entered parliament in 1899. When his ministerial duties involved an inspection of St Helena, the warders and flunkeys were anxious to please with 'Careful, sir' and 'Mind the step, sir' until Hamilton interjected 'I know where the bloody steps are, I scrubbed them for three years'.

After the caucus ballot for the speakership resulted in a tie, Ryan's casting vote went to McCormack. The Premier was wary of the blunt forcefulness and coolness to non-unionists like Hunter, Lennon and himself that made McCormack a potentially disruptive figure, and felt that he would be less threatening as Speaker. McCormack presided sternly over the Assembly in the normal Queensland tradition of partisan speakers, but added a new dimension with the debating suggestions he passed to government members during political warfare and his arbitrary interpretations of standing orders to deflect opposition attacks. Queensland's equivalent of Ted Larkin was Irish-born J.A. Fihelly, a thrusting Rugby League forward who in politics as in football 'attacked the man rather than the subject'. In July caucus agreed to Ryan's proposal that two assistant ministers should be appointed, and added Fihelly and J.A. Huxham, a Brisbane retailer dedicated to improving social welfare for the disadvantaged, to the cabinet.

When delegates assembled in Adelaide for the sixth federal conference they were still jubilant about the Queensland triumph a week earlier. Labor now governed in five states – all but Victoria – as well as nationally. The first item of conference business was a resolution urging the government to resubmit the 1911 and 1913 referenda proposals 'at the earliest opportunity'. Despite Holman's thinly veiled distaste, and opposition from the WA delegates who felt the referenda could only succeed when coupled with a federal election, the resolution was carried overwhelmingly. Conference proceeded to ratify at last the concept of a national executive, which had been under consideration for a decade and shelved by the previous two conferences. Comprising two delegates from each state, the executive was established to administer the party nationally between federal conferences just as the equivalent state executives administered Labor's state branches between state conferences. With its formation Labor's organizational structure was complete. The party had taken shape in accordance with basic principles of democracy and solidarity which, although sometimes broken by powerful groups and manipulated by cunning individuals, have remained fundamental to the party ever since. All party representatives – whether leaders, MPs, organizational office-bearers or branch delegates – are accountable for their actions and subject to regular re-election. Decisions are reached at all party levels by majority vote after full discussion by all entitled participants, who are then required to abide by those majority decisions. By 1915 this creation of the Australian labour movement had achieved remarkable success, far in advance of all equivalent parties overseas. 'This nation has such a chance that to see it reject it will make angels weep', wrote Boote with anguished foreboding in the *Australian Worker*. He sensed prophetically that it all might suddenly fall apart.

After Australians began to be slaughtered in large numbers there was a steep rise in enlistments. However, by mid-1915, with Gallipoli deadlocked in trench warfare like the Western Front, and Britain indicating that every available man was wanted, organized appeals for recruits began. For anti-Labor the situation was straightforward: the war had to be won and the reinforcements had to be obtained by whatever means necessary. For Labor people it was not that simple. Some leading Labor figures, like indefatigable organizer Jimmy Catts, who usually aligned himself with the FPLP's most radical section, involved themselves wholeheartedly in recruiting. NSW minister A.C. Carmichael enlisted aged 49 (he claimed to be 43), and campaigned successfully for a battalion of 1000 recruits to join him. Others were more muted.

A few like Maurice Blackburn challenged the notion that any querying of Australia's commitment was treachery to the AIF. Blackburn, a lawyer who had edited the VSP's *Socialist* newspaper and generously provided legal advice to unions and the Labor Party, was a fearless, principled moralist. Although he supported compulsory military training in case home defence by a citizen army was ever needed, he saw this war as abhorrent. In mid-1915, having entered the Victorian parliament less than a year earlier, he publicly announced that he would not participate in recruiting.

The following month Brennan, another individualistic Victorian lawyer, clashed heatedly with former Victorian Premier W.A. Watt, who accused him of being 'pigeon-livered'. Brennan publicly challenged Watt to enlist with him.. On the nominated day Brennan, a most unlikely soldier, turned up at the recruiting depot with expectant onlookers and journalists, but Watt failed to appear. In this dispute Holman further aggravated the labour movement by inexplicably supporting Watt.

As the casualty lists continued to fill columns of newsprint, some Labor supporters agreed with the sentiments of IWW stalwart Tom Barker. His response to the recruiting campaign was featured in a poster plastered around Sydney:

TO ARMS!!
Capitalists, Parsons, Politicians, Landlords,
Newspaper Editors And Other Stay-at-home Patriots.
YOUR COUNTRY NEEDS YOU IN THE TRENCHES!
WORKERS, FOLLOW YOUR MASTERS!!

Barker was arrested for prejudicing recruiting on the orders of Holman's Chief Secretary, George Black, whose return to political prominence was smoothed by his less controversial private life but not by certain strange ministerial decisions he made, such as the banning of leg-crossing on public transport after he stumbled over some women on a tram.

Fisher was finding the strain difficult to bear. Hughes and Pearce had huge workloads, but Fisher had the ultimate responsibility and it was weighing heavily upon him. He was troubled by widespread discontentment with spiralling price rises as well as the differences within his party over aspects of war policy.

Conscription was beginning to cast its menacing shadow, with influential Australians in growing numbers publicly asserting that voluntary recruiting was insufficient. Fisher was also tormented by a terrible fear about Gallipoli. He was told nothing about the operation beforehand, and the little information he had since gleaned was extremely worrying. When he learned that his journalist friend Keith Murdoch had obtained Pearce's authority to visit Gallipoli in order to investigate the vexing problems in AIF mail there, Fisher urged Murdoch to find out all he could about the campaign and write to him privately. Murdoch did so from London, where he was to begin work as manager and editor of a cable network sending news to Australia. The Murdoch letter became a highly controversial document. This scathing indictment of the 'continuous and ghastly bungling' of inept British generalship, which had wasted the magnificent deeds of the 'indomitable' AIF, was soon circulating in British government circles, and contributed to the decision to withdraw from Gallipoli.

Before the letter reached Australia Fisher had decided to resign. On 30 October 1915 he told caucus that the strain on his health was too severe for him to continue as leader, and that he had been appointed Australian High Commissioner in London. After an appropriately glowing tribute to Fisher's 'long and valuable service', caucus made the fateful decision to select Hughes. He had again stood out clearly as the most dynamic Fisher government minister, attacking complex problems with zeal and devising frequently unorthodox solutions consistent with his assessment of Australia's interests. Volatile, frenetic and administratively chaotic, he had none of Pearce's methodical orderliness. By late 1915 Hughes was more convinced than ever that the Allies, Australia included, had to be galvanized into a desperate prosecution of the war to ensure that they won it. His singleminded pursuit of this objective, together with his personal abrasiveness and chronically turbulent style, made some Labor people wonder whether – despite all his talents – it was wise to entrust Labor's leadership to such a man at such a time. Very soon there were signs that these misgivings were well founded.

Hughes tried to restrict cabinet changes to the election of one new minister to replace Fisher, but caucus insisted on a spill of all positions. Deputations of unionists had received abrupt treatment from Archibald at Home Affairs, and he was dropped together with Spence. Hughes's worst fears were realized when O'Malley was returned; Higgs and Webster became ministers for the first time. Archibald resented his demotion and vented his spleen in an undignified outburst against O'Malley, who replied in the same spirit. Hughes's ministers then had an unpleasant taste of his leadership style. At the last possible moment before the swearing-in Hughes tried to manipulate their agreement to a hastily devised departmental restructuring, which was intended to keep the Treasury, the Attorney-General's department and the important parts of External Affairs all in the new Prime Minister's hands. The ministers objected. When it became clear that Hughes could not get his way, he reverted to the status quo with all previous ministers retaining their former positions (Jensen had been given the newly-created Navy department in July to lighten Pearce's load), plus Higgs as Treasurer, O'Malley back at Home Affairs, and Webster at last fulfilling his great ambition to be Postmaster-General. They trooped off to Government House in a bad frame of mind; Gardiner found Hughes's performance so distasteful that he nearly refused to go at all.

Then within a week Hughes antagonized almost the entire labour movement. Soaring prices – since the outbreak of war meat had doubled in price, and food and grocery items were up 50% – had reinforced the movement's attachment to the referenda, which would enable the national government to control prices and the detested profiteers. After the federal conference in May had instructed the government to reintroduce the referenda as soon as possible, Hughes had introduced the necessary legislation in June; 11 December was specified as polling day. A tornado of seething dissent began to blow. Businessmen were up in arms about government interference with free enterprise. Others maintained that a nation in dire peril should not be divided by such provocative 'party' proposals, conveniently ignoring the fact that these changes had been approved by over 49% of the voters in 1913, Labor was in office in six of the seven state and national governments, and the success of these referenda was the most desired objective of Labor supporters throughout the land. Fisher had assured Labor followers that 'nothing short of an earthquake would prevent the. . .proposals being submitted to the people', but Hughes was now pessimistic about the outcome and the unwelcome blow to his prestige which defeat would bring. Immersed in other problems and keen to visit Britain as soon as possible, Hughes remained publicly committed to the campaign but privately schemed to abandon it.

The way out came from the state governments. Holman was predictably involved. So too, more surprisingly, were Ryan and Theodore. Both had supported the referenda in 1911 and 1913, but sensed that Queensland Labor's attachment to them had waned: the powerful Queensland AWU had requested the FPLP in August not to proceed with them. Theodore was also influenced by the threat posed by one of the referenda to his designs for sweeping reforms to Queensland's labour laws. When Ryan suggested that the referenda could be deferred if the states legislated to surrender the powers in question to the national government for the duration of the war, the other premiers agreed. Hughes ensured that caucus was given minimal time to consider the implications by immediately summoning a late-night caucus meeting, where only six members opposed ratifying his agreement with the premiers. That agreement was superficially attractive, avoiding an expensive referenda campaign which many Labor people suspected would fail; but its glaring weakness was that even if all the premiers could be trusted to introduce legislation to surrender their powers, there was no likelihood whatever – as Anstey sarcastically pointed out – that their Legislative Councils would approve (although Ryan was sincere about tackling Queensland's Council forcefully on this issue). The withdrawal of the referenda induced a widespread sense of betrayal; many in the labour movement interpreted it as confirmation that Hughes could not be trusted. In January 1916 the federal executive moved to censure the government, but this was averted after a threatened resignation by Hughes and some fancy footwork by his executive supporters.

Later that month Hughes departed for England. He felt in the dark in Australia, far from both the war zones and London, where decisions vital to Australia were being made. Only after the decision to evacuate Gallipoli was made did Hughes hear about it in a secret cable, which warned him to expect that half the AIF would become casualties in the process. Hughes had to keep this terrible forecast to himself for some weeks, until the news came through that the evacuation had been a miraculously complete success. Fisher had shown Murdoch's Gallipoli letter to Hughes (and Pearce). Its effect on Hughes was to convince him that Murdoch could be a valuable ally and to reinforce his inclination to visit England in order to ensure that Australia's contribution to the war was properly utilized. There were momentous problems which could best be tackled in London – shipping shortages, disrupted markets for Australia's staple commodities like wool, wheat and metals, and Hughes's suspicions about Japan's strategic aims. Hughes felt that Fisher would be no match for British officialdom and, besides, Hughes wanted to handle these vital questions himself. Before his departure Hughes authorized the establishment of a highly secret Counter Espionage Bureau, to be managed by the official secretary of one of the new Prime Minister's closest advisers and admirers, Munro Ferguson.

Hughes's impact in England was spectacular. His forceful private dealings with British politicians and officials were full of drama, especially in such matters as installing an Australian civilian at the War Office and secretly buying 15 British ships which became the basis of the Australian Shipping Line. Even more striking was the way Australia's wizened walking walnut electrified British audiences as he exhorted them to apply themselves wholeheartedly and remorselessly to the crushing of Germany. Lionized and fêted in a whirlwind of engagements skilfully publicized by Murdoch, he became the celebrity of the hour, acclaimed for fervently spelling out what England had to do just when this was most needed. Despite censorship and news manipulation, Britons sensed that the war was not going well and were beginning to connect this with the indecisive drift of their government.

Hughes was permitted to inspect Britain's top-secret solution to the trench warfare deadlock, the tank, which was to be unveiled in September, but Britain's tunnel-visioned generals were preparing to launch a massive offensive before then. After two years Western Front experience of the futility of throwing men in their thousands against machine-guns, they had placed their faith in a misconceived plan which, in effect, threw men in their hundreds of thousands against machine-guns. In June Hughes visited the AIF, now in France and destined to be slaughtered in the battle of the Somme. As he mixed with these men who were about to confirm the reputation for outstanding bravery, comradeship and endurance they had won at Gallipoli, Australia's gnome-like leader was emotionally stirred: 'his admiration for and identification with them was the deepest and most enduring passion of his life'. While mingling with the First Brigade, Hughes noticed a familiar private in the ranks; it was Labor's former MHR for Robertson, 45-year-old Bill Johnson, who was well aware of the fuss made of Hughes in England and the honorary degrees showered on him. 'Well, Billy', Johnson greeted him, 'have they made you a Doctor of Divinity yet?' The following month Johnson was killed at Pozières, that tiny village whose name was to haunt many other Australian families.

Hughes was welcomed home with tremendous public enthusiasm. Pearce's private greeting was just as heartfelt: 'it seems a long time since you left and I feel that I have lived about 7 years instead of as many months'. As acting Prime Minister Pearce had continued to deal with his multitudinous Defence responsibilities as well as lead a cabinet lacking Hughes and Fisher. He was pleased with Higgs at Treasury but Jensen and Gardiner had 'not developed', Mahon had 'either been ill or dodging responsibility all the time', and Tudor was 'the same loyal painstaking though somewhat weak man that you know him'. As for Webster and O'Malley, they 'have been a perfect nightmare to me. Had I been in charge instead of acting either they or I would have gone out'. Home Affairs had continued to attract damaging criticism over its major undertakings, the east-west transcontinental railway and the development of Canberra. When O'Malley's administration, which had been denounced in caucus, was criticized in parliament by his antagonistic predecessor Archibald and even O'Malley's ministerial colleague Webster, Pearce decided that a royal commission should inquire into the beleaguered department.

Such matters, while understandably annoying to Pearce, were trifles compared to the conscription issue, which had been widely canvassed in Australia during Hughes's absence. Hardly any anti-Labor politician or newspaper did not join the clamour for conscription, and some Labor politicians, including Poynton and Archibald, had publicly lent their support. Opposition to conscription had also gathered momentum while Hughes was away. It was condemned by the annual conference of the AWU and by a specially convened interstate congress of unions (representing 97 organizations and almost half Australia's unionists), which declared its 'undying hostility to conscription of life and labour'. Labor Party conferences in three states – NSW, Queensland and Victoria – firmly ruled that any Labor MP supporting conscription would be denied endorsement. In February Gardiner had ruefully predicted that this issue 'will throw the party back five or perhaps ten years', and Higgs had confided similarly gloomy thoughts in May. Pearce was privately convinced that conscription was necessary, but his repeated response to the mounting agitation on the question was that no decision would be made until Hughes was back home. There was a tense air of expectancy as Hughes returned. 'Welcome Home to the Cause of Anti-Conscription' was Boote's pre-emptive greeting in the *Australian Worker*, and he maintained the pressure: Hughes should 'not mistake the popping of champagne corks for the voice of the people'.

For several weeks Hughes remained publicly neutral on the issue while he worked out how to proceed, but his mind was made up. His decision in favour of conscription was a natural result of his singleminded attitude to winning the war ever since it started. His emotional attachment to the AIF strengthened his resolve, especially after the horrific AIF casualties in the Somme offensive. Furthermore, his suspicions that Japan was intending to confront the White Australia policy after the war was over had not lessened after private consultations in London with the British Foreign Office and the Japanese ambassador. Hughes feared that after the war Britain might not wish – for future strategic reasons – to support Australia in upholding the White Australia policy. He believed Australia could earn the right to Britain's postwar assistance through a devoted contribution in this war.

While he strongly favoured conscription, achieving it in practice was not so straightforward. He consulted widely and considered his options. There were three possible ways. He could bring a bill into parliament as in Britain and New Zealand, but the numbers were not right in the Senate. He could bypass parliament altogether, using a regulation under the WPA, but, as Pearce acknowledged, this was 'altogether distasteful and would have caused turmoil and possibly bloodshed'. The other option was a referendum. He was assured on all sides that there was community support for conscription, and once this was established the recalcitrant Labor Senators would have to accept it. He was made aware of the opposition he faced in the labour movement, but seems to have concluded that with a clear message he could convert many Labor voters to the cause, particularly those with relatives in the AIF. A referendum seemed the quickest way to meet his objective and was consistent with Labor's democratic traditions. Once the referendum had settled the issue, the party could regroup and press onward.

Hughes encountered considerable resistance within the party from the outset.

Sensing correctly that most of his ministers opposed conscription (only Pearce and Webster initially supported him), Hughes avoided the issue in cabinet as long as possible. 'The atmosphere is electrical and a storm appears which is calculated to rend us in twain', observed Higgs on the eve of the first caucus meeting since Hughes's return. It began on Thursday 24 August and continued, with breaks for equally stormy cabinet discussions, for long periods of Friday, Saturday and Monday, before at 2 am on Tuesday – with a significant proportion of members unable to stay the distance – Hughes managed to obtain a tiny majority for his proposal by a vote of 23 to 21. In caucus the Prime Minister castigated the state executives who had threatened to withdraw preselection from conscriptionists as ignorant haters of 'everything that was clean, decent and respectable'. He flourished an official cable just received from London which forecast that the AIF's Third Division, then training in England, would have to be broken up to provide reinforcements for Australia's four other infantry divisions. This cable, which had been timed and phrased with a view to assisting the conscription campaign, added that the only way the Third Division could be saved was if Australia sent reinforcements at a specified rate, which was clearly unrealistic and, as intended, far beyond the capacity of voluntary recruiting. (Afterwards Australia at no stage even came close to the specified rate, but the Third Division was not dismantled.)

Hughes told caucus that he would stake his life on his ability to reverse the stance of Labor's anti-conscriptionist state executives, but he soon found that this was a very rash assertion. He addressed the Victorian executive at length on 1 September, using 'every one of his many oratorical, logical and political tricks', but 'not a single man was impressed in the slightest degree'. When he promised them that he would fight for a 'Yes' majority as if for his very life, the chairman, Hobart-born bootmaker and active unionist E.J. Holloway, replied that his listeners would be fighting just as fiercely against him. Having imposed strict censorship on any reporting of that meeting, Hughes then travelled to Sydney to tackle the PLL executive. To his dismay, he found that Victorian PLC secretary Stewart and Queensland Senator M.A. Ferricks had taken the precaution of making the same journey to prevent him from giving the NSW executive the impression that he had converted the Victorians. Increasingly desperate, Hughes played all his cards in Sydney, even the Japanese one, but his hints about the diabolical consequences for Australia if the referendum failed fell on unreceptive ears. He fared no better at a special meeting of the NSW TLC, where Ferricks and Stewart also spoke. Next was the ULP annual conference in Adelaide. After Hughes's address, conference passed resolutions which supported his government and its decision to hold the referendum but opposed conscription (without making preselection threats to Labor conscriptionists). Premier Vaughan and other Hughes supporters concluded they were as free as their counterparts in WA and Tasmania to campaign for conscription, but Lundie and the militants claimed that the conference 'absolutely binds every member to oppose conscription' as in Queensland, NSW and Victoria. From afar Fisher was increasingly alarmed by developments: 'The motto for the times is "Steady Boys Steady"', he cautioned, but his warning was like a whisper in a cyclone.

Labor's turmoil was publicly exposed when the Military Service Referendum Bill came before the national parliament. On 14 September, the day Hughes moved its second reading in the Representatives, Tudor resigned from the ministry. Pearce, like Hughes and other conscriptionists, bitterly resented the role of Labor organizations in coercing Labor MPs into opposing conscription by threatening them with withdrawal of preselection; he later claimed that Tudor had admitted that conscription was justified but 'Richmond won't stand for it'. Tudor had been publicly non-committal on the great question, until Richmond PLC and other branches in his Yarra electorate gave him a virtual ultimatum. Brennan alluded to Tudor's resignation in a passionate impromptu speech against the Referendum Bill:

> I am not surprised that, as a result of this grave and gross breach of faith on the part of the Prime Minister, his Government is already beginning to crumble. . .This Government should try to realize at once that its policy is foredoomed to failure, that it is driving the country to disaster, chaos, confusion, loss, and, probably, bloodshed. . . Although we were told a little while back that a referendum of the people on proposed alterations of the Constitution could not be taken because it would create strife and ill-feeling, they propose now to throw this country into the vortex of a struggle more acrimonious and bitter than any that has happened in the history of Australia.

Brennan opposed the holding of a referendum at all because it was a 'misuse. . .of a democratic instrument for an undemocratic purpose'. Other caucus opponents of the bill included Anstey, Maloney, Tudor, Catts, Page, Findley, Ferricks and Turley, although most of the FPLP supported placing the issue before the people.

The dam burst in NSW first. In that state a meeting of unionists called by the AWU in November 1915 had formed a new group called the Industrial Section of the PLL, which resolved to organize to deny Holman control of the next conference. They did their work well, and the government found itself censured by the 1916 conference. Holman countered with a theatrical stunt: he and his ministers all suddenly resigned, and Balmain boilermaker Jack Storey presented himself to conference as Labor's reluctant new leader. Meanwhile, behind the scenes Holman and Griffith hammered out a compromise with the industrialists whereby Holman and his ministers were 'returned' to office and the government agreed to run a referendum on the abolition of the Council. The Industrial Section captured control of the executive at this conference, which was also noteworthy for its emphatic resolution against conscription and preselection for conscriptionist MPs. The executive then requested a special federal conference to deal with the conscription question in all states, an initiative quickly supported by Queensland Labor. It expelled Hughes from the party; he reacted dismissively, claiming that conscription was an issue for the party at federal, not state, level and the FPLP platform was silent on the question. The NSW executive also withdrew the endorsements of prominent conscriptionists Holman, Hall and Griffith, and pressured other Labor MPs to clarify where they stood.

So Labor men and women, MPs and supporters alike, had to make a choice. For some of them it was clear-cut; most found it profoundly distressing. Many wondered how long their party would take to recover or whether it ever would. As they made their choice the mad convulsion in Europe careered on like a wild avalanche, indiscriminate in its destruction of bodies, minds, lands and hopes. The future was impossible to predict, even more so with strict censorship stifling vital information. Labor followers who mistakenly presumed that military information was available to their leaders were influenced by the conscriptionist advocacy of men like Hughes, Pearce and Watson who had been involved with the party since its inception. Others who accepted Australia's commitment to the war as a duty to be endured and reluctantly supported saw conscription as too high a price to pay: anti-conscriptionists were fond of saying that it was hardly worth defeating objectionable Prussian militarism if Australia had to be Prussianized in the process. Personal AIF links could also be a weighty factor; many Labor people had husbands and sons in the trenches. Pressure from Labor associates or from electorate branches or state executives was also important. It was, however, obvious that the party was being plunged into the biggest crisis of its existence, one which was likely to rupture friendships forged in decades of comradely endeavour for the downtrodden.

Hughes was not exaggerating when he described the campaign as 'the most severe and bitter Australia has ever known'. He and others with long experience in public life had never seen such crowds or passion. There was violence too: anti-conscriptionist meetings were particularly prone to be physically broken up, often by men in AIF uniforms. The AIF had suffered over 28 000 casualties in only seven weeks at Fromelles and Pozières, and, although any mention of such statistics was censored, it was clear enough that being sent to the Western Front might well prove a death sentence. Ardent conscriptionists, therefore, seemed like murderers to some of their rivals; anti-conscriptionists were liable to be seen as traitors. Hughes had assured caucus sceptics that anti-conscriptionists would have unlimited scope to put their case as long as they stayed within the law, but the activity of the censors made a mockery of this assurance. By special directive from the Prime Minister himself, the censors disallowed any 'hostile personal reference' to him and any 'resolutions or reports of any meetings calculated to prejudice' his campaign. The tiny minority of anti-conscriptionist papers, like Boote's *Australian Worker*, Scullin's *Evening Echo* in Ballarat and E.J.C. Dwyer-Gray's *Daily Post* in Hobart, managed a telling contribution despite harassment from the censorship which was not inflicted on their conscriptionist counterparts. The Irish rebellion a few months earlier also raised the temperature, with anti-conscriptionists highlighting the obvious contrast between Britain's brutal retribution in Ireland and its professed regard for the sanctity of small nations like 'gallant little Belgium'. In a strident speech to the Queensland Irish Association, Fihelly quoted the Welshman about to become Britain's Prime Minister, Lloyd George (though this was ignored in the fuss) in describing England as 'the home of cant, humbug and hypocrisy'. Curtin was a conspicuous opponent of conscription. Along with comrades like Holloway and Hyett, he directed 'with the energy of a tornado' the trade unions' activity against conscription, despite his absorption in a different fight altogether, his personal battle against alcohol, which put him into a convalescent home in 1916. 'Never mind what others say', Anstey encouraged him,

> the man who has carried his crucifix and climbed his Calvary is a better man than he who never touched the stony road of suffering. . . Stand upright, proud of yourself, proud of the conquest that you are going to achieve and the good that you yet will do.

The campaign intensified as Hughes recklessly ranted and raved his way towards his objective. The violent language he formerly adopted in assailing monopolies, employers and other enemies of the labour movement he now used against anti-conscriptionists, Labor MPs included. He accused them of being friends of those menacing Germans who eyed Australia rapaciously. 'If Britain fell, in Australia there would not be warfare but massacre', he thundered. 'We would be like sheep before the butcher'. When 12 members of the IWW were charged on dubious evidence with treason (later amended to conspiracy and arson), Hughes tried to smear all anti-conscriptionists with the IWW brush, citing an intercepted letter of support Anstey sent to Barker. Campaigning in a similar style in WA, Pearce received a stinging rebuke from his old friend William Somerville, a respected Labor activist:

> You and your leader are responsible for blowing the Labor Party to shreds, you are the men who have destroyed the results of a quarter of a century of laborious building. . .I tell you it is a cowardly, mean thing to attempt to associate men, who have worked with you in the past, and whose sense of honour is as keen as yours, with criminals and incendiaries simply because they dare to differ with you on an important question of public policy.

Both sides used inflammatory racist arguments based on concern about alleged Japanese intentions to justify their stance; anti-conscriptionists also claimed that their opponents planned to import coloured labour as workforce replacements for Australians conscripted into the AIF.

As well as maximizing divisiveness, Hughes's political style resulted in some costly errors. The decision to call up for training all single men and childless widowers aged from 21 to 35, in order to avoid loss of time in anticipation of a majority referendum vote, provided a taste of conscription which converted many apathetic voters to anti-conscription. (Curtin, who refused to obey the call-up, was arrested and spent a harrowing few days in gaol.) Also damaging was an extraordinary episode shortly before polling day, which was 28 October. Voting in the referendum had been made compulsory, and Hughes wanted to have suspected call-up defaulters questioned at the polling booths and their votes kept separate. This idea was incorporated in a WPA regulation submitted, without previous cabinet discussion, for authorization by the Executive Council meeting in Melbourne on 25 October. This meeting, attended by Higgs, Gardiner, Jensen and Russell, rejected the regulation. Next day Jensen left for Sydney. There, on the 27th, another Executive Council summoned by Hughes and comprising the Prime Minister, Munro Ferguson, Jensen and Webster approved that same regulation. Gardiner, Higgs and Russell all resigned in protest when they realized what had occurred. They issued a press statement which Gardiner was able to clear with the censor, since he was in charge at Defence while Pearce was on the hustings in WA. Hughes was devastated by the resignations. It was nearly midnight. Needing consolation and someone to confide in, Hughes telephoned the Governor-General, apologized for getting him out of bed, and requested a meeting. Having crossed Sydney Harbour, Munro Ferguson met Hughes in a car, where the 'poor little man asked for advice and sympathy saying he "had not a brainwave left"'. Hughes's choice of counsellor indicated both his isolation in the Labor Party and his closeness to the austere, meddlesome vice-regal custodian of British imperial interests.

The anti-conscriptionists had a narrow victory. Their overall margin was 72 476 in a total vote exceeding 2·3 million. 'Yes' majorities in WA, Victoria and Tasmania were countered by 'No' majorities in Queensland, SA and especially NSW. Hughes had presumed that the AIF would vote overwhelmingly for conscription. He urged Murdoch and the AIF commander to ensure that this occurred, and arranged for the soldiers' voting to be conducted early enough for him to trumpet this anticipated handsome majority before polling day in Australia. However, many soldiers who had experienced the Somme offensive were not inclined to compel others to endure such carnage, and Hughes not only cancelled the advertising space he had booked to boom the soldiers' vote but refused for five months to reveal the figures at all. This only fuelled rumours that the AIF had voted emphatically against conscription. When Hughes belatedly announced details of the small AIF 'Yes' majority, suspicion persisted that he had tampered with the figures. As a perceptive Australian soldier commented, the 'lack of faith in the truth of official returns, statements and good faith is not the least of the legacies the war will have left us'. Another legacy was the devastation of the Australian Labor Party. Even Hughes felt remorse as he surveyed the wreckage: 'I look around today. . .and see the Party to which I have devoted my life hopelessly, irrevocably divided'. Pearce was philosophical: 'I suppose that we cannot wonder that the crisis that is shaking the world has rocked our little boat'. Russell's conclusion was poignant and accurate: 'Things can never be again as they were in Australia. Everything must be recast'.

The climax came at the next caucus meeting on 14 November. After W.F. Finlayson brusquely moved a no-confidence motion in Hughes as leader, Charlton tried to keep the party together with a compromise amendment that the FPLP confer with delegates from each state executive. But the situation was beyond the peacemakers. A group in caucus was determined to remove Hughes, and made this obvious. At the lunch break Hughes conferred with Pearce and Givens, and prepared a surprise. When the meeting resumed Catts was soon in full flight with an anti-Hughes tirade; its target sat outwardly calm, smoking a cigarette. Suddenly he stood and raised a hand. Catts fell silent. Hughes extinguished his cigarette, and picked up his papers. 'Enough of this', he said firmly, calling on all who agreed with his attitude to the war to come with him. He marched out, followed by Pearce, Givens and a third of the others, to a Senate club-room which Pearce had unlocked at lunchtime. The dramatic manoeuvre nearly resulted in more breakaways. Some rose to join them, then hesitantly reconsidered; it seems that Fenton even left the room altogether before returning. If reconciliation was barely possible when this meeting started, it was now unthinkable to those left behind. They proceeded to carry unanimously Finlayson's no-confidence motion in Hughes, and resolved that 'the names of those remaining be recorded and published'.

Hughes formed a 'National Labor' ministry from among the defectors. He chose Pearce, Jensen, Webster, Poynton, Archibald, Bamford, 'Paddy' Lynch, Spence, Russell and Tasmanian MHR W.H. Laird Smith. Jensen had made a late decision to uphold conscription. Russell opposed it, but defected with Hughes because he agreed with Australia's wholehearted prosecution of the war by all means short of conscription. Spence's inclusion, like his alleged advocacy of conscription some weeks earlier, amazed and appalled his many admirers. But he was very ill and seems to have been tricked or, according to his daughter, 'bludgeoned' by Lamond (that daughter's husband), Hughes and Watson into supporting conscription. Other veterans in the Hughes camp included de Largie, Givens and Labor's old man of the sea, Guthrie, who lost two sons killed in action. Thomas, whose son had been killed in the Somme fighting, was not at the fateful caucus meeting. Having represented the Broken Hill militants in state and federal parliament for 22 years, he lost preselection after informing them that he would vote against conscription but would not campaign against it. In all, Hughes's National Labor group comprised 25 defectors, while 46 remained in the FPLP.

The NSW Labor government also swiftly disintegrated after the referendum.

Holman's actions confirmed his waning attachment to fundamental Labor principles; he might well have drifted from the Labor Party irrespective of the war, which could be conjectured with far less conviction about Hughes. Having persuaded all his ministers except ex-miner John Estell to publicly support conscription, Holman had campaigned vigorously himself. Then, immediately the referendum result was known, he commenced negotiations with his anti-Labor foes with a view to forming a coalition government and postponing the next election. By 12 November the unsavoury merger was settled, and three days later a Nationalist administration was sworn in. Holman remained Premier, and his ministers included Hall and three other ex-Labor defectors (or four counting Beeby, who had left Labor in 1912). The Legislative Assembly Continuation Act was whipped through the parliament to shield the motley government from the electors for 12 months. Meanwhile the PLL executive had expelled 18 MPs for either advocating conscription or failing to vote for a parliamentary no-confidence motion against the Nationalist government. The new Labor leader who introduced this motion was Bathurst accountant Ernie Durack. Holman's reply attacked the discipline imposed on Labor politicians by the party's organization, which he had once seen as essential and now, like Hughes, was traducing as control by a 'junta'. Holman expressed his pleasure at being 'free from the pettifogging machine-made tyranny which has done so much to disgrace the Labour movement'.

In Labor's other state parties the position varied. Tasmanian Labor had lost office at the March 1916 election. Its leader, Earle, a staunch conscriptionist, was deposed after the referendum and replaced by Lyons, who had been one of Tasmania's most conspicuous anti-conscriptionists. Only one other Labor MHA accompanied Earle out of the party. A very different situation prevailed in SA, where the entire Labor ministry backed Premier Vaughan's advocacy of conscription and 'No' had a convincing win. Five days after the referendum a special meeting of the ULP council branded the ULP's 31 conscriptionist state and federal MPs as disloyal. Lundie was in the ascendancy. Skilfully harnessing majority rank-and-file disapproval of the conscriptionists, he began the process of ruthlessly forcing them out of the party. In Victoria, where there was more distrust of Hughes before 1916 than in other states, the PLC took a hard line against compulsion. The large-scale trade union opposition was organized in Melbourne by men like Holloway, Hyett and Curtin who had been active in the VSP. Women, too, threw themselves into the campaign throughout Australia. In Victoria their activities were organized and led by Jean Daley and the first woman to graduate from an Australian university, Bella Guerin, and their valuable contribution was recognized by the revival of the Women's Central Organizing Committee – although Guerin claimed that Labor women were still treated as 'performing poodles and pack-horses'. In state parliament three of Labor's 22 MPs were expelled, although Elmslie, in poor health and overwrought, was granted 'leave of absence' after offering his resignation as leader. After many sleepless nights he had decided that he could not join the anti-conscription campaign, but he kept his promise to remain scrupulously neutral until his death in May 1918. Prendergast was then returned to the leadership.

Strife within the party in Queensland was minimized. This was partly attributable to the firm early stance of the state executive against conscription and a general unwillingness to jeopardize the fine start made by the Ryan government, especially after the unhappy precedent of the Kidston split. Ryan's role was also decisive. He was willing to face a fight if necessary, but he was, unlike Hughes, a leader whose conciliatory style with colleagues placated rather than provoked them. When Hughes announced the 1916 referendum Ryan refused to comment publicly on the issue until caucus had considered it. Within the party his main aim was to maintain cohesion. This he achieved despite having on the one hand ministers like Coyne, Adamson, Hunter and Hardacre who were inclined, like several backbenchers, to support compulsion, and on the other militant 'No' advocates like McCormack who wanted to drive conscriptionists out of the party without delay. In the end all but Adamson, who was the only MP to leave the party over conscription, agreed to oppose compulsion. As the only government or opposition leader in state or federal parliament to campaign against conscription in 1916, Ryan was calm, logical and effective, frequently asserting that the labour movement could not be expected to tolerate conscription of men when so little had been done to conscript wealth: it was the last man without the last shilling.

Strife within the ALF in WA was also contained, but altogether differently. The Westralian party's attitude to conscription was discussed at its 1916 congress in a three-day debate involving 60 delegates. T'othersider Don Cameron, who had been lured from Melbourne to the West by the gold rush in 1895 before being radicalized by his experiences in a Boer War contingent, proposed a sweeping anti-conscription motion outlawing all MPs who thought differently. But such notions had gained far less sympathy in the West than in other states, and congress instead declared its willingness to support conscription if the Hughes government considered it necessary. When the tempo quickened on the east coast with expulsions and withdrawn endorsements, many in the ALF were startled; Scaddan described Hughes's expulsion from the PLL in mid-September as a 'joke'. WA was the only state Hughes did not visit during his referendum campaign; the contest there was conducted with spirit but less spite than in the other states. The *Westralian Worker* was even-handed, carrying arguments from each side, and there was a widespread determination not to let the issue split the party.

This determination was reflected in the ALF's approach to the special federal conference on conscription in Melbourne in December. Whereas most delegates attending it – and certainly the executives initiating it – saw the conference as sealing the split and ratifying the action already taken against conscriptionists, the ALF optimistically saw it as a means of healing the breach. Stewart, federal secretary as well as Victorian secretary, told the ALF that he was appalled to learn that half its representatives would be conscriptionists, and doubted whether they would be permitted as delegates. He seconded the crucial motion from Scullin seeking the expulsion of all FPLP members who had either supported compulsory overseas military service or left the FPLP and formed another party. Some delegates including Rae and O'Keefe regretted that the motion combined censure of the advocacy of conscription, which some state executives had permitted, with the greater offence of forming another party in opposition to Labor. Gardiner argued that it was unwise to pass a motion which would result in a state being deprived of some of its properly endorsed delegates. Stocky ALF secretary Alec McCallum, who had been recovering in Adelaide from a nervous breakdown, announced that while he was firmly against conscription himself WA MPs could hardly be blamed for their stance when the ALF conference had given them a free hand. The proceedings were enlivened by the cantankerous contribution of one of WA's conscriptionist delegates, 'Paddy' Lynch, who had not only followed Hughes in the split but was now his Works and

Railways minister. In his Irish brogue he admonished the 'tyranny' of 'parasites' who paraded 'tinpot principles' in order to seize parliamentary seats for themselves. His manner belied his claim that he came to conference 'with an olive branch'; Rae, who clashed heatedly with him, interjected that he waved his olive branch like a shillelagh (the traditional Irish cudgel). When Scullin's motion was passed by 29 votes to 4 (Gardiner and the WA anti-conscriptionists opposing, with the WA conscriptionists abstaining), Lynch made a dignified farewell speech, wished the labour movement good luck, and left the party forever. As Gardiner predicted, many ALF members were outraged that half their delegation had been removed from the conference. Strenuous efforts continued to be made in the West to avert a schism, but by April 1917 the ALF had also split asunder.

Like Holman, Hughes and his band entered a coalition with anti-Labor and tried to have the next election postponed. After extensive negotiations a new National Party was formed, and Hughes, Pearce, Jensen, Webster and Russell joined a ministry containing such avowed enemies of Labor as Cook and Forrest. This fusion provided the Nationalists with a comfortable majority in the Representatives, but did not quite give them the numbers in the Senate which they needed to achieve a postponement of the next election. Hughes was eager to return to London for an Imperial War Conference, but told Lloyd George that the domestic political situation would probably prevent him from attending: 'Unless we can contrive secure support of two or more old Labour party Senators only course open is early election'. The 'contriving' began in earnest.

Hughes and Pearce led the way in the ensuing manoeuvring which debased the political process and created further bitterness. With the extension of parliament about to be considered by the Senate, 'a strange epidemic' struck Tasmania's Labor Senators. Long, 'a man of robust appearance', and Guy absented themselves for health reasons. The Nationalists encouraged Long to take the recuperative voyage he claimed he needed by sending him to Java, having discovered that Australian trade with the East Indies required on-the-spot investigation. Guy refused to budge from his sickbed in Tasmania, and Labor's Senate majority was reduced to one. A third Tasmanian, 38-year-old R.K. Ready, had not been well, experiencing severe stress and fainting fits owing to the combined effect of Labor's turmoil, his view – unsupported by caucus – that the election should be postponed, and criticism of his chairmanship of Tasmania's State Recruiting Committee. His sudden resignation was announced on the evening of 1 March. Obviously forewarned (unlike the FPLP), Hughes had the intricate constitutional procedures well in hand, thanks to the connivance of Tasmania's Governor, its anti-Labor Premier, the Governor-General, Senate President Givens and Hughes's choice as Ready's successor, Earle. The necessary arrangements were rubber-stamped and Earle, the Labor defector and former Tasmanian premier with a penchant for devious politics, was in Melbourne ready to sit in the Senate the very next morning. The effect was like a conjuring trick. It was a typical Hughes exploit, skilfully executed with its shortsighted concentration on the quick fix, and completely ignoring such wider implications as its damaging impact on Australians' confidence in their political system. Labor MPs were devastated. Belton said that nothing had ever made him feel 'so sick', and McGrath, who had enlisted and was in England, wrote feelingly to Fisher that 'it makes my head Ache to think about it'. The uproar, and the sweeping rumours of corruption, were fuelled when Labor's NSW Senator David Watson claimed that Hughes and Pearce had resorted to bribery in order to entice him into the

Nationalists. Hughes and Pearce denied the allegation, which boiled down to uncorroborated different versions of private conversations (which Hughes had ensured would be private by locking the door beforehand). Hughes's reputation for unscrupulous trickery gave Labor supporters little reason to doubt Watson's version, and there would have been even fewer doubts if knowledge had become public of a separate Nationalist plot to bribe a Victorian Labor Senator, which was apparently abandoned because of the risk that he would react just like Watson. Ironically, these sordid attempts to capture the Senate were foiled by two Nationalist Senators from Tasmania, who were so perturbed by Hughes's conduct that they crossed the floor to vote with the FPLP in favour of a royal commission into the corruption allegations (a resolution ignored by Hughes) and to prevent the postponement of the election.

So Hughes and the federal Nationalists had to face the electors after all, and they were relieved when Holman paved the way with another auspicious precedent for them. Having obtained his special extension of parliament until the end of 1917, Holman quixotically announced on 17 February that a snap election would be held. As he knew, Labor was still reeling from the split. Another shock for Labor supporters four days later was the news of Durack's resignation as NSW Labor leader for personal reasons unconnected with conscription. Storey became the new leader and fought gamely against allegations by the Nationalists, including the ex-Labor defectors, that Labor was 'disloyal' and associated with criminal extremists like the celebrated IWW 'Twelve' who had been convicted and given hefty gaol sentences. The election result showed that Labor had retained nearly all its usual voters, especially in its traditionally strong areas, but it had lost the extra support so crucial in the finely balanced seats which have to be secured to win government. Not all the expelled Labor conscriptionists had followed Holman. McGowen, Griffith and Meagher could not stomach Holman's eager embrace of the enemy, and preferred to flirt with political oblivion by standing as 'Independent Labor' candidates. They all lost. Griffith retained his social radicalism and spent much of the next two decades trying to persuade the labour movement that he had been unjustly excommunicated. McGowen, with one son killed at Gallipoli and two others in the AIF, had heart trouble and spent the election campaign in hospital with a broken leg. His successor as member for Redfern – who had not been born when 'Old Jim' first won it – was 25-year-old native-born boilermaker and popular boxer and footballer, Billy McKell, a prominent figure in the Industrial Section. McGowen had taught McKell at Sunday school and closely supervised his political development; their mutual admiration was unscarred by the Redfern contest, which lacked the vilification that was a feature of the election elsewhere.

The federal election took place six weeks later on 5 May 1917. Hughes campaigned 'with even more than usual asperity and lack of restraint', accusing his detractors of being linked to Germany, the IWW or the Irish Home Rule organization Sinn Fein. He was careful to repeat frequently that conscription would not be introduced unless approved at another referendum. Once again sectarianism was rampant, and Labor candidates were mercilessly taunted by their former colleagues as 'disloyal' and controlled by 'outside organizations' or 'secret juntas'. The election result confirmed that a significant number of voters were prepared to endorse the Nationalists' win-the-war policy without accepting conscription. The Nationalists won all 18 Senate seats contested and 53 Representatives seats to Labor's 22, giving them a clear majority in both houses. Nearly all the Labor renegades already in parliament were re-elected. Some seats were captured for the Nationalists by ex-Laborites new to federal parliament like Lamond and – of all people – Mat Reid, the former stern enforcer of socialist principles now reincarnated as a British imperialist, conscriptionist and denouncer of strikes. Reid was joined in the Senate by Thomas, who had always been contemptuous of that chamber but did not fancy his chances of retaining Barrier as a Nationalist. Labor's electoral casualties included O'Malley, Burns, Findley, Mahon, Turley and David Watson. Hughes again charged Murdoch with the task of harvesting the AIF vote. McGrath, who had participated in the clamour about falsifying the soldiers' vote in the referendum, was permitted to act as Labor's scrutineer, and his formal acknowledgement that proper tallying procedures had been followed was sufficient to scotch any allegations of miscounting this time. However, there were widespread complaints that the figures were deliberately distorted by the AIF ballot papers with their anonymous squares marked 'Ministerialist' and 'Opposition': many soldiers understandably unaware of recent political events voted 'Ministerialist' assuming this meant Labor.

For Labor supporters especially, 1917 was a grim year. In April 1916 six of the seven state and national governments were Labor; 15 months later only one, the Queensland government, remained. Many shared Tudor's gloomy assessment that 'we are in for a very bad time, industrially as well as politically, and it is quite possible that the movement will be put back at least 10 years'. He blamed the war for 'a bloodlust among the people', who 'saw red and thought red and were unable to reason' as in prewar days. While Hughes ran the country 'in an atmosphere of almost perpetual crisis', the censors continued their hyperactivity and the various surveillance authorities formed during the war busied themselves in pursuit of Australians – including some of the Prime Minister's former parliamentary colleagues – who questioned or opposed his view of the war. The war itself seemed endless, a raging juggernaut of destruction. There were new names of faraway places to strike dread into Australian families: Bullecourt, Messines, Ypres, Polygon Wood, Broodseinde. Despite the continually optimistic headlines and official dispatches, it was clear to anyone reading between the lines or closely studying a map that the huge losses had not brought the Allies to the verge of ultimate success. State Labor conferences in NSW, Victoria, Queensland and SA endorsed a motion announcing that 'the present colossal struggle' was an inevitable product of capitalism, welcoming the momentous events occurring in Russia, and calling for an immediate international conference containing labour representatives and women delegates to negotiate a peace settlement. The pent-up frustrations of the labour movement were unleashed in a 'general strike' in NSW, involving railway, tramway and road transport workers, miners and maritime employees. The action taken by the NSW and federal Nationalist governments to smash the strike – recruitment of strikebreaking labour, arrest of strike leaders on charges of conspiracy – resembled the methods adopted in the legendary Labor defeats of 1890–91. Afterwards a legacy of sullen bitterness was guaranteed when many strikers were refused re-employment. One of them, a 32-year-old Bathurst engine driver named Ben Chifley, was propelled into politics by this 'harsh and oppressive treatment'.

Nobody was more affected by Labor's agony than Fisher. Australia was to him 'the brightest and best land in the world', and it was constantly in his thoughts. From afar he followed developments with horror as the party disintegrated amid 'the stress of desperate times, which I hoped never to live to see'. As the party's crisis escalated in October 1916, his 'whole hearted wish' was 'that the friends of many fights for right may not be driven apart for the rest of their lives'. After the explosion he was devastated. Former colleagues on both sides of the great schism wrote to him sorrowfully; many criticized Hughes's leadership and emphasized the heartfelt wish of many Labor people, Pearce's wife included, that Fisher had never resigned. When Hughes asked him to endorse a conscriptionist plea from all of Australia's former prime ministers, the High Commissioner excused himself tactfully: for once the chafing restrictions on his ability to speak out in his new sphere came in handy. He had found the adjustment difficult. While ill-health had made his resignation as Prime Minister essential, 'I cannot say I have been really happy since'. Fisher resented being bypassed by Hughes, who preferred to use Murdoch as his London intermediary and emissary; that brash young journalist shared Hughes's willingness to circumvent 'proper channels'. Fisher had several glimpses of the Western Front, and during one visit was almost led right into an unexpected burst of German shelling: it was like being 'in Hell'.

Late in 1917 Hughes plunged Australia further into discord with a second conscription referendum. The campaign was 'more strident, more bitter and even more uninhibited on both sides than before'. At riotous meetings speakers were showered with eggs, fruit and metal. Hughes raised the stakes even higher by declaring that he would resign if the referendum failed. Boote's contribution in the *Australian Worker* was again brilliant, despite the ever-tightening squeeze of the censorship. Archbishop Mannix was a provocative spokesman for Irish-Australians, infuriating conservatives with his ironic taunts. Hughes's main opponent was Ryan, who emerged as a national figure after several celebrated clashes with the increasingly agitated Prime Minister. When Ryan exposed flaws in the conscriptionists' arithmetic which again weakened their claim that voluntary recruiting had failed, his argument as published was flagrantly distorted by the censorship. To counter this, Theodore and McCormack suggested circulating their uncensored views in the Queensland Hansard. Ryan duly outlined his banned arguments in the Assembly, and for good measure Theodore read the text of some heavily censored pamphlets. Theodore and McCormack instructed the Queensland government printer to highlight the previously censored portions in heavy black type and to print 10 000 extra copies. The Queensland censor endeavoured to prevent publication, but was rebuffed by the government printer. Then Hughes intervened, authorizing uniformed soldiers to raid the printing office and seize all copies; the censor prevented any published reference to this unprecedented action. Ryan's rejoinder was the distribution of 50 000 copies of a special government gazette which outlined the remarkable incident and ensured that it received maximum publicity despite the censorship. Hughes soon embroiled himself in another controversy at the Queensland town of Warwick, where he was involved in a physical altercation. This resulted in another exchange with Ryan, who coolly corrected Hughes's hysterical version of the affray. Ryan also acquitted himself well in various legal manoeuvres against Hughes and between their respective governments. The labour movement was jubilant when the referendum resulted in a win for the anti-conscriptionists; the proportion of voters supporting conscription was less than the first referendum, both within the AIF (despite Murdoch's efforts) and overall. Labor people were understandably less thrilled by the ensuing constitutional charade: Munro Ferguson accepted Hughes's resignation, perfunctorily considered alternatives and then re-commissioned him.

In March 1918 the military situation dramatically altered. The Germans launched a vast offensive, smashed through the trench deadlock, and looked like winning the war. In April Munro Ferguson, supposedly detached from party politics, convened a conference of politicians, union leaders and employers which aimed to repair Australia's national cohesion and boost its flagging recruiting. But the labour movement had endured too much to be conciliatory; some labour movement figures refused the invitation. Ryan was there, buoyed by his resounding triumph on 16 March when his government was re-elected with an increased majority and the highest proportion of the vote Queensland Labor has ever achieved. He and other Labor participants at the conference were wary. They made their involvement conditional upon certain grievances being remedied: there had to be an end to conscription, victimization of unionists, and political censorship under the notorious WPA. Even then, they added, any agreement reached by that conference was not binding on the labour movement unless ratified by its own bodies at their own conferences. Debate meandered unproductively and, at times, angrily. Labor's utter distrust of Hughes surfaced frequently, notably when he produced a cable from London about the grave military situation and was told 'We've had enough of your forgeries'. After the conference ended with a nondescript resolution which Hughes described as 'pure piffle', he hastily returned to England for further war talks. Australia was a far less turbulent place without him, as even Pearce and Munro Ferguson admitted.

Labor's 1918 federal conference also signified how much the labour movement's attitude to the war had changed since 1914. In June 32 delegates gathered in Perth. SA and Tasmania, short of funds, sent only three delegates each, but Tasmania boosted its representation by accrediting two proxy delegates, Curtin and McCallum. Curtin was now in Perth as editor of the *Westralian Worker*; his appointment owed much to Anstey's lobbying, which overcame the misgivings of Mahon and others about Curtin's drinking. After adopting the peace resolution carried in four states in 1917, conference turned to Labor's approach to recruiting. With the military situation in the balance, this was a contentious issue. Some members actively supported voluntary recruiting, whereas Rae moved to ban the departure of any more Australian reinforcements. After animated debate this motion was only narrowly defeated, by 15 votes to 13. A sub-committee of 12, two from each state, came up with a compromise. Continued participation in recruiting was made subject to a clear statement by the Allies that they would 'enter into peace negotiations upon the basis of no annexations and no penal indemnities' and to a thorough investigation of Australia's domestic manpower requirements. Conference further decided that this policy would only apply if endorsed by a referendum of all Labor members. This was an unusual procedure, and acutely unsatisfactory to some party activists both at the conference and outside it; but these were unusual times, and without a compromise on this issue another split could not be ruled out. In another controversial debate an attempt to end Labor's commitment to compulsory military training proved unsuccessful after Scullin warned that Australia should be ready to defend itself against the burgeoning 'menace' of Japan. The party exercised some prudent censorship on these delicate issues. Considerable precautions were taken against leaks during the conference, and there were significant deletions from the official report published afterwards.

Labor's 1918 federal conference did not restrict itself to the war. Unification was inserted into the first plank of the fighting platform, although several delegates including McCormack and Cameron mentioned that the administration of the WPA made them uneasy about the extensive powers unification would bestow on the national government. The intense bitterness felt towards Labor's renegades, and the fact that most of them were not born in Australia, had prompted much discussion, especially in AWU circles and the *Australian Worker*, about restricting certain positions to native-born Australians. Boote declared his firm opposition to such notions, unlike earnest native-born shearer Arthur Blakeley, who had risen through the AWU to defeat the exiled Spence at the 1917 election. Blakeley asserted not only that the office of prime minister should be restricted to native-born Australians, but also that its incumbent should never leave Australia while in office. He was not a delegate at the 1918 conference, but a resolution from his Bourke constituents was among those endorsing similar ideas. Conference gave them short shrift. Delegates pointed out that insisting on Australian-born leaders was no guarantee that they would reflect Australia's interests, and also offended a growing (but still moderate) consciousness of Australian Labor as part of an international labour movement.

Two internal party matters received attention. Since its establishment by the 1915 conference the federal executive had met only three times, and not at all since December 1916. Although its functioning had been severely hampered by the split and the financial problems plaguing the party in some states, Curtin expressed his 'grave dissatisfaction' with its 'gross dereliction of duty'. His motion calling on the executive to smarten up in future was carried. The 1908 federal conference report records a motion by Catts that 'the name of the party be the Australian Labour Party', which was carried by 22 votes to 2 but not formally extended to cover the party at state level. A decade later, when a different spelling was becoming more prevalent, the federal conference resolved that 'the name be the Australian Labor Party' and that the states, instead of having different titles such as PLL, PLC, ALF and ULP, 'will be branches of the ALP'.

When the Armistice signalled an end to the carnage on 11 November, staid people in various parts of the globe went berserk with relief. Some Australians, overwhelmed with sorrow by what had been lost in the great madness, found it impossible to celebrate. Labor's wounds were still raw: when the national parliament was recalled especially to salute the Armistice, the occasion was marred by bickering between an ALP Senator and an ex-Labor renegade. The outbreak of peace also took the heat out of the question of Labor's attitude to recruiting, and the ballot of party members lost its significance.

Although peace came to the Western Front there was no sign of it in Australia in 1919. The colossal slaughter in the trenches was quickly followed by a deadly influenza epidemic which swept across the world, spreading apprehension, misery and desolation. The epidemic killed over 12 000 Australians in 1919, and provoked sharp friction within and between their governments as they tried to control it. In April Curtin was profoundly shocked to learn that the epidemic had claimed his closest mate. Hyett, having blossomed relatively late as a cricketer, was on tour with the Victorian team in Sydney when he caught the disease; the labour movement mourned the loss of one of its very finest men. The influenza scourge was not the only concern of unsettled Australians. The extent of industrial unrest was unprecedented: 6·3 million days were lost in 1919, which for over half a century remained the highest tally in one year. Prices, which had risen faster than wages during the war, soared again in 1919; this contributed to the strikes and led to renewed calls to deal with the still-flagrant profiteering. Newspapers and public figures used the language of hate and violence to keep

Australians anxious – stirring up sectarianism, disseminating hysterical nonsense about events in Russia and the threat posed by 'Bolshevism' in Australia, and accusing people of 'disloyalty' on the flimsiest pretext. There was even further volatility when what was left of the AIF came home.

Labor men had joined the AIF in droves. (So many enlisted from the AWU that Holloway unsuccessfully asked Pearce to let the union have its own division.) Some of them were renowned soldiers. Bill Currey distinguished himself at Péronne and became, as Labor's MLA for Kogarah 1941–48, the first VC winner to enter the NSW parliament. Another lifelong Labor man, Jack Carroll, was awarded the VC for exceptional gallantry at Messines, but this breezy WA railwayman kept missing his appointment to receive it; he turned up at the fourth attempt, and amused himself by exercising the VC winners' right to order the Buckingham Palace Guard to parade. Because he rarely said anything but yes or no he was known as 'Referendum' Carroll, a nickname exemplifying the AIF's relatively democratic spirit (for an army) which was largely derived from the labour movement.

The Nationalists were very worried that the returning soldiers might not placidly adjust to competitive, acquisitive civilian life. They were alarmed by the prospect of restless men involving themselves in disruptive radical groups. Conservative forces laboured mightily on a variety of fronts to achieve the sort of soldiers' transition they wanted. Overall their efforts were successful, but not entirely. Dissatisfaction with the quarantine restrictions produced a number of mutinous incidents on returning troopships. A different demonstration by returned soldiers culminated in an inkstand being hurled at Victoria's Nationalist Premier after his office was invaded. In Queensland soldiers encouraged by conservative manipulators to deal with 'Bolsheviks' and 'disloyalists' did so with such commitment that uncontrolled mayhem raged through Brisbane streets. When WA's Nationalist Premier led strikebreaking labour to Fremantle to smash a wharf labourers' strike in May 1919, returning soldiers aboard a passing troopship asked the strikers if they wanted help. Then on top in the pitched battle, the strikers thanked the soldiers but told them their assistance was not needed. If their offer had been accepted, perhaps the conservative conditioning of Australia's returned soldiers might not have been so successful. This conditioning utilized the new national stereotype of the resourceful, sardonic, independent digger. It was subtly and repetitively suggested that after the life-and-death struggles of the battlefield the petty struggles of politics were beneath the digger: 'political' became a word of disparagement, almost invariably applied to Labor politics and 'the machine', which was at odds with the diggers' notorious abhorrence of excessive authority. This process was accelerated when the Nationalists bestowed 'official' recognition on the most conservative organization of the various returned soldiers' groups which had evolved; this favoured organization was eventually known as the Returned Soldiers' League (RSL). Soldiers were also detached from their prewar union affiliations by the notion of preference to returned soldiers in various spheres, especially employment, which some Nationalists promoted, well aware of its incompatibility with preference to trade unionists. No longer was Australian nationalism a forward-looking, progressive sentiment epitomized by the radical AWU bushworker. Nationalistic sentiment now looked backward to the war, had been taken over by the conservatives, and was symbolized by the digger, who disdained 'politics' and therefore supported the Nationalists' preservation of the status quo.

Part of the powerful conservative conditioning of returned soldiers was that the Nationalists claimed an exclusive affinity with the AIF while asserting that the 'disloyal' post-split Labor Party had let them down – despite the fact that several state and federal Labor MPs had enlisted. One of them, J.V. O'Loghlin, became the AIF's first Senator when he was appointed at the age of 62 to command transports carrying Australian reinforcements. Having urged Pearce to place him as close to the action as possible, he returned after the split to find 'there is more war here in Australia than there is at the front, and. . .it is being conducted more bitterly'. The Nationalists made elaborate attempts to discredit three able Labor MHRs – McGrath, Yates and A.T. Ozanne – who had proved their 'loyalty' by enlisting but had not followed Hughes out of the party. After enlisting in March 1916 Charlie McGrath was joined in the AIF by his 16-year-old son Dave, who did valuable and dangerous work as a driver in France. Shortly before the 1917 election Dave was returned to Australia under the impression – shared by his father in London and family in Ballarat – that, like other under-age AIF youths, he was being given a furlough before returning to the front when older. Instead, he arrived home to find that the Nationalists had spread it about that his father had insisted upon his discharge. Charlie McGrath was livid. He was frustrated too, sensing that devious influences were preventing him from getting to the front, so that the Nationalists could sneer that he had done no real soldiering. Like McGrath, Ozanne had enraged Hughes by campaigning against conscription among the soldiers, and he was dealt with even more effectively. With his division under General Monash about to embark for the front, Ozanne had a nasal condition which required medical treatment and resulted in his discharge. Monash was convinced he was virtually a deserter, and told Murdoch so. The allegation caused a storm in Australia during the 1917 election campaign. Ozanne travelled home to participate in it, but his ship was mysteriously delayed at sea, he arrived too late and lost his seat. Yates enlisted in his mid-forties after an incident in parliament, and publicly attributed his delayed departure to scheming by the Nationalists. His return home was even more controversial. When broken undertakings about quarantine procedures riled the soldiers on board his transport, Yates felt that he reduced both the tension and the likelihood of the dreaded influenza spreading. However, he was court-martialled, convicted of mutinous conduct and sentenced to 60 days' detention. The Nationalists capitalized on this by spreading defamatory rumours that Yates had managed to avoid doing his bit while at the front. Different standards applied to those on the other side of politics. Monash had to dismiss a brigade commander for drunkenness and incompetence, but the disgraced general returned to prominence in Queensland conservative politics. There was no everlasting slur for his family (unlike Ozanne's) to endure; one of his children became a minister in federal Liberal governments.

By 1918 many radicals and unionists were convinced that the workers' salvation lay in the One Big Union (OBU) scheme. They welcomed the creation of a single all-powerful giant union which would signal the demise of craft unionism, and were absorbed in agitating for its introduction. Conservatives eyed the OBU's IWW-like rhetoric with a shudder. Boote hailed the scheme in the *Australian Worker* as 'the greatest thing that has happened in the history of this country', but had to change his tune when his employer, the AWU, decided to throw its considerable weight against it. The AWU's decision, which most MPs supported as they considered the OBU too radical to be electorally popular, doomed the OBU scheme to failure and generated profound ill-feeling. The

21. The striking granite memorial to Donald Macdonell at Stuart Mill, Victoria. Macdonell was greatly admired by many, including prominent Victorian unionist and Labor activist Laurie Cohen, who remained alone under a blazing sun for a fortnight while he carved the inscription, which reads:

Erected by members
of
The Australian Workers Union
in memory of
Donald Macdonell
General Secretary A.W.U. 1900–1911
Chief Secy McGowen Ministry N.S.W. 1910
Died October 26 1911 aged 49

He has mounted his horse and smiled
    farewell
And rides where the shadows fall
Honor him, men of the Western Sheds,
Honor him — honor him all!
(Betty Emms)

22. The Fisher ministry, 1910–1913. Standing (from left): J. Thomas, K. O'Malley, G. Pearce, E. L. Batchelor, F. Tudor. Seated: W. M. Hughes, A. Fisher, G. McGregor. Front (on floor): C. Frazer, E. Findley. This cabinet remained unchanged for three years except for the inclusion of E. A. Roberts after Batchelor died in October 1911. *(National Library)*

23. The Earle ministry, 1914–1916. Standing (from left): J. Lyons, P. McCrackan. Seated: J. Ogden, J. Earle, J. Belton. (*State Library of Tasmania*)

24. Andrew Fisher tired of the burdens of office. (*National Library*)

25. Prime Minister Hughes and High Commissioner Fisher watch the AIF marching off to the front shortly before the terrible Somme battles (Fisher is wearing a light-coloured jacket and dark hat; Hughes is closer to the soldiers and holding his hat). (*Australian War Memorial*)

26. 'The Case For Labor'. (by Claude Marquet; *National Library*)

27. Prime Minister Hughes throwing himself into a speech. (*Australian War Memorial*)

28. 'I'll Have You!' (by Claude Marquet; *National Library*)

rivalry was especially bitter in NSW, and guaranteed a lively state conference there in 1919. There was no-holds-barred arm-twisting and head-counting in the brutal tradition that has often characterized Labor's internal struggles. Wild scenes ensued when the results of the crucial conference motions showed that the AWU/politicians group narrowly had the numbers. Arthur Rae, an AWU man for decades, having declared that it was about time that the Labor platform could be distinguished from anti-Labor 'without a microscope', voted with the OBU faction and joined them in a defiant walk-out from the conference. Tudor found it ironical that these breakaways sang 'Solidarity Forever' as they marched out to form their own party. A concerned federal executive authorized Stewart and Ryan to intervene, but their efforts were fruitless. Stewart reported back to the federal executive that this new split in his view was not as damaging to NSW Labor as had been feared, although there was no denying the mutual acrimony of the two factions. The AWU leaders denounced the 'blowfly, maggot-creating, white-ant' tactics of the OBU activists, who replied that the NSW ALP executive was 'a bogus and parasitic growth upon the Labor movement'. The breakaways formed themselves into the Industrial Socialist Labor Party (ISLP).

Another federal conference was held in June 1919. It was severely disrupted by the influenza epidemic, which made some delegates too ill to participate on some days and combined with a shipping dispute to prevent Tasmania's delegates from attending at all. Conference confirmed its belief in unification by endorsing a specific scheme which provided for provinces to replace the states, 'full sovereign powers' for the national government, and the abolition of the Senate. This scheme was similar to the 1910 proposal of FPLP defector Fred Bamford; its assiduous advocate in 1919 was Stewart's assistant secretary in Victoria, Danny McNamara, who was building a reputation as an efficient, dedicated administrator. Conference recognized the spread of an international outlook within the party by supporting the Victorian proposal to insert in the objective 'the maintenance and extension of fraternal relations with Labor organizations of all countries'. A hard line was taken against defecting MPs: 'any member of Parliament or Conscriptionist candidate expelled for advocating overseas Conscription shall not at any time, under any pretext, be readmitted to the Labor Movement'. Conference carried a motion which had been unsuccessful at the 1918 conference when it endorsed the removal of the compulsory clauses from the Defence Act. Gardiner was bound by the NSW branch to vote for the motion and did so; but he spoke strongly against it, raising the spectre of Japan once again and asserting that there was 'a good deal of shallow clap-trap talked about "international brotherhood"'. A motion to end the exemption from land tax of properties worth less than £5000, a recurring party debating topic, was contested by moderates hoping to maximize Labor votes among small farmers. On this occasion the hardliners mustered the required numbers and the exemption was abolished, but the moderates soon initiated moves to reverse the decision: the upshot was a special federal conference in October to review Labor's policy on land taxation.

However, this special conference was more noted for the action it took concerning the federal leadership. Tudor was not a natural leader. 'I know that the position is one of the most difficult to fill in Australia at any time', he had remarked when appointed, 'and it will be particularly hard for some time to come'. In adverse circumstances he had done his best, but his performance had been uninspiring. Although Higgs saw himself as a worthy alternative, there was a dearth of prospective leaders in the FPLP owing to the combined effect of the split and the earlier untimely deaths of talented men like Frazer and Arthur. Acutely conscious of this was the FPLP's secretary and industrious beaver, Jimmy Catts, who was intent on bringing to national politics the only ALP man who had since the split proved more than a match for Hughes. That man was T.J. Ryan, who was attracted by the challenge but realized that the transition would have to be handled delicately. When the Queensland executive asked Labor's other state executives to support its resolution that Ryan should transfer at the next federal election, Catts was instrumental in having Tasmania and his own NSW branch express their agreement. Tudor's home state, Victoria, significantly did not reply. Ryan announced that he would only move to federal politics if this was the 'unequivocal desire' of the labour movement. With a federal election approaching, Catts and his NSW colleagues decided to raise Ryan's transfer at the October special federal conference. When they did so the Victorians sternly objected that the conference was constitutionally unable to discuss any business other than land taxation policy (conference had reinstated the £5000 exemption). They also deplored the unwarranted slight to Tudor. After it became apparent that the numbers were against the Victorians, they even threatened that they would walk out. Ryan, unlike Tudor, was at the conference and his skilful handling of the awkward situation helped defuse the tension. Holloway eventually admitted that the Victorians admired Ryan but could not countenance the unprecedented methods adopted to bring him into the federal sphere. Federal conference supplemented its unique summons to Ryan by appointing him national campaign director.

Election day was 13 December. Concurrently with the election Hughes placed before the voters referenda resembling in diluted form the measures Labor had put to the people in 1911 and 1913; if granted, however, they were only to apply for three years. Labor's dilemma was either to support them as a compromise (but nonetheless desirable) instalment, or to reject them outright as unsatisfactory, makeshift and temporary. Ryan firmly favoured rejection and persuaded the October special conference that the referenda were 'a sham and a delusion'. The virulent election campaign increasingly became a contest between Hughes and Ryan; this was accentuated when Tudor fell ill. Nervous of Ryan's capacity, the Nationalists attacked him at every opportunity, and distributed large posters screeching 'RYAN SPELLS RUIN', 'RYAN AND ROME', and 'LABOR MEANS BOLSHEVISM, IWWISM AND OBUISM'. The way the war had stimulated the dark side of Australian politics was illustrated by a shameful incident involving Labor's former MHR for Wannon, farmer-poet J.K. McDougall. Nearly two decades earlier the Boer War had inspired him to write a bitterly satirical adaptation of one of Kipling's imperial battle-hymns. Although McDougall was not a candidate in 1919, this poem was trumpeted by Hughes and the *Argus* as reflecting Labor's attitude to the men of the AIF. This sordid electioneering culminated in a raid on McDougall's farm by a group of returned soldiers seeking retribution. McDougall was kidnapped, then tarred and feathered.

For Labor enthusiasts the election result was very depressing. The ALP won only a third of the Representatives seats and, disastrously, only one (Gardiner) of the Senate vacancies. This result was influenced by the introduction of preferential voting which, as intended, enabled anti-Labor candidates to contest seats against each other without benefiting Labor and facilitated the arrival of the Country Party on the federal scene with 11 MHRs. Labor's soldier MHRs McGrath, Ozanne, Yates, Con Wallace and E.W. Corboy all lost (although McGrath soon recaptured Ballarat at a by-election). The voters rejected the referenda. The fundamental dismal reality for Labor was that the hated Hughes was back with probably a working majority in both houses for his Nationalists. The FPLP's talent and experience was further depleted when Higgs, having supported the referenda in defiance of the Queensland executive, made a stinging, tactless attack on Labor's executives, was expelled and ultimately joined the Nationalists. Curtin was dispirited too. He had taken on far too much during the election, directing the overall campaign in WA with little assistance and standing as Labor's candidate for Perth when nobody else would, as well as churning out the *Westralian Worker*. Afterwards he plumbed the depths again with a severe breakdown. For the ALP there was bleakness everywhere.

The Great War was a terrible tragedy for Australia. Its people had eagerly embraced the conflict but were profoundly soured and chastened by the anguish, bitterness and authoritarianism it engendered. Australia had lost some 60 000 killed, and many more were broken in mind or body or both. There was a gulf between Australians who had endured the indescribable in the trenches, and those who had stayed home and experienced the curbing of civil liberties and the increased cost of living. The growth in the national debt from £6 million to £350 million was a crippling economic legacy. The war was also disastrous for Labor. Pearce and Givens claimed that the split was unavoidable because the party's organization had become impossible; on the other side of Labor's great schism some saw it as cleansing and beneficial. Both these views betray a blinkered perspective. Leadership was a crucial factor. The combustible elements were already testing a tired Fisher when he resigned, and they became much worse later. Under a leader of Ryan's tact and ability the party might have avoided a rupture. Hughes's leadership made one inevitable.

As Demaine sorrowfully told Fisher, 'I am afraid that the severance of old friendships has come Andy'. In prewar days at Ballarat a close-knit native-born AWU trio, Jack Barnes, John McNeill and Andy McKissock, became known as the 'Three Musketeers of the Trades Hall'. Barnes was a 'breezy unconventional character. . .with a whiff of the shearing-shed about him', who had been a Senator since 1913; McNeill, another bushworker, known for his reliability and integrity, married Scullin's sister; McKissock, involved like McNeill and Scullin in Labor's Ballarat paper the *Evening Echo*, had served a term in both the Victorian and federal parliaments. United in their nationalism, devotion to the labour movement and reverence for Spence as its grand old man, they made a pact that each musketeer and the AWU would ensure that a Cootamundra wattle was planted on each of their graves. When McKissock died in the 1919 influenza epidemic, Holloway and scores of other Labor mourners were huddled together at the cemetery as McNeill and Barnes planted the commemorative wattle. Suddenly they noticed a pathetic old man standing alone and forlorn some 50 metres away. It was Spence. An unbridgeable chasm separated him from them after the ghastly war that had shattered Labor friendships and devastated their party.

6 'There was Crookedness in New South Wales', 1920–1928

MORE THAN A decade after the split the FPLP was still in the political wilderness. Its barren period mirrored the sour, sterile tenor of Australian life during the 1920s. The Great War had permanently damaged the faith in enlightenment and social progress which propels democratic reform. There was a pessimistic, inward-turning greyness of spirit prevalent in the 1920s, as Australians seemed to recoil chastened from the tumultuous years of a war which they had welcomed so exuberantly. They responded to the 1922 federal election with stupefying apathy, over a million eligible voters staying away from the polling booths, a prodigious increase. Compulsory voting was introduced before the 1925 federal election, but the Nationalists mounted a scare campaign and won comfortably. Far from building on its moderate gains of 1922, Labor went backwards, winning less than a third of the Representatives seats and none at all of the 22 Senate positions contested in 1925.

This sorry state of affairs occurred despite the advent of Ryan. He sensibly avoided any antagonizing displays of immediate assertiveness in caucus, which re-elected Tudor as leader and Gardiner as his deputy. Ryan concentrated on adroit parliamentary manoeuvres designed to lure the Country Party away from the arms of Nationalists. While he quickly established himself as the FPLP's most able performer, he was not so consistently outstanding in his new sphere as he had been as Queensland's Premier. With a demanding legal practice and frequent speaking engagements, he was still remarkably busy although less equipped to withstand the strain. In the notoriously draughty Victorian Parliament House he suffered from continuous sniffles and bronchial infections which sapped his vigour, and the extensive travelling he undertook did not help. Even so, he was in better health than Tudor, who was sidelined with heart trouble in August 1920. The choice of Tudor's replacement as acting leader in the Representatives became a controversial question in caucus. The FPLP gave Charlton the position on 12 August when Ryan was away with influenza, but a special meeting to settle the matter on 9 September resulted in Ryan being elected as acting leader.

Hugh Mahon's passionate attachment to Ireland contributed to his singular departure from the FPLP. After losing Kalgoorlie in 1917 to the Labor renegade E.E. Heitmann, he had won it back in 1919. In October 1920 an Irish nationalist with relatives in Melbourne died in an English gaol after a hunger strike. Mahon could no longer contain his burning indignation about the continued British presence in his beloved Ireland, and at a meeting of Irish patriots in Melbourne he unleashed his rage. The British government was 'a gang of false hearted hypo-crites' who ruled over a 'bloody and accursed Empire'; they had sent 'spies, informers and bloody cut-throats' to Ireland, and he 'read with delight that some of those thugs' had been killed. When his speech was extensively reported in the *Argus*, the breastbeating imperial loyalists were predictably inflamed; even some of Mahon's FPLP colleagues found his comments disturbing. Hughes's response was to have Mahon expelled from parliament for making seditious utterances inconsistent with a parliamentarian's oath of allegiance. His FPLP colleagues, with Anstey particularly eloquent, vigorously attacked the government's action, asserting correctly that a court of law was the place to judge Mahon's conduct, not the Nationalists' party room. Anstey described the Nationalists as 'the ac-cusers, the prosecutors, the judges and the executioners, driving this man out of the place into which he was sent by the people of this country'. As some Labor members pointed out, Mick Considine, MHR for Barrier, had reportedly said 'bugger the king, he is a bloody German bastard' in mid-1919, but he had been fined and gaoled by a court without being expelled from parliament. The dif-ference was that the Nationalists had no hope of winning Barrier at any time. Kalgoorlie in 1920, however, was marginal, the Country Party was proving an unreliable group in parliament, and Hughes wanted to bolster his shaky majority in the Representatives. Hughes's gambit was successful. Mahon con-tested the acrimonious by-election, but the stigma of his expulsion prevented him from regaining Kalgoorlie. It was a distasteful end to his political career. No other member has been expelled by the national parliament, and at no other federal by-election has the government managed to capture a seat from the opposition.

The FPLP's declining stocks of ability and experience dwindled further. In June 1921 Labor lost an amiable stalwart with the death of Jim Page, who had held Maranoa in western Queensland since the inception of federal parliament. Another veteran, McDonald, was now the only other Queensland Labor MP in federal parliament; Ryan was determined that Maranoa would not share the fate of other rural seats and fall to the Country Party. Labor's by-election candidate was W.J. Dunstan. Formerly a roving bushworker, Dunstan had risen through the AWU in SA to become secretary of the enlarged, all-powerful Queensland AWU; in the by-election context he was a party official from the city rather than a popular western Queenslander like Page. Ryan felt ill and very tired as he began the long journey (against advice from friends and colleagues) north from Mel-bourne to assist Dunstan's campaign among the people he used to represent in the Queensland parliament. He began coughing blood, but persisted with his schedule. The night before polling day he addressed a meeting at Queensland Labor's spiritual birthplace, Barcaldine. Immediately afterwards he was taken to hospital. Two days after Maranoa voters elected a Country Party member to succeed Page, Ryan died of pneumonia. The Great War had severely shaken ALP supporters' confidence in the inevitability of their party's progress, and their hopes for its revival largely rested on Ryan. His death at 45 was a shattering blow. Five months later Tudor's overtaxed heart finally gave up the struggle, and another loyal party servant was gone.

The FPLP appointed its new leaders at the start of the 1922 parliamentary session in May. There were only two nominations for leader, Charlton and

Gardiner. Like Tudor, Matt Charlton was likeable, honest and diligent, but he lacked flair, imagination and personal magnetism. 'Jupp' Gardiner was one of Labor's giants in more ways than one. It was over 30 years since he had entered the NSW parliament as the youngest of Labor's 35 of 1891. Even then his physique was imposing – he represented NSW as a rugby forward – but it had since become awesome. Tipping the scales at around 18 stone (120 kg), 'generous and manly without a mean streak in him', he had been Labor's solitary Senator since 1920. Caucus refrained from establishing an unusual precedent – the FPLP's leader has always sat in the Representatives – and elected Charlton. Gardiner continued as deputy leader. Blakeley and fellow AWU stalwart Tom Lavelle, the busy MHR for Calare 1919–22, sprang a surprise when they nominated the new member in Tudor's old seat of Yarra, Scullin, to succeed Ryan as assistant leader in the Representatives. At his first caucus meeting since he lost Corangamite in 1913 Scullin modestly declined the nomination. Instead, the FPLP chose Anstey as its assistant leader.

The woeful state of Labor's NSW branch, which plagued the party for a generation, deprived the FPLP of the valuable services of Catts. He had embarked on a crusade to end the scandalous administration of the NSW branch's dominant faction, which retaliated by expelling him in April 1922 without giving any reasons. While Catts had previously been guarded in his public comments, after his expulsion he regaled parliament with lurid allegations of corruption in NSW. He made detailed charges of 'wholesale, barefaced ballot-faking and impropriety and embezzlement in the administration of union funds', and insisted that the state branch was rotten to the core: its 'whole machinery' was 'manipulated to cover up criminality, graft and corruption'. Having formed a separate party called the Majority Labor Party, Catts led it spiritedly into the 1922 federal election, but all its seven candidates were defeated and it faded into oblivion. Catts lost Cook, which he had held since 1906, to E.C. Riley, who joined his father (MHR for South Sydney, 1910–31) in the FPLP. The younger Riley's ordeal in the preselection for Cook illustrated the problems in NSW. He was not the anointed candidate of the dominant faction, and two successive ballots won by him were annulled by the NSW executive. After the FPLP, alerted by Riley senior, resolved that the preselection shambles was 'ruinous to the prospects of the Party', the state executive responded to pressure and endorsed E.C. Riley.

Catts's claims were wayward in some particulars, but his fundamental allegation of widespread corruption was uncomfortably true. The Bailey-Lambert regime in NSW was notorious. Jack Bailey was a rough and tough Tumut shearer who had risen to prominence through the AWU. 'A bare-knuckles fighter, he had literally fought his way upwards.' His lack of educational polish forced him to rely on associates to do his clerical work. Ambitious, cunning and unscrupulous, he was a dangerous adversary. In 1915 Bailey became president of the AWU's powerful central branch and his crony, hard-drinking ex-shearer Bill Lambert, was appointed branch secretary. While furthering the interests of the bushworkers they represented, they also proved most adept at feathering their own nests. Bailey was one of the chief organizers of the Industrial Section which had marshalled the numbers at the 1916 NSW conference, and after the OBU faction left in 1919 the Bailey-Lambert forces were able to dominate the NSW ALP. Preselection ballots were rigged to assist Bailey-Lambert candidates, AWU and ALP finances were misappropriated, funds were received with illicit strings attached, and it seems standover tactics were also part of the repertoire. Bailey himself entered the NSW Assembly in 1918 by winning a by-election in Monaro before switching to Goulburn for the 1920 state election. Catts, the campaign director, investigated the Goulburn preselection ballot and found it 'grossly corrupt'. Lambert became ALP state president, created 'great mistrust' as lord mayor of Sydney with his 'sharp practices', and moved on to the plum seat of West Sydney which became vacant when Ryan died. He had an undistinguished seven years in federal parliament, where he responded to Catts's allegations in the Representatives with vigorous denials and pointed references to his accuser's recent divorce proceedings. Like any organization made up of men and women the ALP is shaped by human frailty, but even the most tolerant Labor visionaries found all this lamentable.

Labor's narrow election win in March 1920, only nine months after the pandemonium of its 1919 conference and the walk-out of the OBU breakaways, was both an indictment of the scandals and disunity of the Nationalist government and a tribute to the trustworthiness of the incoming Premier, Jack Storey. Aware that his Assembly majority was precarious and that the Council was poised to obstruct, Storey immediately offended party militants by declaring that since the voters had given Labor 'only half a mandate', the government would have to proceed on a 'go slow' basis. Among the government's critics within caucus, on the executive and in the wider labour movement was Bailey, who found his omission from the ministry galling. Storey had a difficult time, and not only with politics – he was mortally ill with kidney disease. According to Catts, shortly before Storey died in October 1921 he urged Catts to 'save the old movement from a pack of savages'. The ministerial vacancy arising from Storey's death went to Charlie Lazzarini – there was still no place for Bailey.

All Storey's ministers remained in the new cabinet led by Storey's deputy Jim Dooley. A cheery Irish-born tailor from Lithgow, Dooley was capable, industrious and eloquent; he exerted a strong moderating influence on the government. He did not get on with his deputy, Greg McGirr, who was Bailey's closest associate in cabinet. McGirr, a flamboyant, wealthy pharmacist and land dealer from a family prominent in mid-western NSW, was known as 'Mother McGirr' because of his ministerial responsibility for child endowment. Their cabinet colleagues included Estell (at 58 the oldest minister), Auburn estate agent Jack Lang, altruistic country schoolteacher Peter Loughlin and ex-AIF sergeant George Cann, whose brother was one of the 35 of 1891. Attorney-General was talented barrister Edward McTiernan; his involvement in the ALP had in part been inspired by Hughes's 'The Case For Labor' articles. Minister for Justice was McKell, now embarking determinedly on a law course although his schooldays had ended at 13. The able Agriculture minister was W.F. Dunn, who had rocked the Holman government in 1911 with his shortlived resignation over its land policy. Since the state executive was controlled by the Bailey-Lambert AWU faction, its relations were likely to be frosty with a cabinet which not only excluded Bailey but contained only one minister with an AWU background, Tom Mutch. Mutch had imbibed bush socialism through avid reading and years of toil as a rouseabout at shearing sheds. He became a journalist, joined the *Australian Worker* staff, and developed close links with artists and writers; he was especially supportive of Henry Lawson in his declining alcoholic years. Mutch was a founder of the Industrial Section, but had since fallen out with Bailey.

The Storey government's best-known action was the release of the IWW Twelve. They had languished in gaol since 1917 despite increasing agitation from Boote, Mutch, socialist activist E.E. Judd and many others who were convinced that a travesty of justice had occurred. The sentences were excessive, the convictions for arson and conspiracy were based on concocted evidence, and nearly all the Twelve were innocent. Boote's crusading journalism for the release of the Twelve was superb. He was initially driven by the flagrant injustice suffered by his friend Donald Grant, a striking orator with flaming red hair, who had been gaoled, like seven of his IWW comrades, for 15 years. The case against Grant mainly concerned a speech at the Sydney Domain after Tom Barker was arrested: 'For every day Barker is in gaol it will cost the capitalists ten thousand pounds', Grant allegedly said. Boote declared that his friend had received 'fifteen years for fifteen words'. The Storey government's hand was forced by a group in caucus and, more significantly, Percy Brookfield and P.J. Minahan, who were two of the quartet holding the balance of power in the Assembly. Both insisted that the prisoners should be unconditionally released, and after an inquiry established as a result of their pressure all twelve were freed by the end of 1921. A sincere and greatly admired socialist, Brookfield was the ISLP's solitary state MP. Like Considine, that party's only federal member, he was a dedicated anti-conscriptionist in Broken Hill who had been fined and gaoled during the war: he had publicly cursed the British Empire and called Hughes a 'traitor, viper and skunk'. When he was fatally wounded in 1921 after courageously tackling a gunman who went on a rampage at Riverton railway station, the labour movement mourned one of its noblest sons.

Overall the achievements of the Storey and Dooley governments were limited. McTiernan and McKell were busy in law enforcement issues. Dunn established the Rural Bank. Mutch was a vigorous reformer in education, abolishing high school fees, urging more Australian content in the classroom, boosting educational opportunities in the country and banning war trophies in schools. But the unions were disappointed by lack of action on issues like unemployment, non-union labour on the waterfront, restoration of seniority to 1917 strikers and abolition of the Legislative Council. Labor lost the 1922 state election after a vicious sectarian campaign by its opponents.

An All-Australian Trade Union Congress convened by the federal executive preceded Labor's 1921 federal conference. The aim was to invigorate the ALP and come up with amendments to the party's objective and policies satisfactory to all sections of the labour movement. The congress recommended the replacement of the four-pronged ALP objective applicable since 1919 with a completely new one, the 'socialization of industry, production, distribution and exchange', to be achieved using various specified 'Methods', including nationalization of banking, industry-based organization of unions, dual resort to industrial and parliamentary action, and the readmission of anyone 'officially disconnected with the ALP' who had 'continued fighting for working class interests' and wished to return to the party.

Four months later the ALP federal conference in Brisbane spent several days debating these proposals. Strenuously advocating them were Scullin and R.S. Ross, who had both been conspicuous at the congress. A fine speaker, debater, writer and organizer, Ross was a dedicated socialist propagandist who had been inspired by the pre-Paraguay idealism and writings of William Lane. His tireless and multitudinous activities for the labour movement over three decades had included editing the first daily labour newspaper in the world (the Broken Hill *Barrier Daily Truth*) and being 'the driving force behind the VSP'. Theodore attacked the socialization proposals. 'Wild ideas were not necessary', he contended, predicting a split if Labor was 'prostituted by Communism'; anyway, 'no two delegates would agree as to what socialization of industry meant'. Ross, however, claimed that there was worldwide social upheaval and Australia would not escape. Scullin agreed: 'The capitalistic system was crumbling' and 'chaos' would result, he predicted. By adopting the congress proposals, Ross argued, Labor could avert the threat of violence and 'construct a new society'. Conference voted to accept the congress proposals with some modifications. The argument that the proposals were the key to unity of the labour movement seemed decisive. Delegates from the less populated states voted strongly in favour, while the NSW contingent opposed them. Later in the conference Blackburn tried to qualify the effect of these changes with a motion that Labor would 'not seek to abolish private ownership' where it functioned 'in a socially useful manner and without exploitation'. Despite objections from Ross – 'this would becloud the whole thing in a world of fog' – conference approved this 'Blackburn Declaration', as it came to be known, and provided some compensation for Labor moderates who deplored the socialization objective as lead in the ALP saddlebags at election time.

The return to the ALP of A.C. Willis guaranteed further intense factionalism in NSW. Born in 1876 in Wales, Willis had been a miner since the age of 10. Four years after he migrated to Sydney in 1911 he emerged as the general secretary and leader of the Miners' Federation. Burly and bald, Willis was just as ruthless, capable and ambitious as his arch-rival Bailey, and just as solicitous for the needs of his miners as Bailey was for the AWU bushworkers. However, Willis was puritanical and proud of his profound knowledge of radical social and economic literature, whereas Bailey was boorish and mocked educational pursuits. At the tempestuous 1919 NSW conference Willis led the OBU faction which walked out of the ALP after being unable to outvote Bailey's AWU group and its supporters. But the ISLP did not live up to his expectations. Like some other ALP members who have from time to time during the party's existence left it because they were frustrated with its moderation and channelled their radicalism into an alternative left-wing organization, Willis found political irrelevance even more intolerable. He was prominent at the All-Australian Trade Union Congress and travelled to Brisbane to observe the ALP federal conference with his close colleague Jack Baddeley, the Miners' Federation president. Together they rejoined the ALP.

A colourful participant in NSW Labor's kaleidoscopic factionalism was Jock Garden. He was born in Scotland, where he was an apprentice sailmaker with evangelistic inclinations. After migrating to Australia in 1904, he was variously a clergyman, sailmaker, Defence department clerk and unsuccessful ALP candidate. During the Great War he became prominent on the NSW Labor Council. Like Willis, he was inspired by the Russian revolution, was conspicuous in the OBU movement and the ISLP, and was no friend of Bailey, who ridiculed him as 'an addle-headed Pommie'. In 1920 Garden was one of the founders of the Communist Party of Australia, and the following year played a leading role at the All-Australian Trade Union Congress. In 1922 Garden was elected to the executive committee of the Communist International at its congress in Moscow, where he made extravagant claims about Communists' influence in the Australian labour movement. Such exaggerations were typical of Garden, and gratefully quoted by conservatives to embarrass the ALP.

Labor's defeats at both the federal and NSW elections in 1922 and Bailey's manipulation of that year's NSW conference stimulated attempts to do something about the parlous state of the NSW branch. In December the FPLP leaders Charlton and Gardiner, both from NSW, joined state leader Dooley in endorsing a plan to clean up the state organization which was distributed to unions and party branches. The state executive summoned Dooley for an explanation, and then censured him for a Legislative Council appointment made 18 months earlier. Dooley retorted with a stinging attack on the 'selfish intriguing of uncouth crooks and their hangers-on'. The executive promptly expelled him, and appointed McGirr as the new leader. A majority of the NSW caucus, however, pledged their support to Dooley. The situation in NSW was naturally harming the party beyond that state, and at a special meeting in Sydney in April 1923 the FPLP recorded that it viewed with alarm the dissension in NSW, which was detrimental to the party nationally, and asked the federal executive to intervene.

For the federal executive this was an unwelcome invitation. It lacked confidence in its ability to confront successfully the recalcitrant NSW branch, especially when NSW's delegates on the federal executive were Bailey himself and one of his closest associates, J.M.Power, who had succeeded Lambert as NSW ALP president. The executive had responded to Catts's allegations with a tepid statement claiming that 'ample means of remedying any evil that may exist' lay with the rank and file through the choice of delegates to attend state conference. Yet this was hardly a satisfactory remedy if the party's internal balloting procedures had been grossly corrupted. On 11 April 1923 the federal executive debated how to handle the situation. The SA delegates Yates and Bob Richards urged their fellow delegates to assume control at the next NSW conference, but the majority preferred to discuss the situation with various NSW representatives. Eventually, however, the SA formula for federal executive management of the next NSW conference was carried. That evening, Friday the 13th, the NSW executive met and refused to tolerate any such notion. Siege warfare set in. Ultimately the federal delegates forced the issue, threatening that if the NSW executive did not agree to a modified version of the Yates formula 'negotiations will cease and the Federal Executive will take charge of Labor activities in NSW'. They were relieved when the state executive capitulated. As agreed, the state conference was to be supervised by federal delegates, Dooley was guaranteed the right to appeal to conference against his expulsion, and the discredited McGirr was replaced as state leader by his deputy Dunn.

Although NSW conferences had been consistently turbulent since the election of the McGowen government in 1910, probably none had been as stormy as the 1923 gathering. The Bailey forces were routed. Not even their expedient alliance with the group of militant unionists led by Garden (notoriously known as the 'Trades Hall Reds') could prevent their demise. This became clear when conference elected Bailey's old foe Willis to the party presidency and a shrewd pair of moderate union leaders, E.C. Magrath of the Printers' Union and Jim Tyrrell from the Municipal Workers, as the vice-presidents. Lilian Fowler, the redoubtable organizer and Bailey opponent who reigned supreme in Newtown branch, was elected to the executive. So too were Garden and his close associates J.J. Graves, Jack Kilburn and 27-year-old electrician Jack Beasley. In another telling blow to the Bailey-McGirr group, conference responded to the exhortations of Dooley's supporters, including Lang and Fowler, by voting to readmit Dooley to the party.

The most damaging issue for Bailey at the boisterous conference was his alleged involvement with 'crook' ballot boxes. Enrolling non-existent members, impersonating voters and multiple voting on union tickets was hardly without precedent, and not only in NSW – Wren and his associates were seasoned practitioners of such tactics. But the systematic use of ballot boxes with sliding panels was another dimension altogether. Their existence in NSW had been known to senior party insiders for some time, and an investigation had been meandering along quietly. Bailey and his cronies were not the only culprits, but Willis and Lang skilfully brought the accusations into the open to denigrate Bailey at the conference, which established a committee of inquiry, chaired by Willis, to examine the charges against the Baileyites. Together with three associates, Bailey was found guilty and expelled 'as a menace not only to the Labor Movement, but also to the body politic'.

Caucus had regained the power to choose its own leader. Dooley still had strong caucus support, but the affable ex-leader had had enough of the corrosive factionalism and withdrew. McGirr also ruled himself out, but he had no chance anyway; having alienated most of his colleagues, he resigned from the party and disappeared from parliament at the next election. Dunn was competent and experienced, but somewhat tarnished in his colleagues' eyes by being imposed on them as the federal executive's choice. Another leading contender whose mild temperament contained no thrustful yearning for the top job was Loughlin. Thoughtful, intelligent and a devout Catholic, he lacked empathy with the powerbrokers jostling for control of the party, and had regretted in 1922 that 'the movement is full of corruption'. NSW Labor in the 1920s was a forbidding environment for his idealism.

So, almost by default, Jack Lang became the new leader. He had in abundance the fanatical hunger to get on that was absent in Dunn and Loughlin. Unlike them, he had lived nearly all his life in Sydney and was at home in the big city. He was 19 and his wife 17 when they married three months before their first child was born. They had four more before Lang left to live with Nellie Louisa Anderson; he was devastated by her tragic death in 1911. He returned to his wife. Already streetwise and climbing to affluence through his Auburn estate agency, he was further hardened by this domestic turmoil. He entered parliament in 1913 and during the war served as caucus secretary and whip. As NSW Treasurer 1920–22 his administration was a model of prudent, unimaginative orthodoxy and 'sane finance'. Although he met his wife at the celebrated radical bookshop run by her mother, Bertha McNamara (his wife's sister also met her future husband, Henry Lawson, at this shop), 'Lang's reading had been desultory' and his 'social ideas were meagre'. He was

> a large, solid man, 6 ft 4 ins (193 cm) tall. His black moustache spread as his hair receded, making him more striking in appearance, formidable to men and not unattractive to women. His auctioneering produced a crude but effective public speaking style: rasping voice, snarling mouth, flailing hands. . .Lang seldom laughed; his rare smiles highlighted his jutting jaw. He was insecure with people, but they were attracted by his appearance of strength. He gained many followers, but no real intimates. . .he was ruthless, calculating and shrewd, adept at short-term judgements that fostered his own interests. . .

He characteristically grasped the opportunity to fill the leadership vacuum in 1923.

There was also a new Prime Minister in 1923. After the 1922 federal election the Nationalists did not have a majority in the Representatives without the Country Party's assistance, and under Earle Page the Country Party was adamant that its price for joining the Nationalists in a coalition was the replacement of Hughes as Prime Minister. His successor, S.M. Bruce, a complete contrast in background and style, was born to the purple. Bruce's appearance, dress, speech and priorities in office reflected his privileged upbringing in England and Melbourne. Anstey, who found Bruce's imperturbability frustrating, summed him up as 'brains, breeding and business'. Australia has known no national government more devoted to business interests than the Bruce-Page government. It introduced a variety of incentives designed to encourage business to flourish, including reduced taxation for the wealthy, in accordance with Bruce's belief that if business prospered so would the nation. Tariffs had been substantially increased to aid Australian manufacturing in 1921, and the Country Party's presence in cabinet ensured greater assistance to farmers. This 'protection all round' combined with immigration and further overseas borrowing (despite the intimidating national debt incurred during the war) to underpin the government's economic policy of 'men, money and markets'.

Australia's postwar mood helped the Bruce-Page government. Norman Lindsay considered that uninhibited hearty laughter, common before 1914, had all but disappeared. Novelist Martin Boyd observed that 'before the war we hoped that things would happen, whereas now we hope that they won't'. This chastened pessimism turned many Australians away from broad social goals and aspirations for reform, which perfectly suited Bruce. He aimed to deliver what he felt the Australian people wanted 'above all things, a period free from political turmoil'. Australia now had a Prime Minister prepared to waive £1·3 million of land tax arrears owed by wealthy property-holders, and simultaneously claim that an overdue increase in pensions was impossible because his government had no funds to spare. This typified the government's record on welfare. Never again would Australia be an advanced social laboratory attracting overseas interest and acclaim.

Few of Labor's wartime defectors remained politically prominent for long. Hughes expected the Bruce-Page government to flounder quickly. When this failed to occur he became a restless maverick, resentful of Pearce for agreeing to serve in Bruce's cabinet. Pearce, the only ex-Labor minister in it, had, wrote Boote, 'ratted with Hughes and then ratted on the rat'. Besides Hughes and Pearce there were only five renegades still in federal parliament after the 1922 election. Whereas two of them, Queenslanders Bamford and Givens, remained on reasonably friendly terms with their former colleagues, another, Paddy Lynch, became a bitter public opponent of the ALP. Others who had displayed intense hostility to old comrades before disappearing from public life included Archibald, Poynton and de Largie, who at the height of the wartime cataclysm snapped at Labor Senators 'like an old grey wolf that's been fed on nothing for a week'. Not all adjusted easily to the transition. Some who apparently found it hard to live with the consequences of their defection included Russell and Nielsen, who were both admitted to a hospital for the insane during the 1920s, and Adamson, who died in 1922 in circumstances which strongly suggested suicide. Among the leading state politicians who left the ALP over conscription the only one to have much of a political career afterwards was Scaddan, who was in anti-Labor WA cabinets in both the 1920s and 1930s. W.A. Holman lost his seat as Premier in 1920 and did not return to the NSW parliament. Shortly before that election his close colleague Hall, who could see the writing on the wall for the Holman government, was appointed Agent-General in London; the enduring bitterness of the split was exemplified when the incoming Storey government promptly revoked the appointment.

There were many other echoes of the Great War in the decade that followed it.

The treatment of the returned soldiers was a potent political issue. The FPLP embarrassed the Nationalists by contrasting the postwar reality with the extravagant promises the Nationalists had made about how they would look after the soldiers when they came home. At the same time Labor was nonplussed by the way returned soldiers' needs tended to obscure the fact that other Australians were being denied social justice; with the deserving digger missing out it was unlikely that others' claims for assistance would find a sympathetic ear. Few Australians begrudged the RSL's activities when it involved itself in repatriation and the welfare of the returned soldiers, but its grandstanding on defence and security questions was a different kettle of fish and many returned soldiers left the organization. While supposedly non-political, the RSL claimed that its endorsement of conservative candidates with 'sound' views on defence was justified because such matters were above party politics. Surveillance agents retained their exclusive focus on radical and revolutionary individuals and organizations. They showed little or no concern about the sinister activities of secretly organized semi-military groups.

The Nationalists continued to accuse Labor of wartime disloyalty and to smear FPLP men who had enlisted. This backfired when Yates, who was understandably incensed when a minister's remarks in parliament implied that he had evaded front-line duty in 1918, sought redress for this slur. Although Yates was then out of parliament, his former colleagues were active on his behalf, notably Norman Makin, the studious and courteous MHR for Hindmarsh since 1919. Blakeley and Ryan wanted to extend the FPLP's agitation to cover what happened to Ozanne (then engaged in pursuing his grievance in a defamation action against the Geelong *Advertiser*) and McGrath, but caucus decided to concentrate on the injustice to Yates. A committee of inquiry completely supported Yates's version, but the government denied that he was entitled to any compensation. After Yates returned to the Representatives at the 1922 election he resumed his fight for justice, and a select committee which included Charlton and Makin awarded him £200 compensation.

Although the early 1920s provided little joy for Labor supporters, their party had continued to hold sway in Queensland. Theodore, formerly Ryan's deputy, took over as Premier in 1919 after convincingly defeating Fihelly in the leadership ballot by 37 votes to 4. Fihelly, the new deputy, had a variety of ministerial responsibilities. Although occasionally erratic, he was as acting Premier an impeccable host during the visit of the Prince of Wales, one of a succession of imperial emissaries dispatched to ensure that Australia emerged from war and influenza without any fraying of its ties to the mother country. McCormack was at last elevated into cabinet, where he was an influential Theodore supporter. With Theodore in charge, his forceful mate McCormack beside him, and Ryan, Hunter, Lennon and Hardacre no longer in cabinet, the powerful AWU machine had strengthened its representation in the government. The meticulous, hard-nosed administration of Queensland ALP secretary Lewis McDonald and Queensland AWU secretary W.J. Dunstan, together with Collings's tireless organizing, kept this well-oiled machine functioning smoothly.

The dominant figure in the government was 'Red Ted' Theodore. His years as Ryan's Treasurer had given him valuable experience in government administration and a sound grasp of public finance to add to his profound understanding of the union movement. While he was at least as capable and industrious as Ryan, he differed significantly in temperament. Ryan's genial nature and conciliatory manner contributed to his high standing in the party. Theodore's ability was respected, but his cold, blunt approach meant that he was not warmly admired like Ryan. Although Theodore's ministerial colleagues observed many instances of his comradeship and humanity, these characteristics were hardly ever displayed in public. He was simply not very gregarious, preferring the company of a book to convivial ales with a crowd. Because of his temperament, heavy workload and self-assured manner, he developed a damaging reputation in Labor circles for aloofness.

Queensland Labor in government was as busy and innovative under Theodore as under Ryan. Improvements in housing were achieved through the Fair Rents Act, the Workers' Homes Act and amendments to the Savings Bank Act. There was more good news for workers in the Profiteering Prevention Act, changes in the Safety and Accommodation Acts and the compulsory scheme of unemployment insurance which, although designed to cushion toilers from the effects of seasonal breaks in work rather than long-term unemployment, was a useful palliative and the only systematic provision for the unemployed in Australia for many years. Labor under Theodore continued and extended Ryan's commitment to developing Queensland's agriculture through orderly marketing and controls on price fluctuations. The Theodore government established a Wheat Board, a Cheese Pool, a state cannery, a cold store, an Agricultural Bank and involved itself in the marketing of Queensland fruit produce; the Main Roads Act, the Irrigation Act and the Agricultural Education Act further testified to the government's purposeful agricultural policies. It introduced adult franchise in local government elections before any other state. Its requirement that judges had to retire at the age of 70 resulted in the removal of three elderly Supreme Court justices; for some time the court's decisions on Labor legislation had hardly 'been either fair or sound in law'. The new Chief Justice, 40-year-old Thomas McCawley, was a complete contrast to his predecessor not only in age (he was the youngest chief justice in the British Empire) but also in the brilliance and humanity he brought to his judgements. Sadly, he died suddenly only three years later.

The Theodore government also achieved one of Queensland Labor's most cherished objectives when it abolished the Legislative Council. When Queensland's wartime Governor ended his term of office, Lennon was appointed in January 1920 as Lieutenant-Governor to succeed him. On 11 February the Council, true to form, amended two important bills and completely rejected a third. Cabinet then recommended the appointment of 14 extra MLCs which Labor needed to obtain a clear majority in the upper chamber and, on 19 February, the 14 selected by caucus were duly appointed by Lennon. This 'suicide squad' included Collings, Dunstan, ex-MHR W.F. Finlayson and a Queen Street pieman. Already in the Council and just as intent on its abolition were Lewis McDonald, AWU president W.J. Riordan, rumbustious journalist Randolph Bedford and 'Bolshevik Billy' Demaine, who was still pumping out his *Alert* in Maryborough. With the key to abolition at last in their hands, some Labor people seemed temporarily hesitant but in October 1921 the anachronistic chamber of privilege was consigned to oblivion, and what was but a distant dream in the 1890s for men like Demaine and Hinchcliffe had become a marvellous reality.

In some spheres, however, the Theodore government's record was not distinguished. As education minister Huxham showed his concern for the disadvantaged in important initiatives benefiting the isolated and the handicapped, but Demaine was one of the party's few leading identities to show an awareness that a more visionary approach to education could benefit Labor by producing a more enlightened community. The government's treatment of Aborigines was scarcely visionary either. Even if more funds were directed to Aboriginal affairs in Queensland than elsewhere in Australia, and its compassionate Chief Protector of Aborigines compared favourably with his equivalents in other states – such as the man 'with absolute power to inspect Aboriginal homes and children [who] was feared and hated by two generations of Aboriginals throughout New South Wales' – the government's attitude, as McCormack conceded, was that 'of course, the aboriginal was a decaying race, and was not given much consideration'.

With the Council's abolition one of the major impediments to reform in Queensland had disappeared, but the Theodore government's biggest problem had not. Its activities in rural development, public works and railway construction required loan finance. After the federal government relaxed its wartime control of state borrowing, Theodore visited the customary source for borrowing by Australian governments, the London finance market, only to find it hostile. The London moneymen took a dim view of various Theodore government measures, particularly its amendment of the Land Act authorizing rent increases on Queensland properties leased by British investors, and refused to make loans unless his government changed its policies. Returned to office with a reduced majority, Theodore proceeded to obtain alternative finance from New York, arranging the first American loan to any government in Australia. His defiance of dictatorial British financiers was commended as 'courageous statesmanship' by the 1921 federal conference; nevertheless it was a costly victory. The New York loans he raised in both 1921 and 1922 carried expensive charges and contributed to Queensland's mounting public debt and unemployment. When Theodore returned to London in 1924 in search of loan finance, even Queensland businessmen, who had sabotaged his 1920 visit, supported his endeavours and wished him well. This time he was successful. In negotiating the deal he made one concession, agreeing that pastoral rents would not be increased after May 1924. Also possibly significant was the New York cable offering loan terms which Theodore 'accidentally' left behind at a preliminary meeting; the cable was recent and genuine, except that the interest rate had been carefully erased and a lower figure inserted. The London financiers were more accommodating after that meeting.

Queensland had its own scandal in 1922 which even surpassed NSW's ballot boxes with sliding panels. Theodore's narrow parliamentary majority after the 1920 election was reduced to one (after providing a Speaker) when a Labor backbencher defected to the Country Party in September 1921. With rumours of further ALP defections and Labor's opponents ready to try anything to snatch power, the Theodore government looked decidedly vulnerable. Anti-Labor refused any pairs to the government despite an influenza epidemic which laid low both McCormack and Ipswich MLA David Gledson. In August 1922 Theodore had Gledson carried in on a stretcher; with the Speaker's casting vote, this gave the government the numbers to obtain an adjournment. It was 'impossible for the government to continue business without seriously endangering human life', asserted Theodore. The government faced a testing no-confidence motion when parliament resumed, but the situation was transformed by the bombshell that two journalists had been arrested for attempting to bribe a Labor backbencher, F.T. Brennan, to vote against his party. Brennan, MLA for Toowoomba since 1918, had been frequently critical of the government in caucus and was known to be in financial difficulties; as the only lawyer in caucus, he was peeved that he was not Attorney-General. The corrupters offered Brennan bonds and cash worth nearly £3500 to cross the floor, but they misjudged their man. He told Theodore, who arranged to have detectives and shorthand experts secreted at Brennan's subsequent meetings with the conspirators. With the revelation of this scandal Theodore regained the initiative. In his clinical style he denounced the bribery attempt, added that he himself had been approached to desert his party, then dramatically assisted his sick mate McCormack into the Assembly so that the no-confidence motion could be defeated. The following day he offended the purists and outraged the opposition by introducing proxy voting in parliament. Brushing all objections aside, 'Red Ted' asserted that this unprecedented step was justified to counter the opposition's unprecedented denial of pairs when members were seriously ill. The bribers were gaoled, the opposition was humiliated, the government increased its majority at the 1923 election, and Theodore's reputation as a shrewd, tough political operator was confirmed. Brennan benefited from the episode too, when caucus chose him to fill the first available cabinet vacancy.

Despite Theodore's ascendancy he had some fierce critics within the ALP. They were appalled by his endorsement of the Arbitration Court's decision to reduce the basic wage by 5·3% in February 1922 (McCawley found that the cost of living had decreased 11·9% during 1921). Theodore considered that the lower basic wage would enable the government to employ more workers who could not find a job. The expenditure cuts arising from his government's loan-raising difficulties had resulted in unpopular retrenchments, especially in the railways, which angered the already hostile officials of the militant Australian Railways Union (ARU). That union's Queensland leaders George Rymer, Tim Moroney and Bill Morrow were ardent socialists, contemptuous of cautious Labor politicians, and eager to pursue the ARU's industrial objectives through direct action. They were poles apart from Theodore and McCormack, who had in their AWA days been strenuous advocates of selective direct action but now regarded the doctrines of militant socialists with undisguised intolerance. Like many others in the labour movement with AWU connections, Theodore and McCormack insisted that the arbitration machinery established by Queensland Labor in government had rendered strikes unwise and unnecessary. Theodore had been the leading opponent of the socialization objective at the 1921 federal conference, and argued strongly at the 1924 federal conference that Communist Party members should be ineligible to join the ALP. 'You cannot mix oil and water', he told the 1924 delegates, who supported his stance by a large majority. Theodore ensured that it was rigorously implemented in Queensland by drafting an anti-Communist pledge which all ALP members were required to sign. He claimed that despite Labor's desperate opponents and acute financial problems 'we have made Queensland the best country in the world for the bulk of the people'. That militants felt very differently became clear at the Queensland ALP's 1923 convention. Despite Theodore's opposition the convention directed the government to introduce the 44-hour week, and a motion ordering the government to end the expenditure cuts and restore the decrease in the basic wage was only narrowly defeated. Theodore was further attacked in the *Advocate* and elsewhere for his concession to the London financiers on pastoral rentals in 1924; Fihelly, Agent-General in London, resigned in protest against this 'undignified climb down'. Theodore returned from England to a mutinous caucus, which was mollified only when he agreed to legislate promptly for the 44-hour week.

Before Theodore had even left Queensland on his 1924 loan-raising mission he had decided to transfer to federal politics. Not yet 40, he would clearly be a tremendous acquisition to the struggling FPLP; but first he had to find a seat. Charlie McDonald was still MHR for the safe seat of Kennedy despite being so afflicted with Parkinson's disease that sometimes his speech could barely be understood. There were moves to replace him but Morrow, the suggested alternative, was reluctant, and the sentimental loyalty very characteristic of the ALP in such circumstances prevailed. McDonald, one of the party's heroes in 1891 and since, was re-endorsed but died the day before polling day, giving the Nationalists a walkover in Kennedy. Theodore opted for Herbert, the seat held since 1901 by popular ex-Labor Nationalist Fred Bamford, who was retiring from politics. Theodore resigned as Premier in February 1925, left the Queensland parliament in September, and agreed to lead Labor's campaign throughout Queensland. His opponent, well-known locally as the mayor of Mackay, stayed in Herbert, where he kissed babies and ostentatiously shouted beers – things Theodore could never bring himself to do – and ran a slick, amply funded, anti-Theodore campaign. Many railwaymen in Herbert heeded Rymer's call in the *Advocate* to abstain or vote informal. Theodore's defeat by a mere handful of votes was one of the biggest sensations in Australian political history.

Theodore's successor as Premier was his kindly, hard-working deputy and Agriculture and Stock minister, W.N. Gillies. Backbenchers with militant connections voted for him in the leadership ballot, which he won by one vote from McCormack. F.T. Brennan, still restlessly ambitious, promised his ultimately crucial vote to whichever contender would appoint him to the judiciary; McCormack scorned him and Gillies was receptive, so Gillies became Premier and Brennan immediately became a judge. However, Gillies had an unhappy time in his new position. After a short railway strike in August 1925 the ARU had a great victory when Gillies agreed to their demands for wage increases without consulting cabinet. This episode confirmed that he lacked the necessary tough-mindedness under pressure to be an effective leader. McCormack, who possessed this quality in abundance, took over as Premier when Gillies resigned in October.

McCormack lost no time in showing who was boss. In November Rymer and Moroney were removed from the state executive for failing to sign the anti-Communist pledge. They attended the 1926 convention intending to protest against this action, having signed the pledge under protest in the meantime, but were thwarted by McCormack's swift counter-attack. Signing the pledge under protest was improper, he argued, and warranted the removal of Rymer and Moroney from the convention. Out they went. The strong man was in control and the 1926 state election, with Theodore back in harness as the ALP's astute campaign manager, was a triumph. But McCormack was not yet finished with the ARU, which had disaffiliated from the ALP along with other similarly disenchanted unions. In 1927 a complicated dispute arose at a north Queensland sugar mill, which came to involve other unionists transporting the mill's sugar. McCormack, just back from an overseas trip, elbowed aside his Railways minister, Jim Larcombe, seized personal control of the Railways department, dismissed all the railway workers, and announced his intention to set up an alternative transport service with several businessmen. For a Labor premier it was an extraordinary performance, which earned him the enmity of large sections of the astounded labour movement.

Meanwhile a separate controversy was smouldering. Rumours had been circulating that there was something shady about the purchase by the government some years earlier of north Queensland mines at Chillagoe and Mungana. In the

Advocate Rymer publicized suggestions that McCormack himself was somehow implicated, which seemed to gain added veracity when it was discovered that he had been a shareholder in Mungana Mines Ltd. The demonstrable unprofit-ability of the mines since the government acquired them also left it vulnerable to criticism of its state enterprises policy. When this criticism together with the innuendoes of corruption threatened to harm the government's 1926 election prospects, McCormack issued a defamation writ which, as intended, muzzled further discussion of the matter until the campaign was over, when the re-elected Premier quietly discontinued his action. Afterwards further evidence came to light of fraud and mismanagement in the operation of the mines. McCormack and his well-meaning, honest Mines minister Alf Jones blamed a former man-ager, and denied any impropriety by anyone else. Sweeping rumours to the contrary persisted. In the *Advocate* Rymer supported the opposition's renewed call for a royal commission. At the 1928 convention Demaine called for party unity, and the delegates gave McCormack a vote of confidence and a rousing refrain of 'For He's a Jolly Good Fellow'. Rymer was unconvinced. Mungana, according to the *Advocate*, still 'stinks in the nostrils of the Labour Movement'.

In 1923 Queensland was the only state with an ALP government until Tas-manian Labor under Lyons unexpectedly took office in October. Since the war Labor had not distinguished itself in Tasmania, and the crucial factor in the advent of a Labor government without a majority in the Assembly (or any mem-ber at all in the Council) was the state's desperate financial mess, which a succession of inept anti-Labor governments had been unable to fix. 'We absol-utely don't know where to look for a shilling', remarked Lyons's Attorney-General, lawyer A.G. Ogilvie, who had 'a razor sharp mind, a choleric temper and a low frustration tolerance'. Other Lyons government ministers included the Premier's friends Allan Guy, a butcher who had risen through the union move-ment to become an MP like his father, and Labor veteran Jim Belton. But Lyons was the dominant figure. Under his genial and effective consensus leadership the state's finances were overhauled – partly through the special financial aid he managed to obtain from the Bruce-Page government – and Labor became more acceptable to Tasmanians. Lyons relied on advice from Tasmanian businessmen and economists like his friend Giblin; he even welcomed suggestions (and ac-claim) from his political opponents, referring to the Opposition Leader as his 'colleague and mate'. For the 1925 state election Theodore was imported to bolster the campaign; when Labor won 16 seats on 3 June, it was the first time the party had obtained an Assembly majority in Tasmania.

Labor supporters were disconcerted to find that Lyons's priorities were essen-tially unchanged despite the election triumph. He refused to legislate for the 44-hour week and preference to unionists, insisting that these objectives in the party platform had not been specified in his policy speech at Deloraine. Pro-ceeding with them, he argued, would be a breach of faith with the electors which would harm the party, and the Council would not let them through anyway. The unions and radicals were angry, and 'Deloraining' entered the Tasmanian pol-itical vocabulary as a scornful reference to cautious Labor policy speeches. When legislation was introduced to reduce land taxation for large landholders, radical unionist and Denison MHA Charlie Culley attacked the bill and voted against it. Tasmanian militants were also nettled when their party contravened federal conference and granted ALP endorsement to a conscriptionist defector, Jensen, who had won an Assembly seat in Bass in 1922 as an independent. Lyons's approach did not simply reflect the canny assessment of a practical premier who knew his electorate; his cancellation of his longstanding subscription to the *Australian Worker* was one of many signs that he was becoming more conservative himself.

Ogilvie was also a controversial figure in the party. In 1927 it was alleged that his legal firm had been involved in a scandalous relationship with the Public Trust Office, and Lyons insisted that Ogilvie should stand down pending a royal commission. From then on Lyons and Ogilvie were bitter enemies. Lyons's action seemed vindicated when Ogilvie's legal partner suicided, although after the inquiry and ensuing litigation Ogilvie emerged with a qualified exoneration. At the 1928 state election he made a strong appeal to voters who 'favour fair play and are opposed to persecution'. His plea was answered when he topped the poll in Franklin, winning more votes than anyone except Lyons had ever received in a Tasmanian election. 'Our Tasmanian Trotsky' (this was the *Mercury*'s preposterous label) was unable to return to ministerial office after the election, however, since the Lyons government was defeated at the polls. The incoming Nationalist Premier praised Lyons's statesmanship and offered to serve under him if, as the *Mercury* repeatedly recommended, he happened to leave the ALP.

Another state ALP government came into existence when Labor under Collier was victorious at the 1924 WA election. The new ministry was seasoned and cohesive. Collier, his deputy Angwin, Drew and McCallum all provided extensive political experience as well as proficiency. Collier was an effective speaker and a good administrator, strong-willed and 'unchallengeably in command'. Under its uniquely integrated structure the WA labour movement continued to be relatively harmonious, which contributed to the government's image of steady competence, and the electors rewarded the government's sound performance by returning it to office in 1927 with precisely the same 27 seats.

Politics in WA during the 1920s was dominated by rural development. Since the isolated West still lacked private capital, only the government could do something about the widely felt belief among the citizenry that their state's future depended upon how quickly it could be opened up for wider settlement. No one epitomized this drive more than Collier's predecessor as Premier, the Nationalists' 'Moo-cow' Mitchell, who committed WA to ambitious schemes to promote dairying and to attract thousands of prospective farmers from Britain. After initial hesitation, the Collier government retained both schemes. Angwin, the minister for Lands, Immigration and Industries, shared Mitchell's keenness to see WA self-sufficient in dairy products, and continued the group settlement scheme, even though the recruitment of rurally inclined Britons had to run the gauntlet of Labor's opposition to immigration when there were not enough jobs for workers already in Australia. This hostility was outlined in the party platform, and frequently expressed during the 1920s by FPLP members; in WA it was also prevalent but, for most Labor people, overridden by what they saw as the special needs of their state. During a visit to England in 1925 Collier secured a new agreement with the British government, which provided that WA would receive further migrants and low-interest loan finance from Britain. His government took pride in its achievements in rural development, which outshone even Mitchell's. Its Agricultural Bank made generous advances to farmers, water supply in agricultural areas was increased, and railways, roads and bridges were constructed at a great rate. Under the Collier government both the annual wheat harvest and the area under crop more than doubled.

137

The Collier government also had other achievements to its credit. Industrial safety requirements were made more stringent, and workers' compensation entitlements and benefits were increased. The only new state enterprise, the State Government Insurance Office, was a distinct success. In an overhaul of the WA arbitration system, a state basic wage award was introduced and a new court of arbitration established under Walter Dwyer, a cultured Irish-born lawyer who had been Labor MLA for Perth 1911–14. Firm, fair and thorough, Dwyer was president for nearly two decades; the widespread confidence in his court did much to make the arbitration system function effectively and reduce industrial disputes. Working conditions were regulated for coal miners, timber workers and employees in other designated industries. All this lay within the ministerial province of McCallum who also reorganized the Public Works department and was responsible for an innovative Town Planning Act. Curtin, Collier's close associate and still editor of the *Westralian Worker*, was pleased with the government's overall record, although he was embarrassed when his Victorian friends challenged him about the hanging of two men sentenced to death for murdering two policemen. There was considerable opposition to capital punishment within the ALP – the Theodore government had abolished it in Queensland – and Collier's determination to proceed with the death penalty caused a stir in WA. The government's record was affected by the rough treatment some of its legislation received in the Legislative Council. Controls on prices and rents, a lottery to aid hospitals, and jury service for women were all rejected. Although the Council knocked back the 44-hour week and preference to unionists, the government managed to introduce both for most of its own employees by administrative action. Like Lyons in Tasmania and some other Labor premiers before and since, Collier was well aware that he could use the Council as a convenient scapegoat when party militants grumbled that more radical measures should have been enacted.

One of the Collier government's backbenchers was unique. J.B. Holman, the Timber Workers' Union (TWU) secretary and Daglish government minister, died in 1925 while MLA for the safe Labor seat of Forrest. His eldest daughter May had been her father's assistant at the TWU and in his constituency work since the Great War. She assured her dying father that she would look after his widow and the eight other children. She kept her promise. WA produced more timber for export than any other state, and there were more of its mighty timber-yielding forests in Forrest than in any other WA electorate. When May Holman contested preselection for Forrest against 10 men, the support of the TWU was decisive in her success. Unopposed at the by-election, she became Australia's first woman Labor MP. Her maiden speech was a stirring account of the primitive, dangerous conditions endured by the timber workers.

May Holman's trailblazing did not herald a surge of women rising to prominence in the ALP. Plenty of women contributed energetically and invaluably at branch level in organizing functions and fundraising, but few Labor women emulated Lilian Fowler's iron control of her Newtown branch or were conspicuous in the upper echelons of the party. The exceptions included Kate Dwyer, still a frequent conference delegate, and nowadays factionally linked to Bailey; at the 1921 federal conference she had voted against the socialization objective and failed to convince her fellow delegates (all men) that in future one representative from each state should be a woman. Also in Sydney was Bertha McNamara, now in her seventies but still managing a radical bookshop, attending Labor Party conferences and leading women's deputations to her son-in-law, Jack Lang. In

Melbourne Muriel Heagney and Jean Daley were members of the ALP's Victorian executive during the 1920s and organized a national conference on maternity allowances in 1923. Heagney continued her ardent advocacy of equal pay for women, and established the Labor Guild of Youth in 1926. Daley became the Victorian ALP women's organizer in 1926. She was the first woman in Victoria to stand for federal parliament as an endorsed ALP candidate: the seat was Kooyong, and practically unwinnable. Similarly, Gertrude Melville broke the ice as an endorsed candidate for the NSW parliament in 1925, having been on the state executive for three years. Jean Beadle was still busy in a host of worthy pursuits for WA women. In Tasmania Joe Lyons's wife Enid not only exerted a powerful influence through the private advice and support she gave her husband; despite bearing and caring for a succession of children, she mustered the time and energy to attend Tasmanian ALP conferences and to contest the 1925 state election. As expected, Tasmanians were not ready to elect a woman, but her folksy campaigning style was popular and effective. But such women were not typical. At a time when the gradual introduction of compulsory voting – by 1928 only the state parliaments of SA and WA were without it – had made the women's vote even more important, there was increasing support in the ALP for the notion that special machinery should be created within the party structure to promote issues particularly affecting women voters.

Remarkably, the Collier ministry was not the only state Labor government to take office on 16 April 1924. ALP supporters in SA were also savouring their first Labor election victory since the conscription split. Whereas Collier had plenty of administrative experience in his cabinet, all the men in the SA wartime ministry had left the party during the split; the new SA Premier, Gunn, had not previously handled the reins of government. Nevertheless, the 1924 SA ministry was not without experience. Attorney-General W.J. Denny had held that portfolio in the Verran government. The venerable Andy Kirkpatrick had been in Price's cabinet and, even further back, had been prominent in the party's very origins in SA. 'Kirk' was now 76, 'a wonderful old man, honest, and as straight as a die'. After Gunn's political baptism in the VSP alongside Curtin, Hyett and Anstey and his militant leadership of the Drivers' Union which had halted Adelaide's commercial traffic in 1910, his eight years in parliament had made him more patient and ready to compromise in striving for his political goals. Since the wartime rupture he had shown persistence and ingenuity in rebuilding his shattered party and restoring its standing in the electorate, especially in country areas to counter the rural gerrymander. In office Gunn 'won his colleagues' affection, his opponents' respect, the grudging commendation of the press, and a public popularity rarely achieved before or since by a Labor leader in South Australia'.

The Gunn government was imaginative and purposeful. The Legislative Council was, of course, a daunting obstacle – Labor only had four MLCs, and was not to exceed this tally in SA for half a century. It was no surprise when the Council refused to tolerate Gunn's plans to make the state's electoral system more democratic. When it also rejected his proposed state government insurance commission, Gunn introduced it by administrative action instead. To improve the supply and quality of housing for needy families, Gunn launched the Thousand Homes Scheme. Although this enlightened project was dogged by financial controversy, one of the nation's earliest planned suburbs, Colonel Light Gardens, was the pleasing result. The Gunn government lifted expenditure on education, providing more scholarships, higher wages for teachers, new junior technical schools and better medical facilities. A state bank was established.

Working conditions for public servants were improved. Rural areas were not neglected, with a visionary reafforestation programme in addition to better roads and improvements in access to bore water and technical expertise in agriculture.

Gunn's resignation in August 1926 staggered Labor supporters. Prime Minister Bruce knew a talented rival when he saw one, and he plotted to remove Gunn by dangling a tasty carrot in the form of a position on his Development and Migration Commission at £2500 per year (twice Gunn's salary as Premier). Gunn's reluctance to support the 44-hour week – because he thought it would harm Labor's prospects in crucial rural seats – had cost him some admirers, and the economic portents were adverse. His wife felt he should accept Bruce's offer. Nevertheless, Gunn's departure from public life aged only 41 remains curious. His successor was former union official Lionel Hill, who had held three portfolios in the Gunn government. 'Slogger' Hill had been a famous footballer in Adelaide, an MP since 1915, and president of the Anti-Conscription Council in SA during the war. Although he had plenty of self-confidence, Hill was a slow thinker and no orator. His undistinguished leadership until the 1927 election, which Labor's reunited opponents won convincingly, sharpened the sense of loss felt within the ALP after Gunn's abdication.

Problems of membership and finance have bedevilled the party throughout its existence, and the SA branch during the 1920s was no exception. Membership fluctuated, but in 1927 comprised almost 30 000 in SA. Only about 10% were members of local ALP branches; the remainder belonged to unions affiliated with the party. Easily the largest affiliated union (as in Queensland and WA) was the AWU, where Lundie still ruled the roost as secretary. As a vital contributor of members and funds, the AWU provided many party office-bearers and pre-selected candidates. The most regular source of income to cover the state branch's ordinary running costs was the annual sustentation fee paid by the members. Formerly a shilling per member, the fee was raised to 1/3d in 1918 and 1/6d in 1927. Election campaigns were a hefty additional burden, financed by a fighting fund raised in the prelude to the election and usually a debt liquidation appeal afterwards. The SA branch spent over £900 on the 1924 state election, £2475 on the 1925 federal election and almost £1500 on the losing battle to retain the state Labor government in 1927. Despite creating an extra source of income by imposing a levy on Labor MPs' parliamentary salaries, the branch was financially in dire straits. In an attempt to reduce its debts, the sustentation fee was increased temporarily to 2/6d. As in other states, there were allegations that party funds had been supplemented by donations with strings attached from liquor interests.

Yet another state Labor government followed the Collier and Gunn governments into office in 1924. This one was in the least likely state – Victoria, which previously had been governed by Labor only once for a mere 13 days in 1913. During the 1920s ALP membership in Victoria increased both in affiliated unions and local branch members, and the party was relatively harmonious with a stable state executive and cohesion between the industrial and the political wings. Because of the outrageous gerrymander, however, Victorian Labor could not make much electoral headway at state level, and Labor's opponents could concentrate on squabbling among themselves. Years of mean-spirited neglect under a Treasurer whose 'one idea of statesmanship was to sit on the treasury chest' culminated in an alarming strike in 1923 by the 'wretchedly underpaid' police. Melburnians were shocked by a wave of looting, rioting and anarchy. At the next state election Labor for the first time won more seats than any other party, only six short of a majority. The Nationalists and Country Party could not agree on a coalition, and on 18 July Labor's 70-year-old leader, 'Windy Mick' Prendergast, was surprised to find himself Premier. His ministry contained fellow veterans from the *Tocsin* days, Tom Tunnecliffe and J.P. Jones, two highly regarded country members in E.J. Hogan and H.S. Bailey, able ex-AIF lawyer Bill Slater, and Danny McNamara, who, when Arch Stewart died the following year, was to succeed him as Victorian and national ALP secretary. Also included was John Cain, a former VSP stalwart and professional spruiker who had been prosecuted for his anti-conscriptionist oratory; Cain had assiduously transformed Jika Jika (later Northcote) into a safe Labor seat after capturing it from the Nationalists in 1917 with the help of his shrewd, stuttering 17-year-old friend, Pat Kennelly.

In the circumstances the Prendergast government did well. As a minority government it was unlikely to last long, and the Legislative Council would inevitably reject any radical legislation. Yet Prendergast could claim to have largely achieved his dual aim of showing that Labor could govern competently and – as he promised applauding delegates at the 1924 federal conference – 'not sacrifice any principles while in office'. The government immediately acted to provide shelter for the unemployed. It set up royal commissions into flour and bread prices and the causes of the police strike. It announced its intention to abolish capital punishment. Its removal of militarism from school textbooks and refusal to make Anzac Day a holiday or commit funds to the proposed Shrine of Remembrance were controversial measures consistent with the 1923 Victorian ALP conference resolution proclaiming Labor's opposition 'to war and militarism in all its forms'. Very different policies, designed to maintain Country Party support, included a compulsory wheat marketing pool (rejected by the Council), reductions on rail freights and fares, increased funding for rural roads and a royal commission into the soldier settlement scheme. After Prendergast's budget uncompromisingly raised income and company tax on the wealthy and reduced the tax burden on the poor, the Nationalists and the Country Party agreed to resume their uneasy marriage. The Labor government was defeated in the Assembly on 11 November 1924. After the Governor refused Prendergast's request for a dissolution, Victorians had to endure the atrophy of the bickering 'do-nothing' coalition government until relief came at the 1927 election.

Labor returned to office in May 1927. It was again a minority government, dependent this time on two metropolitan Liberals and a breakaway Country Party group under A.A. Dunstan known as 'the four black crows'. Prendergast had stepped down as leader in mid-1926, and was Chief Secretary in the new government. Imbued with the importance of Labor maximizing its rural support, he backed Hogan as his successor, and caucus agreed. Of striking appearance with his lanky, athletic frame and probing blue eyes, Ned Hogan was a son of the soil and devout Catholic who had been impressive in administering the portfolios of Agriculture, Railways and Markets in 1924. Now a farmer like his father, Hogan had spent much of his twenties at the WA goldfields where he felled timber and helped form a Firewood Workers' Union, as well as achieving renown as a caber-tosser, weight-putter and hammer-thrower. Much of the Hogan government's legislation was wrecked by the Council. Bills dealing with workers' compensation, fair rents, assistance to the unemployed, stamp duties on various commercial transactions and improved marketing arrangements for agricultural products were all mutilated. The government's positive achievements were few. At least John Lemmon, who was again minister for Public Instruction and Labour as in the Elmslie and Prendergast governments, accomplished his goal of establishing an apprenticeship authority. The government made a notable appointment, initiated by J.P. Jones and Slater, in choosing Alf Foster to fill a County Court vacancy despite the usual outcry whenever someone with radical credentials becomes a judge. Interestingly, Victoria's most distinguished public servant, Sir John Monash, concluded after his experience of managing the State Electricity Commission under the Hogan government that he much preferred Labor in office than their opponents. Less satisfactory was the mutual antagonism that developed, as in Queensland, between the ARU and Labor in government.

Disillusionment spread within the party over Labor's ineffectiveness in office without power. One of the strongest advocates of Labor refusing government unless it had a majority in the Assembly was one of the Victorian branch's most dedicated activists, Arthur Calwell. A clerk in the Victorian Treasury, Calwell had been attending Victorian ALP conferences for over a decade, was on the party's federal executive and had positioned himself as Maloney's heir apparent in the safe federal seat of Melbourne. It was Calwell's motion in 1928 which resulted in the state conference direction to the government to conduct a redistribution. Later that year Hogan introduced a redistribution bill, and his government predictably lost the support of Dunstan's Country Party rebels. The one thing all Country Party members had in common was their attachment to the existing electoral distortions which gave their party its power and Victorian politics its instability. Unable to control the Assembly, Hogan resigned on 21 November 1928.

John Wren was doing very nicely. He had amassed great wealth and power. Outside Victoria his most extensive operations were in Queensland, where he monopolized horse-racing, controlled the Brisbane *Daily Mail* and formed a significant relationship with Theodore. Racing, newspapers and Labor politics also dominated his interests in Sydney; he carefully observed the Willis versus Bailey contest over the sliding-panel ballot boxes, and allegedly sought to influence it. Wren's associates in SA included Labor's extraordinary firebrand Bert 'the King' Edwards, hotelier, MHA for Adelaide, flashy friend of the destitute, and reputedly the homosexual illegitimate son of former premier C.C. Kingston. But Wren still exercised his greatest political influence in his home state. He knew Prendergast well, and was very close to Hogan, who apparently paid the shadowy wire-puller a special visit before allocating portfolios to his ministers. Other ministers in both Victorian governments who were freely labelled as Wren men were W.J. Beckett, a well-known racing identity, and deputy Premier Tom Tunnecliffe.

The 1925 Fitzroy by-election showed that Wren's scheming did not always go according to plan. After the incumbent of this safe Labor seat died, 31 aspiring candidates contested preselection, including Maurice Blackburn, who had been out of parliament since losing Essendon in 1917 following his forthright refusal to participate in AIF recruiting. Blackburn was agnostic, principled and at the 1924 federal conference had opposed Theodore's outlawing of Communists from the ALP. Wren, however, was Catholic, sternly anti-Communist and had involved himself in AIF recruiting. He decided that Blackburn had to be stopped. After a bitter preselection battle which saw numerous breaches of party

rules, Blackburn managed to defeat the Wren candidate and all the other aspirants (including Calwell, who had not yet decided that succeeding Maloney was to
be his destiny). But Wren was not done yet. A Fitzroy councillor was prevailed
upon to stand against Blackburn in the by-election as an Independent Labor
candidate. The Wren camp engaged in large-scale intimidation and imperson-
ation of voters, and resorted to bribery in an attempt to paint Blackburn as a
Communist, but Blackburn won easily. Such electoral abuses were also prevalent
in other ballots in Melbourne's inner suburbs where Wren forces (and other
obnoxious manipulators like the Loughnans and O'Connells) exerted their influence. These episodes, together with the infamous incidents in NSW, led some
Victorian party strategists to agitate for reform of the preselection process. Leaving it to the rank and file was nice and democratic in theory, but only a small
proportion participated and the system too often produced fraud and mediocre
candidates; a central panel, they argued, would perform the task much better.
Ultimately, however, this agitation failed. Stronger safeguards were instituted in
Victoria against corrupt practices, but there was no departure from the party's
democratic traditions.

During the 1920s, a decade when the FPLP was in eclipse, there were periods
when five of the six states had Labor governments. This discrepancy between the
performance of the FPLP and its state counterparts was partly attributable to
leadership: Theodore, Gunn, Collier and Lyons were all more effective leaders
than Charlton. Also significant in the accession to office of Labor governments in
four states between October 1923 and July 1924 was their opponents' internecine warfare. Much of this was due to the emergence of the Country Party, and
its awkward early relationship with the Nationalists. Prime Minister Bruce
realized this, and tried to strengthen the federal links between the two parties. At
the next federal election in 1925 the tightly knit coalition campaigned hard on
industrial relations at a time when the FPLP was on the defensive about strike
activity, and won well. Another telling factor was the different impact of issues in
state and federal politics. The accusations of 'disloyalty' and 'Bolshevism' which
so damaged the FPLP in the aftermath of the war did not have the same bite at
state level. Defence and security issues were far less important in state politics
than competence in administering agricultural development in WA, economic
recovery in Tasmania and the sugar industry in Queensland.

The scandal of the ballot boxes with sliding panels dominated the 1924 federal
conference. The findings of the Willis-led inquiry, which had pronounced Bailey
and three associates guilty, had been challenged: the AWU conducted its own
inquiry, exonerated them, and then requested the federal executive to intervene
in the matter. The federal executive formed its own investigation committee
which, although hampered by the unco-operative NSW executive, eventually
found in favour of the Baileyites. On that committee was WA engine driver and
unionist J.J. Kenneally, who concluded that undoubtedly 'there was crookedness
in New South Wales'. Willis was among the NSW delegates to conference; he
referred to scurrilous Bailey-inspired circulars about him with such titles as 'A
Welsher From Wales', and told conference that he had threatened Bailey that he
'would break his neck' if they continued to appear. Strife seemed likely to keep
poisoning the party. Conference ultimately decided that another overriding
inquiry was required to settle it once and for all, and that one or three of the
Labor premiers should sit in judgement. Theodore, the only premier attending
the conference as a delegate, responded frankly: 'He was not seeking to be an
arbitrator in the case, nor did he think anyone else would'. Despite his misgivings

about the task, he acknowledged the seriousness of the dispute and agreed to adjudicate if necessary. He commenced his one-man inquiry in November 1924, and quickly showed that he would not tolerate any nonsense. Theodore's AWU background had given the Baileyites confidence that he would see things their way, but after weighing the evidence he crisply delivered a verdict that stunned them. He found the case against one of the four appellants not sustained, but upheld the charges against Bailey and the other two. Garden and others surmised that Theodore's verdict was at least partly motivated by his ambitions in federal politics, which would presumably be assisted if he aligned himself with Willis and the ruling faction in NSW. That was open to conjecture, but there was no doubt at all that the malevolent Bailey was now Theodore's sworn enemy.

NSW Labor returned to office at the May 1925 state election with a lift of nearly 8% in its overall vote, which brought nine extra seats and an Assembly majority of two. Among the new members were 34-year-old J.J. Cahill, a fitter dismissed from the railways like Chifley for his role in the great strike of 1917, and 31-year-old H.V. Evatt, a brilliant barrister with a breathtaking academic record and enough ambition and effrontery to hustle immediately for a cabinet spot. It was no surprise when caucus did not give Evatt a guernsey in the solid-looking ministry, which included Loughlin as Lang's deputy, W.F. Dunn, Baddeley, McTiernan, McKell, Mutch, Charlie Lazzarini and G. Cann. It did include one novice parliamentarian, however – Willis, who was whipped quickly into the Legislative Council by Lang along with the new Premier's other key unionist supporters, Magrath and Tyrrell.

The labour movement applauded the government's achievements. One of Lang's first actions in office was to keep the promise he had made to Chifley and other railwaymen that he would restore seniority and related entitlements to the 1917 strikers. Legislation soon followed, providing for the 44-hour week, changes in the industrial arbitration system and improvements in rural workers' accommodation. There were extensions to workers' compensation and the applicability of the Fair Rents Act. The Marketing Of Primary Products Act introduced compulsory marketing along Queensland lines. Widows' pensions and family endowment were much-vaunted initiatives in social policy; although the labour movement received the endowment scheme frostily because it was used to justify wage restraint, it did assist large families, especially if a breadwinner was not in work (and unemployment remained high in NSW, as throughout Australia, during the later 1920s). Adult franchise was introduced for local government elections. A Government Insurance Office was established. There was legislation to protect native flora and to penalize ships for discharging oil. Parliament itself was transformed. Sittings began at 10 am, instead of the traditional 4 pm start which had enabled non-Labor members to maintain business and professional careers outside parliament. Women were made eligible for appointment to the Legislative Council, despite the *Sydney Morning Herald*'s objection that it was inappropriate for ladies to 'enjoy the rather unfeminine privilege of wielding the executioner's axe'. After the Council's axe left its mark on the government's legislation, Lang's pressure on the Governor for additions to the Council paid off when the viceroy reluctantly authorized 25 ALP nominations. This was trumpeted as a magnificent coup, and of course Labor's strength in the chamber of privilege was substantially boosted, but Lang knew as he pressed on theatrically with legislation for its abolition that he had not made enough appointments to achieve this. To reinforce his image as a dauntless fighter, he sent McTiernan on an otherwise pointless trip to London to complain about the Governor.

144

Even Labor newspapers became embroiled in the 'seething mass of vendettas, dogfights and double-crossings' that engulfed the NSW branch during the 1920s. One of the most grievous war casualties for the NSW labour movement had been the postponement of its plunge into daily journalism. After comprehensive planning directed principally by Chris Watson, by mid-1914 the AWU-established Labor Papers Limited had everything in readiness – the finance collected, the staff chosen (Keith Murdoch was associate editor), the premises built (Macdonell House in Pitt Street, Sydney) and the machinery ordered. At long last NSW Labor's dream of its own daily paper – Boote's *Australian Worker* was admirable, but not a daily – to combat the antagonism and misrepresentations of the Sydney dailies seemed on the verge of fruition. But the outbreak of the Great War delayed delivery of the machinery, the price of newsprint rose, and Watson decided to postpone the launch until after the war. When that time came he had parted company from the labour movement, which had developed grander visions of a chain of Labor dailies in all the capital cities. However, the necessary extra capital could not be raised from the unions. There was more bad news for Labor Papers Limited in 1924 when the *Labor Daily* was born and two existing Labor dailies, the *Daily Herald* in Adelaide and the *World* in Hobart, ceased publication for financial reasons. The *Labor Daily* was conceived when Willis grasped the opportunity to take over the struggling *Daily Mail*. He formed a company with Lang and Baddeley as directors, himself as chairman and managing director, and his Miners' Federation comprising most of the shareholders. Other unions like Magrath's printers were also very involved; the AWU, however, with its heavy investment in Labor Papers Limited and factional hostility to Willis, stayed aloof. The virulence of the Willis-Bailey feud was reflected in the reciprocal sniping of the *Labor Daily* and the *Australian Worker*. The *Labor Daily* virtually became Lang's own publicity vehicle, extolling his virtues at all times and denouncing his opponents within the ALP and outside it. Lang greatly benefited from this idolatry, but the *Labor Daily*'s financial health was precarious; it owed its survival to the excellence of its sporting pages, especially the horse-racing tips. When the NSW Labor Council founded one of Sydney's earliest radio stations, Lang also made good use of this new propaganda medium.

Lang's domineering tendencies became increasingly apparent. Never one for close friendships, the 'Big Fella' had always treated most of his caucus colleagues like political opponents; any who crossed him, even slightly, received 'constant insults and taunts' in return. In mid-1924 his shortcomings as leader resulted in a challenge by Mutch; Lang escaped by one vote. His habit of claiming all the credit for the government's achievements was galling to his ministers and to others like Evatt, whose outstanding expositions of government measures smoothed their passage through parliament. The 1925 industrial legislation which had so delighted the labour movement was primarily the work of Baddeley, with help from Willis, Magrath and Tyrrell; apart from endorsing it Lang played a minimal part, but this would not have been apparent to *Labor Daily* readers. Nearly all Labor supporters were unaware of Lang's defects and held him in high esteem. He emerged from the typically uproarious 1926 conference with added stature and the right to choose Labor appointees to the Council; it had previously been up to caucus to make the selection from the applicants approved by the executive. One of the many disgruntled delegates remarked that the deviousness displayed at this conference made Bailey look like a saint.

Later in 1926 Loughlin acceded to requests from disaffected caucus members to challenge Lang for the leadership. He and Lang, 'the scheming suburbanite', were chalk and cheese. Loughlin, a 'generous, genial and trusting countryman' and a devout Catholic, was affronted by Lang's abrasive, self-centred style and disturbed by his closeness to militant unionists like Willis and Baddeley. Other union leaders left caucus in no doubt that they wanted Lang to stay leader; the AWU was the only union to prefer Loughlin. The ballot was extremely close. There was intense excitement as efforts were made to contact McTiernan, then at sea on his way back from London. His vote for Lang brought the rivals level at 23 votes each; this was adjudged an endorsement of the status quo, so Lang scraped home. Loughlin continued as deputy, only to resign two months later after a special conference not only barred caucus from replacing Lang as leader before the next election, but approved in addition the 'Red Rules' which Loughlin interpreted as paving the way for an influx of Communists into the party. When two ALP rural backbenchers indicated that they were prepared to cross the floor with Loughlin, the Lang government's position became desperate. The outcome was still uncertain when the opposition brought on its no-confidence motion on 22 November, but all three dissidents abstained by leaving the chamber. It was another uncomfortably close call for the 'Big Fella'.

When Bruce held a referendum seeking enlarged powers for the national government in industrial relations, Lang and the NSW branch joined other influential ALP identities in displaying a regrettably short-sighted approach. Not for the first or last time, pretensions about state rights and concern about increased power being acquired by the national government when Labor's opponents were in office overrode the merits of the referendum proposal and its consistency with ALP platform objectives. The labour movement was hopelessly divided over the referendum. Faced with this situation, the federal executive declared that ALP members were free to campaign for either side if they wished. The referendum was defeated.

During 1927 there was utter chaos in NSW. In March the executive split into two groups, which each purported to control the party. The W.H. Seale executive was supported by Lang, Willis and a majority of the rank and file. The F. Conroy executive had the backing of all the other ministers then in the state and most of the caucus, together with Theodore, Bailey and the AWU. An uncontrollable Easter conference rapturously greeted Lang as usual, suspended the Conroy group and directed Lang to reconstruct his cabinet. Caucus by a majority vote repudiated the Easter conference. Baddeley and McKell, both overseas, struggled to make sense of what was happening. In May separate delegations endorsed by the rival executives turned up at the first federal conference to be held in Canberra, where the federal executive, meeting prior to the conference, ruled in favour of the Conroy executive; so did the conference itself, which recommended that a special state conference be held to resolve the crisis.

Meanwhile the bizarre situation continued. Later in May there was a federal by-election for a NSW electorate, and both executives endorsed an ALP candidate. It was a safe Nationalist seat, and their candidate won easily; but Lang's vigorous campaign was rewarded when the Seale executive candidate finished ahead of his Labor rival, who had been actively supported on the hustings by Theodore and some of Lang's ministers. With cabinet government at a standstill, Lang dismissed all his ministers except Willis and Baddeley (and, briefly, McKell, who was sacked 10 days after the others), and promoted his caucus supporters to fill the vacancies. McTiernan was incensed. Evatt described Lang as 'the biggest crook in the labour movement'. The Premier 'will die without a friend', added Mutch. The *Labor Daily* claimed that Lang was supported by 95 unions and 155 party branches, while only three unions and 22 branches opposed him. The federal executive, striving to achieve a reconciliation while sensing that Lang's rank-and-file backing would ensure his side's eventual ascendancy, organized a special conference on 9 July. It was another triumph for Lang. He was welcomed with wild enthusiasm, the legitimacy of the Seale executive was ratified, and Willis engineered more power for the controlling faction over pre-selections. This enabled Lang to settle old scores by denying ALP endorsement to some of his caucus critics. After all this, Labor predictably lost the ensuing election. Lang emerged with a far more compliant caucus. Two who lost their endorsement, Mutch and Evatt, retained their seats as Independent Labor candidates. Evatt's win in Balmain was assisted by the zealous organizing of unemployed timber worker J.S. Rosevear, and Mutch defeated New Zealand-born unionist R.J. Heffron in Botany.

Earlier in 1927 Theodore had belatedly managed to enter federal parliament. After his shattering loss at the 1925 federal election, Theodore had involved himself in NSW politics, where he hoped to obtain both a safe seat and a support base to propel himself towards the FPLP leadership. Although he had to contend with Bailey's enmity and Lang's chronic suspicion of potential rivals, he found a seat: W.G. Mahoney, MHR for Dalley since 1915, agreed to resign to make way for Theodore, who won the by-election on 26 February 1927.

After Charlton swallowed his disquiet at the prestigious newcomer's presence and welcomed him to the FPLP, Anstey announced his resignation as assistant leader. For public consumption he gave ill-health as the reason (he had recently returned from a New Guinea trip with malaria), but privately he confessed to being motivated by his disgust at the undermining of Charlton that was occurring. Theodore publicly quashed the inevitable speculation that his caucus colleagues would immediately make him their deputy leader; he knew that this was an unlikely eventuality, and any presumptuousness on his part would annoy them and be counter-productive. In the ballot caucus preferred Scullin, who had used his outstanding debating skills to good effect since returning to the Representatives in 1922. Popular with Labor MPs, he was a fervent, industrious orator who had displayed a sound grasp of important contemporary issues, especially finance. With the ALP tainted by the antics of its NSW branch, Scullin's abstemious tastes and spotless integrity were also appealing virtues. Scullin was appointed deputy leader. Gardiner, who had been the FPLP's second-in-command for nearly a decade, was not re-elected to the Senate in 1925.

A year later Scullin became leader. With a federal election approaching, Charlton, now 62, had been placed under renewed pressure to step down, and he announced his resignation to caucus on 29 March 1928. Scullin had given further proof of his capacity by a series of prophetic speeches analysing the glaring inadequacies in the Bruce-Page government's economic policies and the disastrous consequences for Australia. Theodore had not been idle either. While he neither denigrated Charlton nor openly lobbied caucus for support – it was not his style to cultivate or ingratiate – his obvious ability, controlled assurance and forceful thrusts in parliament needling Bruce all sent clear signals to impressed FPLP onlookers. However, his one year as a federal MP and the influence of his enemies (who now included Charlton) would, it was anticipated, prevent him from overtaking Scullin. The widely-predicted new partnership was expected to be Scullin as leader with Theodore the vice-captain. Scullin was duly elected on 26 April, but the deputy leadership result was a bombshell: a caucus section opposed to Theodore managed to procure his defeat by Blakeley by 14 votes to

13. McGrath, a committed Theodore supporter, was furious that after the FPLP's long years in the wilderness it could spurn 'one of the best men we have ever had in our party' because of 'personal jealousy and ill-feeling'; he told the *Argus* that the rank and file desired Theodore at the forefront, and he wanted caucus to review its decision. The next caucus meeting was long, acrimonious and, it seems, violent: there were rumours afterwards that the tensions erupted into a fist-fight between McGrath and Bert Lazzarini (brother of one of Lang's ministers), and that furniture was broken. Further murky intrigue emanated from NSW when Theodore's supporters there circulated suggestions that if Blakeley did not resign as deputy there would be an inquiry into alleged irregularities in his narrow preselection win over Considine.

Just at the psychological moment dramatic allegations surfaced about Theodore's own preselection. This was a masterstroke by the venomous Bailey. He used his alcoholic crony Lambert, who was sour about losing his endorsement for West Sydney to Jack Beasley in yet another notorious NSW preselection contest. In May 1928 Lambert alleged that his preselection defeat was assisted by Theodore forces as revenge for Lambert's earlier refusal to accept £8000 as an inducement to step aside for 'Red Ted'. Bailey also masterminded George Cann's corroborative statement two days later. The accusations that £8000 was offered on Theodore's behalf to Lambert, Anstey and another Sydney MHR (later identified as former clerks' union leader Percy Coleman) effectively stymied the agitation to reconsider the deputy leadership. The Nationalists, wary of Theodore, quickly formed a royal commission to investigate the allegations. Earlier rumours that Mahoney had been recompensed for handing his seat to Theodore seemed well-founded when he unconvincingly testified at the commission that the large sum of money he acquired upon resigning his seat had been obtained by backing the Melbourne Cup winner two months earlier. Having pleaded ill-health as his reason for retiring from politics, he had made such a miraculous recovery that he was intending to stand for the Senate in 1928. The commissioner found that Mahoney had been given about 5000 reasons for resigning by an unspecified donor acting in Theodore's interests. It was widely believed that the money came partly or wholly from John Wren, although he denied any involvement in a brief appearance before the commission. Far more entertaining in the witness box, but no more forthcoming about the matters at issue, was Anstey. Neither he nor Wren referred to Anstey's substantial shareholding (donated by Wren) in a New Guinea goldmining venture, but it may well have been irrelevant to the inquiry and to Anstey's resignation from the deputy leadership as soon as Theodore arrived in federal politics. As well as discrediting Mahoney, the commissioner disbelieved Coleman's denial that he had been offered £8000 to vacate his seat for his friend Theodore; five witnesses, including Hinchcliffe, testified that they had heard Coleman refer to such an offer.

Newspapers unfavourable to Labor had a field day with their pious effusions about 'deep humiliation', 'disgraceful transaction' and 'sordid scandals'. The Nationalists wanted to maximize Labor's pre-election discomfort by prosecuting individuals, but were unable to find a specific offence that would result in a probable conviction. Anstey lashed their hypocrisy in a withering counter-attack. Addressing his Brunswick constituents, Anstey claimed that Victorian Labor's

> history is one of unblemished honour. If it has not been distinguished by the brilliance of its leaders, at least it has been distinguished by their integrity. . .The same can be

said of the other states. If we have one tinge of regret it is for a little section in New South Wales. I shall not apologize for it, nor explain it away. As members of the party we must all accept responsibility. What, however, is the record. . .of our opponents. . .

His audience was then treated to vintage Anstey as he outlined in his inimitable style the Ready-Earle scandal of 1917, the donation of £25 000 to Hughes in 1920 by grateful admirers of the Prime Minister, the payment of £3000 to a Nationalist Party official in 1922 for standing aside in North Sydney when Hughes wanted to switch to a safer seat, the attempt to bring down the Theodore government by blatant bribery, and the more sophisticated corruption which succeeded in maiming the Gunn government by seducing its leader.

In the 1928 federal election, which occurred during a particularly turbulent waterfront dispute, the Nationalists tried hard to reproduce the formula which provided their sweeping 1925 victory by adopting a provocative stance in industrial relations. Nevertheless, Labor improved its strength in the Representatives by eight seats to put itself within striking distance: similar inroads at the next election would result in a national ALP government. Three of the eight gains occurred in NSW, where Theodore was an enterprising campaign director. Two notable newcomers captured seats they had failed to win in 1925, Curtin in Fremantle and Chifley in Macquarie. For Labor's idealistic saviours of humanity the 1920s had been heavy going, with the depressing awareness of the war's catastrophic legacies, the FPLP's decade in the doldrums and the vicious internal fights in NSW. But the ALP still retained the allegiance of a 'multitude of footsloggers' who, like Curtin and Chifley, had not lost their faith in Labor's great vision of a fairer and more humane society for all Australians. Their faith was about to be tested as never before.

7 'Spitting upon the Altar of Labour'? Floundering in the Great Depression, 1929–1932

IN 1929 THE FPLP maintained the momentum generated by its pleasing advance at the polls the previous November. In August Scullin was stricken with influenza and pleurisy, but during his absence there was no respite for the Nationalists since Labor's acting leader was the redoubtable Theodore, who had replaced Blakeley as Scullin's deputy in the customary post-election review of leadership positions in February. The FPLP's attacks on the Nationalists received assistance from an unexpected quarter when Hughes, sensing that the Bruce-Page government was cracking, met secretly with Theodore to plot the downfall of the men who had supplanted him in 1923.

The Bruce-Page government was preoccupied with industrial relations policy. It had tried a variety of coercive methods to curb strikes, with little success. Bruce and his Attorney-General, the austere J.G. Latham, were fed up with the structure of Australia's industrial relations system, with its overlapping state and federal awards. Their frustrations were intensified in 1929 by three major disputes involving wharf labourers, timber workers and coal miners. The timber workers were mutinous about a federal award (handed down by a reactionary judge appointed by Bruce and Latham) which cut their wages, increased their working hours and curtailed their union's powers. Disturbances in Sydney during the dispute resulted in Garden and Eddie Ward being arrested, but even more controversy attended the government's prosecution of Holloway, who was fined in Melbourne for encouraging workers to strike against the detested award. The coal miners had been locked out when they refused to accept wage reductions imposed by colliery owners in contravention of the award. In an effort to get the colliery owners to the conference table, the Bruce-Page government abandoned its announced prosecution of one of the perpetrators, the legendary union-hating capitalist John 'Baron' Brown, who had vowed to make the miners eat grass; but the lockout continued. The labour movement was indignant about this brazen display of double standards, since Holloway and other unionists had been pursued remorselessly through the courts. The withdrawal of the Brown prosecution was not the only evidence that under this government there was one law for the rich and powerful, and another for the workers. Bruce and Latham, irked by their inability to deliver industrial peace, made the stunning decision in May to remove the national government altogether from the industrial relations sphere;

29. 'Labor and Loyalty'. 1917 federal election poster. (*National Library*)

[PASTE UP.] [READ OTHER SIDE.]

LABOR AND LOYALTY

In the Homes of Labor there is
Patriotism and Love of Country

LABOR SENATE CANDIDATES:

PETER BOWLING

HAS

Five Sons on Active Service.

ARTHUR RAE

HAS

Two Sons on Active Service.
One Son in Camp Training.
One Son on Home Service.

SENATOR

DAVID WATSON

HAS

Two Sons on Active Service.

It is an insult to Australia's Soldiers to insinuate that Labor
is disloyal. The above named Soldiers have not come from
disloyal homes.

Vote for Labor No-Conscription for the Senate

Written by J. H. Catts, M.H.R., Director Labor Election Campaign.
Authorised on behalf of the P.L.L. Executive by P. C. Evans, General Secretary.
Worker Print, Sydney. Macdonell House, Sydney. [Over

30. 'The Spoils Are Heavy'. (by Claude Marquet; *National Library*)

31. Matt Charlton.

32. Maurice Blackburn. (*National Library*)

33. Percy Brookfield. (*State Library of Victoria*)

34. John Gunn. (*Old Parliament House*)

35. The Prendergast ministry, 1924. Standing (from left): J. Lemmon, J. Cain, W. Slater, T. Tunnecliffe, G. Webber. Seated: E. J. Hogan, J. P. Jones, W. J. Beckett, G. M. Prendergast, J. H. Disney, D. McNamara, H. S. Bailey. (*National Library*).

36. Jack Lang. (*John Fairfax*)

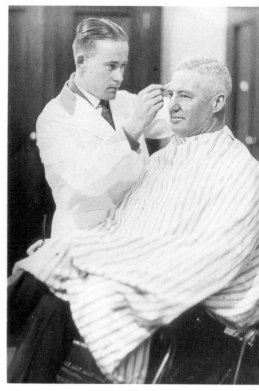

37. Jim Scullin. (*Alison McNeill*)   38. 'Red Ted' Theodore. (*National Library*)

they proposed to repeal all federal legislation and give responsibility for industrial regulation to the states. There was uproar. Some Nationalist backbenchers were critical. A few government MPs nursed other grievances. Hughes fuelled the discontent, and on 10 September 1929 five rebels crossed the floor with him to deprive the government of its majority in the Representatives. It was close: if the sitting MHR for Indi had not mistaken the deadline for nominations at the previous election and thereby handed his seat to Labor, the Bruce-Page government would have survived and Australia's political history during the next few years might have been very different.

On 12 October 1929 Labor captured 15 seats in its biggest election victory in the Representatives since federation. When it also gained Franklin in a mid-December by-election, the FPLP held 47 of the 75 Representatives seats. (Labor also had fiery ex-AWU organizer H.G. Nelson as the non-voting member for the special seat of Northern Territory, which he had held since the seat was created in 1922.) Scullin found election night 'exhilarating'. He brushed aside the observation of a friend, J.L. Cremean, that his majority was so large that it might adversely affect the FPLP's cohesion. For Theodore, who had again been a tireless campaign organizer in NSW, the results represented 'success beyond even his wildest dreams'. Six of the 15 gains were NSW seats. 'Australia Is Ours!' exulted the *Labor Daily*.

Those 15 gains provided the FPLP with some notable acquisitions. Scullin had long been concerned about the quality of Labor candidates in Tasmanian federal seats, and before the 1928 election he had approached Lyons and Guy to stand. Both had declined, although ex-MHA Charlie Culley won Denison in that election. A year later Culley was joined in federal parliament by both Lyons and Guy. During the 1929 campaign Lyons attacked Bruce's somersault on arbitration, called for increased federal aid to Tasmania, and became a father for the tenth time. Labor men retrieving seats they had formerly held in federal parliament comprised AWU stalwart L.L. Cunningham in Gwydir, Scullin's brother-in-law John McNeill in Wannon, and quirky Methodist greengrocer J.M. Gabb – who was nicknamed the 'Gawler Bunyip' – in Angas. Theodore arranged for McTiernan to contest Parkes, where he defeated one of the five government ministers who were unseated. The most remarkable result was the defeat of Bruce himself, seemingly impregnable in Flinders, by none other than Holloway, the unionist prosecuted by the Bruce government earlier that year. There has been no other instance of an incumbent Australian prime minister losing his seat. This exquisite result was soon followed by success at the Victorian state election, when Labor under Hogan won more seats than ever before.

The trend to Labor was far from uniform across the nation. Queensland actually recorded a significant decline in Labor's voting share, although it managed to provide an additional MHR, former AWU official and ex-MLA 'Darby' Riordan. The campaign in Queensland had featured additional allegations about corrupt dealings in mining shares which irreparably damaged McCormack's credibility and integrity, but he was no longer Labor leader in Queensland, having stepped down after leading his party to ignominious defeat at the state election the previous May. A swing of nearly 8% had lost Labor 16 seats including those of two ministers, and ended 14 years of unbroken ALP rule in Queensland. This debacle was partly attributable to drought conditions affecting the pastoral industry, but many Queenslanders, including unseated Railways minister Jim Larcombe, had no doubt that McCormack's unpopularity with radical unionists had been crucial. For Queensland Labor 1929 was not a good year.

In Melbourne, however, thousands of excited wellwishers flocked to Spencer Street station when Scullin and his men boarded the train to Canberra to take over the reins of government. Since the transfer of parliament to the 'bush capital' in 1927 Victorian members had gradually adjusted to the tiresome travelling which federal MPs from other states had endured since 1901; certainly no Labor parliamentarian begrudged this memorable journey. Crowds turned out to cheer them at stops along the way, and when the fêted travellers arrived at their destination on the Limestone Plains they were greeted not only by the customary magpies, currawongs and legions of flies, but also by some 600 people and the Canberra City Band playing 'See The Conquering Hero Comes'. Accommodation was limited in sparsely developed Canberra – when Lyons the following year sought a house for his family he could not find an available one big enough – and most Labor members stayed at the Hotel Kurrajong. Their boisterous behaviour in the wake of such a heady victory was regarded by Pearce with unconcealed distaste, and another conscriptionist renegade, Lynch, even complained in parliament about high-spirited refrains of 'The Red Flag' at the Kurrajong.

The FPLP's understandable hilarity overlooked the stark reality that the 1929 election had been for the Representatives alone. The numbers remained unaltered in the Senate, where the FPLP was in a hopeless minority with seven Senators out of 36. All seven had been elected in 1928. Representing SA were genial former MHA Mick O'Halloran, ex-labourer A.A. Hoare and talented lawyer J.J. Daly. A carpenter's son, Daly had left school at 13 to serve at a pie and saveloy stall. Later he worked as a rouseabout while attending evening classes. In 1914 he joined the AWU and became articled to W.J. Denny's legal firm in Adelaide. Prominent in Irish Catholic circles in the 1920s, Daly had a solid grounding in the SA labour movement including legal work for unions and stints on the state and federal ALP executives. The solitary Labor Senator from Victoria was Jack Barnes, who had carried books by Henry George and Henry Lawson in his bushworker's swag during his party's early days. Now 61, gnarled and shrewd, he had been AWU president since 1924 and was an influential figure in caucus. The remaining three Senators were all from NSW. J.B. Dooley (no relation to the NSW Premier Jim Dooley) had a wide-ranging background in manual work and union organization in Sydney, Newcastle and rural NSW before winning preselection under AWU auspices. Similarly varied experience of manual toil had comprised the working life of flamboyant ex-AIF identity 'Digger' Dunn (no relation to shortlived NSW leader W.F. Dunn). 'Digger' Dunn pursued issues relating to defence and returned soldiers with a vigour that unsettled the array of generals among the opposition Senators who were accustomed to a monopoly of concern in such matters. Labor's third NSW Senator was the irrepressible stalwart Arthur Rae, one of the ALP's most dedicated socialists. Since siding with the Willis OBU faction in 1919 he had involved himself in a variety of activities, including writing for the *Labor Daily* and challenging the hegemony the moderate AWU leaders enjoyed over organized bushworkers. Two of his sons had died while overseas with the AIF, and his wife died in 1929, having never recovered from these wartime shocks. Now 69, Rae was back in the Senate making his presence felt after nearly four decades of militant commitment to the labour movement.

It was a jubilant caucus that assembled on 22 October. Scullin's entry into the party room was marked by cheering and singing, and there were more cheers when he and Theodore were unanimously confirmed in their leadership positions. Caucus opted for a cabinet of 13 ministers, 11 MHRs and two Senators. In earlier Labor governments headed by Fisher and Hughes there had been only 10 or 11 ministers, yet three had been Senators. The ALP platform still called for the abolition of the Senate, although a motion to repeal this plank had been defeated by one vote at the 1927 federal conference. The ballot for the two Senators to sit in Scullin's cabinet resulted in Daly and Barnes being elected. The Senate's declining status within the FPLP was confirmed when neither was given a department of his own to administer.

Caucus then elected nine MHRs to join Scullin, Theodore, Daly and Barnes in the ministry. The first ones chosen were the experienced pair of orators from Victoria – Brennan, who became Attorney-General, and Anstey, who was given Health and Repatriation. Then came Fenton and Queenslander Frank Forde, both fanatical protectionists; Scullin gave Fenton Trade and Customs, and appointed Forde his assistant. Next was 'Texas' Green, a rough diamond who became a popular identity in the Westralian goldfields labour movement and sturdily represented it in state parliament for almost a decade before becoming MHR for Kalgoorlie in 1922. He was allocated Defence, although after his experience as a postal clerk and founder of the Kalgoorlie branch of the Post and Telegraphists' Union he would have preferred the Postmaster-General's department. That portfolio, along with Works and Railways, Scullin gave to the next minister elected, Lyons. The last three chosen were Parker Moloney, Blakeley and Beasley. Moloney was a cultured schoolteacher who represented Indi for two terms before crossing the border into NSW to contest Hume which he had held since 1919. 'A calm, dignified man of medium height. . . with a piercing, reedy voice', Moloney was a devout Catholic who prayed silently before delivering an important speech and suffered a nervous reaction after each election campaign. His familiarity with rural concerns equipped him for the Markets and Transport portfolio. Blakeley had been critically ill during 1929, but had recovered sufficiently to handle Home Affairs. The militants at the Sydney Trades Hall were delighted by the inclusion of 33-year-old Beasley. Despite his boyish, meek appearance Beasley was – as Sydney unionists already knew – astute, tough and nobody's fool. He became Scullin's assistant in the Industry portfolio, which the Prime Minister retained for himself along with External Affairs. Eight of the ministers were Catholics, and Scullin was Australia's first Catholic prime minister. Although only Theodore and Lyons had previously been ministers, there was plenty of parliamentary and administrative experience in the cabinet. 'No body of men', commented Boote, 'were ever better qualified for the task that confronted them'.

Some caucus members were disappointed by their omission from the ministry, but Curtin was heartbroken. There was so much for the Scullin government to do, and he yearned to be at its forefront, alongside Anstey, using his talent and energy to make life better for Australians in need. In his brief span in parliament his intellect and brilliant oratory had made a striking impression on those not already aware of his contribution to the labour movement on the *Westralian Worker* and in the wartime fight against conscription. He had been elected to the FPLP executive in opposition and he was the only member of the executive as it stood prior to the federal election not to become a minister (apart from Makin who, as caucus secretary, was automatically on the executive; he was Speaker during the Scullin government, and continued the Labor tradition of dispensing with the wig, gown and parliamentary mace). Two voting tickets had circulated before caucus chose the cabinet, one from the AWU and the other from the NSW executive. Curtin was the only one of the ten men listed on both tickets to be omitted. There was dark speculation in some quarters about Wren's role in the ministerial selection; Curtin hated Wren and his influence in the labour movement. Curtin himself blamed Theodore, who had spread his damaging assessment of Curtin as unreliable before the caucus meeting and then during it, just before the vote, had remarked meaningfully 'One Anstey in the Cabinet is enough'. Scullin, devoutly religious and a teetotaller, found Curtin's craving for alcohol repugnant, and he made it known that he preferred Green to Curtin as WA's representative in the ministry. In fact Curtin had waged his perpetual battle against temptation more successfully since moving to Perth, where a stable family life and fulfilling work had combined to form an effective antidote. Now, however, his wife and children were far away at Cottesloe, his caucus colleagues had rejected him, and he was unable to shrug off his frustration and despondency. Before long he was drowning his sorrows. 'Lend me a fiver', he would ask a friendly journalist, 'Frank Anstey and I want to go on the scoot'.

The incoming Scullin government was immediately faced with a range of pressing problems, but the most fundamental was Australia's dire economic position. The government inherited a heavy budget deficit and a balance of payments crisis with declining prices for Australia's staple exports, wool and wheat. Even worse, the comfortable hammock of British loan funds which had underpinned Australian development had been suddenly cut away. The outgoing Treasurer, Page, had been complacent about both the budget deficit and Australia's overseas borrowing. In Australia and London sombre men in dark suits had been shaking their heads disapprovingly about the burgeoning national debt and burdensome interest repayments, and the London moneymen had decided that Australia had to mend its ways. Access to loan finance was tightened, causing a decline in capital inflow, which in turn led to cuts in expenditure on public works and gave added impetus to Australia's climbing unemployment. In opposition Scullin had cogently attacked the Bruce-Page government's economic policies, emphasizing their damaging consequences, but when he discovered the real nature of Australia's economic plight he was 'staggered'.

Scullin's briefing about the disastrous economic position had come from Australia's quintessential sombre man in a dark suit, Sir Robert Gibson. A Scottish-born businessman of stern disposition, Gibson was chairman of the Commonwealth Bank Board. From the bank's creation by the Fisher government it had been managed in autocratic but effective style by Labor's appointee as governor, Denison Miller, until his death in 1923. The Bruce-Page government had then altered the management structure of the bank, leaving the governor a far more limited role as the bank's chief executive officer. The bank was now to be managed by a board comprising the departmental head of the Treasury, the new governor and six other directors 'actively engaged in agriculture, commerce, finance or industry'. The labour movement attacked these changes, suspecting that they would enable powerful capitalists to take over control of 'the people's bank'. Gibson was precisely the sort of person they had in mind. One of the bank's inaugural directors, Gibson was steeped in conservatism: he possessed indomitable rectitude and blinkered views on finance. A gaunt, sad-looking man approaching his 66th birthday when Scullin became Prime Minister, Gibson loathed indulgence in any form. He became the bank's dominant figure when his fellow directors elected him as chairman of the board in 1926, the same year a newspaper listing the most influential men behind the scenes in the Nationalist Party named Gibson among the powerbrokers right at the very top.

Anstey advocated a bold solution to the Scullin government's problems. Two days after the cabinet was sworn in, the New York Stock Exchange spectacularly collapsed, adding another dimension to the Scullin government's difficulties. At one of its earliest cabinet meetings Gibson 'piled on the horrors and notified us that unless the government indicated the methods by which it would reduce expenditure the bank could not finance the government beyond the end of November – *five weeks*'. He made it clear that as chairman of the Bank Board he considered himself loftily independent of the elected government, which he despised. Anstey reacted to this stunning ultimatum aggressively, accusing Gibson of blatant bias: 'you financed Bruce so long as he remained in office and close down on us as soon as we become a government'. After Gibson left the meeting Anstey delivered his assessment:

> That puts the lid on us. We are going to be blockaded not only by a hostile Senate but by a hostile Bank Board. There is only one way to save our lives – force a double dissolution before the tide of popularity runs from under us.

Anstey insisted that there were appropriate issues they could utilize, and it was better to take the gamble than face disgrace through their 'inability to do anything but carry out the policy of our opponents'. His forceful advocacy did not persuade his colleagues then or later when he returned to this theme. Wider soundings within the party revealed that there was considerable resistance to Anstey's urgings. There had been two federal elections in quick succession, and another would acutely strain the financial resources of the party and its candidates, who frequently contributed their own funds to campaign expenses. Some caucus members who had won unlikely Labor seats or prestigious positions in the first national Labor government for 13 years were reluctant to risk losing them. An argument favoured in particular by some influential union leaders was that in tough times even a hamstrung Labor government would provide sympathetic administration, and this was preferable to risking the return of a harsh anti-Labor government.

Theodore's rashness had contributed to Scullin's worries about the turmoil in the Hunter Valley coal mines. The timber workers' resistance had waned as the federal election approached, but the coal miners remained intransigent after being locked out for eight months. Theodore's eagerness to maximize Labor's vote and donations to the party's campaign funds had induced him to make some extravagant promises on the hustings, but none was ultimately more damaging than his repeated claim that an ALP government would have the mines reopened within a fortnight on the miners' terms. While not contradicting his deputy, Scullin made no such claim himself during the campaign. After the election Theodore moved quickly to achieve a resolution of the conflict through negotiation and compromise between the parties, but the colliery owners remained obdurate, insisting that the mines would stay shut unless there was a wage reduction. The miners, equally adamant, refused to accept less pay. Scullin organized further conferences, but they too proved abortive. The federal government's constitutional power to intervene more fundamentally in the dispute was limited, and – despite urgings from Beasley and others that a bold stroke was politically imperative – Scullin would not countenance any step which contravened the Constitution. Attorney-General Brennan affirmed that the ministry would govern 'in the interests not of any particular class but of the people as a whole', without being 'stampeded into taking illegal and unconstitutional

155

action'. Considering the miners' destitution and misery, they had managed to contribute with magnificent generosity to Labor's campaign funds in 1929, and they were not interested in anguished hand-wringing in Canberra about constitutional niceties. Their government was in, and they looked forward to decisive action to keep Theodore's promise. When this was not forthcoming the fury in the Hunter Valley knew no bounds.

This angry mood was soon animating some government backbenchers. There was a lengthy debate on the coal dispute in the party room on 28 November, when 'Digger' Dunn and Rae wanted the government to set aside £25 000 to ease the suffering of unemployed miners and their families. Five days later Rowley James, the former miner who had succeeded Charlton as Labor's MHR for the stricken coalmining electorate of Hunter, publicly admonished the government. 'My people were deserted by the party which proposed to protect them', he declared in parliament; the Hunter Valley donations to the ALP campaign funds had been acquired 'practically under false premises'. The government should have taken over the mines, even if the High Court later ruled this step unconstitutional: 'Far better. . .to die fighting than to go down without a fight'. Watkins and Bert Lazzarini also rebuked the government, although more mildly. While acknowledging the distress in James's electorate, Scullin defended the government, in some respects dubiously: 'Never have we said that we could end the trouble'. James argued the case for the £25 000 emergency grant in parliament on 3 December and again nine days later: 'There are 36 000 of my constituents absolutely on the verge of starvation'. Scullin had resisted these appeals, but relented just before Christmas and authorized a £7000 grant to the coalfields communities.

Unlike Scullin, the NSW Nationalist government was prepared to open the mines by force. It was willing to use police and strikebreaking labour to have the coal mined on the owners' terms, and it chose to begin at Rothbury Colliery. Rothbury was invaded by police and thousands of angry striking miners. On 16 December there was a violent clash, some policemen began shooting, and a ricochet fatally wounded a miner, Norman Brown, who was playing cards well away from the confrontation. Other miners were injured, but it was Brown's death which emblazoned Rothbury on the national consciousness and profoundly shocked the labour movement. The following day Lang launched a ferocious censure debate in the NSW Assembly, linking the incident to the notorious military order 'Fire low and lay them out' issued during the maritime strike in 1890. A committee of NSW FPLP members recommended that all involved sections of the labour movement confer in Sydney. Again the militants demanded drastic action, and once more Scullin and his ministers refused. McTiernan reminded the participants that Scullin had a different option in the form of another referendum to extend the national government's power over industrial disputes, which might have a better chance of success in the highly charged atmosphere. But this suggestion did not bear fruit, and the conference degenerated into stalemate and abuse. A strident miners' leader labelled Theodore 'a two-up spieler'. Around 10 pm Lang made a belated and theatrical appearance. Scullin had not wanted him there at all, and was discomfited by the Big Fella's blunt assessment:

> Seize the mines. . .Your government was elected to govern. . .I do not ask lawyers whether I am right or wrong. I tell them I want to do something. It is then their job to tell me how to do it. If I were the Prime Minister, with a mandate from the people to

open the mines in a fortnight, I would seize them and work them under the conditions of the lawful award. . .Who is to tell us in the absence of High Court decisions what restrictions the Constitution imposes? Seize your mines and, if necessary, pass your law later.

The proceedings of that conference confirmed that the Scullin government was likely to have a troublesome relationship with NSW Labor under Lang. The sordid struggle for control of the NSW branch throughout the 1920s had been followed with distaste by nearly all the FPLP and federal executive delegates. The federal bodies had intervened resolutely in 1923, and also the following year when the federal conference overruled a NSW attempt to control its state and federal MPs by making their preselection conditional upon the receipt by the NSW executive of their signed undated resignations. In 1926, however, when consistency with Labor's platform necessitated strong support for Bruce's referendum which the FPLP leaders provided, Lang's truculent opposition was instrumental in the federal executive's decision to abstain from directing party members how to vote. Two years later there was a referendum ratifying changes in the financial relationship between the federal government and the states, and Lang again opposed (this time unsuccessfully) the FPLP's support of the 'Yes' case. Also in 1928 the NSW executive declared that it would 'maintain the right of autonomy in all domestic matters'. In mid-1929 Scullin ventured into these domestic matters in an attempt to end the rift in NSW between the Langites and the AWU, but he was firmly rebuffed by Lang. The NSW branch's hostility to the party's federal bodies was aggravated by the 1929 caucus election of ministers. NSW had provided nearly half the FPLP throughout the 1920s (more than half for one term), and some senior NSW Labor identities felt their state had been harshly treated when its representation in cabinet comprised Blakeley and Beasley, who both scraped in, and interstate imports Theodore (who was loathed by many Langites) and Parker Moloney (who was still really a Victorian with his home and political base in Melbourne).

It was not surprising therefore that some NSW ALP activists publicly attacked the Scullin government over the coal dispute. In mid-January 1930 J.C. Eldridge, the newly elected MHR for Martin, went so far as to describe the situation on the coalfields as 'impending civil war', and implied that he and others might not remain loyal if Scullin did not act. Eldridge was reacting to the formation of a labour defence army organized and drilled by ex-AIF miners, and the violent clashes which had occurred between it and the NSW police. When the embittered miners obtained no relief after pursuing their cause through the courts, alarming forecasts began to circulate: 'for months, Canberra dreaded tidings of a major uprising'.

However, the Scullin government pleased Labor supporters with its tariff policy. The government hoped that tariff assistance to local manufacturers would result in increased employment opportunities; the parlous balance of payments would also be aided by any brake on imports. Moreover, on tariffs the government could act unhindered. This freedom contrasted sharply with any attempt to use monetary policy, which had to overcome Gibson's stern resistance, and any legislative reform, which had to run the gauntlet of the Senate. When the government's commitment to tariffs became clear Scullin, Fenton and Forde were overwhelmed by manufacturers clamouring for assistance; backbenchers were also inundated by 'tariff touts' – 'wherever two or three people were gathered together in a quiet place, it was an easy wager that one of them was a Labor member, and the others high tariff advocates'. Scullin announced that any protected manufacturers who exploited the public would lose their tariff advantage, but despite all the broken promises of increased employment and wages there is no record of this happening. With tariffs being implemented at such a rapid rate, shady rackets were plentiful. One of the more notorious was the 'Whisky Tariff', which was very lucrative for Wren and his company Federal Distilleries Pty Ltd.

The labour movement was also satisfied with some of the Scullin government's expenditure reductions. Australia's immigration programme was pruned and the Development and Migration Commission abolished (a job was found for Gunn at a reduced salary in the Prime Minister's department). Theodore summoned the Defence department secretary and asked him how much could be slashed from departmental expenditure (then £6·54 million). The secretary estimated £1 million at the most. Theodore said it had to be £2 million. Compulsory military training was abolished, a step unambiguously sought in Labor's platform since 1919. It produced howls and insults from the opposition, but plenty of congratulatory resolutions from the union movement. Anger and dismay among Australia's defence fraternity greeted other cuts affecting specialist training institutions at Duntroon and Jervis Bay, together with the cessation of construction work at the Australian War Memorial. By 1932 defence expenditure had been reduced to £3·86 million.

Federal parliament met briefly during November and December 1929. During this period the only significant legislation was a sensible change to the Commonwealth Bank's powers which was approved by Gibson and bastions of financial orthodoxy in Britain. Nevertheless Australian conservatives reacted with a frenzied outburst which presaged their hysterical attacks on the Scullin government throughout its existence. The economy was the subject of a long debate in caucus on 13 November. Several backbenchers led by 'Gunner' Yates argued that the critical situation justified the then unorthodox remedy of an inflationary note issue. Theodore was dismissive, scorning such impracticable notions, and only a small FPLP minority directly challenged cabinet's economic policies. After the introductory parliamentary sittings caucus, unlike the cabinet, did not meet again until parliament resumed in March. By then Labor backbenchers were realizing what Scullin's ministers with their greater access to information and expertise had already grasped: they were dealing with a catastrophe of unprecedented magnitude.

The Great Depression was a worldwide phenomenon, but Australia was hit harder than most countries. At the peak of the Depression probably 'as many as one million people in a total workforce of a little over two million lacked fulltime employment'. Many breadwinners became itinerant battlers, scrounging provisions and improvising shelter before trudging away in search of a nonexistent job at the next town along the track. Ingenuity and comradeship eased the burden for some, but to hundreds of thousands of Australians the Depression represented dashed hopes, worry and wretchedness.

It was common for men who had been out of work, upon eventually resuming employment, to collapse after trying desperately to keep going on an empty stomach – and there were plenty of others to take their places. Teachers in working-class areas reported a high degree of malnutrition among their pupils. The weakened state of mothers was reflected in an increase in infant mortality. Every town and city had its shanty camps, with primitive shelters made of packing cases, hessian and corrugated iron, lacking sanitation and infested by vermin.

How to alleviate the effects of the Depression was the preoccupation of all governments during the early 1930s. Labor politicians and activists groped for solutions with added urgency because they were all too aware that it was their people who were suffering most. Many Depression victims experienced a heightened sense of powerlessness and insecurity induced by yet another calamitous visitation so soon after the Great War. At election times they tended to vote governments out on the basis that no alternative could be worse. This was already evident in April 1930 when a change of government in SA saw Labor return to office and a week later WA voters removed the Collier government.

In the circumstances, only an outstanding leader blessed with good fortune in tackling the crisis could have emerged with an enhanced reputation. Jim Scullin was a principled, humane man devoted to his church, his party and his country. As a leader he was able to inspire loyalty through admiration, but the capacity to command loyalty through fear was something he lacked (unlike Theodore and Lang). Although Scullin was not short of resilience and fighting qualities, the strain of the extraordinary difficulties he faced was soon affecting his health and his sandy-coloured hair was rapidly turning white. The restoration of 'confidence' in Australia's economy he saw as vitally important. 'There is no need for panic', he announced, while privately continuing his frantic efforts to obtain funds to pay Australia's debts as they fell due. His repeated assurances to the British money moguls included a joint statement with Theodore denying that Australia would have to postpone its interest payments, and stressing that Australia had always met its obligations (although he was well aware that it was perilously close to its inaugural default). Scullin then followed the lead of Victorian Premier Hogan in appealing to Australia's wheatgrowers. 'We must grow more wheat, and we must export more wheat', he declared in a speech broadcast in all states. Labor would assist wheatgrowers in their 'urgent national service'. with a guaranteed price and improved marketing arrangements.

This assistance to wheatgrowers was one of several important Scullin government initiatives slaughtered by the Senate. By mid-1930 the opposition Senators were prepared to show their true colours, convinced that the economic gloom had cost the government electoral support. The rejection of the Wheat Marketing Bill was quickly followed by obstruction of the Central Reserve Bank Bill, which represented another moderate reform in line with good sense, Labor's platform and recognized banking practice in Australia and overseas. Conservative interests opposed the bill because it weakened the stranglehold they enjoyed over the Scullin government's financial policy via the Commonwealth Bank Board. The Senate also dismissed bills for three referenda: two involved sorely needed enlarged powers for the national government in industrial matters and in the realm of trade and commerce, the third was a radical attempt to empower the parliament itself to amend the Constitution. The Senate also mutilated initiatives in industrial relations, notably the government's bill overhauling the conciliation and arbitration system and the regulations restoring primacy at the waterfront to the Waterside Workers' Federation rather than its scab union rival which the Bruce-Page government had encouraged.

The worsening economic crisis and the patent inability of the Scullin government to do much about it cast a sombre air over the federal conference which began on 26 May 1930. Scullin, Brennan and Daly urged their fellow delegates to keep in mind the financial and constitutional constraints preventing the government from acting more comprehensively. Collings, the experienced and energetic Queensland organizer, confessed that he was very moved when Scullin said how much he had been worried by the tribulations of office, and recounted his own horror at seeing a destitute man fossick through a rubbish bin for food which he put into his pocket presumably for others even more hungry. But to concede that the problems were 'unsolvable' was, according to Collings, 'preposterous'. They had to look for unorthodox solutions. It was Collings who suggested that Frank Locke, who had written a book about the national- ization of credit, should address conference. This proposal was supported by a majority of delegates, but not Curtin, who correctly pointed out that listening to Locke was pointless, since the Scullin government could not possibly do what he advocated.

Delegates discussed measures to alleviate the 'widespread and terrible unem- ployment', which 'has been a nightmare to every member' of the FPLP. They endorsed a well-intentioned but impracticable statement prepared by six del- egates, one from each state. Declaring that the restoration and freeing of credit was 'indispensable' and calling on the Scullin government to find £20 million as 'a first contribution' was all very well, but conference failed to advise the govern- ment how to achieve this despite the parlous state of the country's finances and the hostility of both the Commonwealth Bank Board and the Senate.

The 1927 federal conference had approved a proposal to integrate the labour movement's political and industrial wings nationally like the ALF structure in WA, but this was overturned by the 1930 conference after Victorian unionist W.J. Duggan claimed that the formation and progress of the Australian Council of Trade Unions (ACTU) – Duggan was its inaugural president – had made such a fusion of the two wings no longer possible. The 1930 conference also streng- thened the hand of the federal executive in dealing with a recalcitrant state branch. Collings remarked how pleasing it was to hear NSW delegates acknowledge the supremacy of the federal conference and federal executive.

The 1930 federal conference also ratified the establishment of the Labor Women's Interstate Executive (LWIE), which had been provisionally formed in March 1929. As WA delegate May Holman explained, it was envisaged that conferences would be held every three years, with three delegates from each state. Between conferences the organization of ALP women would be administered by the LWIE, 'subject to the control and supervision of the federal executive'. One of the functions specifically outlined in the LWIE's constitution was the repre- sentation of Labor women at appropriate forums. At the 1930 federal conference May Holman, who was the inaugural president of the LWIE, sought approval for LWIE representation at the next Pan-Pacific women's conference at Honolulu, but federal conference sided with the view brusquely articulated by Collings: 'Let them do their job and focus the Australian women's attention on problems in Australia and not talk about extending their operations to Honolulu. . .' The Scullin government instead appointed May Holman a delegate to the League of Nations Conference in Geneva. While overseas she was extremely busy, attend- ing the British Labour Conference and visiting constituents' relatives in England, Scotland and Ireland. Sadly, her enthusiasm aggravated her asthma and chronic heart condition, and she became seriously ill.

Scullin made a fateful decision to visit London in 1930. The Imperial Con- ference in October and November would involve vital discussions about the economic and constitutional links between Britain and its dominions. Further- more, Scullin believed that his ability to give the London moneymen assurances in person about Australia's finances and his government's intentions in econ- omic policy would assist in the restoration of confidence, which he regarded as crucial. Another issue he was keen to pursue personally was his determination to appoint an Australian as the next Governor-General. Every other nation attending the Imperial Conference was represented by its prime minister except for India and the Irish Free State, and Scullin felt that his own presence was necessary in London, even though Brennan and Moloney would be away with him and Fenton was just returning after spending several months in England. Early in July Scullin confirmed that in his absence Australia would be led by Theodore, then immersed in deliberations about a forthcoming budget of greater than usual significance in the critical economic climate.

These plans were sensationally disrupted later that same week by the explosive findings of a Queensland royal commission. At last the relentless striving of Labor's opponents to nail Theodore had paid dividends. The Queensland Nationalists, now in government, had established an inquiry into the Mungana allegations. To conduct it they overlooked all their own state's judges, and handpicked a retired 71-year-old NSW judge, J.L. Campbell, who had been an active conscriptionist in the Great War. His hastily compiled report, publicized with alacrity by the Nationalists, concluded that Theodore was implicated with the already disgraced McCormack in fraud and dishonesty and was 'guilty of the grossest impropriety'.

Theodore resigned as Treasurer after consulting Scullin. In a fervent declaration of his innocence, Theodore blasted the findings as

the most dastardly piece of partisanship. . .The whole thing reeks of politics. For years my political enemies in Queensland have spread rumours of scandal. . .and have persisted in the calumnies against me personally with peculiar malignancy. The Mungana inquiry is just another phase of that same campaign.

His powerful parliamentary speech two days later was remembered by witnesses long afterwards. 'I've heard nothing like it', commented Hughes, who described it as 'a masterpiece'. Theodore told the Representatives that he had 'been the victim of a hired assassin', and he demanded the opportunity to vindicate his name in proper proceedings 'before an unimpeachable tribunal'. As he left his office, bound for Queensland to expedite this process, he farewelled his secretary confidently: 'Good-bye, it will only be for two months'. Scullin showed that he too believed Theodore's absence would be brief when he informed caucus that there was no need for a cabinet replacement and he would temporarily act as Treasurer himself. Nonetheless, the loss to the government was immense. Theodore was easily the most able treasurer since federation, and his departure deprived the government of his experience, toughness and outstanding intellect when it desperately needed these qualities.

Theodore's denials adroitly sidestepped some disturbing questions. Campbell had concluded that Theodore was McCormack's undisclosed partner in the Mungana affair (which also involved two other men not actively involved in politics). This finding was essentially based upon an inspection of the private financial transactions of the two former premiers, which revealed that McCormack, who was indisputably incriminated, regularly paid Theodore roughly half his share of the periodic proceeds of the illicit scheme. In the commissioner's acerbic opinion there was only one reasonable inference to draw in the absence of an alternative explanation, and none was forthcoming from McCormack. He had declined to appear before the commission, accepting his lawyer's advice that his best course would be to refrain from testifying and then assail the findings as politically biassed. This was in effect precisely what Theodore did also, saying that he was not available until his work on the budget was completed. This was a compelling justification, but the commissioner refused to wait and speedily issued his scathing report. While McCormack's payments to his closest mate are clearly suspicious and were never explained, by themselves they constitute no absolute proof of Theodore's guilt. Theodore's unwavering reiteration of his innocence helped to convince many Labor supporters that the whole thing was a conservative stunt to ruin their champion and undermine their government. These suspicions seemed well founded when the Queensland government did not promptly give Theodore an opportunity to clear his name.

While Mungana was monopolizing the headlines a British banker, Sir Otto Niemeyer, was on his way to Australia. Scullin 'invited' Niemeyer to make the visit, which was in fact instigated, with Gibson's full support, by the Bank of England. Its senior bankers were appalled by the prospect of Australia defaulting, but before authorizing the provision of emergency assistance they wished to obtain first-hand detailed information about Australia's financial position. Their chosen emissary, Niemeyer, was a typical conservative product of the British establishment with impeccably orthodox views on finance. Arriving at Fremantle on 14 July, Niemeyer spent the following three weeks confirming his preconceptions about the Australian economy as he perused documents and met businessmen, politicians and public servants. His discreet affability and the government's reticence about the purpose of his visit did not prevent uneasiness spreading through the labour movement. In an unguarded moment Niemeyer revealed the wisdom of these suspicions when he met Labor's Speaker in the Representatives, Makin. Ever polite, Makin said he hoped Niemeyer was finding his visit satisfactory. 'That depends on whether you do as you're told', the banker barked back.

Scullin followed his invitation to Niemeyer with another controversial decision when he reappointed Gibson to the Commonwealth Bank Board. Once again the need for confidence was uppermost in the Prime Minister's mind. Not to reappoint the domineering Scot, Scullin reasoned, would put at risk the delicate negotiations with British moneymen which – supplemented by his own representations in London – he hoped would advance Australia's financial recovery. Moreover, a new chairman would come from and be chosen by the remaining directors, and since nearly all of them were Bruce's capitalist appointees their choice would inevitably be someone with views like Gibson's. (While this pessimistic view was understandable, Scullin was about to please the labour movement by appointing M.B. Duffy, a Victorian Labor identity, THC secretary and financial specialist, to succeed one of Gibson's fellow directors, and another's term would expire in 1931. Death or retirement might create further vacancies. In addition, the director who was representing the Treasury on the board was presumably susceptible to a direction to follow government policy.) Cabinet approved Scullin's recommendation that Gibson should be reappointed, although not without some dissent. Many Labor backbenchers were amazed by Gibson's reappointment, and they were furious that Scullin had broken his promise to them that no decision would be made without being discussed in caucus beforehand.

Gibson applauded Niemeyer's harsh medicine when it was unveiled at a conference of federal and state ministers in Melbourne on 18 August. Niemeyer had already outlined his gloomy conclusions privately, but this Melbourne conference presented them for the first time to the Australian people. It was not so much his analysis of the economic position that caused sparks to fly, but his blunt criticism of Australian characteristics like their unhelpful 'natural optimism', faith in 'sheltered trades' protected by high tariffs, and unwillingness to cut 'costs' (which was, as the labour movement recognized, a euphemism for wages). With Scullin confined to bed with a severe bronchial cold and recurring pleurisy, his government was represented at this conference by Fenton, who was about to become acting Prime Minister when Scullin departed for London, and Lyons, who would then take over as Treasurer. Despite his illness Scullin managed to chair a cabinet meeting at his Richmond home attended by Gibson. This meeting paved the way for the Melbourne Agreement, whereby all state governments concurred with the Scullin government on the desirability of strict economies and balanced budgets as stipulated by Niemeyer and Gibson. Labor's two premiers, Ned Hogan from Victoria and 'Slogger' Hill from SA, fell into line with the rest, convinced of the necessity to display their sound intentions under the gaze of the British banking representative. Radicals found the whole proceedings outrageous. 'It made one hang one's head in shame', the *Australian Worker* commented, to witness 'the ignominious spectacle' of Australia's leaders 'sitting like a class of schoolboys to be lectured by an emissary of British moneylenders, and told how they should govern their own land'. The proposal that Australian workers should put up with less in the interests of 'Britain's wealthiest loafers' was offensive at any time, but especially repugnant when there was such widespread unemployment and 'heartrending distress'. 'Niemeyerism' entered the political vocabulary as a scornful label for deflationary reductions.

Scullin rejected advice that in the circumstances he should cancel his trip. Beasley and others could see problems ahead for the FPLP if Scullin was absent for over four months at such a difficult time when Theodore was out of action and Brennan and Moloney were also away. At the first caucus meeting following Theodore's resignation Gabb and Hoare unsuccessfully moved that only Scullin should journey to England. (Alternatively, and perhaps more prudently, Brennan and/or Moloney could have represented Scullin there, and Scullin could have kept in touch with them using the cable service and the new telephone link to London which had just been opened.) But after agonized analysis, Scullin remained adamant that all three ministers should go: 'I firmly believe that there never was a time when it was more important that Australia's financial and economic position should be properly interpreted in Great Britain'. Possibly also influencing him was the prospect of a relaxing convalescent voyage after his months of worry had culminated in illness. While wishing him well in his travels, Anstey frankly told him his departure was a mistake and that the Melbourne *Herald* cartoon of a captain deserting his sinking ship was uncomfortably accurate. 'Scullin is leaving his government behind him', observed Beasley. 'He may not find it here when he returns'.

The strongest ALP hostility to the Melbourne Agreement came from NSW, where Lang made Niemeyer a special target during the state election campaign in October. At the same time Lang was careful to stress that Labor 'sets its face against all repudiation'. The NSW Labor Council had recently called for the cancellation of Australia's remaining war debt obligations to Britain, but Lang and the state ALP executive rejected this proposal. They knew that most of the electorate, including ALP voters in large numbers, adhered to the financial orthodoxy that made inflation and repudiation such alarming concepts to so many. Lang had developed a masterly ability to read his audience and hone his populism accordingly. Sensing that hordes of bewildered battlers were yearning for someone to arrest the pervasive doom and gloom, he gave them hope that salvation was possible. He projected toughness by vehemently flaying his enemies, his terse rasping demagoguery implied that straightforward solutions were at hand, and he convinced hundreds of thousands of Australians during the worst of the Depression that he alone had the strength, the answers and the commitment to overcome the powerful forces that had produced such deprivation and misery. The Langites reinforced his message. 'There is one man, and only one man, who can save you', exhorted Garden, 'and that man is John T. Lang'. One of the Big Fella's enraptured followers was a struggling 27-year-old barrister from the wrong side of the tracks, Garfield Barwick, who had been shattered when ruthlessly forced into bankruptcy by oil companies earlier in 1930 after his brother's garage failed. Lang's campaign overcame the customary unbridled hostility to his party of all but a very few newspapers, and Labor won comfortably with 55% of the vote and 55 of the 90 Assembly seats.

Lang's victory seemed to ignite the potential for storm and tempest within the FPLP. His campaign had received conspicuous support from FPLP members – 35 of them including six ministers, according to Beasley. This partly reflected the large proportion of FPLP members connected to the AWU, which had reaffiliated with the NSW branch of the party in August 1930, but it also signified the willingness of an FPLP contingent to associate itself with Lang's aggressive denunciation of Niemeyerism. Anstey, characteristically uninhibited on the hustings, included Niemeyer in his condemnation of 'these cormorants and vultures of finance'. When the FPLP met two days after the NSW election triumph, Lazzarini's motion congratulating Lang for this 'magnificent success' was carried. Fenton and Lyons then presented to caucus a range of financial measures in line with the Melbourne Agreement. These proposals were subjected to spirited criticism, and the FPLP confirmed its different mood by carrying Beasley's motion that 'this Caucus disagrees with. . .Sir Otto Niemeyer. . .and affirms that the Tariff and Industrial Policy of Australia are domestic matters to be determined by the people of Australia'. This marathon meeting lasted from early afternoon on Monday 27 October until 6.20 pm on the following Thursday. Cabinet and caucus gatherings during the Scullin government had always been lively affairs, but from this meeting onwards they became notoriously abusive and rancorous. Fenton was unable to control proceedings, and journalists and staff based in Parliament House found it almost impossible to escape the tumult. This draining turbulence added to the disillusionment enveloping many Labor MPs.

Fenton and Lyons were in an unenviable position. Now 66, determined and experienced but unimaginative, Fenton was essentially 'an old-fashioned dull man who would have looked in place behind the counter of a little grocer's shop'. Out of his depth during his trying months at the helm, he was on the phone to Scullin so often that it became a standing joke in Canberra. Fenton was altogether overshadowed by Lyons, who had more ability, personal warmth and strength of character. Lyons had struggled to adjust to the unfamiliar ruthlessness of federal politics after being largely responsible for the Tasmanian parliament's friendlier consensus style. Before Scullin's departure he had concentrated almost exclusively on administering his allotted departments, but his promotion to Treasurer during the economic crisis unavoidably thrust him onto centre stage.

His economic conservatism and amiable temperament instinctively inclined him towards a repetition of the methods he had used to improve Tasmania's parlous economy; but instead of the co-operative approach which seemed to him natural and logical in such circumstances, he found Labor's opponents inflexibly unco-operative and a growing proportion of his caucus colleagues prepared to renounce fiscal orthodoxy in favour of radical alternatives. He was dismayed to find at the marathon FPLP meeting following Lang's election victory that the financial heretics had captured the numbers in caucus. Lyons was feeling increasingly out of step with most of his colleagues at a time when he acutely missed his wife, children and family life in Tasmania.

The crucial factor in this transformation in caucus was Theodore's return to prominence. Since his resignation as Treasurer he had been absent from parliament and caucus, but his presence at the caucus meeting of 27–30 October indicated that he was ready to assert himself once again. While out of the limelight he had discussed Australia's economic plight with R.F. Irvine, a former economics professor who was in 1930 the only credentialled economist propagating the virtues of expansionary remedies. Although his conversion to these ideas was partly influenced by Irvine, Theodore was familiar with all facets of economic thought and required no tutoring in how to formulate and advocate a plausible scheme that provided for a controlled injection of mild inflationary stimulus. This conversion also suited Theodore politically. Since the Melbourne Agreement, sections of the labour movement had been outspoken in their hostility to Niemeyerism. FPLP members upholding the merits of expansionary measures – principally Anstey and Yates, but also Lazzarini, Beasley and Curtin – had lacked cohesion, and the emotional fervour of their arguments had sometimes detracted from their substance. Theodore's economic knowledge and analytical clarity gave these arguments added credibility which convinced many well-meaning waverers in caucus. In the process he attracted the support of the growing number of Labor supporters intolerant of Niemeyerism, as well as reminding everyone of his obvious ability which had already prompted calls for his reinstatement as Treasurer. At the same time there were implications for the ongoing power struggle in NSW between the two titans, Lang and Theodore. Lang had stolen a march with his electoral triumph, but Theodore was now countering with a sophisticated policy comprising a feasible alternative to Niemeyerism; all Lang had so far managed was well-chosen words of abuse of the banker and his views.

After protracted debate Theodore's proposal was carried by caucus on 30 October. Under the proposal the Commonwealth Bank would 'be required to create sufficient credit' for several purposes: to finance all federal government 'services covered by Parliamentary appropriations', to provide £20 million for works programmes and further funds for 'productive purposes in primary and secondary industries', and to meet all internal loans maturing during the 1930–31 financial year. This proposed credit was to be made available at an interest rate no higher than 5%. During the lengthy debate there were stages when Labor MPs were hurling such impassioned vilification at each other that Daly and Curtin felt impelled to remind their colleagues that maintaining unity was essential, and after Theodore's proposal was carried caucus passed a conciliatory motion expressing 'its appreciation of the services rendered' by Fenton, Lyons and the other ministers.

But the following FPLP meeting on 6 November only aggravated the wounds. Fenton began it by reading to caucus a cable from Scullin critical of the Theodore plan. Scullin asserted that 'all this talk about creating credit and inflation is most damaging' to Australia's reputation in London financial circles, and added that 'Government cannot deliberately coerce the administration of the banks'. Lyons then referred to a £27 million internal loan maturing in December and, ignoring the FPLP's endorsement of Theodore's plan, recommended that caucus authorize the loan's conversion by public subscription as usual. Curtin and Yates countered with an amendment – in line with the Theodore plan – that the Commonwealth Bank be required to meet the loan when it fell due. Anstey suggested that when the Commonwealth Bank directors refused the government's instruction, as they surely would, redemption of the loan should simply be postponed for 12 months. The Curtin and Anstey proposals were merged into a single amendment, put to the vote, and carried by 22 to 16.

The FPLP's approval of the Curtin-Anstey amendment was the last straw for Lyons. He was not the only one to regard postponement of redemption as perilously close to repudiation. Pale and 'trembling with anger', he silenced the effervescent party room as he dramatically shouted:

> I will not do it. . .I will go out of public life first. I will cable the Prime Minister and if he wants it done then he must get someone else to do it.

Fenton added that he too would have to 'consider his position'. Green saw Lyons's hurried departure from Parliament House, and feared that he was about to resign. 'Texas' anxiously rushed after him to Canberra railway station and saw Lyons's train pulling out of the station; he ran alongside it yelling desperately 'For God's sake, Joe, don't do it!'

Lyons was indeed contemplating drastic action. He repeated publicly that he had cabled the Prime Minister, and pending Scullin's reply he would refuse to act as caucus had directed, thereby defying not only caucus but the party's tradition of decision-making by the majority. Like other financial conservatives in the party, Lyons firmly believed that anything smacking of repudiation would irreparably besmirch Australia's national honour, which was not only morally repugnant to him personally but would also jeopardize Australia's prospects of obtaining future loan finance. Lyons and others elevated this conviction above their allegiance to their party and the workers. It was ominously clear that the crisis threatened to split the party.

All this was of course distressing news for Scullin. His health had been slow to recover during his journey, but by the time he reached England he was back to full strength. En route he had stopped at Geneva, joining Brennan at the League of Nations and making a speech in favour of disarmament. The Scullin government's tribulations were reflected in Brennan's 'state of high nervous tension', but he was able to inform his chief that his address to the League had been very favourably received. Brennan had described his government as 'deeply committed' to 'ultimate disarmament and outlawry of war':

> Australia tells the world, as a gesture of peace. . .that she is not prepared for war. . .we have given practical proof of our earnestness. . .We have drawn our pen through the schedule of military expenditure with unprecedented firmness. . .

The Imperial Conference later in London, which yielded disappointingly few tangible benefits for Australia, was nearly over when Lyons's cabled ultimatum arrived. Scullin handled the crisis decisively. He gave Lyons his unqualified support in both a public statement and a private cable to his acting Treasurer: 'I do not approve and will not support resolution of the party, which I agree is repudiation, which is dishonest and disastrous. Brennan and Moloney concur. . .' He also cabled a message for Fenton to read to caucus.

The FPLP next assembled on 12 November. At this meeting caucus responded to the conservative clamour about repudiation by unanimously carrying Makin's motion that the FPLP 'strongly deprecates and emphatically denies any suggestion of, or association with, the repudiation of any financial obligation, and will faithfully discharge all lawful commitments'. Fenton informed caucus of cabinet's view that the party 'should not precipitate a crisis while the Prime Minister and his two Ministers were absent'. When Yates and Lazzarini disagreed, Fenton produced Scullin's cabled message and read it aloud. It described the Curtin-Anstey amendment of 6 November as 'appalling', 'disastrous', and amounting to repudiation. 'No self-respecting Government could agree to it.'

> Our Government floated a loan and guaranteed the public a safe investment. Thousands of people withdrew their savings from the Savings Bank to assist the Labour Government. To default on this loan would weaken the value of their investments, would destroy public confidence, and would delay for years the restoration of economic prosperity.

Scullin's appeal had the desired effect, transforming the mood in the party room. Anstey suggested that the whole question should be put aside until Scullin's return and, with Curtin and Yates concurring, this suggestion was promptly accepted by a chastened caucus intent on averting a split.

Scullin had another success in a confrontation with the King and the British Labour government. Scullin's determination that the next Governor-General would be an Australian had influenced cabinet's recent choice of native-born Sir Isaac Isaacs, a High Court judge and a Jew, but Scullin was soon aware that Isaacs was considered unacceptable by the British authorities. Undeterred, Scullin managed to persuade the Imperial Conference to ratify the principle that the dominions could directly approach the monarch concerning a vice-regal appointment. He also made it clear to British Prime Minister Ramsay MacDonald and the King's private secretary that he was not going to budge on the question of Isaacs's appointment. The King was not amused. A letter was sent to Scullin containing the monarch's firm opinion that the AIF commander General Birdwood would be a better choice than Isaacs. At a private meeting with the King the tenacious railwayman's son stuck to his guns as they traversed the subject for 45 minutes. Eventually the King yielded and ungraciously announced the appointment of Isaacs. Scullin had managed to dent significantly the machinery of Empire. The Victorian *Labor Call* rejoiced: 'Australians are equal, if not superior, to any imported pooh-bahs!'

Although caucus had agreed to shelve consideration of economic policy until Scullin's return, he discovered on his way home that the FPLP was not so compliant in other matters, notably the filling of High Court vacancies. Since 1913 the court had comprised seven judges. One resigned in 1929. Another resigned in March 1930 after inheriting a fortune in the will of the hated millionaire coal magnate John 'Baron' Brown. The Scullin government decided, as an economy measure, not to fill these vacancies, contending that the remaining judges could handle the volume of court business. Yet another vacancy arose when Isaacs became Governor-General. This time the FPLP was more inclined to take the opportunity to dilute the conservative complexion of the court, especially as there was pressure from the NSW and Victorian branches to do so. Scullin first realized caucus was discussing the matter when wireless messages reached his ship. He and Brennan, who was also vitally involved as Attorney-General, sent Fenton a strongly worded cable of protest. On 11 December cabinet accepted the recommendation of acting Attorney-General Daly that any decision should be postponed until Scullin and Brennan had returned. However, caucus apparently refused to tolerate any delay and cabinet decided on 18 December to implement the FPLP's instruction.

The two new judges were Evatt and McTiernan. There was the normal howl of frenzied protest about the appointment of judges with Labor affiliations. Evatt was an outstanding barrister, and his suitability on legal grounds was rationally indisputable. The choice of McTiernan, a competent but less ostentatiously brilliant lawyer, was more controversial. Scullin and Brennan were understandably peeved that caucus ignored their wish to 'express strongly held views' before the decision was made, but they had contributed to the discord themselves by waiving Labor's first opportunity since 1913 to influence the composition of the court. It was incorrectly surmised that these 'strongly held views' amounted to Brennan coveting a judgeship himself. They more likely concerned his loathing of Evatt's naked ambitiousness. Although Lang's reminiscences are unreliable, he claimed that Wren and Theodore were instrumental in organizing the numbers in caucus and that Theodore wanted to maximize his chances of a favourable hearing if Mungana ever came before the High Court. However, the man Scullin primarily blamed for the judicial appointments going ahead in his absence was Daly. Interestingly, Lang claimed that Daly was close to Wren. It may be entirely coincidental that before entering the Senate Daly had come to the aid of Mahoney (and presumably Theodore and Wren) concerning the 1928 royal commission with an affidavit supporting Mahoney's discredited story of a Melbourne Cup windfall.

Scullin glimpsed Australia again in the first week of 1931. Like Hughes in 1916, he returned after a long absence in England to a taut, expectant party. As in 1916, the acting Prime Minister was greatly relieved at his leader's return: 'Thank God Scullin has come back' was Fenton's fervent reaction. As in 1916, not only his anxious party but the politically informed section of the whole electorate were keenly awaiting the Prime Minister's lead on the dominant policy issue of the day: in 1931 Scullin had to decide whether to adhere to the traditional economic methods he had advocated or switch, like Theodore, to the more radical measures which had attracted the support of a caucus majority while he was away. Like Hughes in 1916, Scullin consulted widely before committing himself. NSW party officials strongly pressed Scullin to support the Theodore plan during the by-election for McTiernan's federal seat of Parkes. They were not pleased when Scullin kept his options open in launching the by-election campaign and, furthermore, briefly deprived NSW of some of its most prestigious campaigners by scheduling a FPLP meeting five days before polling day.

The main business of that meeting on 26 January was Theodore's position. His manoeuvring to be restored to cabinet had been assisted by powerful NSW elements with Beasley, state secretary Graves and 'Digger' Dunn particularly assiduous. Although the stigma of Mungana was a profound obstacle, Theodore's supporters argued that this should be overlooked because, firstly, the beleaguered Scullin government needed its best man back in a key position rather than on the interchange bench, and secondly, the Queensland Nationalists' conduct showed that the whole exercise was a political stunt to get Theodore. The laws of evidence distinguishing between royal commissions and other cases made a successful prosecution unlikely, so the Queensland Nationalists seemed content to let the mud of the commission's findings stick. They belatedly decided on civil proceedings, then changed the laws of evidence to assist their chances of a conviction, but even this civil case was still six months away.

Scullin was one of the many who found the delay absolutely unjustifiable. He had to choose a Treasurer. Lyons had asked to be relieved of that unpalatable burden, and Scullin felt that to take it on himself was a guarantee of further ill-health. Theodore remained head and shoulders above any other candidate for the position. Besides, Scullin had taken into account the clear signals that his own leadership might become vulnerable if he remained unreceptive to the growing support within the labour movement, especially in NSW, for the Theodore plan. If Theodore was reinstated there would certainly be an almighty outcry from conservative newspapers, but they could hardly be more critical than they were already. A more difficult problem arising from any restoration of Theodore would be the reaction of Lyons, Fenton and other economic conservatives in caucus.

The caucus vote on Theodore was extremely close. After hours of contentious debate the motion to reinstate him was narrowly carried when some FPLP members changed their minds at the last minute. The concerted pressure applied by the NSW branch paid dividends when that state's federal MPs voted overwhelmingly in favour. Scullin's strong support for Theodore was also vital. Fenton, Lyons and their fellow thinkers remained opposed, but Anstey, Yates and Lazzarini 'would not have Mr Theodore at any price' either: they had seen Theodore commandingly belittle their expansionary arguments in caucus, only now to propound them partly as a calculated means of climbing back to office. However, Theodore was supported by Curtin, Eldridge and others who accepted the need to look beyond traditional financial remedies. The Mungana proceedings 'have been unduly protracted' and Theodore was 'incomparably capable', explained Curtin, who welcomed the return of the man he blamed for his omission from cabinet: 'At last this Government will fight for something', he privately concluded. Makin, who supported expansionary remedies, considered that returning Theodore to office would be unethical while he was still tarnished by such damaging findings, as did a number of others.

The repercussions came swiftly. Gabb was so enraged that he left the party, contending that a minister should be 'above suspicion'. The Gawler Bunyip had some harsh parting words for Scullin. 'I have lost faith in your judgement as a leader, and in your possession of gratitude, when I noticed how the advice and appeal of Mr Fenton and Mr Lyons were received by you'. Those two ministers felt betrayed. They had fought hard in trying circumstances to prevent the FPLP from defying its leader's wishes, and now they considered that he had dumped them. Even Yates criticized Scullin's 'ingratitude and apostasy', and described him as 'a most mystifying enigma'. Lyons went back to Devonport to discuss the situation with Enid. Shortly afterwards, just before polling day in the Parkes by-election, he and Fenton announced their resignations from cabinet. The likelihood of an ALP win in this normally anti-Labor seat was already slim, and the resignations did not help. Nor did the announcement on 22 January of the Arbitration Court's 10% reduction in the basic wage, which only underlined the powerlessness of Labor MPs to safeguard the interests of the people who elected them. The result in Parkes was a massive swing to the Nationalists: one-third of the electors who had voted for McTiernan in 1929 refused to support the Labor candidate less than 16 months later.

Nine days later Lang rocked the FPLP with a staggering blow. The Big Fella had shrewdly not participated in the Parkes by-election. The control he and his Inner Group exerted over the NSW branch continued to be a perversion of the party's ideals of participatory democracy, although he had allowed caucus to choose his ministers (except for Attorney-General A.A. Lysaght). Lang had quickly acted to ease the plight of evicted tenants and the hardships of house-holders and other debtors struggling to meet repayments, and he agreed to provide boots for battlers who had worn theirs out looking for work in rural areas. He also resumed hostilities with the Council. But he soon had to face up to the harsh financial reality that NSW was short of funds and he could not rectify the situation by borrowing. Even if the London money market was receptive, the combined effect of Gibson's stubbornness and the 1927 Financial Agreement between the national government and the states meant that NSW could not borrow independently. He reluctantly supported Theodore's reinstatement because the Theodore plan did promise some succour for NSW's depleted finances, unlike the rigid Niemeyerism of Lyons and Fenton; but the Big Fella was concerned that his control of the NSW branch might be threatened by Theodore's resurgence, and he was finding his state's financial difficulties suf-focating. Furthermore, a movement dedicated to promoting Labor's socializ-ation plank was spreading through the NSW ALP with such rapidity that Lang and his Inner Group were hard pressed to contain it. He decided that a bold stroke was required and at a premiers' conference early in February 1931 he provided it. After Theodore had delivered on Saturday the 7th a brilliant speech outlining his proposals for a mild stimulus to the economy, Lang spent the next day cloistered with his advisers. On the Monday he stunned onlookers by unveil-ing his own plan. The Lang plan tilted clearly at Theodore with its radical veneer and 'artful simplicity' designed to appeal to the masses. The Big Fella's plan proposed assertively that Australia should abandon the gold standard (this had in fact already occurred), reduce all interest on government borrowing within Australia to 3%, and refuse to pay interest to British bondholders until Britain agreed to an arrangement about Australia's debt obligations as America had with Britain's.

The launching of the Lang plan may also have been related to the need for another federal by-election. For the safe ALP seat of East Sydney the NSW executive chose Eddie Ward as the candidate, and announced that he would campaign on the Lang plan. The NSW branch had once again thumbed its nose at the ALP's federal bodies and the party's national structure. There was no olive branch in response this time. Having endorsed the Theodore plan, the federal executive declared firmly that the by-election campaign would be opened by Scullin, and Labor speakers during the campaign could not diverge from author-ized federal executive policy. If Ward refused to comply, the federal executive would not acknowledge him as a valid ALP candidate. The NSW executive replied with a similarly uncompromising resolution demanding that all NSW members of the FPLP support Ward and campaign on the Lang plan. Scullin told caucus that he 'was not going to take dictation from any one section of the movement', and threatened expulsion for anyone promoting the Lang plan. 'Here's one who's going to do it', retorted Eldridge, 'put me out now'. Beasley had also publicly associated himself with the Lang plan in supporting the candidacy of his pugnacious mate Ward.

The FPLP conducted a re-election of the ministry and other office-bearers on 2 March. In view of the resignations of Lyons and Fenton, Beasley's conduct and the generally chaotic atmosphere, it was no surprise when the motion for a spill of all positions was carried. Beasley challenged Scullin for the leadership, but polled poorly. Theodore was confirmed as deputy. The ballot for the two Senate ministers retained Barnes and added J.B. Dooley to the cabinet. The first ballot for MHRs resulted in the re-election of Blakeley, Brennan, Forde and Parker Moloney. Further ballots produced a quartet of new ministers in Holloway, McNeill, Culley and Chifley. The last place went to 'Texas' Green after a close contest against Curtin and Yates; Curtin would probably have won it if he had not discouraged potential supporters by saying he did not wish to serve in the cabinet because of Anstey's relegation. As well as dispensing with Beasley's Langite tendencies and Anstey's erratic maverick qualities, caucus had demoted the absent Daly. The talented SA Senator had been away from Canberra, either working in WA or ill, almost since the start of the year. His omission was allegedly a product of Scullin's retribution for the High Court appointments, coupled with Theodore's hostility derived from Daly's absence from the caucus meeting which restored Theodore to cabinet. Theodore settled another score from that occasion when he organized the defeat of McGrath as caucus nominee for the position of Chairman of Committees. A vigorous Theodore supporter in 1928 but an opponent of his reinstatement in January 1931, McGrath intensely resented Theodore's display of vindictiveness.

Upheaval in the FPLP continued in the wake of Ward's by-election victory. Lang involved himself fully in Ward's campaign, attracting huge crowds (as he did in Sydney's inner suburbs throughout his second term as Premier). Accompanied by Beasley, Rae and 'Digger' Dunn, Ward journeyed to Canberra where the first caucus meeting since his election was held on 12 March. Scullin reminded that meeting of the federal executive's instruction regarding Ward, and ruled that because he had shunned federal Labor's policy during the by-election campaign he was ineligible to join the FPLP. Beasley objected strongly, arguing that if Ward was excluded then other FPLP members who campaigned alongside him should meet the same fate. Rae and Lazzarini moved dissent from Scullin's ruling. As pandemonium broke out around him, Ward remained completely silent. Maloney and Curtin urged that any action be postponed until the forthcoming special federal conference which had been called to deal with the recalcitrant NSW branch, but Scullin stood firm, fortified by a cabinet decision the previous day authorizing Ward's exclusion. Eventually the Rae-Lazzarini motion was put to the vote and convincingly defeated. The FPLP's split with the Langites was thereupon dramatically sealed when Beasley, Eldridge, Ward, Lazzarini, Rae and 'Digger' Dunn marched out of the party room. They gathered in Dunn's room at Parliament House and formed their own party. With the later acquisition of James, who was then absent ill, Beasley's Lang Labor Group comprised five MHRs and two Senators.

This walk-out with its overtones of 1916 was sensational, and especially so because of its timing. Just then parliament was debating a no-confidence motion, which the Nationalists had introduced knowing that several other FPLP members were about to formally signal their defection from the ALP. Since early February there had been secret negotiations between Lyons and six business and political identities who were intent on enticing him to leave the ALP and join the Nationalists. The Group, as these conspirators labelled themselves, was headed by an old Tasmanian friend of Lyons now in charge of Australia's leading firm of stockbrokers and investors. The Group also included R.G. Menzies, a Victorian

171

MLC who had never experienced hunger and deprivation but did not allow this to interfere with his wonderful insights into Australia's economic malaise:

> If Australia were to surmount her troubles only by the abandonment of traditional British standards of honesty, justice, fair play and honest endeavour, it would be better for Australia that every citizen within her boundaries should die of starvation within the next 12 months.

Lyons was distressed by the notion of leaving the ALP, and briefly contemplated quitting politics completely. But he felt driven to join Labor's enemies because of his firm belief that without Niemeyerism Australia was endangered. Enid nurtured and steeled his resolve. The Group offered encouragement, support and, according to rumour, promises of financial aid in the event of Lyons losing his seat. Still he hesitated. While in this unsettled mood, unable to make the break, he attended the Tasmanian ALP conference. There, instead of the comradely warmth of old friends, he encountered a withering blast from Ogilvie and a vote of censure for disobeying federal caucus. Being subjected to such treatment in his home state, when his crime was to carry out what he saw as a moral duty, finally pushed him over the brink. His faithful henchman in all things political, J.A. Guy, agreed to follow him. Fenton had indicated that his defection from the ALP was imminent, and the Gawler Bunyip had already left. If the Langites were prepared to cross the floor as well, the Scullin government would be without a majority in the Representatives.

In the debate on the no-confidence motion Lyons made the speech of his life – emotional, straightforward and sincere. The Group hoped to make Lyons leader of the anti-Labor forces instead of the uncharismatic Latham, and this speech, which impressed Nationalist MPs, gave a boost to the campaign already under way through the Group's links with Murdoch, now Australia's most powerful press magnate. Murdoch had used the newspapers under his control to boom Lyons throughout the nation as its saviour 'Honest Joe' in such a blatant promotional drive that the Melbourne THC banned Murdoch journalists from its meetings and recommended that workers should boycott his newspapers. 'Honest Joe' was joined by Fenton, Gabb, Guy and another FPLP defector, Jack Price, in voting for the parliamentary motion that threatened the Scullin government's existence. Price's father Tom had been a popular Labor leader and premier in SA, but Price the younger was not as capable or prominent, was a staunch financial conservative, and was allegedly piqued at being overlooked for the ministry in the recent reshuffle. The Scullin government survived the no-confidence motion, as Beasley's Lang Labor contingent received their instructions from Sydney to vote against it – the Big Fella had decided that keeping the Scullin government in office best suited his delusions about controlling the ALP throughout Australia. The conservative plotting to elevate Lyons continued, and the pressure mounted on Latham to step aside. Eventually Latham reluctantly did so, and after the anti-Labor forces were hastily revamped Lyons presented himself to parliament early in May as the leader of the United Australia Party (UAP).

Late in March 1931 Labor's special federal conference took the drastic step of exorcizing the NSW executive. During the preceding fortnight the NSW ALP had expelled Theodore from the party and the Lang government had defaulted on interest repayments owing to the Westminster Bank in London, events which buttressed the determination of nearly all federal conference delegates to take strong action against the NSW branch. A few of them were inclined to favour conciliation in the hope of averting a major schism, but the mood of the overwhelming majority was epitomized by Curtin's contention that 'the story of previous efforts at conciliation in the past was the story of continued humiliation for those endeavouring to maintain the solidarity of the Movement'. Delegates voted 25 to 4 to pass Curtin's motion that the NSW executive, 'having refused to acknowledge and accept the Federal Platform, Constitution and Rules' of the ALP, 'is hereby declared to have automatically placed itself outside' the party. Conference then proceeded to create an alternative party structure in NSW which would be loyal to the party's federal bodies.

Adding to the pressure on Labor politicians was their awareness that profoundly disturbing undercurrents were developing in response to Australia's economic breakdown and the inability of its political system to fix it. Unemployment continued to skyrocket. Although its impact on the many workless tended to induce an individualistic response with feelings of isolation and demoralization commonplace, there were occasions when the unemployed took direct collective action. Scullin happened to be passing through Adelaide when an angry demonstration about dole rations culminated in a savage mêlée between police and demonstrators. Ten days later there was an explosive encounter in central Melbourne when police broke up a march of protesting unemployed. Evictions of tenants were resisted in brutal confrontations.

A sinister contribution to the heightening tension was the formation or reactivation of clandestine paramilitary organizations ostensibly to safeguard law and order. Their most visible presence was in Sydney, where the New Guard was formed shortly after the Lang plan was announced as NSW government policy. The New Guard drilled, plotted, assaulted Communists, and made threats against other labour movement activists, Lang in particular. Gibson typified the ruthless class allegiance and impatience with democracy of many New Guard sympathizers; he accosted its leader in a Sydney street and declared that it was 'high time the New Guard did something' because 'Lang has got to be stopped'. The New Guard was an offshoot of the even more sinister Old Guard, which had more powerful connections, stronger rural roots and tighter secrecy. The Old Guard had equivalents in other states. In Victoria the White Army turned out in force on 6 March 1931 when the preposterous rumour circulated that Communists had seized Sydney and were marching to Melbourne. In the Mallee, the Wimmera and Gippsland 'the farmers and local businessmen turned out with firearms, dug trenches, laid sandbags and kept watch all through the night' in their pointless vigil. The activities of these private armies contributed to the palpable air of menace pervading Australia between 1930 and 1932, and imposed further tension on Labor politicians struggling with their Herculean burdens of office.

Without its breakaways the FPLP was smaller but more cohesive. Meetings in cabinet and caucus were less fractious and traumatic. (The ex-Labor recruits to the UAP, who now also included McGrath, were amazed by the tranquillity of party meetings in their new surroundings after their experience of recent FPLP gatherings.) Having lost many of its divisive influences, the FPLP seemed to have generated a sense of revitalized purpose as it introduced several items of legislation related to the Theodore plan. The new mood dissolved all too quickly, however, when the Senate mutilated the legislation, Gibson intervened with the breathtaking notification that the Commonwealth Bank was about to withdraw its financial assistance from the government, and the prospect of imminent default became more alarmingly likely than ever.

Scullin felt that he now had no alternative but to acquiesce in the deflationary Niemeyerism preached by the conservatives. He believed that default would result in far more severe hardship for Australians in need than mild deflationary measures administered sympathetically by a Labor government. A proposed scheme was submitted with his approval for consideration by a premiers' conference attended by all state leaders, even Lang, who had prevented any NSW participation in some of the preliminaries.

The other Labor premiers, Victoria's Hogan and Hill from SA, had already signalled their unwillingness to emulate Lang's defiance of traditional fiscal policies. Hogan had antagonized party members by refusing to abide by the directive of a special state conference that Victorian Labor MPs sign a pledge not to support any reductions in wages or pensions. The Depression admittedly imposed daunting demands on the economic expertise of politicians, but 'Slogger' Hill was proving to be one of the worst ALP leaders in the party's history. Shrewd anti-Labor identities in SA had foreseen that losing the 1930 state election might be a blessing in disguise, and Hill's ineptitude, vanity and swift abandonment of Labor principles helped vindicate these predictions. After scab labour backed by a citizens' militia had been utilized to defeat striking waterside workers in a savage dispute at Port Adelaide in 1928, the oppressed wharf labourers looked forward to relief from the Hill government. Instead, Hill latched onto exaggerated reports of Communist activity on the waterfront as justification for rushing through a Public Safety Preservation Act which gave the government and the police extraordinary powers to repress the strikers. Hill was the puppet of conservative interests, easily manipulated by such men as the editor of the *Advertiser* (a close associate of Murdoch), leading SA businessmen and the SA Governor.

The premiers' conference in mid-1931 was a protracted affair. In contrast to Scullin, who, as so often during his prime ministership, was to be seen 'walking in short, nervous steps, and always worried', Lang maintained his authoritative image with terse, forthright contributions. Only occasionally did he relax the aloof, abrasive manner that so offended ALP stalwarts like Chifley who were imbued with the comradely ideals of the labour movement. 'Slogger' Hill tended to be grumpy and dithering. Asked for his views by Theodore during the deliberations, Hill replied 'I can't really make up my mind...I don't know'. 'You bloody old woman', Theodore snapped, 'you haven't got a mind to make up'. The Premiers' Plan emerging from the conference was said to embody 'equality of sacrifice'. Scullin and all the premiers (Lang grudgingly) agreed to 'bind themselves to give effect promptly to the whole of the resolutions' incorporated in the Premiers' Plan, which provided for increased taxation, reduced interest rates, relief for holders of private mortgages, and a 20% reduction in all adjustable government expenditure including wages and pensions. From the ALP's viewpoint, being coerced into approving cuts in wages and welfare was the crowning humiliation.

Scullin moved quickly to persuade the FPLP to endorse the Premiers' Plan. He repeated at various party forums that acceptance was the government's only alternative to imminent default, which would impose larger cuts on pensioners and public servants than the Premiers' Plan. To abdicate by calling an election 'would have been traitorous to the labour movement', since it would have left the conservatives free to implement the retrenchment they had long advocated. Scullin's initial task was to convince cabinet to reverse its opposition to reduced pensions affirmed as recently as 19 March and 27 May. He managed to achieve this at a meeting on 6 June when Culley was absent and Holloway dissented. Five days later he tackled caucus, uneasy about his reception there. Only a week earlier the FPLP had asked to be consulted before any plan involving reductions was ratified. Scullin had ignored this request. He and Theodore began on the 11th with lengthy dissertations. The ensuing debate continued that afternoon and evening and much of the following day, with Yates, Makin, Holloway, Riordan and others up in arms about the cuts in welfare. Scullin and Theodore challenged their critics to suggest an alternative way to avoid default. Coleman and Makin moved that the government call a double dissolution election and campaign on the expansionary plan previously promulgated by Theodore. After rejecting this motion, caucus voted by 26 to 13 to endorse the Premiers' Plan.

The federal executive met on 18 June to consider the Premiers' Plan, having received protests against it from the Victorian and WA executives and such far-flung local branches as Cairns, Fremantle and Franklin. The SA branch instructed its delegates Makin and H. Kneebone to oppose the Premiers' Plan, which they did, along with Curtin, Tasmanian leader Ogilvie and Don Cameron, who had been at the forefront of the anti-conscription fight in WA but since 1919 had been back in his birthplace Melbourne immersed in working-class activism. A compromise formula was devised. The executive released a statement which 'definitely opposed' the cuts, attacked the banks and the Senate, and claimed that 'during this time of crisis' it was 'of the greatest importance' that the ALP should remain in office instead of an 'abhorrent', 'disastrous' anti-Labor government. The executive left FPLP members free to vote as they wished on the Premiers' Plan, which, with UAP support, was approved comfortably in federal parliament despite the opposition of 17 FPLP members and the Lang Labor group.

The labour movement collectively seemed dazed by the powerlessness of Labor in politics during the previous 18 months, and there was not the veritable storm of dissent that might have been expected for such an abrogation of party principles. Nevertheless the hostility of some state executives continued unabated, and many local branches were incensed. Holloway and Culley resigned in protest from Scullin's cabinet (caucus chose Daly and Cunningham to replace them). A few backbenchers expressed their disapproval publicly, including Makin, Riordan and Yates, but the most incisive outbursts came in parliament from Anstey and Curtin. Both passionately disputed the argument that it was better for Labor to administer the Premiers' Plan cuts than their heartless opponents. Anstey was at his most emotionally compelling:

This is the annihilation of everything that the Labour party has produced during two long generations. . . This government has, since it took office, pursued a policy of drift. It has suffered ignominy upon ignominy. . .But are we justified in spitting upon the altar of Labour simply because others may desecrate it worse than we may?. . .That is not the path of salvation. . .this Government is crucifying the very people who raised its members from obscurity and placed them in power.

Curtin divulged his deep fears that his party's endorsement of the Premiers' Plan 'will bring about the demoralization of the Labour movement', handing 'its enemies. . .an era of political mastership', because 'the faith that it has built up in the minds of its supporters will be destroyed'. Previously, he contended, the ALP was 'at least noted for its consistent adherence to its principles', but the Premiers' Plan had punctured this reputation and he despaired for Labor's future.

Throughout the party's history the preselection process has influenced the

175

calibre of Labor parliamentary candidates. The difference between capturing the preselection numbers and making a wider contribution in the formulation and articulation of uplifting policies has resulted in some Labor seats being held by politicians of little vision, whose focus has rarely diverged from the honing of support in their local bailiwicks. Preselections have commonly been fiercely contested, and have sometimes featured glaring infringements of party rules. There have also been instances when chance or a notable individual contribution has been decisive, and both occurred in Melbourne Ports in 1931. Jim Mathews, who had battled ill-health for years, was retiring after a quarter of a century as the local member. Holloway was planning to relinquish his frail hold on Flinders electorate by switching to much safer Melbourne Ports. The preselection took place on the Saturday when the Melbourne *Sun* mistakenly reported that Holloway had approved the Premiers' Plan. Holloway was appalled by the error, which contradicted assurances he had given to party members in Melbourne Ports and 'could very easily have ruined my political career'. Frantically trying to retrieve the situation, he managed to obtain a newspaper retraction, but this would not have been enough without the quick thinking of feminist party stalwart Jenny Baines, who had fought for women's suffrage in Britain alongside the Pankhursts, later became a VSP activist, and after being gaoled for her radical activities was reputedly the first prisoner in an Australian gaol to go on a hunger strike. She had the presence of mind to take this retraction to a nearby football match, aware that many of Holloway's disillusioned supporters had adjourned there after disgustedly abstaining at the preselection because of the *Sun*'s mistake. She rounded them up and herded them back to the polling booth, and their votes enabled Holloway to win. He remained MHR for Melbourne Ports nearly as long as Mathews, and played a crucial role in the narrow election of Scullin's successor as FPLP leader.

After the Premiers' Plan was ratified the FPLP was

> beaten and broken. . .they drank their tea or their whisky amid gloomy and despondent self-criticism. Regretting the lost chances of the past, they clicked the balls around in the billiard room, or paced the long, lighted lobbies with saddening eyes. . .

Anstey was bitterly disillusioned and 'merciless in his criticisms'. Some FPLP members 'came to dread the appearance of this grim apostle of the class war, wandering through the parliamentary corridors like a grey ghost from their own more vital past, accusing, scorning, jeering'. Scullin tried to generate some optimism by talking up the economy. He told a crowd in Melbourne that at last he could 'see daylight ahead in Government finances', but was stopped in his tracks by an interjector's quip: 'You must have very good eyesight'. At least there was good news for Theodore when the jury in the Mungana case cleared him in August. Naturally he and his supporters ecstatically trumpeted this result as proof that the allegations against him were politically inspired, but the jury found only that the circumstantial evidence was not strong enough to sustain a guilty verdict; while it was not up to Theodore to establish his innocence, doubts lingered about his involvement.

While continuing to swap insults freely with their former colleagues, the Beasley group holding the balance of power in the Representatives seemed unwilling to bring down the government. However, Lang was always alert for opportunities to strike at Theodore. Since the Premiers' Plan agreement the Big

Fella had been trying to distract his disciples from realizing that he had actually signed it and that NSW's disastrous financial position verged on bankruptcy. He and his Inner Group had been attempting to extend Lang Labor's influence into other states; although this infiltration met with minimal success in Queensland and Victoria, there were encouraging developments in SA. Forcing an early federal election suited Lang's objectives, especially as 'Digger' Dunn had informed him that some federal Langites might try to rejoin the FPLP. The Beasley group had made further allegations of impropriety against Theodore, accusing him of manipulating a Scullin government programme of unemployment relief to favour his political supporters in NSW. On 25 November Beasley moved that these allegations should be fully debated in parliament. Lyons and the UAP agreed. Theodore denied the charges, reiterating that the Langites were guilty of similar conduct themselves. After the FPLP was defeated by 37 votes to 32, Scullin recommended an election to Governor-General Isaacs, and it was scheduled for 19 December. The brevity of the shortest federal election campaign so far was partly intended to frustrate Lang Labor plans to stand some state MPs as federal candidates.

It was a rowdy campaign, especially in constituencies held by ex-FPLP breakaways. There were wild scenes in NSW contests between Scullin's followers and the Langites, who disrupted Theodore's meetings by chanting their adaptation of a popular contemporary song 'Yes, We Have No Munganas'. Electioneering in Sydney was also marked by the pernicious assistance the UAP received from the New Guard. On polling day the FPLP was routed. Its strength in the Representatives shrank to a dismal 14 out of 75 (46 in 1929) with a derisory voting share of 27·09%. In NSW Lang Labor easily outpolled federal Labor to gain a quarter of the votes and four seats; the FPLP emerged with three seats, having won 20 NSW seats in 1929. No fewer than seven Scullin government ministers were defeated. Theodore was thrashed by his 1929 campaign manager in Dalley, J.S. Rosevear, and Chifley, Moloney and Cunningham all lost their rural NSW seats. Culley was defeated in Tasmania, where Labor won no seats at all. The FPLP lost half its WA representation with the defeat of Curtin. In Victoria McNeill lost Wannon, but the biggest shock of all was Brennan's narrow loss after a swing of over 30% in seemingly impregnable Batman. Labor's only bright spot was its performance in Queensland, which as in 1929 sharply contrasted with the overall trend. There Labor retained its three MHRs and gained two others, as well as winning all three Senate vacancies. No Labor candidate for the Senate was successful in any other state. It was 'a staggering blow' to the party, admitted Scullin. But after all the turmoil and torment of his approximately two years in office – it 'seemed like twenty' to him – he confessed to understandable feelings of relief. Asked how he felt after handing power formally to Lyons, Scullin replied 'I feel like a school kid going on holidays'.

Labor Tasmanians had endured an equally shattering catastrophe in May at a state election which was dominated by national issues and closely followed the sensational defections of Lyons and Guy. Tasmanian Labor managed a woeful voting share of 34·92% and a third of the Assembly seats in its worst performance since the introduction of the Hare-Clark voting system in 1909. This dismal effort occurred at a uniquely propitious time for oppositions: there was hardly a democratically elected government in the world that managed to survive an election in the early 1930s. Labor in Tasmania was hampered by local divisions which mirrored the FPLP's trauma over economic policy. The majority in the party supported Theodore's expansionary plan, and its creator was invited by Tasmanian ALP leader Ogilvie to participate in the campaign. This was intolerable to Ogilvie's deputy Ben Watkins, a Lyons admirer who resigned in protest and accused Ogilvie of 'most diabolical intrigue'. At the election Watkins regained his seat as an independent. Lyons's prestige in Tasmania and his adherence to straitening economic views, supported by Guy and Watkins, no doubt influenced potential Labor voters in a state where conservative attitudes had always flourished. As 1931 drew to a close Tasmanian Labor was at its lowest ebb ever.

In WA 'Moo-cow' Mitchell's limitations as Premier were being exposed. Before the 1930 election campaign he had given bluff guarantees about reducing unemployment through further agricultural development, and he was baffled that the ills of the Depression refused to yield to his simplistic cure. The ALP in WA continued to be relatively cohesive and, unlike its Tasmanian counterpart, did not have to contest an election between mid-1930 and mid-1931 when any strongly held differences about economic policy would have been difficult to submerge. Collier's shrewd leadership was instrumental in preventing the ructions that scarred the party elsewhere. From the opposition benches he could criticize aspects of the Premiers' Plan although he and some senior colleagues were inclined to favour the conservative economic views advocated by Lyons.

As in WA, Labor in Queensland benefited from being in opposition under an able leader while its opponents grappled in vain with the insuperable problems of the Depression. McCormack had been succeeded as leader in 1929 by capable and determined William Forgan Smith, who as a 24-year-old Scottish painter and decorator had been impressed by Prime Minister Fisher's oratory during his 1911 visit to Britain and had resolved to emulate his emigration to Queensland and involvement in Labor politics; settling in Mackay, Forgan Smith joined the AWU, entered parliament in 1915 and became a minister in 1920. In reviving his party's fortunes after the 1929 defeat Forgan Smith was greatly assisted by the unpopularity of Queensland's Nationalist government. Led by an apostle of Niemeyerism, the Nationalists abolished the rural award, sharply reduced the basic wage, increased working hours from 44 to 48 hours per week, and ardently upheld the Premiers' Plan. Formulating his own response to the Premiers' Plan was a thorny task, but Forgan Smith handled it superbly. His qualified support ensured that Queensland under a future Labor government would not suffer from differential treatment while his expressed willingness to amend its cuts in wages and welfare accorded with his own inclinations and the Queensland labour movement's stated preference for expansionary remedies. His astute, decisive style was also evident in the way he and the like-minded state ALP executive ruthlessly crushed the attempts to organize a Lang Labor offshoot in his state.

Queensland Labor approached the state election in June 1932 confidently. With restored unity and an air of renewed purpose, it achieved a swing of nearly 10% which returned it to office. Especially gratifying was the downfall of the Attorney-General, who had declared his intention to 'ringbark the Arbitration Court' and had claimed that the huge legal fees he received in the Mungana proceedings were justified because that controversy 'smashed the Labour Party in Australia almost beyond mending'. This obnoxious opponent was defeated in South Brisbane by a 31-year-old Railways department clerk, Vince Gair.

The situation was very different in SA. Labor enthusiasts there were so appalled by the performance of 'Slogger' Hill that he and other ALP supporters of

the Premiers' Plan were expelled on 13 August 1931. At a special federal conference shortly afterwards a motion to expel other state MPs supporting the
Premiers' Plan was defeated. This cut no ice in SA, where the expulsions of
13 August were confirmed at the annual conference in September. The aggrieved
outcasts appealed to the federal executive, which eventually allowed all these
appeals. Meanwhile the Hill government had remained in office, sustained by
the guidance, encouragement and funds of conservative powerbrokers.

The internal party strife in SA extended to local branches and was further
complicated by the activities of a Lang Labor faction. This was headed by
brothers Doug and Ken Bardolph, and owed its origins to Doug's cantankerous
involvement in several bitter disputes in the SA ALP well before the Lang plan
was conceived. He and Ken had retained close links with the ALP in their birthplace, Sydney, and Doug's proprietorship of the *South Australian Worker* provided a useful propaganda medium for themselves and Lang. In March 1931 the
Bardolphs arranged for Lang (accompanied by Beasley, Ward, Rae and 'Digger'
Dunn) to visit Adelaide to promote the Lang plan. Prominent trade unionists
and several state Labor MPs gave their imprimatur to Lang Labor, which
enjoyed a triumph at the July 1931 by-election for Adelaide. The vacancy had
arisen because Lang sympathizer Bert Edwards had been gaoled after being
allegedly framed for a homosexual offence; Edwards's defenders blamed his bitter enemy, Attorney-General Denny, who had been labelled a 'rogue' by Niemeyer for asking about the effects of repudiation but was now one of those
expelled for being a Premiers' Plan apologist. But the SA Langites, who were
expelled from the party the next month, followed their success at the Adelaide
by-election with failure at another state by-election and the federal election, and
themselves split into warring groups after these setbacks.

There was also upheaval in the Victorian ALP after some of its leading MPs
refused to disown the Premiers' Plan. Like the Scullin government, the Hogan
ministry had a powerful upper house to contend with – its attempt to obtain
more funds for unemployment relief by increasing taxation was sabotaged by the
Council – but Hogan had the additional problem of depending on an unreliable
group of independents for his majority in the lower house; as he knew, any outlandish measures would result in the withdrawal of their support. In July 1931
there was a second directive from a special state conference (the Hogan government had ignored the earlier one issued in September 1930) to Labor MPs
instructing them to oppose Niemeyerism but Hogan dismissed the instruction as
'stupid and unpatriotic' and announced that the government would carry on
regardless with Premiers' Plan legislation. When the Victorian executive still
refused to discipline the offending Labor MPs, outraged unionists retaliated by
planning to take control of the executive. State president Calwell, whose firm
action had made it difficult for the infiltrating Langites to gain a footing in Victoria, hit back hard against the unionists, and the escalating tensions seemed
likely to produce a destructive schism. Divisions on the Premiers' Plan extended
to branch level. It was opposed by many urban branches; Hogan, a farmer representing a country electorate, was supported on the issue by various rural
branches and by Wren-controlled urban ones in Collingwood and Clifton Hill
(but not by the MLA for Clifton Hill, Blackburn, who was outspoken in his
criticism of both Wren and the Premiers' Plan).

But the hotheads stepped back from the brink, and the federal election disaster
had a profoundly sobering effect. The annual Victorian conference, brought

forward from Easter to January, made some changes to the executive, with Blackburn among the inclusions, and most of the politicians fell into line with the conference's renewed hostility to the Premiers' Plan. The exceptions included Hogan, Bailey (who was another minister holding a country seat) and J.P. Jones, who associated himself proudly with the creation of the Premiers' Plan and had changed considerably since his involvement with the *Tocsin* group in the 1890s. The strain of office undermined the health of Hogan and Jones, who both embarked on recuperative voyages. While Hogan was away his deputy Tunnecliffe was non-committal about Labor's continued adherence to the Premiers' Plan, and consequently the independents withdrew support from the government. At the ensuing election Labor was crushed. Its listless campaign was not helped by the great tension generated by Lang's sensational activities across the border, but Victorian Labor only contested 32 of the 65 Assembly seats, winning 16 (30 in 1929). Jones had been expelled before the election, and four other ministers including Hogan and Bailey were excommunicated after it. Younger members of talent and promise like H.M. Cremean, Attorney-General Slater and assistant minister of Agriculture Reg Pollard lost their seats. Morale in the Victorian ALP was shattered.

Meanwhile Lang, 'as resourceful and reckless and magnetic as ever', was careering on with his unique brand of defiance, demagoguery and desperate scrambling to keep NSW solvent. The federal election results gave the Langites no cause for comfort – except for Theodore's defeat – and Lang now had to joust with Lyons and Latham in Canberra instead of the more conciliatory Scullin. When Lang admitted that NSW was once again unable to meet its interest repayments, the Lyons government paid the debt and commenced legal proceedings against NSW for the amount owing. Scullin had taken similar action when Lang defaulted earlier, but the Lyons government went further and pushed through parliament the Financial Agreement Enforcement Act, which required banks to remit to the federal government any money they possessed or received that belonged to NSW. Lang responded theatrically by sending NSW public servants, escorted by police, to transfer large amounts from banks to the NSW Treasury. He also challenged the Enforcement Act in the High Court. Lang was relying on Evatt and McTiernan siding with the Chief Justice, a renowned state-righter, to form a majority in favour of disallowing the act. Evatt and the Chief Justice agreed with NSW that the act was invalid, but they were the dissenting minority as the remaining judges, including McTiernan, held that it was validly within the national government's constitutional powers. Many Langites simplistically cursed McTiernan as a traitor, muttering that 'we picked the wrong man', but during his long term on the bench McTiernan remained a supporter of extensive national government powers consistent with Labor's ultimate aims. After his setback in the High Court, the Big Fella was sustained by an enormous rally of ecstatic Langites at the Sydney Town Hall. He had convinced them that he was their sole defender against attempts to reduce their living standards to the level of 'Argentine gypsies'.

For some time the NSW Governor, Sir Philip Game, had been under pressure from diehard conservatives to deal with Lang. As early as March 1931 the SA Governor was urging Game to have no qualms about dismissing Lang: 'when all this scum is out of the way confidence will be restored and we shall go ahead'. Fortunately for Lang, Game did not (unlike his would-be advisers) see Lang as a vulgar vagabond, and to the chagrin of society right-thinkers he approved the Premier's request for 25 additional appointments to the Legislative Council.

But Game had to consider the escalating likelihood of civil war in NSW. In March 1932 the New Guard sabotaged Lang's official opening of the Sydney Harbour Bridge. More subversively, it was contemplating a coup d'état against the Lang government. 'The time is finished for talk', its leader declared ominously. Bills, proclamations and circulars were the instruments of war in the battle between the federal government and the Langites for control of NSW's finances, but paper ammunition seemed likely to give way to more lethal weaponry. The *Labor Daily* warned the Lyons government that 'civil war was the logical outcome of its mad purpose', and commented menacingly when the High Court validated the Enforcement Act that 'the war is on. Labor takes up the challenge'. Burly unemployed timber workers were assigned to guard the NSW Treasury, and Lang authorized the recruitment from the state public service of an army of 25 000 special constables. 'If it is fight they want we will give it to them', threatened 'Digger' Dunn. Wild rumours swept through Sydney and Canberra, and panic-stricken citizens feared bloodshed. Early in May Garden was bashed at his home in the middle of the night by eight members of a New Guard inner section, the Fascist Legion. More significant were the activities of the Old Guard, which was preparing – apparently in concert with the Lyons ministry – to shed its cloak of strict secrecy and intervene in the crisis. When the Lyons cabinet sanctioned an audacious raid on the NSW Treasury, the Old Guard was involved in the proposed operation, but it was cancelled because of the Langites' certain resistance. Within a fortnight the Old Guard was poised to mobilize, and the prospect of carnage in Sydney streets was imminent. Game, who was aware of these sinister developments, found a legal pretext to justify Lang's dismissal on Friday 13 May, the day before the Victorian election. The Big Fella went quietly. He did not want blood to stain the wattle either.

The election was fought with passionate commitment. Conservatives made hysterical predictions of the consequences if the Langites won, and some newspapers banned Lang Labor advertisements. The Langites retaliated by plastering posters throughout Sydney:

LANG IS RIGHT
DON'T READ THE DAILY TELEGRAPH

Zeal and resilience marked the Big Fella's campaign. Its highlight was an amazing gathering at Moore Park of over 200 000 people who rapturously agreed that 'LANG IS RIGHT'. He ignored a Lang Labor conference instruction to make socialization his main campaign theme. The New Guard distinguished itself by kidnapping a Lang supporter and branding the word 'RED' into his forehead with nitrate of silver. The Langites were annihilated at the polls. They won only 24 of the 90 seats (55 in 1930), and for the first time since Labor's formation in 1891 it held no rural non-mining seat. Not even W.F. Dunn could withstand the flood; his defeat caused the only break in the four decades he represented the electors of Mudgee. Cahill lost Arncliffe with a swing of over 20%. The makeshift federal Labor organization was outgunned, managing a voting share of only 4·26% and no seats, although Coleman, having been unseated by a Langite in December, ran Lang uncomfortably close in his own seat. A tremendous surge of relief, extending well beyond NSW, greeted the demise of the Langites. The Old Guard melted into the shadows.

Labor was devastated by the Great Depression. The Scullin government was dreadfully unlucky to take office when it did, but its wretched record underlined crucial shortcomings in the ALP. Party members' theoretical control of Labor MPs was again shown to have acute limitations in practice, and the ALP's fundamental objectives were called into question. The notion that Labor's role was to build a fairer society by civilizing capitalism, and maybe abolishing it eventually, crumbled when capitalism itself foundered and Labor not only had no coherent overall strategy ready to implement but was unable unitedly to fashion one during the crisis. The bankruptcy of ALP ideas was again apparent. Denunciations of the 'Money Power' and bogeymen like Niemeyer, Gibson, Bruce, 'Baron' Brown and Murdoch were no substitute for concentrated analysis of the system Labor was striving to change. 'We, as a party, in Australia write no books, produce no pamphlets and set up no research', lamented R.S. Ross. In mid-1932 the unions were powerless, and unemployment, poverty and insecurity plagued the lives of hundreds of thousands of the Australians the ALP was supposed to protect. The party's leaders were scarred by their ordeal during the Depression. Brennan's astonishing defeat in Batman was like a 'bereavement' in his family. Beasley was adjusting to the nickname 'Stabber Jack' which was to haunt him for the rest of his life. Parker Moloney's notable achievement of negotiating the first Australian trade treaty with Canada seemed ancient history when 'he was left virtually destitute' after losing his seat. 'I'm finished', wrote Anstey, totally disillusioned with his party and 'the hopeless, spineless mob you try to serve'; his 'hopes. . .had turned to ashes and everything was sour'. Years later Scullin was asked if he would pen some memoirs of his government. 'It nearly killed me to live through it', he replied. 'It would kill me to write about it.'

39. Niemeyer's medicine. (by George Finey)

40. John Curtin with Frank Anstey. (*National Library*)

41. The Beasley Langite group bring down the Scullin government. (by Will Donald)

42. 'Stabber Jack' Beasley. (*National Library*)

43. Premier Lang dismissed by Governor Game. (by George Finey; *National Library*)

44. John Curtin, with his private secretary Eric Tonkin (left) and press secretary Don Rodgers (right), on the campaign trail in Adelaide. (*National Library*)

45. Premier Forgan Smith in control in Queensland. (by Noel Lambert; *Oxley Library*)

8 'There is a Huge Job to Do': Gradual Recovery, 1932–1941

BOTH AUSTRALIA AND the ALP recovered slowly from the Depression. Unemployment descended sluggishly from its Everest peak of 1932. In 1939, when the outbreak of the Second World War betokened grisly new employment possibilities, there were still around 300 000 Australians without work. The social devastation of these years produced the 'Depression generation', a label covering those long-suffering Australians – Labor's traditional supporters in the main – who emerged from the 1930s with deep scars and warped expectations. After the FPLP's distressing time in government under Scullin, it spent a decade in opposition while Australia was ruled in an increasingly undistinguished manner described by one of Lyons's own ministers as 'government of the feeble for the greedy'. As in Canberra, each state government by the end of 1933 had the same political complexion as five years before. From mid-1931 each of the seven governments then in office was removed by the voters at the next opportunity, and in each instance the losers remained a long time in the wilderness. In the states where Labor's internal ructions over the Premiers' Plan were most severe, SA and Victoria, the ALP remained out of office for over a decade afterwards. For Labor in NSW the 1930s were stormy and barren years as the individualistic, destructive reign of Lang and his followers continued to bedevil the ALP in his own state and beyond.

The anti-Lang federal ALP organization made little headway in NSW. The Langites retained the allegiance of all major unions apart from the AWU. The fledgling federal NSW branch struggled to obtain adequate finance and to make an impression on the voters in Labor strongholds. Politics were raw, crude and unsophisticated in Sydney's inner suburbs, where Lang 'maintained popularity by his capacity to coin a phrase of revolt and to manufacture dramatic confrontations'. Langite 'basher gangs' violently disrupted federal Labor meetings. The general secretary of federal Labor's NSW branch, lifelong ALP activist Bill Colbourne, was on a harbour ferry on his way to a public meeting when he heard five bruisers, who had not recognized him out of context, discussing their plans to assault him and wreck the meeting. Prominent among Colbourne's colleagues in the unequal fight in NSW was an unlikely assortment of outcasts united in their hostility to Lang. Bailey was one, working alongside such former enemies as Catts, Gardiner, Griffith and even Willis, who had fallen out spectacularly with

Lang. Theodore lent low-key support, while resisting repeated entreaties to stand again for parliament. Much of the drive, idealism and commitment came from Coleman and Chifley. Coleman was temperamentally unsuited to the role of factional warrior, but selflessly immersed himself in the hostilities. He flayed the Langites' 'graft, patronage and corruption' orchestrated by the 'vicious, mercenary, arrogant and immoral' Inner Group. Coleman's endeavours contributed to his sudden death aged 41, and Chifley, who had resolved in 1931 'to fight Lang until I had seen him out of the Labour Movement', succeeded Coleman in the stressful, unrewarding position of president of the federal ALP in NSW.

Chifley and his frail, embattled organization enjoyed one memorable highlight in their war against the Langites. At the 1934 federal election Lang Labor boosted its strength in the Representatives to nine when Garden defeated E.C. Riley in Cook and Joe Clark overcame Blakeley in Darling. The solitary NSW MHR left in the FPLP was the Newcastle veteran David Watkins, but he died in 1935 after over 40 consecutive years as a Labor MP in state and federal parliament. Federal Labor endorsed Dave Watkins junior for the by-election, and he managed to triumph over his Langite rival despite the FPLP's meagre assistance and Lang's confident involvement in the campaign. Chifley was jubilant. He had campaigned so vigorously against the Langites that he permanently damaged his vocal cords and spoke huskily for the rest of his life. In the by-election his significant tactical contributions included using recorded speeches by Labor's successful Queensland Premier Forgan Smith, and asking Charlton, a respected figure in the electorate, to come out of retirement and support Watkins.

The struggle between federal Labor and the Langites extended to the newspaper world. When the Depression engulfed Australia the capital, machinery and Macdonell House premises of Labor Papers Limited were still awaiting the AWU's decision to proceed with its own chain of newspapers. The vociferous support the Big Fella derived from his *Labor Daily* and the parlous state of the AWU-backed anti-Lang NSW branch induced Bailey and others to argue within the AWU that at last the time had come to roll the presses. The *World* commenced publication as a Sydney afternoon daily in October 1931. Boote wrote its inaugural editorial, promising that it 'will combat with all its strength attempts to disrupt and defeat the party, both within and without the gates of the movement'. The *Labor Daily* was scornful. The *World* had well-credentialled staff, but attracted insufficient advertisers, and was soon in trouble. Theodore was approached for help. His nifty scheme to sell the *World* netted him a tidy profit and left the AWU with a large overdraft and its great dream in ruins, yet nonetheless relieved not to emerge even worse off. Having decided not to pursue a political career further, Theodore was in the process of amassing a fortune from business activities in cahoots with men like John Wren and newspaper magnate Frank Packer. In mid-1933 the machinery that printed the *World* was used by the Packer-Theodore company to launch the *Australian Women's Weekly*. Later that year the *World*'s initial editor confessed sorrowfully to Boote that 'I feel utterly hopeless regarding the future of Labor'.

Scullin's poor health during the winter of 1935 forced him to resign as FPLP leader. Since the 1931 débâcle he had carried Labor's banner nobly, without emulating the hardhitting vitality he had displayed in opposition during the later 1920s. He was aware that his unhappy experience of the difficulties and pressures Lyons was facing had induced him to moderate some of his criticism of the government, whereas a new leader who did not possess that painfully acquired knowledge might be more effective. On 23 September, at the first FPLP meeting after his decision was announced, Scullin was absent ill when caucus unanimously requested him to reconsider, but he confirmed that his colleagues would need a new leader. It was generally assumed that the experienced, energetic and likeable deputy FPLP leader, Forde, would be chosen. Political pundits felt his election was even more assured because the man regarded as his strongest rival, Makin, happened to be then representing the FPLP at an international parliamentary gathering in London. It was a great surprise when Forde lost the leadership ballot by one vote to Curtin.

This unexpected result was the culmination of Curtin's remarkable comeback since losing his seat in 1931. 'What's the bloody good of being here?' he had snapped during his ordeal as a Scullin government backbencher when he felt cooped up in Canberra, powerless to prevent that ineffectual government bleeding to death. Despite his attempts to escape into alcoholic binges, some of his colleagues retained their faith in him. He was a different man after resuming family life at Cottesloe, where he recovered his stength, zest and belief in the party's future. 'What do we do now?' Calwell asked him after the FPLP had been decimated in 1931. 'The Labor Party has to be reincarnated', Curtin replied firmly. Like Chifley, he urged Theodore to return to active politics, writing fervently that the workers are yearning for someone 'to inspire them with hope and guidance' and 'the hour is now'. Theodore, however, made clear that although his self-confidence was undiminished, his 'faith in the intelligence of the workers is sadly shaken' while they were still 'deifying the charlatan Lang'. Curtin found congenial employment as the *Westralian Worker*'s sport reporter, and kept in touch with political developments, reading the Commonwealth Hansard avidly. After the 1933 WA election returned Labor to office, Premier Collier appointed Curtin to a committee charged with preparing WA's complex case for greater federal government assistance. A senior Treasury official raved about Curtin's contribution, enthusing to Collier that he was 'a genius with figures'. 'There is not one thing he could not master if he put his mind to it' was Collier's rejoinder. This glowing tribute from an old friend was vindicated by Curtin's success in putting his drinking days behind him.

He recaptured Fremantle in 1934 and returned to Canberra. Back in parliament he was in fine form, eloquent and analytical without the erratic tendencies of his previous term. Holloway felt that the party would be best served if Scullin's successor had, unlike Forde, opposed the Premiers' Plan. Furthermore, Holloway believed that Curtin, who had worked alongside him as long ago as the hectic days of the anti-conscription fight, possessed outstanding talents which Forde lacked. Holloway headed a caucus group including 'Texas' Green and Riordan which began to gather support for Curtin. But nagging doubts gnawed. Had he conquered the grog? An emissary approached Curtin. After perfunctorily confirming that alcohol had not been a problem for years and never would be again, Curtin asked the purpose of the inquiry. He was stunned when he heard. Armed with the vital promise, the Holloway group mustered the numbers.

The crucial vote they needed came from an unlikely source. With Anstey retiring, the safe ALP seat of Bourke became vacant. Curtin tried to persuade Anstey to continue but to no avail, and had the mortification of seeing the preselection for a watertight seat that had been offered to him (as a less precarious alternative to Fremantle) go to Maurice Blackburn, a man he disliked. Blackburn came into the Representatives with his close friend Arthur Drakeford, a former engine driver who defeated Fenton in Maribyrnong. As head-counting proceeded prior to the leadership ballot, Drakeford, who was in the pro-Curtin camp, approached Blackburn about voting for Curtin. 'It's the last thing I'll do' was Blackburn's sharp reply. Next day, however, Blackburn notified Drakeford that if he really believed in Curtin he could lodge a proxy vote for Curtin on Blackburn's behalf. Drakeford did so. Without his proxy the ballot would have been tied at 10 votes each.

Curtin took over the leadership of a party well and truly in the doldrums. Its federal and Victorian secretary was his old friend Danny McNamara, who had Curtin as best man when he married on May Day 1915. Curtin and McNamara were acutely aware of Labor's dismal record since 1915. No longer could ALP members take pride in the knowledge that their party was leading the world. The British Labour Party had broken through in 1924 to form its first shortlived government, and formed another in 1929, before the pressures of governing during the Depression produced a split with several leaders defecting like Lyons. In New Zealand the Labour Party took office for the first time in 1935; unfettered by such hindrances as a constitution reserving vital powers to regional authorities, it introduced a wide range of reforms and governed with sufficient competence to be re-elected. Furthermore, although few other countries possessed Labour parties comparable to the ALP in that trade unions were affiliated, in two nations that did – Sweden and Norway – Labour parties broke through in the 1930s and established themselves as the natural governing parties.

Why did the ALP struggle after promising so much in its initial quarter-century? The calamities of the Great War and the Depression were partly responsible. Also, the unwieldy, three-tiered Australian system of government, with its outdated apparatus of upper houses and inflexible constitution, posed a profound obstacle to reform. But Labor's own shortcomings had contributed to its decline since 1915. The most glaring weakness – in sharp contrast to the British Labour Party – was the ALP's intellectual bankruptcy. Practical men predominated in the Australian labour movement, where intellectuals were distrusted as flighty and unreliable and education tended to be downgraded even during the party's more enlightened and successful eras such as the Ryan government in Queensland. There were a small number of newspapers preaching to a proportion of the party faithful, but little systematic effort was made to inform wavering or potential ALP voters about Labor's viewpoint. The damaging consequences were clearly evident during the Depression, when Labor had no blueprint ready to implement, very few of its MPs had alternative ideas to the manifestly inadequate precepts of orthodox finance, and large numbers of its disillusioned supporters were unaware that the Senate and the Commonwealth Bank board had rendered the Scullin government virtually powerless. The exchange of ideas with equivalent parties overseas continued to be minimal – apart from New Zealand, they were too far away and contact was too expensive. The ALP platform was still headed by the objective inserted in 1921, the 'Socialization of Industry, Production, Distribution and Exchange', although the accompanying 'Methods' had been watered down in 1927. Sincere Labor socialists thought far too many party luminaries ignored the objective. This lip-service was symbolized in NSW, where the socialization units had prospered with increasing momentum until they were ruthlessly crushed by Lang's Inner Group. Lang's hatchet man, the controversial ex-Communist Garden, proclaimed the units' demise in a typically outlandish peroration which became paraphrased for posterity as 'Lang is greater than Lenin'. Labor enthusiasts critical of their party's insufficient radicalism often blamed the pervasive influence of the AWU. That giant union dominated the party in Queensland, SA and WA, and also in the federal sphere. At least half the FPLP during the Scullin government was at some stage connected to the AWU.

Even worse for Labor idealists was the flagrant graft and chicanery practised by some prominent party identities. The municipal council in the Melbourne inner suburb of Richmond, an ALP stronghold with reputedly the largest party branch in the nation in 1931, was involved in a series of scandalous incidents during the 1930s. Much of the opprobrium attached to the notorious Loughnan family, who were allegedly closely linked to Wren and 'Squizzy' Taylor. Con Loughnan, irascible and hard-drinking, was mayor of Richmond during the 1930s. While controlled by the Loughnans and their associates, the council displayed a weird sense of priorities as Richmond residents were being devastated by the Depression. Ratepayers' funds were frittered away on lavish functions, hired cars and ostentatious town hall renovations. Unemployment relief was channelled to a privileged few known to the ruling clique, who appointed themselves to council sinecures and public housing. Council meetings were riotous, and police attended regularly. Ballot-rigging was rife, and Con Loughnan's brother Jim frequently displayed his dexterity as a returning officer. After Con Loughnan's re-election to the mayoralty was prevented when a councillor changed his vote, the smouldering ex-mayor nursed his grievance for years before bludgeoning the twister with an axe. In 1935 the Victorian ALP executive could no longer ignore the goings-on in Richmond, and enforced tighter procedures. It was too late for some Labor idealists who had already withdrawn heartbroken from the party.

Sleaziness permeated Victorian politics during the 1930s. In 1935 Wren influenced the Country Party to withdraw its support from the UAP in order to form a government itself with Labor support. Calwell later claimed that it 'was my idea, and mine alone', and that Wren had reacted enthusiastically when Calwell suggested it to him. It was a reflection of Victoria's distorted electoral system that the Country Party's voting share of 13·71% not only gave it 20 of the 65 Assembly seats but enabled it to form a minority government, while Labor could win only 17 seats with 37·93% of the vote. Labor's alliance with the Country Party was also a tribute to Wren's influence. He was close to the new Country Party Premier, Dunstan, and some of his ministerial colleagues including ex-ALP renegades Hogan and Bailey, as well as Labor's leader Tunnecliffe and a number of his followers. Dunstan made a few calculated gestures to ALP objectives and remained Premier with Labor's support for seven years. A crafty miser who proudly boasted that he had never read a book, Dunstan was no doubt assisted by the prevailing mood in the aftermath of a depression attributed to lavish borrowing and grand development schemes. In such circumstances frugality was never more likely to be judged virtuous, but Dunstan's unscrupulousness and penny-pinching made his lengthy reign disastrous for Victorian education, health and welfare. Corruption also reared its ugly head, with Labor MPs mentioned in bribery allegations; Dunstan's cynical and belated reaction to the accusations was influenced by Wren. Cain succeeded Tunnecliffe as leader in 1937 despite his abhorrence of Wren's influence in the party. Like many other ALP Victorians, Cain felt that Labor's subservience to Dunstan was distasteful, unproductive and betrayed party traditions. He was at loggerheads with his deputy, H.M. Cremean. A devout Catholic, Cremean was a close associate of Wren and Calwell, had been mayor of Richmond, and was MLA for Wren-controlled Clifton Hill for over a decade. Wren, Dunstan and Cremean formed a powerful triumvirate.

Curtin did not underestimate the task ahead of him.

There is a huge job to do. . .The Leader of the Party should be a young snoozer of thirty or thirty-five. He should not have his inner force dissipated by ten thousand conferences with all their silk tearing. However. . .I know what I want to do and I am going to try and do that.

Soon after he became leader he embarked on a crusade 'to revive the spirit and unity of the Labor movement'. During parliamentary recesses and at other available times Curtin toured diverse regions of his vast country, addressing cynical executives and meagerly attended meetings of local branches, encouraging, persuading, cajoling and instilling much-needed confidence. His only assistant on these trips was press secretary Don Rodgers.

Staying in second-rate pubs, a different room every second night, travelling by train [in the evening], Curtin and Rodgers travelled thousands of miles around Australia. No expenses were allowed. They had no car – Curtin had a gold pass for free travel on the railways. The Party was broke and there were very few ways of attracting money.

Although he was still feeling his way as leader, his integrity, dedication, knowledge, agile mind and straightforward manner made a fine impression on party members who met or heard him during his travels.

Curtin's other immediate priority was to make peace with the Langites. Although he regarded Lang with distaste, it was clear that Labor could not hope to prosper nationally without some resolution of the internecine strife in the oldest state containing the most federal seats. There was significant support for Lang emanating from ALP elements in Victoria, SA and Tasmania. To the chagrin of Chifley and his gallant band fighting Lang in his own state, some Victorians including Blackburn visited NSW to appear alongside the Big Fella on the hustings. In order to bring the Langites back into the ALP, some of the appeasers outside NSW were even prepared to weaken the authority of the ALP's federal bodies, but Curtin regarded that proposal as an unjustifiable price to pay for unity. While welcoming the Langites' desire to rejoin, the new leader declared that the ALP 'rules are not capable of special interpretation for any special group'. A special federal conference in February 1936 readmitted the Langites, who gave appropriate assurances of loyalty and submission to federal ALP authority. They had their own sound reasons for approving the rapprochement after a severe defeat at the state election on 11 May 1935, the very day Queensland Labor under Forgan Smith had a pointedly contrasting electoral triumph. Although Chifley's federal Labor organization had only captured 5% of the overall votes in 1935 (Chifley himself contested Lang's seat of Auburn, polling respectably but unsuccessfully), Lang and his cronies realized that they needed every one of those votes to have any prospect of regaining office. Chifley and his associates understandably resented the return to the ALP of their detested adversary. They knew the Big Fella too well to expect anything other than vindictive retribution now that control of the official NSW branch was to be ceded to him.

Despite disheartening episodes and eras the ALP has displayed an admirable resilience throughout its history. With the party's disappointing performance since 1915 very much in mind, one observer concluded that the ALP

has been burdened with careerists, turncoats, hypocrites, outright scoundrels, stuffy functionaries devoid of sense and imagination, bellowing enemies of critical intelligence, irritatingly self-righteous clowns bent on enforcing suburban points of view, pussy-footers, demagogues, stooges for hostile outside groups and interests, aged and decayed hacks and ordinary blatherskites.

Nevertheless, that same observer noted, Labor had retained its idealism and purposefulness. Another commentator, a journalist who witnessed the destruction of the Scullin government at close quarters, was struck by

the zeal and sacrifice of scores of thousands of humble little people who work for nothing but their faith in 'the movement'...the truly incredible thing is how staunchly and unendingly this adherence to a political faith goes on blossoming, in the face of betrayals and treacheries, greedy self-seekings, avarice for place and power, arrogance and money-pride.

One local party branch renowned for the verve of its enthusiasts was Coburg. Activists in this northern suburb of Melbourne were committed and radical, and it was appropriate that they were represented by MPs of the calibre and idealism of Anstey, Blackburn and Frank Keane MLA. But time and again Coburg branch members felt let down by the state executive. They were appalled by its reluctance to take action against Labor MPs who ratified the Premiers' Plan. Workers were 'getting tired of paying money to unions and ALP branches to put Labor men into parliament to cut wages', asserted a Coburg spokesman. During the 1930s Coburg was one of a number of Victorian ALP branches increasingly disenchanted by the state executive's lack of dynamism, indifference to rank-and-file concerns and intolerance of views at odds with its own.

Much of the ALP's renewal came from young Australians determined to prevent a recurrence of the hardships of the Depression. Fred Daly grew up in comfortable circumstances on a farm at Currabubula NSW, but his father's death threw his family into poverty. Daly was told that the ALP was 'the only way to a better way of life for those without wealth, power or influence' (although that advice from Daly's cousin would have been vehemently disputed by devotees of the Communist Party, which was then flourishing in industrial areas as a direct result of Labor's failure during the Depression). After joining the ALP Daly became 'dedicated to the cause...and gave it preference at all times over all other activities'. On the west coast of Tasmania Eric Reece, a miner like his father and grandfather, covered so many miles on his bicycle searching for work during the Depression that he had to stuff straw into the tyres in place of inner tubes. He later joined the AWU and won ALP preselection for a federal seat in 1940. Gil Duthie grew up on a Wimmera wheat farm where the Depression was 'a nightmare of debt and insecurity'. As a trainee Methodist minister, he glimpsed even more harrowing effects of the Depression in Melbourne slums, and he decided to join the ALP although he 'knew only a handful of ministers had made such a decision'. Clyde Cameron imbibed labour history from his mother before leaving school in 1928 aged 14 to become a bushworker like his father. During the Depression he 'was among that army of unemployed which was forced to live on a miserable dole of 4 shillings and 10 pence a week'. By 1940 he was state AWU secretary in SA and the youngest office-bearer to attend the AWU federal convention since 'Red Ted' Theodore. This quartet was typical of many others whose activity in the labour movement was initiated or intensified by the Depression.

These newcomers looked up to Labor veterans who were still active, like Dr Maloney. Throughout the 1930s Melbourne's less fortunate citizens continued to benefit from the humanitarianism of the popular 'Little Doctor', who had represented them in parliament since 1889. His eightieth birthday was commemorated in 1934 at a celebrated affair at Melbourne Town Hall. The following year he made a film advocating milk for creches and free kindergartens. At the age of 83 he visited Russia. In 1940 he led the eight-hour-day parade in Melbourne. Since he showed no inclination to retire, the 1930s were frustrating years for a person with Calwell's parliamentary ambitions. Calwell was already referring to the electors of Melbourne presumptuously as 'my constituents', and trying to ignore the jibes that the mourners at his funeral would include the effervescent, seemingly ageless 'Little Doctor'. Meanwhile Calwell maintained his pre-eminence as an ALP powerbroker. Schoolteacher and award-winning debater Frank McManus attended his first state ALP conference in 1932:

> For two days I gazed and wondered. On the third day Arthur Calwell introduced me to one of his supporters and said to him 'Take Frank for a drink'. I was taken to a union office, given two beers, taken to the door of the polling room and instructed to go in and vote for the candidates on a list handed to me. It was my first lesson in political organisation.

In August 1940 Dr Maloney finally died, and Calwell duly succeeded him. Bound for Canberra at last, he was 'strutting around like a "peacock with two tails"' now that he had 'realized his life's ambition'.

Other legendary veterans from the 1890s were still inspiringly busy, notably Labor's outstanding propagandist, Henry Boote. In 1934 Maloney warmly saluted the fortieth anniversary of Boote's Labor journalism: 'I wish there were a thousand like you', he enthused. Another anniversary tribute to Boote came from Demaine, who in his seventies had extended his activities beyond the production of the Maryborough *Alert* each week and the presidency of the Queensland ALP executive he had held since 1916. He became mayor of Maryborough at the age of 74, and was the oldest MP to enter the Queensland Assembly when he became MLA for Maryborough aged 78. When he died in August 1939 he was still secretary of the Labor Party's Maryborough branch as he had been at its inception nearly half a century earlier. His old comrade Silver Collings was another Queenslander defying advancing years. A sprightly 67 when he entered the Senate in mid-1932, Collings managed to combine his Senate duties with his role as Queensland ALP organizer and much of the state secretary's responsibilities when Lewis McDonald's health deteriorated. Collings had also assisted with the organization of the federal ALP's troubled NSW branch in its early days. In 1935 he became FPLP leader in the Senate.

Collings was part of the Queensland ALP machine which reigned supreme in that state throughout the decade following its return to office in mid-1932. At Queensland's 1935 election Labor annihilated its opponents, gaining its second highest voting share ever and 46 of the 62 Assembly seats. The next two elections reduced this overwhelming ALP majority only slightly, and Labor still held 41 seats in 1941. Forgan Smith was Premier throughout this period, directing affairs with a masterly grip that established him as one of the party's finest leaders and prompted frequent rumours that he would transfer to federal politics. The AWU remained more in control in Queensland than ever. All the Forgan Smith ministers elected in 1932 had close AWU connections except former railwayman and grocer Ned Hanlon, and nine of those initial 10 ministers were still in cabinet in 1939. The Premier enjoyed a close rapport with Queensland AWU secretary

Clarrie Fallon, a tough, astute political operator who succeeded Demaine as state ALP president. Forgan Smith and Fallon dominated the increasingly powerful executive committee which managed the Queensland ALP. Between them they kept the ALP machine humming so smoothly that towards the end of Johnny Mullan's second lengthy term as Queensland's Attorney-General he began spending considerable time at his Surfers Paradise home where there was no telephone, disarmingly explaining that if the Premier really needed him the local police would let him know.

Forgan Smith's achievements in economic development underpinned Labor's revival in Queensland. His successful challenge to the pessimism of the Premiers' Plan reinforced the spreading realization that the conservatives and traditional economists had been mistaken in advocating it, and that more expansionary remedies – such as Theodore had advocated and Forgan Smith implemented – would have generated a more humane and effective recovery from the Depression. Like Theodore, Forgan Smith had a profound concern for the unemployed, and alleviating their lot was one of his highest priorities in politics: 'If the Labor Movement cannot deal with the problems of unemployment, then the movement will have failed', he told the 1930 federal conference. As Premier he raised the weekly payments received by relief workers to the basic wage, financing this through a graduated income tax. He initiated a vigorous public works programme which boosted employment opportunities and provided Queensland with major constructions of lasting worth. One of the most notable was the decision to transfer the University of Queensland from its cramped temporary accommodation to a new site at St Lucia. Forgan Smith had founded a faculty of Agriculture at the university when minister for Agriculture in 1926, and the government he led established further new faculties in Medicine, Veterinary Science and Dentistry. The creation of these new faculties was part of the co-ordinated development of the university and Queensland's health services. As the inaugural minister for Health and Home Affairs, Hanlon displayed energy and skill in revitalizing Queensland's administration of health and welfare. In 1938 Forgan Smith claimed that Queensland had 'the highest wage system, the best conditions of labour and the lowest unemployment' in Australia.

A feature of Forgan Smith's reign was his willingness to clamp down firmly on any ALP dissidents. At times in the ALP's history the virtue of solidarity has been a smokescreen purporting to justify excessive conformism. Forgan Smith and Fallon defended their rigid control by pointing to the destabilization of Queensland Labor governments during the 1920s by the actions of disaffected sectors of the labour movement. Under the Forgan Smith government the activities of Communists, reputed Communists and other militants in the unions and unemployed groups were closely scrutinized, and drastic emergency powers were inserted into the State Transport Act; Labor MPs sensed as troublesome had their ministerial ambitions blocked and were sometimes confronted with a preselection contest. Backbenchers out of favour included Gair, postal worker and active unionist Frank Waters and experienced ex-minister Larcombe, who was responsible for a caucus motion carried against the wishes of Forgan Smith and Fallon directing that awards and other rights removed while Labor was in opposition should be restored by legislation. Claims that Forgan Smith had dictatorial tendencies were understandable when his ministers lined up in deferential guards of honour at the railway station as the Premier began or ended trips outside Queensland, and when he customarily doled out their servings in the parliamentary dining room. Yet he kept consulting, aware of the hazards of losing touch with party and electorate. When a decision was made, however, he demanded loyalty and obedience.

Although Forgan Smith's authority was rarely challenged, he was unable to prevent the erosion of ALP support at the 1938 state election by the newly formed Protestant Labour Party. The Protestant activists complained that Catholics enjoyed a disproportionate influence in the Queensland government. They were critical of Archbishop Duhig's closeness to the Premier, who was reared as a Presbyterian but had long ago forsaken his religious beliefs. They also contrasted the proportion of Catholics in the general population (less than one-fifth) with the proportion of Catholics in caucus (27 out of 46) and cabinet (7 out of 10). Sensing trouble, Forgan Smith brought the 1938 election forward. Even so, the Protestant Labour Party gained 8·75% of the vote, slashing Gair's majority, giving Hanlon a fright, and capturing the seat of Kelvin Grove from Frank Waters. But in 1941 the ALP recaptured Kelvin Grove (with a different candidate after the executive refused to endorse Waters) and the sectarian offshoot faded into oblivion.

Labor was also well on top in Tasmania in the later 1930s. As in Queensland, Labor returned to office in Tasmania at the next state election after the Scullin government's downfall and performed so impressively in government under a charismatic premier that it received a resounding endorsement from the voters at the following election. Ogilvie governed Tasmania with style and panache, although a continuing succession of controversies during his public career endowed him with a Theodore-like reputation for unscrupulousness as well as brilliance and fluent oratory. His deputy, E.J.C. Dwyer-Gray, MHA for Denison since 1928, was another colourful character. Born in Dublin in 1870, Dwyer-Gray was the son of a politician, and involved himself in Irish journalism and politics before migrating to Australia, where he became a flamboyant propagandist for the labour movement, although his prickly personality and bursts of heavy drinking made his career in Labor journalism a chequered one. After one row resulted in his temporary expulsion from the party, he moved to Sydney where he worked for Lang. Returning to Hobart in 1925, he edited a new Labor weekly the *People's Voice*, later the *Voice*, for the next 20 years, and was prominent in the serious internal strife (over Langism and the Douglas Credit movement) which bedevilled the Tasmanian ALP during the early 1930s. The Ogilvie ministry also included grocer Robert Cosgrove, who had been in and out of the Assembly as MHA for Denison since 1919, and west coast identity Tom D'Alton.

As Premier, Ogilvie broadened Tasmanian horizons with the most progressive government the island state had ever experienced. Even an unfriendly newspaper conceded that his record in education was 'exceptionally good'; among his reforms in this sphere was the spectacular removal of high school fees within 24 hours of taking office. His government improved health care and modernized hospitals. Housing loans were provided at minimal terms for the needy. Hydro-electric and papermaking development was accelerated. Unemployment relief was increased, much of it devoted to public works including the road to Mount Wellington, an outstanding tourist attraction. Ogilvie was keen to boost Tasmania's tourist potential, and showed a visionary sensitivity to environmental concerns with his condemnation of excessive tree-felling and his legislation (rejected by the Council) to curb advertising hoardings. He even banned unnecessary tooting by motor vehicle drivers, a measure that intrigued Boote, who visited Hobart in 1937 and was amazed by how quiet it was. Ogilvie anticipated other later trends in his skilful use of broadcasting and in his government's ministerial structure: 'Ogilvie dominated cabinet, taking no one portfolio but overseeing all'. According to the Premier, his most significant achievement was to create 'a psychological change' which enabled Tasmanians to discard their 'inferiority complex' and to see themselves and their state no longer as second-class Australians. His overseas trips and incisive comments back home about European leaders and international relations encouraged Tasmanians to widen their outlook. His verve, supremacy and wide-ranging reforms achieved in spite of Legislative Council sabotage were rewarded at the polls in 1937 when his government attracted a tremendous 13% swing and captured 58·67% of the vote, a proportion that Tasmanian Labor had previously never even approached.

Not all Labor Tasmanians revered Ogilvie. His 'abrasive, hedonistic and sometimes cynical personality...created numerous bitter opponents', prominent union leader Jack O'Neill among them, but Ogilvie's greatest foe in the labour movement while he was Premier was an interstate import. Bill Morrow's dedicated leadership of Queensland railway workers had been interrupted by a breakdown induced by overwork, but in 1936, refreshed and recovered, he was persuaded by ARU president Tim Moroney to become Tasmanian ARU secretary in Launceston. Morrow found that 'the industrial outlook and the class consciousness of the workers of this state are approximately twenty years behind the workers of the mainland'. His efforts produced the encouraging response from Ogilvie that cabinet would redress some of his unionists' grievances and pay all railway employees an extra sixpence per day from mid-1937. Morrow's campaigning skills assisted Ogilvie's electoral triumph in February 1937; but later that year they fell out badly when Ogilvie claimed that a federal basic wage award giving all adult male toilers a rise of two shillings a week justified a backdown on the sixpence a day increase for railway workers. Morrow became an outspoken conscience of the Tasmanian labour movement, attacking Ogilvie for deficiencies in the treatment of some of the unemployed and his advocacy of increased defence expenditure as well as the broken assurance to the ARU. But Ogilvie was a formidable adversary, and Morrow found himself expelled from the party in 1938. The Premier persisted with determined efforts to undermine Morrow's principled leadership of the ARU, even offering him the position of Railways Commissioner, but Morrow brushed aside all Ogilvie's subterranean scheming and continued to be a thorn in the government's side.

In 1939 Tasmanians were shocked when their most famous citizens and sparring partners, Premier Ogilvie and Prime Minister Lyons, died of heart trouble within nine weeks of each other. Lyons's death was partly attributable to the stress of combating the restless intrigue of men in his own party, and after his demise the divisiveness in the UAP and Country Party ranks flourished malignantly. The Tasmanian ALP handled its succession very differently. Dwyer-Gray, now 69, was elected stopgap leader on condition that he step down six months later. Cosgrove defeated D'Alton for the deputyship, and duly became Premier when Dwyer-Gray honoured his pledge in December and reverted to deputy and Treasurer. Cosgrove took over a party in high standing with the voters and, thanks to Ogilvie's 1936 reform providing for five-year terms, the next election was not due for another two years.

Compared to the flair of Ogilvie and the mastery of Queensland Labor under Forgan Smith, the only other state Labor government during this period was lacklustre. Collier was past his best in 1933 when he returned to power in WA, where he and the departing Premier, Mitchell, 'went in and out of office like cricket teams going to bat and bowl'. Mitchell not only lost office but his own seat of Northam to Bert Hawke, a lanky 32-year-old ALP rural organizer. Hawke had served a term as MHA for Burra Burra in his native SA while it was governed capably by Labor under Premier Gunn (whose sad decline gathered momentum when the Lyons government dismissed him from the public service; financially embarrassed, separated from his wife and children, he suffered a nervous breakdown and disappeared into obscurity). The influx of talented ALP back-benchers in 1933 also included Queensland-born agricultural expert Frank Wise and schoolteacher John Tonkin. Collier dampened expectations straightaway by declaring that the primary task of recovery from the Depression precluded extensive reform. Although he cleverly defused an agitation animating many WA Depression victims who felt that their state should secede from the rest of Australia, Collier's grip gradually loosened as he became increasingly prone to solitary bursts of heavy drinking. It was rumoured that the secretary of the Premier's department covered his absences by imitating his signature and telephone voice. Six months after Labor scrambled back into office in February 1936 Collier accepted the verdict of his caucus colleagues that he should resign after nine years as Premier and an unbroken 19 years as state ALP leader. He was succeeded by his deputy Jack Willcock, an amiable ex-railwayman with a ponderous, guileless manner. Willcock was no orator and seemed the image of solid, unimaginative respectability with his spectacles, heavy moustache and watchchain, but he was sharper than he looked. After the massive jolt of the Depression the WA electorate valued stringent budgeting rather than grand visions, which suited Willcock's cautious temperament perfectly. His government was re-elected in 1939.

The WA labour movement generally tolerated its sluggish ALP government during the 1930s. Crucial to this attitude were the strong links between the cabinet and the powerful AWU, which recovered from the grievous buffeting of the Depression much more successfully than other WA unions. By 1935 the AWU had over 20% of the votes at the WA branch's general council. The AWU controlled the influential *Westralian Worker*, which contended in 1938 that the Willcock government should be assessed 'not altogether in respect of what it has failed to do. . .but what it has prevented being done'. The government's inactivity provoked no widespread anger, partly because many WA Labor people concluded after having to put up with Mitchell during the Depression that even a pedestrian ALP government was much better than any anti-Labor one.

A shortlived challenge to AWU supremacy came from the Relief and Sustenance Workers' Union (RSWU) headed by T.J. Hughes. RSWU members felt that the AWU was insufficiently aware of issues concerning part-time workers, especially in expecting them to pay the full union fee. In implementing government policy of preference to unionists Employment minister J.J. Kenneally effectively crushed the RSWU by refusing to recognize it. He also assisted the moderate AWU leadership by transferring rebellious militants engaged on relief work to projects in more isolated areas. But disgruntled unionists had their revenge when Hughes successfully stood against Kenneally in East Perth at the 1936 election. Hughes also had some bitter clashes with a longstanding adversary, McCallum (who retired from politics in 1935 when he was Collier's logical successor), but while the AWU held sway it was not easy for even a determined maverick with a long memory like Hughes to defy the cohesively integrated WA labour movement.

WA Labor lost its pioneering woman MP, May Holman, at the 1939 election. She had emerged from her serious 1931 illness with a strengthened commitment to feminist issues within the ALP. After a proposal to have women represented at the party's supreme forum in proportion to their membership in each state was defeated at the 1936 federal conference, May Holman was one of the WA Labor women who urged the following year that each state delegation should be required to include at least one woman. But reforms to federal conference representation, although mooted for decades, still lay well into the future. Although the LWIE had functioned productively during the Depression, another disappointment for feminist ALP activists was that the interstate Labor women's conference had to be postponed because of lack of funds and the turmoil in NSW. But such reverses did not deter May Holman from involving herself in the 1939 election campaign with her customary zest. However, on the way to a campaign meeting the evening before polling day she had a car accident, and her injuries proved fatal. The Holman dynasty in Forrest continued when Ted Holman succeeded his father and sister, and he retained the seat until his retirement in 1947.

During the 1930s Muriel Heagney had no peer in advancing the cause of women in the labour movement. She established the Unemployed Girls' Relief Movement, which formed suburban sewing centres where women received a relief allowance for making clothes for other Depression sufferers; she also set up a jam factory. Her continued efforts to promote equal pay included writing a book *Are Women Taking Men's Jobs?*, helping to found the Council of Action for Equal Pay and appearing before arbitration tribunals. From 1936 the objective of equal pay was included in the ALP platform. Heagney had left Melbourne to live in Sydney before ALP women had their first parliamentary breakthrough in her state of origin when Fanny Brownbill succeeded her husband as MLA for Geelong in 1938. But many years were still to pass before a woman represented Labor in the Tasmanian parliament. When Bill and Kate Morrow attended their initial ALP fund-raising gathering after moving to the island state, Kate thought she was the only woman there until a female platoon marched in from the kitchen armed with the evening's food and then departed, leaving the men to eat it. North Queensland was hardly a trailblazing region for feminism, but the Morrows were not accustomed to such universally accepted rigid segregation.

SA Labor went from bad to worse in the 1930s. 'Slogger' Hill completed his apostasy by relinquishing the premiership just before the 1933 state election and departing for England to take up the position of Agent-General on unusually lucrative terms. Eighteen months later he was forced to resign after scandals concerning those financial arrangements and his administration of the London office. Labor, hopelessly divided, was decimated at the 1933 poll. The official ALP won only six seats, the Langites picked up three and four were taken by the expelled group of Premiers' Plan upholders led formerly by Hill and now by Bob Richards, a devout Methodist from Moonta who represented Wallaroo from 1918 to 1949. The following year Richards and others managed to bring these groups together as a reunited force under the leadership of A.W. Lacey, who had been an affable AWU organizer at Port Pirie from 1916 until he became MHR for Grey in 1922 when he wrested it from the conscriptionist renegade Poynton. As a Scullin government backbencher Lacey had opposed the Premiers' Plan before losing his seat in the FPLP's electoral débâcle of 1931. In state parliament he achieved the unusual feat of being chosen party leader as a newly elected MHA, but after another heavy defeat in 1938 Richards took over the party leadership with Lacey as his deputy. They looked forward to improving Labor's stocks when the SA Premier resigned in 1938 to contest a federal by-election and was replaced by a relatively unknown and seemingly undistinguished orchardist, Tom Playford, but Playford was to remain Premier for the next 26 years.

The 1930s also saw the gradual erosion of Lang's power in NSW. For nearly a decade he had ruled his caucus with such an iron hand that anyone stepping out of line was promptly denied preselection and often expelled from the party as well. The extent of his one-man control was frankly illuminated by a senior minister in his 1930–32 government, Mark Gosling:

> The Cabinet has one Leader, who announces its policy. When he announces it, we follow, and as soon as he announces it we know where we stand. We do not seek to know what he is going to do, and are prepared to surrender our judgement, if necessary, in advance.

Chifley was not the only Labor activist nauseated by such a perversion of party ideals and traditions. It was after the Langites were trounced at the polls in 1935 that some NSW MPs, notably Heffron and Charlie Lazzarini, began defying the Big Fella. Some unionists began querying the wisdom of supporting a leader who could not win elections when unemployment was still high. His unsuccessful scheming to increase his control of the *Labor Daily* and radio station 2KY lost him supporters. His Inner Group was a declining force. Garden theatrically broke with him. Other former close associates including Magrath and even Gosling were now, like Willis, among Lang's greatest enemies.

Nevertheless a long struggle lay ahead before the Big Fella was tamed. Curtin handled the continuing eruptions in NSW patiently, although at one stage he exploded privately that every time he visited NSW he had 'to attend a bloody unity conference'. He was not intimidated by Lang, but he sensed that any imprudent or premature move against the Big Fella risked the emergence of another breakaway Langite party, which would once again set back the ALP cause nationally. The rebellious anti-Lang faction headed by Heffron gradually strengthened, attracting increasing support from influential unionists including some Communists, and received a further boost when Lang suffered another defeat at the 1938 state election. The climax came in 1939 when the Heffronites had the numbers at a rowdy special NSW conference at Newtown convened by the federal executive; prominent Heffronites became the NSW ALP branch's new office-bearers, including vice-president Jack Hughes and secretary Bill Evans. Both were present at a special caucus meeting the following month to supervise the election of Labor's parliamentary leader (a prerogative the recent conference had restored to caucus). In this ballot McKell defeated Lang and Heffron to become NSW Labor's new leader.

Curtin also had to tread warily in another sphere threatening ALP unity. Developments in international relations became more and more alarming during the 1930s. Curtin took over the leadership when the League of Nations' doctrine of collective security faced a stern test with the Italian invasion of Abyssinia. Countries affiliated to the League, like Australia, had to decide whether or not to support the imposition of sanctions (military or economic) against the aggressor. Both the British and New Zealand Labour parties supported action against Italy, but the FPLP – then led, with Scullin absent ill, by Forde – called for 'non-participation' by Australia. 'The control of Abyssinia by any country is not worth the loss of a single Australian life', and Labor 'wants no war on foreign fields for economic treasure', Forde told parliament in a speech reflecting the isolationism pervading the labour movement since the horrors of the Great War. After Curtin became leader the FPLP's basic response did not change, but the nuances did. While affirming Labor's 'perfect loyalty to the League of Nations and support for its high purposes', Curtin justified Australia's 'non-participation' on the basis that 'major powers were not participating and Australia. . .did not have the resources to warrant. . .the grievous risk' of involving itself in a war against Italy.

Uppermost in Curtin's mind was the need for party unity. Without it, Labor's aim of attaining office in order to improve the lot of the common people would remain unfulfilled. Curtin was acutely aware that deeply felt attitudes to communism and Catholicism, together with the ever-present factional feuding, frequently determined the various responses within the labour movement to developments in external affairs during the 1930s. Russia's affiliation with the League in 1934 had induced many staunch anti-Communists in the labour movement, Catholics especially, to take a more jaundiced view of the League's activities. Isolationist tendencies within the ALP were strengthened by pro-Mussolini utterances by Catholic spokesmen and fears that sanctions might involve Australia in full-scale war. On the other hand, sanctions were supported by Ogilvie, Collier, Blackburn, Boote, prominent SA unionists and some ARU leaders in NSW. Blackburn was conspicuous in the Movement Against War And Fascism (MAWAF), which comprised Communists and others more worried by the threat to peace posed by the fascist dictators than concerned about belonging to an organization containing Communists. Although Blackburn's activities were applauded by the MAWAF activists in the Coburg ALP, they were regarded unfavourably by the anti-sanctions Victorian ALP executive, which possessed a fiercely anti-Communist complexion during this period. In September 1935 it ruled that 'no loyal member of the ALP' could be associated with the MAWAF. Blackburn's defiance of the edict resulted in his expulsion by the Victorian executive in December 1935. As usual in such circumstances, the FPLP accepted the state branch's decision, and Blackburn was barred from attending caucus.

Curtin had even more reason to be careful about the Spanish civil war. In that country the reforms of a republican government angered powerful groups including the wealthy, the army and the Catholic church. The army under General Franco revolted against the government in 1936. Radicals from throughout the world, Australia included, volunteered to join the International Brigade fighting alongside the Republicans against Franco's army. In Australia numerous Labor supporters and MAWAF enthusiasts devoted themselves to the cause, which acquired even more virtue in their eyes when Franco received support from Hitler and Mussolini. Australians animated about Spain – which inspired them as Vietnam was to galvanize a later generation of radicals – included people of such varying backgrounds as Andrew Fisher's son, John Wren's daughter, J.G. Latham's son and W.A. Holman's daughter. Within the labour movement, however, Spain was a potentially explosive issue. Many ALP Catholics were reluctant to oppose Hitler or Franco because the greater evil in their eyes was the spread of atheistic communism in Europe which they hoped the fascists might curb. The intensity of feeling on both sides convinced Curtin, a Republican sympathizer, that if he said anything about Spain he might split Labor from top to bottom. He stayed silent. So too did other senior ALP figures. Accordingly, the FPLP responded to the supreme issue for many idealistic radicals in the 1930s by having no policy on Spain at all.

Australia's national security was a vital issue at the 1937 federal election. Curtin avoided focussing on international relations and concentrated on defence, which had far less dangerous connotations for ALP cohesion. At the 1936 federal conference he had influenced a reassessment of his party's defence policy. He had long been impressed by the merits of upgrading Australia's air force as part of an effective self-reliant defence capacity; unlike Labor's opponents, Curtin did not accept that Australia's protection was guaranteed by Britain's much-vaunted Singapore base and navy. Outlining Labor's new defence policy directions to the electors in 1937, Curtin called for greater emphasis on air defence, specifically in aviation development, airport construction and oil exploration, while reiterating Labor's unchanged hostility to conscription and to Australia's involvement in overseas conflicts unless approved by a referendum. His resolute campaign was hampered by Labor's chronic internal strife in NSW. Anti-Labor maximized the spectre of Lang by warning voters to 'look behind the Curtin'. The results were most encouraging for ALP supporters in the Senate, where their party won 16 of the 19 seats contested under the preferential system which still made a winner-take-all outcome likely in each state: on this occasion Labor gained no seats at all in SA, yet scooped the pool in the other five states. Four seats were contested in NSW, where smart ALP operators further exposed the defective Senate voting system by maximizing Labor's harvest of the 'donkey' vote (apathetic electors voting straight down the ballot paper) through the endorsement of the 'Four As'–Amour, Armstrong, Arthur and Ashley. Less encouraging was the result in the Representatives, where Labor secured only 29 of the 74 seats. Still, the party was exhibiting a keener vigour under Curtin, and further electoral improvement was likely provided that the NSW ulcer could be healed.

The later 1930s were years of darkness when another world war became increasingly likely. In 1935 Curtin described the world as 'deranged'. 'All the visible portents are of evil', he added. The situation did not improve. The struggle in Spain ended in defeat for the Republicans, and appeasing the fascist dictators produced only illusory pauses in their frightening strutting towards war. It was an awful time for many radicals, with memories of the Great War and the Depression all too fresh and another holocaust threatening. 'Eyes are only to weep with now' lamented a Melbourne poet, exemplifying the widespread despair.

During this gloomy descent into global warfare Curtin pursued his goal of moulding Labor's policies closer to his perception of Australia's defence requirements without undermining his primary objective of maintaining a united party. When the federal government sharply increased defence expenditure in April 1938 Curtin conceded that the increase was justifiable, but not the government's priorities in spending it. In September 1938 he reiterated that Australia

> should not be embroiled in the disputes of Europe. . .we have not the power to solve or appease them. . .The wars of Europe are a quagmire in which we should not allow our resources, our strength, our vitality to be sunk. . .

In May 1939 yet another federal conference was dominated by debate about Labor's NSW problems, but Forgan Smith gave Curtin valuable support when delegates turned to consider defence policy after wrangling for two days about NSW. The Queensland Premier pushed through a resolution which assertively restated Labor's defence priorities, denied allegations that the party was anti-British and isolationist, and attacked Labor's opponents for Australia's 'lack of preparedness'. When the Menzies government passed legislation to introduce a census and national register, the ACTU wanted the FPLP, which had opposed the bill, to join the unions in non-compliance. But Curtin replied that defying the law 'was treading dangerous soil', and invited comparisons with the activities of the New Guard; furthermore, he 'would not allow the bankers or the Chamber of Manufacturers to disobey the law were a Labor Government in power'.

The diversity of views within the FPLP made Curtin's task difficult and delicate. Brennan's idealistic pacifism had stirred audiences since 1914, and he repeatedly scorned the idea that Australia might be attacked and ought to spend more on defence. His scathing reference to the government's increased defence expenditure in April 1938 as a 'calculated panic' was supported by Eddie Ward, the former boxer who had acquired a reputation since 1931 as a stormy petrel with a mind of his own. Compulsively aggressive, Ward was frequently the centre of fiery parliamentary exchanges, and his independent spirit sometimes caused his leader anxious moments; his admirers saw him as a genuine, hardhitting working-class representative, whereas others wished that there was more vision and humour in his make-up to accompany his unbridled hatred of Labor's enemies. Other senior FPLP members reluctant to face the unpalatable reality included Collings and also Holloway, who in May 1939 told parliament he was 'certain that there will not be a war'. Blackburn, who had been readmitted to the party in March 1937, continued to propagate an anti-war philosophy, denying in April 1938 that a Japanese invasion of Australia was possible; but a year later he reluctantly accepted that war was likely and conceded the necessity 'to make some preparations'.

The range of opinions in the wider labour movement also presented problems for Curtin. In NSW the Langites, while accusing Heffron Labor of being dominated by Communists, promulgated a strident isolationism designed to appeal to Catholics; the Heffronites denounced isolationism as an impractical policy that endangered Australia's security. Boote's authoritative *Australian Worker* upheld collective security and trenchantly opposed isolationism and appeasement. In Victoria, where the foreign policy tensions were most acute, the executive continued to advocate isolationism, being more concerned about communism than fascism. In supporting Forgan Smith's resolution at the 1939 federal conference, Calwell claimed that 'those who advocated collective security only discovered its virtues when Russia joined the League of Nations'. However, whereas Hanlon contended, in also supporting Forgan Smith, that northern Australia (meaning Queensland) was practically undefended, Calwell's view was 'that there was not enough mercantile marine afloat' for a successful invasion of Australia. There was no more ardent anti-Communist than Calwell's colleague on the Victorian executive, Dinny Lovegrove, himself an ex-Communist; Lovegrove was so committed to isolationism that late in September 1939 he was contending that this new world war was as imperialist a conflict as the Great War. Also adding to Curtin's difficulties in presenting a cohesive ALP defence policy were the ACTU's advocacy of collective security, the Tasmanian branch's call for the return of compulsory military training (rejected by the 1939 federal conference), and the variant of collective security propagated by sections of the SA union movement.

On 3 September 1939 the UAP Prime Minister, Menzies, announced that Britain had declared war on Germany because of Hitler's invasion of Poland

'and that, as a result, Australia is also at war'. Curtin responded swiftly, preparing a policy statement which was approved by the FPLP executive and ratified by the full caucus before being announced by him in the Representatives when parliament reconvened on 6 September. Once again Curtin demonstrated his skill in compiling a manifesto broadly acceptable to the diverse strands in his party. After affirming Labor's 'traditional horror of war', Curtin told the Representatives that his party would 'preserve its separate entity' while doing 'all that is possible to safeguard Australia'. He declared that the government should take 'immediate control. . .of all essential raw materials' and munitions factories, institute 'a rigid control of commodity prices and house rents so that war-profiteering will become impossible', keep a tight rein on interest rates, and readjust 'the monetary system. . .so that the National Debt be kept as low as possible'. Furthermore, in a pointed reference to his (and some of his colleagues') own trying experiences during an earlier world war, Curtin added that such measures should be implemented with the 'very minimum of interference with the civic liberties of the people'. In a radio address on 10 September Curtin elaborated on the manifesto, emphasizing two differences which clearly distinguished his party from the government – Labor's 'traditional opposition to conscription', and its hostility to dispatching Australian soldiers and materials to Europe when all the nation's resources should be kept in Australia in case it was attacked. After certain Labor figures aired their personal responses to the advent of war – Lang made a mischievous somersault from his extreme isolationism, and advocated maximizing assistance to Britain – Ward and Blackburn protested in caucus against these 'embarrassing' statements. The federal executive, which had become a far more significant entity in the party's structure over the preceding two decades, not only endorsed Curtin's exposition of ALP policy, but adopted as well the suggestion of Forgan Smith and NSW secretary Evans that the leader's radio address should be printed and distributed as a leaflet.

For some time the continuing hostilities within and between the government parties overshadowed the news from the war zones. After Lyons died in April 1939 'the smouldering animosities and barely suppressed rivalries' within the coalition government could no longer be concealed. Menzies, Lyons's logical successor, had the requisite ambition and intellectual equipment in abundance, but made enemies in displaying them too ostentatiously. Remarkably, he was nearly toppled in the UAP leadership ballot by Hughes, now 76. Then Page, heading the UAP's coalition partner, launched a savage personal attack on Menzies, accusing him of disloyalty to Lyons and unsuitability to be prime minister because he had shirked enlistment in the Great War despite being fit, trained and a conscriptionist. The Country Party then split over the propriety of Page's outburst. Menzies soldiered on without the Country Party, implementing some preliminary wartime measures without ever being convincing in the role of war leader. He retained the barrister's knack of arguing a case with ability and style, but behind the pretentiousness he was essentially a shallow politician who invariably associated himself with Labor's enemies. Unlike the fighting within the Menzies government, the Second World War was slow to generate momentum. There was no large-scale involvement in battle by the Second AIF prior to 1941, although Australian sailors and ships saw action before then and Australian airmen participated in the Battle of Britain.

Early in 1940 a federal by-election was created in Corio when Menzies appointed one of his senior ministers, R.G. Casey, to the newly created post of Australian ambassador to the United States. Menzies was pleased to have removed one of his leadership rivals, but the ploy backfired. In the by-election the voters ignored his fatuous claim that the UAP candidate should be returned because 'Hitler's eyes are on Corio', and J.J. Dedman won the seat for Labor. This result prompted Menzies to revert to the tattered coalition with the Country Party. Scottish-born Jack Dedman had served with the British army at Gallipoli, the Western Front and, after the Great War, in India, before migrating to Australia in 1922 to take up dairy farming. He had an intense but shortlived involvement in the Country Party, before concluding that the ALP was more genuine about his particular objective of a milk board and about furthering the interests of primary producers generally. The Depression hastened his realization that the whole economic system was flawed. He sold his farm, and plunged into a comprehensive study of banking and finance. Convinced that Labor's socialization objective – or, in his preferred term, 'social control' – was the answer, he earnestly lectured ALP branches in his dour Scottish burr about the virtues of a planned economy, and unsuccessfully contested several seats for Labor during the 1930s. At the outbreak of war Dedman was 43, tall, strong and fit, and offered himself for enlistment. But the army did not require him, and he returned to his job at the Forestry Commission and the economic studies he was pursuing at Melbourne University. A few months later came his success in Corio, and he was bound for a different battlefield in Canberra, where his commitment and considered, intelligent contributions quickly impressed his colleagues.

The uplifting Corio result was followed by developments in the NSW ALP which were anything but pleasing to Curtin and the FPLP. The outcome of the Newtown unity conference and the dethroning of the Big Fella had reinvigorated the party in NSW, but the struggle for supremacy in the state branch was far from over. At the 1940 Easter state conference the Langites duped some prominent Communist-connected factional enemies – notably Hughes and Lloyd Ross, who was a talented writer and historian, son of R.S. Ross, and the NSW secretary of the ARU – into giving their hearty support to a resolution which was not merely at odds with Curtin's declaration of ALP policy at the outbreak of war, but specifically expressed hostility to any pre-emptive strike against Soviet Russia. Some Langites even voted in favour of this 'Hands Off Russia' resolution to ensure that conference ratified it by a large majority, thereby lending weight to their later protests that Communists and Communist sympathizers had captured control of the state branch. On 18 April Lang announced the formation of his breakaway Non-Communist Labor Party, claiming nine MLAs and six MLCs in NSW and, in Canberra, five MHRs (Beasley, Rosevear, J. Gander, T. Sheehan, and D. Mulcahy) and two Senators, Amour and Armstrong.

To express open sympathy for Russia has been to invite political controversy in Australia ever since 1917, and rarely more so than in the threatened, uncertain atmosphere of March 1940. Russia had signed a non-aggression pact with Germany, together they had partitioned Poland, and Russia had invaded Finland; but it was still unclear what role Russia would play in the war. Conservatives outside the ALP and some Catholics within it were very antagonistic to Soviet Russia and still saw it as a more natural enemy than Nazi Germany. The official Communist line (until mid-1941) was that Britain and its allies were waging an unjustifiable imperialistic conflict, and the Menzies government banned the Communist Party in June 1940. But besides avowed Communists who followed the party line, there was within the Australian labour movement – despite the ALP's explicit hostility to communism – a measure of goodwill for what seemed from afar to be the noble experiment of Soviet Russia. Boote, for example, was

201

no Communist but he remained a staunch admirer of Russia, and he welcomed the 'Hands Off Russia' resolution. When his article applauding it was removed from the *Australian Worker* by AWU officials concerned that pro-Russian sentiments would harm Labor electorally, Boote was outraged and threatened to resign.

After Curtin's painstaking efforts to re-establish Labor as a united and credible alternative government, he was naturally appalled by the developments in NSW. Initially he reacted warily to the 'Hands Off Russia' resolution, but he lashed out angrily when the Langites broke away once more to form their own party. 'Again Labor has been stabbed in the back', he declared; Lang and Beasley have 'wrecked the solidarity of Labor at a time of great crisis'. Curtin contrasted the alleged concern of Lang and Beasley about Communist influence in the ALP with their decidedly different attitudes in earlier years when it suited their factional objectives to be more hospitable to Communists.

Resentment of the Langites' action was bitterly aired at a federal executive meeting which repudiated the 'Hands Off Russia' resolution and confirmed the ALP policy Curtin had announced when the war began. This stance was also publicly upheld by the NSW MHRs and Senators who had not followed the Langites out of the FPLP. When 'Stabber Jack' Beasley rose in the Representatives on 2 May to justify his conduct there were heated interjections from Makin and Pollard. There was also a sharp clash with Ward, who was not the only Langite from the previous split unwilling to follow Lang and Beasley in this one. Rowley James and Joe Clark remained in the FPLP, and so did Bert Lazzarini, whose brother had been one of the first state MPs in the NSW parliament to defy Lang in the 1930s. Lazzarini answered Beasley in parliament on 2 May with a slashing broadside, and Rosevear, who had apparently agonized for some time before once again joining a Langite breakaway group, lived up to his reputation as one of the national parliament's most rugged performers with a hardhitting counter-attack against Lazzarini.

Meanwhile the European situation had altered dramatically. Nazi Germany swept through Norway, Denmark, the Netherlands, Belgium and France. Italy entered the war alongside Germany. It was obvious that Britain was in great peril, and would be unable to provide much assistance if Australia needed it. The long-held concern felt by Australians about the prospective enemy they most feared, Japan, was revived. Like Ward, Curtin had urged that all possible avenues to peace should be explored; but after Germany surged through Europe he seemed to accept that there would be no peace until the fascists were defeated. Curtin's assessment of what was best for Labor combined with party policy to make him unreceptive to the clamour for an all-party government like the one Churchill had just formed in Britain, but caucus supported his call for a special federal conference to clarify Labor's policies relating to the war, Australia's defence, and 'the necessity of an early outline of the general principles of postwar reconstruction'.

France had succumbed to Germany and was negotiating an armistice as sombre ALP conference delegates commenced their deliberations in Melbourne on 18 June. Conference endorsed a seven-point defence policy as its response to 'the gravity of the world situation and the imminent danger' to Australia by 24 votes to 12. This resolution, which originated in a proposal from Forgan Smith, affirmed Australia's 'complete and indissoluble unity with the Allies', and called for the 'entire resources of Australia' to be utilized by the government with maximum efficiency 'in the urgent and adequate defence of Australia'. But the manifesto made clear that this process was not to occur at the expense of the labour movement's hard-won advances in working conditions; the trade unions were to be recognized and involved. A tax of 100% was also sought on excessive war profits. 'Necessary provision for reinforcement of the AIF divisions, the extent of European participation by volunteer army to be determined by circumstances as they arise' was the flexible solution to a problem that vexed Curtin during the Corio by-election campaign. Sensing community hostility to Labor's continued opposition to dispatching Australian soldiers overseas, Curtin had angered some ALP activists by modifying Labor's policy at Corio to the extent that contingents already departed would be reinforced if necessary. The 12 delegates who opposed the Forgan Smith proposal were probably the delegates from NSW and Victoria, who had been instructed to oppose the deployment of Australian military forces other than for the defence of Australasia.

There was vigorous debate at the conference about the merits of an all-party government. Ward insisted that Labor should avoid any entanglement with the discredited Menzies government, which should be attacked remorselessly until it fell, and the sooner Labor replaced it the better. Some Tasmanian delegates completely disagreed. Dwyer-Gray went so far as to move that the next federal election should be postponed, Labor should enter an all-party government, and Forgan Smith should resign as Queensland Premier in order to become a minister in it. Several delegates expressed concern about Australia's security. Hanlon felt that an attack 'could take place within six months', and 'Australia would have no chance if Britain went down'. Such comments made NSW state secretary Evans conclude that he was 'witnessing the capitulation of the ALP' caused by 'panicky' delegates gripped by 'war hysteria'. Curtin and Makin affirmed the unsuitability of joining Menzies in a composite government – Labor 'should maintain its integral identity in the people's interests' – but advocated a joint-party advisory War Council, which would enable Labor to make a valuable, informed contribution to the war effort. Curtin said that he had been endeavouring to achieve this himself by maintaining a good personal relationship with Menzies and discussing developments with him frequently. An advisory War Council would extend and formalize these worthwhile talks, he assured delegates, as well as meeting the 'demand' in the community for Labor to involve itself directly in 'the conduct of the war and in preparing for the post-war reconstruction'. Conference proceeded to ratify this Curtin-Makin proposal, although Ward truculently reiterated his hostility to an association of any sort with Labor's enemies.

There was no respite for Curtin. The very next day Menzies introduced to parliament an important amendment to the National Security Act giving the government greatly increased powers over employment, taxation and property. It authorized industrial and military conscription on the home front (although conscription for service beyond Australia and its territories was still prohibited). Curtin considered the amendment appropriate in the circumstances, and a large caucus majority agreed with him. But a small FPLP group (Ward, Blackburn, Brennan, Maloney and, for one of the parliamentary votes, Pollard) joined Beasley's Langites in opposing the amendment, mainly because they felt the Menzies government could not be trusted with such all-embracing powers. Evans's attempts to persuade other FPLP members from NSW to join Ward in opposing the amendment seems to have convinced Curtin and ALP federal president Fallon that further surgery was essential in NSW, despite the likelihood of an imminent federal election. Curtin's overtures to Menzies about an advisory War Council had been rejected; Menzies was only interested in an all-party government, which Curtin adamantly ruled out.

This time the federal executive did take drastic action. Hughes, Evans and the rest of the NSW executive were suspended. Some of them were reinstated when a provisional executive was appointed, but emotions again ran high in the NSW labour movement. Boote and Fallon had a blazing row about the federal executive's decision. Curtin came to Sydney and addressed union leaders at the Trades Hall. He spiritedly defended the suspensions and his stance on the National Security amendment; Boote, who disagreed with Curtin's arguments, conceded that it was a 'fine speech'. In this address Curtin also made an emphatic appeal for unity, although he knew that the federal executive's action had made unity in NSW even less likely in the short term. There were now three warring groups in that state. The Langites had considerable support in ALP branches but hardly any union backing. As the federal executive had hoped, some Heffronites declined to side with the exiled members of the state executive and their supporters, although this Hughes-Evans faction retained the loyalty of many branches and some unions. The third faction, official Labor, had considerable union backing but little initial support in the branches. The federal executive was presuming that, in time, official Labor in NSW could attract ALP members and voters who wanted their party to support Australia's war effort without being led by the discredited Lang or susceptible to the allegation of having Communist sympathizers among its leaders.

These NSW problems probably prevented Labor from winning the 1940 federal election, although it went within a whisker of government. In the Representatives the UAP and Country Party together totalled 36 seats, which exactly matched the combined tally of the ALP's 32 and the four Beasley Langites. The balance of power was held by two Victorian independents. One, A.W. Coles, was inclined to favour the UAP, and the other, Alex Wilson, tended to support the Country Party. The election also produced an almost evenly balanced Senate. In NSW the Senate voting shares were official Labor 29·65%, Langites 19·73% and Hughes-Evans faction an acutely disappointing 5·03%. The tension naturally following a photo-finish election was increased by uncertainty about Curtin's own seat, Fremantle, which he had neglected in his arduous campaigning throughout Australia. Eventually, however, he received from his daughter a heartening telegram – 'Batting on a sticky wicket, but you will get the runs' – correctly predicting that he would be returned after all to lead the FPLP, which had been bolstered by two illustrious acquisitions.

One of them was Chifley. The bitter fight with the Langites had cost him his parliamentary seat (Macquarie) and membership of his engine drivers' union, as well as severely affecting his vocal cords and peace of mind; but once he had made up his mind about the correct course he was not one to waver because the going was tough and the struggle long. However, he later came to regret his support of the Premiers' Plan. At the time he was motivated by the Labor principle of displaying solidarity in upholding an unpopular majority decision made by the body (in this case cabinet) authorized to make it. His ministerial experience during the Scullin government's depressing final months had been brief, but by the end of 1931 Scullin, Theodore, Curtin and Lyons all held him in high personal and political regard. In his years out of parliament he deepened his involvement in the Bathurst community he cherished. He developed a worldly wisdom and sound commonsense approach, and also brought to politics a naturally warm, attractive personality which endeared him to his colleagues. In 1935

Chifley was appointed by the Lyons government as a Labor voice on its royal commission into the Australian banking system. Chifley and his five fellow members recommended a range of reforms, including increased central banking powers for the Commonwealth Bank, and insisted – conscious of Gibson's conduct during the Scullin government – that monetary policy should be the preserve of the national government, not the Commonwealth Bank Board. Chifley emerged from the commission with a deeper understanding of public finance but, as he outlined in his separate additional report, an undiminished faith in the nationalization of private banking. During the early months of the Second World War Chifley's acknowledged ability induced the Menzies government to appoint him to responsible positions in wartime agencies, but there was never any doubt about his devotion to the labour movement. At the May Day social at Bathurst in 1939 Chifley, who was never consumed by ideology, referred to his vision of Labor's goals as the 'light on the hill'. The admiration of the party faithful for him prompted dedicated canvassing which ensured his success in Macquarie in 1940, although he spent nearly all the campaign in a Sydney hospital stricken with double pneumonia.

An even more prestigious ALP candidate in 1940 was Bert Evatt. After a decade on the High Court bench he had forged an enviable reputation as a learned, compassionate and sound judge, but he was chafing with frustration. His country was at war, it was being led ineptly by a squabbling government, and Labor in his state was yet again in turmoil. Seeing his natural rival Menzies become Prime Minister was an added irritation. Evatt and Menzies were the same age, had both achieved dazzling academic results and an illustrious career in the law, and had a strong mutual dislike. Evatt had delighted the labour movement with his judgements in the Kisch case in 1934, when the High Court disallowed the clumsy attempts by Menzies, then Lyons's Attorney-General, to prevent a European writer entering Australia to address a MAWAF congress. With his towering intellect and relentless energy Evatt was not content with a cloistered judicial existence. While on the bench he contributed prolifically to legal journals, and somehow found the time to write four distinguished books on aspects of Australian history. One of them was his reworked Doctor of Laws thesis. Another was *Australian Labour Leader*, his fine study of W.A. Holman written while Evatt was contemplating the unprecedented step of relinquishing a judgeship for the hurly-burly of Labor politics. Insatiably ambitious, utterly self-confident, and convinced that his country needed him in its hour of crisis, Evatt seemed to many Labor enthusiasts like a conquering knight on a prancing white charger, but overturning preselection arrangements for even the most glamorous candidate was no easy task. Eventually he was invited to stand in the UAP-held seat of Barton. The announcement of his candidacy generated a surging sense of expectancy (although Menzies reacted sourly); even the incumbent MHR, who had held Barton for nine years, accepted the inevitable when he learned that Evatt would be opposing him. 'Then I'm done for', he said, and he was right.

Evatt's prominence continued during the election aftermath. With Curtin distractedly silent while vote-counting proceeded in Fremantle, Evatt took the lead in announcing Labor's terms before any collaboration with Menzies could be agreed. He was fanatical about getting into power, not so much for the plums of office but because he had the utmost faith in his ability to provide the best possible direction for his party and his country. He had not left the High Court to sit in opposition. About a year before the election he had raised with at least two government ministers the startling and unrealistic proposition that he could step

205

down from the court to lead an all-party government. In sheer intellect he had no peer, but in political astuteness he had much to learn. Soon there were rumblings in ALP ranks about Evatt's presumptuousness. He was on the point of contesting the deputy leadership against Forde, until Boote and others discouraged him. At the first caucus meeting after the election Evatt was included in the FPLP executive, and then persuaded his colleagues to take the initiative in the uncertain parliamentary situation. His motion, carried by caucus, turned Menzies's revived advocacy of an all-party government on its head by stressing ALP objectives, and inviting co-operation and support for Labor's 'substantial aims' from members of the other parties and the independents. Negotiations commenced the following day at an all-party conference. Evatt, representing the FPLP with Curtin and Forde, was appalled to hear Menzies address Curtin as 'Jack' and Forde as 'Frank'; the general tenor of the discussions convinced Evatt that Curtin was 'woefully timid' and 'afraid to press for power'. Evatt's intense activity and sense of frustration culminated in a severe bronchial illness verging on pneumonia, which forced him away from the deliberations. Makin replaced him as the FPLP's third delegate in the protracted negotiations, where ALP obduracy prevented the emergence of an all-party government, although Menzies agreed to create an Advisory War Council as advocated by Labor. Evatt was absent ill on 23 October when caucus elected Curtin, Forde and Makin as its representatives on the Council, which also comprised Menzies, Hughes and P. Spender (all UAP) together with Beasley and Country Party leader Fadden.

However, Evatt was back and fighting fit during the political crisis over the budget later in 1940. Before the budget was presented to parliament it was unveiled to the Council, where Labor representatives registered objections. The FPLP executive in consultation with caucus produced some amendments which Curtin duly moved in parliament. On 4 December Curtin informed caucus of the concessions the Labor representatives had managed to wring from the government during hours of gruelling haggling in the Council earlier that day. He was dismayed to find a strongly held caucus view, vigorously promoted by Evatt, that these concessions were insufficient. During this stormy caucus meeting, which lasted five hours, Curtin became so upset that he threatened to resign and walked out of the party room. There was such uproar in caucus that Beasley and his Langites, meeting next door, had to adjourn their gathering. Senator Don Cameron had never participated in such bitter discussions, and feared a split. Blackburn also concluded that 'the Party will not come thro' 1941 unbroken'. Eventually caucus carried a motion from Evatt, seconded by Scullin, which sent the FPLP's representatives back to the Council 'empowered to do their best in negotiating for further improved conditions in the Budget'. They had little success. Another lengthy debate ensued in caucus before the amended budget was narrowly approved by 24 votes to 19.

Such traumatic discord arose because much more than the particular budget items was at stake. Evatt, Ward, Cameron and others were intensely critical of Curtin's attitude to the Menzies government. They saw him as insipid and ineffectual, when decisiveness and strength were required to push the fragile coalition over the brink. A caucus group, mostly comprising NSW MPs close to and influenced by Evatt, kept urging that Labor should seize the initiative, and if the best result in the circumstances was an all-party government then at least Labor would have more influence over the destiny of the country in possibly its gravest crisis than the FPLP could exert in opposition. Ward and Brennan were prominent in a separate caucus section antagonistic to Curtin because they felt there should be no co-operative dealings with the Menzies government what-soever. A third group backing Evatt's tactics on the budget were individuals like Drakeford, Holloway, Dedman and James, who, although usually supportive of Curtin, were opposed to aspects of the budget, including its treatment of pensioners, soldiers and wheatgrowers and the lowering of the income tax exemption level.

Curtin argued that an all-party government was not in the best interests of Australia or his party. Referring to Menzies's difficulties in achieving a united approach from the UAP and the Country Party, Curtin remarked more than once that the only thing worse than government by two parties was government by three. Furthermore, he argued, it would leave an opposition vacuum which would be filled by the Communist Party and miscellaneous malcontents with an increased likelihood of subversive activities that would hamper the war effort. Nor should Labor endeavour to govern on its own, contended Curtin, citing the recent history of the Scullin government; in this view he was fortified by Scullin himself. As Curtin's closest confidant in caucus, Scullin was exerting an important elder statesman influence behind the scenes just as another former leader, Watson, had done for his successor. Chifley agreed that attempting to govern without definitely having the numbers in either chamber (at least the Scullin government started with a clear majority in the Representatives) was asking for trouble. But there was another factor behind Curtin's hesitancy. He had severe misgivings about his suitability to lead Australia during a world war. This anxiety was undermining his health. He tended to worry chronically in times of stress, unlike Chifley, who could unwind after a harrowing day with an escapist book, usually a Western.

No episode more starkly exemplified the contrasting approaches of Curtin and Evatt to the political situation following the 1940 election than the Swan by-election in December. This federal seat in WA had been held for nearly two decades by a Country Party veteran until his recent death. If Labor could capture it, an ALP government would surely follow. Evatt was straining at the leash, itching to head for the West and launch the campaign of his life. Curtin, however, did not go. His health was poor after the succession of tumultuous events, and he also had to cope with the news of Anstey's death: 'I find it very difficult to speak about Frank Anstey', he confessed as he began his moving obituary speech in parliament. Curtin was concerned about suggestions that the Labor candidate in Swan, Jim Dinan, was connected to the Communist Party, and his worries about becoming Prime Minister if Dinan managed to win the by-election only made him feel worse. Some ALP supporters concluded that it was no mere coincidence that no other prominent party figure except Evatt made the long journey to help Dinan. Evatt, whose solitary assistant on this trip was former Heffron aide and publicist Allan Fraser, was undeterred, even when he learned on arrival in Perth that all the state branch's senior office-bearers were unenthusiastic about Dinan. Despite Evatt's superhuman endeavours the campaign was a shambles owing to the state branch's poor organization; eventually Evatt organized his own meetings and paid for the advertising himself. By this stage Evatt's hypersensitive conspiracy detector was on red alert, but he pressed on nevertheless with his whirlwind campaign. He was optimistic about the result when he and Fraser began the return rail journey. As the train pulled in at Kalgoorlie Fraser was abruptly woken by Evatt, who was triumphantly asserting 'We've won! We've won! Listen to the cheers!' There was indeed a large, excited crowd on the platform; Evatt had concluded that they must be saluting him as the Labor hero who had singlehandedly won a famous victory that would usher in a Labor government. Alas, the heroes the crowd was welcoming were sportsmen returning after a famous victory. Labor had lost in Swan, and there was a controversial sequel when the WA branch expelled Dinan after he publicly denounced Curtin and others for their halfhearted support.

The Langite MPs in the Non-Communist Labor Party rejoined the ALP in February 1941. There had been tough bargaining on both sides. The banning of the Communist Party by the Menzies government and the federal executive's removal of the Hughes-Evans executive in NSW had largely removed the raison d'être of the Non-Communist Labor Party, and the 1940 federal election indicated that the defectors faced a limited future outside the ALP. Even Lang signed a pledge of loyalty to the official ALP, and both the FPLP and the NSW caucus readmitted all their Non-Communist Labor Party breakaways. Each of them was promised ALP endorsement at the next election. 'Stabber Jack' Beasley in particular was keen to return to the fold and a senior cabinet post in the Labor government he felt was close at hand. He soon formed a close alliance with Evatt, who a year or so earlier had frequently referred to Beasley scathingly as an unscrupulous political operator.

The reunited NSW ALP had a magnificent victory at the May 1941 election. Labor's opponents had been lethargic and unimaginative in government ever since Lang's dismissal in 1932, and they now blamed the war for their inactivity. The government was also publicly divided and scandal-prone, and a number of its more able and experienced members were not recontesting their seats. Labor seized its opportunity. McKell campaigned well. He countered the claim that in a crisis the electors would refuse to 'change horses in mid-stream' by retorting that it would be 'pitiful' and 'rank lunacy' not to switch to a fresh horse when the old one was 'broken-winded. . .and never had been good for a hard gallop'. Labor also benefited from McKell's shrewd 'horses for courses' strategy. He persuaded the executive to allow him to decide Labor's candidates, and used this power astutely. He convinced Billy Sheahan, who had been prominent in events leading up to the memorable 1939 Newtown unity conference, that he should stand in the electorate where he had grown up, Yass, which Labor had not even contested in 1938. Sheahan, a Catholic public servant and returned soldier who had qualified as a barrister in his mid-thirties, would have preferred a less daunting task, but agreed to tackle Yass and won it. Another notable selection was Eddie Graham, a butcher and pig-breeder prominent in Wagga Wagga, which he captured for Labor. Other successful McKell choices included farmer Roger Nott (Liverpool Plains), wealthy hotelier and racehorse owner Bill Gollan (Randwick), and 31-year-old farmer and Coonabarabran shire councillor Jack Renshaw (Castlereagh). The only clear misjudgement McKell seems to have made was in Murrumbidgee, where he preferred former Timber Workers' Union official and minister in Lang's first government, J.J. Fitzgerald, to well-known local orchardist A.G. Enticknap who, as an Independent Labor candidate, defeated Fitzgerald; but Enticknap made peace with the ALP in 1942 and was admitted to caucus. With Dubbo snared in a by-election, Labor held 56 of the 90 Assembly seats at the end of 1942. The Hughes-Evans faction contested 27 seats in 1941, but confirmed its impotence by winning none and managing a meagre overall vote of 5·64%.

The new Premier was given the ministers he wanted. Lang made no effort to muster the numbers for a cabinet spot, and the election of the ministry was relatively straightforward. Baddeley was confirmed as McKell's deputy. Heffron was given National Emergency Services, a new portfolio created by the war. W.F. Dunn was back at Agriculture and Forests. Bert Evatt's younger brother Clive had Education. Housing and Local Government was allocated to Greg McGirr's younger brother Jim, the only minister from the ranks of the recently returned Non-Communist Labor breakaways. Health went to Chifley's friend Gus Kelly, who had found employment as a turnstile attendant at the Sydney Cricket Ground after the 1932 landslide when he lost Bathurst for the only time in 42 years. Others in the cabinet included Cahill and Charlie Lazzarini. The senior Legislative Council minister was lawyer and former union official Reg Downing, close associate of Chifley, cousin of Sheahan, and a shrewd moderate who was to exert a powerful influence in the NSW ALP for many years.

During the first half of 1941 there was continued dissatisfaction in the FPLP and the wider labour movement with Curtin's unassertive leadership. He especially frustrated some of his colleagues by honouring his assurance to Menzies that the FPLP would not take advantage of the Prime Minister's lengthy absence overseas. Meanwhile, the increasing concern about Japanese intentions aggravated Bert Evatt's restlessness. His great fear was that a sudden Japanese drive southwards would unite Australia in desperate necessity behind even such an inept war leader as Menzies, and Labor would never get in. With Curtin's acquiescence Evatt had been appointed to an inter-departmental advisory committee on postwar reconstruction – just as Chifley was assisting the Labour and National Service department on industrial relations matters, and Holloway and Drakeford were involved in a survey of manpower and resources – but it was not enough for Evatt, who pressed his claims for inclusion in the Advisory War Council. That body had received highly secret information a month earlier about aggressive Japanese intentions so disturbing to Curtin that he persuaded Council members to issue a joint statement warning Australians about the 'utmost gravity' of the situation and calling for 'the greatest effort of preparedness this country has ever made'. At the first FPLP meeting in 1941, which was spread over three days, Curtin was criticized for both this warning and his approval of FPLP members' involvement in government-related activities. At times the meeting was tempestuous, and there were virulent clashes between Ward and Curtin. Ward, who had already attacked the Council's warning in parliament as a baseless hoax intended to deflect tension from domestic scandals, urged caucus to withdraw its representatives from the Council and to initiate moves to have the Menzies government defeated in parliament without delay. Again Curtin resisted any such action, and a caucus majority supported him; far from seceding from the Council, the FPLP enlarged its contingent by adding Evatt to it and endorsing Beasley's continued membership. 'There are going to be difficult times ahead', predicted Fallon, 'and to have a Labor government in power then, with Jack Curtin at its head, would be a bloody calamity'.

In June 1941 Hitler invaded Russia, changing the course of the war and dramatically altering the attitudes of Australian Communists to the conflict. As the Russians tenaciously defended their homeland, Communists everywhere earnestly supported their struggle. In Australia the opposition of Communists to the war effort gave way to enthusiastic support in a year when the involvement of AIF divisions in battle also generated a heightened emotional commitment to the cause.

Russia's emergence as a wholehearted ally cut no ice with the Victorian ALP executive. With fanatical anti-Communists like Lovegrove and H.M. Cremean prominent on it, the executive intransigently retained its ban on any association by ALP members with Communist groups. Cremean's profound concern about the growing influence of Communist union leaders in Australia led him to approach Catholic Action activist B.A. Santamaria about forming an organization to combat them. That organization, which came to be known as the Movement, came into existence when a quartet including Cremean and Santamaria met in Melbourne on 14 August 1941, Santamaria's 26th birthday. That same evening another member of the Victorian ALP executive, Maurice Blackburn, openly defied it by attending meetings of a very different organization, the Australian-Soviet Friendship League, one of many groups established in Australia to express support for Russia following Hitler's invasion. A federal executive meeting in September issued a statement, which recognized Russia's 'magnificent fight against Nazi aggression' but threatened to expel any ALP members who involved themselves in the activities of 'Communist subsidiaries' like the Friendship League. This 'reactionary decree' incensed Boote, who was vice-president of a Sydney Aid to Russia committee: 'We must lend all possible aid to Russia, the ALP agrees, yet if we belong to any organization devoted to that purpose, we are excommunicated!' Blackburn's response was similarly unyielding, and he was expelled on 3 October. Within a further month two MLAs were driven out of the ALP in Queensland for retaining their links with an association providing medical aid to Russia.

In Coburg and nearby suburbs in northern Melbourne, Blackburn remained a widely admired figure among Labor's rank and file, who had launched their own revolt against the Victorian executive in 1940. When the safe state seat of Coburg became vacant after Frank Keane died, the executive cancelled the preselection contest and appointed Don Cameron's son (who lived in Glen Iris, a south-eastern middle-class suburb) as Keane's successor; but the rebellious Coburg branch endorsed Charlie Mutton instead as their Independent Labor candidate. Mutton, well-known locally as an amiable former ironworker who had taken over his father's poultry farm, defeated Cameron at the by-election.

The Menzies government sank into disarray after its leader returned to Australia in May 1941. By now Hughes was saying that Menzies 'couldn't lead a flock of homing pigeons'. Menzies twice repeated his unsuccessful overtures for an all-party government. In May Curtin's response was a superb caucus-approved statement of Labor's consistent, principled approach under his leadership since the outbreak of war. When Menzies tried again in August Curtin's reply, again ratified by caucus beforehand, reiterated that Labor had not impeded the prosecution of the war and suggested that since Menzies clearly could not give Australia stable government he should resign. When caucus met two days later Calwell moved that the FPLP should bring down the Menzies government in parliament immediately. Curtin disagreed, and contended that the budget a month or so away would be the appropriate time to strike. Still personally apprehensive of office, he was also determined to avoid any suggestion of political opportunism, since a Labor government without a majority in both chambers would need every ounce of moral legitimacy. Calwell's motion was defeated by 35 votes to 15. He was stunned when Evatt, who had persuaded him to move it, voted against it. That evening Menzies resigned, and was replaced as Prime Minister by Fadden.

In mid-September a fresh scandal emerged to further discredit Labor's opponents. A journalist who had worked for Menzies and had a grudge against Fadden handed Curtin documents incriminating senior government ministers in sensational allegations, which concerned the improper disclosure of budget information and the attempted procurement of industrial peace through secret payments of public funds to union officials. The material was in typed carbon copies, which meant – as Curtin realized – that there were probably copies in the possession of other Labor members who would be less circumspect than Curtin in using the information. Curtin reacted cautiously. He showed the material to Fadden, consulted the FPLP executive about how to proceed, and referred to the documents in parliament with deliberate vagueness. Later, however, Ward publicized the substance of the allegations and the FPLP moved to censure the government, but the decisive votes of independents Coles and Wilson enabled the coalition to survive.

The day after this debate Fadden introduced his budget. Labor's motion challenging it was drafted by Evatt, and caucus left the parliamentary tactics to Curtin. Tension mounted as the debate proceeded, with everyone waiting for the independents to declare themselves. For some time Evatt, a notoriously unsubtle intriguer, had been assiduously cultivating Wilson, and Coles had let Curtin know privately that he was prepared to vote with Labor. Eventually both Coles and Wilson confirmed that the government no longer had their support, and Fadden resigned. On 3 October, the day the Victorian executive expelled Blackburn, Curtin accepted the Governor-General's commission to form Labor's first national government for 10 years. ALP enthusiasts throughout Australia were thrilled. Amid the euphoria there was a chilling reminder of the dark side of Labor politics. The Victorian executive had decided to order a second ballot after alleged irregularities in a fiercely contested preselection for the safe ALP state seat of Richmond. After this second ballot reversed the first result and gave the endorsement to the sitting member by 410 votes to 407, Pat Kennelly, the Victorian ALP's assistant secretary, was leaving the counting room with the ballot box containing the votes when an assailant wielding a gun forced him to hand over the ballot box and then took off with it.

9 'Dangers and Problems Unprecedented and Unpredictable': The Curtin Government, 1941–1945

THE NEW MINISTRY was elected on 6 October. Caucus accepted Curtin's recommendation that cabinet should comprise 14 MHRs and five Senators. Scullin moved that the leader allocate the portfolios among the ministers chosen by caucus, which was traditional ALP procedure, and added the proposal – most unconventional for a Labor government – that 'the Prime Minister be empowered to remove a Minister' if necessary. The FPLP carried Scullin's motion, and then confirmed Curtin and Forde as leader and deputy.

After the 17 other ministers were elected by caucus, Curtin's allocation of portfolios exemplified his repeated early statements as Prime Minister that the wholehearted and uninhibited prosecution of the war would be his government's paramount concern. He retained for himself Defence Co-ordination and gave Army to Forde, who had expected to become Treasurer. That portfolio, and the ranking of senior minister after the leadership pair, went to Chifley. Evatt received the heavy but welcome load of Attorney-General and External Affairs. Beasley was allocated Supply and Development, Makin Navy and Munitions, and Drakeford Air and Civil Aviation. These ministers constituted the war cabinet, which made the most vital decisions. Dedman, who was added to the war cabinet in December, had War Organization of Industry and ministerial responsibility for the Council for Scientific and Industrial Research. His department had been established by Menzies in mid-1941 but nothing had been done, and all Dedman inherited was some sheets of blank paper and an otherwise empty office. Curtin gave Ward – despite their frequent bitter clashes in opposition – the challenging and important portfolio of Labour and National Service. Lithgow tobacconist Bill Ashley, one of three Boer War veterans in Curtin's cabinet, became Postmaster-General and Information minister. Genial, gargantuan Dick Keane had Trade and Customs, Holloway was well suited to Social Services and Health, Home Security went to Bert Lazzarini, 76-year-old Collings had Interior, Cameron was allocated Aircraft Production, prominent Tamworth identity and former NSW MLA Bill Scully became Commerce minister, WA Senator J.M. Fraser had External Territories, Repatriation went to the sole Tasmanian, Charlie Frost, and Transport was taken over by Queensland Carters' Union founder George Lawson, who had served in the Boer War and the suicide squad that abolished the Queensland Legislative Council. Only the four who had served under Scullin (Forde, Beasley, Chifley and Holloway) had been ministers before, but this inexperience was partly offset by the valuable insights into wartime administration afforded by participation in the Advisory War Council.

Some members felt their omission keenly. It had been assumed that Rosevear's inclusion was certain, especially after Curtin chose him as one of Labor's seven speakers when the Fadden budget was challenged. He narrowly missed a place owing to lingering animosity arising from his temporary defection to the Non-Communist Labor Party. Most aggrieved of all was Calwell. He had only been in parliament for a year, but after waiting so long to get there he was indignant about being overlooked when men he considered inferior were promoted. He abused Evatt in the parliamentary foyer about his omission, but decided that Curtin's 'slumbering resentment' was primarily responsible for it: certainly his bitter reaction provoked Curtin's hostility afterwards. In the Representatives Calwell sat as far away from the ministry as he could, with Rosevear alongside, and became a troublesome focus for backbench discontent. Of the other unsuccessful aspirants, Pollard had strong claims. Scullin did not accept a cabinet post because of his variable health, but nonetheless exerted a profound influence in the upper echelons of the government: it was no accident that he was allocated the office between Curtin and Chifley. Brennan's omission from the ministry was no surprise, since his colleagues had not included him in the FPLP executive in 1940. He was gradually succumbing to Parkinson's disease, which made speechmaking increasingly difficult for him. His utter revulsion of war was undiminished, and he was an unsettling presence in caucus and on the backbench. Brennan's wartime priorities were frequently supported in parliament by Blackburn, who had not sought readmission after his second expulsion from the party, even though rank-and-file pressure forced the Victorian executive to back down on its ban on the Australian-Soviet Friendship League.

Despite a few disaffected individuals the Curtin government began with impressive zeal, dedication and cohesion. All the accumulated frustration and rancour concerning the right approach in opposition vanished overnight now that there was important work to be tackled urgently. Suspicions about Evatt's craving for office became grudging admiration for the incredible 'Doc' who maintained a cracking pace during long working hours, juggling numerous complex problems simultaneously. Curtin was soon raving about Evatt's ability to dictate word-perfect legislative clauses and cable messages on complicated issues. The youngest minister, 42-year-old Ward, applied himself with such fervour to the task of minimizing industrial disruption of the war effort that his wife became concerned about the risk to his health. On 18 November he told parliament proudly that there were no industrial disputes anywhere in Australia. The misgivings in the party about Beasley had only concerned his devious scheming with Lang; there was never any doubt about his acumen, as he showed in grappling ably with the vast organizational problems of supply. Makin quickly had the head of the Munitions department replaced by a talented public servant whose technical knowledge and experience had been undervalued by the Menzies government, and this change paid handsome dividends.

Chifley too burned plenty of midnight oil as he recast Fadden's budget, placing his own proposals before the ministry only 10 days after the government was sworn in. Following extensive cabinet deliberations, the revised budget was presented to caucus on 29 October. Fadden's plans to derive more revenue from all taxpayers were scrapped. Instead, Chifley levied higher income taxation on the wealthy, and increased company, sales and land tax. Soldiers' pay and allowances were lifted. These proposals were broadly acceptable to caucus as a short-term overhaul, but Calwell and Rosevear spearheaded an agitation on pensions which – by a margin of only one vote in caucus – resulted in special legislation being introduced to raise pensions by more than Chifley initially proposed. On this issue Ward voted against his cabinet colleagues in caucus. Whereas Dedman and other ministers had decided that in caucus they would never breach the principle of cabinet solidarity, Ward indicated that he would not be at all averse to persuading his caucus colleagues to reverse cabinet decisions he disagreed with. Chifley was also quick to utilize National Security Regulations to implement banking reforms consistent with his own recommendations in the prewar royal commission on banking.

The minister most transformed in government was Curtin. His adjustment to office surprised himself and others aware of his fears that he would not measure up as a war leader. In his integrity, oratory, commitment and his ability to get quickly to the core of a problem, he had displayed ample aptitude for the position: in office he also found the inner strength to sustain him through difficult, momentous decisions and the endless administrative grind. At times he still worried terribly, but the doubts and diffidence of opposition days disappeared. Instead he was soon unexpectedly assured in his new role. His anxiety about the parliamentary position eased when his government's resolute performance was rewarded by the continued support of Coles and Wilson in the Representatives and some independently inclined opposition Senators. Curtin made sure that despite the rush of pressing business he set aside time to think, lying on his office couch, either alone or trying out ideas on a trusted confidant like Chifley, Scullin, Holloway or his influential press secretary, Rodgers. Curtin's sincerity and modesty appealed to Australians. To them he conveyed – in a manner that was beyond Menzies – a genuine concern for the nation and its people, and a willingness to ensure that in Australia's time of trouble his government would take the drastic measures that were appropriate.

Curtin's relationship with the press was unique. No Australian prime minister has been more open with journalists than Curtin. He decided that the best way to handle highly secret wartime information was to take the newspapers into his confidence so that they would understand what could and could not be published, and why; having been a pressman himself, Curtin had a higher regard than most politicians for journalists' trustworthiness. His normal practice was to have an informal gathering twice a day with the 'travelling circus' of senior correspondents who accompanied him during the war. However, he was disappointed to find that his faith in working journalists was not always justified. Furthermore, Curtin was angered by the occasional misuse of privileged information by newspaper proprietors, especially Murdoch, whose anti-Labor tirades in the newspapers he controlled were interrupted on one occasion by a humble apology when Curtin threatened to sue him for defamation and £20 000 damages. Rodgers played a vital supporting role as press secretary, speechwriter and general adviser; he moulded the favourable image of the Prime Minister by providing journalists with suitable information and being prepared to beguile and bully them if necessary. As Rodgers knew, Curtin was much more troubled by criticism from the press and elsewhere than most public figures and suffered periodically from severe depression. Chifley arrived one evening at the Kurrajong after a long car journey from Bathurst to find a message from his chief

46. Albert Ogilvie. (by Alex Gurney; *State Library of Tasmania*)

47. Muriel Heagney. (*State Library of Victoria*)

48. A group of WA premiers. From left: Phillip Collier (Labor), 'Moo-cow' Mitchell (Nationalist), Frank Wise (Labor), Jack Willcock (Labor). (*Battye Library*)

49. Bert Evatt laying down the law, tie characteristically askew. (*National Library*)

50. Prime Minister Curtin exhorting Australians to contribute wholeheartedly to the war effort. (*John Fairfax*)

51. The killer of Father Christmas. (by John Frith; *Australian Consolidated Press*)

"Mr. Dedman Scrooge has banned Christmas advertising, the words 'Yuletide' and 'festive season' and the employment of Santa Claus in shops."

"*It's nae use waitin' for Father-r-r Chr-r-istmas, ye ken. Ah've r-r-rationalised him.*"

52. Five ALP premiers of Queensland. From left: 'Red Ted' Theodore, Frank Cooper, William Forgan Smith, Ned Hanlon and Bill McCormack. (*Oxley Library*)

53. John Curtin feeling the strain.

summoning him to the Lodge: 'Come over whenever you arrive; I'm spiritually bankrupt tonight'.

Despite Japan's pact with Germany and Italy it seemed during the Curtin government's early weeks that the likelihood of imminent Japanese attack had eased. Australia received numerous assurances from Britain and America that there was nothing to worry about for at least three months. Accordingly, while the Curtin government concentrated on galvanizing activity on the home front and explored ways to increase Australia's involvement in strategic decision-making, it made no dramatic move to bring the AIF divisions home immediately. However, when Churchill argued that the remaining weary 'rats of Tobruk' should stay in the beleaguered garrison they had long maintained in North Africa, Curtin and his war cabinet promptly showed that they would not be browbeaten and, as Curtin politely insisted, the relief was completed.

Curtin also resisted pressure from a different source concerning some appointments made by the Menzies government. Calwell and Ward, whose unbridled combativeness in tandem had earned them the joint sobriquet of 'the terrible twins', were angry that Curtin did not dismiss ex-Senator Pearce from his chairmanship of the Defence Board of Business Administration. Similarly, Curtin retained the drive and organizational genius of BHP's Essington Lewis, whose appointment by Menzies as Director-General of Munitions with extraordinary powers had been assailed by Ward. Far from reversing it, Curtin in fact responded to the slow manufacture of warplanes under Menzies by appointing Lewis to the additional post of Director-General of Aircraft Production. Curtin's response to the death of Labor's first national leader, Watson, also raised some eyebrows. Traditionally the party has not treated its defectors like Watson and Pearce generously, but Curtin, who as Brunswick branch president had defended Watson's leadership in 1907, gave him a warm obituary tribute in caucus and parliament in November 1941.

Later that month Japan's intentions became unmistakably ominous. A few days later it launched the Pacific war with a devastating attack on the American navy at Pearl Harbour, and followed up with an invasion of Malaya, air raids against Singapore, and the destruction of two powerful British battleships which had just arrived in a blaze of publicity after being dispatched by Churchill to assuage repeated Australian entreaties that Singapore should be fortified. Curtin reacted decisively. Appropriate emergency measures were swiftly taken, and Curtin made a straightforward yet inspiring national broadcast: 'Men and women of Australia', he began. 'We did not want war in the Pacific', but we 'are now called upon to meet the external aggressor' in 'the gravest hour of our history':

> We Australians have imperishable traditions. We shall maintain them. We shall vindicate them. We shall hold this country, and keep it as a citadel for the British-speaking race, and as a place where civilization will persist.

The sinking of the British battleships confirmed Curtin's longstanding misgivings about reliance on the capacity of Singapore and the British navy to safeguard Australia: 'Enemy striking-power in the air has given to the enemy an initial momentum, which only a maximum effort can arrest', declared Curtin, adding – to counter any despondency – that 'nobody worries about being a few goals down at half-time'.

The Curtin government had continued the efforts made by its predecessors to obtain assurances of support from Britain and America in the case of attack from Japan, and these efforts were now redoubled. Just before Christmas 1941 Churchill met US President Roosevelt in Washington to discuss how to distribute the forces at their disposal to meet the Japanese threat and maintain satisfactory activity in other war zones. Aware that these discussions were critical to Australia's security, Curtin and Evatt bombarded both leaders with cables. Over Christmas the 'cables in and out have just been staggering', observed Curtin. On 25 December Evatt was urged by his wife to have a break for Christmas dinner, but it was nine o'clock before he stopped for a meal; he wolfed it down, and returned immediately to work.

The limited replies the Australians received gave them no comfort. In fact Churchill and Roosevelt had decided that their strategy would be to 'beat Hitler first', with the Pacific remaining a subsidiary theatre of operations, but Curtin and his senior ministers were unaware of this decision. They were receiving ominous reports from their representatives in Malaya and Singapore, and concluded from the little they were told from Washington that both America and Britain were unable or unwilling to aid Australia properly although the situation was critical and most of Australia's soldiers and airmen were far from home helping Britain. The meagre aid offered by Churchill only confirmed to Australia's leaders that he underrated the Japanese, overrated the strength of Singapore, and was inclined to give over-optimistic assurances he could not fulfil.

Accordingly, Curtin decided that 'the stage of gentle suggestion has now passed'. He told Churchill bluntly that the measures proposed to bolster Singapore were 'utterly inadequate'. About this time he read a draft article prepared by Rodgers in response to a request from the Melbourne *Herald* for a New Year message about the challenge facing Australians in 1942. After Curtin amended and strengthened the draft, Rodgers sent it to the *Herald*, and one sentence in it was soon being flashed around the world: 'Without any inhibitions of any kind, I make it quite clear that Australia looks to America, free of any pangs as to our traditional links and kinship with the United Kingdom'. Although Australia had been privately looking to America for some time, this public plea – coupled with its directness, shorn of diplomatic linguistic subtleties – was highlighted in Australia and overseas as a dramatic shift in foreign policy. Menzies and the British were predictably displeased, but so was Roosevelt: 'in Washington Curtin's appeal was seen as almost treason against the major ally, Britain, as an unpleasant ditching of that ally in time of stress'. Hardly any notice was taken of Curtin's ambitious attempt in the same statement to obtain Russia's assistance in the Pacific war against Japan and to stir Australians not yet jolted out of their complacency:

> The position Australia faces internally far exceeds in potential and sweeping dangers anything that confronted us in 1914–1918...Australia is now inside the fighting lines ...Australians must be perpetually on guard...against the possibility, at any hour without warning, of raid or invasion...

The relentless Japanese advance showed no sign of faltering. The Eighth AIF Division was involved in a brave but unsuccessful attempt to stem the tide in Malaya, where its efforts were hampered by the undistinguished contribution of some of the British and Indian forces there. The defenders fell back on Singapore, but that much-vaunted linchpin – as Churchill had belatedly discovered after the repeated assurances Australia had received of its invulnerability – was only designed to meet a naval attack, not a southward thrust down the Malay peninsula. Sensing the inevitable, Churchill contemplated withdrawing Allied forces from Singapore, but decided against it after receiving a cable from Australia which contained a stinging sentence inserted in Curtin's absence by Evatt: 'After all the assurances we have been given, the evacuation of Singapore would be regarded here and elsewhere as an inexcusable betrayal'. The surrender at Singapore on 15 February dismayed Australians and was one of the darkest days in British military history. Over 15 000 Australians were included in the Japanese haul of about 130 000 prisoners, who were to suffer horribly at the hands of their captors.

Four days later the war reached Australia. On 19 February the Advisory War Council was meeting in Sydney when Beasley, having been called away from the Council's discussions, burst back into the meeting and blurted out 'The Japs have bombed Darwin!' Hundreds were killed in the biggest single air attack by Japanese bombers since Pearl Harbour. Suspicion of Japan's intentions had been a longstanding concern in the Australian labour movement, and now it seemed that the so far invincible Japanese forces could well be about to invade Australia as some Japanese strategists were advocating. No prudent Australian government could ignore the possibility. Although Curtin himself was so exhausted that he was admitted to hospital for a brief rest and some of his ministers apparently became temporarily unnerved by the alarming turn of events, the government responded rapidly and resolutely to the desperate situation facing Australia. The strength of the Australian militia – the force created by the government's exercise of its power to conscript Australians for home defence – was boosted when additional categories of men were called up. An Allied Works Council was created to undertake the wide-ranging construction projects required on the home front; Theodore was appointed its Director-General, with such sweeping powers over employment and administration that he could make and vary contracts, compulsorily acquire property and spend up to £250 000 without prior authority. A Civil Construction Corps, comprising volunteers and conscripts, was established to provide the workforce for these projects. The manufacture of various unnecessary commodities was prohibited, so that those producing them could be transferred to war work. An identity card for each citizen was introduced. Restrictions were brought in or tightened on trade, employment, supplies and travel. Chifley had already imposed sharp increases in taxation additional to the changes he had made in October.

Among the all-embracing regulations gazetted during this hectic period was one requiring Australian residents to perform any specified service to further the war effort. In the Representatives Brennan described such a measure as 'absolutely foreign and hostile to the whole of the theory, origin, genesis, history and tradition of the Labour movement'. Ward, Rosevear, Calwell and Charlie Morgan also made critical speeches in parliament, as did Blackburn, who used his freedom as an independent to the full and moved to disallow the regulation. Curtin, however, persuaded a caucus majority that Blackburn's motion should be opposed. Caucus solidarity prevailed when the vote was taken in parliament, and no Labor MHR voted with Blackburn. 'I envy him', Morgan admitted, 'because on this occasion he can not only speak but also vote as he honestly thinks proper'.

In this crisis the deployment of the AIF became a controversial issue. The decision to transfer the Sixth and Seventh Divisions from the Middle East to the Pacific theatre had already been taken, but their particular destination was in dispute. Churchill and Roosevelt were concerned about the situation in Burma, especially the Japanese threat to the Burma Road, a vital supply route to China. Since the Seventh AIF Division then on the water comprised the only available force in the vicinity, both leaders requested Curtin's approval of the use of this division as a temporary stopgap in Burma. Support for this proposed diversion came from Bruce and Page, who were then representing the Australian government in London, and the opposition members of the Advisory War Council. The Australian war cabinet had other ideas. With Australia itself endangered, its army should be brought straight home. Besides, the ministers correctly sensed, another fiasco like Malaya (and an earlier one in Greece) would be on the cards in Burma, especially as the men of the Seventh Division lacked air support and were detached from their arms and equipment. Curtin informed London that the Australian government was opposed to the diversion and wanted all its three divisions in the Middle East to return home immediately. Churchill and Roosevelt redoubled the pressure. On 22 February Curtin repeated his government's insistence that the Seventh Division had to come home. However, Churchill – unlike Roosevelt – still refused to accept the Curtin government's decision as final, and took the extraordinary step of diverting the convoy anyway. When the Australian ministers realized this, they were understandably enraged. Curtin rebuked Churchill for treating Australia's clear wishes so cavalierly and increasing the risks to the convoy of Japanese attack en route. Australia should be saved 'not only for itself, but to preserve it as a base' for a later counter-offensive against Japan, Curtin declared; it was 'quite impossible to reverse a decision which we have made with the utmost care, and which we have affirmed and reaffirmed'. Churchill grudgingly backed down, redirected the convoy to Australia, and remained under the mistaken impression that the Seventh Division could have prevented the fall of Burma.

Curtin then had to endure an agonizing wait while the AIF moved defence-lessly through Japanese-controlled waters. The acute burden of responsibility he felt for ordering Australia's soldiers home disturbed his sleep for weeks. Night after night he spent pacing about the grounds of the Lodge. 'How can I sleep while our transports are in the Indian Ocean with the Japanese submarines looking for them?' he explained to a friend. Another evening, when Curtin had to make an overnight train journey, journalist Alan Reid happened to get up in the middle of the night and found the Prime Minister staring out of the window with sweat trickling down his forehead. Reid asked what was the matter. Curtin replied, his hands shaking, that he had just had a ghastly nightmare about the returning troopships being torpedoed. Reid woke two other passengers, and together they played bridge with the Prime Minister until morning. When Boote heard that Curtin was overtaxing himself with work and worry, the veteran journalist asked him in the national interest to 'have mercy on yourself, and save up your energy for the truly big things'. In his letter Boote described Curtin as the irreplaceable 'mental and spiritual incarnation of Australia in this hour of peril'. Curtin replied that

> I am feeling much better although I must admit the strain is very heavy. . .Nothing gives me greater pleasure than the constant evidence that those whose friendship I have valued through all the years have been with me in my work in this present terrible time. I confess that if I did not have those the job would be intolerable. . .

He was tremendously relieved when the troopships arrived home safely.

Curtin received further good news on 17 March. That day he was informed that Douglas MacArthur, the celebrated American general, had landed in Australia after a dangerous secret journey from the Philippines, and that Roosevelt hoped that Australia would accept MacArthur as Supreme Commander of the South-west Pacific. Curtin readily agreed to the appointment. He was delighted that America had decided to make a genuine commitment to the defence of Australia. Roosevelt and Churchill had agreed on a zonal division of responsibility, which left the Americans in charge of the South-west Pacific region including Australia. Senior American policy-makers, influenced in part by Australia's representations, had modified the 'beat Hitler first' strategy, having concluded that it was in America's interests to respond to Japan's aggression more sternly and swiftly than previously envisaged.

Australians welcomed MacArthur enthusiastically. He was a charismatic commander with a massive ego which had been dented by the defeat of the forces he had led in the Philippines. As his train neared Adelaide he made his famous public declaration that 'I came through, and I shall return' to the Philippines, a characteristic utterance by a master of the theatrical flourish and the studied gesture. On 26 March he arrived in Canberra and met Curtin. A strong rapport quickly formed between the Supreme Commander and the Prime Minister. In strategic matters Curtin relied completely on MacArthur, which was fine at the beginning of their partnership when their objectives were identical. Later in the war, however, when Australia's interests did not always coincide with MacArthur's, Curtin was criticized for being too prepared to accept MacArthur's priorities.

In May 1942 there was a critical battle in the Coral Sea when a Japanese force intending to attack Port Moresby was intercepted. Parliament was sitting when news reached Curtin that the battle had commenced, and his impromptu remarks electrified the Representatives.

> The events that are taking place to-day are of crucial importance. . .As I speak, those who are participating in the engagement are conforming to the sternest discipline and are subjecting themselves with all that they have – it may be for many of them the last full measure of their devotion – to accomplish the increased safety and security of this territory. . .I put it to any man whom my words may reach. . .that he owes it to those men, and to the future of the country, not to be stinting in what he will do now for Australia. Men are fighting for Australia to-day; those who are not fighting have no excuse for not working.

This speech was considered by Rodgers, who saw hardbitten journalists moved by it, as Curtin's finest. At Coral Sea Japan experienced its first setback in the Pacific when its force was turned away from its objective. That engagement was followed by a major battle a month later at Midway, where the American navy inflicted some telling blows on the enemy.

These naval battles became more telling in retrospect than they seemed at the time. Japanese planes continued to bomb northern Australia, Japanese submarines made disturbing raids along the east coast, and Curtin and others remained extremely concerned about Australia's vulnerability to invasion. However, by mid-1943 only the most pessimistic refused to accept that the phase of acute crisis to Australia had passed. Yet there was no relaxation for Curtin. Australia remained on a total war footing, committed to removing the Japanese menace from the region. The government kept urging Britain and America to provide the necessary resources, and Curtin kept stressing to the Australian people the need for 'austerity'. He regarded drinking, horse-racing and betting as especially obnoxious activities at such a time, and was irritated by the reluctance of Victorian Premier Dunstan, that shifty cynic and Wren man, to curb horse-racing in his state. By contrast, when Wren telephoned Curtin to protest about one of Chifley's taxation measures – 'This Bill hits Mr Theodore and myself very severely, and I want you to do something about it' – Curtin replied, after consulting Chifley, that the legislation would proceed, and Wren should 'let Mr Theodore know that the Senate rejected a similar provision introduced by him in the days of the Scullin government'.

While Curtin and MacArthur kept striving for an increased allocation of resources to the Pacific and a greater role in strategic decision-making for Australia, Evatt reinforced these messages personally during a three-month trip to Britain and America. Evatt, like Curtin, hated flying, but he reluctantly agreed to run the Japanese gauntlet in the Pacific to press Australia's claims in the highest quarters. Beasley was full of admiration for him: 'poor bloody Evatt' would 'be crawling aboard those little planes at night, without lights, no heating, freezing to death, the stink of petrol everywhere, and sit for hours in a roar that would knock your ears off, with the plane trembling all round him'. With his untidy appearance, tie perpetually askew, Evatt, 'the Ayers Rock Australian nationalist', was bound to prove a jarring presence in the polished corridors at London and Washington. Never one to beat about the bush, Evatt saw his task as 'to bang on closed doors' to get Australia's viewpoint across, especially as he felt Australia had been kept in the dark about the formal agreement to 'beat Hitler first'. Curtin was delighted that Evatt managed to persuade Churchill to part with three squadrons of Spitfires, and the top-level strategic information the Doc acquired was also beneficial to Australia. Outside the closed doors Evatt also served his country well by vigorously publicizing its war effort and defence needs. Even Bruce, no admirer of Evatt, conceded that he 'worked unceasingly both day and night'. Although the Doc made minimal progress in Australia's perennial striving to obtain a meaningful voice in the big decisions, nobody else could have done more.

During the worrying months of mid-1942 the government accomplished a major breakthrough in the sphere of taxation. With Australia imperilled, the government was looking for ways to finance the war effort. It also wanted to remove the inequality and inefficiency created by the states' independent collection of varying rates of income tax. Chifley and Scullin were convinced that a uniform system of centralized direct taxation was necessary; when the premiers refused to accept a voluntary scheme, Chifley introduced legislation in May 1942 for a national takeover of all income tax. The legislation comprised four bills and was not founded only on the national government's defence power (which was far-reaching in wartime), thereby endowing the reform with a lasting significance. Sufficient opposition members supported the legislation to ensure its passage through both chambers, but all the premiers were antagonistic, some of them livid. Although the scheme provided that the states would be reimbursed to compensate for their lost revenue, even Labor premiers resented this intrusion on their autonomy: 'I will not be a vassal to anyone', declared Forgan Smith. He and McKell contended that this reprehensible change would jeopardize future social reform by the states, but ALP advocates of state rights had a difficult task when unificationist tendencies were entrenched not only in many Labor minds but in the party platform as well. McKell's intention to contest the constitutional validity of the scheme in the High Court was overwhelmingly overruled at the 1942 NSW ALP conference. Victoria's Dunstan also condemned the scheme, which convinced the Victorian ALP executive that its state MPs should withdraw their support from the Country Party Premier. Cain led Victorian Labor into opposition. Dunstan, who continued as Premier with UAP backing, and Forgan Smith aligned their states with SA and WA in a judicial challenge to the scheme, but the High Court, to the immense satisfaction of Chifley and Scullin, upheld the legislation.

Dedman was gradually making a name for himself. His admiration for Curtin was reciprocated, and the Prime Minister initially envisaged Dedman as his assistant, organizing the country for war. He had a rough early passage in the War Organization of Industry portfolio owing to the unprecedented administrative problems arising from such extensive departmental co-ordination, together with resentment from some cabinet colleagues at his rapid rise. But this awkward start was nothing compared to the reception awaiting him in the Australian press. He was completely dedicated to diverting Australia's non-essential resources to the war effort, but in public he was earnest and humourless: public relations techniques were a closed book to him, and he had no one like Rodgers to polish his image. Curtin could proclaim – as he frequently did – the virtues of austerity, without losing any of his lustre as a noble war leader exhorting the unpalatable in the interests of victory; it was completely different when Dedman, inspired by identical ideals, announced that women's clothing would be restricted to three basic sizes, men's clothing would be standardized to the basic 'Victory suit' and shirts with shortened tails, and a variety of other commodities would be rationed or banned altogether. Especially notorious was the attempt to curb excessive consumer spending by banning Christmas advertising: this decision made Dedman the killer of Santa Claus and, as far as even the less frivolous newspapers were concerned, it was as if Scrooge had been resurrected to torment the masses. Dedman became the most unpopular man in Australia. Although occasionally bruised by the intense criticism, he remained essentially undeterred. 'Like everyone else I want to win the war', he observed in September 1942. 'Unlike some other people, I am prepared to take the action which is necessary if we are to have a chance of winning it'.

While Curtin had complete faith in Dedman, his attitude to his other controversial minister, Ward, was very different. The Prime Minister was frequently troubled by Ward's conduct during 1942. Ward's propensity to divulge his disagreement with certain government decisions did not endear him to Curtin, whose adherence to the traditional notions of collective responsibility for cabinet decision-making was epitomized by his reverence for 'mateship'. Ward was also one of the FPLP members who revived old animosities by attacking Theodore's exercise of his all-embracing powers: Curtin, who supported Theodore, described Ward privately in July 1942 as 'a bloody ratbag', but refrained from criticizing him publicly.

Ward's most bitter clash with his chief came late in 1942 when Curtin initiated a significant change in party policy. There had been an increasing clamour about the unwisdom of having two Australian military formations, the volunteer AIF force, which could serve anywhere, and the militia, which had a more limited role since conscripts could only be directed to fight in Australia and its adjacent territories. During 1942 Labor's opponents kept trumpeting Australia's need for one army which could be utilized wherever appropriate. They knew this would mean in effect the introduction of conscription for overseas service, the very issue which had smashed the ALP during the previous world war; they were hoping for a repetition, but claimed that the interests of national defence were uppermost in their minds. Murdoch pressed for it so vehemently that Calwell, who was never one to shirk a confrontation with the press, suggested that he should be interned. While Australia was desperately defending against the Japanese the question of one army was irrelevant, but Curtin acknowledged that there might be a case for it when the process of driving the aggressor back commenced. MacArthur, whose strategic assessments greatly influenced Curtin, was eager to expedite the counter-offensive that would ultimately enable him to return to the Philippines. It seems that pressure from MacArthur was crucial in Curtin's decision to seek an extension of the area where the Australian militia could serve. There was also the sharp contrast between American conscripts coming so far to defend Australia and Australian conscripts being restricted to service in Australia and its nearby territories. If Australia did abolish this limitation, Curtin believed, the United States would be likely to look more favourably on Australia's continued requests for the men and equipment necessary to push Japan back. But it would be an explosive issue for the men and women of his party: 'many viewed conscription through spectacles made in 1916', even though the circumstances in 1942 were very different.

Curtin decided that his best option was a direct appeal to his party's federal conference in November 1942. He discussed his intentions beforehand with Chifley, perhaps Scullin and maybe nobody else. Evatt and Drakeford were among the ministers attending conference as observers to hear Curtin's address. Although they were in his war cabinet they were as stunned as all other onlookers except Chifley when the Prime Minister declared bluntly that there was 'no argument against one army'; it was an anomaly that 'a man could be sent to Darwin, where he could be bombed, but not to Timor to save Darwin from being bombed'. However, by placing a motion before conference that stopped short of creating a homogeneous army, Curtin implicitly acknowledged that he would be risking a massive upheaval like 1916 if he attempted a complete reversal of Labor's traditional policy. Instead he asked conference to agree that in this war a larger region was vital to Australia's security than the area defined in the legislation authorizing conscription for home defence. Accordingly, he moved that the provisions of the Defence Act should be extended beyond Australia and its territories to include also 'such other territories in the South-west Pacific area as the Governor-General proclaims as being territories associated with the defence of Australia'. Calwell protested. This matter was 'not properly before conference', he contended, and it should be 'remitted to State branches before Federal conference committed the Labor Movement to what was conscription for overseas service'. After Curtin stated that he had no objection, conference adjourned to enable state branches to consider the question.

A spirited debate began within the party. When cabinet discussed Curtin's idea on 24 November Ward and Cameron expressed their antagonism in the fiercest terms, and Holloway, usually a strong Curtin supporter, was also opposed. Three days later Curtin and Ward resumed hostilities at a meeting of the NSW ALP executive, which voted in favour of Curtin's proposal. Ward's conduct was condemned from a different quarter when Federated Ironworkers' Association secretary Ernie Thornton, one of the prominent Communist union leaders whose influence was perturbing Santamaria and H. M. Cremean, derided Ward contemptuously as a 'cheer-chaser'; the Communists were still right behind the war effort. In Victoria Dedman and Keane, who supported Curtin's proposal, were on the state executive, but they were in the minority as Calwell and Cameron organized the numbers. At the executive meeting on 4 December Curtin 'was kept waiting outside for some time and on the conclusion of his hour-long address was curtly told that the meeting no longer required his presence'. Dedman protested against this discourtesy to the Prime Minister.

Caucus met only twice more before federal conference resumed on 4 January. At the first meeting there was a rowdy debate when Curtin ruled an anti-conscription motion from Calwell out of order, since the matter was being considered by the federal conference. Calwell moved dissent, and was supported by Ward and Brennan, but they failed to persuade more than a quarter of the FPLP members present to vote for the dissent motion. Feelings continued to run high. Shortly afterwards Calwell, still smarting, sparked a major row on this emotional issue when he contravened an FPLP decision and seconded an anti-conscriptionist amendment moved in parliament by Blackburn.

Curtin emerged with a green light after all the state ALP branches committed themselves. WA and SA supported his proposal convincingly and Tasmania very narrowly, so its success was assured although the Queensland executive agreed with Fallon that it should be opposed. When the conference reconvened each delegate voted as instructed, and Curtin's motion was accordingly carried by 24 votes to 12. From his viewpoint it was a notable achievement. Not for the first time he had faced up to his conception of contemporary strategic realities and steered his protesting party away from longstanding defence attitudes. By adopting a flexible approach he obtained the maximum possible change while maintaining all-important party unity. The end result was well short of his ideal objective of a homogeneous army, and the extra flexibility he gave MacArthur and other strategists in their utilization of Australia's armed forces affected the future course of the war only slightly, but Curtin believed, with justification, that the extension of conscription yielded significant diplomatic benefits for Australia. His achievement reflected the fact that his party respected and – in direct contrast to Hughes in 1916 – fundamentally trusted him.

Curtin paid a price, however. The poisonous remarks flung at him during the controversy by the most vitriolic FPLP anti-conscriptionists – principally Ward, Calwell and Cameron – distressed the Prime Minister and damaged the government's cohesion. Curtin responded to one of Cameron's outbursts with dignified resignation:

> Rabaul is further from the Australian mainland than Timor. It is not possible for me to be a good Labor man when I conscript men for Rabaul and New Guinea and to become a suspect Labor man for doing the same thing in respect of Timor...The strictures of the Minister for Aircraft Production upon myself make me unhappy, but what is irrelevant can be endured.

But it was a different story when Ward bluntly accused Curtin of 'putting young men into the slaughterhouse, although thirty years ago you wouldn't go into it yourself'. After that barb Curtin apparently broke down and wept. Later, when Ward attended the reconvened federal conference (although not a delegate), Curtin was sufficiently nettled by his presence – despite having the numbers sewn up – that he challenged Ward's right to be there. There was no way that delegate Calwell's presence could be challenged, and he used the occasion to direct a bitter diatribe against Curtin, charging him with frequently violating

Labor principles in office. 'Why', he cried, 'we had to line you up against a wall to get you to agree to twenty-five shillings a week for old age pensioners, and even then we only won by one vote!' Boote, who had vigorously opposed conscription in 1916 like Cameron, Ward and Calwell (and also Curtin), conceded that the 'Curtin proposal was brought forward in all sincerity', but his uncompromising opposition to it in the *Australian Worker* and elsewhere especially saddened the Prime Minister.

Curtin's relationship with Ward and Calwell further deteriorated. He had a bitter exchange in caucus on 24 March 1943 with Calwell, who later claimed that he was sneeringly described by Curtin as 'the hero of a hundred sham fights'. Always an instinctive counter-puncher, Calwell instantly hurled back a wounding retort: 'It's all very well for you to say that, but the way you're going you'll finish up on the other side, leading a National Government'. Curtin responded angrily, and left the meeting. Amid uproar Tasmanian Senator Lamp rushed up to Calwell threatening to fight him, and Lazzarini tried to have Calwell expelled from caucus. A hastily written letter from Curtin was read to the meeting, inviting the FPLP 'either to dissociate itself from the accusation or appoint another leader'. Calwell apologized and withdrew his allegation, and caucus unanimously confirmed its 'complete confidence' in Curtin.

The evidence of Curtin's declining confidence in Ward was unmistakable the following month when sharp differences between them emerged in the handling of an important waterfront dispute, but a much bigger controversy initiated by Ward was capturing the headlines. He was infuriating the opposition by repeatedly alleging that the Curtin ministry's predecessors had been derelict and defeatist in adopting the Brisbane Line concept in their planning to counter the threat of a Japanese invasion. The details of his allegations lacked precision and consistency, and were based on confidential advice from an informant whose identity Ward never publicly disclosed. Ward was inadvertently encouraged in his campaign by some loose remarks by MacArthur, who claimed in March 1943 that when he arrived in Australia a year earlier he had altered the existing home defence plan based on the Brisbane Line. This plan recognized that Australia's most vital strategic centres lay in its south-east corner, and it was not realistic to expect that the whole of the vast continent could be held by the available forces against a determined invader possessing overwhelming superiority in trained soldiers, equipment and air cover. Therefore the idea was to concentrate Australia's forces south of Brisbane, and to maintain elsewhere only scattered garrisons which if attacked would not be reinforced. This plan was presented to Curtin and his war cabinet (which did not include Ward) as an appreciation by its military advisers in February 1942, and was rejected. Army minister Forde was appalled by the inference that much of Queensland (including his electorate) was to be abandoned, and the war cabinet accepted his recommendation that all populated areas of Australia should be defended. As the controversy stirred up by Ward escalated, searches were made in official records, which purportedly established that no government had ratified the Brisbane Line plan. So, according to these records, the Brisbane Line concept was submitted to Curtin and his colleagues, not their predecessors; it was rejected, not supported, by the government; and this occurred before, not after, MacArthur arrived in Australia.

It was a delicate situation for Curtin. He had no fondness for Ward, and no desire to embroil MacArthur and other senior military figures in political mudslinging. Nor did Curtin want Australia's highly secret defence plans to be divulged, a concern shared by other war cabinet ministers who were angry with

Ward, believing that he was 'ill-informed' in these matters and had 'blundered badly'. Beasley was especially irate with Ward. At the same time, however, the opposition's heated response showed that Ward's claims had touched a raw nerve. Curtin's awareness of the opposition's discomfort seems to have influenced him not to curb Ward until it became politically imperative. That stage was reached in June 1943, when Ward declared that if there was nothing in official records to substantiate his charges then a document must have been removed from the files. Checks were made and assurances given that this was incorrect, and Ward conceded in a private conversation with Curtin that his informant might have confused the dates. In public, however, Ward enraged the opposition by stating that he was 'satisfied' that a document which would verify his claims was 'still in existence' and insisting that his 'charges still stand'. Whenever in a tight corner Ward would instinctively counter-attack with redoubled aggression, but it is possible that he had acquired information, which he believed genuine, about decisions or attitudes not disclosed in the official records that were searched. When the opposition's call for a royal commission was supported by Coles, whose support was still crucial to the government's survival in parliament, Curtin agreed to an inquiry.

The royal commission proved unenlightening. Ward refused to step down from the ministry, so Curtin suspended him until the inquiry was over. Ward also protested about the commission's narrow terms of reference, contending that they prevented him from proving his claim that Menzies and Fadden were responsible for the 'defeatist' Brisbane Line concept. Curtin, however, wanted to avoid a wide-ranging probe into Australia's defence secrets in wartime, and restricted the inquiry to Ward's allegation of a missing document. At the inquiry Ward used parliamentary privilege to absolve him from giving evidence, and the commission's findings were predictably inconclusive. Meanwhile the opposition had felt sufficiently emboldened to make threats about blocking supply, and Curtin had responded by calling an election.

The election was a triumph for Curtin and his party. With his fine leadership the campaign centrepiece, Labor won more Representatives seats then ever before (more than twice the opposition's tally), and its clean sweep in the Senate gave it a clear majority in that chamber, its first since 1914, as well. For the first time the voters had re-elected a national Labor government. The 15 ALP gains in the Representatives were offset only by Labor's solitary reverse in Maranoa. Blackburn contested Bourke as Independent Labor but was narrowly defeated by ALP candidate Bill Bryson, a postal unionist. In Curtin's own seat, almost lost in 1940, the Prime Minister quadrupled the vote obtained by his closest opponent. Having publicly confirmed that the danger of invasion had passed, Curtin summarized Labor's policy in the slogan 'victory in war, victory in peace'. He reviewed his government's performance with pride:

> We faced an era of dangers and problems unprecedented and unpredictable. We met them unwaveringly. We had a trusteeship to and for Australia. Our country has now withstood the direct trials; it has lived through its darkest hour; it is now confronting the dawn of a victorious and a better day. The Labor Government has done its duty.

Labor's disunited opponents complained that they had received insufficient credit for establishing the foundations of the war economy which was now in full swing; there were undoubtedly distortions in the election atmosphere, but

Labor could be justifiably proud of its achievements under Curtin's distinguished leadership. Aircraft and munitions were being manufactured speedily, and Theodore's Works Council had accomplished miraculous feats of rapid construction.

A feature of the campaign was the newspaper coverage. Murdoch was more belligerent than ever. During the campaign he 'wrote a number of incoherent and venomous articles, accusing Labor of being defeatist and pacifist'. Despite Murdoch, Labor was treated more favourably by the press than ever before. Even the *Sydney Morning Herald* declared its admiration for the performance of Curtin, Chifley, Evatt and Beasley, although it withheld its approval from some other ministers including Ward. A year earlier it had extravagantly praised Curtin's leadership. 'Thank God, we may all say fervently', it gushed, that he managed to hang on to Fremantle in 1940.

> For John Curtin has since his (and our) critical hour become Australia articulate. . .In every race, someone arises at its direst extremity, with the gift of the very best in that race. Sometimes he is a poet, but rarely. Today we are fortunate in having him a Prime Minister.

Among the FPLP's acquisitions in 1943 was *Australian Women's Weekly* news editor Les Haylen, who was demoted by Frank Packer for seeking ALP preselection. A witty, talented livewire who had written plays and novels, Haylen was never inclined to submit to injustice, and a major controversy developed. Haylen won his point and also the preselection contest for the safe UAP seat of Parkes, held since 1919 (except for McTiernan's brief tenure) by a decorated soldier who had been a minister under Bruce and Lyons. Haylen was also a veteran of the Great War, having enlisted under-age and served at the Western Front, where his brother was killed. During the Depression Haylen's acclaimed play *Two Minutes' Silence* became one of Australia's first 'talkie films'. In the 1943 campaign he regretted Curtin's promise not to socialize any industry in wartime (a response to alarmist opposition pressure), and there was consternation at NSW ALP headquarters when the novice in Parkes described its election propaganda as poorly written and printed. Using his own material instead, Haylen capitalized on the general swing to Labor, and won a famous victory. His unconventional approach continued in parliament when he used his maiden speech, with war still raging, to call for measures to stimulate Australian culture.

Haylen was not Labor's only talented acquisition in the 1943 landslide. Adelaide was won by railwayman's son Cyril Chambers, a dentist and former SA ALP president who pioneered dental services in the Northern Territory while serving with the army. The FPLP's two newcomers from Tasmania provided further evidence that Labor was endorsing more candidates with tertiary educational qualifications. Into the Senate came Nick McKenna, who had left his birthplace, Melbourne, to practise law with A.G. Ogilvie's firm of solicitors, and Denison was prised from the UAP by Doctor Frank Gaha, who had served in Ogilvie's cabinet. Labor's new MHR for Martin, boyish-looking 30-year-old clerk Fred Daly, had more modest educational attainments but was second to none in zeal and determination, as he showed in winning a difficult preselection and then dislodging the wealthy, well-entrenched UAP incumbent. Another unlikely NSW Labor seat, semi-rural Eden-Monaro, was won by Allan Fraser, whose preselection was aided by a batch of faked unionist votes sent in by an obliging union secretary at Goulburn. Another new member from NSW was Senator Donald Grant, one of the IWW 'Twelve' controversially gaoled during the Great War.

Labor's gains in WA enabled it to hold all Representatives seats in that state for the first time. Becoming MHR for Perth was a superb 33rd birthday present for Tom Burke, a former wood carter who had qualified as an accountant. The large WA rural seat of Forrest was captured by Nelson Lemmon, who had a proud pedigree in the labour movement. His father John had been MLA for Williamstown in Victoria since 1904, and was to retire in 1954 as the Australian and British dominion record-holder for uninterrupted tenure of a parliamentary seat. Nelson was an able, down-to-earth character who enjoyed living in the country and brought to the FPLP a valuable knack of devising solutions to rural problems. At his farm he arranged a signalling system with his wife: one teatowel alone on the clothes line meant a snake about; two indicated another hazard; and three signified 'Come home quickly', the signal that brought him thrashing home in the tractor one June evening in 1943, to be told that Curtin had unexpectedly called the election and there was not a moment to lose in starting his campaign.

There was another notable newcomer from WA, Perth-born schoolteacher Dorothy Tangney, who became Labor's first woman member of the federal parliament. Daughter of an engine driver, Senator Tangney had an early involvement in the labour movement and formed the Labor Club at the University of WA, before unsuccessfully contesting the state seat of Nedlands in 1936 and 1939 and the Senate in 1940. A second Labor woman, redoubtable feminist Jessie Street, having lost the Eden-Monaro endorsement to Allan Fraser, switched her sights to Wentworth and almost pulled off an improbable victory. Another woman well known to Labor voters was elected: Enid Lyons won a Tasmanian seat for the UAP and became the first woman MHR. The sharp increase in women candidates at this election flowed naturally from the wide-ranging activities and employment opportunites for women arising from the demands of the war and the decisions of the Curtin government. The creation of the Women's Employment Board, with Judge Alf Foster as its chairman, resulted in increased wages for some women during the war but not equal pay, which was the objective of indefatigable Muriel Heagney (and the ALP platform). The Curtin government benefited women in other ways, notably with the long-overdue introduction of pensions for widows and deserted wives. Curtin himself found the time during a hectic period to honour Jean Beadle, who died in May 1942, with a generous tribute published in the *Westralian Worker*.

However, the status and prominence of women within the ALP had scarcely changed. At the 1908 federal conference Andrew Fisher had expressed the hope that the presence of two female delegates signalled an increasing involvement by women in the party. Yet no federal conference since then had been attended by more than two women delegates, and Tasmania was the only state to include a woman in its delegation between 1936 and 1953. Jessie Street had believed that the party 'stood for equality of women, but. . .found by experience the Labour stalwarts were as loyal to the status quo of male preference and male domination as their opponents'. Jean Daley terminated decades of dedicated service to her party with a parting blast to her male comrades along similar lines.

After the 1943 election caucus made only one change in Curtin's ministry. It was not surprising that the large number of newcomers tended to support the existing ministers, who were not only the most familiar names but had also contributed to such a slashing victory. Before the ballot there was speculation that Ward's prospects had been damaged by the Brisbane Line affair, and it was known that Curtin did not want him included; nevertheless, he was re-elected. Calwell was desperate to be elevated into the inner circle, a promotion he considered overdue on account of his ability, seniority in Victoria, long service and experience, and he scraped in on the last ballot just ahead of Pollard and Lawson. Rosevear was not a contender, preferring the position of Speaker, although his aggressive debating style was more suited to the role of protagonist than detached judicial umpire.

Curtin made few changes in allocating the portfolios. He consulted with Rodgers on the alterations, which included Holloway taking over Labour and National Service from Ward, J.M. Fraser transferring to the vacancy left by Holloway at Health and Social Services, and Dedman rising in seniority while retaining his previous responsibilities. Curtin could not resist a smile as he told Rodgers

> I've given Calwell Information. He's been fighting with the newspapers all this time, now he can learn to live with them. I've given Ward External Territories and Transport. The Japs have got the external territories and the army's got the transport.

These ministerial arrangements continued the dual burden Chifley had carried since December 1942, when in addition to his heavy duties as Treasurer he was appointed minister for Postwar Reconstruction (PWR). Proper planning for the adjustment to peace was a high ALP priority, affirmed and reaffirmed at wartime federal conferences. Although there was a strong feeling in the party that PWR should be headed by a minister with no other responsibilities, Curtin made a shrewd choice. His appointment of Chifley clearly showed the importance the government attached to PWR, and provided the new department with a minister possessing the political clout to win demarcation disputes with other departments. The PWR department attracted a variety of talented visionaries who were preoccupied with creating a better social climate than Australians had previously known. They wanted to avoid the dislocation of the previous transition from world war to peace and to help create international financial structures which would prevent the devastating economic crashes of the past. Above all they wanted to ensure full employment, despite the massive problems generated as hundreds of thousands of Australians in the armed forces and other war work returned to peacetime activities. They were confident that the doctrines of Keynesian economics would be the key. Under the benevolent eye of Chifley (himself a wholehearted Keynesian), and with Curtin's full support, the idealists flourished at PWR, plunging into exciting research and formulating their optimistic plans for the future.

An important PWR objective was to improve welfare provisions for Australians in need, and the Curtin government did not wait until peacetime to act. Its prompt action to increase the pension rate for the elderly and the infirm and to introduce pensions for widows and deserted wives was followed by legislation providing workers with unemployment and sickness benefits, and other initiatives included funeral benefits and extended maternity allowances. Reciprocal arrangements with New Zealand were introduced concerning old age and invalid pensions. Aboriginal Australians were given significantly increased entitlement to welfare benefits. The Curtin government also made a start on a comprehensive health scheme, but the first step, the Pharmaceutical Benefits Act, was declared constitutionally invalid. Under this legislation certain medicines prescribed by doctors could be supplied by chemists to patients free of charge, the national government paying the cost, but some doctors claimed to detect in this legislation a blow to their professional status. Their challenge was successful in the High Court, which underlined the Constitution's obvious shortcomings by ruling (Mr Justice McTiernan dissenting) that the scheme was beyond the government's power. Although health reform initially faltered, the war and the reforms enacted during it resulted in a measure of economic improvement for working-class Australians after the grim 1930s.

Attaining PWR objectives would naturally be easier if the constitutional obstacles could be removed, and Evatt embarked on a bold attempt to shift them. In 1942 he introduced a bill for a referendum to endow the national government with greatly enlarged powers to facilitate postwar reconstruction. Without appropriate constitutional amendments, he asserted, there would be 'social and economic disorganization, chaos in production, mounting unemployment, widespread social insecurity – in short, anarchy'. The bill was greeted with animated protest from all sides, including senior state Labor politicians. Forgan Smith even managed to claim that 'this proposal involves not only the danger of a Fascist dictatorship, but also a Communist dictatorship'. As in the Great War, opponents of constitutional change argued that the divisive distraction of a referendum would hamper the war effort. The government responded by organizing a constitutional convention, to be attended by federal and state MPs of all the major parties, to discuss the proposed changes. Evatt's fanatical desire to achieve fundamental constitutional reform was very apparent. He summoned about two dozen hand-picked lawyers, writers and advisers to a secret meeting in Melbourne one Sunday, and told them they were to produce a book within a month. The result, *Post-War Reconstruction: A Case For Greater Commonwealth Powers* (188 pages), was distributed to convention participants.

The discussions at the convention confirmed that strong opposition to Evatt's proposals would persist, and agreement was reached on an alternative approach. This compromise involved the voluntary transfer by the states of specified powers for the duration of the war and five years afterwards. Curtin – whose 'superb leadership' in Dedman's opinion prevented the convention from ending in utter failure – apparently concluded that this avenue was the government's best option if it wanted to avoid a fiercely contested referendum in wartime. However, the Prime Minister was not alone in having misgivings about repeating the procedure pursued unsuccessfully in the Great War as an alternative to the referendum. Besides, Australians might never be more inclined to support a referendum on increased national powers. In those critical, anxious months of 1942 Australians regarded Curtin and Evatt as the key men, and the state political leaders in comparison were of minor significance. In November 1942 a public opinion poll asked Australians whether state governments should be abolished, and only 22% supported retention with no fewer than 60% favouring abolition.

There was hardly any change in the political complexion of the states during the Curtin government. The thriving economy, with low unemployment and improved welfare provisions, contributed to the re-election of incumbent state governments as well as the Curtin government. Forgan Smith's fury with the uniform taxation scheme contributed to his resignation in 1942, and he 'retired' to an important and well-paid position supervising the sugar industry. His successor was courteous, capable theatre enthusiast, AWU activist and MLA for Ipswich since 1915, Frank Cooper, who became the first Queensland ALP premier from an electorate outside his party's traditional strongholds in the north and west of the state. The Queensland ALP retained its authoritarian aura. It did not soften its stern attitude to pro-Russian organizations, which led to the birth of rebellious offshoots like the North Queensland Labour Party headed by colourful Mundingburra MLA Tom Aikens. Labor's other premiers, Willcock (WA), Cosgrove (Tasmania) and McKell (NSW), remained in office throughout the Curtin government, and there was no change in SA, where Labor under Richards continued in opposition although it improved its position at the 1944 election.

The only state where a change occurred was Victoria. Cain had been plotting with UAP leader T.T. Hollway to end the electoral distortions perpetuated by the Country Party government led by Dunstan and supported by Wren. Cain's scheming paid off when Labor and the UAP combined to defeat the government in September 1943 on a no-confidence motion based appropriately on the electoral system and Dunstan's neglect of education. Hollway had expected to become the new Premier, but the Governor commissioned Cain as Labor was numerically stronger in the Assembly than the UAP. In these circumstances Hollway patched up a hasty agreement with Dunstan, and the Cain government was in office for only four days.

Curtin and Evatt continued their strenuous efforts to safeguard and promote Australia's interests at the highest international levels. Evatt returned to the Northern Hemisphere in 1943, again spectacularly displaying his unease as an aircraft passenger and making himself an unpopular visitor by pressing Australia's viewpoint with bluntness and vigour. Curtin journeyed to America and England in 1944. He stirred British audiences with brilliant impromptu speeches, but he did not enjoy his stay in London. The constant strain he had endured since October 1941 was severely affecting his health. He handled the business part of his sojourn capably, but reduced his social engagements to the bare minimum, preferring to rest at his hotel alone or with his wife or Rodgers. In America Curtin met Roosevelt and soothed his hosts' chagrin at the Evatt-inspired treaty between Australia and New Zealand. This agreement asserted the signatories' common interests, including the right to participate in decisions and arrangements affecting postwar security, especially in the Pacific region. It was the product of a conference in Canberra in January 1944, and arose from Evatt's angry reaction to faraway talks between representatives of America, Russia and Britain which seemed to indicate that the great powers were shaping the peace and postwar settlement without consulting Australia.

While Curtin was overseas in 1944 Calwell was involved in a bitter censorship controversy. Senior ALP identities reacted differently to Labor's problems with adverse press treatment. In the range of responses Evatt at one extreme tried sedulously to cultivate the proprietors, and at the other Calwell counter-attacked ferociously. Calwell claimed in 1941 that the press was 'owned for the most part by financial crooks and. . .edited for the most part by mental harlots'. In 1942 he and Ward were involved in separate bitter clashes with Packer's notorious *Daily Telegraph*. As differences over the administration of censorship arrangements gathered momentum early in 1944, a cool ministerial head might have avoided a major confrontation. Instead Calwell was inflammatory, referring to the Australian newspapers' wartime role as 'inglorious' and describing their hostility to censorship as 'insincere and unpatriotic'. In mid-April 1944 the smouldering dispute erupted when Calwell authorized the suspension of the *Daily Telegraph* and *Sydney Morning Herald* for censorship breaches. In the ensuing uproar four other newspapers were suspended, there were dramatic accounts and photographs of police seizing newspapers at gunpoint, and the newspapers concerned obtained a High Court injunction restraining the censors. NSW Premier McKell, who was concerned that the controversy might harm Labor's prospects at the imminent state election, incurred Calwell's lasting wrath for publicly accusing him of a 'rash and ill-considered approach typical of conduct which has already seriously embarrassed my government'. In Curtin's absence Forde told Calwell that he should 'pipe down on the whole question'. The censorship differences between the newspapers and the Curtin government were further aired in the High Court before a compromise was found, but there was no truce in the hostilities between Calwell and the press: Calwell began to appear in *Sydney Morning Herald* cartoons as 'Cocky', an old bird with a big beak whose only words comprised the repetitive screech 'Curse the press!'

McKell need not have worried about that election. The large majority Labor enjoyed at the end of 1942, 56 of the 90 Assembly seats, was retained after NSW voters had their say on 27 May. This superb result was a tribute to the McKell government's performance, which attractively combined sound administration with visionary touches. Fundamental to the Premier's leadership style was his firm faith in the benefits to be derived from prudent planning. He also demonstrated shrewd insight into rural problems, a willingness to commit NSW wholeheartedly to the war effort, and an enlightened approach to conservation concerns, consumer protection and cultural pursuits. A strong leader in cabinet, McKell was not averse to riding his ministers hard when he considered it necessary. He was often perturbed by the impetuosity of Clive Evatt, and after the election he demoted Evatt to assistant minister and allocated Education to Heffron, who had been a purposeful minister for National Emergency Services. McKell was the first NSW Labor premier to serve a full term and be re-elected for another. His government was productive without the bombast and fireworks characteristic of NSW Labor under Lang. The Big Fella's slide continued when his disruptive behaviour led to an irrevocable break with Beasley and expulsion from the party in 1943. He continued his sniping from the sidelines and endorsed 23 Lang Labor candidates at the 1944 NSW election, but the only successful one besides himself was Lilian Fowler, the forceful Newtown personality who had become the first woman mayor in Australia.

The McKell government, unlike nearly all its equivalents in other states, fulfilled its obligations arising from the constitutional convention. All state governments had agreed with Tasmanian Premier Cosgrove's suggestion that they should do their utmost to pass a bill drafted at the convention providing for a voluntary temporary transfer of powers to Canberra, but only the NSW and Queensland governments had passed the bill in its original form. In Victoria the Dunstan government inserted a condition that the transfer would be inapplicable unless all states agreed. In SA the Playford government watered down the bill with amendments. So did the WA government, reflecting ALP Premier Willcock's hostility to the transfer. Tasmania's intransigent Legislative Council embarrassed Cosgrove by refusing to pass it at all.

Since the procedure for a voluntary transfer had obviously failed, the Curtin government decided to proceed with a referendum. It asked the electors on

19 August 1944 to provide the constitutional power – until the war ended and for five years afterwards – to legislate on rehabilitation of returned soldiers; employment and unemployment; organized marketing; companies; trusts, combines and monopolies; profiteering and prices; production and distribution of goods; overseas exchange and investment; air transport; uniform railway gauges; national works; health; family allowances; Aborigines. The voters were also requested to approve the insertion into the Constitution of clauses protecting Australians' freedoms of speech, expression and religion. All the proposals were grouped together, which meant that anyone disliking one of them was almost certain to reject the lot. This approach repeated the error made by the Fisher government in 1911. Evatt of all people should have realized this, as he had written about it himself in his biography of Holman. While Evatt was researching that book Hughes had told him that the 'only way to win a referendum is to frame the question so that you win when they vote No'. Nonetheless Evatt raced around Australia in a campaign 'strenuous even by his standards'. Curtin was exhausted and had to restrict his involvement severely, and some other Labor luminaries displayed a lack of enthusiasm about the referendum. Although all the powers sought were possessed by the national parliament in Britain, Canada, South Africa and New Zealand, the hysterical negativism of Labor's enemies 'was carried to extraordinary lengths of misrepresentation'. The national mood had changed since 1942. Despite 'Yes' majorities in SA and WA, the referendum was defeated.

By late 1944 an end to the war seemed in sight with Japanese and German forces being driven back, and the Curtin government was giving increasing consideration to peacetime issues like banking. The validity of the regulations introduced by Chifley very early in the government's life derived from its wide defence powers in wartime. The government was now looking to formulate permanent controls which did not exceed its constitutional limitations in peacetime. A group of ministers including Ward, Calwell, Dedman, Cameron, Holloway and Drakeford wanted complete nationalization; Chifley had advocated nationalization in his royal commission recommendations in 1937, but had concluded on the basis of wartime experience that it was not essential to achieving the government's objectives; Curtin was too ill to attend the lengthy cabinet discussions on the question, but his ministers knew that he opposed nationalization. Chifley's arguments prevailed in cabinet, and were also endorsed by the FPLP. The 1945 legislation strengthened the Commonwealth Bank's central banking functions, abolished its board (which had thwarted the Scullin government so effectively) and restored management to a governor, while keeping ultimate control of policy firmly in the government's hands. There was also a requirement, inserted against Chifley's wishes after Calwell had advocated it and Evatt had approved its constitutional validity, that in accordance with ALP policy all state governments and semi-government authorities had to transact their banking business with the Commonwealth Bank. While these measures were under consideration Curtin received some unsolicited advice about banking reforms, as Chifley had in 1941, from King O'Malley, now an 86-year-old living legend fond of describing his occupation as 'death dodger'.

Other significant initiatives also looked to the postwar era. Interstate airline operations were nationalized, with the establishment of an Airlines Commission and the government-owned Trans-Australia Airlines. The government participated actively in plans to revive the building industry. Ward was impressing transport experts with his energetic commitment to uniform Australian railway gauges. Evatt's zeal and intellect dazzled delegates attending the prestigious San Francisco conference which established the charter of the United Nations. No Australian had ever been as prominent at a global gathering, and the Doc's virtuoso performance secured for his country and himself an international reputation. Back in Australia Dedman released on 30 May 1945 the government's White Paper entitled 'Full Employment in Australia'. This document, a product of extensive consultation over a long period and eight separate drafts, was a detailed blueprint of the government's primary PWR goal and the foundation of Labor's aspirations for 'a new social order' in peacetime Australia.

However, while these plans for 'victory in peace' were gathering momentum it was becoming apparent that Curtin might not be able to lead Labor into the post-war era. In November 1944 he was hospitalized with heart trouble. Recovery was slow. He returned to duty on 22 January 1945, but too soon; he was more tired, more temperamental and more tormented than ever. It was a difficult time for his staff and colleagues, especially Chifley. Some judgements the Prime Minister made during this period were questionable: his decision to send Forde to San Francisco with Evatt in a joint delegation, for instance, caused friction between them and intense annoyance on Evatt's part. In April Curtin returned to hospital. Shortly afterwards Germany conceded defeat and the war in Europe was over. In June Curtin was transferred to the Lodge; 'I'm too tired to live', he remarked. On 5 July he died.

Curtin was fortunate that during his government the opposition was in disarray, but posterity has confirmed contemporary assessments of his greatness. In tackling a relentless stream of the most daunting problems – with notable success – he not only kept his party united but left it in its best shape for decades. He applied himself totally, although he knew that the incessant strain, his inability to relax and his sensitivity to criticism might make him a war casualty; he had in fact predicted in February 1943 that he would not survive the conflict. Curtin's stirring broadcast to the Australian people in response to the sudden Japanese onslaught in December 1941 contained some words quoted from Swinburne:

> Hasten thine hour
> And halt not till thy work be done.

They became a fitting epitaph to the man who read them.

10 'The Hope, the Inspiration and the Saviour of the Australian People': The Chifley Government, 1945–1949

FORDE, WHO HAD just returned from the United Nations conference, was sworn in as Prime Minister on 6 July 1945 pending the caucus election of Curtin's successor. He was certainly experienced, and had been a conscientious and loyal deputy to Scullin and Curtin, but there was a widespread feeling that he did not possess the necessary qualities to inherit Curtin's mantle. During May and June, in Forde's absence at San Francisco, Chifley had acted capably as Prime Minister following Curtin's readmission to hospital, but he was reluctant to contest the leadership until urged to stand by a number of colleagues, notably Scullin. Chifley told Forde of his decision to stand during an amiable conversation over a cup of tea, and that night they each issued a statement announcing their candidature. Makin subsequently announced that he too would nominate.

When caucus made its choice on 12 July Chifley had the numbers. Forde had discovered this beforehand when he invited Haylen to his office:

> He asked me about his chances. I told him frankly what the position was. It was brutal, but it was the kindest thing to do...His face went deathly white, the veins on his neck stood out in an effort to suppress his emotions...After a while he said, 'I must say a little prayer for Ben. It's not an easy job'.

Haylen had already established himself as the FPLP's irreverent imp, but even he was deeply touched by Forde's 'dignity and humility' during this crushing conversation. When caucus assembled, James proposed that the FPLP should postpone its decision because illness and overseas travel had caused so many absentees, including Evatt who was still in America; but caucus resolved to proceed with the leadership ballot, and the result was a convincing win for Chifley. Caucus again re-elected Forde deputy leader.

The FPLP's choice recognized Chifley's vital role while Curtin was Prime Minister, when Chifley took responsibility for the economy and PWR, allowing Curtin to concentrate on defence and war strategy. Chifley's personal and political support had been crucial to Curtin, and the party had benefited from their close association and complementary blend of attributes. Whereas Curtin was a fine orator, Chifley was an indifferent speaker, repeatedly mispronouncing certain words in his 'slow hacksaw of a voice'. However, Chifley's natural aptitude for dealing with people enabled him to shield Curtin from some of the tasks which Curtin found so draining. He received deputations and skilfully managed parliamentary business on Curtin's behalf. Curtin and Chifley had in common close friendship, devotion to the labour movement, the capacity to maintain gruelling working hours and the ability to absorb quickly the gist of lengthy tightly-reasoned documents. Rodgers always regretted that Curtin had not relinquished the leadership before his health was irreparably damaged. If he had done so, Rodgers believed, he could have been for Chifley the valuable elder statesman Scullin had been for him, and Australian political history after the Second World War might have followed a different course.

Chifley continued as Treasurer after becoming Prime Minister, but despite his heavy workload he was always approachable and never seemed flustered or hurried. Evatt could be a difficult colleague: the value of his unique talents and tremendous capacity for sustained high-pressure intellectual exertion was sometimes tarnished by his brusqueness, erratic tendencies and suspiciousness of others' motives. Although Curtin admired the Doc's ability, drive and intense nationalism, there had been intermittent tensions in their relationship. Yet Evatt had an unqualified regard for Chifley. Ward and Calwell were also fond of 'Chif'. Curtin was often withdrawn, preoccupied with war problems, and at times uncomfortably distant from his backbenchers; Chifley, in his everyday dealings with people, genuinely and effortlessly symbolized the ideals of the labour movement more than any other Labor leader. While Curtin was greatly admired by his party, Chifley was greatly loved.

A feature of Chifley's leadership was his skilful handling of caucus. When there were fiery exchanges in stormy FPLP meetings he was adept at soothing the tensions. He also frequently managed to steer caucus in the direction he wanted on particular issues which involved the perennial conflict between principle and pragmatism. In summing up after a lengthy debate when everyone who wanted a say had been given one, Chifley would often remark that it was all very well to be practical, but the ALP believed in principles and there were times when they had to be upheld irrespective of the cost. Alternatively, he would sometimes say that he admired Labor members with ideals, but there were times when common sense must prevail. It was rare for him not to get the result he desired.

Curtin's death enabled two West Australians to make a significant political advance. At the FPLP meeting on 12 July James and Scullin moved that there should be no change in the composition of the cabinet other than the elevation of one minister to replace Curtin, but this motion was carried only narrowly, since a number of ambitious ministerial aspirants desired a spill. Thirteen MPs nominated for the vacancy, but it quickly became a contest between Pollard, Lawson and 'Texas' Green's successor as MHR for Kalgoorlie, Vic Johnson. Pollard, the able Victorian who missed out in 1941 and 1943, was again unlucky: Johnson defeated him narrowly, preserving WA's dual representation in the ministry and underlining the influence of the AWU. A veteran bush unionist and formerly a champion shearer, Johnson had been national AWU president since 1942; initially a reluctant politician and an unconfident public speaker, he was much happier reciting bush yarns and verse. Curtin was succeeded as Labor MHR for Fremantle by 27-year-old schoolteacher Kim Beazley, and before long pundits were predicting big things for this handsome, knowledgeable and articulate newcomer. Tonkin and Hawke had been approached to stand for Fremantle, but both had misgivings about transferring to Canberra. Hawke's decision was later to gnaw at him, but Tonkin had no regrets. As if to confirm their more assured future in state politics, Willcock retired later that month. Caucus chose Wise as the new Premier; Hawke became deputy leader and Labor's heir apparent in WA.

Chifley settled into his new job smoothly. Totally immersed in his work, he spent long hours at his office before sauntering back – often alone and after midnight – to his small room at the Kurrajong. He used the Lodge only for distinguished guests, and continued to eat sparingly, making his own toast and tea. In May 1945, as acting Prime Minister, Chifley had announced the Allied victory in Europe, and one of his most pleasant tasks shortly after being sworn in was to broadcast officially the news that Japan had surrendered. If anyone needed a break at the end of 1945 it was the Prime Minister, but instead he made a surprise trip to New Guinea to spend Christmas with Australian soldiers awaiting discharge there.

Labor's national government maintained its reform momentum under Chifley. Returned soldiers were provided with a war gratuity and entitlement to vocational training, loans, special unemployment allowances and preference in employment for seven years. Every effort was made to avoid the mistakes made in arrangements for soldiers returning from the Great War. Soldier settlement schemes this time were organized much better than their earlier equivalents, which had produced such tragic hardship in the 1920s and 1930s. Returned soldiers benefited along with other Australians from the creation of the Commonwealth Employment Service. For the first time Australia's national government involved itself firmly in education, acknowledging its responsibility to returned soldiers as well as introducing a scheme of university scholarships and establishing in Canberra the Australian National University (ANU) for specialized research and postgraduate training. Lengthy discussions and negotiations about a planned revival of peacetime construction culminated in a housing agreement binding all state governments. This agreement complemented the National Works Council's carefully chosen priorities for major construction activity outside the housing sector. Australia's vital export industries, wool and wheat, were given firm postwar foundations. Plans were advanced for the establishment of an Australian motor vehicle industry. Life insurance was comprehensively regulated. Labor's hostility to the distortions perpetrated by the capitalist press prompted the government to legislate that the Australian Broadcasting Commission (ABC) had to establish its own news service and broadcast proceedings of the national parliament. The Hospital Benefits Act established free public ward treatment by introducing hospital subsidies to the states. Chifley told federal conference delegates that expenditure on social services had quadrupled since the Curtin government came to office in 1941.

In September 1946 the Chifley government was re-elected with a reduced but still comfortable majority. Although Chifley was sceptical about the effectiveness of last-minute electioneering, he spread Labor's message far and wide in a punishing campaign schedule. Despite the discouraging precedent of 1913, the government decided that concurrently with the election it would put to the voters three referendum proposals seeking greater national powers in social security, employment and marketing: the social services referendum was successful, and the other two proposals were nearly carried also. Labor lost seven Representatives seats held since the record-breaking triumph of 1943 and captured one. In the Senate Labor won every state but Queensland, an outcome which meant under the winner-take-all system that when the newly elected Senators entered the parliament no fewer than 33 of the 36 Senators would be representing the FPLP. It was a very pleasing result, although Labor's casualties in the Representatives included two ministers, Frost in Franklin and Forde in Capricornia.

Labor's vote was lower in Queensland than any other state, and in addition Forde suffered from his unpopular tenacity in refusing, on Curtin's instructions, repeated appeals from individuals desiring early release or other special treatment from the army.

Two ALP MHRs were defeated by Labor-leaning independents. One was Lang, who at last made the move into federal parliament which had been predicted for so long. In 1943 he had stood for Reid against Morgan unsuccessfully, but in 1946 he turned the tables. The other newly elected independent was Blackburn's widow Doris, who defeated Labor's Bryson in Bourke. Her success in her husband's former seat was another exquisite triumph for the ALP radicals in and around Coburg who were still at odds with the Victorian executive and still supporting their Independent Labor candidate Mutton in state parliament.

Labor's solitary gain in the Representatives was a most unexpected triumph. The Tasmanian seat of Wilmot was a sprawling electorate which covered nearly half the state and included its most inaccessible areas. Since federation Labor had held Wilmot for only three years, and Allan Guy, the well-known and experienced ex-ALP political shadow of Joe Lyons, had held it for anti-Labor since 1940. After Labor's slashing 1943 victory some disgruntled conservative Methodists in South Gippsland (Victoria) had decided to take revenge on their enthusiastic and popular local minister, Gil Duthie, because of his active support of the ALP. Using outrageously trumped-up charges, the troglodytes had Duthie transferred by the church to Latrobe in north-west Tasmania, where he characteristically plunged into the community life of the district, becoming active in the football and cricket clubs and president of the re-formed Latrobe ALP branch which had been defunct for nine years. With no other candidate offering to stand in seemingly unwinnable Wilmot in 1946, the Tasmanian ALP executive decided to take a punt on 33-year-old Duthie, and was promptly ridiculed for endorsing a mainlander who was unknown outside the Latrobe region. Duthie embarked on the most gruelling personal campaign ever conducted in Tasmania: during its most severe winter for 20 years he visited isolated mining and construction areas, tackling dangerous roads in heavy snow, and toured tiny hamlets in the backblocks where no politician had ever been. He was rewarded with an exhilarating victory over his opponent, who had contemptuously dismissed him as 'chicken feed'. But Duthie was not content to rest on his laurels: he amazed cynical Wilmot voters by making another extensive tour of his large electorate only four months after polling day. Duthie remained the energetic and committed MHR of this unlikely Labor seat for three decades.

Duthie was not Labor's only notable Tasmanian success in the 1946 federal election. Bill Morrow's success as a Senate candidate climaxed a remarkable resurgence after his expulsion from the ALP in 1938. His efforts to return to the party had failed repeatedly until mid-1942, when the state conference agreed to his readmission as a gesture to conciliate the powerful Tasmanian ARU. Back inside, he galvanized the party's radical unionists into a more cohesive force and spearheaded criticism of the uninspiring Cosgrove government, which scraped back to office at the 1946 state election after its lacklustre performance produced a swing away from Labor of 11·5%. Morrow's enemies in the party were appalled when he managed to win Senate preselection in 1946, and some AWU stalwarts withdrew their nominations in disgust, thereby boosting the preselection prospects of another left-winger, Justin O'Byrne. A former fighter pilot who had been a prisoner of war in Germany, O'Byrne accompanied Morrow into the Senate.

The Labor ministry guiding the nation's destiny after the 1946 election was significantly different from Curtin's 1941 cabinet. Unavailable were Curtin, Forde, Frost, Collings, Keane, Beasley and Makin. Collings, although still remarkably alert for an 81-year-old, was persuaded by Chifley not to stand. Dick Keane had died in April 1946. Beasley and Makin both had diplomatic posts, Beasley in London and Makin in Washington (Ward was offered an equivalent posting to Russia, but refused it). Evatt, after abundant achievements in power and with the war over, was tempted to return to the High Court, but Chifley persuaded him that he was still greatly needed and he stayed, perhaps also attracted by the possibility of following 'Chif' as Prime Minister. Inevitably, other ministers also aspired to the succession. Dedman, after his fine record in ministerial administration (if not in public relations), concluded that with Forde, Beasley and Makin all departed he had become a possible future leader. He nominated for the deputy leadership at the first caucus meeting after the election, encouraged by promises of support volunteered by Chifley, Scullin and others. Also standing were Evatt, Ward, Calwell and Drakeford. In the final ballot Evatt defeated Ward 43–33.

The caucus ballot for the remaining ministerial positions followed. Again there was no official leader's ticket, but Chifley had made clear to colleagues that he wanted Lemmon and Pollard to be among the new ministers. Both accordingly made it in the first ballot, along with nine re-elected ministers including McKenna, who had been promoted to cabinet after Keane's death. Later ballots restored Don Cameron and elevated five newcomers. They were Chambers, former Bundaberg cane farmer Ben Courtice, ex-Langite publican John Armstrong, Claude Barnard, who (like Chifley and Drakeford) was formerly an engine driver and prominent unionist, and Bill Riordan, a lawyer from a well-known north Queensland ALP family. Barnard followed Frost as Tasmania's representative in cabinet, and requirements of state balance affected other choices; Lemmon and Johnson were both successful in the first ballot, which meant that fellow Westralian J.M. Fraser was out and neither Burke nor Beazley would get a post despite the promise they had shown. The only minister dropped besides Fraser was Lazzarini.

The most disappointed aspirant was Haylen, who failed by one vote. His talent and experience in journalism had resulted in his appointment as publicity director of Labor's ill-fated 1944 referenda campaign, and he was looking forward to bigger and better things. Like Calwell in 1941, Haylen felt that the 1946 ministry was very able at the top but possessed a long tail of undistinguished performers. His chagrin was sharpened by the discovery on the party room floor afterwards of two discarded pro-Haylen ballot papers. Haylen concluded that skulduggery had robbed him of a ministry, and that Rosevear, the returning officer in the ministerial ballot, and other ex-Langites were the culprits.

Lang himself was a big drawcard in federal parliament. Nursing his hatred of Chifley, who had dared to challenge the Big Fella's supremacy in the 1930s, Lang was an implacable critic of the government. While providing the opposition publicly and privately with ammunition to attack the Chifley government, Lang in his parliamentary broadsides postured as an anti-Communist conscience of the labour movement. 'Probing and harassing at every opportunity, he inhabited the House like a huge monument of stone dug from a prehistoric quarry, alone, aloof, ignoring virtually all his past associates, cutting many of them dead'. Like other younger FPLP members, Duthie was fascinated to observe the legendary Big Fella in action:

His small dark moustache seemed to snap defiance with each word. The scars of battle were not visible on his face, but they were implanted in his soul as he flayed the ALP with unbelievable intensity. . . He spoke staccato – a human machine gun. He spat his words out. He emphasized his message with a disdainful shrug of his massive shoulders. I was amazed how well preserved he was at 71 years of age. . .

Lang's attacks induced Rosevear to leave the Speaker's chair and assail his former chief with one of the fiercest diatribes ever heard in the Representatives. It reminded Haylen of 'the hungry huskies in the Arctic Circle eating their fallen comrade in the traces so that the remainder could survive', but through it all Lang 'just sat rocklike, silent and unmoved. It was uncanny and awesome. . .The verbal bullets bounced off him as if he was armour-plated'.

Arthur Calwell was tackling the new Immigration portfolio with vigour and vision. Now that he had become a senior minister under a leader he revered, his forcefulness and impulsiveness were unchanged but his earlier embittered frustration had evaporated, and his more appealing qualities came to the fore. He was erudite, articulate and dedicated to his party, and the warm-blooded temperament responsible for those vitriolic outbursts also made him a likeable, witty companion. He wholeheartedly embraced the Immigration portfolio, which involved constructive, creative activity with long-term national implications. For years he had been an outspoken advocate of an extensive immigration scheme consistent with the White Australia policy, and soon after being appointed he sent a fact-finding mission headed by Haylen to Europe. Its recommendations included a promotional campaign overseas to emphasize Australia's attractiveness and another one back home to assure Australian citizens that the migrants would make jobs, not take them. Calwell was assiduous in breaking down trade union suspicions on this score, and he was greatly aided by the government's continued commitment to full employment. Despite shipping shortages and other problems the scheme prospered and grew, and by 1949 the government was bringing in annually 150 000 'New Australians' (which was Calwell's welcoming term intended to discourage insulting alternatives). The immigration programme became a great national success which benefited Australian life in a variety of ways.

SA Labor's endeavours to remove the Playford government were frustrated by a distorted electoral system. Whereas Labor's voting share increased from 42·52% in 1944 to 48·64% in the 1947 election (and the party contested five fewer seats in 1947), its MLAs decreased from 16 to 13. The capture of those three seats by the Playford government gave it 23 MLAs from a voting share of 40·38% (45·84% in 1944). Playford was benefiting from the electoral structure introduced by his predecessor, who had boasted that it would keep Labor out for 20 years. Under this notorious scheme Adelaide and its surrounding suburbs, with over 60% of the state's population, had only one-third of the parliamentary seats. Richards, who had led Labor since 1938, resigned, remarried and repaired to Nauru as the Chifley government's Administrator. He was succeeded as SA leader by Mick O'Halloran.

Meanwhile the SA branch structure had been significantly altered. Chiefly responsible were two tough and skilful political operators, AWU state secretary Clyde Cameron and Jim Toohey of the Vehicle Builders' Union. At the 1946 state conference, which elevated Cameron to the state ALP presidency, he managed to push through an important reform enabling party affiliates to utilize via their conference delegates a card vote equivalent to their members' sustentation fees paid to the state branch. This change naturally strengthened the unions' influence in party decision-making. Cameron realized that the key to party unity – which was so crucial to electoral success – was to acknowledge the inevitability, within a broad-based party like the ALP, of strong differences about the pace and priorities of change, and to ensure that no sections within the party felt excluded from its decision-making processes. By consulting, persuading and astutely utilizing the card votes at their disposal he and Toohey, who became state ALP secretary in 1947, provided SA Labor with a consensus-based cohesion which at times contrasted sharply with the situation in other state branches.

SA became the only state without an ALP government when Victorian Labor gained eight Assembly seats at the November 1945 state election and returned to office. The Victorian ALP's share of the primary vote had increased by nearly 5% since the previous election. Menzies's endeavours to unify diverse anti-Labor elements in a new national political force had culminated in the formation of the Liberal Party, but Cain continued to benefit from his opponents' splintering tendencies in Victoria. At the polls Labor won 31 of the 65 Assembly seats, a commendable result under the biassed electoral system. Many Victorian ALP enthusiasts had concluded that never again should Labor attempt to govern without a clear Assembly majority of its own, but the Victorian ALP executive supported Cain's acceptance of a commission to form a government although Labor lacked a majority in both chambers. H.M. Cremean had died suddenly in May, aged 45. While acknowledging Cremean's ability, Cain was relieved when Cremean's successor as deputy was a more congenial and unthreatening colleague – Frank Field, a lawyer and MLA for Dandenong since 1937. Cain's ministry also included Pat Kennelly, who had been the Premier's closest political friend for three decades; Carlton MLA and Wren associate Bill Barry; Attorney-General and Chief Secretary Bill Slater, who had spent part of the war in Russia as the Curtin government's diplomatic representative; likeable ACTU president Percy Clarey, who had climbed to prominence in the labour movement despite a permanent disability which forced him to get about on crutches; and two prominent ARU identities, Bill Galvin from Bendigo and Clive Stoneham from Maryborough.

One of Cain's new backbenchers was Frank Crean. After growing up in Hamilton Crean moved to Melbourne, where he was employed at the Taxation department and studied part-time in Commerce (and later Arts) at university, acquiring academic qualifications in finance rare in the ALP. A quiet, bookish Presbyterian Sunday school teacher, Crean was an amiable, tolerant man of calm temperament with an air of solid purposefulness about him. As a youngster he had listened to his father and friends talking about their dreams of Australia leading the world in social justice, and in Melbourne he joined the Albert Park ALP branch. In 1944 he was appalled by his first taste of a Victorian state conference with its cynical number-crunching and manipulation of the agenda, and he outlined his criticisms in *Labor Call*. Before the 1945 state election he sought preselection for Albert Park, which was not then a Labor seat and not regarded in ALP circles as very winnable. With the Movement's activities contributing to an increase in unedifying sectarianism which was no help to Labor, especially in Victoria, Cain and Kennelly judged Albert Park as unsuitable for a Catholic, and Kennelly – the crafty fixer with the most notorious stutter in the labour movement – decided to visit this stranger he only knew as Francis Daniel Crean. He took his time before delicately approaching the vital question: was Crean a Catholic? Greatly relieved by Crean's negative answer, Kennelly blurted out 'From now on you're Frank Crean, you've g-g-g-gotta cut out the Francis b-b-b-bloody Daniel!' Crean won the seat, and before long his unostentatious capacity was impressing Premier Cain.

The Cain government soon had severe problems with industrial unrest. No longer could strikers be accused of sabotaging the war effort; the wartime shackles restraining most unionists were off, and the Communists could resume direct hostilities with Australian capitalism now that Soviet Russia was safe from the fascist menace. It was estimated that between the armistice and the end of 1947 nine Communist-controlled unions representing 26% of unionists were responsible for 84% of the time lost in strikes. Victorians experienced a succession of strikes covering the building, transport, waterfront and fuel industries. Cain was racked with worry. He spent long nights with Kennelly in the Premier's office trying to find solutions. Eventually Cain urged rank-and-file unionists not to follow their Communist leaders, and he publicly attacked 'the communist minority which seeks to disrupt the social structure of this country and cause chaos to the whole community'.

This surge of industrial unrest was not confined to Victoria. There was an unsettled industrial mood throughout the nation as unions revived deferred objectives at a time when the economy was in transition from war to peace and the predictions of a new social order had stimulated unionists' expectations. This situation was especially pronounced in WA, where the prewar hegemony of the AWU was being challenged by urban trade unions growing in size, power and militancy. In 1935 the AWU had provided about one-third of all unionists who were affiliated members of the ALP; by 1944 this proportion had decreased to less than one-fifth. This decline was mainly attributable to the increasing mechanization of farming and construction work and the termination of unemployment relief projects. The militants wanted the new order to arrive more quickly than the WA government seemed willing to allow. They also desired to break the moderates' control of the integrated WA labour movement by creating a separate organization to co-ordinate trade union activity such as existed in every other state. The culmination of their growing influence was a bitter strike in November 1946 when the Locomotive Engine Drivers, Firemen and Cleaners' Union defied the WA Railways. The Wise government condemned the strike, the Arbitration Court president declared that the union 'had broken all rules and principles of law and morality', and by the time the dispute was settled the state economy had been crippled. Many WA unionists were now contemptuous of their state government, and this attitude contributed to its narrow defeat at the election four months later which ended 14 unbroken years of ALP government in WA.

There was another major strike in 1946. It occurred in Queensland shortly after Cooper retired as Premier and was succeeded, as expected, by Hanlon, whose enlightened initiatives at Health and Home Affairs, coupled with the Chifley government's health reforms, had given sick and needy Queenslanders the most advanced hospital system in Australia. Hanlon – like his Labour and Employment minister, Gair – loathed communism, and when he concluded that Communist influence was behind the widening of a three-month-old meatworkers' strike there was nothing enlightened about his reaction. Invoking a state of emergency under the Forgan Smith government's Transport Act, Hanlon announced tough measures designed to uphold the arbitration system and end the dispute. The strike quickly folded.

The influence of communism in the labour movement was becoming a potent political issue. It was the beginning of the 'Cold War', when Soviet Russia was no longer seen as a glorious wartime ally but as a hated foe. Labor's opponents have always tried to persuade the electorate that the ALP is infected with odious and dangerous doctrines, but never more stridently than just after the Second World War, a period when Communist influence in the Australian union movement was at its peak and the Communist Party sought to supersede the ALP as the party representing the Australian working class. The most notable Communist union leaders were Thornton of the Federated Ironworkers' Association and Jim Healy of the Waterside Workers' Federation, but the Communists' control of the mid-1945 ACTU congress showed that their significance extended far beyond a couple of prominent tough officials. The industrial activities of Thornton's union were disconcerting the McKell government in NSW – all state ALP governments were being troubled by militant unionists. The Communists had even managed to obtain direct parliamentary representation: Fred Paterson, barrister, ex-soldier, Queensland Rhodes Scholar and sometime pig farmer, had represented the north Queensland seat of Bowen since 1944. In another first, from 1944 to 1947 the municipality of Kearsley on the northern NSW coal-fields had the only Communist-controlled council to have ever been elected in Australia.

Some ALP enthusiasts were relaxed about the Communist Party's advance over the preceding decade. While recognizing that it might at times be a political nuisance to Labor, they accepted that it might also at other times be a useful ally in Labor's struggle against the excesses or the very existence of capitalism. They detected no Communist threat to Australia's social fabric other than the danger to Australians' civil liberties arising from any excessive clampdown on Communists. Other ALP stalwarts were not so sure, and many of them welcomed the establishment and activities of the industrial groups. Although the battle between the Communists and their foes had been for some years especially vicious at the Trades Hall in Melbourne – the state capital where ideological ferment has traditionally been most pronounced – it was the 1945 ALP conference in NSW which created units to tackle Communist influence in the labour movement directly by campaigning for ALP-backed candidates against their Communist rivals in union elections. The idea spread the following year to Victoria, SA and also to Queensland, where the meatworkers' strike was crucial in the state executive's decision to authorize groups in that state. Attempts to create industrial groups in WA and Tasmania foundered because the potential for significant Communist influence in those states was meagre. 'The Groupers', as devotees of the groups became known, were supported by Santamaria's burgeoning Movement, which kept its involvement secret at the insistence of his earliest unionist ally, Melbourne THC secretary (and Protestant) Vic Stout, who understandably wanted to avoid handing the Communists the opportunity to tar their opponents with the Catholic Action brush. The Movement had utilized the Catholic Church (with Archbishop Mannix's blessing) to involve Catholic workers in their unions, organizing their attendance at meetings and voting at elections. By 1946 the Movement had blossomed into an effective national force to confront the Communists.

Chifley's skills in managing his party were tested in the long-running Bretton Woods controversy. He was convinced of the wisdom of establishing the kind of international economic co-operation embodied in the 1944 Bretton Woods Agreement, which created an International Monetary Fund to supervise exchange rates and help nations with balance of payments problems and a World Bank to provide loan capital in appropriate circumstances. However, Labor's traditional antipathy to the practitioners of high finance ensured that Chifley would have difficulty persuading his party that Australia should ratify the agreement. He decided to put the matter quietly aside. When debate resumed in 1946 a crucial convert was Dedman, who changed from initial wariness to whole-hearted approval. He became the leading ministerial advocate of ratification, and even had a pamphlet on the subject printed partly to persuade his own colleagues. Leading the opponents in public was Ward:

the Agreement will enthrone a World Dictatorship of private finance, more complete and terrible than any Hitlerite dream. It...quite blatantly sets up controls which will reduce the smaller nations to vassal States and make every Government the mouth-piece and tool of International Finance...World collaboration of private financial interests can only mean mass unemployment, slavery, misery, degradation and final destruction.

Ward and other non-ratifiers such as Calwell, Don Cameron, Holloway and Lang sought to revive memories of the Great Depression and the role played by powerful financiers in the downfall of the Scullin government. Supporters of Bretton Woods, who included Scullin and McKenna, argued that international economic co-operation was the best means of averting the devastating crashes of the past and therefore Australia should ratify the agreement even though its provisions were not perfectly suited to Australian requirements.

Late in 1946 Chifley grasped the nettle firmly. The federal executive met in November with half the delegates instructed to oppose ratification, but after Chifley addressed the meeting the WA pair decided to override their instructions and vote in favour of the agreement. With the Victorian delegation divided (Calwell voting against ratification), Chifley was supported by the slender margin of seven votes to five. Later that week caucus began a lengthy debate on the question, which continued for three meetings before Chifley found that he did not quite have the numbers: by 29 votes to 26 caucus resolved to refer the question to a federal conference. As Chifley knew, the federal executive's decision could be overruled by federal conference, the party's supreme body; however, a special federal conference could only occur if at least four of the six states requested it. While Ward and Dedman were debating the question publicly, Chifley privately tried to persuade the state executives to see things his way. He was delighted when NSW, WA and Tasmania declared themselves against a special conference on the question. With that option ruled out, Chifley shrewdly returned the matter to the FPLP early in March 1947 when caucus members were still glowing with the news of the tax reductions and pension increases he had just announced to them. This time, despite the reported opposition of six ministers including Holloway, Chifley obtained by 33 votes to 24 the approval of Bretton Woods he had laboured so long and patiently to achieve. When the ratification legislation came before parliament Chifley declared fervently that 'the Bretton Woods agreement is justified':

Perhaps the experiment will fail; but no country which has any regard for the cause of humanity can, for some selfish reason, or because some ghosts of the past happen to walk, or because of fears created by their experiences of a financial and economic depression, refuse to become parties to this agreement. If we have any love for man-kind and a desire to free future generations from the terrible happenings of the last thirty years, we must put our faith in these organizations...

243

Holloway demonstrated his commitment to Labor's traditional principles of solidarity by voting for the legislation in parliament, but Ward and a few others preferred to signify their undiminished abhorrence of Bretton Woods by absenting themselves when the vote was taken. For Chifley, this issue was the equivalent of Curtin's struggle to extend the area where the militia could be directed to serve. Chifley's tact, patience and acute grasp of the nuances and sometimes unwieldy processes of the ALP enabled him to obtain the result he wanted with the least possible disturbance to party cohesion.

In February 1946 McKell stunned Labor's rank and file when he announced that he wished to retire from politics before the next NSW election. He was then in his mid-fifties, hardly elderly for a politician, but he had almost completed three busy decades in the Assembly and five years as Premier, and he was tired. Major reforms were either completed or under way, and guidelines for future administration were clearly established. He was also irked that some of his ministers were becoming restless under his tight restraining leash. His announcement produced a chorus of dismay in party circles. Great pressure was applied to persuade him to continue, and he conceded that the decision was 'not irrevocable', but he remained keen to retire at an appropriate moment. He was staggered when Chifley offered him the post of Governor-General. Chifley was looking for an Australian without 'pomp and plumes and social glitter', 'a man of the people' familiar with Australia's needs and aspirations. His friend McKell fitted the bill; moreover, Chifley had admired McKell's tenacity in a protracted battle with British authorities about the appointment of an Australian as NSW Governor. Eventually McKell decided to accept. One of Chifley's ministers sparked an uproar and embarrassed McKell by prematurely leaking the decision to the press. This minister was presumably Calwell, who even decades later referred to the appointment in contemptuous terms and admitted that he was the only minister opposed to it. Calwell had made no secret of his hatred for McKell since their public clash in 1944; he did not attend McKell's inauguration and refused all invitations to Government House while McKell was in residence. The labour movement warmly approved the appointment, but conservatives were apoplectic about the prospect of an ex-boilermaker and Labor premier being installed as the King's vice-regal representative. When the appointment was officially confirmed Menzies described it as 'shocking and humiliating'.

McKell was one of Labor's finest leaders. The last dozen years of Lang's leadership had been a barren period of turmoil for NSW Labor, but under McKell the party enjoyed six years in government which were full of achievement and paved the way for the future. McKell's success lay in his combination of pragmatism and vision. Two outstanding far-sighted personal initiatives were the Kosciusko State National Park, which rescued and preserved for future generations – despite furious opposition – a superb environmental treasure devastated by overstocking and erosion, and the Snowy Mountains engineering scheme. Even before McKell became Premier he had envisaged the immense development potential of diverting the Snowy waters, and in office he formed a committee of experts to appraise the possibilities. The Chifley government became involved in the planning, and was still evaluating the project when McKell was appointed Governor-General. Later, during a conversation at Government House Yarralumla, Chifley mentioned that one of the problems causing delay was the grave doubt that his government would be constitutionally entitled to undertake it, and McKell advised him to use the defence power. With that difficulty solved and other problems capably dealt with by Chifley's Works minister

Lemmon, the great Snowy scheme was launched in October 1949. Enlightened McKell government initiatives also occurred in workers' compensation, child welfare, education and soil conservation, and there was increased funding for libraries, art galleries and the Sydney Symphony Orchestra. In the ballot for his successor McKell's preferred candidate was Heffron, but caucus chose Jim McGirr. With NSW Labor in such good standing with the electorate, it was no surprise when three months after the leadership change the McGirr government was comfortably re-elected.

Internationally the Chifley government was active in the transition to peace. The ministers most concerned were Evatt of course, Chifley himself, and also Dedman, who now had Defence as well as the PWR department he had taken over from Chifley in 1945. By and large Chifley gave Evatt a free rein in global matters which did not affect Australia's immediate interests. However, Chifley involved himself closely in the postwar overhaul of Britain's relationships with its dominions and colonies. He visited London for important conferences in 1946, 1948 and 1949, and formed a strong sympathy for the British people's continuing hardships caused by the war. He established close relationships with ministers in the Attlee Labour government which was then transforming Britain. When in government British Labour retained the traditional custom of the prime minister selecting the cabinet; the Australian practice (eventually also adopted by New Zealand) of caucus election of ministers was regarded by Attlee as 'totally wrong'. Chifley also visited New Zealand in 1947, and maintained the close relationship with that country's Labour government exemplified by the 1944 agreement which had disturbed the United States. While Chifley and Evatt were both abroad for a while in 1949 the acting Prime Minister was Holloway. This promotion crowned the fine career of a devoted servant of the labour movement who had entered parliament so spectacularly two decades earlier by toppling Prime Minister Bruce.

Evatt was maintaining his individualistic contribution as External Affairs minister. He was, as ever, difficult to work for – restless, demanding, exhausting, liable to telephone subordinates in the middle of the night. Yet he could be exhilarating, unpredictably endearing, and admirably courageous and tenacious on matters of principle. He spent lengthy periods outside Australia and, while deferring to Chifley, tended to keep foreign policy matters to himself; they were rarely discussed in caucus. In cabinet Evatt, as deputy Prime Minister, Attorney-General and the government's finest legislative draftsman as well as External Affairs minister, was given informal priority; ministers with important cabinet business had to wait if the Doc had matters to raise. The courage and idealism Evatt displayed in directing Australia's independent and principled contribution to international relations was rewarded by his election as President of the United Nations General Assembly in 1948. When crowds gathered in Paris to witness the dignitaries arrive for the General Assembly, they observed a glittering array of formally dressed diplomats alight from the back of gleaming limousines, each attended by an impressive entourage.

One car and its occupant were different. It was a modest, late-model Ford; there was nobody in the back; and a heavy, tousle-headed man in a baggy lounge suit, his tie off-centre, sat next to the chauffeur. Muttering a nasal 'see you later' to the driver, the passenger let himself out and shambled up to the official entrance – only to be barred by a gendarme whose instructions were to admit dignitaries only. Later the policeman was flabbergasted to learn that he had delayed the President of the General Assembly himself, Dr Evatt.

245

In this prestigious position Evatt laboured resourcefully to achieve desirable outcomes in the world's trouble spots, and also to maximize individual liberty and social justice in international law and charters like the Declaration of Human Rights.

While Evatt was a crusading figure on the international stage, back home his government was being thwarted by his former colleagues on the High Court. Latham, the solemn, austere conservative who had facilitated Menzies's entry to federal parliament by agreeing to move from Attorney-General to Chief Justice, still held that position; two of his fellow judges were crusty veterans who, although aged 84 and 76 in mid-1947, refused to retire because they did not want to give a Labor government – especially one with Evatt as Attorney-General – the opportunity to select their replacements. The court had followed its disallowance of the Curtin government's Pharmaceutical Benefits Act by invalidating the legislation nationalizing interstate airline operations. In the latter case the decision was based on a dubious interpretation of Section 92 of the Constitution persuasively argued by the ambitious barrister opposing the government, Garfield Barwick, who had climbed from bankruptcy to eminence, shedding along the way the political views which had once inspired him to hand out leaflets for Lang. In 1947 Barwick also convinced the court to disallow (Mr Justice McTiernan forcefully dissenting) the provision in Labor's 1945 Banking Act prohibiting the trading banks from accepting the accounts of state governments and semi-government authorities. The unsatisfactory result in this case was another in a series of decisions during the 1940s by the High Court which frustrated the Curtin and Chifley governments. From Labor's viewpoint the court had displayed since its inception a disconcerting tendency to reserve its most restrictive interpretations of the national government's constitutional powers for the times when the FPLP was ascendant.

In fact the Labor government had contributed to its own difficulties. During one of Evatt's overseas trips Ward and Calwell had pushed through cabinet a proposal to enlarge the High Court and appoint three new judges, but Evatt on his return opposed this idea because it would invite damaging accusations that Labor was packing the bench. The ensuing cabinet debate was stormy and the vitriolic attacks Calwell and Ward directed at Evatt drove the Doc to tears. Evatt, however, managed to persuade cabinet to make only one appointment to the court. His uninspiring choice of Queensland Chief Justice Webb was apparently influenced by Catholic lobbying headed by Archbishop Duhig; Calwell reckoned that Evatt picked Webb 'because he wished to court the Catholic vote'. Chifley, presumably following advice from Evatt, believed that Webb would help the government overcome its predicament with the High Court, but during his lacklustre career on the bench Webb gave no sign that he sympathized with Labor's approach on constitutional questions.

The Chifley government's momentous reaction to the adverse High Court decision on its banking legislation came soon after the judgement was announced on 13 August 1947. Cabinet met to consider its response on the following Saturday morning. During the intervening days Chifley had already discussed the implications of the judgement with Evatt, McKenna (who acted as Attorney-General during the Doc's frequent absences abroad), and senior public servants and advisers. Evatt and McKenna knew what Chifley was contemplating, but the other ministers present at that fateful Saturday cabinet meeting did not. Chifley himself had not wanted to include in the 1945 Banking Act the particular clause

54. The Chifley ministry, 1946–1949. Standing (from left): J. Dedman, H. C. Barnard, W. Riordan, N. Lemmon, B. Courtice, C. Chambers (partly obscured), R. Pollard, D. Cameron, N. McKenna, W. Ashley, E. Ward. Seated: A. Drakeford, H. V. Evatt, B. Chifley, E. J. Holloway (partly obscured), W. Scully, V. Johnson, J. Armstrong. Absent: A. Calwell. (*National Library*)

55. Immigration minister Arthur Calwell welcomes a newly-arrived migrant to Australia. (*National Library*)

56. Senator Bill Morrow. (*Fryer Library*)

57. Launching the Snowy Mountains scheme. Standing (from left): Prime Minister Ben Chifley, Governor-General Bill McKell, Works and Housing minister Nelson Lemmon. Seated on the right, partly obscured, is Allan Fraser MHR. (*Department of Foreign Affairs and Trade*)

that the court had just invalidated, but he told his ministers that it was clear that the private banks planned to challenge other more vital aspects of the legislation. In his view the government could either wait and respond to these challenges as they arose or they could knock them out beforehand by acting boldly, in accordance with party policy, to nationalize banking. When Chifley's ministers realized that their leader was recommending nationalization, McKenna saw his colleagues react with 'complete stunned shock' followed by 'a good deal of jubilation'. Chifley asked each minister in turn for his views. All favoured nationalization. 'Well, that's the decision then', concluded Chifley. Pollard interjected 'Wait a minute, what about you Chif – where do you stand?' 'With you and the boys, Reggie', Chifley replied, 'to the last ditch'.

Chifley's reversion to his previous advocacy of nationalization was the crucial factor in this bombshell. He was a warmly admired leader, and on financial questions his technical knowledge, long experience and political judgement were profoundly respected: he was the party's recognized authority in such matters. After the tribulations of the Scullin government there was a determination in Labor ranks to ensure that no subsequent ALP government would be so powerless to control the banks and the national economy; once Chifley showed that he had lost his faith that Labor's objectives in banking reform could be achieved without nationalization, it was understandable that his ministers should so readily follow him.

The decision was political dynamite. When Rodgers showed journalists Chifley's brief statement announcing it, one pressman was so startled that he apparently bit through the stem of his pipe as he read its sensational tidings:

> Cabinet today authorized the Attorney-General (Dr Evatt) and myself to prepare legislation for submission to the Federal Parliamentary Labor Party for the nationalization of banking, other than State banks, with proper protection for shareholders, depositors, borrowers and staff of private banks.

Dedman, who was in Geneva attending the United Nations Conference on Trade and Employment, 'flatly refused to believe it' when an adviser told him that the decision had been announced. Calwell and Ward, who were also overseas on government business, met Dedman later in London, and together the three ministers chuckled over the irony that such a decision had been taken in their absence although they were the most committed nationalizers in cabinet. Parliament was in recess when the announcement was made, and FPLP backbenchers were as surprised as their constituents when the news broke. Some MPs initially felt resentful that they had to cope with the hysterical aftermath without any warning of the decision or say in it, but when caucus gathered a month later nationalization was upheld unanimously.

The private banks recovered quickly from their initial shock. They swiftly hired as many top barristers as possible to restrict the expertise available to the government in the looming legal battle, and began a massive, orchestrated propaganda campaign which continued relentlessly for over two years. Chifley's brief statement of 17 August played into their hands. He presumably believed that a storm of outrage was inevitable whatever form the announcement took, and the government simply had to batten down the hatches and sail through it. But the abruptness of his statement squandered a valuable opportunity to publicize a reasoned case justifying the controversial decision, and left the government vulnerable to charges of high-handedness. Chifley's terse statement, which was not supplemented for weeks, in effect handed Labor's opponents the initiative in the vital propaganda war and they never lost it.

No ALP reform in the history of the party has produced greater hostility than the nationalization bombshell. As Duthie observed, 'all hell broke loose': Labor was deluged by an avalanche of protest and fury. Nationalization of the banks was heralded as the prelude to a Communist takeover and the onset of every imaginable evil. Funds for this campaign were unlimited. Hundreds of bank clerks were seconded to it or coerced by their employers into maintaining a united front. The agitators doorknocked assiduously, compiling petitions, distributing leaflets and warning pensioners and other needy Australians that nasty Mr Chifley was plotting to steal their savings. The thousands of organized telegrams and roneoed petitions to Parliament House became such a torrent that swamped FPLP backbenchers in marginal seats needed their colleagues' help simply to open their mail.

This agitation was the death-knell for the Cain government in Victoria. Cain supported the decision to nationalize the banks, but Kennelly – now the ALP's national secretary as well as Victorian state secretary and one of Cain's senior ministers – tried to persuade Chifley to delay the legislation until after the next federal election. The Prime Minister's refusal to postpone it made Kennelly conclude that the Cain government was history. As an MLC himself, Kennelly was well aware that the anti-Labor MPs holding a majority in the Victorian Legislative Council had been emboldened by Cain's problems with industrial unrest, and the banks' awesome counter-offensive further encouraged them. In October 1947 they blocked supply and forced an election. Cain's endeavours to highlight the impropriety of withholding supply seemed to have little impact on the voters; the nationalization issue dominated the campaign although it was irrelevant to his government's performance. Moreover, the prevalence of industrial disputes, the tensions inflamed by the formation of the industrial groups, and persistent rumours of corruption involving his Wren-linked ministers Bill Barry and Archie Fraser overshadowed the Cain government's achievements. It had emulated the McKell government in constructive initiatives in soil conservation and adult education. It had increased eligibility to workers' compensation and provided long-service leave to railway workers. It had reformed public service administration and wage determination procedures. Despite these accomplishments the Cain government was routed at the election on 8 November. Labor lost 14 of its 31 Assembly seats, including Albert Park where Crean, who supported nationalization publicly and privately, was swept away by the tide.

The parliamentary debate on the nationalization legislation was long and impassioned. Menzies echoed the banks' fervent denunciation by describing it as 'the most far-reaching, revolutionary, unwarranted and un-Australian measure' ever introduced in the national parliament. Numerous FPLP speakers recalled that the banks had worsened the miseries of the Depression by their own financial policies and also by determinedly blocking the Scullin government's attempts to ease the suffering. Chifley reiterated that control of the banks was necessary to maintain the stable economy and full employment that were essential to Labor's continued progress towards its fundamental objectives, which Chifley again referred to as the 'light on the hill'. Bank nationalization thrilled party activists like Clyde Cameron, who declared that 'Labor is doing more to implement its policy than at any time in our history', and 'we now see our party in its finest hour'; he called on Labor supporters to ignore 'the ill-informed rantings of certain over-fed prelates'. The rank and file overall may not have been quite so enthusiastic, although Fallon told Chifley that his soundings in Queensland indicated widespread support in the labour movement for nationalization, and a north Queensland stalwart sent warm congratulations to Chifley:

> you alone of all Labor leaders since T.J. Ryan really meant business. You have made the mighty tremble and my heart goes out to you as one who has worthily carried the banner.

The banks challenged the legislation in the High Court even before it received the Governor-General's assent. When the case opened on 9 February 1948 during a Melbourne heatwave the court was more cluttered with legal heavyweights than ever before. Barwick headed the banks' challenge, with a large team of top-ranking barristers in support. Carrying the government's banner in court was Evatt. It was unthinkable to him that anyone else should argue the case for the government, even though it added a huge burden to his already staggering workload. He was of course Labor's best-credentialled lawyer, but his skills as a courtroom advocate were rusty and he would be encountering judges who intensely disliked him. His first return to the court he had left in 1940 began inauspiciously when he suggested that since one judge owned shares in two private banks and another judge's wife was also a shareholder, the judges concerned should disqualify themselves from the case. After both refused to do so, Chief Justice Latham ordered the case to proceed. Things did not improve for Evatt. In the sweltering weather he displayed a neurotic concern about catching a chill, ordering the court windows shut (Latham promptly had them reopened) and demanding a rug to keep the 'cold' at bay. The Doc was repeatedly baited by a veteran judge who loathed him. Barwick's opening argument took seven days, and then Evatt addressed the court for 18 days. No High Court case had ever lasted longer. The judgements delivered four months later revealed that once again Barwick's view of Section 92 of the Constitution had prevailed over what was commonly regarded as good sense and sound law in the form of Evatt's alternative interpretation, which had underpinned the Doc's own 1930s judgements and was to be upheld by a later generation of High Court judges. In dissenting judgements Latham and McTiernan indicated that they agreed with Evatt on the meaning of Section 92.

Their dissent encouraged Chifley and his cabinet to fight on with an appeal to the Privy Council. The appeal was heard in London between March and June 1949, attracting an even bigger array of eminent barristers and lasting even longer than the record-breaking High Court hearing. Evatt covered every possible angle, taking 14 days to present the appeal before rushing away to preside at the United Nations, where the ominous Berlin blockade, the difficult Middle East question and the crisis in Greece were pressing problems. After Barwick took six days to outline the defence, the amazing Doc raced back from New York to respond with another eight days of argument. Two venerable law lords hearing the case died during it. Their surviving colleagues found against the government in an oddly reasoned judgement which demonstrated that the Australian legal structure would have been healthier if the Privy Council had no role in it.

So, after two years of hysteria and headlines, the Chifley government seemed to have suffered a severe defeat. In the propaganda sphere this was certainly correct, but the banks made a significant concession when a spokesman publicly admitted that they would now accept the 1945 banking reforms. In that sense

Chifley could claim to have won the war. Yet the price of victory had been high. The propaganda offensive unleashed by Labor's enemies had considerably damaged the Chifley government's standing in the electorate.

A similar campaign was being waged by doctors. Their extraordinary efforts to frustrate the Chifley government's goal of 'a national health and medical scheme which was free, comprehensive and of the highest technical excellence' were again supported by an unsatisfactory High Court majority decision (McTiernan once more dissenting). In 1949 McKenna had to admit that the combined objections of the doctors – understandably labelled 'conservative shellbacks' by Chifley – and the High Court had defeated his strenuous attempts to establish a viable scheme of free medicine. Nevertheless the Chifley government did succeed in making arrangements with the states to upgrade the quality and availability of hospital treatment, and it conducted a magnificently effective campaign to reduce the incidence of tuberculosis.

The Chifley government was also increasingly troubled by the relentless anti-Communist campaign orchestrated by Labor's enemies. Murdoch's *Herald* was characteristically at the forefront, as it had been on bank nationalization and the immigration programme. In 1949 the *Herald* boomed its publication of the 'memoirs' of a once-prominent Communist as a dramatic scoop full of revelations of insidious Communist influence, and the Hollway government obligingly established a royal commission into them. Labor's opponents, especially the resurgent Liberal Party, lost no opportunity to make cheap sneers and smears about Australians with alleged Communist affiliations or sympathies. A typical outburst from a Victorian government backbencher in April 1949, which implied that a number of named Melbourne University academics were Communists, was described as 'character assassination' by Frank Crean (now MLA for Prahran); having been on the university staff himself, Crean defended some of the academics, who included historian Manning Clark and a 34-year-old economic history lecturer, Jim Cairns.

In fact the Chifley government had displayed a preparedness to take strong action against Communists in Australia. As well as prosecuting Communist union leaders for sedition, it challenged their power by including in its extensive reforms to the Conciliation and Arbitration Act provision for court-controlled ballots where illegalities had occurred in union elections. Furthermore, when Communist-led unions threatened to disrupt the construction in central Australia of a defence facility planned in association with the Attlee government, Evatt pushed through parliament an act which introduced severe penalties for any action that prevented, hindered or obstructed the project. The federal executive congratulated Chifley and Evatt 'on the firm stand taken', which had quashed Communist disruption aimed at 'defeating Australia's Defence Policy in the interest of a foreign power' (Russia). Another initiative was the creation of the Australian Security Intelligence Organization (ASIO), which was reluctantly established by Chifley after pressure from the British and American governments and trumped-up allegations of security breaches unscrupulously dramatized by Fadden.

Within the ALP, however, the majority view was still firmly against outlawing the Communist Party. Recognizing Australian Communists' support of Australia's war effort since 1941, the Curtin government had in December 1942 reversed the Menzies government's decision to ban the Communist Party. Now, however, in the tense Cold War atmosphere, there were elements in the ALP, especially in some rural Queensland AWU strongholds, keen to reinstate the ban.

They received a clear rebuff at the 1948 federal conference, where delegates agreed that the proposed ban would be 'a negation of democratic principles'. At the same time conference delegates reiterated the unequivocal hostility the ALP had consistently displayed to the Communist Party since 1924. Earlier in 1948 some FPLP backbenchers including Burke had made no headway in caucus when they argued that the Communist Party should be suppressed. Such action was strongly opposed by Chifley, who affirmed in parliament that Labor 'does not propose bans on any class of political philosophy or thought'.

Communist influence in the industrial arena was the area of greatest concern, and this was accentuated by another viciously fought Queensland dispute. The major union involved in this strike, the ARU, had been renowned for its frequently frosty relationship with Queensland ALP governments, notably while McCormack was Premier during the later 1920s. McCormack's 1927 measures had seemed astonishingly repressive for a Labor premier, but in 1948 Hanlon – who had been one of the leaders in the memorable Brisbane general strike of 1912 – implemented even more drastic anti-strike action which exceeded his own draconian response to the 1946 meatworkers' strike. In February 1948 Hanlon proclaimed a state of emergency under the Transport Act, authorized the arrest of strike leaders and rank-and-file picketers, and portrayed the dispute in a state-wide radio broadcast as a civil war directed by the 'high command of the communist party'.

Nonetheless the dispute continued, and Hanlon rushed through parliament (only Paterson and Aikens objecting) the Industrial Law Amendment Act, which gave police even wider powers than the state of emergency. They could now take action against anyone they considered might be prolonging the strike; they could arrest without warrant, prohibit picketing, enter union offices or meetings at any time, and use force whenever they considered it necessary. On St Patrick's Day a small, orderly demonstration protesting against Hanlon's extreme legislation was brutally attacked without warning by a large police contingent. Communists in the demonstration were punched and kicked, arrested and gaoled, and the lightly-built Paterson suffered permanent head injuries after being savagely bashed from behind while observing police conduct from the sidelines and making notes of what he saw. The following month a compromise settlement was achieved, but the strike inevitably generated intense bitterness. 'If ever there was a weak collection of salary-chasing opportunist humbugs devoid of even a semblance of working-class principles, it was the members of the Labor Party led by Hanlon', asserted the ARU's Queensland secretary. He concluded that no anti-Labor government 'could have been more vicious'.

Another big strike a year later provided further impetus to those demanding action against Communists in Australia. Like the Queensland dispute, the 1949 coal strike was widely claimed to have been plotted and directed by the Communist Party. While both disputes arose because large numbers of toilers who were not at all linked or sympathetic to the Communist Party had genuine industrial grievances, as the strikes proceeded Communists became increasingly identified with prolonging them and using them to discredit the ALP. The Communist Party involved itself in the coal strike, which began on 27 June 1949, more fully than it had in any previous large Australian dispute. The strike's significance was sharpened by the extent of the Australian economy's dependence on coal, and the consequences were severe and nation-wide. NSW, the state hit hardest, also had to contend with devastating floods. Heavy restrictions on gas and electricity affecting the workplace, transport and domestic use resulted in hundreds of thousands of workers losing their jobs and the national economy being suddenly thrown into chaos. 'Within a fortnight industry was brought almost to a standstill, unemployment reached half a million and soup kitchens dotted Sydney's industrial suburbs.'

History and tradition played an important part in the struggle. Events during the Scullin government had generated in coalmining communities a legacy of ill will towards Labor governments. While Curtin was Prime Minister he was acutely troubled by the frequency of disputes in the coal industry. Chifley and McKell felt that they had gone a long way towards constructively resolving many of the industry's difficult problems when their governments enacted complementary legislation in 1946 to establish a Coal Industry Tribunal to deal with industrial disputes and a Joint Coal Board with wide powers and responsibilities to supervise and regulate the industry, its workforce and communities. The miners had already achieved significant gains under these new arrangements, and further benefits were in the pipeline when the strike was declared.

In these circumstances Chifley felt that the strike was unjustified. Although he acknowledged the hardships of a miner's life, Chifley felt that the pursuit of such a strike at such a time smacked not merely of ingratitude after what Labor governments had done for the miners, but also of deliberate Communist-inspired troublemaking intended to sabotage the ALP's carefully planned economic achievements. Many Labor activists agreed with the Prime Minister, but some of them had misgivings about his government's strong action against the strike. Evatt rapidly prepared legislation which made any donation of funds to the striking unions illegal. This unprecedented measure was endorsed by caucus despite fierce objections from Ward, Morrow and some others, and pushed through parliament. Ward denounced it as 'monstrous', and Holloway later admitted to a union delegation that it was 'terrible': 'I never thought I would be associated with such a thing'.

As the strike continued the Chifley government sought to detach non-Communist miners from their union leaders. In this struggle, unlike bank nationalization, the government laboured assiduously to win the propaganda battle. Labor MPs ran the gauntlet of stormy meetings in mining townships to explain the government's viewpoint, but sometimes adopted an aggressive tone which was counter-productive. Remarkably, the sons of R.S. Ross were leading propagandists on opposite sides: Edgar Ross was committed to the Communist Party and the strike, while the government's role was supported by his brother Lloyd, who had left the NSW ARU and the Communist Party and had become a senior public servant and adviser in the Curtin and Chifley governments. Defiance in the mining communities hardened when the Arbitration Court imposed severe gaol sentences under the government's special legislation upon miners' union leaders and other prominent Communist unionists. The judge responsible for most of these stiff sentences was Alf Foster, who felt thrust into a painfully invidious position and was never forgiven by some previously friendly militants. The gaol sentences appalled many Labor activists. Especially critical were some inner-urban Sydney ALP branches, notably Paddington, which had already expressed their outrage at the emergency legislation. Allan Fraser MHR, whose independent instincts on matters of principle had already irked some of his colleagues, criticized both the legislation and the gaol sentences in radio broadcasts to his electorate.

By consulting widely Chifley kept ALP dissent within acceptable limits. Throughout the dispute he discussed developments regularly with his cabinet sub-committee on the strike, which comprised himself, Evatt, Ashley, Calwell, Lemmon, Johnson and Chambers (but, significantly, not Holloway, although he was the Labour and Industry minister). The prime minister also frequently met other identities with far-reaching connections in the labour movement. He obtained the approval of party officials representing the federal and NSW executives before taking the grave step of sending in the army to revive coal production, a decision made (despite Ward's condemnation) at a joint meeting of the Chifley and McGirr cabinets and announced on 27 July. This highly controversial decision – the ALP platform specifically denounced the use of the armed forces in industrial disputes – was justified as unique action in unique circumstances to counter a political strike engineered by enemies of Labor. Shortly afterwards an overwhelming majority of the striking miners, convinced that it would be fruitless to continue the strike, overruled their leaders' recommendation and voted to return to work. After seven weeks of drama, disruption and hardship the strike was over and the Communist Party had suffered a severe setback, but the biggest impact on most voters was the considerable inconvenience they had endured during a harsh winter.

As the 1949 federal election approached, Labor enthusiasts had good reason to feel proud of their party's achievements in its last eight years as the national government. Labor had inspired an appropriately greater national commitment to the war without neglecting ALP priorities in social reform. Its success in managing the massive transition to peace without the widely feared adverse effects on employment and the economy was a magnificent feat. Chifley and Dedman were the two ministers primarily responsible. Chifley had kept a vigilant eye on the national economy to ensure that it came through these vast changes with minimal strain, and was now prepared to relinquish the Treasury reins to Dedman, whose ministerial load would be reduced after the election when the PWR department, having fulfilled its objectives splendidly, was abolished. Since 1946 the Chifley government had passed more acts and more significant legislation than had been enacted in any other national parliament. As well as maintaining economic growth and full employment, it had played a visionary role in the establishment of the immigration programme, the Snowy Mountains scheme, the ANU and the Holden car manufacturing industry. Pension levels had doubled since 1941. Labor had done more for farmers since 1941 than the Country Party had managed since its genesis. A ringing salute to the ALP's achievements came from Henry Boote, Labor's supreme journalist, during a speech he made at a function in his honour in May 1949 shortly before he died aged 84:

> I will now conclude these few remarks with a toast I have often drunk in the privacy of my heart: 'Long live the Australian Labor Party – the hope, the inspiration and the saviour of the Australian people'.

However, Labor's outstanding performance since 1941 in these important areas was overshadowed by subsidiary and ephemeral issues. The constant barrage levelled at the Chifley government since 1947 by the banks and other powerful vested interests had created a nebulous irritation with the Chifley government's 'controls' and, from Labor's viewpoint, a dangerous expectation that they should be lifted. This growing feeling was clearly demonstrated by the dismal failure of Labor's 1948 referendum seeking to equip the national government with the power to control prices and rents.

Labor had provided its opponents with some handy ammunition. Allegations of corruption placed Ward's ministerial administration under a cloud, and a royal commission incriminated one of his advisers, the controversial ex-Communist Jock Garden. Although Ward was completely cleared of impropriety himself, his reputation was nevertheless harmed by his unwise decision to appoint in the first place someone with Garden's already proven lack of integrity. As Immigration minister, Calwell had made some controversially inflexible rulings affecting individuals which were highlighted gratefully by Labor's enemies. Chifley, too, had made some fateful decisions. His close contact with British Labour leaders convinced him that his government should help Britain's adjustment to peace after its far more severe war than Australia experienced. The FPLP endorsed his recommendations for generous donations to Britain amounting to £35 million. Furthermore, having assured the British leaders that he would assist them to overcome Britain's shortages of commodities by restricting Australian petrol consumption, he reintroduced petrol rationing in Australia a few weeks before the election. There was a predictable howl of protest, but Chifley was unfazed. Colleagues and friends of the Prime Minister warned that just before an election he should be relaxing controls, not increasing them; 'Stabber Jack' Beasley had pointed out that running simply on Labor's record in office – however outstanding – might have worked in 1946, but it would be a risky manoeuvre to repeat in 1949. But Chifley was sceptical about the worth of electoral sweeteners, determined not to relax his tight grip on the economy, and very hard to shift once his mind was made up. In the policy speech he pointedly reviewed social conditions in the grim 1930s compared to the improved 1940s under Labor, emphasized that his party was striving 'to see that our less fortunate fellow citizens are protected from those shafts of fate which leave them helpless and without hope', and repeated that this objective was Labor's 'beacon, the light on the hill'.

After the election was fixed for 10 December thousands of Labor enthusiasts threw themselves as usual into the campaign, which was the longest before a federal election since 1910. Once again there was more activity at the local branch level at election time. There were meetings to organize and attend, leaflets to prepare and print. Other important tasks for the rank and file included the grinding slog of individual canvassing or letter-boxing, stout defence of their party at workplace or pub, and, on polling day, distribution of how-to-vote cards and scrutineering. Fund-raising was crucial. From Albany to Zeehan there were chook raffles, appeals for donations and a variety of other devices to boost campaign funds. Although party finances were healthier than ever before – the decades when the federal executive 'lived on budgets which would have shamed an outer-suburban football team' were thankfully in the past – the ALP still relied heavily on donations to finance its costs in a national election campaign. Labor's total expenditure in the 1949 campaign was probably around £100 000, and a large proportion of these funds came from voluntary levies on unionists and ALP members.

All efforts were unavailing, however. The Chifley government's opponents had at their disposal an election budget probably more than ten times Labor's. The banks, doctors and other anti-Labor zealots were out in force to support Menzies, who promised to put value back into the pound, ban the Communist Party, abolish petrol rationing and provide child endowment for the firstborn (the Menzies government had introduced it – as a means of avoiding a basic wage increase in 1941 – for every child in a family after the first). Labor was also harmed by the claim of some influential Catholics like Archbishop Duhig who revived the old notion that voting ALP was inconsistent with Catholic doctrines. All the same, if Chifley had heeded the advice he received to match his opponents' pledges on petrol rationing and child endowment, Labor would surely have won. For Labor supporters it was a sickening defeat. It probably even surpassed 1913 as an election that should never have been lost, and the pain of this perception was to be sharpened by events in future years.

Labor had not been helped by a significant enlargement of the national parliament. The number of Senators had been changed from 36 to 60, and from 1949 they would be elected under a proportional representation system. The Representatives had been increased from 75 fully-fledged MHRs to 121 (along with the member for the Northern Territory and a new member for the Australian Capital Territory who both had restricted rights in parliament). While the previous winner-take-all method in the Senate had produced clearly unsatisfactory results, proportional representation coupled with more Senators tended to increase the likelihood of political instability with smaller parties holding the balance of power. As well, increasing the Senate hardly sat comfortably with Labor's platform plank seeking abolition of it (although the party's federal conference had twice approved an increase in the Representatives, and the Constitution stipulated that concurrently with any such increase there had to be a proportional enlargement of the Senate). These reforms were instigated by Calwell. Rosevear correctly disputed Calwell's confident assurances that the changes would be advantageous to Labor, but Calwell eventually obtained majority FPLP support for them and the necessary legislation was passed in 1948.

It was a clearcut defeat. In the greatly enlarged Representatives Labor increased its strength by only four to 47, while the Liberals and Country Party · soared from a combined tally of 29 in 1946 to 74 three years later. In the Senate Labor also won fewer seats on polling day, but its high proportion of the Senators not due for re-election in 1949 enabled it to retain a majority in the upper chamber. (Doris Blackburn was defeated, and Lang also lost after making false poisonous allegations against Chifley regarding Bathurst financial transactions which the Prime Minister angrily refuted.) Afterwards Chifley wryly quipped that his government fell because people who could not afford a bus ticket when Labor came to office were now up in arms about petrol rationing. It was true that in Australia (and also New Zealand, where the Labour government was defeated nine days earlier) the relative prosperity enjoyed by the workers under Labor had disadvantaged the party by encouraging some of them to develop middle-class aspirations. But Chifley characteristically did not dodge responsibility for the defeat. He was especially disappointed that two of his favourite ministers, Dedman and Lemmon, lost their seats along with Scully, Barnard and seven backbenchers. For Dedman in particular it was a stunning blow. He had been very confident of Labor's overall success, and took for granted his own seat, generously campaigning for other candidates and ignoring warnings from some colleagues to pay more attention to Corio. After the shattering result he loyally refused to blame his chief, observing that if he and other ministers felt that the decision to campaign solely on Labor's record was mistaken, it was up to them to change Chifley's mind. Dedman made several attempts to re-enter parliament, each without success, and remained bewildered by what was, to him, Labor's inexplicable loss in 1949.

255

11 'Sad Days for the Party': Another Big Split, 1950–1960

THE INITIAL FPLP gathering after Labor's electoral disaster naturally lacked the jubilation of the post-election meetings of 1943 and 1946. Enduring the return to power of Menzies, Fadden and Page was an unpleasant experience for Labor supporters everywhere. On 21 February Chifley was re-elected unopposed as FPLP leader, and Evatt defeated Ward comfortably in a ballot for the deputy leadership. Ashley and McKenna were re-elected as Senate leader and deputy. A few days after this meeting the Attlee government was defeated at a British general election; Labo(u)r governments in Australia, New Zealand and Britain had all been removed within three months.

The 1949 result aggravated the uneasiness growing in Chifley's mind about the future of the party. Even before the election he had confessed privately that the Groupers' activities were troubling him. He kept in close touch with federal ALP secretary Kennelly – the supreme organizational figure in Victoria – who shared his concerns. Chifley and Kennelly were aware that the frustration of being in opposition might stimulate a burst of infighting, especially in view of some of the FPLP's acquisitions after the 1949 election. There were eight new MHRs from Victoria; another, Bryson, was returning after losing Bourke in 1946. Seven of these nine men were Catholics noted for their singlemindedness about communism, which exemplified the Movement's strong influence in the Victorian ALP. Some of them soon made their presence felt, notably Bill Bourke, a lawyer, and Stan Keon and Jack Mullens, who had both represented Labor strongholds in the Victorian Assembly.

Mullens was 'a large, genial, urbane but furiously bigoted man given to florid eloquence and anti-communist zeal'. A former Footscray mayor, he had succeeded former ALP Premier Prendergast as MLA for Footscray in 1937, and in 1949 won preselection for the new federal seat of Gellibrand by defeating Hec McIvor, a likeable stalwart and Presbyterian who was in 1949–50 also mayor of Footscray. The Movement's dedicated and thorough campaigning was instrumental in Mullens's victory over McIvor. In Footscray and nearby suburbs, as in other electorates, party members who regularly attended local ALP meetings were liable to find their branch suddenly inundated with purposeful strangers intent upon supporting the Movement or Grouper candidate. Improper practices in preselection contests were of course not confined to the Movement; but

McIvor was told that in the Gellibrand preselection dead people voted, Catholics who were not eligible to participate received ALP tickets in the mail from their church and were encouraged to use them to record a vote for Mullens, and at least one local unionist was bashed when he tried to exercise a valid vote for McIvor. Kennelly did not want Mullens's abrasiveness in Canberra, and urged McIvor to protest against the preselection abuses, but McIvor refused, not wanting to damage his party by publicizing these unsavoury incidents.

Keon was a product of a traditional Labor storm centre, Richmond. His formal education ended early but by 1945, when he entered state parliament as Richmond's 30-year-old MLA, he was already a formidable politician. Keon was 'an intense, extremely ambitious man of penetrating intelligence and rapier wit, dedicated to and consumed by politics'. Voracious reading had further developed his sharp intellect. His combative temperament and utter self-confidence produced a brash bravery which made him unafraid to take on anyone. The 1945–47 Cain government had ended the monopoly Wren had long enjoyed over trotting, and when that government fell during the bank nationalization uproar it was rumoured that Wren's vengeful influence had contributed to the electoral defeats suffered by Slater, the Attorney-General who drafted the Cain government's Trotting Control Board legislation, and Field, the deputy Premier who introduced it into parliament. Keon had made no secret of his determination to purify the ALP of corruption, and there was no love lost between the Richmond crusader and Wren. Having unsuccessfully stood (aged 32) for the deputy leadership following Field's defeat, Keon demonstrated his fearlessness with an astonishing attack on Wren in July 1948. He alleged in parliament that Wren had 'financed the campaign of the Country Party' in order to 'destroy' the Cain government because of its trotting legislation. Keon's denunciation of the shadowy wire-puller's methods was devastating:

> Those who can be bought will be bought. Those who can be intimidated will be intimidated. . .What is badly needed is a Royal Commission to investigate Mr Wren and his ventures.

Yarra, the federal seat based on Richmond, became vacant when Scullin retired in 1949. Wren opposed Keon's candidacy without success; Keon, supported by the Movement, won the preselection battle, and was bound for Canberra. Although Kennelly was wary of Keon's Movement and Grouper connections he greatly admired Keon's ability, and even regarded him as a potential prime minister.

Menzies quickly introduced a Communist Party Dissolution Bill, which Chifley described as 'a political measure aimed at splitting the Labour Movement'. Under the bill the Communist Party became an illegal organization; its members were ineligible to become union office-bearers and were liable to expulsion from the public service. If the government 'declared' someone to be a Communist, the legislation placed the onus on that person to prove non-membership of the Communist Party. The dangerous implications for Australians' civil liberties were starkly illustrated in parliament when Menzies himself nominated 53 union officials as Communists and later had to admit that he had been mistaken about five of them. The bill was repugnant to Chifley and Evatt, and federal conference had in 1948 firmly pronounced that Labor was opposed to the banning of political parties. However, for Keon, Mullens and others more animated about the menace of communism than the evils of capitalism, the bill was a test of their credibility as anti-Communist warriors. Considerations of political tactics were uppermost in some FPLP minds. Labor's Senate majority meant that the FPLP's response would determine the fate of the bill; there was considerable concern that rejecting it outright risked handing Menzies a double dissolution election with communism as the main issue.

Reconciling the divergent attitudes within the labour movement was not easy. During the late 1930s an advisory committee had been established to improve co-ordination between the FPLP, the federal executive and the ACTU, but it subsided into disuse before being revived in 1948. On 3 May 1950 Chifley informed caucus that the ACTU representatives on the advisory committee were 'thoroughly opposed to all the provisions in the bill'. Although Chifley agreed with the ACTU, in the interests of devising a response which all caucus members could support he fell in behind the FPLP executive's recommendation that Labor should use its Senate majority to amend the bill by modifying its more obnoxious features, placing the onus of proof back on the government and introducing further safeguards to protect civil liberties. Prolonged debate followed. Only a small group of MPs sided with Keon and Mullens (and the Movement) in supporting Menzies's bill as a worthy measure. Others advocated vigorous and absolute hostility. There was also some support for a more passive opposition that would allow Menzies to dig his own political grave when he attempted to enforce such unworthy and unworkable legislation. Caucus eventually voted 34 to 27 to accept the recommendation as the best possible compromise in the circumstances. Labor's amendments were duly introduced in the Senate. The Menzies government rejected these amendments, and parliament went into recess.

The potency of communism as an anti-Labor campaign weapon, which had been crucial at the 1949 election, increased even further during 1950. The Victorian royal commission into communism attracted renewed publicity. Also significant was the outbreak of the Korean War in June and the early success of the Communist North Korean forces, all the more when some maritime unionists refused to co-operate in sending supplies to South Korea. There was also industrial unrest directed against the Communist Party Dissolution Bill itself. At every opportunity Menzies dramatized anxiety about the Communist threat, predicting that Australians would soon be at war against the Communists. International surveys revealed that Australians had relatively high expectations of another world war, and an Australian opinion poll in May 1950 revealed 80% support for banning the Communist Party. This was sobering news for some FPLP backbenchers uncomfortable about the prospect of a double dissolution on the Dissolution Bill. There were signs, too, that many in the labour movement were having second thoughts about the bill, but Chifley firmly adhered to his abhorrence of it. While outlining Labor's response to it in the Representatives on 9 May, he made his own attitude clear: 'I do not want anybody to think I see any virtue in this legislation'. In Labor circles Chifley stressed that a cynical policy switch to avoid an election would cost the party dearly in political credibility. He also observed that elections were sometimes not decided on issues emphasized at the start of the campaign, and Labor could make much of Menzies's inglorious failure to keep his promise to 'put value back into the pound'.

Despite Chifley's influence the party made an ignominious backdown on this issue. Having endorsed the FPLP's amendments to the anti-Communist bill in May, the federal executive, the ultimate decision-making body between federal conferences, reviewed the situation in September. The 12 delegates had before them a motion from the Victorian executive – which believed that the FPLP numbers were now in favour of letting the bill pass – that the FPLP should be allowed to formulate its own attitude to the bill without direction from the federal executive. The Queensland and Tasmanian delegates supported the motion and the vote was deadlocked at six-six, which meant that the federal executive's determination back in May still prevailed – until 40-year-old Tom Burke, the influential MHR for Perth, persuaded his state executive to change its mind. 'Chif' was particularly fond of Burke and entertained high hopes for his future in the party. When Burke telephoned with the news that the WA branch had switched its position, Chifley was stunned. 'You couldn't have done a worse thing to the party', he told Burke. Hindmarsh MHR Clyde Cameron, in Chifley's office during this conversation, saw his leader's face go 'white with anguish and shock'. When Cameron learned why, he exploded. 'That bastard ought to be expelled', he thundered, 'you've treated him like a son!' But Chifley, although still upset, urged Cameron to be tolerant of Burke's viewpoint. Burke was very distressed himself. On 16 October, the day the reconvened federal executive by eight votes to four directed the FPLP to allow the bill through the Senate, Burke offered to resign in a private letter to Chifley. 'I honestly feel that I have helped to save your leadership', wrote Burke, 'and to have helped to save the Labor movement from humiliation, devastating defeat and possible destruction'. The enclosed letter of resignation was torn up by Chifley. He and Senator McKenna, who had supported him firmly on this issue, had the task of announcing to parliament the backdown which, Menzies gloated, 'must surely be the most abject surrender in the history of the once great Australian Labor Party'. In caucus on 18 October Chifley did not hide his personal dismay at the débâcle, but urged a united front: 'Accept your humiliation and we can go forward', he told them, 'recriminate, and we shall split'. The Labor MPs who responded to this moving appeal with loud cheering were appalled to learn the following month that 'Chif' had suffered a severe heart attack.

Shortly before Chifley collapsed Evatt had startled the labour movement when he appeared as counsel for a Communist-controlled union challenging the Dissolution Act in the High Court. Evatt had no sympathy for communism, as he had amply demonstrated during the Chifley government, but he regarded this legislation with distaste and was confident that the High Court could be persuaded to invalidate it. His decision to handle the case was another instance of his unwillingness to leave in other hands tasks or causes that were important to him. However, many Labor people thought Evatt's action was unwise, and the Victorian ALP executive expressed its disapproval. Evatt had resolved to take the case without obtaining FPLP assent or even discussing it with Chifley beforehand. In public Chifley loyally defended Evatt when one of Menzies's senior ministers, Harold Holt, pounced quickly with a predictable smear that sought to link Evatt in the minds of politically unsophisticated voters with support for the Communist Party. In private Chifley warmly praised the Doc's record as a fighter for civil liberties and upheld his right to appear in the case as a barrister, but concluded that his involvement was political folly. The case was a fortnight old when Chifley's heart attack occurred. While he lay critically ill in Bathurst hospital the acting FPLP leader was once again locked in courtroom combat with Barwick. At least Evatt did not have to contend with the two judges who had delayed their retirement in order to deny him any role in choosing their replacements. That pair of ancients had left the bench soon after Labor's 1949 defeat. This time Evatt had a gratifying win when a majority of the judges agreed with him that the Dissolution Act was not a valid exercise of the government's defence power.

This judgement did not shake Menzies's conviction that anti-communism was an election winner. He decided to seek a double dissolution, and obtained advice from Barwick about how to go about it. Chifley, now 65, had returned to Canberra in February 1951, undeterred by medical warnings that he should not overtax himself. He attended Labor's federal conference in March and endorsed the presidential address by his close friend Jack Ferguson, who was, like him, a former NSW railwayman. Ferguson, like other leading Labor figures who had initially welcomed the Groupers' intention to attack communism in the unions, had become concerned that, as he told conference delegates, 'too many of our people are encouraged to believe that hatred of Communism is the only condition to good membership in the Labor Party'. The following day Chifley made a speech in the same vein as several others he made during 1950–51, emphasizing Labor's fundamental principles and the need to fight for them even at the cost of short-term unpopularity. Despite these remarks and his criticism at the conference of the Menzies government's reintroduction of compulsory military training, conference narrowly (19 votes to 17) altered Labor's defence policy and directed the FPLP to allow the National Service Bill through the parliament. Labor's Senators duly obeyed this instruction and allowed the bill to pass, rendering that potential double dissolution trigger unavailable to Menzies. However, conference also congratulated the FPLP for blocking the Menzies government's attempt to emasculate Chifley's banking reforms and, furthermore, approved an amendment to the platform, moved by Duthie with Chifley's full support, opposing the reinstatement of the Commonwealth Bank Board as provided for in the government's legislation. Here was Menzies's opportunity. When Labor's Senators stalled his banking legislation by referring it to a Senate select committee, the Prime Minister visited Government House and asked for a double dissolution.

For some months there had been intense speculation about how the Governor-General would react when Menzies approached him. Evatt and McKenna were apparently convinced that the FPLP would not be risking an unwanted double dissolution if it referred the banking bill to a Senate select committee. Menzies and Barwick had other ideas. They and other Liberals asserted that Labor's handling of the bill was tantamount to a 'failure to pass' under the Constitution. There was no precedent: the only previous double dissolution had been in 1914, when the Senate had unambiguously rejected legislation. It seems that Chifley accepted, not unreasonably, the assessment of his two senior legal lieutenants, until he received alternative private information from an impeccable source. Reg Downing, minister for Justice in the McGirr government and a crucial backroom figure in the NSW ALP, was close to Chifley and McKell personally and also to McKell geographically – his rural property near Goulburn adjoined McKell's. With rumours circulating wildly about the Governor-General's intentions, Downing happened to be working on his farm when McKell came across for a yarn and dropped what Downing interpreted as an unmistakable hint that he was inclined to comply with Menzies's request. Downing relayed this information to Chifley, who was therefore not surprised – unlike some other Labor figures – when McKell gave the Prime Minister the answer he wanted. Although the Governor-General could plausibly have insisted upon a more rigorous definition of 'failure to pass' and rejected Menzies's request, his decision was a sensible recognition of the political realities. Some ALP partisans grumbled that it was damaging to their party's immediate prospects, but any enlargement of

Senate power and vice-regal prerogatives was hardly in Labor's longer-term interests.

Pessimistic predictions in the ALP camp about a replay of 1949 were proved correct when the Menzies government was returned to power on 28 April 1951 with a majority in both houses. Attempts by Labor advocates to focus the campaign on the government's inadequacies in economic policy and other areas were overwhelmed as anti-Labor kicked the Communist can with gusto; 'Menzies or Moscow' was the Liberal slogan in Tasmania. Dedman and Lemmon both failed to get back, and Evatt narrowly managed to hold Barton. Labor could gain only five Representatives seats to hold 52 against their opponents' 69. The result of this first election for the whole of the enlarged Senate was Labor 28, Liberal and Country parties 32. Labor MHRs who had captured seats included accountant Bob Joshua (Ballarat, Victoria) and AWU official Pat Galvin (Kingston, SA). Condon Byrne, a Queensland lawyer and experienced public servant, was the only Senate newcomer.

Holloway had retired, and his successor as MHR for Melbourne Ports was Crean. Having been encouraged by Kennelly to stand, Crean was appalled by the bitterness of the preselection campaign, especially the way his Grouper rivals freely used the Communist slur against him. His preselection success owed much to a team of assistants mostly from Melbourne University, including Jim Cairns and Law student Clyde Holding, who were determined to overcome the Groupers.

Kennelly was pleased with Crean's success, but not at all thrilled that the Tasmanian executive decided its Senate candidates' positions on the ballot paper by arranging for Premier Cosgrove to draw their names out of a hat. Morrow, who was well aware that his conservative enemies in the Tasmanian branch including Cosgrove wanted him to fill a low and unwinnable position on the ballot paper, smelt a rat when the draw was over half-way and his name had not been called: Morrow suddenly grabbed the hat, inspected it, and found the paper with his name on it stuck inside the hat band. The draw began afresh after this discovery, and Morrow's name was the first one removed, which assisted his re-election to Canberra.

Chifley battled gamely throughout the campaign. He had not been the same man since his heart attack five months earlier. His doctor had pleaded with him to curtail his campaigning. Together they arranged a reduced schedule which avoided the West and restricted him to the other capital cities only, with the exception of a visit to Geelong to help Dedman. But to the doctor's horror Chifley, having presented his most dynamic and forward-looking policy speech since taking over as leader, embarked upon a gruelling nation-wide campaign which included Perth, Tasmania and north Queensland. 'He was pale, tired and drawn, but kept going', recorded Duthie, 'amazing us with his stamina'.

After the election Chifley made a memorable speech at the NSW state conference on 10 June. He began by expressing the hope that the defeats of 1949 and 1951 had 'not discouraged members of the Labor Movement from fighting for what they think is right, whether it brings victory to the Party or not'. This was his main theme, although along the way he attacked 'the slander and calumnies of the Press', 'the mean and vicious propaganda' of Labor's opponents, and the 'sheer and complete rubbish' propagated about communism. He accused some ALP members of

> trying to get over as far as possible to the right without becoming opposed to the Labor Party...We have had examples in the past 15 months...of people shifting their

ground. No one has any admiration for people who shift ground. . .You have to be quite clear about what you believe in, whether popular or unpopular, and you have to fight for it. . .if I think a thing is worth fighting for, no matter what the penalty may be, I will fight for the right, and truth and justice will always prevail.

Three days later, 13 June, he was back in Canberra. He attended a gathering to celebrate Fred Daly's 38th birthday, but told colleagues that he would not attend the grand ball that evening in Parliament House to mark the jubilee of the inauguration of federal parliament. Chifley had never owned a dinner jacket, and avoided events that required him to wear one. 'Oh no', he told Daly, 'you can go and trip the bloody light fantastic, I'm going home to read a couple of westerns'. Later that night the revelry was in full swing when the news spread that Chifley had suffered a heart attack in his room at the Kurrajong. He was rushed to Canberra hospital, but died soon after arrival. Menzies interrupted the ball to announce the news of 'the passing of a fine Australian', and suggested that the festivities should cease. Doc Evatt, Duthie, Dorothy Tangney and many others could not hold back the tears. At well-to-do Geelong College a saddened 17-year-old named John Button wore a black tie to school in Chifley's honour. 'I know Mr Chifley is in heaven', remarked another admirer when she heard the news, 'because Labor leaders have their hell on earth'. The whole of Chif's beloved Bathurst seemed to stop for the state funeral there on 17 June. Thousands of mourners attended, some travelling to Bathurst on specially scheduled planes and trains. Among them were numerous dignitaries, including a visibly affected Governor-General McKell. Haylen wrote a moving poem, 'Chifley's Grave', about the final resting place. A monument was later erected, inscribed with the last words of Chifley's Sydney speech just three days before his death. 'I never saw his like before and will never see it again', wrote Calwell four months later, 'there never was, and never will be another Chifley'. 'We've never had his like since', Clyde Cameron reverently agreed nearly four decades later. Fred Daly concluded that 'Ben Chifley was the most impressive personality I have met in my life time'.

The new leader was Evatt. Elected unopposed by caucus on 20 June, he became Labor's first national leader without experience in the trade union movement. The ballot for the deputy leadership was won by Calwell ahead of the other contenders, Clarey (who had been MHR for Bendigo since 1949), Ward and Allan Fraser. The Evatt-Calwell partnership was not a happy one. Within a few weeks Calwell was feeling sufficiently slighted about Evatt's lack of consultation to rebuke the Doc sternly. 'Ben Chifley, I am sure, never treated you as his deputy in that discourteous fashion and you must not do it to me', warned Calwell. Rodgers was another who found Evatt's methods intolerable; he soon resigned. Evatt had great compassion for humanity in the mass, but his suspiciousness and whirlwind approach to tackling multitudinous problems contributed to the insensitivity which frequently marred his everyday dealings with individuals. Shortly before his death Chifley had privately conveyed to a few colleagues his lack of confidence in Evatt as a prospective leader, especially in the fundamental task of keeping the party united amid the pronounced strains generated by the Groupers' activities.

Misgivings about Evatt's leadership style were brushed aside, however, when he had a stunning triumph in his first campaign as leader. As foreshadowed during the 1951 election campaign, Menzies introduced a referendum to give his government the power to deal firmly with communism which, according to the recent High Court decision, was not authorized under the existing Constitution. On 5 July, the day Menzies introduced the referendum legislation into the Representatives, the ALP federal executive was meeting in Canberra. Determining a united party response on the issue of communism once again proved a difficult process; eventually, by eight votes to four (the Victorian and WA representatives comprising the minority), the delegates upheld the motion of federal president Ferguson that ALP members were 'required to oppose the Bill both in. . .Parliament and throughout the country'. Evatt was delighted. In caucus on 6 July he reminded his colleagues that this directive 'was binding on all members of the Party'. Some Victorians defied it, and Chambers declared that he 'could not in conscience associate himself with the campaign'. A larger group of caucus members were not fanatical but simply unenthusiastic, feeling that the 'No' case was certain to lose after Menzies had just won an election convincingly on the Communist threat. Indeed, an opinion poll in August measured community approval of the referendum at 73%. But Evatt, again animated about the renewed danger to civil liberties in Australia, propelled himself into a superhuman campaign. While he was not totally without support – some FPLP colleagues including Ward, Drakeford, McKenna, Pollard, Haylen, Morrow and a few others were committed to the fight – it was essentially Evatt who turned the situation around, assisted for once by the Australian reluctance to pass referenda which had frustrated him in the past. Many observers who heard his speech at Bondi just before polling day regarded it as one of the finest he ever made. On 22 September the referendum was rejected by the voters, and the large 'No' majority in NSW, Evatt's home state, was crucial. In caucus on 26 September Evatt's colleagues saluted his 'splendid leadership'. Evatt replied that the principles at stake made the referendum result more important in his view than a general election, and added that he had treated the campaign as a crusade associated with the name of Ben Chifley.

In the wake of this spectacular triumph, which enhanced his leadership stature, Evatt declined to enforce disciplinary action against the FPLP's anti-Communist zealots. Retribution against the disruptive Victorians was a distinct possibility. Keon and Mullens had refused to support party policy during the referendum campaign; the state executive had tried to force the FPLP to allow the Communist Party Dissolution Bill through the Senate; and Evatt's appearance in the High Court as counsel for Communists had not only been condemned in caucus by Victorian MHR E.W. Peters but also attacked publicly by the Victorian branch, which had even repeated its criticism during the 1951 election campaign. Within Victoria there were also severe ructions. One episode concerned the Toorak branch, which included Jim Cairns and barrister Sam Cohen among its members and was not sympathetic to the Groupers' viewpoint. After it publicly censured its local member, Bourke, for his attitude to the referendum, the Victorian executive retaliated by suspending the Toorak branch. We 'sternly rebuke those guilty' of 'unjustifiable disregard for Federal Conference decisions and democratic principles', pronounced the federal executive at its first post-referendum meeting, when it also proscribed the Movement's strident publication *News Weekly*. But that was all. Evatt, who was now keen to cultivate the Groupers, opted for conciliation. He recommended against any specific penalty for Keon and Mullens, and the SA branch followed suit in December 1951, deciding that no action should be taken against Chambers beyond the federal executive's stern rebuke.

The turbulence in Victoria had been aggravated by the publication of *Power Without Glory* by Communist author Frank Hardy. This sensational novel outlined the seamy career of a shady businessman and political puppeteer named John West, who was, nearly all readers concluded, a thinly disguised representation of John Wren. The novel's one-sided account of West's life, which involved murder, corruption and other criminal activities, revived old arguments about Wren's role in the labour movement. His antagonists cited the book as 'proof' of their conviction that Wren's influence had been evil. His defenders argued that Wren might not be pure, but he was not the unmitigated villain portrayed in the book; they pointed to Wren's generosity to impoverished battlers and donations to charities and other worthy causes. Some Wren supporters who shared his Catholic faith regarded the book as a scandalous Communist plot intended to desecrate their church. *Power Without Glory* did not flatter the ALP either, depicting many of its leading identities as weak-kneed, unprincipled and corrupt.

The impact of *Power Without Glory* was heightened by its treatment of contemporary events. The novel covered the struggle for power between West's forces and the Movement, and even included extracts from a secret Santamaria memorandum to the Catholic bishops which had been accidentally left on a train by Archbishop Duhig. In 1950 the book made its surreptitious appearance in Victoria, where Wren and Santamaria's Movement had commenced their activities and the Groupers had made their most significant progress in the ALP. Astonishingly, part of its second edition was printed secretly at the Victorian ALP's printery. The book was soon circulating in the labour movement, and readers began matching characters in the novel with real people (Thurgood for Theodore, Ashton for Anstey, Kiely for Keon, and many more). In the Victorian parliament some MPs started calling their opponents by the fictitious names used in *Power Without Glory*. The book's notoriety escalated when Hardy was arrested, charged under a rarely used statute with criminal libel, and acquitted after a sensational trial.

Late in 1951 there was a stark public demonstration of the tensions which had developed within the FPLP since the 1949 election when proceedings in the Representatives were enlivened by an unseemly clash between Mullens and Pollard. These two Victorians, who had both been MLAs before entering federal parliament, represented opposite extremes of their state branch's factional spectrum. In November Mullens used an adjournment debate to attack in his characteristically florid style both Hardy and a pro-Communist journalist, Wilfred Burchett. It was after midnight when Pollard rose to dissociate himself from Mullens's remarks. During Pollard's speech Mullens repeatedly accused him of 'defending the Coms'. 'I am defending the right of free speech', Pollard insisted. Mullens continued to interject and Pollard boiled over, calling Mullens 'a narrow-minded skunk'. Mullens leaped from his seat and rushed wildly towards Pollard. 'He is a man who is prepared to do violence', added Pollard amid the uproar, while Pat Galvin tried desperately to restrain Mullens. Order was eventually restored, but this wild parliamentary scene revealed the dangerous cracks undermining the FPLP's cohesion.

Victorian Labor's internal fissures were much less apparent than their opponents' disarray, however, and Cain became Premier for the third time after the 1952 state election. The Menzies government's inability to control inflation was also a significant factor in the Victorian ALP's victory. In a splendid result for the party, Labor won more seats than ever before in Victoria and formed a government with a secure Assembly majority for the first time. Cain's ministers included a Wren faction of Barry, Archie Fraser, wealthy publican Les Coleman and ex-railwayman Tom Hayes. These men, together with Bill Galvin, Slater and Stoneham, had all been in Cain's previous cabinet. Two of the new ministers were Sunshine MLA Ernie Shepherd, a former Footscray footballer and mayor, and lawyer Jack Galbally, who had represented the Wren family during part of the *Power Without Glory* courtroom drama. The most interesting newcomer was Francis Scully, who had succeeded his close friend Keon as MLA for Richmond when Keon transferred to federal politics. Scully was an intense Movement and Grouper ideologue who had shown marked capacity and tremendous energy as a parliamentarian. His 'tireless organising produced a youngish, aggressively Catholic, Movement-inspired faction, militantly opposed to Cain'. Naturally, Cain did not relish Scully's presence in cabinet, and Kennelly loathed him.

Kennelly's absence from Cain's cabinet represented a major triumph for the Groupers. They detested the stuttering kingmaker's intuitive, anti-intellectual wheeler-dealer style: his legendary preference to have the numbers in a party fight rather than the logic, if he could not have both, was anathema to the Groupers. His influential positions in the party and parliament, his network of contacts, and his conviction that the Groupers had become too powerful for the ALP's good combined to make him their arch-enemy. Although the party had belatedly introduced a salary for its national secretary in 1950, only a relatively small amount was provided because of Kennelly's remuneration and allowances as ALP leader in the Legislative Council. The Groupers reasoned that if they could deprive him of his main source of income by unseating him at the preselection for West Melbourne they would significantly dent both his influence and his capacity to intrigue against them. The campaign to defeat Kennelly orchestrated by the Groupers, the Movement and their allies was in full swing when their target was rocked by a terrible personal blow. His 13-year-old son (whose twin brother had died some years previously) was killed when thrown from the back of a truck during an outing to collect a Christmas tree. Kennelly was desolated. For weeks he paid little attention to the battle in West Melbourne, and lost the preselection ballot.

> Kennelly's distress and rage at defeat while he was grief-stricken was never likely to be forgotten by those who experienced it. He swore vengeance, and the differences in the party intensified more than ever.

He bounced back quickly by obtaining preselection for the Senate, which enabled him, as before, to supplement his moderate income as national secretary with a parliamentary salary. However, after becoming a Senator he acceded to a widespread feeling in caucus that it was inappropriate for a member of the FPLP to be federal ALP secretary; before stepping down he made sure that Queensland ALP secretary Jack Schmella would take over from him as national secretary.

Cain missed Kennelly acutely. Without him Cain, now 71, was less effective. Nonetheless his government settled into its stride capably, introducing a range of reforms including changes to the Landlord and Tenant Act, workers' compensation and the Shops and Factories Act. Long-service leave was introduced. Legislation was enacted to penalize rogues who resorted to fraudulent misrepresentation in soliciting corporate investment from the public. The most significant measure was a long-overdue electoral redistribution to reduce the scandalous distortions which had retarded Victorian Labor in the state sphere for so long. Cain continued to benefit from opposition disunity which was very patent, whereas only ALP insiders were aware of the extent of the factional and sectarian tensions affecting the party in Victoria.

There was, however, a public glimpse of Labor's internal problems when an amendment to a seemingly innocuous Land Settlement Bill was debated in the Assembly. A cherished objective of Santamaria and the Movement was the establishment of industrious independent farmers on rural land, and Santamaria had asked Cain to grant the Movement some unused mediocre government-owned land in Gippsland. Cain agreed to this request. But when the Land Settlement Bill amendment authorizing the government to grant land to unspecified 'organizations' came before tired MLAs at about 4 am on 11 December 1953 Cain's Lands minister, R.W. Holt, amazed onlookers by tearing up the bill and marching dramatically out of the chamber. Holt, who was a solicitor, a friend of Kennelly and son of a Presbyterian minister, resigned his portfolio shortly afterwards. This incident gave 'another twist to the sectarian spiral'.

NSW also had a change of premier in 1952. McGirr had not been a successful leader. Although humane and popular, he was indecisive, lacked McKell's grasp of administrative detail, emulated Bert Evatt in his excessively suspicious nature, and also possessed an impulsive streak which often brought trouble to himself and his government. His outlandish promises during the 1947 election campaign returned to haunt Labor at the following state election in 1950 when the government narrowly escaped defeat. McGirr's extravagant public works promises had been followed by an unco-ordinated construction programme which contrasted sharply with McKell's carefully planned development. There was severe internal discord in both cabinet and caucus. In April 1952 McGirr resigned, and Cahill took over as Premier with Heffron as his deputy. During the McGirr government Cahill had been vigorous and impressive in tackling the serious problems affecting NSW electricity supplies. As Premier he was equally decisive. Cabinet decisions were made promptly, the public works programme was placed under tighter control with a system of development priorities, and some astute Canberra-bashing highlighting the Menzies government's deficiencies helped improve the NSW government's fragile parliamentary position. Unlike McGirr, Cahill made no rash promises when he called a shrewdly timed election early in 1953. With anti-Labor lacking cohesion in NSW, the ALP gained a remarkable swing – especially for a government in office for 12 years – of over 8% and won 57 seats (46 in 1950).

Coinciding with that NSW poll on 14 February 1953 was a state election in the West where Labor achieved a swing of similar magnitude. A singular facet of this WA election was that as many as 22 of the 50 Assembly seats were won by candidates who were unopposed on polling day. The ALP was unopposed in 12 electorates, and did not stand a candidate of its own in 11 seats. In a close result Labor was returned to power when it won 26 seats (23 in 1947 and 1950), despite the failure of reformers' efforts to overcome the hostility and indifference of WA unionists which had been instrumental in the 1947 defeat. The *Westralian Worker* folded in 1951, and attempts to launch a new paper were unsuccessful. A proposed rise in affiliation fees, which would have injected the extra funds necessary to employ a full-time organizer and establish an industrial bureau to assist unions with their Arbitration Court cases, was opposed so strenuously that it had to be abandoned. For the 1953 election campaign the unions provided less than half their modest 1947 contribution, with the AWU registering its protest against the proposed increase by making no offering at all. Nevertheless Hawke, who had become leader (with Tonkin as his deputy) when Wise resigned to become Administrator of the Northern Territory, drew up a blueprint for the election which emphasized development and welfare, and he campaigned on these themes to good effect. In office his government's worthwhile initiatives included increases in workers' compensation payments, accelerated construction of schools and houses, and the gradual easing of some of the more obnoxious controls which had been imposed on Aborigines in WA.

In 1952 there was also a change at the head of government in Queensland. 'I'll never resign – they'll have to carry me out with boots on', Premier Hanlon had retorted when friends sugested that he should consider retiring from politics because of his frail health. True to those defiant words, Hanlon in January 1952 became the first Queensland premier to die in office for over half a century. During his ministerial career the vision and sympathy for the needy evident in his fine achievements in public health contrasted sharply with the toughness and ferocity he displayed in industrial relations. He was also responsible for the innovation of a notorious zonal system of electorates brazenly inconsistent with Labor's traditional commitment to one vote, one value. Hanlon's scheme divided the state's electorates into four zones. Within each zone there was a uniform quota of voters for each electorate, and this quota varied considerably from zone to zone: for example, each metropolitan zone was allotted over 10 000 voters, while each electorate in the western zone was given less than 5000 voters. To help him maintain Queensland Labor's remarkable record since 1915 (which had occurred under electoral arrangements at least as fair overall as elsewhere in Australia), Hanlon evidently concluded that some creative engineering was required. This institutionalized electoral inequality assisted the re-election of the Hanlon government in 1950. In January 1952 Hanlon was succeeded by Gair, who had been acting Premier for the previous 4½ months owing to Hanlon's ill-health. Like Cahill and Hawke, Gair obtained a large swing to Labor at his first state election as leader early in 1953.

While premiers were coming and going in other states, Tasmania's Premier Cosgrove was still clinging to power. His career in public life seemed over when he had to stand down in December 1947 – exactly eight years since he first became Premier – after being charged with bribery and conspiracy for allegedly accepting contributions to his secret leader's fund from transport companies hoping to avoid being nationalized. Ted Brooker, a Hobart engineer, succeeded him. Two months later Cosgrove was acquitted of the charges, Brooker resigned, and Cosgrove was re-elected leader. The Tasmanian Liberals, sensing that this Cosgrove scandal would prove an election winner despite his acquittal, blocked supply in the Legislative Council and forced an election. Cosgrove nervously nursed his own electorate, leaving his able but relatively inexperienced Attorney-General Roy Fagan, who had become deputy leader when Brooker died, to lead Labor's campaign elsewhere in the state. Labor lost a seat (although Cosgrove held his) to lose its Assembly majority, and three independents held the balance of power. Labor managed to continue in office. The parliamentary instability produced another election in 1950, but the situation remained essentially unchanged – Labor 15, Liberals 14, and one of those three independents, who continued his support of the Cosgrove government, returned to hold the balance of power.

Cosgrove adopted a right-wing position on most issues. Associated with the Movement, he ardently supported the Groupers, the referendum to ban the Communist Party and the Menzies government's revival of compulsory military

267

training. When he was attacked by party critics for his attitude to the Communist Party referendum, he threatened to bring down the government if replaced as leader. Cosgrove was right behind the Tasmanian executive's decision not to endorse uncompromising left-winger Morrow for the 1953 Senate election, although it produced widespread anger in the labour movement. Doc Evatt, trying to build bridges with both left and right wings of the party and impressed by Morrow's sincerity and ability, offered the 63-year-old Senator a position on his staff, but Morrow 'didn't want to fire other men's bullets'. When two of Morrow's friends were expelled by the state executive after agitating for his re-endorsement, Morrow was stung into resigning from the ALP and standing as a Tasmanian Labour Group candidate in the Senate. He polled under 6%, and for the rest of his life channelled his political activity into the peace movement. Cosgrove was delighted by the departure from Labor politics of his most prominent critic in the labour movement. But in 1954 the Premier encountered more trouble from even moderate unionists like AWU officials and Hobart TLC strongman Jack O'Neill when his government suspended the system of automatic inflation-adjusted wage increases. Without an absolute parliamentary majority in either chamber, with continued disruption from cabinet dissidents and with a state election due in 1955, even a tenacious survivor like Cosgrove had his problems.

In 1952 the FPLP acquired an arresting newcomer. When Labor's Lazzarini brothers, Bert MHR and Charlie MLA, died in successive months, the by-election for Bert's seat of Werriwa was won by 36-year-old barrister Gough Whitlam. Unusually tall and confident, Whitlam had a brilliant mind and a dazzling wit. No stranger to Canberra, where his father had been a senior public servant for two decades, Whitlam grew up in a teetotal home environment which exalted intellectual endeavour and eschewed frivolity. His mother's partial deafness and his father's linguistic fastidiousness endowed him with an attachment to clear and precise speech, and he was inclined to be irritatingly pedantic when others did not meet his exacting standards. Thirst for knowledge remained an enduring Whitlam characteristic, and so was his propensity to flaunt his erudition. Most caucus traditionalists initially treated him with reserve: not only was he arrogant – he came from an affluent background, was fussy about his appearance and speech presentation, and had not developed an active allegiance to Labor until his late twenties. The main single spur to Whitlam's involvement in the ALP had been the Labor government's ill-fated 1944 referendum and the cynicism exhibited by the opposition in fighting it; Whitlam campaigned vigorously for 'Yes' among his Royal Australian Air Force (RAAF) unit, and joined the ALP the following year. Whitlam's maiden speech in March 1953 highlighted the difficulties with housing, schools, telephones and other amenities faced by residents in the outer suburbs which were developing rapidly since the war. He was familiar with these problems from his young family's experiences as residents in Werriwa. Whitlam's parliamentary debut was so effective that a government minister broke the convention against interjections during a maiden speech. Clyde Cameron was also stirred by it. He congratulated Whitlam effusively, and predicted that Whitlam would become Prime Minister. That prophecy did not seem to surprise Whitlam.

Whereas Whitlam was ridiculed by some colleagues for his dashing white tie and tails at a parliamentary reception for the Queen during her first visit to Australia, Eddie Ward attracted notoriety of the opposite kind when he turned up in a lounge suit. He was uncomfortable wearing a dinner suit and too sensitive to the reactions of his East Sydney constituents to be seen in it at a public function. He had been representing them for over 20 years, but his uncompromising rebelliousness was undiminished. To the delight of Labor's rank and file, he generally refused to follow the common practice of MPs to give no quarter inside the chamber and fraternize with the enemy outside it. He maintained his unforgiving hostility to Labor rats, explaining his refusal to attend a function honouring Hughes's 50 consecutive years as a parliamentarian with the comment that he did not eat cheese. Although he had displayed in government a capacity for constructive achievement which surprised his detractors, his slashing style of machine-gun oratory was naturally more suited to opposition. Even one of the many anti-Labor MPs who intensely disliked him acknowledged that he was 'a formidable antagonist, a supremely confident demagogue, and an outstanding rabble-rouser' who 'spat out his vituperations as lava erupts from a volcano'. Menzies had always been a special target. Ward relished taunting Menzies that his promising military career had suddenly halted when the Great War began, and on one occasion described him as a 'posturing individual with the scowl of a Mussolini, the bombast of Hitler and the physical proportions of Goering'.

The Groupers had achieved considerable success in reducing Communist influence in the union movement. Their most celebrated victory was in the Ironworkers' Association, where the Thornton Communist regime was toppled after a protracted battle in the union and in the courts by a determined team headed by well-known anti-Communist Laurie Short, who received a useful public commendation from Evatt, crucial organizational support from Santamaria and the Movement, and sage legal advice from solicitor Jim McClelland and barrister John Kerr. The Groupers had also notched up other significant victories, and their activities had contributed to the marked decline experienced by the Communist Party in Australia since its zenith around the end of the Second World War. The Groupers had become a powerful force within the ALP as well as in the union movement. At the 1951 federal conference Kennelly and Ferguson ensured the defeat of a motion recording the party's 'appreciation of the splendid work performed by ALP Industrial Groups' and seeking their establishment on a national basis. The Groupers were present at the 1953 federal conference in greater strength – although Clyde Cameron had in the meantime managed to have the groups disbanded in SA – and Kennelly was concerned that they might make another attempt, with a good chance of success, to place the groups on a formal national footing. He was relieved when this did not eventuate.

Evatt was understandably delighted about the succession of excellent electoral results Labor had achieved around Australia. His personal triumph at the 1951 referendum had been followed by pronounced swings to Labor at state elections in Victoria, NSW, WA, Queensland and also SA, the only state without an ALP government in 1954. At the 1953 SA election the ALP won only 15 of the 39 Assembly seats despite managing to capture 50·97% of the vote, its largest voting share since 1927. There was also pleasing success at the half-Senate election in May 1953 when Labor outpolled the coalition government by over 6%. Although opinion polling indicated that the Menzies government might have recovered some ground in the ensuing months, in April 1954 Evatt had good reason to feel confident that the imminent election for the Representatives would crown Labor's nation-wide resurgence and make him Prime Minister. Even the *Sydney Morning Herald* had concluded that Menzies would need to pull a rabbit out of the hat to win the election on 29 May.

On 13 April Evatt travelled to Sydney in a buoyant mood. He was looking forward to being guest of honour at that evening's annual reunion at Fort Street, the famous school he had attended. Federal parliament was still sitting, but it was about to wind up for the election. Journalist Alan Reid has claimed that he intuitively guessed that something big was about to break and advised Evatt to check before leaving for Sydney. According to Reid, Evatt consulted Holt and Menzies and was assured that he would not be missing anything significant in parliament. Haylen, one of Evatt's closest FPLP colleagues, accompanied the Doc to Canberra airport. They discussed literature, a great common interest. Haylen felt that Evatt was 'more happy and relaxed than I had seen him for some time'.

While Evatt was relaxing at Fort Street, Menzies theatrically announced in the Representatives that a Russian spy had defected and supplied ASIO with oral and documentary information concerning Soviet espionage in Australia. The announcement was initially to have been made that afternoon, but the information that Evatt would be away from parliament in the evening induced Menzies to change his plans. He deliberately dropped his bombshell in Evatt's absence, which conveniently coincided with the peak audience for the radio broadcast of parliament. This conduct flagrantly breached both precedent and parliamentary conventions concerning security questions. It was Chifley's custom in office to brief Menzies as Opposition Leader about such matters. Although the Menzies cabinet was sworn to secrecy about the impending sensation, some ministers could not resist urging friendly journalists to make sure they were in the Representatives at 8 pm. 'I can't tell you more than that', Fadden advised a correspondent, 'but the big white bastard will be making an announcement and it's a winner'. Another journalist was told by A.G. Townley to expect 'the biggest story of the century' which would 'destroy Evatt'. From the moment Evatt first heard about Menzies's dramatic announcement he remained convinced that it was nothing more than a shabby stunt concocted by desperate men seeking to rob him of his rightful destiny. The government's blatant duplicity in making the announcement was crucial to Evatt's opinion of the controversy and his handling of it.

Labor publicly backed the establishment of the royal commission announced by Menzies, although Evatt was privately scornful of it. A special caucus meeting early on 14 April unanimously endorsed a press statement already made by the Doc declaring that Labor 'will support the fullest inquiry into all the circumstances connected with the statement made by Mr Menzies'. It added that Labor would aim to ensure 'that no guilty person escapes, that no innocent person is condemned and that the whole matter is dealt with free from all questions of party politics and on the basis of the established principles of British justice'. Unfortunately for Labor and especially its leader, these worthy aspirations proved to be wishful thinking.

Many Labor partisans have agreed with Evatt's assessment of the circumstances of Vladimir Petrov's defection, but the notion that it was simply a Menzies plot to steal the election has taken a battering since the mid-1980s release of extensive archival records (but not, some have contended, absolutely all the significant official material) relating to the affair. Menzies initially claimed that he had no knowledge of Petrov before 11 April, but subsequently backdated this initial awareness to 4 April and, many years afterwards, to 10 February, the date of his first ASIO briefing about Petrov documented in the records. Even if one allows for the unlikely possibility that Menzies was given an unofficial inkling before 10 February 1954, the long and fluctuating process of cultivating the erratic, hard-drinking Soviet intelligence agent was hardly compatible with forward planning for a precisely timed election.

However, Menzies exploited the situation to the full. He introduced a bill on 14 April to establish a royal commission and piously declared that he wished that the need for such an inquiry had not arisen just before an election. Yet he and his government were well aware that in Petrov they had a lethal campaign weapon. Menzies apologists have lauded his 'propriety' in not mentioning the Petrov commission specifically during the campaign (although Fadden and other anti-Labor candidates did); but altruism did not inspire this decision. It arose from the government's fear that too much emphasis on the Petrov issue on the hustings might be counterproductive. Furthermore, in the prevailing atmosphere, with the Communist menace once again trumpeted incessantly as the conservatives' main theme, the hysteria accompanying the sensational developments of the Petrov saga guaranteed its electoral potency irrespective of any help from Menzies. Amid dramatic and emotional scenes at airports in Sydney and Darwin, Petrov's wife was intercepted at her request while in the process of being escorted back to Russia. In graphic photographs and riveting newsreel footage Australians 'saw an attractive young blond woman, weeping and vulnerable, one foot bare, being dragged across the tarmac by two formidable, scowling Slavic gorillas'.

There was another blaze of publicity when the royal commission proceedings began – most conveniently for Labor's opponents – during the second-last week of the election campaign. The three judges carefully chosen by Menzies to be the inquiry's commissioners and W.J.V. Windeyer, the barrister selected to act as their assisting counsel, formed a quartet 'as deeply rooted in conservative society as could be found'. Lush carpet and velvet curtains rapidly transformed Canberra's Albert Hall from a venue for concerts and dances into a large courtroom. To maximize publicity the arrangements for numerous observers included communications facilities for journalists better than correspondents with international experience had seen anywhere. Windeyer gave an outline of Soviet espionage in Australia and made titillating references to the material Petrov had given ASIO, especially the notorious Documents H and J. The commissioners and Windeyer made it publicly clear that their inquiry would catch spies, and inspired rumours circulated that some spies might even be operating close to certain politicians. Menzies prevented any pre-election disclosure that ASIO had paid £5000 to induce Petrov to defect. He had also instructed the Director-General of ASIO – and later denied in parliament that he had done so – not to discuss the defections with Evatt, although ever since ASIO's creation its chief had routinely discussed security matters with Evatt and his predecessors as opposition leader, Chifley and Menzies himself.

The election was bitterly contested and the result was very close. Evatt's policy speech on 6 May unveiled a number of lavish proposals in welfare, health and housing which were denounced as recklessly imprudent by Labor's enemies in the government and the press. These critics attacked the vagueness of Evatt's analysis of how these costly measures would be financed – the Doc's intellectual prowess was least evident in economics – and highlighted a damaging intervention by one of his own backbenchers. Bill Bourke was not the only FPLP member disturbed by Evatt's promise that a Labor government would abolish the means test on pensions; only Bourke, however, took the grave step of undermining his leader during the campaign, and his disparaging remarks at a Prahran meeting were gratefully publicized by government speakers. Evatt's bid for power failed narrowly. Labor candidates polled more first-preference votes throughout the country than all other candidates combined (although the ALP's

271

proportion of 50·03% slightly exaggerated its real voting share, since there were a number of uncontested anti-Labor seats), but not enough ALP votes were in the vital marginal electorates. Two seats were captured by returning former ministers. Makin won Sturt after spending five years in the United States as Australia's ambassador, and Nelson Lemmon was victorious in St George, which he had unsuccessfully contested in 1951 after Chifley had encouraged him to leave WA and find a NSW seat. Teacher Lance Barnard won the Tasmanian seat of Bass held by his father Claude, a Chifley government minister, from 1934 to 1949. But there was a net gain of only one other seat, leaving the FPLP with 57 and the coalition government 64.

Evatt was shattered by the election result. At one stage during the campaign he had counter-attacked his traducers in a fervent radio broadcast, lashing 'the sneerers, the slanderers. . .the people who dare to criticize me because I want a new deal for our people'. After the election he issued a surly statement:

> The Government did not win the election fairly. . .Throughout the campaign it resorted to the smear and hysteria technique. . .In spite of that, Labor outnumbered Government votes by more than 250 000. . .a clear majority of Australians. . .have given a popular verdict in favour of Labor's positive programme.

Although it is naturally impossible to ascertain with certainty the voting motives of electors, Evatt understandably felt that without the Petrov upheaval the small number of extra ALP votes in a few vital seats could have been attained and he would have become Prime Minister. It could be surmised with no less validity that Evatt could have satisfied his yearning to defeat Menzies and become Prime Minister if his election promises had been less vulnerable to attack or if there had not been a successful pre-election royal tour, but Evatt was intent on blaming what he saw as the Petrov conspiracy. 'His mind seethed with plots and conspiracies', wrote a newspaper editor who lunched with Evatt in the wake of the election and was 'appalled' by his frame of mind.

Evatt was soon reeling from another devastating blow. It came from his press secretary, Fergan O'Sullivan. On 3 June O'Sullivan told Evatt that he was the author of Document H, which he had written as a 23-year-old *Sydney Morning Herald* journalist in 1951 before joining Evatt's staff. Evatt was furious, and sacked him immediately. Sinister thoughts about O'Sullivan and his possible connections began to perturb the Doc. In mid-July O'Sullivan publicly admitted authorship at the Petrov commission. He claimed to have compiled Document H, which was three pages of pithy personal profiles – mostly unflattering – of journalists in the Canberra press gallery, at the request of a representative of the Soviet news agency Tass in order to assist international relations by helping Tass to get more Russian news items into Australian newspapers. O'Sullivan denied that he had ever belonged to or supported the Communist Party. He was also questioned about Document J, a 37-page 'farrago of facts, falsity and filth' according to Windeyer. Attributed to an Australian journalist who was a Communist, Document J contained a miscellany of 'information' including details of donations to the ALP and erroneous material about Evatt purportedly obtained from 'sources' mentioned in it. O'Sullivan was asked about his inclusion as one of these sources. He admitted contact with the alleged author of Document J, but denied any knowledge of the 'information' contained in it. During O'Sullivan's evidence the names of the rest of Evatt's staff were mentioned, and one of them was specified as another of the sources listed in Document J. These developments were predictably emblazoned in eye-catching headlines.

To Evatt, still smouldering after the election result, all this was intolerable. The commissioners had breached the inquiry guidelines stipulating that names would not be mentioned publicly until those concerned had been given an opportunity to see and challenge the evidence involving them. Evatt sent a blistering telegram to the commission 'to protest at once at the making of defamatory and injurious imputations reflecting upon members of my staff'. Each member of his present staff, Evatt assured the commission, 'has unequivocally denied having given at any time any such confidential information to the alleged author of Document J or to any person'. Clive Evatt offered to travel immediately to the commission and represent the staff members, but the Doc insisted that he himself would act as their counsel. He was motivated not merely by the way the reputations of his staff, and by inference his own, had been blackened. He wanted to blow the entire commission out of the water by exposing it as a naked and sordid conspiracy. Sensing correctly that many caucus colleagues would disapprove, he resolved not to tell them.

The commissioners' treatment of the references to Evatt's staff in Document J contrasted with their handling of certain other allegations in it. Document J also claimed that a senior anti-Labor minister, who was in both the wartime Menzies cabinet and the ministry formed after the 1949 election, had acted as a Japanese agent early in the Second World War, and that the minister and the UAP had been paid money by the Japanese after the minister warned them that the Australian government was about to freeze Japanese funds in Australia. Any reference to these allegations during the inquiry was avoided by the commissioners, and they only came to light many years later.

The resumption of federal parliament in August raised the FPLP temperature to boiling point. At the first post-election caucus meeting on 3 August there was a surprise when Evatt was opposed for the leadership by Chifley's former protégé Tom Burke. Despite minimal canvassing, Burke managed to attract 20 votes to Evatt's 68. In the exhaustive balloting for the FPLP office-bearers and executive Ward antagonized some of his colleagues by his manipulative conduct. He was given proxies by four absent members, and therefore voted five times each ballot. 'Terrible display of intrigue, powerdrunkenness, pressure, double crossing' with 'Ward influencing people between ballots', noted one (anti-Grouper) MHR who was there. Eight days later tempers became frayed in caucus during a protracted debate about the Petrov commission. Haylen told Ward to stop 'beating his own chest as if he was running the party'. Ward lashed out at Haylen with a punch that struck an unsuspecting Senate colleague. Haylen swung back at Ward before they were separated. 'All this tenseness is playing havoc on members' nerves', Duthie recorded in his diary, and 'it's a sad time and sad days for the Party'. With all 'the crosscurrents and bitterness' in caucus, he ruefully concluded, Labor was 'not fit to govern'.

The following day the mutual hatred of Menzies and Evatt sparked a venomous public exchange. Evatt presented his interim conclusions about the Petrov conspiracy in a press release, and Menzies responded in parliament with anger and scorn but not – as far as his first claimed knowledge of Petrov was concerned – the truth. Evatt followed Menzies and repeated his conspiracy allegations despite a hail of derisive taunts from government backbenchers which a correspondent described as 'one of the most merciless spectacles the House of Representatives has ever seen'. It was 'probably the most bitter personal debate', another observer concluded, between two party leaders ever seen in the national parliament.

Evatt dominated the Petrov inquiry from the moment he entered it directly on 16 August. Not until the morning of his appearance as counsel for his staff did he send his caucus colleagues an explanatory telegram. Before morning tea on his first day the Doc had accused Windeyer of smearing and uttering propaganda, and had lectured the commissioners on constitutional law and the conduct of the inquiry. 'Bad-tempered, dishevelled and flamboyant, Evatt dominated the proceedings' as he beavered away for days in cross-examination, attempting to show that Document J was a forgery. At first the commissioners refused his repeated requests to inspect Document J in its entirety, but his persistence and persuasion changed their minds.

In September there was a discernible shift in the commissioners' attitude to Evatt. Menzies was worried that the Doc's 'considerable measure of success in the public mind' might result in 'the ultimate public reaction' to the Petrov affair being harmful to the government, and he persuaded Barwick to come to the rescue as counsel for ASIO. It seems that Menzies may have also resorted to pressure on the commissioners to be much tougher on Evatt. The commissioners' changed approach was evident when they instructed Evatt to provide precise charges pinpointing the alleged conspirators instead of further long-winded pursuit of vague inferences. In reply Evatt named Petrov and O'Sullivan as the key figures in 'one of the basest conspiracies known in political history'. Evatt then made an application to call an independent handwriting expert to testify about the authenticity of Document J, but the commissioners refused this request.

That same week a newspaper reported that Madame Ollier, a French diplomat serving in Australia, had been arrested after being allegedly implicated in Soviet espionage by the Petrovs. On Friday 3 September the commissioners agreed to release a transcript of the evidence against Madame Ollier provided by the Petrovs in a secret hearing in July. Evatt was furious. She had been given no opportunity to provide evidence herself or to have the Petrovs cross-examined. During the weekend the Doc jumped to her defence with a forceful statement: 'Today she will find herself defamed throughout the world as a spy apparently on the say so of two paid informers who, on their own admission, have been treacherous to both Russia and Australia'. When the inquiry reconvened on 7 September the commissioners, clearly nettled by Evatt's statement, asked him to justify such grossly improper remarks. He replied that they were perfectly proper from the Leader of the Opposition. The commissioners maintained that his political position and his legal role at the commission were incompatible. Evatt hotly disagreed. Eventually he conceded that if he could not do both he would drop his political hat for a while; he guaranteed that there would be no repetition of his controversial weekend remarks. He was stunned, then devastated, when it dawned on him that the commissioners were withdrawing his leave to appear at the inquiry. He pleaded desperately, to no avail. Outside the courtroom he defiantly gave his conspiracy fixation another airing before returning to Canberra.

FPLP turbulence had continued in Evatt's absence. In caucus on 25 August his participation at the inquiry had been criticized by Daly, Pat Galvin, Burke, Johnson, Peters and the 67-year-old MHR for Port Adelaide, Salvation Army enthusiast Bert Thompson. Ward had clashed fiercely with Keon, accusing him of allowing Santamaria to dictate policy to him. By now Ward was demonstrating the extent of his intolerance of the Groupers by chanting 'Santa, Santa' during their speeches in parliament.

On 8 September Evatt addressed caucus emotionally and at length about developments at the Petrov commission. His account continued beyond the scheduled end of the meeting, and pandemonium broke out when he finally finished. Ward tried to move a vote of confidence in Evatt's leadership, Evatt declared the meeting closed, and some of his critics including Keon and Thompson loudly demanded the right to speak against Ward's motion. Amid the uproar Ward and Thompson shaped up to each other before being separated. When newspapers next morning carried graphic accounts of this stormy meeting Evatt called a press conference and denounced 'the treacherous liars' and 'paid informers' responsible for leaking distorted reports to the press. After this outburst FPLP passions cooled somewhat, and the following caucus meeting was conducted in a good-humoured and conciliatory spirit.

However, this FPLP tranquillity was shortlived. Labor MPs were appalled to learn soon afterwards that Evatt had applied to reappear at the Petrov inquiry in contravention of an implicit commitment that some of them thought he had given caucus. The commissioners refused Evatt permission, even when he asked to appear not for his staff but on his own behalf (and until then anyone mentioned in the inquiry proceedings had been allowed to appear). They indicated that they were not prepared to spend any more time on wild-goose chases to satisfy Evatt's obsession about a conspiracy, especially when they had unquestioning faith in the integrity of ASIO and its officers. Evatt had to restrict himself to loud whispered directions to his legal team from the public gallery. Back in Canberra Evatt's unpredictable actions were scathingly attacked in caucus on 22 September by Bill Bourke, who was supporting a motion requiring Evatt to obtain FPLP approval before making any further appearances at the Petrov commission or public statements about it. Bourke's remarks were so vitriolic that even the proponent and seconder of this motion, Peters and Tom Burke, distanced themselves from them. Pollard, not for the first time, was quick to return the Groupers' fire. 'There are some here not fit to lick the Doctor's boots!' he thundered, recalling Bourke's sabotage of the last election campaign and unwillingness to oppose the anti-Communist referendum. Duthie and Ashley also strongly attacked Bourke. When it was alleged that there was a plot to replace Evatt with Calwell the meeting became wilder still. Calwell tried to hose down the flames, denying knowledge of any such plot and supporting Evatt's recommendation that Peters should withdraw his motion. Peters did so. Evatt, who had promised during the meeting that he would make no further attempt to act as counsel at the commission, began to consider the merits of a drastic counterattack against his caucus detractors.

On 5 October Evatt issued a statement which was headlined throughout the country and rocked the ALP to its foundations. At the recent federal election, asserted Evatt in what Alan Reid described as his 'hydrogen bomb', 'the self-sacrifice of tens of thousands of voluntary workers' for the party was undermined by

> the attitude of a small minority group of members, located particularly in the State of Victoria, which has, since 1949, become increasingly disloyal to the Labor Movement and the Labor leadership. Adopting methods which strikingly resemble both Communist and Fascist infiltration of larger groups, some of these groups have created an almost intolerable situation – calculated to deflect the Labor Movement from the pursuit of established Labor objectives and ideals. . .It seems certain that the activities of this small group are largely directed from outside the Labor Movement. . .The Melbourne *News Weekly* appears to act as their organ. . .

Issuing such a statement at such a time was like putting a match to tinder-dry scrub in a heatwave.

There was an immediate angry response to Evatt's statement from several party spokesmen, including the Victorian secretary Lovegrove, and the ALP became ravaged by internecine conflict of a bitterness not seen before or since, except in 1916. The upshot was that Menzies was entrenched in office and the Cain government in Victoria was smashed when some of the Grouper and Movement enthusiasts left the ALP and formed a separate party, which eventually became known as the Democratic Labor Party (DLP). The choice for some Labor supporters was straightforward. However, as in 1916, others found it difficult, and many individuals were terribly scarred as families and lifelong friendships were ruptured by the split. With many Labor Catholics defecting to the DLP, especially in Victoria where the ferment was most pronounced, some Catholics who stayed with the ALP endured abuse and ostracism at the church they had attended all their lives. Other ugly manifestations of the conflict included brutal violence by enforcers, dispatch of dead rats to rivals through the mail, and calculated haranguing and harassment of the children of detested opponents.

The lasting enmity between the ALP and DLP helped to shape a subsequent ALP tradition that the split was inevitable and justified. According to this doctrine, Evatt was a principled radical who decisively exposed the treacherous conduct and connections of minority elements which were like boils on the body of Labor and had to be lanced sooner or later. This tradition is flawed. Evatt was a tremendous fighter for civil liberties and had other outstanding radical credentials, but he also dabbled in intrigue and power plays. During his first three years as leader he had consistently cultivated Labor's right wing, and his flirtation even extended to secret meetings with Santamaria before the 1954 election. At a time when knowledge of Santamaria and his role was restricted to informed political and religious circles, Evatt invited suggestions for the ALP policy speech from him and enthused about the prospect of having Keon in the forthcoming Labor cabinet. It was the Petrov controversy, and Evatt's response to it, that made a continuation of this cosy concord impossible. Later, when Santamaria had become famous, Evatt implausibly denied having been aware of the extent of his influence.

Evatt's leadership aggravated the split. His increasingly erratic behaviour during 1954 – combined with unsettling Evatt characteristics observable for years, such as his acute suspiciousness – intensified muted speculation about the Doc's mental stability. During the 1960s Evatt suffered from severe mental and physical deterioration, and some of his detractors have claimed that the initial signs of this tragic decline were evident years earlier. Irrespective of one's conclusion on that delicate issue, it is clear that the narrow election defeat and the Petrov affair contributing to it caused Evatt intense frustration which accentuated the ALP's internal strains. Whether the split would have been more contained or avoided altogether under another leader, and whether or not it would have occurred in some form under Evatt if Labor had won the 1954 federal election, are tantalizing questions. If Labor had won in 1954, some Evatt apologists have argued, the split would never have happened. Evatt's hunger for the prime ministership would have been sated, he would have avoided being racked by the Petrov and election defeat torment which warped his judgement, the elixir of power would have eased Labor's internal tensions, and Evatt's intellectual brilliance and reformist instincts justified an expectation that he would have followed his fine record as Opposition Leader between mid-1951 and 1953 with an impressive performance in government. On the other hand, even if Evatt had won in the Representatives in 1954 he would have had to contend with an opposition majority in the Senate, he would have been faced with the dilemma of how to implement his extravagant election promises without disrupting the economy, Labor's factional stresses would not have disappeared just because of an election victory, and some observers were asking awkward questions by the mid-1950s about Evatt's temperament and balance under pressure.

FPLP meetings became even wilder after Evatt's bombshell. On 13 October Johnson, Peters and Tom Burke vehemently condemned their leader's conduct and G.R. Cole, a Tasmanian Senator, moved for a spill of all FPLP leadership positions. The anti-Evatt ranks wanted to make Calwell leader and had in mind as his deputy Allan Fraser, who had criticized Evatt for delivering a public blast instead of utilizing internal party mechanisms to deal with dissidents. The numbers may well have been there for a leadership change, but Evatt shrewdly ruled that a week's notice was needed. During the intervening week MPs were pressured by the pro-Evatt forces, and in the general whirl of events the mood and momentum of the 13th had evaporated by the 20th. Cole nevertheless proceeded with his spill motion. Keon and Bill Bourke again attacked Evatt, and Mullens flayed the Doc as a 'smear merchant' and 'phoney' with a 'colossal ego': 'If you want Evatt', he bellowed over the interjections, 'then you are gluttons for punishment!' When the vote was taken, by hand as usual, Evatt clearly had the numbers.

Ward mischievously called for a division. Evatt instantly adopted Ward's suggestion and clambered up onto a table to get a clear view. Tom Burke demonstrated his distrust of Evatt by climbing up alongside him. 'Take down their names!' exclaimed Ward, who sometimes compiled lists of how FPLP members voted on important issues. Evatt took up Ward's cry. There was pandemonium. Armstrong, who had joined the majority group opposing Cole's motion, was provoked by Evatt's conduct to respond that if names were being taken then they could include his, and he marched dramatically across the room to join the smaller group. Other NSW members followed, including Tony Luchetti and Frank Stewart; so too did Fred Daly, who 'crossed over in rebellion against the worst action I have ever seen from a Labor leader'. These late additions, who also included Riordan, boosted the minority group to 28, while 52 ended up opposing Cole's spill motion. In the following day's newspapers and during the ensuing stormy months the names of those 28 members were widely publicized. Some of them later joined the DLP, but most did not.

On 27 October the federal executive decided that it would begin an inquiry into the Victorian branch a fortnight later. This decision was taken after consideration of a submission from Evatt and a number of others as well, including a letter from former Victorian Lands minister Holt which contained the bald allegation that 'the Victorian branch is controlled and directed through Mr B. Santamaria'. During its lengthy inquiry, which lasted over 100 hours during November and December, the federal executive questioned 26 witnesses, including Evatt, Keon, Mullens, Bourke, Kennelly, Cain, Scully, Holt and Lovegrove. Another witness, assistant Victorian ALP secretary Frank McManus, who was described by one of the 12 federal executive investigators as 'no doubt the ablest of all' the prominent Groupers, admitted his strong support of the groups but unconvincingly denied any connection with the Movement. Some non-Victorian delegates were appalled by the rancour revealed in the Victorian branch. At the conclusion of the inquiry the federal executive announced that it would supervise a special Victorian conference, which would elect a new state executive. The rules stipulated for that special conference, to be held in February, were framed to maximize the likelihood that the Victorian contingent for the federal conference in Hobart in March would comprise committed anti-Grouper delegates. McManus afterwards maintained that this inquiry result was only approved by a seven-five vote, and that if Kim Beazley had not been replaced as a WA delegate the numbers would have been tied at six-six, which would have made that outcome impossible for the anti-Groupers to achieve.

Beazley was overseas at a Moral Rearmament conference. His interest in that organization was genuine and deep, but McManus believed that his unavailability during the federal executive's inquiry was suspiciously convenient to the anti-Grouper forces. Beazley's temperament had prevented him from living up to his initial sparkling promise. Austere, opinionated and highly moral, Beazley exuded profound intelligence, but had made himself unpopular in caucus by displaying his intolerance of excess in drink, smoking, profanity and bawdy anecdotes. Not a Catholic but implacably anti-Communist, Beazley had sided with his closest political friend (and best man) Tom Burke and the Keon-Mullens section during the FPLP's turmoil over the anti-Communist bill and referendum.

Another Westralian, F.E. 'Joe' Chamberlain, played a crucial role in formulating the outcome of the inquiry. Born in London in 1900, Chamberlain had known abundant hardship and adversity in his earlier years. Conscripted into the British army at the end of the Great War, he surveyed his unpromising prospects after demobilization and decided to become one of the immigrants to WA enthusiastically recruited by 'Moo-cow' Mitchell's government. Arriving in mid-1923, he found it heavy going. He spent many years employed in a variety of arduous rural pursuits before rising to prominence in Perth through the Tramways Union during the Second World War. In 1949 he was elected state ALP secretary. Tall and meticulously attired, dogged and attentive to detail, by 1954 he had honed the tactical skills that equipped him to succeed Kennelly as the party's most significant backroom powerbroker nationally. Chamberlain was masterly in committee. Always well prepared and concentrating singlemindedly, he kept 'a terrier grip on the essential point of an argument', and had 'a steely eye for the weakness of an opponent's case'. Previously an unsuccessful ALP preselection aspirant himself, he became – like the tough, uncompromising pre-1910 Mat Reid – the scourge of MPs too willing to be flexible about sacred Labor principles. For years he had been urging action against the industrial groups, encouraging the growing attitude in the ALP that whether or not the initial decision to establish them had been sound, they had become a malignant influence within the party.

The Victorian branch cracked wide open amid fierce debate about how to respond to the federal executive's investigation. On one side were McManus, Keon, certain industrial group leaders in the unions, and the factions in state caucus headed by Scully and Barry, with vigorous behind-the-scenes backing from Santamaria. Important support came from Evatt and Kennelly for the other side, which comprised Cain, Clarey, other anti-Grouper MPs and unionists and, significantly, Lovegrove. Members of the McManus group wanted to boycott the special Victorian conference imposed by the federal executive. They did not trust Chamberlain to conduct it fairly, and believed that to attend it would endow it with legitimacy; it would be better, they concluded, to pursue a legal challenge in the courts and preserve their anti-Communist virtue which

58. Arthur Calwell addressing a meeting in the Sydney Domain during the 1949 miners' strike. (*National Library*)

59. One of many cartoons hostile to Labor during the 1949 election campaign. (by Ted Scorfield; *Australian Consolidated Press*)

60. Ben Chifley (and his ever-present pipe) with ALP federal secretary Pat Kennelly (left) and federal president Jack Ferguson during the 1951 federal conference. (*National Library*)

61. Bert Hawke. (*National Library*)

they were confident would be rewarded at the polls if Labor divided into two warring camps. Lovegrove, previously one of the most committed Groupers, argued that challenging the federal executive's authority was unwise, and a more prudent course would be to lie low for a while and look to the realistic hopes of a long-term victory for the Groupers even if they suffered a few casualties along the way. In an atmosphere of increasing distrust and sectarian animosity there was a split on the Victorian executive, and Lovegrove, Cain, Clarey, Bill Galvin, Peters and several others all resigned. A leading representative of the McManus group sought an injunction to block the Victorian special conference, but was unsuccessful. Chamberlain described this airing of the party's dirty linen in the Supreme Court as 'the most shocking thing to happen in the Labor Party for years'.

There was another public exhibition of Labor's turmoil at the federal conference in Hobart. The special Victorian conference had elected a new executive and federal conference delegation possessing a predictably strong anti-Grouper complexion, while the 'old' McManus executive sent its own six representatives to Hobart to plead their legitimacy as the proper Victorian delegation. The McManus group was hoping to have the choice between the two delegations determined by a vote from the 30 non-Victorian conference delegates. The anti-Grouper forces agreed that the McManus delegation had a good chance of winning such a vote, and did their utmost to prevent it from taking place. Utilizing their numbers on the federal executive, they forced a ruling at its pre-conference meeting that the properly accredited conference delegates from Victoria were the anti-Grouper six headed by Lovegrove and Kennelly. Nevertheless McManus and his five colleagues turned up at the conference venue and demanded admission. They were thwarted by a carefully chosen doorkeeper, a massive AWU stalwart, who insisted that only credentialled delegates were allowed in. The McManus team retaliated by doing some blocking of their own outside the door, so that if they could not enter nobody else would either. There was no resolution of the angry stalemate, which prevented the conference from beginning at all on its scheduled opening day.

After a hectic round of meetings and abundant plotting and persuasion amid extraordinary tension, 19 of the 36 accredited delegates gathered at an alternative venue the following day to begin the conference. In attendance were all six delegates from SA led by Clyde Cameron and Senator Toohey, the Lovegrove-Kennelly six from Victoria elected by the new state executive, four Tasmanians, one Queenslander and, from WA, Chamberlain and Ruby Hutchinson MLC. The absent 17, who included Beazley, Tom Burke, Cole, Queensland's Premier Gair and all six NSW delegates, had decided to defy the federal executive and boycott the conference unless the 30 non-Victorian delegates were authorized to decide which Victorian delegation was eligible to attend it. These 17 delegates would have had the numbers (over the other 13 non-Victorians) to have the McManus six admitted to conference, the Groupers would have won the day, and the Evatt-Chamberlain-Kennelly forces would have been trounced. When the 17 boycotters met the McManus six to discuss tactics, however, there was a lack of unanimity about their next move. Meanwhile the truncated official conference proceeded to carry a resolution moved by Chamberlain and seconded by Clyde Cameron officially withdrawing ALP endorsement of the groups. About a third of the 19 at the official conference were Catholics, whereas the proportion of Catholics among the 23 gathered elsewhere was around two-thirds.

On the last day of conference Calwell flew to Hobart and addressed the delegates. It seems that his prepared speech was very critical of Evatt – and even went so far as to assert that Labor could not win under Evatt's leadership – but he was influenced (apparently by a standing ovation arranged by Clyde Cameron) at the conference to moderate his remarks. Federal conferences were still closed to the press, and some newspapers in possession of Calwell's prepared speech published it as if he had actually delivered it. Evatt (who was not a conference delegate) denied these reports, but apparently added that if they were true he would give his deputy a 'hiding'. Calwell refused to make any public comment, but one newspaper quoted him as retorting that Evatt 'couldn't flatten an egg with a shovel'.

Calwell's ambivalence in Hobart was typical of his attitude throughout the split. Being Evatt's deputy would have been a difficult job for anyone at any time. Yet during the crisis Calwell was neither the selfless loyal party servant submerging his own leadership ambitions and trying to minimize internal disruption, nor the decisive aspirant prepared to take the plunge with a bold stroke which would probably have won him the leadership. Some MPs felt that there were occasions – notably the FPLP meeting on 13 October 1954 – when he would have secured the prize he coveted if he had seized the initiative and forced a vote. Instead he seemed intent on maintaining his position as the logical successor, warding off rivals like Ward and continuing to be scathingly critical in private of Evatt, while hoping that the Doc's erratic conduct would deliver the leadership to him before long. When Evatt neglected to renew his 1955 ALP membership on time Calwell was exultant, confidently anticipating that this oversight would hand him the leadership on a technicality. However, he had to wait just as impatiently for the leadership in the 1950s as he had been forced to wait agonizingly for the seat of Melbourne in the 1930s. His own relationship with Evatt at one stage descended to the point where they were not on speaking terms and Crean had to carry messages between their adjacent offices. After October 1954 Evatt was a marked man and mercilessly savaged in public by DLP partisans, yet Calwell, who was like them a devout Catholic and fervent anti-Communist, probably had an even more painful time: for remaining loyal to the ALP he endured many years of wounding personal slights and vindictiveness in private and religious contexts as well as criticism in the public domain.

In the month following the federal conference the split in Victoria moved rapidly to a climax. Mullens released a statement lashing the 'cloak-and-dagger procedure and Moscow technique shown at Hobart' by 'the pro-Evatt minority junta', and claimed that the 'bogus Victorian executive' was 'honeycombed with Communists and fellow-travellers'. Evatt in reply attacked the 'treacherous record of Mullens', who 'has been a disloyal man from the beginning to the now-approaching end of his political career'. Santamaria publicly accused Evatt of emulating Hitler's 'weapons of racial bitterness and religious sectarianism'. After the conference the McManus 'old' executive continued to regard itself as the validly constituted Victorian executive. The opposing executives marshalled their forces in preparation for battle, and in April each side expelled dozens of its most active opponents. Seven MHRs and 17 state MPs including four ministers (Scully, Coleman, Barry and Hayes) sided with the McManus section. Cain, who had remained oddly optimistic that the troubles would quickly subside, swiftly reconstituted his cabinet without the defecting quartet, but he lost control of the Assembly as soon as parliament reconvened on 19 April. There was a no-confidence motion from the inexperienced Liberal Opposition Leader, Henry Bolte, who had unexpectedly become leader – and was widely seen as merely a stopgap

– when his predecessor perished in a plane crash. The ex-ALP breakaways supported Bolte's motion in a lengthy exchange of abuse with their former colleagues. At 4.20 am on 20 April Bolte's motion was carried when Barry led the defectors across the chamber, and the Cain government fell. The upshot was a state election on 28 May.

This debate on Bolte's no-confidence motion coincided with the resumption of federal parliament. As in Victoria, MPs aligned with the McManus section left caucus and began trading insults with their former colleagues. These breakaways comprised all but one (Peters) of the seven Catholic Victorians the FPLP had acquired at the 1949 election. The seventh ex-FPLP renegade was Joshua, the Ballarat accountant first elected in 1951 who was an Anglican himself although his wife and six children were Catholic. Joshua was clearly less effective as a politician than Keon or Mullens or Bill Bourke, but was appointed their notional leader in a cynical manoeuvre which unsuccessfully sought to refute criticism that their little band was a Catholic party. When they were later joined by Cole, their first Senate recruit, O'Byrne remarked that his fellow Tasmanian would 'become known as Senator Maria'.

The extreme mutual hatred displayed during the 1955 Victorian election campaign by the ALP and the breakaways handed power to Bolte and the Liberals. The split extended to local branch level, where the rank and file bitterly divided on primarily sectarian lines.

> Those who took part in the campaign were never likely to forget it. Everybody has his story of being insulted and even spat upon, of doors shut in the face, of scuffles, whispering campaigns and. . .angry or threatening telephone calls. . .Political sermons thundered out from many pulpits, both Catholic and Protestant. . .The feeling engendered was so intense that it took many years to die away.

The most bitter and violent contest in the state was the battle for the seat of Carlton, which Lovegrove managed to wrest from Barry. While Barry was frequently labelled as a rat by supporters of the ex-Communist Lovegrove, Barry asserted that his rival had 'ratted on the communists, ratted on the Labor Party and ratted on his mates'. Nearly all the branches in Richmond followed their local members Keon and Scully out of the ALP, and Kennelly had to preselect someone to oppose Scully from a meagre pool of local talent. He later concluded that his choice of an undistinguished member of the notorious O'Connell clan instead of legendary footballer Jack Dyer was one of the greatest errors of his long political career. Scully defeated O'Connell narrowly to become one of only two MPs ever to win a lower house seat for the DLP in any state or federal election. Cain, who campaigned with public dignity and private resignation like the seasoned trouper he was, had predicted that the best that Labor and the ex-ALP breakaways could expect was 21 seats between them. That was precisely the outcome. Whereas the Liberals trebled their Assembly representation at the polls to win the election in their own right, Cain Labor managed 20 (37 in 1952, and 25 since the April defections).

The NSW branch was unable to avoid being embroiled in Labor's turmoil. In that state the key figures included Jack Kane, a fervent anti-Communist possessing great organizational skills and zeal, and blunt AWU powerbroker 'Big Tom' Dougherty, once a supporter of the groups but now an ardent advocate of a purge of the Groupers. Premier Cahill was relaxed about having Groupers in control of his state branch; his nickname of 'Old Smoothie' was in part a tribute to his manoeuvring to minimize the disruption to his government arising from Labor's great schism. Kennelly's attempts to lessen the friction were channelled through the close association he established with Downing, who was still a powerful NSW figure. Under a compromise which emerged from an April 1955 meeting between NSW branch representatives and federal executive officers, a special NSW conference was held in August to elect a new state executive and deal with vague 'charges' that Dougherty insisted should be brought against Kane and a Newcastle Grouper and Movement activist F. Rooney. At that conference most of the important ballots were won narrowly by Grouper supporters, including one on Dougherty's attempt to have Kane and Rooney suspended. Afterwards the anti-Groupers muttered sourly about the large number of informal votes, and friction broke out anew later in 1955 over the appearance of a mysterious 'bodgie' how-to-vote ticket allegedly used to induce informal anti-Grouper votes at the August conference.

Cahill was desperate to keep caucus united and out of the fight as the best means of preserving his government. Although Clive Evatt directed a caucus section of primarily coalfields MPs (including Rex Connor) who were keen to align themselves publicly with the anti-Grouper forces, Cahill insisted that 'purposeful unity has always been the keystone of Labor's success'. 'Old Smoothie' was vindicated when his government was returned to office at the March 1956 state election despite continual glaring publicity about Labor's fissures in and beyond NSW. He was assisted by the disunity and unattractiveness of the NSW Liberals and the proven capacity of his ministry. Also important was the attitude of the NSW Catholic leaders who, unlike their Victorian counterparts, were keen to prevent their state Labor government being sacrificed.

On 23 April 1956 the federal executive began an investigation into the strife-torn NSW branch. Two days earlier the NSW Labor women's conference had broken up in uproar after organized disruption and intimidation by Grouper delegates. As in Victoria, the federal executive's inquiry uncovered plenty of acrimonious insights into the tensions within the state branch. After a witness claimed that Kane and Rooney had been involved in distribution of the allegedly 'bodgie' ticket, that besieged pair heatedly denied the charge and Kane issued a libel writ claiming £25 000 damages from the witness and two NSW MHRs, Ward and Charlie Griffiths. Chamberlain, now national ALP president, conducted the inquiry in an authoritarian manner which enraged the Groupers. After protracted tactical shuffling the federal executive announced its decision to intervene directly in the state branch. It declared that the NSW executive was 'over-ruled' and 'no longer exists', and set in train arrangements to establish a new state executive; a resentful victim of the reshuffle complained that it was 'a shocking thing that people from hillbilly states could come over and tell the New South Wales Labor Party what to do'. It was becoming widely accepted that there had been an overreaction in Victoria when the Groupers were excommunicated and too much control had been handed to left-wing unions; accordingly, the new executive was more 'balanced' than its Victorian equivalent. But there was no room for Kane and Rooney under the new regime and they were driven out of the party, although the new executive's first expulsion was in fact Clive Evatt after his clashes with the Premier culminated in the Doc's controversial brother voting against the Cahill government on public transport fare increases. Another expulsion involved Alan Manning, who was very hostile to the Movement but also outspokenly critical of the anti-Groupers' power plays during the party's strife. Kane, Manning and Rooney were the prime movers and senior office-bearers when the DLP was formed in NSW in September 1956.

The split was contained in NSW and its state Labor government preserved, but circumstances in Queensland were very different. There was intense and fairly widespread dislike of Premier Gair in the Queensland labour movement, partly on personal grounds. There was a deep mutual hatred between the pudgy, jaunty Premier and domineering AWU state president Joe Bukowski which dated back to their childhood days in Rockhampton when Bukowski had been, as he still was, an incorrigible bully. Their enmity had helped to end the cosy relationship the AWU had enjoyed with previous ALP governments. Gair had rejected both the AWU's offer of membership and an invitation to open its 1953 conference. He affiliated himself with the Grouper-controlled Federated Clerks' Union, and engaged as his private secretary one of the most senior Movement activists in Queensland. When the AWU did not make its customary handsome donation to ALP campaign funds prior to the 1956 state election, Gair was able to finance the campaign himself by contributing £12 000 which he had acquired from undisclosed sources and handed over in a brown paper bag. This was not the only instance of mysterious donations allegedly finding their way to the heart of the Gair government. Experienced, pragmatic and a capable administrator, Gair was inclined to be stubborn and devious, but had demonstrated a preparedness to introduce measures to assist workers and their families. His government had introduced long-service leave together with reforms in annual leave, sick leave and workers' compensation. The government's price controls enabled Queensland workers to have the highest real wages (adjusted for prices) in Australia. But the Gair government had been slow to respond on other issues of concern to the labour movement, and there was spreading unease among rank-and-file unionists about the future directions of the purposeful Groupers now that they had succeeded in their primary aim of reducing Communist influence in the unions. The undercurrents generated by the 1954–55 explosions in the ALP outside Queensland aggravated personal animosities towards Gair and union dissatisfaction with his government, particularly when Gair twice invoked a state of emergency to crush major strikes. Emotions were heightened by the similarities between one of these disputes and the 1891 shearers' strike which had such legendary links with the ALP's origins in Queensland.

The road to ruin for Queensland Labor was the Gair government's refusal to abide by a state executive instruction to legislate promptly for an extra week's annual leave. The conflict generated by this issue – a genuine industrial grievance which united Gair's opponents in the AWU and at the Trades Hall – was a symbol of the deep-seated divisions in the Queensland branch. The intense bitterness, distrust and sectarianism came to a head when the leading belligerents arrived at the 1956 state ALP conference in an aggressive mood. This convention did not possess the strong majority in favour of the groups apparent at the previous conference in 1953, primarily because of tireless preparation and lobbying by Bukowski, Schmella, and especially by ambitious Boilermakers' Society secretary Jack Egerton. In 1948 Bukowski had been on the three-man committee which supervised the establishment of the industrial groups in Queensland, but he had followed 'Big Tom' Dougherty in making a spectacular recantation and had become a strident critic of the Groupers. Schmella disliked Gair, and as state and national party secretary he was an influential figure. Egerton combined painstaking organization with unsubtle ruthlessness and was close to militant Frank Waters, a veteran of many clashes with Queensland ALP premiers. Gair told the convention that there were compelling economic reasons why he could not comply with the demand for extra leave. The next speaker, Egerton, knowing he had the numbers, conceded that the Premier's argument was not without logic,

283

but bluntly declared that 'the time for logic has passed'. Deputy Premier Jack Duggan skilfully but unsuccessfully sought a compromise. Initially Gair refused to budge, but later modified his attitude to the extent that he was willing to give private assurances that he would enact the necessary legislation, although he remained vague about when and refrained from actually doing anything about it.

The feuding continued after the convention. Bukowski, more powerful than ever now that he was the state's AWU secretary and ALP president, engaged in some acerbic public exchanges with Gair. Egerton continued to whip up a 'Gair Must Go' agitation at the Trades Hall. 'We haven't got a Labor government now', he claimed. 'They are only masqueraders and the Tories couldn't be any worse'. Schmella was equally adamant, and those counselling caution like Duggan were swamped. Bukowski was not the only protagonist who behaved as if he felt that Labor could not be defeated in Queensland. In April 1957 the state executive carried a vote of no confidence in Gair by a narrow margin, and summoned him to show cause why he should not be expelled. Invited to provide an undertaking about precisely when he would introduce the required legislation, Gair once again refused, apparently owing to a combination of his pigheaded nature, the extent of caucus support for his stance on this issue, and a mistaken belief that the federal executive would come to the rescue if necessary. After his expulsion (by 35 votes to 30) the federal executive considered intervention, but the delegates from Victoria and SA were all firmly anti-Grouper with no fondness for Gair, and the executive heeded the forceful views against intervention of its Queensland delegates Bukowski and Schmella.

After Gair's expulsion there was no turning back. Before his final confrontation with the state executive Gair had locked in his entire cabinet behind him in unqualified support except for Duggan, who opposed Gair's expulsion but refused to promise to stick with Gair, as the other ministers had, if the executive did expel him. Gair, who continued as Premier, formed the Queensland Labor Party (QLP) on 26 April in association with 15 backbenchers and all his ministers other than Duggan. Amid savage public recriminations the ALP began expelling Gair's followers. As in Victoria and NSW, the split penetrated to local branch level. The introduction of an Appropriation Bill when parliament resumed on 11 June triggered probably the most virulent debate ever seen in the Queensland Assembly. 'For two days the QLP and ALP shouted, sneered, abused and impugned each other', using all the vile labels in Labor's lexicon commonly unleashed during a split. Cries of rat, scab, traitor and much more were hurled with tremendous hate across the chamber. At the end of this venomous debate the ALP voted with the opposition parties to deny supply to the Gair government.

The ensuing election on 3 August abruptly ended Labor's long reign in Queensland which had lasted, except for a brief period during the Depression, ever since the famous triumph of 1915. Under the first-past-the-post system reintroduced in Queensland during the Second World War the ALP, which entered the election with 24 MLAs after the departure of Gair and his supporters, emerged with 20 members while 11 QLP MLAs were re-elected, including Gair and six of his ministers in the outgoing government. The Liberals and Country Party profited from Labor's war, gaining 18 seats between them and forming a coalition government despite obtaining a smaller combined voting share than at the previous state election 15 months earlier. Both Duggan, the new ALP leader, and his deputy Dr Felix Dittmer lost their seats, although Duggan regained the leadership after returning to the Assembly via a by-election (at the second attempt) in May 1958. The ALP also lost another possible leader when 67-year-old former Prime Minister Frank Forde, who had re-entered the Queensland parliament in 1955 after a long stint as Australian High Commissioner in Canada, lost the seat of Flinders by one vote. Labor's tale of woe did not end there. Of the ALP celebrities imported to bolster the campaign, Evatt contracted severe influenza and spent most of his visit feeling miserable inside a Bundaberg hotel room, while Cain, the 75-year-old Victorian warhorse who had led Labor in his state for two decades, suffered a heart attack while in Queensland and died late on election night. So the successful political edifice of Queensland Labor came tumbling down. The pioneers had laid the foundations, Ryan and Theodore had been the chief builders, Forgan Smith and Fallon had added extensions, Cooper and Hanlon had attended to maintenance, and Gair and his ALP enemies had made a bonfire of it.

The effects of Labor's split were far less catastrophic in Tasmania, where Premier Cosgrove managed to insulate the state branch from the damaging fallout. Reading the political winds astutely, he distanced himself from the Movement before the 1954 eruption and, realizing that there would be fireworks at the Hobart federal conference which would alienate some prospective ALP voters, arranged for the Tasmanian election to precede it. Retaining office at that election despite his government's undistinguished recent record, Cosgrove confirmed his reputation as a political survivor. His government was again threatened when one of his ministers, C. Bramish, defected not to the DLP but to the Liberals, providing them with a parliamentary majority. However, Cosgrove and his able Attorney-General Fagan persuaded the Governor not to commission a Liberal government but to call an election instead, and, to the Liberals' chagrin, Cosgrove scraped back again for his sixth successive election victory as Premier. Afterwards Cosgrove's tolerance of cabinet disunity was again tested when Fagan clashed heatedly with R.J.D. 'Spot' Turnbull, who had been named in a bribery allegation. Fagan became so fed up that he eventually resigned in July 1958, even though he was Cosgrove's logical successor and the Premier was in poor health. It was only a month later that Cosgrove had to resign after major surgery. His 19 years in charge of his state made him the longest-serving Australian premier other than Playford, but they were years of cynicism and drift rather than vision and direction. The DLP made little headway in state politics in Tasmania partly because Cosgrove was so conservative himself and his low-key style of leadership helped to cushion the state branch from the shock waves on the mainland.

The repercussions of Labor's split were also limited in WA. The four WA federal conference delegates including Beazley and Tom Burke who had sided with the McManus section in Hobart were charged by the WA executive with 'deliberate and defiant disobedience'. In recent times WA delegates on national party bodies had rarely received instructions unless there were issues of concern to their state, but according to Chamberlain the state executive had firmly instructed their Hobart delegates to support the Lovegrove-Kennelly group as the Victorian delegation. The carpeted quartet argued that these instructions did not preclude them from acting upon their independent assessment of the justice of the Lovegrove-Kennelly six being allowed to vote on which Victorian delegation was legitimate. Beazley defended himself in his characteristic lucid and learned style by stressing the 1927 precedent when two NSW delegations had arrived and the non-NSW delegates had decided which six would represent NSW. The state executive's desire to minimize internal strife in WA was evident in its decision, influenced by Premier Hawke, to inflict the trifling penalty of banning the four from representing WA at federal conferences for three years.

The Hawke government even managed to increase its majority at a state election held within a year of Labor's massive ructions. This success reflected the sound leadership of Hawke and Tonkin and the state branch's shrewd campaign barbs attacking the Menzies government. An anti-Communist Labor party had, as in other states, been formed, but it was still in its infancy, lacked well-known leaders and did not field any candidates. But the DLP was a far more effective force at the next election in 1959. It stood candidates in 17 seats, directed its preferences away from the ALP, and these preferences of DLP voters were crucial in four of the six seats lost by Labor in a swing of almost 5% which caused the defeat of the Hawke government. During the campaign the government was heavily attacked for its commitment to WA's state enterprises and its legislation tilting at improper commercial practices. The government's other achievements in office included raising the school leaving age to 15, regulating hire purchase transactions and allowing women to sit on juries, although the Legislative Council had blocked attempts to widen its own franchise as well as various other reforms such as the granting of automatic citizenship rights to most Aborigines.

The state least affected by Labor's split was SA. After the withdrawal of ALP endorsement for the groups in that state in 1951, SA delegates on the party's national bodies consistently supported the anti-Groupers. In the state political sphere Labor was still finding the gerrymander maintained by Playford an insuperable obstacle. O'Halloran was a genial leader capable of rousing oratory, but his effectiveness was reduced because of his inattention to publicity; most Labor MPs seemed torpidly content to remain in opposition. Labor's most dynamic MHA was lawyer Don Dunstan, who had captured Norwood from the government in 1953 when aged 26. Unlike most of his colleagues, Dunstan was from an affluent background (St Peter's College and Adelaide University), hardworking, cultured, very articulate and attuned to the need for SA Labor to improve its publicity. When Playford sought to refine the gerrymander in 1954 so that the imbalance between the value of votes in country and city electorates was even more pronounced, Dunstan deliberately caused a stir in staid, conformist Adelaide by contending that the Premier responsible for such outrageous electoral arrangements was 'immoral'. Dunstan's resulting suspension from parliament – the only instance in his career, and the first in the gentlemanly SA parliament for years – ensured that the issue captured headlines it would not have otherwise received.

Evatt continued as FPLP leader after the split. In a surprise ploy at the first caucus meeting following the Hobart conference, he resigned the leadership and recontested it. Catching his rivals unprepared, he won easily: Evatt 52, Calwell 22, Burke 5. Even after the departure of the DLP defectors there were plenty of Evatt critics still in the FPLP. There was lingering animosity and distrust in caucus, with some members feeling that men like Daly, who had voted for Cole's spill motion in October 1954, and Beazley, who had sided with the Grouper boycotters at the Hobart conference, were fortunate to be still in the ALP. The Menzies government relished the predictable stormy exchanges between the FPLP and the breakaways, with Ward and Haylen prominent on one side and Keon and Mullens on the other. In one heated debate all four were suspended from parliament.

There was more drama in October 1955 when the Petrov commission findings were debated. After all the publicity and expenditure, Evatt declared, no spies had been uncovered and no prosecutions were recommended. Reiterating his allegations of conspiracy and fabrication of documents, he stunned onlookers by informing the Representatives that he had written to Molotov, the Soviet Foreign minister, and had received confirmation from Molotov that the documents Petrov handed to ASIO were forgeries. It was not politically prudent, to say the least, to place weight on Molotov's opinion, especially in the Cold War era, and Evatt's revelation of this correspondence was greeted with derision. Menzies made a stinging speech in reply, and decided to take advantage of Labor's disarray by holding an immediate election for the Representatives although it was not due for over 19 months. McKell's successor as Governor-General, Sir William Slim, accepted the spurious reasons Menzies offered in justification of an early election, and 10 December was chosen as polling day.

It was no surprise when the election result showed a sizeable swing away from Labor. The most pleasing feature from the ALP's viewpoint was that the seven Victorian breakaways all lost. Mullens vacated his seat to stand against Calwell in a quixotic gesture against 'fence sitters', and was succeeded in Gellibrand by McIvor, who had controversially lost preselection for that seat to Mullens prior to the 1949 election. Ebullient 41-year-old teacher, unionist and Second AIF veteran Gordon Bryant defeated Bryson in Wills, and Cain's former Lands minister Holt defeated another ex-FPLP defector in Darebin. Far less satisfactory for Labor was that Drakeford, Burke and Lemmon all lost their seats and ended their parliamentary careers. As in 1951, Evatt had a close shave in Barton. In the concurrent election for half the Senate the renegade party which had not yet named itself nationally as the DLP had sufficient strength in Victoria for McManus to win a seat. The ALP won 12 of the 29 other Senate seats contested.

The election's closest and liveliest contest between an ex-FPLP renegade and an impressive ALP candidate was in Yarra. After the sour experience of Scully's. success against O'Connell, Kennelly decided against anointing a Richmond local to challenge Keon. Instead he swallowed his aversion to ALP 'intellectuals' and selected Dr Jim Cairns, the former policeman and champion athlete who had become a Melbourne University lecturer. Cairns vindicated the kingmaker's choice with a strong campaign which included 72 street meetings and tireless door-knocking. He received valuable support from university contacts like his campaign manager Clyde Holding and law student John Button. Another useful source of assistance was the Communist Party, especially in providing enforcers to be on hand for the sporadic skirmishes, although this backing was not public knowledge and even Cairns was kept in the dark about the full extent of it. Polling day, 'bloody Saturday', was particularly violent, and the diminutive Button was placed on standby to whisk a carload of Communist bruisers to the hot spots when ALP advocates needed rescuing. This tough battle for Yarra ended in victory for Cairns by 791 votes. He quickly made an impression in Canberra, delivering knowledgeable speeches 'in a measured, unemotional, coldly courteous, irritatingly logical way'. Conservatives soon found Cairns an unsettling opponent. His manner was purposeful, his commitment to radical change was clear, and he was able to discuss economic issues with academic expertise and compelling fluency.

So the Menzies reign continued. Lucky to win in 1949, he had used hate and fear campaigns against Communists to stay in office, but seemed to be on the way out when the Petrov affair dropped conveniently into his lap. That controversy and the great Labor brawl that followed kept him in power, endowing him with an enviable but undeserved reputation as a national leader. His eloquence, magisterial eyebrows and baggy double-breasteds gave him a veneer of stylish statesmanship, but too often his actions were dictated by shallow opportunism. He presided over years of easy economic growth with occasional ham-fisted interventions in the national economy, but improving its competitiveness was apparently not a priority. Menzies was unduly subservient to Australia's 'great and powerful friends', the American and British economic imperialists. His willingness to subordinate Australia's national interests to British foreign policy produced the scandalous British nuclear weapons tests at Maralinga in SA and the absurd folly of the Menzies mission to Suez to resolve the international crisis which he completely misinterpreted (unlike Evatt, who grasped the essentials despite having access to far less information about it). Evatt's courageous and effective opposition to the anti-Communist legislation and referendum prevented the Menzies reputation in posterity from being tainted by the damage that such an illiberal measure would have inflicted upon Australia's social fabric. Menzies was supposed to revere the sacred traditions of parliament, yet he lied in the Representatives, and not just about the Petrov affair; he also made a false statement when he denied that Australian applicants for the modest writers' grants provided by his government were vetted by ASIO. His worthwhile achievements – very thin for a leader in power for so long – were limited to the expansion (after the Chifley government had paved the way) of national government involvement in tertiary education, and the accelerated development of a beautiful national capital. Even the eulogies about his mastery and command of his own party, based upon his dexterity in shunting possible leadership rivals to a judicial post here and an ambassadorship there, have overlooked that the fundamental reason for the leadership vacuum then prevalent in many aspects of Australian life besides the Liberal Party was the loss of so many of Australia's brightest and best – like two of Bert Evatt's brothers – on the battlefields of the Great War.

Echoes of Labor's convulsion continued to resound. There was implacable public hostility between the ALP and DLP, especially while the FPLP was still led by Evatt. Following the 1955 election he had been confirmed as leader by a large margin after the main alternative contenders Calwell and Ward declined to stand. Allan Fraser, taking the same view as Tom Burke had earlier about the inappropriateness of Evatt being unopposed, stood against him because nobody else would. Calwell was re-elected deputy. The disquiet within the FPLP about Evatt's leadership flared openly in August 1957 when Chambers claimed publicly that Labor had no hope of winning the next election unless Evatt was replaced. McManus praised Chambers's courage, Tom Burke privately sent him a congratulatory telegram, and Victorian ALP spokesmen denounced his breach of unity and the comfort he had given to Labor's enemies. Another MHR certain that the FPLP would never recover under Evatt, Vic Johnson, having already unsuccessfully tried to persuade Premier Hawke that he should take over Johnson's seat with a view to replacing Evatt, publicly supported Chambers. Both Chambers and Johnson were disciplined by their state executives. Johnson's penalty was mild – the WA executive refused to re-endorse him for Kalgoorlie, but knew the 67-year-old veteran was going to retire anyway – yet Burke strangely made a vigorous protest about his friend's 'particularly vicious and sadistic' punishment, and was expelled for this outburst.

The 1958 federal election indicated that the effects of Labor's split would not be shortlived. While the voting largely returned the parliamentary status quo, the DLP's voting share was bad news for Labor. The DLP now possessed a nation-wide organization covering all states except Queensland, where it formed a close alliance with the QLP until their merger in 1962. The ALP was clearly the mainstream Labor party, but the 1958 election confirmed that the DLP was not going to disappear overnight; its direction of preferences away from the ALP delivered vital votes to the Menzies government, making the ALP's task of defeating that government that much harder. During the campaign Evatt tackled this predicament directly with a bold gesture. After delivering his most impressive policy speech so far, Evatt announced, apparently with minimal prior consultation, that he would 'undertake to vacate the leadership' after the election and not recontest it if the DLP behaved like a Labor party and directed its preferences to the ALP instead of Menzies. After some disagreement within the DLP, its hardliners prevailed and Evatt's startling offer was rejected. Hardliners in the ALP were also critical of it. Ward was furious that Evatt had decided 'to go crawling for DLP votes', and after the election he made his long-awaited bid for the leadership. Calwell did not stand and supported Evatt. While Ward and Calwell, the terrible twins of the 1940s, were still close during the 1950s, they were wary rivals in the jockeying for the inside running to succeed Evatt. Their mutual unwillingness to assist each other helped Evatt retain the leadership. On 16 February 1959 Evatt won the ballot against Ward by 46 votes to 32, and Calwell, McKenna and Senate deputy Kennelly also retained their FPLP leadership positions.

Yet within a year Evatt was out of politics altogether. When he had decided in the wake of Labor's 1949 electoral defeat to end his political career and return to the judiciary he had his eye on an appointment to the NSW Supreme Court before the NSW Attorney-General stymied his plans. History almost repeated itself. Again Evatt hankered after a spot on the Supreme Court, and again a Labor Attorney-General refused to co-operate. In 1950 the stumbling block had been Clarrie Martin; in 1960 it was Downing, who was convinced that Evatt's mental stability had so deteriorated that he might prove an embarrassment as Chief Justice. Since Cahill's sudden death from a heart attack in October 1959 Downing had become the strongest figure in the NSW government. The new Premier, Heffron, would have been a better choice than McGirr to succeed McKell in 1947, but he was now 69 and the elevation had come too late. He had lost his vitality, and was unable to provide assertive and capable leadership. As Premier he was renowned for procrastination, and his government displayed a rudderless drift typified by its handling of the Evatt appointment. Heffron backed it himself but Downing had his supporters on the issue, and it was the subject of interminable cabinet discussions which were copiously leaked to the press. Eventually Renshaw, who had been elected Heffron's deputy by one vote ahead of Sheahan, was induced by his concern that the impasse was severely damaging the government to switch his vote in cabinet in order to enable the appointment to proceed. Evatt was sworn in early in 1960, but serenity eluded the mercurial Doc even in his final years. He suffered a serious collapse in 1962, and was an invalid until his death in 1965. At the funeral one of the pallbearers was Menzies.

12 'Doomed to Indefinite Opposition'? 1960–1966

THE FPLP CHOSE a new leader and deputy on 7 March. Calwell, who had for years been Evatt's most likely successor, attained the leadership as expected, defeating Pollard by 42 votes to 30. More surprising was the voting for the deputy's position, which Ward was generally expected to win. He was ahead on the first ballot, but after Jim Harrison was eliminated, then Haylen, the final result was Whitlam 38, Ward 34.

Whitlam's elevation was in part an acknowledgement of his obvious ability. In his seven years in parliament his splendid intellect and hard work had impressed even the caucus traditionalists suspicious about his background and repelled by his personality, and he had been elected to the FPLP executive in February 1959. One of his more notable contributions in opposition had been his presence on a committee of inquiry established to formulate desirable amendments to the Constitution. The recommendations of this inquiry were largely ignored by the Menzies government, but it was a valuable exercise for Whitlam. He was initially discouraged and exasperated that the realization of Labor's objectives seemed so impeded by the Constitution and judicial interpretation of it, but he eventually concluded that a potential means of surmounting these obstacles lay in conditional grants to the states under Section 96.

Other factors besides Whitlam's conspicuous talent influenced his promotion to the deputy leadership. One of the few friends he had made in caucus, Lance Barnard, had urged Whitlam to contest the ballot and had been extolling Whitlam's merits to FPLP colleagues. Another backbencher actively canvassing for the Whitlam camp was former clerks' union organizer Les Johnson, who had helped Whitlam win the Werriwa by-election in 1952 before entering parliament himself in 1955 as MHR for the neighbouring seat of Hughes. Whitlam had other influential backers. Veteran kingmaker Senator Pat Kennelly had concluded that 43-year-old Whitlam would provide a youthful, forward-looking element in Labor's image, whereas Ward was (like Calwell) in his sixties and prone to dwell on the battles and hatreds of the past. Kennelly and FPLP Senate leader McKenna quietly reminded members that electing Ward as deputy leader would give the FPLP a leadership group of four Catholics, which would make Labor vulnerable to damaging anti-Catholic sectarianism. The Calwell-Whitlam partnership, with its initially smooth blend of contrasting attributes, was soon attracting favourable notice, but some ALP sympathizers regretted that an archetypal working-class fighter like Ward had not been preferred to Whitlam, whose background and manner were so untypical of Labor.

Ward was devastated by this reverse, and he was a changed man afterwards. He was especially bitter that a sectarian argument had caused him to be 'sacrificed'. He contended that if four Catholics heading the FPLP really was a problem – which he disputed – then McKenna and/or Kennelly could have solved it just as easily by resigning their Senate leadership positions. Ward unleashed his resentment at subsequent caucus meetings. He moved that it should be a party rule that any member using sectarianism to influence the result of a ballot should be expelled; Calwell, despite Ward's angry protests, ruled the motion out of order. Ward's further attempts to retaliate against McKenna, the hard-working lawyer who had lived in Sydney for years while representing Tasmania in the Senate, included resolutions (both rejected after stormy caucus debates) seeking to compel FPLP members to reside in their electorates and to discontinue any other business or professional activities while they were MPs. Ward's loathing of Whitlam the usurper knew no bounds. During a meeting in October 1960 Ward was stung by a Whitlam remark into throwing a punch at the deputy. By this time Ward's previously robust health was beginning to show the effects of his wholehearted approach to politics and decades of devotion to the constituents who customarily crowded his Paddington home. Heart trouble resulted in an enforced rest on doctor's orders for several months during the summer of 1960–61. He made light of his illness, claiming that his first inkling that his health was not the best came when 'I took a swing at Gough Whitlam and missed'.

At the closest-ever federal election in December 1961 the FPLP almost pulled off an unlikely victory. The crucial factor in the swing to Labor was the Menzies government's inept economic management, especially its credit squeeze which had severely affected manufacturing industry and employment. The conservatively inclined men controlling the *Sydney Morning Herald* were so disgusted with the government's financial policies that they publicly endorsed Labor in their paper's editorials, and offered Calwell the services of shrewd advisers and talented speechwriters. This valuable assistance from an unexpected quarter greatly benefited Labor's campaign. Menzies in his policy speech promised the voters next to nothing. 'There was something shocking', frowned the *Sydney Morning Herald*, 'in the Prime Minister's lofty paternalism, his unshaken complacency, his bland dismissal of a major social and economic problem as "some temporary unemployment"'. In contrast Calwell proposed increased government expenditure to revive the economy, reduce unemployment and boost welfare. He promised that a Calwell Labor government would nationalize no industry during its first three years. The election was so close that the result was still in doubt more than a week after polling day.

A talking point in ALP circles was the swing's lack of uniformity. It was easily weakest in Victoria, where Labor did not improve on its tally of 10 out of 33 Representatives seats and the DLP voting share increased to over 15%. In Queensland, where Whitlam concentrated his efforts, Labor did superbly. In 1958 it had only won three of the state's 18 seats, but this time it secured eight more, over half the party's nation-wide gains, and very nearly captured a ninth. One of the new Labor seats was Oxley, where the Menzies government's Health minister was defeated by 28-year-old policeman Bill Hayden. Eventually it was announced that the government had been re-elected with 62 seats to Labor's 60.

To be so near and yet so far was disappointing, but it was heartening to feel that Labor was on the way back. Moreover, the combined effect of Evatt's departure and the influx of MPs who had not participated directly in the mid-1950s explosions helped to reduce the lingering animosities in caucus. Both Beazley and Daly were elected to the FPLP executive after being out of favour since the split. They were later to share a room which reflected their different interests and priorities. Beazley's table and bookshelves were lined with learned tomes on international affairs and politics in other lands, while Daly concentrated on maintaining files with labels like 'Liberal Disunity' and 'Country Party', full of useful gems to toss into the hurly-burly of debate. Just as the ideal Test batting line-up consists of the right blend of dour solidity and brilliant flair, the ALP has always done best as a parliamentary force with a balanced combination of the visionary reformer fertile with ideas and the shrewd practical type attuned to what the voters will tolerate. Only a few gifted individuals have excelled as both.

Some experienced FPLP tacticians became concerned in the aftermath of the 1961 election that Labor was not being tough enough in opposition. Haylen, Daly and – predictably – Ward were among those dismayed that pairs were granted too readily to absent government MPs, and that Labor members were too inclined to accept opportunities for trips enticingly dangled by Menzies. These critics felt that Labor was in a position to make life difficult for the government, but the FPLP was not using its parliamentary numbers properly. Meanwhile Menzies had brazenly filched the ALP economic policy he had denounced at the election as irresponsible and inflationary, and this prescription was vindicated when the ailing economy recovered after being treated with Labor's medicine.

Labor hopes that the 1961 election signalled the start of an ALP resurgence were dashed when Menzies called an election prematurely in November 1963 and won easily. With the economy in much better shape, the *Sydney Morning Herald* controllers were no longer alarmed about declining revenue from advertising in their paper. There was no complacency from Menzies this time, and during the campaign he exploited issues where Labor was vulnerable.

One of them was funding for schools. The question of state aid to church schools had been perplexing governments in Australia throughout the ALP's history. The Catholic church had long complained that its schools were entitled to special assistance, but even in the ALP, with its high proportion of Catholics (especially between 1916 and 1955), advocates of state aid struggled. They had to overcome sectarian feeling (or the fear that state aid would produce it), and the low priority which the labour movement generally accorded to education. In addition, many non-Catholics felt that Labor should be aiming at one universal school system providing equality and excellence, rather than furthering a hotchpotch structure with government schools co-existing with 'independent' schools of varying quality, wealth and religious emphasis. In the DLP, however, with its preponderance of Catholics, state aid was in the party platform from the outset. Between the 1961 and 1963 elections Santamaria had stressed the desirability of state aid in several discussions with Harold Holt, Menzies's lieutenant and Treasurer. These representations paid dividends when Menzies announced in his November 1963 policy speech that his government if returned would provide grants to schools for science facilities and introduce scholarships for students in their final two years at school. These two unexpected proposals were completely at odds with the attitude to state aid held for over half a century by the Australian Establishment, which has always been overwhelmingly Protestant. While these measures were in small part a recognition of the increasing cost of education, they were initiated primarily to keep the vital DLP preferences – which had saved Menzies from defeat in 1961 – flowing to the coalition government.

Menzies was well aware that his state aid proposals also capitalized on internal ALP strife. In the early 1950s the Groupers had achieved the inclusion of 'financial aid for all forms of education' in the ALP platform, but after the split the 1957 federal conference resurrected Labor's traditional hostility to state aid for non-government schools. In mid-1963 the ALP state conference in NSW requested its Labor government to provide science facilities for all schools, government and independent. In August, however, federal conference approved a new addition to the party platform proposed by Chamberlain, an unwavering opponent of state aid, that Australians had 'the absolute right' to opt out of the government school system 'provided they do so at their own cost'. Next month the Heffron government unveiled in its budget a proposal to provide means-tested allowances to parents of children in non-government secondary schools. Calwell, who had been forewarned, publicly endorsed it as consistent with party policy, but Chamberlain's reaction was swift and very different. At a federal executive meeting a few days later he pushed through a motion critical of the budget initiative for contravening the ALP platform, and afterwards called on the NSW government 'to recast its present plans'. Delicate negotiations were required to resolve this embarrassing public imbroglio. Fine distinctions were drawn between permissible aid to students irrespective of their school and forbidden aid direct to non-government schools. During the controversy there was pronounced friction between Chamberlain and senior figures in the NSW ALP, which at its 1964 state conference repeated its call for the state Labor government to increase state aid. The ill feeling intensified when this policy was stolen by Menzies and became a significant factor in his successful re-election campaign.

Foreign policy was another issue which Menzies highlighted to Labor's detriment at the 1963 election. In May 1962 he had announced that a United States base would be constructed at North-west Cape in northern WA. According to the government, this base was merely a communications facility. Barwick, now the Menzies government's Attorney-General and External Affairs minister, described it in parliament as 'a wireless station, nothing more and nothing less'. In fact the primary function of North-west Cape was to direct the activities of American submarines carrying nuclear weapons, a function which placed Australia in the front line in any global nuclear war. Although this real purpose was initially kept secret, some FPLP members like Haylen were critical of the decision to construct the base. Especially prominent was the MHR for Reid since 1958, Tom Uren, a likeable harsh-voiced NSW left-winger who was an outstanding swimmer and heavyweight boxer before enduring 3½ years as a prisoner of the Japanese; his maiden speech had praised the primitive socialism practised by Australian prisoners which had enabled so many of them to survive their wartime ordeal. North-west Cape was an awkward issue for Labor. Traditionally the party had opposed foreign bases on Australian soil, and it was now committed to a nuclear-free Southern Hemisphere; but some of its leading MPs were strong advocates of the Australian-American alliance. Furthermore, Labor's critics would certainly accuse the ALP of jeopardizing Australian security if it rejected the base outright.

Calwell and Whitlam argued that North-west Cape was not in conflict with ALP policy provided that Australia retained joint control. This stance was narrowly upheld in March 1963 by a special federal conference convened to overhaul the ALP's platform on foreign affairs and defence. All the delegates from NSW, SA and Tasmania supported the Calwell-Whitlam position, and all the delegates from the other three states opposed it except one man – Queensland Opposition Leader Duggan, who had shown in the 1957 split that if necessary he was prepared to paddle his own canoe. But the contentment which Calwell and Whitlam derived from this outcome was dashed when Alan Reid arranged for a photograph to be taken of them standing outside Canberra's Hotel Kingston awaiting the verdict of the conference delegates. This photograph, and the ensuing allegation that the ALP was ruled by '36 faceless men' rather than the politicians heading the FPLP, proved very damaging to Labor. Menzies and other anti-Labor propagandists also made much of the government's recently signed agreement with the United States to purchase advanced supersonic F111 aircraft for the RAAF. The loopholes in this agreement, which had been hastily finalized by a seriously ill minister so that the Menzies government could trumpet it during the campaign, later proved immensely costly to Australia when problems emerged in the planes' manufacture and performance. Labor's rank and file felt that the damage their party suffered at the hands of Menzies, the DLP and the media on defence and foreign policy issues was unwarranted. It was the Menzies government, not the opposition, which had reduced Australia's defence capacity sharply. The ALP, in fact, throughout its history (including both world wars) has generally performed much more soundly – and in Australia's best interests – on defence and foreign policy questions than the conservatives.

Unsettling overseas events also contributed to the swing away from Labor at the 1963 election. The traditional Australian anxiety about Japan, which peaked in the dark days of 1941–42, had since been transferred to other Asian nations, notably China in the aftermath of the Communists' victory there in 1949. Developments in Korea culminating in the Korean War had also caused concern. More recently, Indonesia's belligerence under Sukarno had led to the removal of the Dutch from West New Guinea and confrontation with Malaysia, and the consequent regional instability had threatened to involve Australia; supporters of the F111 purchase welcomed its capacity to take off from Australian soil and bomb Jakarta. There was also a conflict under way in Vietnam, which was attracting increasing American interest and involvement. Most dramatic of all was the Cuban crisis in October 1962 when the United States and Soviet Russia seemed on the brink of nuclear war before Russia backed down. With this background, the assassination of America's charismatic President Kennedy in November 1963 only a week before polling day in Australia significantly influenced the election result. To some voters disturbed by the insecure international environment it seemed best to play safe and stick to the coalition government, rather than flirt with the alternative which had not known the responsibility of office for 14 years.

One ALP candidate defied the overall swing to the coalition government. For some years Bob Hawke had seemed to many of his admirers to be destined for greatness. His mother, an extraordinarily strong-willed, forthright and energetic model of Methodist rectitude – she considered it sinful even to knit or play cards on Sunday – had openly declared her belief that he would become Prime Minister. His father Clem had been ALP branch secretary at Kapunda (SA) and aspired to a political career, but became a minister in the Congregational church instead. Clem's brother Bert Hawke, the former WA Premier, became Bob's mentor, attending to his political education and sharing the family dream that Bob would lead Australia some day. The talented protégé possessed charm and vitality, a razor-sharp intellect inclined more towards pragmatic problem-solving than abstract philosophical questions, and a tendency to alternate work and play in bursts of fierce concentration and rollicking hilarity. He had rejected his parents' intense attachment to formal religion while retaining a respect for Christian values in general. He had also turned his back on the strict teetotalism preached and practised by his mother; not one for doing things by halves, he was notorious for his exploits during wild drinking sprees, and was mentioned in the *Guinness Book of Records* for downing 2½ pints of beer in 12 seconds. At Oxford University as WA's 1952 Rhodes Scholar, he supplemented his earlier degrees in Law and Arts with a Bachelor of Letters for his thesis on Australian arbitration. In 1958 Hawke joined the ACTU as its research officer. The sneers of traditionalists at the appointment of an 'academic' who had never had a real job by their reckoning turned to admiration when he proved an astonishing success as their advocate at wage tribunal hearings. In 1963, when the approach came to stand for the seat of Corio, he was 33 years old and becoming a celebrity; articulate and occasionally truculent, he was in demand to speak at public functions and on television.

In 1963 Victorian ALP powerbrokers had earmarked Corio as a seat Labor could capture with a good candidate. The swing needed was 3·4%. Corio's MHR was H.F. Opperman, Australia's champion cyclist of the 1920s, conquerer of Dedman in 1949, and a minister in the coalition government since 1960. The approach to Hawke came at a difficult time: in August his fourth child had not survived a premature birth, and both Hawke and his wife Hazel, who was an invaluable source of private support to him, were profoundly distressed. Hawke tried to drown his sorrows, and shortly afterwards was admitted to hospital with alcoholic poisoning. Corio ALP insiders airily described his dicey health to others as 'a bit of a chest problem'. Once their candidate had accepted the challenge and agreed to stand, his awesome competitive instincts were aroused and he mounted a fine campaign. His renowned debating skills were highlighted when the Menzies policy speech was televised live at an ALP rally in Corio, and Hawke and Whitlam provided impromptu responses to it. During that lively meeting Whitlam exaggeratedly told the crowd that Hawke had 'greater industrial experience than any man in Australia'. Opperman was cycling around the electorate denouncing the 36 faceless men, but Hawke was well ahead with a week to go. Then Kennedy was assassinated and the whole picture changed. The insecurity was palpable. While Australian electors in these unnerving circumstances 'clung to Menzies as a child to its father's leg' and the ALP voting share declined nationally by 2·43% (in Victoria by 1·12%), Hawke achieved a swing of 3% to Labor in Corio and ran his opponent uncomfortably close.

Hawke had been denied victory in Corio by DLP preferences, and that minor party was still helping to keep the FPLP in opposition. Feeling at the grass-roots level remained intense, especially in Victoria. When Hawke and Kennelly attended the opening of a Catholic church hall in the Corio electorate, they were greeted by crowds of Catholic children pointing at them and screaming 'Communists, Communists, Communists'. The DLP was hoping to keep its vote high enough for long enough to force an ALP starved of office back to the negotiating table; the DLP would then seek a merger on favourable terms. In 1963 the DLP voting share nationally was 7·44% (8·71% in 1961); in Victoria it was 12·38%

(15·09% in 1961). The DLP had two successes at the 1964 Senate election after missing out completely in 1961. Gair, having lost his state seat, became a Queensland DLP Senator, and Victorian voters re-elected McManus, who had been defeated in 1961. These encouraging 1964 results had not shaken Santamaria's regretful conclusion that the DLP vote was 'essentially a wasting asset', so he was cautiously amenable when he received an overture from Kennelly suggesting peace talks.

In mid-1965 Santamaria, Kennelly and McKenna spent six consecutive Saturday evenings in highly secret negotiations. Santamaria found Kennelly 'full of worldly wisdom, both likeable and amusing', and a basis of agreement for a merger was established. McManus, Gair, Kane and very few others knew about the talks beforehand; those in the know kept them confidential. For Kennelly and McKenna these discussions were an extremely risky manoeuvre: any attempt at a merger would outrage powerful elements in the ALP and might lead to another split. Some years earlier Allan Fraser and others had urged Calwell to accept an offer of possible co-operation from DLP Senators McManus and Cole. McManus claimed that Calwell's rejection of this proposal was influenced by a blistering telegram sent to him by Chamberlain, who also issued a forceful statement ruling out any pact with the DLP. Yet Calwell had often displayed a strong hostility to any proposed arrangement with the DLP. In February 1965 he had reacted angrily when Kennelly publicly recommended that the ALP and DLP should settle their differences. But neither Calwell's response nor the rebuke Kennelly then received from the Victorian ALP executive had caused the king-maker to reconsider. He and McKenna told Santamaria in their secret talks that they were prepared to pursue an amalgamation and risk a split; the FPLP Senate leaders believed that the regained allegiance of DLP supporters would more than offset any lost votes in the event of a left-wing faction departing from the ALP. Their ambitious scheme was feasible, they felt, if the other two FPLP leaders approved, and they approached Whitlam and Calwell. They later told Santamaria that Whitlam was prepared to explore it further, but Calwell remained passionately intransigent. The talks with Santamaria ceased, and public animosity between the ALP and DLP continued as before.

One of the most frequently aired policy differences between the two parties concerned unity tickets in union elections. The withdrawal of ALP backing for the groups had increased the prevalence of unity tickets, which comprised how-to-vote material bracketing ALP members with non-members (mostly Communists) in mutual support. This practice was vehemently condemned by the DLP. ALP policy was against unity tickets, but enforcement varied. In NSW, where some Grouper sympathizers remained on the state executive, unity tickets were actively discouraged. They were much more tolerated by the staunchly anti-Grouper controllers of the state branch in Victoria, where the practice was instrumental in the removal of Grouper-DLP elements from power in important unions. In the late 1950s Evatt believed that the ALP was being harmed by allegations that it condoned unity tickets, and he had urged the federal executive and conference to take action against party members implicated in the practice; but he had little success, partly because Chamberlain exerted his considerable influence in favour of the Victorian approach. Calwell expressed himself against unity tickets in principle, but he considered that the DLP's strength in his home state made the Victorian situation a special case. However, others including Kennelly were less indulgent, and federal intervention against the Victorian executive over unity tickets was narrowly averted.

Since the split the Victorian ALP had exuded an authoritarian, uncompromising left-wing aura. Unity tickets had assisted left-wingers to regain control of ALP-affiliated unions and use their influence in the state branch, which had lost thousands of members as well as thousands of pounds and party records and furniture to the DLP in the split. A Trade Unions Defence Committee (TUDC), formed in 1961 ostensibly to counter DLP leverage in the unions, became a powerful vehicle in internal ALP affairs. By the mid-1960s the TUDC was controlling state conference through its 'official ticket', which predetermined conference ballots with a regularity that party moderates were unable to prevent. With left-wing unionists in the ascendancy, hardline attitudes were adopted and enforced by the state executive. There was unremitting hostility to the DLP; apart from Calwell, Kennelly and Labor's leader in the Legislative Council, Jack Galbally, Catholics were not endorsed as candidates and at times, it seemed, hardly wanted in the party at all. The virtues of 'ideological purity' were proclaimed. There was an unyielding hostility to state aid, even after the Menzies government's implementation of it made this attitude difficult to sustain politically. Intellectuals and middle-class radicals were suspect and barely tolerated.

The Victorian executive kept its federal and state MPs on a tight rein. It sometimes attempted to coerce them before important votes in caucus, and its control over their preselection endowed it with significant intimidatory power. Throughout the ALP's history preselection procedure has varied from state to state, but it had been most commonly performed, as in Victoria prior to 1955, by local branch members and affiliated unionists in the electorate concerned. The post-split state executive, however, had decided to choose the candidates itself. Initially this step was justified as an emergency measure, but a decade later it was still in operation, modified only by the votes of three token and heavily outnumbered local members. Very few Victorian MPs were willing or able to challenge the state executive's control.

Electorally the Victorian ALP had not distinguished itself since the split. No federal seat had been captured from anti-Labor since 1952, and in three state elections since Labor's great convulsion handed power to the Liberals the Bolte government had – with the crucial support of tightly directed DLP preferences – consistently doubled Labor's tally of Assembly seats. Cain was followed as Victorian ALP leader by Shepherd, who died suddenly in September 1958 aged 57. Shepherd's successor, Stoneham, was decent but lacked verve. No match for Bolte or the controllers of the state branch, Stoneham did not get on with his deputy, Lovegrove, who was a much abler politician but was tainted in the eyes of powerbrokers in his state because of his pre-split Grouper activities. By the mid-1960s numerous ALP activists dissatisfied with the situation in Victoria had resolved to do something about it.

Labor was also struggling in NSW. The Menzies government's economic mismanagement had enabled the Heffron government to increase its majority at the 1962 state election, but three years later the situation was very different. Events in the interim such as the state aid saga, the loss of seven NSW Labor seats in the Representatives in 1963 and the election of only two NSW senators at the 1964 Senate poll indicated that the 1965 state election might be a tough proposition for Labor. Heffron had been succeeded in April 1964 by 54-year-old Renshaw, who was popular in caucus and had been a competent minister in a variety of portfolios since 1950. The eldest of eight siblings, Renshaw had left school at 11 to keep the family farm going when his father was killed in an accident. During the stormy 1930s he crossed swords with the Old Guard at his home town Binnaway and later with the Langites after he joined Heffron Labor. His rural background was useful in a state where Labor's ability to win seats in the country has been particularly significant in its overall electoral performance, but he inherited a fractious caucus and a generally old and stale ministerial team. Early in 1964 the Mosman ALP branch condemned the 'uninspiring' recent record of the state government and caucus, and was particularly critical of their 'inactivity, procrastination and opportunism'. Furthermore, the NSW anti-Labor forces had for once produced a doughty opponent, R.W. Askin, who was projecting himself as an alternative leader attuned to contemporary concerns.

Renshaw performed well in the lead-up to the election, but was not blessed by good fortune. Shortly before the campaign began in earnest, headlines blared that Labor's Speaker had been implicated in an indecent exposure incident; he was later acquitted, but not until after the election. The Renshaw government was also disadvantaged by the sort of unscrupulous press conduct that has often harmed the ALP. The state political correspondent of Frank Packer's notorious *Daily Telegraph* filed a carefully researched article outlining Labor's bold plan to make more land available to meet the pressing demand for housing. This initiative, a key element in the government's re-election strategy, was to be unveiled in Renshaw's imminent policy speech. After receiving the journalist's copy, the *Telegraph* editor telephoned Askin. Next morning the journalist was amazed to find his article transformed into a front-page lead story booming Askin's dramatic new move to provide land for housing. The election on 1 May was close, and the result was in doubt for some time. Eventually it became clear that a swing against the government of over 5% had ended 24 years of uninterrupted ALP government in NSW. The 'full effect of the Chamberlain carnage has now been felt', concluded the outgoing Health minister, Sheahan, in a blistering outburst which reflected widespread NSW animosity towards the federal executive strongman.

The NSW branch continued on its firmly moderate path under its vastly experienced senior office-bearers, Bill Colbourne and Charlie Oliver. Colbourne spent over two decades altogether as state secretary in two widely spaced periods, 1930–36 (when he stood firm alongside Chifley against the overwhelmingly superior Langite forces) and 1954–69. Colbourne's deputy was another long-serving right-wing party official, ex-railwayman Tony Mulvihill, who was assistant state secretary from 1957 until he entered the Senate in 1965. Oliver was one of the ALP's legendary AWU products – big and blunt, rough and tough, and contemptuous of the middle-class professionals who were becoming much more numerous in the party. After a brief stint as a Labor MP in WA, he became secretary of the NSW AWU, and retained that position for nearly three decades; throughout the 1960s he was president of the NSW ALP as well. He had followed Dougherty in opposing the Groupers before the split, but after the storm broke he became part of the dominant right-wing faction in NSW comprising other moderate anti-Groupers like himself as well as surviving Groupers like Colbourne. As state president he gave warm public support to unradical Labor governments, advocated reconciliation with the DLP, and exerted tight control over the NSW annual conference.

Although the right wing dominated throughout the 1960s in NSW in both the parliamentary party and the state branch generally, the minority faction was not excluded with the same rigour as in Victoria. A measure of power-sharing was traditional in NSW, and it was increased by Mulvihill's reforms in Senate preselection. Under the new system Senate candidates were chosen on a multiple preferential basis by a panel comprising the state executive and two local representatives from each federal electorate. Mulvihill described 'this most democratic selection system' as his 'major administrative achievement'. However, Armstrong, the former Chifley government minister who had been one of the 'Four As' first elected in 1937, was less complimentary about the new system after he was dumped when it was first used in 1960. Two of the candidates endorsed for the 1961 election had been close to Doc Evatt. Former MHR Joe Fitzgerald had been Evatt's secretary, and Doug McClelland had been Evatt's electorate minder in Barton. Both were successful at the election.

Labor's third NSW Senator elected in 1961 was 39-year-old barrister Lionel Murphy. His father was born in Tipperary, and there was a strong Irish streak in the Murphys. Lionel Murphy grew up in Sydney, where one of his contemporaries, another Lionel, attended the same kindergarten, the same school, also studied and practised law, and even entered parliament as a Labor MP in the same year as Murphy. This close friend was Lionel Bowen MLA, a solicitor and former mayor of Randwick. At Sydney University Murphy involved himself in student politics, obtained a Science degree, and then turned to Law: 'I was concerned even then about civil liberties and public affairs', he later recalled. Murphy graduated with first-class honours in Law, but lacked the right social background and contacts for instant success at the Bar. An important early association was with Ray Gietzelt, a left-winger dedicated to removing the Groupers from control of the Miscellaneous Workers' Union. Gietzelt achieved this goal, with Murphy as his barrister, following a long legal battle. It was Gietzelt who organized the numbers to get Murphy preselected. By this time Murphy's 'outstanding grip of the law' was acknowledged by his peers. The protracted feud between Clyde Cameron and other AWU powerbrokers had again reached the courts when Cameron reported to his solicitor Clyde Holding (who became MLA for Richmond in 1962) that he had recently seen his great foe Dougherty in conversation with 'a chap at the airport with a long nose and a Homburg hat – who would that be?' 'Christ, that's Murphy', replied Holding, 'I hope he's not doing the case, he's bloody good'.

Murphy possessed remarkable qualities. He had extraordinary vitality, and could fire on all cylinders at work and play for longer, and with less sleep, than his confrères. Always a restless searcher for fresh approaches, Murphy dazzled lesser mortals with his agile and penetrating mind. His scientific training and fascination with new ideas enabled him to make scintillating lateral leaps in conversation that left other well-endowed intellects gasping. He had a generous, charming and warmly effusive personality, a free-wheeling optimistic outlook, and a genuine desire to help the disadvantaged.

Despite the modicum of power-sharing that facilitated Murphy's preselection, NSW left-wingers like Haylen felt suffocated by the prevailing right-wing hegemony. Haylen had offended majority opinion in the NSW ALP by maintaining his strong opposition to state aid and also by writing a glowing book about China, a country he had twice visited. In 1963 he lost Parkes, the marginal seat he had done well to retain for 20 years. The following year he overcame powerful resistance to win the number three spot on the ALP Senate ticket. Only twice since the 1948 enlargement of the Senate has NSW Labor failed to get three Senators elected, but the 1964 election was one of those instances and Haylen missed out. He and his supporters claimed that an underground campaign by certain ALP figures had sabotaged his candidature. When he then lost preselection for Parkes he was reduced to expressing his frustration in caustic anti-Oliver doggerel, like his verse about a NSW conference entitled 'Labor Sheep':

> It was a great big muster – seven hundred in the fold,
> And to my great amazement, they all did as they were told...
>
> The man on top gave voice again: 'I declare the motion passes'
> They nodded with their empty heads and wagged their woolly arses,
> 'I need a seconder' he cried, 'for item umpty-three',
> 'Oh, let me move it Charlie, I'm from the DLP'.

In Queensland the split proved a watershed for the ALP. The breakaway of the QLP had left the AWU and the Trades Hall unionists led by Egerton in uneasy alliance and there was a leadership vacuum in the Queensland ALP which Egerton was eager to fill. The Trades Hall group, which felt aggrieved at being kept out of power for so long by the AWU, shared the widespread dislike of Bukowski, the abrasive AWU secretary. After an incident at the 1958 Trades Hall Christmas party, Bukowski was removed from the state ALP presidency by the Queensland inner executive. Bukowski retaliated by taking the AWU out of the ALP. Following Bukowski's death in 1961 the AWU soon reaffiliated, but events at the next state conference confirmed that the Trades Hall militants under Egerton were firmly in command. Just as the AWU had done for decades, the new controllers showed that they were prepared to use their possession of the numbers to maintain their dominance, install their nominees in parliament and discipline factional opponents.

However, the low priority the Trades Hall regime gave to maximizing the Queensland ALP's electoral performance was very different from the traditional AWU approach. Its hostile actions against Labor MPs perceived to be close to the AWU predictably harmed Labor's standing in the electorate, and moved the parliamentary leader, Duggan, who was an advocate of organizational power-sharing among the factions, to comment angrily that certain people 'couldn't care less if the Labor Party is in power or opposition'. Egerton publicly criticized Duggan for rarely visiting the Trades Hall and being insufficiently attentive to the concerns of industrial unionists. Accordingly the Queensland ALP was wide open to taunts about faceless men at election time, with Egerton depicted as Duggan's evil puppeteer. Moreover, the anti-Labor coalition had been quick to modify Queensland's electoral arrangements to suit itself; at the 1963 election Labor achieved a swing of 4% but could only raise its tally of seats by one to 26, whereas the government, although its voting share was almost identical to Labor's, won 46 seats. A significant element was the QLP, which delivered nearly all of its 7·22% of the vote to the government under the recently reintroduced preferential system. Following a similar result at the 1966 election Labor sank to an even lower ebb when Duggan, its only prestigious MP and an orator of unsurpassed fluency, resigned in embarrassment after his repeated understatement of his taxable income became known.

In the mid-1960s there was no joy for state Labor in WA either. After able and popular Bert Hawke had piloted Labor to victory at state elections in 1953 and 1956, the party suffered three successive losses under his leadership in 1959, 1962 and 1965. Especially disastrous was the last defeat, when Labor won its lowest number of seats for over 40 years and there were acrimonious exchanges between Hawke and state ALP secretary Chamberlain during and after the campaign. Six days before polling day, after Chamberlain had been more prominent than Hawke as a spokesman for the ALP in the campaign, Hawke publicly associated himself with Kennelly's call for a reconciliation between the ALP and DLP. Chamberlain made his hostility clear. After the election Hawke was summoned by the state executive to explain his remarks, and later rebuked (together with Kennelly) by the federal executive. Hawke continued to speak out, insisting that he had committed no offence. The dispute widened with Hawke denouncing Chamberlain's 'campaign of disruption and treachery', the two antagonists accusing each other of being primarily responsible for the election débâcle, and state caucus passing a motion of no confidence in Chamberlain. Despite this motion, which referred to his 'evermounting widespread unpopularity', the redoubtable Chamberlain continued as state secretary. It was his subsequent absence through serious illness that was crucial in the reversal of WA Labor policy on state aid engineered by Tonkin who, as expected, became party leader when Hawke stepped down late in 1966.

The organizational structure of the WA branch was overhauled in the early 1960s. The push for the establishment of a separate TLC to co-ordinate industrial activity as in every other state was at last successful, and the integrated political and industrial structure established as long ago as 1906 was replaced. The district councils were abolished. An enlarged and more powerful state executive with direct union and local branch representation now acquired absolute control over the preselection of candidates and the choice of both party officers and delegates to national ALP forums. Chamberlain's eventual acceptance of the changes was denounced by the AWU, which felt disadvantaged by the new arrangements. Having supported Hawke in his feud with Chamberlain, the giant union withdrew from the ALP in mid-1965 – adding to the party's financial problems – and refused to reaffiliate while Chamberlain remained state secretary.

Amid all the doom and gloom generated by the electoral failures of state Labor in Victoria, NSW, Queensland and WA, there was a long overdue breakthrough in SA. Despite the monstrous Playford government gerrymander the Labor opposition had managed to become electorally competitive, chipping away at vulnerable government seats and clinging to its own marginals. At the 1962 election Labor managed to win more seats than the government, but was kept in opposition by two independents who supported Playford. Labor's 19 MHAs represented seats containing some 312 000 voters altogether, whereas the government's 18 members represented around 205 000 voters. The wily Premier tried to shore up his position by tinkering further with the gerrymander and arranging for parliament to sit for only 37 days in 1964, but Labor's vigorous campaigning was rewarded by victory at the state election on 5 March 1965. The two vital gains were Barossa, where Molly Byrne became the first woman to win a seat for Labor in SA, and Glenelg, where one of Playford's ministers was unseated by a university lecturer in economics, Hugh Hudson. Playford's record-breaking period of 26 years as Premier had ended at last, and Labor formed its first SA government since the early 1930s. The new Premier was 67-year-old former stonemason Frank Walsh, who had become leader after O'Halloran died in 1960. A conservatively inclined Catholic unionist, Walsh had been deputy leader since 1949 but had his limitations. He was an awkward speaker and ill at ease with more educated party members, notably Dunstan, who, now 39, was the only minister aged less than 50. Five of the eight ministers were over 60.

The new government soon encountered difficulties. It had to overcome ministerial inexperience and an entrenched public service accustomed to serving a conservative government. Walsh's lack of administrative and media skills and his inability to provide cohesive direction were significant handicaps. The government was predictably but mistakenly blamed for a downturn particularly affecting the SA economy: early in 1965 SA unemployment was lower than any other state's, but a year later it was higher than every state except Queensland. Legislation was stalled, altered and sometimes rejected altogether by anti-Labor MLCs, who had the effrontery to claim that they were acting 'impartially in the interests of the people' and representing the electorate's 'permanent will' as distinct from its temporary Labor-leaning aberration. The measures they knocked back included legislation to close death duties loopholes and a bill which sought to correct the undemocratic features of the electoral arrangements covering both chambers.

Despite these problems the Walsh government's reform achievements were impressive, and the driving force behind most of its accomplishments was Dunstan. He had told SA citizens for years that under the Playford government their state had the worst health, education and welfare services in Australia, and he was keen to rectify that situation without delay. With cyclonic zeal he tried to galvanize other ministers in cabinet, and practised what he preached in his wide-ranging responsibilities as Attorney-General and minister for Social Welfare and Aboriginal Affairs. Under his impetus outmoded social welfare procedures were transformed, and his pioneering Prohibition of Discrimination Act and other Aboriginal Affairs legislation were 'far ahead of anything else in Australia at that time'. He initiated sweeping town planning legislation, the abolition of flogging and capital punishment, and a variety of other legal reforms affecting maintenance, wills and jury service. His burning desire to make changes rapidly, his dexterity in handling the media, and the prickliness and hauteur which sometimes surfaced when he felt thwarted all made him a very newsworthy figure. Even his arrival at a cabinet meeting on a blazing summer's day in shorts captured extensive publicity. Although the ministry was not a one-man band, Walsh and the other ministers were completely overshadowed, so much so that there were jocular references to 'the Dunstan government'. Instrumental in Dunstan's monopoly of publicity was his public relations officer (initially Dunstan was the only minister to appoint one), David Combe, a breezy, energetic 22-year-old Arts graduate who had been recruited into the ALP by Dunstan.

Tasmanian Labor had continued to hold the reins of government in the island state. Reece succeeded Cosgrove as state ALP leader and, like his predecessor, remained Premier for a lengthy period. To the leadership Reece brought seasoned political skills, and a background that was once quintessentially Labor but becoming less so – schooling finished at 13, youthful hardship in a variety of manual jobs, unemployment in the Depression, then permanent work as an AWU organizer. He had been in cabinet ever since entering parliament in 1946, had been state ALP president throughout the period 1948–58 except for one year, and had handled his daunting responsibilities as national party president during the split carefully and capably; unlike Cosgrove, Reece was no friend of the DLP and the Groupers. He established himself firmly in command when he clashed with 'Spot' Turnbull soon after taking over from Cosgrove in 1958. When Reece obtained caucus approval to have him removed from the ministry, Turnbull resigned from the ALP and became an independent MP, initially in the Tasmanian Assembly and later in the Senate. Reece strengthened the ministry by persuading Fagan to resume his political career which had been voluntarily curtailed largely because of disenchantment with Turnbull. After the May 1959 election Reece was Premier and Treasurer with ministerial responsibility for Racing and Gaming and also Mines; Fagan was deputy Premier, Attorney-General and minister for Industrial Development. It was a most effective partnership.

Another capable member of Reece's cabinet was Education minister Bill Neilson. He had entered parliament alongside Reece in 1946 as a 21-year-old clerk and the youngest MP in Australian history. In sharp contrast to Reece, Neilson had to endure a frustrating apprenticeship as a backbencher for a decade before achieving promotion to cabinet. Neilson had literary aspirations, a keen interest in the theatre, and a propensity to burst unpredictably into song in a rich baritone voice. His early political career was rapturously followed from the parliamentary visitors' gallery by a girlfriend dressed in school uniform; she became his wife in 1948 after eloping with him to Melbourne. Her parents' initial reservations about him later turned to such warmth that his mother-in-law, Phyllis Benjamin, followed him into parliament as a Labor MP. By 1965 she had spent nine years as deputy leader of the small ALP minority in the upper house. The only woman to precede her (by nine months) as a Labor MP in Tasmania was Lucy Grounds MLC, who took over her husband's seat after he died in 1951. The first ALP woman elected to the Assembly was Lynda Heaven in 1962.

The Reece government extended Tasmania's economic reliance on industrial development powered by hydroelectricity. Tasmanian Labor leaders as far back as Ogilvie and even earlier had shown an awareness that capital could be enticed to their state by the availability of cheap energy. With the support of Reece and Fagan the Hydro-Electric Commission (HEC) continued to grow in size and importance during the 1960s. There were occasional queries and criticism about the placement of too many of the state economy's eggs in the HEC basket, but this disquiet was brushed aside by Reece, who managed to get away with the contention that the role of state conference was to advise or request but certainly not to bind or direct. While Reece, like some of his predecessors, was quick to exploit opportunities to attack Canberra for its allegedly unfair treatment of Tasmania, he maximized its entitlement to grants from the federal government. The ALP in Tasmania continued to be fundamentally very moderate.

The Reece government's increased reliance on hydroelectric-powered industry exemplified a significant change affecting the ALP in and beyond the island state. Initially, although there were variations from state to state, Labor derived its support mainly from bushworkers (who were mostly affiliated to the mighty AWU) and the urban working class. The early Labor governments often cemented their support in the country by accentuating rural development; the distribution of jobs, patronage and influence created prospective Labor voters. This process was elevated to a fine art in the AWU-dominated Labor governments in Queensland and WA, but the disaffiliation of the AWU from the ALP in both states in the 1960s confirmed other signs that this traditional state Labor government approach had outlived its usefulness. To the Tasmanian Labor government, however, hitching its wagon to the HEC star seemed a viable alternative. It boosted the state's economic buoyancy and provided a useful injection of likely Labor voters in rural areas wherever HEC workers were engaged on major hydroelectric projects. SA had followed a different direction. The Playford government had actively encouraged manufacturing industry to grow and prosper after the Depression had shown how vulnerable SA was because of its dependence on international demand for its primary products. However, SA's new emphasis on the manufacture of household goods – motor vehicles in particular

– made it susceptible to sudden falls in consumer demand, such as the 1965–66 slump which affected the state economy severely.

In the rapidly changing 1960s there was a growing feeling that the ALP might have been left behind. Prophets of Labor's doom in the 1930s had been proved very wrong by the Curtin and Chifley governments, but to their 1960s counterparts there seemed more reason for gloomy pessimism than ever. Local branch membership of the ALP had been steadily declining for years, and its financial position was grim. Overseas Labour parties had been much more successful than the FPLP since 1949. The British Labour Party was in office, New Zealand had a Labour government from 1957 to 1960, and equivalent parties had been dominant in Sweden and Norway since the 1930s. Many observers familiar with the ALP believed that it had not adapted well to modern social conditions. They felt that the shibboleths of the post-Depression era no longer appealed to uncommitted voters in the 1960s. Although there was still abundant hardship and inequality in Australia, Labor's traditional supporters in regular employment had grown accustomed to household appliances like washing machines, refrigerators, television sets and other material possessions which added to the comforts of home life in ways scarcely imaginable to battling workers not so long ago. 'Labor still lives in the past when the misery of the proletariat was evident to everyone', asserted the Mosman ALP branch. 'Nowadays most people not only have bread and butter but some have cakes and jam as well.'

The party platform was still headed by the socialist objective. Socialism still meant different things to different people, and some Labor supporters did not see themselves as socialists at all. The massive propaganda assaults on the Chifley government had prompted some Labor figures to proclaim the Blackburn Declaration of 1921 as a significant qualification to the ALP's objective. That qualification was formally incorporated in the objective in 1951, removing the doubts about its ambiguous status and explicitly committing Labor to an appropriate extension of public ownership where the Australian people were being exploited or otherwise oppressed. In the amended platform emerging from the 1957 conference all references to socialization and socialism in the objective were qualified by the adjective 'democratic', enabling Labor figures to distinguish themselves as evolutionary and parliamentary socialists from the revolutionary socialists of the Communist Party.

There had also been very little change in the ALP's federal organization, although a new face was administering it. Each state was still equally represented on the party's national bodies when the membership in each state was manifestly unequal. The development of a cohesive national outlook was still hampered by having six largely autonomous state branches, even though the party's national bodies did have overriding powers at their disposal in exceptional circumstances. Women were still disproportionately underrepresented in the upper levels of the party (although few male activists showed concern about this). After Schmella's death in mid-1960 the duties of national party secretary had been performed by Chamberlain, who emulated Stewart, McNamara, Kennelly and Schmella in combining the roles of national and state secretary. When a full-time salaried national secretary was belatedly appointed in 1963 the position went to the applicant Chamberlain supported, 33-year-old Cyril Wyndham, a former British Labour Party employee who had accepted Evatt's invitation in 1956 to become his press secretary. Wyndham later became state ALP secretary in Victoria, and the administrative skills, industriousness and dedication he displayed in Victoria had much to do with his appointment to the newly created national position. Sharp, short and taut, Wyndham was known variously as the Cockney Sparrow, the Mighty Atom and Cerebral Cyril. The benefits of having a full-time national secretary of Wyndham's calibre were soon evident, although he could have achieved much more with adequate support staff. In 1964 the federal executive authorized him to review the party's national structure; meanwhile he was succeeded in Victoria by a protégé of Chamberlain's, Bill Hartley, who had gravitated to the left of the ALP after a peculiar earlier period as a Liberal activist.

The status of women in the ALP remained low. 'In the Labor Party women are not first-class citizens' and yet Labor 'has always sided with the under-dog', a Queenslander observed in 1960. If women in the ALP did not get a fair go soon, she warned, the party 'might find the under-dog is prepared to adopt good Labor militant tactics and insist upon their right to strike – they won't make cups of tea and wash up'. Similarly, Phyllis Benjamin MLC told Tasmanians that women in the party were 'sick of being kitchen angels' and feeling excluded from the positions that mattered. The situation was similar in NSW: after Edna Roper MLC made a speech which touched on some industrial matters, a prominent union official berated her and made it clear that in his view she should stick to 'women's issues'. In Victoria the state branch did find a new function for women, but it hardly constituted a step in the right direction. Early in 1966 Victorian ALP spokesmen announced with a flourish that Labor would recruit attractive women to act as glamorous ALP 'hostesses', who would form 'a feminine flying gang to assist Labor leaders and members where necessary in their contacts with the public'.

During the 1960s there was an unprecedented accent on youth. The advent of young people with more leisure, more financial resources and broader horizons than any equivalent generation had known created tremendous possibilities for advertising agencies and marketing gurus, and the cult of the teenager spread rapidly. An integral part of the new youth culture was popular music, and Australian teenagers were encouraged to regard artists from abroad as supreme. This development was hardly surprising at a time when Australia was deluged by American merchandise aimed at the Australian youth market. Music from the Beach Boys and the Monkees came to Australia along with Kentucky Fried Chicken, Muzak and, a little later, Uncle Sam deodorant. Labor was slow to react to this focus on youth. 'I am absolutely sick of going to meetings where a lot of Boer War veterans talk about pedestrian crossings', complained the Mascot ALP branch secretary, who felt that 'the encouragement of young, intelligent and dedicated people to join the party' was crucial to its future.

However, although the party was in the doldrums it was still managing to attract young, intelligent and dedicated people like Paul Keating. Born in 1944, Keating had grown up in a close Irish Catholic and staunchly pro-Labor family in Sydney's western suburbs. Before entering his teens he was contributing to the ALP cause himself, helping his father, a likeable boilermaker, with rank-and-file chores like the distribution of party leaflets in Bankstown letterboxes. He left school aged 14, obtained a job as a clerk, attended evening classes to supplement his education, and joined the Labor Youth Council (later renamed Young Labor), which gave him a valuable grounding in factional politics and the cut and thrust of debate. Keating was consumed with politics. He and other politically preoccupied Youth Council friends from similar backgrounds like Laurie Brereton and Bob Carr yarned endlessly, earnestly planning their future careers. In their dreams of future glory they imagined Keating as Prime Minister, Carr as his External Affairs minister, and Brereton as NSW Premier. Keating also used to yarn regularly with Jack Lang, then well into his eighties but still churning out his newspaper the *Century* from a Sydney office. Keating spent his lunch hour with the astonishingly well-preserved Big Fella at least once a week, soaking up political wisdom and ALP history. At one stage Keating was considering establishing himself as a rock music entrepreneur, and for a while he managed a promising young band, the Ramrods; eventually he suggested that it was time for the Ramrods to consider becoming full-time musicians. 'If you do, I'll stay', he told them, 'if not, I'll do politics'. When some of them decided that they were unwilling to take the plunge, Keating dedicated himself to a political career.

Young Australians were at the forefront of the growing hostility to the war in Vietnam. Murky duplicity had characterized Australia's involvement in this undeclared war from the outset. Australia made its initial contribution in 1962, sending 30 military 'instructors' to supplement America's support of the fragile government of South Vietnam in its struggle against the North Vietnamese Communist force of insurgent guerillas, the Viet Cong. The Menzies government's decision to participate was primarily taken not – as it claimed – to help prop up South Vietnam, but to impress the United States that Australia was an earnest and committed ally. Over the next few years America increased its commitment, and repeatedly pressured Australia to do likewise. The Menzies government complied, in the sustained expectation that it was accumulating credit with its powerful ally which might be useful if Australia ever needed assistance. There was undiscriminating support in Canberra – from the External Affairs department in particular – for America's simplistic attitude to the conflict in Vietnam. Indonesia's aggressiveness and the situation in Vietnam influenced the Menzies government late in 1964 to strengthen Australia's defence capacity through the introduction of selective conscription for 20-year-old Australian men chosen by ballot. 'If Sukarno rattles the sabre', Calwell observed, 'the Prime Minister will shake the lottery barrel at him'.

The culmination of the Menzies government's deceit over Vietnam was the announcement in May 1965 that a battalion of Australian soldiers would be dispatched to the region. This decision was taken not merely without any request from South Vietnam, but even before any approach came from the United States, which had not then decided to send combat units of its own. It did make that decision eventually, but only after the Australian government impatiently urged the Americans to intensify their participation. When news of the decision to send a battalion of Australians was leaked, the Menzies government resorted to frantic messages to the United States and South Vietnam in order to substantiate the fictional claim that the battalion was being conveyed at the request of the beleaguered South Vietnam government.

Before May 1965 Labor speakers displayed a marked ambivalence about Vietnam. Ward was the first to be consistently and publicly critical of government policy, predicting that disastrous consequences might ensue for Australia, but he did not see his prophetic words vindicated because he died suddenly of heart failure on 31 July 1963. The firebrand from East Sydney remained truculent and uncompromising to the end, being suspended from the Representatives after a row on his last day in parliament. The widespread admiration in mid-1960s Australia for all things American deterred some Labor MPs from expressing their misgivings about American-Australian policy in Vietnam. This applied particularly to Calwell, who in addition had a strong personal attachment to America arising from the fact that his paternal grandfather had grown up there.

When the United States administration headed by Kennedy's successor, President Lyndon Johnson, commenced heavy bombing raids against North Vietnam, the FPLP executive declared that the Americans' stated 'aim of shortening the war and achieving a negotiated settlement' was 'unexceptionable'. However, some MHRs like Cairns, Cameron and Hayden were more critical of American policy. Cairns, who had read widely about Vietnam, was particularly authoritative.

The task of formulating ALP policy on Vietnam became even more difficult after April 1965. There was instinctive opposition within the FPLP to the decision to send an Australian battalion, but it was not easy to express this without sounding unpatriotic or inconsistent with recent FPLP endorsement of intensified American operations. Outlining the FPLP's response in a significant speech on 4 May, Calwell assured Australian soldiers bound for Vietnam that although the ALP disagreed with their departure it would support them logistically as long as they were there. He correctly predicted that the government would in due course include conscripts in the contingents it sent to Vietnam. Awareness that the party's stance would not be generally popular was reflected in the remarks in Calwell's speech addressed to ALP supporters:

> I offer you the probability that you will be traduced, that your motives will be misrepresented, that your patriotism will be impugned, that your courage will be called into question. But I also offer you the sure and certain knowledge that we will be vindicated: that generations to come will record with gratitude that when a reckless Government wilfully endangered the security of this nation, the voice of the Australian Labor Party was heard, strong and clear, on the side of sanity and in the cause of humanity, and in the interests of Australia's security.

Later, after Australian conscripts were sent to Vietnam, Calwell became increasingly trenchant about conscription. He had upheld the cause of anti-conscription in 1916-17 against Hughes, in 1942-43 against Curtin, and once again he espoused it uncompromisingly. By concentrating on this aspect of the Vietnam controversy he could circumvent the perplexing difficulties Labor faced in attacking Australia's participation alongside America without criticizing the American-Australian alliance.

Labor's standing in the electorate slumped further when Calwell and Whitlam became bitter enemies. After the 1963 election, at the request of the NSW executive, Whitlam compiled an analysis of the reasons for Labor's crushing defeat. His sweeping criticisms of the party included attacks on its 'archaic' and 'rigid' organizational structure, its inability to attract and preselect good candidates, and its inadequate policies:

> The Party's failure to devise modern, relevant and acceptable methods of formulating and publicizing policy is the fault of members in all sections and at all levels of the Party, including leaders and members of the Federal Parliamentary Labor Party.

Calwell took umbrage at his inclusion not just in that sentence but in other deprecatory remarks in Whitlam's report:

> we were defeated not merely because of revulsion in the last week caused by the assassination of President Kennedy or our inferior campaign performance in the month before the election but largely because of our performance in the two years before the election...Mr Calwell did not speak or act as impressively as Sir Robert

Menzies, the Labor members of Parliament did not show the same cohesion and solidarity as the Liberal ones and the Labor organization and its affiliated bodies were not so self-effacing and discreet as the Liberal organization and its backers.

Whitlam assumed that 67-year-old Calwell, the oldest leader the FPLP had ever had, would step down some time before the next election due in 1966. But when Whitlam privately approached Calwell early in 1964 and asked him about his retirement plans, Calwell scornfully replied that he would never be a caretaker leader and he was going to lead the party at the 1966 election. The drastic deterioration in the relationship between Labor's leader and deputy soon became public knowledge.

Calwell was not the same man who had impatiently bustled to Canberra in 1940. Back then

> he could not control his exuberance. He courted trouble and disputation. . .with uninhibited relish. He spoke first and thought later – often ruefully. . .He had hates, strong hates, and enjoyed indulging them, with healthy candour.

After two decades in parliament he measured his words more carefully. The enduring bitterness of the split and an even more excruciating episode, the death of his only son, had profoundly scarred him, and after the near miss of 1961 the defeat of 1963 had been a severe blow. Nevertheless his abundant self-confidence was undiminished. He was contemptuous of suggestions that his age made him an anachronistic party leader in the mid-1960s. Dr Maloney was 86 before Calwell inherited his seat, and Evatt had made him wait for the leadership too: 'Evatt had three goes and so will I', he said bluntly.

Whitlam had no doubt that he could do a better job than Calwell. He was also certain that it would be disastrous from the party's viewpoint for Calwell to lead it at the 1966 election. Whitlam had tremendous ability, energy and drive to achieve reform, even if – or especially if – it meant dragging his creaking and protesting party into the modern era. His willingness to stake all in bold manoeuvres was epitomized in a later comment which became a personal testament: 'When you are faced with an impasse you have got to crash through or you've got to crash'. Calwell, for all his belligerence and courage, tended to falter when confronted with a hazardous step which could well prove ultimately decisive, but not Whitlam. As leader, Calwell felt motivated not to jeopardize party unity; Whitlam was prepared to risk short-term disruption in order to gain long-term benefits. Many Labor enthusiasts were attracted by Whitlam. At the Labor Youth Council in Sydney Keating, Brereton and Carr thought Whitlam was marvellous, and so did Combe and others in the Young Labor group in Adelaide. He gained more supporters when he spoke to gatherings of Labor women with genuine conviction about the need for more Australian women in employment and public office, the injustice of denying women equal pay, and the disgrace of the ALP's failure to endorse more women candidates. Some of Whitlam's admirers may have had reservations about his superiority complex or some of his political attitudes, but they all recognized that he was their best hope of creating the sort of Labor Party and Labor government they desperately wanted after so long in the political wilderness.

Articulate, learned and stylish, Whitlam was a superb media performer, but he was prone to impulsive lapses which made him seem petulant, arrogant and lacking in self-control. Early in 1965 a newspaper report claimed that Whitlam had described Calwell as 'too old and weak' and predicted that Labor would lose the election due in 1966 if it was led by an 'old-fashioned 70-year-old'. Whitlam claimed that he had been talking off the record and had been misquoted as well, but Calwell was livid, and some Whitlam admirers were appalled. After this incident there was frequent public conjecture about the FPLP leadership. Although Whitlam avoided making any open challenge to Calwell, he also refrained from making the earnest expressions of loyalty to the incumbent leader which have become ritualistically expected of ambitious deputies; instead he made subtle but pointed remarks which undermined and infuriated Calwell. While Whitlam's frustration and reprehensible outbursts created unprecedented public animosity between an ALP leader and deputy, Calwell's own conduct at times under Curtin and Evatt gave his complaints about Whitlam's excesses a hollow ring.

Whitlam's disruptive conduct after 1963 enlarged a widening gulf within the party. This schism has been described as the struggle between the traditionalists and the modernists like Whitlam, although in a large broad-based party like the ALP this division was of course not clearcut. The modernists advocated reform of the party's organizational structure, a green light for state aid, and an end to the downgrading of MPs who – rather than machine officials – should be the party's accredited senior expounders. Modernists also welcomed the involvement of academics in developing more up-to-date policies, and did not regard the socialist objective as sacrosanct. The traditionalists wanted the party to retain the purity of the socialist objective and Labor's longstanding hostility to state aid, and saw no need for drastic changes to the ALP's structure. Nearly all traditionalists disliked and distrusted intellectuals, saw trade unionists as the hallowed core of the party, and advocated a continuation of vigilant machine control over potentially expedient MPs. The traditionalists resisted Whitlam's impetus for a combination of reasons. Some regarded the modernists as opportunists hungry for office, some felt attached to the old ways, and some were conscious that their power and status within the party were under threat. The most prominent and influential traditionalist was Chamberlain, and the Victorian executive was a powerful traditionalist stronghold. The pressure of events drove Calwell increasingly into their camp, although from the traditionalists' viewpoint he was wobbly on state aid and out of step in seeing the need for an organizational overhaul. In 1964 he rejoined the Victorian executive. This action, he felt, would reduce the 'faceless men' stigma. But he made himself vulnerable to the accusation that he was 'a prisoner of the left', especially when he accepted nomination as one of Victoria's six 1965 federal conference delegates with firm instructions on controversial issues like support for unity tickets.

That conference in August 1965 was a crucial battleground, and unity tickets, state aid and ALP structural reform were expected to be the most controversial issues. Whitlam was jubilant about the Victorians' backdown on unity tickets just before the conference; partly because of Calwell's invidious position, they even accepted tighter rules against the practice. On state aid the modernists had less cause for celebration. The NSW branch, which still felt aggrieved that the federal executive's hardline interpretation of policy on this question had contributed to the defeat of its state government, unsuccessfully tried to remove the party's opposition to state aid. Both Chamberlain, who clashed angrily with Oliver and Downing during the debate, and Calwell suggested that Labor should advocate a referendum on state aid. However, the outcome was a compromise – accepted by all delegates except the NSW six – which confirmed Labor's opposition to state aid while upholding benefits already introduced. Another potentially contentious issue before conference was the organizational reforms proposed by Wyndham and strongly supported by Whitlam. The Wyndham Plan recommended the enlargement and reconstruction of both the federal conference and the federal executive, and advocated various other measures designed to improve the party's finances, internal co-ordination, branch membership and appeal to younger Australians. It was known that Chamberlain and the Victorian executive vigorously opposed the Wyndham Plan. Although some aspects of it had strong NSW support, conference decided to shelve it for further consideration.

Developments in those three controversial issues tended to overshadow the wide-ranging constructive overhaul of the platform at the 1965 conference. 'This Conference has played its role superbly', enthused Whitlam, who claimed that it 'has done more than any of its predecessors. . .to rewrite its Party's policy'. According to one estimate, as much as 60% of the detailed platform had been rewritten. Whitlam observed that there were radically changed policies in health, housing, transport, immigration, broadcasting and television, labour and industry, foreign affairs, welfare, Aboriginal affairs, science and national development. He praised the contribution of the ALP's standing committees, an innovation by Chamberlain designed to generate more informed analysis and debate of proposed policy reforms, and welcomed the ALP's affiliation with the Socialist International, the admission of the press to the conference and the involvement of intellectuals in party policy-making: 'It is the first time for 50 years that a bearded man has taken part in its deliberations'. Whitlam also vigorously praised the Wyndham Plan: 'state rights are. . .not a Labor concept'. In very different vein was Calwell's conference speech. He lashed out at the 'vicious, vile and violent campaign' against him by the controllers of the media, who believed that 'the only good Labor man is a dead one'. Calwell also denounced 'this horrible war' in Vietnam, defended the 'unjustly attacked' and 'savagely misrepresented' Victorian branch, and reiterated 'to the press of Australia, and to others whom it may concern' that he would lead Labor at the next election.

Among the alterations to party policy made at the 1965 conference was the deletion of Labor's historic attachment to White Australia. There had been mounting recent pressure within the party from activists who felt that this provision was offensive and had long ago lost whatever justification it once had. Leading the charge was Dunstan, who had spent much of his pre-parliamentary life in Fiji and loathed racist overtones of any sort. Calwell was vehemently opposed to any deviation from White Australia, and often said so with characteristic bluntness. He maintained that he was not racially prejudiced at all, simply concerned that significantly increasing the proportion of non-white people in Australia would generate racial strife. Calwell had lobbied successfully to prevent any change in 1961, and the reformers had no joy at the 1963 conference either. The basis of the compromise formula which replaced White Australia in the platform in 1965 was a focus on the prospective immigrant's ability to assimilate. Calwell, Daly and other supporters of White Australia believed that assimilation for non-whites was barely possible, but Dunstan and the reformers had completely different views.

Six months after the 1965 federal conference the ALP was in more turmoil

62. Menzies the matador. (by John Frith; *National Library*)

63. If Pat Kennelly could not have both the logic and the numbers in a party fight, he preferred the numbers every time. (by John Spooner; *Age*)

64. The photograph which prompted the 'faceless men' stigma: Gough Whitlam (back to camera) and Arthur Calwell (right) wait with Frank Waters outside the Hotel Kingston, Canberra, while Labor's federal conference delegates inside determine party policy.

65. 'Joe' Chamberlain (left) and Charlie Oliver.

66. One of Victorian Labor's aspiring 'hostesses', Mary Elliot, daughter of a television personality well known in Victoria, Doug Elliot MLC. (*National Library*)

than ever over state aid. In February 1966 the federal executive, with Chamberlain at the forefront, controversially decided not only that ALP members had to oppose any state aid measures introduced after August 1965, but also to investigate whether existing benefits were constitutionally valid. The latter decision particularly riled the modernists, who could argue persuasively that it was inconsistent with the compromise outcome at the previous federal conference that no 'benefit which is currently established shall be disturbed'. Furious MPs sent telegrams of protest to the federal secretariat, and some expressed their anger publicly. Whitlam did not hide his predictable reaction. Allan Fraser forthrightly announced that he would defy the direction to oppose state aid, as did Kennelly. NSW state MPs called for the federal executive's decisions to be reversed, and declared that when NSW Labor returned to office state aid would be continued and extended. Other critics included Bert Hawke, Fagan, Dunstan, Duthie and Luchetti. Another legacy of that contentious federal executive meeting was the resignation of Calwell's speechwriter, Graham Freudenberg. According to Freudenberg, Calwell had entered that meeting with a prepared submission in favour of state aid; whereas Whitlam passionately opposed the decisions during the meeting, Calwell, once he had assessed the executive's majority view, kept his real opinions to himself and the submission in his pocket.

This crisis over state aid was ignited during a by-election campaign for the north Queensland seat of Dawson. The by-election was Prime Minister Holt's first electoral test following Menzies's retirement early in 1966. Dawson had been since its creation in 1949 a Country Party stronghold. The ALP candidate Dr Rex Patterson, who had degrees in Commerce and Science and a doctorate in Agricultural Science, had recently resigned in frustration from the post of regional director of the department of National Development. Patterson was precisely the sort of quality candidate Whitlam wanted the ALP to endorse more often, and he campaigned vigorously alongside Patterson in Dawson. Together they concentrated on regional matters, northern development in particular. Patterson was an expert on the coalition government's neglect of this issue, and Whitlam had the good barrister's knack of mastering unfamiliar subjects rapidly and effectively. In sticking to a theme of significant local importance Whitlam was reproducing the campaign formula which had proved so successful for him in Queensland in 1961 (and would again in WA later in 1966). Patterson insisted that Calwell was not to divert the campaign by discordantly introducing other issues like Vietnam and conscription; Calwell made a brief appearance at the outset before departing, convinced that Labor had no hope. Patterson was most aggrieved that the federal executive had disrupted his campaign with controversial pronouncements, and he angrily joined the critical chorus. Most pundits concluded that the revived state aid commotion had dashed whatever chance Labor had of an unlikely win in Dawson, but Patterson and Whitlam – who frequently had to interrupt his campaigning to dash south as the drama over state aid unfolded – persisted with their gruelling schedule. The result was a swing to Labor of over 12%, an unprecedented ALP victory in Dawson, and a marvellous personal achievement for Patterson and Whitlam.

During the campaign Whitlam continued with his scathing criticism of the federal executive. He released a statement attacking the 'extremist controlling group' for using the party 'as a vehicle for their own prejudice and vengeance'. He issued a call to arms for the modernists, reviving his agitation for structural reform: 'It is now urgent to reorganize the party', or else 'the greatest political party this country had known' would be doomed to irrelevance as 'a sectional rump'.

> The issue is not the Right and the Left. It is between those who want a broadly-based Socialist and radical party and petty men who want to reduce it to their personal plaything. . .This extremist group breaches the party policy, it humiliates the party's Parliamentarians, it ignores the party's rank-and-file. It is neither representative nor responsible. It will and must be repudiated.

After this forceful statement Whitlam further fuelled the flames of controversy during a television interview on 15 February. It was Whitlam at his most recklessly impulsive. He blasted the 'incompetent and irresponsible' federal executive members who 'don't seem to be able to understand policy', and described the decision to investigate a High Court challenge on state aid as a 'preposterous proposition'. Even more provocative was his aside that 'we've only just got rid of the 36 faceless men stigma to be faced with the 12 witless men'. Whitlam made several snide remarks attacking Calwell's leadership, especially his vacillation over state aid, and asserted that 'I've been destined to be leader of the Party for at least a year, as soon as there was a ballot for the position'. At the end of the interview Whitlam declared that Labor 'led by me would beat the coalition' at the 1966 election; asked to predict the result if Calwell remained leader, Whitlam answered 'No comment'.

Whitlam was soon fighting for his political life. Early in March the federal executive charged him with gross disloyalty, and the vital numbers were ominously poised seven-five against him. Chamberlain and others were keen to inflict the maximum penalty of expulsion. 'We've got the numbers to get rid of the big bastard', Calwell told Allan Fraser. Patterson, who had publicly praised Whitlam as 'a tower of strength' during the Dawson by-election and condemned the moves to discipline him, learned in a chance conversation that the guillotine was about to fall. Patterson urgently passed on this information, and desperate attempts were made to contact Egerton and other senior Queensland ALP figures, so that their state's delegates (J. Keeffe and F. Whitby) could be instructed to reverse their declared intention to 'knock him off'. It seems that Egerton and state secretary Tom Burns were primarily responsible for the direction received by Keeffe and Whitby to vote against expulsion, and at the last minute Whitlam was saved.

Before the 1966 election there were further twists in the struggle between the modernists and the traditionalists. With a Whitlam leadership challenge certain and imminent, FPLP meetings became tense and vituperative as the rival camps held secret meetings and began head-counting in earnest. Whitlam supporters like NSW MPs Mulvihill, Connor and Luchetti believed that their man might topple Calwell in a secret ballot, but could not win if the vote was by show of hands. They tried to engineer a secret ballot on the leadership, but were unsuccessful. The fate of the Whitlam bid was determined in caucus on 27 April; Whitlam's conclusive defeat by 49 votes to 24 showed that he would not have succeeded even in a secret ballot. Calwell announced that he would not seek the leadership after the next election if Labor lost. Meanwhile a lengthy consultative process was under way to resolve Labor's problems with its state aid policy. The culmination came in July at a special federal conference where the numbers were delicately balanced. The traditionalists had moderated their opposition to state aid; Chamberlain was absent in hospital for a crucial period, and missed his first federal conference since 1948. The result was a victory for the modernists when a motion favouring state aid was passed by 19 votes to 17. The vital vote came from Calwell who, again attending as a Victorian delegate, switched sides to provide the modernists with their narrow victory.

A month earlier there had been drama for Calwell of a different kind when he was the target of an assassination attempt in Sydney. The shooting occurred just before 11pm on 21 June 1966 following a rowdy meeting at Mosman Town Hall on the theme of Vietnam and conscription. 'You can't defeat an ideal with a bullet', Calwell had assured the audience in his forceful speech. Afterwards he mingled with onlookers outside the hall, then strolled to his car and climbed in. The car's side window was closed when the gunman, Peter Kocan, approached. The darkness prevented Kocan from aiming properly and Calwell from appreciating any danger; Calwell assumed Kocan was another wellwisher and was winding the window down to shake hands when the shot was fired, shattering the window and spattering glass and bullet fragments in all directions. An ambulance was called, and Calwell was taken to hospital. He was understandably severely shocked, but escaped serious injury and afterwards showed great compassion to Kocan and his mother. Australians awoke the next day to learn from screaming headlines that their assimilation of American culture now extended beyond yo-yos and Kentucky Fried Chicken. The assassination of President Kennedy had partly inspired Kocan's act. A disturbed loner seeking notoriety, he hoped that shooting Calwell would 'set me aside from all the other nobodies'. Among the town hall audience were Les Haylen and his son Wayne, a university student. Wayne Haylen was one of an increasing number of draft resisters defying the conscription process, and had appeared in court after publicly burning his ballot notice. Immediately after the shooting Kocan ran away, but Wayne Haylen chased him, caught up to him, and with assistance apprehended him. There was a bizarre sequel 17 years later when Kocan, having blossomed into a talented writer during his decade in a psychiatric hospital, was awarded a literary prize for a novel based on his experiences by a Labor Premier, Neville Wran, who had been Wayne Haylen's barrister in 1966.

The 1966 election was disastrous for Labor. Holt's assurance that Australia would go 'all the way with LBJ' was rewarded when Johnson made the first visit by a reigning American president to Australia. The President attracted huge crowds of admirers during his stay, but protesters against conscription and the Vietnam War also made their presence felt. When a group of dissenters lay in the path of the presidential calvalcade in Sydney, Premier Askin distinguished himself and pleased Johnson by urging his driver to 'ride over the bastards'. These protests strengthened Calwell's conviction that strident attacks on Vietnam and conscription would pay electoral dividends. He retorted to an elderly interjector that 'I will not allow you or Holt or Menzies or anyone to plunge your arthritic hands wrist deep in the blood of Australian youth'. Other Labor figures like Whitlam and Patterson doubted the wisdom of Calwell's emphasis. After all, Australians had been treated only a month before the election to the full panoply of presidential grandeur and glamour which, as intended, showed clearly that the Holt government and its Vietnam policy had the endorsement of Australia's most powerful and important ally. Furthermore, when Calwell proudly proclaimed his honourable opposition to conscription in 1916–17, 1942–43 and 1965–66, the reaction of uncommitted younger voters was not to commend him for his principled consistency but to regard him as an ancient relic from a different era. Labor's problems were aggravated when voters were reminded of two years of internal ALP strife by a public dispute between Calwell and Whitlam during the campaign. The difference of opinion arose from the lack of precision in ALP policy about how and when Australian combatants would be withdrawn from Vietnam. The devastating upshot on polling day was that the ALP voting share slumped to 39·98% (45·47% in 1963) and the coalition government won twice as many seats as Labor. FPLP casualties included Les Johnson and Pat Galvin as well as two fine veterans, Pollard and Allan Fraser. In SA there was a staggering anti-Labor swing, and the ALP's proportion of the primary vote fell by 12·48%. Three SA seats were lost. All had long been held by Labor, Kingston since 1951 and Adelaide and Grey since 1943. Even in Hindmarsh Clyde Cameron only survived after a close contest. Labor's voting share increased solely in WA, where Whitlam campaigned extensively.

It was a dismal end to the ALP's 75th year. Two decades earlier Labor had seemed Australia's natural national party of government. Yet the FPLP had now occupied the opposition benches for 17 years consecutively, and seemed further away from office than ever. Even the narrow defeat of 1961 seemed more clearly in retrospect an aberration caused by the government's economic incompetence. The DLP was still a significant irritant with a national voting share of 7·31%; in Victoria it obtained more than one vote for every three Labor gained in 1966. The frustrating 17 years in opposition endured by Beazley, Cameron, Daly, Duthie, O'Byrne, Tangney and Willesee had seemed an eternity. Other gifted MHRs like Whitlam and Crean had been waiting almost as long to utilize their skills in government to benefit Australia's disadvantaged. The wait was too long for some of their colleagues, notably Fraser, Haylen and Pollard (whose brief terms as a minister under Hogan in Victoria and Chifley in Canberra were inadequate for a stalwart of his quality and 37 years' parliamentary service). It was profoundly depressing for Labor MPs and the rank and file, and there was little comfort in the state sphere. Labor was in the wilderness in all three eastern mainland states and in WA. Although it was holding its own in the smallest state, many Labor enthusiasts regarded the Tasmanian ALP as so conservative and lightweight in the overall national picture that their only consolation was the vigorous start being made by the long-awaited government in SA. But the crushing swing against Labor in SA at the 1966 federal election was widely interpreted as dissatisfaction with the state government, so even that solace seemed likely to be short-lived. Wyndham, who had earlier in 1966 acknowledged the existence of an 'impression' that the FPLP appeared 'doomed to indefinite opposition', did not beat about the bush when assessing Labor's plight in December. 'A very large task lies ahead of us', he admitted dolefully.

13 'Whose Party is This – Ours or His?': Resurgence under Whitlam, 1967–1972

CALWELL DID NOT resign immediately after Labor's 1966 débâcle. On the contrary, he remained vigorously in the public arena, blasting the South Vietnamese leader then visiting Australia as 'a quisling gangster', 'a butcher', 'a moral and social leper' and 'a pocket Hitler', and leading demonstrations against the visit. He also compiled a lengthy report to the ALP federal executive. It covered in considerable detail the controversial incidents involving Whitlam since early 1965, and asserted that 'only real unity can give us victory'. Although Whitlam's prediction that Labor would be devastated if Calwell led it in 1966 had been vindicated, Calwell clearly felt that Whitlam's own actions had been the main cause, and his resentment lingered: 'I have not had a single conversation with Mr Whitlam since the 1966 elections on matters of policy, on organizational questions, or indeed on anything of importance', Calwell affirmed in his memoirs published in 1972. However, the report he submitted in February 1967 concluded positively:

> I believe the Labor Party is not down and out anymore than it was in 1917 and 1932. My political faith in its future success remains undiminished. . .I can still see the light on the hill.

Calwell ended speculation about his intentions when he honoured his April 1966 undertaking and did not contest the leadership at the first FPLP post-election meeting.

Whitlam was expected to succeed Calwell, but for some years ALP left-wingers, especially in Victoria, had seen Cairns as a possible future leader. Articulate and erudite, principled and humane, Cairns had become a renowned national figure, advocating an independent Australian stance in international relations and upholding a variety of radical causes. His greatest admirer was Uren. Sensing that Cairns was sometimes too gullible and vulnerable, Uren attached himself to his hero as a political minder. Cairns's other close FPLP friend was Hayden. They had in common a disadvantaged upbringing, left-wing views and previous employment in the police force; Cairns helped Hayden, who was studying Economics at university part-time as Cairns once had, with his course work.

It was no surprise when Cairns contested the FPLP leadership – he regarded Whitlam as egocentric and excessively confrontational. Crean, Daly and Beazley also nominated. Likeable, solid and highly respected, Crean had Calwell's backing; the outgoing leader felt that because of Crean's more diverse sources of FPLP support he was more likely than Cairns to be Whitlam's biggest danger in the ballot. Whitlam, however, won easily.

The new leader's preferred candidate for deputy, Barnard, also won. This was a much closer contest, with eight contenders and the margin between Barnard and his closest rival Cairns in the final count being only two votes. Loyal, hardworking and unostentatious, Barnard mixed with his FPLP colleagues more than Whitlam, and accordingly could provide his chief with valuable information about their attitudes, although some MPs were concerned that he would not put a strong enough brake on Whitlam's extravagances. Left-wingers had much more cause for satisfaction with the Senate leadership ballots. With McKenna retired and 66-year-old Kennelly not standing, Murphy defeated Willesee for the top Senate position, and Sam Cohen, a 53-year-old Victorian barrister also linked to the left, won the ballot for Senate deputy. Barnard, whose father had been a minister under Chifley, had been a schoolteacher before entering parliament; the other three in the new-look FPLP leadership group were all QCs.

Whitlam began with characteristic vigour and zeal, as if there was not a moment to lose. In his first statement as FPLP leader he claimed that the immediate future was critical for the ALP: 'the next few years must determine whether it continues to survive as a truly effective parliamentary force, capable of governing and actually governing'. Freudenberg, now working for Whitlam, frequently and fervently declared that the next three years would determine whether the ALP would continue to exist at all. Overhauling the party was Whitlam's earliest priority, and he was prepared to apply all the prestige of his leadership to the task. He was soon skirmishing publicly with Chamberlain. Their most bitter clash followed Barnard's reported remark – he later claimed that he had been misquoted – that Labor should consider reviewing its policies on Vietnam; Chamberlain implied that Barnard had collected his information about Vietnam from 'the cocktail circuit and bars of Saigon'. Whitlam denounced Chamberlain's 'disgraceful and disloyal insinuations':

> Until he apologizes to Mr Barnard, I shall have no further communication with him. . . His conduct. . .establishes how essential it is that in matters concerning the Federal Parliament, the ALP should be based on the rank and file and not on State bureaucracies. If other state secretaries were as autocratic and idiosyncratic as Mr Chamberlain, the party's membership would be as reduced and frustrated in other States as it is in Western Australia. . .

In mid-1967 Whitlam persuasively presented his arguments for structural reform of the party to several state conferences. In WA, where he had a public reconciliation with Chamberlain, Whitlam told conference delegates that every socialist party in the rest of the world had an effective national organization, but all the ALP had was a national secretary and two typists; despite Chamberlain's opposition, he gained a substantial majority vote in favour of organizational reform. Whitlam's arguments were supported at the NSW state conference, but rejected in SA. In Victoria he threw down the gauntlet in an uncompromising speech:

Let us have none of this nonsense that defeat is in some way more moral than victory
. . .This conference, comprising a greater percentage of union delegates than any democratic socialist party on earth, must reject any idea that constant defeat and permanent
opposition do not matter, that the labour movement can be strong and effective industrially, while being weak and ineffective politically. On the narrowest industrial views
this is patently false. . .I did not seek and do not want the leadership of Australia's
largest pressure group. I propose to follow the traditions of those of our leaders who
have seen the role of our party as striving to achieve, and achieving, national government of Australia.

The crescendo of boos and jeers in the audience during his speech delighted
Calwell, and confirmed his expectation that Whitlam's tenure of the leadership
would be brief. 'You won't be working for your new boss for long now', he
assured Freudenberg afterwards.

Whitlam's attack on the Victorian branch had been sharpened by the Bolte
government's easy victory at the recent state election, which occurred not long
after Bolte defied community outrage and persuaded his cabinet to authorize the
hanging of a man convicted of fatally shooting a prison warder during an escape
from gaol. 'If you want to win an election have a hanging', Bolte later commented. The Liberals won 44 seats to Labor's 16 and the Country Party's 12. To
the electorally impotent state executive's chagrin, history repeated itself in the
Labor stronghold of Coburg, where ALP activists endorsed a local stalwart as
their Independent Labor candidate and helped him to triumph on polling day
over the Victorian ALP president and official Labor candidate, Bill Brown. This
successful candidate was Jack Mutton, son of Charlie Mutton who had won
Coburg in similar circumstances in 1940 and retained it – initially as Independent Labor, but from 1956, when he was readmitted to the party after the split, as
official ALP – until his retirement before the 1967 election. After the election
Labor's state caucus elected a new leader, Clyde Holding, and deputy, Frank
Wilkes. The rapid rise of 36-year-old Holding was primarily due to the combativeness he had displayed in attacking Bolte in parliament; the MPs who voted
for Holding hoped that he would provide the toughness which his predecessor
Stoneham lacked, and they were not disappointed. Wilkes had served as Cain's
campaign manager and succeeded him as Northcote's MLA in 1957, defeating
Cain's 26-year-old son who had contested the preselection at Kennelly's
request.

An electoral triumph for Whitlam occurred soon after his calculated confrontation with the Victorian branch. A by-election was created in Corio when
Opperman resigned. Whitlam encouraged Bob Hawke to contest the seat again,
but Hawke, who was then more interested in becoming president of the ACTU
than a parliamentarian, declined. Labor chose Gordon Scholes, a 36-year-old
engine driver and former Victorian heavyweight boxing champion who had contested the seat at the election eight months earlier. A councillor and THC
president in Geelong, Scholes was well known locally. Whitlam based himself
and his staff in a Geelong motel and launched an intensive campaign. As in the
Dawson by-election, he concentrated on local issues while relating them to
Labor's national policy objectives. Scholes had a tremendous win, obtaining a
swing of over 11% and a voting share of 50·28%. For Whitlam it was a superb
vindication of his approach. Only three months after Victorian Labor had been
thrashed in a state election, he had spearheaded Labor's first capture of a Victorian seat from its opponents since 1952. The moral of Corio, he pointedly

declared, was 'that with good candidates, campaigning on relevant and clearly-stated issues, we can enlist the support of more than half the people'.

The Corio by-election was immediately followed by an ALP federal conference, which would be crucial to the outcome of Whitlam's drive to restructure the party. He was hoping to capitalize on the reform momentum established after the Corio result and the state conferences in NSW and WA. The Tasmanian branch had also declared itself in favour of organizational reform. With Victoria and SA opposed, the Queenslanders' attitude would be decisive. Whitlam lobbied their delegates vigorously, but they ultimately resolved, after countervailing pressure from Cameron and Chamberlain, not to support Whitlam, so there was deadlock. A compromise was negotiated whereby the federal executive was enlarged from 12 to 17 by the addition of the four FPLP leaders and a delegate from the Northern Territory, and the federal conference was increased from 36 to 47 with the inclusion of the four FPLP leaders, a Northern Territory representative and an extra delegate from each state, with the additional requirement that each state delegation to federal conference now had to include that state's parliamentary Labor leader. In making these concessions, Cameron, one of Whitlam's most influential opponents on this issue, reasoned that the left-wing majority on the federal executive would be unaffected by the changes, since the votes of Murphy and Cohen would cancel out those of Whitlam and Barnard on vital questions.

The reforms were swiftly and unanimously endorsed by conference. Although they fell short of the thorough overhaul Whitlam was seeking, they did represent a significant breakthrough; they were, he claimed, 'the greatest change in the framework of our party on a national scale' since the formation of the federal executive in 1915. Further changes were needed, Whitlam admitted, but Labor

> has now demolished the cry of the 36 faceless men. . .It could hitherto be said that the Australian Labor Party, alone among Socialist parties, did not trust its leaders. This can never be said again.

In his speech Whitlam also praised the reform achievements of the SA Labor government, which had recently acquired a new leader. Concern in SA Labor ranks about deficiencies in Walsh's leadership had been compounded by the retirement of 70-year-old Playford as Liberal leader and his replacement by 37-year-old Steele Hall. Something had to be done, and Cameron, the consummate political operator who was the most influential machine figure in SA, was just the man for the task. At a meeting in January 1967 Cameron made a speech eulogizing Walsh's contribution and, building to a climax, especially commended him for leading Labor into government in SA for the first time in over three decades and making the noble decision to relinquish the premiership to make way for a younger successor. Walsh, nonplussed, was given a standing ovation. Immediately afterwards he bluntly reiterated his refusal to step down, but a few weeks later announced his resignation.

Walsh, reflecting the antagonism created by Dunstan's impatience with less talented and less radical colleagues, was determined to do all he could to prevent Dunstan from succeeding him. He pinned his hopes on his most junior minister, Des Corcoran, a 38-year-old Catholic and former military officer who had resigned from the army to succeed his father as MHA for Millicent in 1962. Walsh preferred Corcoran primarily because he wanted – like Calwell in Canberra a few months earlier – to throw his weight behind someone who had a realistic chance of thwarting the talented man he disliked. Walsh's vigorous lobbying ensured that Corcoran had strong backing from a caucus section possessing, like Walsh, a trade union background and disapproval of Dunstan, who could seem cold and aloof because 'he lacked the gift of easy conviviality'. These Corcoran supporters were not blind to Dunstan's abilities, 'but found his style – his accent, his dress, his interests, his aggressive modernity – quite alien'. In the caucus ballot Dunstan had a narrow win over Corcoran.

Dunstan took over the premiership in June 1967 with an election due within nine months, and the necessity for speedy improvement was obvious. A deliberate decision was made to use Dunstan's superb media skills to the full in generating positive publicity for the government. There was no slackening in the government's momentum with Dunstan at the helm, and among the more notable and popular reforms were liberalized drinking and entertainment arrangements; these changes removed limitations which had restricted social life in SA for generations. For the first time in Australian politics, sophisticated advertising and market research techniques were used, with Dunstan's full support and participation. State ALP secretary Geoff Virgo, a shrewd and experienced labour movement administrator, was initially unenthusiastic; although he greatly respected Dunstan, Virgo believed that there was no substitute for traditional grass-roots campaigning. But Virgo's scepticism faded as the emphasis on Dunstan and willingness to use unconventional techniques proved very worthwhile. The research surveys confirmed Dunstan's extraordinary popularity – his approval rating climbed to 83% – and provided valuable information about the strengths and weaknesses of Labor's campaigning. The ALP polling confirmed that the government had regained support and could look forward to the election with some hope of success, which had less than a year earlier seemed unlikely.

The countryside proved to be the Dunstan government's Achilles heel on 2 March 1968. Labor's opinion surveys had been entirely conducted in urban and fringe metropolitan areas, leaving party strategists unaware that the government had not managed in rural regions to achieve the recovery that had occurred elsewhere. In another costly oversight, Labor's main campaign pamphlet was almost totally devoid of agricultural content. After his herculean labours Dunstan desperately needed a rest, but had to wait anxiously for weeks while protracted vote counting determined the fate of his government. Eventually it was confirmed that Labor had lost Chaffey and Murray, but Corcoran had scraped home by a single vote in Millicent. Although the overall ALP voting share had held up well at 52%, Labor and their opponents would each have 19 seats in the new Assembly and a non-Labor independent would hold the balance of power. The writing was on the wall for the government, but Dunstan exercised his right to remain in office until he was defeated on the floor of parliament. In the meantime he launched a vigorous campaign to maximize public awareness of the gerrymander. His fervent oratory was buttressed by demonstrations, a huge petition, and supportive denunciations from Whitlam, Murphy and the union movement. Parliament reconvened on 16 April. The government immediately lost an Assembly ballot, and Dunstan resigned. But the election drama was not yet over. Because of various irregularities in the voting at Millicent as well as the knife-edge result itself, a fresh poll was ordered in that seat. This by-election was held on 22 June. Dunstan and Virgo marshalled their forces, the Corcoran clan swung into action, and their candidate was returned with a convincing majority.

319

It was an important win for Labor – defeat would have given the Hall government a clear majority in both chambers.

A year later Labor lost its only remaining government when Tasmanian electors removed the Reece government. Among the reasons for the electoral defeat, which ended 35 years of unbroken ALP government in the island state, were an economic downturn and dissatisfaction with the performance of some of Reece's ministers. There was criticism – largely, it seems, unwarranted – of government ineptitude in administering compensation payments after the tragic 1967 bushfires. Also instrumental, and a sign of things to come, was conservationists' fierce opposition to the HEC project at Gordon River, which involved the flooding of beautiful Lake Pedder. The Reece government's all-embracing faith in hydro-electric-powered development left no room for environmental concern or sensitivity. Its attitude to conservation was epitomized by the hunters, trappers and traders of fur and skins appointed by the government to its Animals and Birds Protection Board; the chairman of this board was also president of the Shooting Clubs Association. Another factor in Labor's 1969 defeat was the Liberals' improved campaigning. Especially during Cosgrove's reign, Labor's opponents in Tasmania had displayed a tendency to snatch defeat from the jaws of victory, but not this time. With a swing away from Labor of 3·62%, the ALP won 17 seats (19 in 1964). The Liberals also had 17 seats, and the balance of power was captured by ex-Liberal rebel and Prime Minister's son Kevin Lyons, who now represented the Centre Party. Lyons formed a coalition with his former colleagues. So Labor had to adjust to opposition, no easy task after the longest continuous period in office enjoyed by any party since the ALP was founded. With the fall of the Reece ministry there was no Labor government anywhere in Australia for the first time since 1910.

Meanwhile a representative of the Tasmanian branch had become the centre of a row which had convulsed the ALP nationally and even threatened Whitlam's leadership. Brian Harradine was neither the first nor the last import from the mainland to make a bigger splash in the small pond of Tasmania than he had in his state of origin (SA). Harradine was able, intelligent, fanatically anti-Communist, and a fine orator and debater. During the 1960s he rose to prominence in the Tasmanian labour movement as a skilful right-wing union organizer, and in 1968 he was accredited by the state branch as one of its federal executive delegates. With the factional composition of the federal executive the focus of even more intense scrutiny than normal, rumours about Harradine's past links with the DLP in SA began to circulate. Cameron became convinced that Harradine's transfer to Tasmania and emergence there had been orchestrated by Santamaria's National Civic Council (which had taken over the role of the Movement in 1957). Harradine issued a defiant statement alleging that 'the friends of the Communists intend to try and silence me' because 'they know that on the federal executive I will support Gough Whitlam if he seeks an inquiry into the Victorian ALP executive'. The first federal executive meeting attended by Harradine began on Wednesday 17 April, and was stormy from the outset. Harradine was subjected to an intimidating interrogation; Murphy, present in his capacity as Senate leader, was one of the chief prosecutors. After the inquisition, which lasted a day and a half, the executive ruled that Harradine's credentials as a federal executive delegate were unacceptable, and banished him from the meeting.

Harradine's departure was a setback for Whitlam, who had hoped that the enlargement of the federal executive would generate more congenial outcomes from his perspective. Whitlam found the vindictive hostility to Harradine repugnant, but agreed that the comment about 'friends of the Communists' was indefensible and should be withdrawn. Yet, as Harradine's statement underlined, the fundamental issue to Whitlam was not Harradine but the Victorian executive. The recent half-Senate election had provided further evidence of Labor's electoral problems in Victoria, where the DLP continued to prosper. The ALP's voting share was nearly 5% less in Victoria than its overall nation-wide proportion. 'Victoria has the smallest percentage of Labor branch members and Labor parliamentarians because branch members and parliamentarians are accorded a disproportionately small role in Victoria', wrote Whitlam in a letter to Hartley inviting suggestions aimed at improving the 'grave and disappointing. . . situation'. Whitlam and Barnard had submitted their own reform proposals at subsequent meetings with Hartley and Brown. Whitlam had also aired them on television. At the federal executive meeting which barred Harradine, Hartley defended the state executive, denied that it was unrepresentative, and criticized Whitlam for publicly attacking it; the meeting then carried Murphy's motion which implicitly rebuked Whitlam. In a separate development Calwell had complained to the federal executive about Whitlam's 'maliciously false' comment in a recent television interview that Calwell had 'debauched' the debate on the Vietnam War during the 1966 election campaign. 'I deeply resent' it, wrote Calwell, 'and charge him with disloyal and unworthy conduct'. On this issue the federal executive also found against Whitlam, and reprimanded him.

By now Whitlam was disillusioned and angry. The inclusion of FPLP leaders on the federal executive seemed to have made no difference; he was especially nettled that MPs on it like Murphy, Cohen and national ALP president Senator Keeffe had consistently opposed him. Whitlam felt that reform of the Victorian branch might be as far away as ever unless he took drastic action. He decided to resign the leadership and recontest it at a special caucus meeting on 30 April. He outlined his reasons to caucus members in a letter which stressed that reform of the Victorian branch remained his paramount concern. 'The issue is not Mr Harradine personally', Whitlam asserted. It was the conduct of a number of federal executive delegates who, he alleged, were determined to exclude Harradine with a view to keeping a majority of the federal executive opposed to reform in Victoria. This 'direct and deliberate affront' to the Tasmanian branch had created 'a well and deservedly publicized impression of intransigence, factionalism and bitterness'. Whitlam claimed that the FPLP had been 'successfully rehabilitating' the party under his leadership, but the 'great gains and immense labours over fourteen months' had now been 'nullified in two days'. He again stressed Labor's 'appalling and declining electoral performance in Victoria', and attacked the state executive's 'unrepresentative character. . .its alienation of many scores of earnest members', and 'the influence of an outside and secret body upon it' (the TUDC). Whitlam declared that he would construe his re-election to the leadership as approval of his pursuit of reform in Victoria.

Most FPLP members were startled by Whitlam's unprecedented action. Even supporters of his objectives felt this step was rash and unduly disruptive. Barnard had pronounced misgivings about the resignation, but assured Whitlam of his support. When he received invitations and encouragement to contest the vacated leadership himself, Barnard refused them. However, Whitlam did have a rival: after mounting speculation Cairns announced that he would be a contender. His attitude was also summarized in a letter to his FPLP colleagues. Whitlam had displayed 'intellectual arrogance and dangerous folly', asserted the

321

Cairns letter, and had violated Labor traditions by his 'continued refusal to accept majority decisions when they go against him'. The essence of the letter was contained in a single question: 'Whose party is this – ours or his?'. Cairns had very capable numbers men in Cameron and Uren organizing support for him. Barnard and Rex Connor were Whitlam's main backers. Connor was born and grew up in Wollongong and had represented it for nearly two decades, initially as an increasingly discontented backbencher out of favour with the NSW branch controllers and, since 1963, in federal parliament. Now 59, Connor was 'a massive, shambling hulk of a man' with 'a grand vision for Australia's future as the powerhouse of the Southern Hemisphere'. Although he 'had nothing in common with Whitlam in terms of temperament, style, attitudes or background', Connor believed that Whitlam could lead Labor to government and give him the chance to turn his dream into reality.

Whitlam's sensational resignation gave Calwell another opportunity to vent his spleen against his successor and adversary. He drafted a pungent reply to Whitlam's letter slating Whitlam as 'a careerist and an opportunist' trying to impose 'a personality cult' on the party. 'I think you are no more capable of leading the Labor Party to victory than you would be in leading a crippled, blinded, wing-clipped duck to a water hole', contended Calwell before adding, as his parting shot, 'wishing you a long retirement'. Calwell lobbied hard for Cairns. An experienced MP pressured by Calwell 10 minutes before the special caucus meeting described Calwell's malevolence towards Whitlam as 'frightening'.

Whitlam won the ballot by 38 votes to 32. This margin was smaller than generally expected, and much smaller than Whitlam had anticipated when he announced his resignation. Clearly some MPs felt that Whitlam was being too reckless and disruptive. He was fortunate that Barnard had resisted the pressure from Cameron and others to stand against him. Cairns, who would not have challenged Whitlam if Barnard had, came so close that if there had been a Barnard-Whitlam contest on 30 April Barnard would surely have won. Cairns was satisfied that the narrowness of Whitlam's victory would make him mend his ways and modify his approach in future; Hartley, along with Whitlam's other Victorian opponents, drew similar conclusions. Whitlam and Freudenberg, however, have claimed that the federal executive was more chastened than Whitlam, who maintained his endeavours to achieve reform of the Victorian branch. Nonetheless observers sensed that the closeness of the result had jolted Whitlam. Never again did he place his leadership so rashly at risk.

Later in 1968 Cairns emerged emotionally bruised from a different contest. His electorate, Yarra, was abolished in a redistribution, and many of its voters were included in a geographically expanded electorate of Melbourne. The sitting member for Melbourne as it existed before the redistribution, Calwell, announced that he would stand for new Melbourne, which would clearly be one of Labor's safest seats. Cairns was quietly angry. He felt entitled to new Melbourne, not only because it contained a large proportion of Yarra voters, but also because Calwell, Cairns believed, had previously encouraged him to feel that he could take over Melbourne when Calwell retired. (The ALP had now instituted a compulsory retirement age in three states, but Victoria was not one of them.) Cairns was annoyed that 72-year-old Calwell showed no awareness of the obvious reality that he was past his prime. Encouraged by Uren and others, Cairns announced that he too would nominate for Melbourne. The prospect of a public brawl between the Victorian ALP's two most nationally prominent MPs posed an awkward dilemma for the party. Attempts to find a compromise were unsuccessful, and the Victorian executive was unwilling to arbitrate. Although the traditional party reluctance to unseat a sitting member worked in Calwell's favour, majority opinion in the party supported Cairns in the dispute. Chamberlain was among the Labor figures who respectfully tried to persuade Calwell to vacate Melbourne, but he refused to budge. 'With all due modesty', Calwell declared, 'I know of nobody in the party who has done as much as I have for it and for Australia'. Eventually Cairns grudgingly backed down and agreed to stand for Lalor, a sprawling electorate in Melbourne's outer western suburbs. He retained Lalor with little difficulty for the rest of his parliamentary career. Calwell continued as MHR for Melbourne until he retired aged 76.

Whitlam and the FPLP were adjusting to a new prime minister. During 1967 Whitlam had established a clear ascendancy over Holt, but at the end of that year Holt disappeared while swimming in strong surf at a Victorian beach. This sensation and the ensuing canvassing in anti-Labor ranks for a new prime minister under the scrutiny of the media marked a turning point in the style and coverage of Australian politics. Developments in Canberra have always been reported by journalists writing for their newspapers with varying expertise, accuracy and fairness, but before 1968 the political whirl had not, by and large, generated books of substance, stature and literary merit; apart from a superb short volume written by a journalist about the ill-fated Scullin government, there was little published besides occasional anecdotal books. However, Alan Reid broke new ground with *The Power Struggle*, an absorbing account of the contest for the prime ministership after Holt's disappearance. All the drama was unveiled, including the Country Party leader's veto which dashed the hopes of one of the leading Liberal contenders, William McMahon. *The Power Struggle* became a best-seller, and before long there was a spate of books about Australian politics.

This proliferation was related to the increased coverage of politics on television. The handling of the media by senior politicians had been significant before 1960 and important since (notably in SA under Dunstan), but from 1968 onwards the ability of party leaders to acquit themselves well on television became absolutely crucial. The new Liberal leader, J.G. Gorton, owed his success primarily to the effective television and radio appearances he made while his parliamentary colleagues were evaluating the various contenders. But the increased importance of television had serious implications, especially for the ALP as a party committed to reform, because of the medium's tendency to accentuate personal, trivial and gladiatorial aspects rather than the substantial issues. Being able to look good and sound good in two-sentence 'grabs' for the television news became all-important.

Cairns's fortunes continued to fluctuate in 1969. He enhanced his reputation as the left's leading intellectual activist, willing to endorse and promote radical causes as patron (never organizer). He remained the hero of the draft resisters and demonstrators who were opposing conscription and the Vietnam War with increasing momentum and growing support from the rest of the community. This made Cairns anathema to the conservatives. His image as the embodiment of rational and moral non-violence lent a sickening irony to the brutal bashing inflicted upon Cairns and his family in their home in August 1969. 'Who do you think you are, God?' sneered one of the intruders before clobbering Cairns into unconsciousness. Cairns and some relatives and friends were taken to hospital. He did not recuperate quickly. Years later Beazley wondered whether Cairns ever did quite recover fully. 'There is no doubt that the assault originated from deep within Richmond; the motives and the actors are known but lips are sealed'.

In March 1969 Wyndham resigned as national ALP secretary. He was tired and very frustrated that after six years the grand plans for an adequately staffed national secretariat for the party still seemed so far from fruition. Also significant was the marked coolness which had recently developed between him and Whitlam. When 71-year-old Colbourne stepped down at last as NSW secretary, a position he had first filled 39 years earlier, Wyndham was offered it and accepted. With more support staff and a more directly influential role in the party's administration, Wyndham saw this switch as a promotion rather than the opposite. However, queries surfaced about his administration of party finances in Canberra. His sympathizers considered that these queries could be answered easily and any problems were simply a reflection of the excessive workload he had shouldered for too long, but they were the last straw for Wyndham. Although Whitlam and others were prepared to support his cause, Wyndham disappeared and refused to defend himself or work for the ALP again.

A new national secretary was appointed by the federal executive on 2 April. Private discussions beforehand had paved the way for Burns to fill the position on a part-time basis while continuing with his duties as Queensland state secretary. Burns, however, had misgivings about becoming national secretary, and Virgo informed his fellow SA delegate, 32-year-old Mick Young, that there had been a change of plan and the job would now go not to Burns but to Chamberlain. Young was horrified. In view of the previous disharmony between Whitlam and Chamberlain, Young believed that to revert to 68-year-old Chamberlain as national secretary 'would be an absolute political disaster'; he said he was prepared to stand against Chamberlain himself. Oliver nominated Young, the delegates voted, and the result was a tie, seven votes apiece. Another ballot was held, with the same outcome. Chamberlain then withdrew his candidacy. Young had won the position, but was well aware that his support had been derived from delegates voting against Chamberlain rather than for him. As the meeting ended, Young reflected that a federal conference was three months away, a federal election was expected in about six months, and the party was in desperate financial straits. 'After locking up the meeting venue, I found myself standing alone on the foot-path on Ainslie Avenue late at night wondering what the hell I had allowed myself to get into.'

Fortunately for the ALP, Young met the challenge superbly. Having left school at 15 and taken up shearing, he had become a union representative as a 20-year-old. At that age he also made an eye-opening overseas trip, which provided a glimpse of Russia and sparked a lasting fascination with China. In mid-1964 he was elected, with Cameron's firm support, as organizer of the SA state branch. In 1968 he progressed, in the orderly promotion which was by now customary in the SA branch, to the state secretary's position vacated by Virgo, who had succeeded Walsh as MHA for Edwardstown. Young possessed dedication and superb organizational skills, although he was sometimes guilty of a lack of attention to detail. He was astute, enterprising, resourceful and receptive to fresh ideas and approaches. When the SA branch broke with tradition and chose as its organizer and his assistant not a unionist but Combe, a university graduate who had attended a privileged private school, Young's firm endorsement of Combe was crucial to the appointment. Young was close to Cameron, Toohey and Virgo, and absorbed much from them – notably an attachment to the power-sharing ethos of the SA branch, and the principle that the secretary should serve all sections of the party – but he was his own man. During the dramatic federal executive meeting which barred Harradine and triggered Whitlam's resignation, Young drafted a cleverly phrased compromise motion which, if carried (and it very nearly was), would have handled the Harradine problem by censuring him while accepting his credentials as a delegate, whereas Cameron wanted to drive Harradine out of the party without delay.

As national secretary Young quickly became a popular and respected figure. In an era when the ALP was adjusting to having in its ranks more highly educated middle-class members like Whitlam and Dunstan, Mick Young's classic bush union background was a pleasing reminder of the party's traditional roots. Whereas Wyndham was somewhat introverted, unmistakably English and slightly built, Young was extroverted, unmistakably Australian, and possessed the burly frame of an ex-shearer who had almost been a 200 sheep a day man. Whitlam's Napoleonic tendencies had been encouraged by Wyndham – who had supported Whitlam's decision to resign and recontest the leadership – but Young strongly recommended to Whitlam that sensible consultation and discussion represented the best way to overcome difficulties. Initially Young had reservations about Whitlam's imperiousness and was closer to FPLP left-wingers like Murphy and O'Byrne, but he gradually became an admirer of Whitlam's intellect and immense drive for work. The admiration was mutual, and the pair formed a most productive partnership. Whitlam came to rely increasingly on Young's down-to-earth advice based on attributes Whitlam lacked – an ability to mix widely and easily within the labour movement, and an intuitive understanding of the electorate's likely reaction to particular events and policies.

The 1969 federal conference was one of the ALP's most constructive. Young's keenness to make it a success was infectious, and the enlarged conference, with the inclusion for the first time of the parliamentary leaders in each state and the FPLP as fully-fledged delegates, functioned effectively. The tendency of state delegations to vote in rigid blocks, so frequent at previous conferences, was less apparent, and the contributions from MPs like Whitlam, Dunstan, Holding, Beazley and Murphy kept debate lively and constructive. However, there were some tense moments. Cameron made a fervent last-ditch stand against state aid, and later in the same debate Downing clashed heatedly with Murphy and Senator John Wheeldon, a WA delegate. There was another reminder of past internal controversy when Chamberlain successfully resisted Whitlam's attempt to obtain maximum flexibility for a future Labor government concerning the extrication of Australian soldiers from Vietnam. Chamberlain's amendment, seconded by Virgo, required an incoming Labor government immediately to 'notify the United States government that all Australian forces will be withdrawn from Vietnam'. Another potential bone of contention was Harradine's endorsement as a Tasmanian delegate, but Young successfully moved that federal conference should follow the federal executive's recommendation that Harradine was 'not a fit and proper person' to be a credentialled conference delegate. The generally productive, cohesive and forward-looking tone of the conference boosted Labor's stocks substantially (especially since the proceedings were open to the media, and some sessions were televised). Whitlam's performance enhanced his stature within the party and the nation as a whole. Suddenly the pundits began to acknowledge that Labor had regained political credibility.

The ALP was now committed to a wide-ranging programme of reform much more comprehensive than it or any other Australian party had ever devised. The creation of this blueprint was a fine collective achievement, involving important contributions from MPs, staffers and party officials together with activists, academics and other expert advisers; but Whitlam's role far exceeded anyone else's. He was personally most closely associated with the new policies in education, health and urban development. The 1969 conference had endorsed the concept of needs-based grants to schools irrespective of religious affiliation, and approved the establishment of an Australian Schools Commission to administer this funding. Labor's main objectives in health policy were to replace the existing inequitable health insurance arrangements with a comprehensive universal scheme, and to reinstate the free hospital care introduced by the Chifley government and dismantled under Menzies. Ever since his maiden speech in 1953 Whitlam had insisted that the national government should take responsibility for urban development so that Australians, especially in outer suburban areas, were not deprived of adequate transport, sewerage, local welfare centres and a host of other community services.

Whitlam's brilliant advocacy of Labor's reform programme was an important ingredient in the remarkable ALP resurgence at the October 1969 federal election. He had gained the same mastery over Gorton in parliament and on the hustings that he had established over Holt. The Liberal campaign was slipshod, and Labor did well even though, as Young admitted, campaign planning

> was pathetic. . .and fund-raising was non-existent. However, we did the best we could. We patched things up and struggled through that period only to witness on election night results beyond our wildest dreams.

Labor's voting share had climbed from under 40% in 1966 to nearly 47% and the coalition government's majority had been slashed from 39 seats to 7 in the greatest anti-government swing since 1931. It was all the more astounding because the government had not seemed vulnerable: the economy was thriving, with strong growth and relatively low unemployment. This result was of course a tremendous fillip to Labor morale; coming in the election after Labor's nadir of 1966, it was another reminder of the ALP's resilience and capacity for renewal. Whitlam's unassailable stature in the party after his fine campaign was acknowledged by his former leadership rival, Cairns:

> Mr Whitlam has passed the test of leadership. . .We have functioned extremely well over the past twelve months in the Opposition. His conduct of the campaign was first rate. I think his presentation has been more articulate and successful than any since the war-time days of John Curtin.

Labor's buoyant mood after the election was coupled with a firm resolve to gain the extra ground necessary to win government. It was obvious to Young that there was room for improvement in Labor's campaign preparation and management, particularly in the way Labor traditionally ran detached campaigns in each state with different styles and priorities. There had to be better co-ordination and nation-wide direction in future. Also, it was clear that Labor had done much better in some states than others. The ALP had won four of the five Tasmanian seats and six out of nine in WA. Labor had also bounced back superbly in SA after the disastrous result there in 1966, obtaining a swing of 11·66% and winning five more seats (eight in all out of 12). However, Labor did not have a majority of seats in NSW despite winning an additional five, and in Victoria the ALP had not even managed to win a third of the seats.

68. Les Haylen and wife Silvia watch as their son Wayne receives from the NSW Police Commissioner a bravery award for chasing and apprehending Peter Kocan. (*National Library*)

67. Arthur Calwell, bloodied but unbowed after the attempt on his life, points to his coat lapel where bullet fragments left their mark. (*Herald and Weekly Times*)

69. The new-look FPLP leadership quartet, 1967. From left: S. Cohen, L. Barnard, G. Whitlam, L. Murphy. (*National Library*)

70. Jim Cairns exultant at the Moratorium. (*Age*)

71. 'Electric Eric' Reece. (*Mercury*)

72. Paul Keating and Jack Lang. (*Mitchell Library*)

73. The stirring Blacktown campaign launch, 1972. Bob Hawke and Clyde Cameron watch as a Whitlam admirer makes a personal tribute. (*John Fairfax*)

The transformation of the Vietnam War from a damaging issue for Labor into the reverse was well under way. Television reportage had reinforced a growing perception in Australia not only that it was a grisly conflict but that the Americans, along with their South Vietnamese and Australian allies, were scarcely making any headway at all towards winning it. By 1969 the Americans themselves were reconsidering their involvement, and Labor's opposition to the war was clearly being vindicated. Since taking over the FPLP leadership Whitlam had been more restrained in his pronouncements on Vietnam than Calwell. While Cairns and others continued to associate themselves with demonstrators fulminating against conscription and Australia's presence in Vietnam, Whitlam did not repudiate them but, despite pressure from Chamberlain and Calwell, did not join them either. Some Labor MPs felt that by mixing with raw and diverse groups of dissenters on the streets they were running a risk of being unwittingly involved in – and, therefore, tarnished by – a demonstration that went violently wrong.

The anti-war movement in Australia organized a day of protest on 8 May 1970. This was Australia's first Vietnam moratorium, and there were large rallies across the nation. Easily the biggest was the spectacular march Cairns led in Melbourne, where 70 000 participated. The peacefulness of the Melbourne demonstration was a great relief to many, and a triumphant vindication for Cairns in particular. It was perhaps the most exhilarating experience of his life to see this vast assemblage sit down together in Bourke Street and observe two minutes' silence. 'Nobody thought this could be done', he assured them exultantly.

On 30 May 1970 two important state elections were held, in Victoria and SA. Before the campaign began in Victoria Labor people sensed that the Bolte government seemed more vulnerable than ever before. A series of episodes had given them good reason to conclude that Bolte was losing his appeal, and Labor was attracting more support from special-interest groups, notably teachers. There was also optimism in Labor ranks in SA, where Premier Hall had felt obliged to modify the worst effects of the gerrymander after Labor's crusade on that issue in 1968. The new electoral arrangements still fell far short of one vote one value, but they were notably fairer than the previous inequitable system, and Labor was accordingly confident of returning to office at the early election called by Hall. The special problems SA citizens experienced intermittently with their water supply had convinced Hall that dam construction could provide him with a winning issue. ALP strategists disagreed, and their view was reinforced by the results of Labor's opinion polling.

Labor's campaign in Victoria was marred by a fiasco over state aid. The precise wording of Labor's state aid policy had been the subject of lengthy debate by senior Victorian ALP figures. Bitter animosity between Hartley and Holding exacerbated the situation. Hartley and others wanted to devise a formula consistent with their hostility to state aid without infringing the 1969 federal conference's endorsement of it (which Holding had supported); ultimately they proposed a form of words which advocated temporary financial assistance for schools prior to the ultimate 'phasing out' of state aid. Holding and the caucus executive protested that this would be electoral suicide, but the state executive, particularly Hartley and state ALP president George Crawford, stood firm. Holding contacted Whitlam and Dunstan. Both were angry about the Victorian executive's intransigence. Dunstan was concerned that it might harm his campaign in SA. Whitlam intervened by directly contacting Hartley, as did other non-Victorians including Young, Barnard and Keeffe. When the press picked up the essence of the dispute and emblazoned and embellished it, Labor's morale sagged and the whole ALP campaign faltered. Eventually Whitlam publicly dissociated Holding, Dunstan, Young and himself from the 'phasing out' reference, and the Labor leader in the Legislative Council, Galbally, followed suit in a separate statement. Despite the shambles over state aid, Labor managed to increase its parliamentary strength on polling day, winning 22 seats in the 73-member Assembly (16 in 1967) with a voting share of 41·42% (37·90% in 1967).

In the other election on 30 May 1970 SA Labor was victorious. The lessons of the 1968 rural oversights had been learned. This time the countryside was not excluded from opinion surveys, and there was a special rural policy speech by Corcoran. Although Dunstan and Young expressed concern that the upheaval in Victoria might disrupt the smooth ALP campaign in their state, their objective of a low-key, undramatic campaign was basically met. The Liberals were flummoxed when Labor refused to match their singlemindedness about water supply and declined to make Dunstan the dominant focus of the ALP campaign as in 1968. Instead, Labor highlighted a range of issues, and emphasized the competence of its entire aspiring ministerial team, not just the leader. One of these alternative ministers was not yet even in parliament. Dunstan had informed caucus that he would not be able to carry any longer the burden of the Attorney-General's portfolio in addition to being Premier, Treasurer and Development minister. He persuaded caucus to allow him to approach a top lawyer who had been a longstanding but relatively inactive ALP member, Len King QC, with an offer of guaranteed preselection and immediate promotion to cabinet. Despite the substantial loss of income this step represented for King, he accepted Dunstan's offer:

> The answer's yes. You've jogged my conscience. My family could not have afforded to send me to law school and I only went through because of Ben Chifley's provision for training allowances for returned servicemen. I owe my career to the Labor Party...

Labor's electoral strategy was vindicated when the Liberals' focus on water ran out of steam, and Labor cruised to a predictable victory by seven seats even though its voting share declined marginally. Labor under Dunstan now had a secure Assembly majority, and could resume the transformation of SA which had been interrupted in 1968.

The mid-1970 state conference in Victoria was predictably fiery after the state aid controversy during the election campaign. In the vengeful atmosphere there were recriminations aplenty. Whitlam was censured, and a complaint about his conduct was forwarded to the federal executive. Galbally was suspended from the ALP for 12 months, and appealed to the federal executive against this penalty.

Coincidentally there was also upheaval at the NSW state conference in June 1970. Some left-wingers seemed content with the token crumbs of power in the state branch bestowed by the dominant right-wing faction ruled by Oliver, but Ray Gietzelt and his brother Arthur were not. The Gietzelts were also furious that Murphy was under attack in some right-wing NSW ALP quarters for representing unions as a lawyer, and they vigorously pursued allegations of improper administration by state secretary Peter Westerway, who had been appointed to that position (to follow Colbourne's very long stint in it and

Wyndham's very short one) after a varied background in academia, television and advertising. At one point during the acrimonious conference there was uproar when the microphone was switched off as left-wing MHR Uren rose to speak. Even before the conference the extent of the factional feuding had prompted widespread representations for a more balanced power-sharing structure in the state branch. Among these lobbyists were a factionally diverse group of FPLP members including Whitlam, Murphy, Daly, Uren and Stewart. Some state MPs also associated themselves with this pressure, although their influence in such matters had declined during the five years Labor had spent on the NSW opposition benches since 1965 while corruption flourished under Premier Askin. Nevertheless, all the overtures and pressure cut no ice with Oliver. At the conference he bluntly indicated that any notion of power sharing was out of the question.

However, Oliver was on his way out after a decade as NSW ALP president. Now 68, he had distracting internal ructions to deal with in his power base at the once-mighty AWU. Poised to succeed Oliver as the commanding machine figure in NSW was John Ducker. Yorkshire-born Ducker arrived in Australia in 1950 aged 18, and found work in an iron foundry. He quickly became one of Short's Grouper activists in the ironworkers' union, and began his ascent in the NSW labour movement. By mid-1970 he had become assistant secretary of the NSW Labor Council with a seat on the ACTU executive, and vice-president of the NSW ALP with a seat on its state executive. His Yorkshire accent and difficulty in pronouncing 'th' gave his speech a distracting quaintness which induced some observers and opponents to underestimate him, but they did so at their peril. 'Bruvver' Ducker possessed ambition, charm, toughness and a penetrating mind. In debate he was a formidable rival with a quick-witted and aggressive style; his slashing denigration of Ray Gietzelt at the 1970 NSW conference was 'an electrifying speech'. Ducker was to reign supreme in the NSW machine during the 1970s as Oliver had during the 1960s.

Important talks were held in Adelaide to determine the SA branch's attitudes to these controversial developments in Victoria and NSW. For years Cameron had generally supported the Victorian executive, and SA's federal executive delegates (although he had not been one himself) had done likewise. However, Dunstan, who believed that the Victorian executive had flagrantly breached Labor's state aid policy and outrageously humiliated Holding in the process, was intent upon persuading Cameron that a different approach was now warranted. Virgo, Toohey and Combe agreed with Dunstan, and were present at these crucial private discussions with Cameron. Young, then overseas, was the only significant SA Labor figure absent, and he too had been singularly unimpressed by the Victorian executive's conduct. The persuaders wanted Cameron not merely to endorse action against the Victorians, but to spearhead the operation himself at the next federal executive meeting in August. They reminded him of certain recent episodes. There was the Calwell-Cairns fight for the seat of Melbourne, when Cameron had supported Cairns and denounced the Victorian executive after its failure to do likewise had resulted in Cairns's humiliating backdown. There was also the federal executive's censure of Cameron for publicly attacking Oliver in the course of Cameron's long-running war with the Dougherty-Oliver AWU regime; Cameron had been infuriated when Hartley and Brown supported this censure motion. The ignominious contribution Hartley had made in facilitating, through inept drafting, the 1966 policy change on state aid still rankled with Cameron, who was contemptuously dismissive of

Hartley as a political operator. Eventually Cameron told the others that he was prepared to move against the Victorian branch, but only as part of a package deal involving intervention in the NSW branch as well. Although Dunstan was initially firmly opposed to action against NSW, a consensus was reached that NSW would be tackled first and Victoria afterwards.

Various considerations shaped Cameron's reaction. The Victorians had antagonized him recently, but a far higher priority for him was NSW. By pursuing intervention in NSW Cameron could strike a blow against Oliver (a longstanding enemy), curb and hopefully eradicate the rumoured administrative abuses and improper preselection practices in that state, and create a less stifling environment for NSW left-wingers whose views were more acceptable to Cameron than the state branch controllers like Oliver. There were other factors too. Having introduced a system of shadow portfolios for the FPLP executive, Whitlam had appointed Cameron as shadow Labour minister. Becoming minister for Labour in an ALP government was Cameron's supreme ambition, and the 1969 election result suggested that after over two decades in opposition his great goal was tantalizingly close – provided Labor could get its own house in order.

The crucial federal executive meeting began in Broken Hill on 3 August 1970. Hartley soon became suspicious because Cameron, attending his first federal executive meeting since 1947, 'kept on furtively looking at pieces of paper' and 'was very abrasive' about Victoria. Hartley's suspicions were confirmed when the meeting came to consider complaints lodged about the situation in NSW by the Gietzelts and other aggrieved activists. Murphy proposed a mildly worded motion directing federal executive officers to investigate the complaints, and also 'to initiate discussions. . .and to recommend what steps if any should be taken to advance the interests of the Party in New South Wales'. In a remarkable but characteristically shrewd manoeuvre, Ducker seconded the motion authorizing intervention in his own state branch. He and Westerway, Ducker asserted, had nothing to hide, and welcomed any procedures that would improve the administration and performance of NSW Labor. The motion was carried comfortably, although Hartley, Brown and the Victorians' firm ally Chamberlain – aware of the implications in the motion for identical action against Victoria – voted against it. During debate on matters arising from the Victorian election Cameron moved a similarly worded motion proposing intervention in Victoria. Hartley and Chamberlain both spoke heatedly against it. Brown followed them and went berserk, threatening to split the party by leading a breakaway faction. After this tirade certain delegates who had agreed to support Cameron changed their minds, and he had to make a tactical withdrawal.

The Victorians' reprieve was shortlived. Next morning Cameron and Young overheard Brown jubilantly telephoning Crawford back in Melbourne to gloat about his success in making Cameron retreat. The Victorian chiefs indulged in further provocative conduct, notably when Crawford publicly announced that 'we are not going to be told what to do' and described the federal executive meeting as a 'Mad Hatter's Tea Party'. After these and other instances of inflammatory defiance by the Victorians, Cameron was soon convinced that the Broken Hill waverers – including Beazley, Don Willesee (who was on the executive as Senate deputy after Cohen's fatal seizure during the 1969 campaign), Burns and the Northern Territory's delegate Jock Nelson – were back in the pro-intervention camp more firmly than ever; Cameron himself was determined to make certain that there would be no escape for the Victorians next time.

Cameron's painstaking planning ensured that this operation was much better organized than any previous intervention in a state branch in the ALP's history. He used a wide range of legal expertise, and absorbed the lessons of the intervention precedents. Among his legal advisers were senior members of the Participants, a Victorian ALP faction dedicated to reform of their state branch. Cameron even consulted appraisals of the technicalities of intervention prepared by Barwick and Kerr in the mid-1950s. From his research he concluded that a number of steps were necessary. Specific charges had to be formulated. The Victorian controllers had to be given adequate time to prepare a defence. When the charges were heard it would be prudent to inflict a separate penalty for each proven offence; otherwise, in the event of a collective penalty being imposed to cover a number of substantiated offences, even if only one of those findings was reversed on appeal the entire penalty might be set aside. Cameron's ultimate aim was not merely to replace the Victorian executive, but to dissolve the entire state branch. This action would avoid some of the problems the interveners experienced in the mid-1950s, when the DLP after the split won litigation entitling it to ownership of funds, records and other property. Whitlam and other federal executive delegates were restless about the time-consuming path Cameron had chosen, but sensibly acknowledged that no one was better equipped than Cameron to mastermind an operation of this nature and it was best to let him do it his way. Meanwhile Cameron and Young continued with their exhaustive preparations. Young was compiling a detailed list of controversial public statements by the Victorian chiefs, and sifting the comments he had received after inviting Victorian ALP members to complain about their state branch. One of these appeals for intervention came from Frank Anstey's son Daron. 'Clean it up and we can march again', he wrote, 'I am 79 and would like to see a Labor Government before I kick off'.

At the federal executive meeting on 29 August Cameron's motion authorizing intervention was carried comfortably. Young sent each Victorian executive member a list of 13 charges to be investigated at an inquiry beginning in Melbourne on 5 September. Cameron directed the proceedings proficiently despite being deluged with abuse. The upshot was that four of the charges were sustained, and on 14 September the federal executive carried Cameron's crucial motion 'that the Victorian Branch of the ALP no longer exists'. This motion also installed Burns (who had succeeded Keeffe as federal president) and Young as temporary administrators of the ALP in Victoria, appointed Crean and Hawke as Victoria's federal executive delegates, and created an advisory council to make recommendations along stipulated guidelines about the reconstruction of the state branch. All this was something to savour for the Participants, who included lawyers John Button, John Cain (junior), Frank Costigan and Michael Duffy, and also for their allies such as Whitlam staffers Freudenberg and Race Mathews. Among the deposed regime Brown had become increasingly subdued, seemingly concerned about preserving his Senate seat, but Hartley, Crawford and some associates like organizer Bob Hogg fought bitterly to the end. Some state executive members with left-wing connections like Cairns, Hawke and influential unionist Ted Innes were ambivalent about intervention. All three, together with Holding, eventually indicated that they would accept the outcome, and agreed to serve on the advisory council alongside Button, other Participants and Peter Redlich, co-partner with Holding in a firm of solicitors.

Cameron's motion abolishing the Victorian branch stipulated a proportional representation voting system for the structure to replace it. What seemed to be envisaged was an enforced variant of the sort of informal power-sharing arrangments which had served the SA branch well for over two decades. However, the SA branch had traditionally been more tranquil than ideologically turbulent Victoria, and the upshot in Victoria was accentuated factionalism. The evicted Hartley-Crawford-Hogg forces licked their wounds, and came out fighting as the tightly organized Socialist Left faction. The Participants retained their separate identity in a small group which was seen as occupying a right-wing position on most issues. In the centre was the Labor Unity faction led by Holding, Hawke, Innes, Redlich, historian Ian Turner and Bill Landeryou, the 29-year-old secretary of the Storemen and Packers' Union. When the new proportional representation and power-sharing arrangements were implemented at the 1971 state conference, the initial composition of the 18-member administrative committee, which was created to take over most of the old state executive's functions, was nine places for Labor Unity, Socialist Left seven, and two positions for the Participants (later known as the Independents). A mild surprise was the election of Crawford as state ALP president, with Innes and Hawke as vice-presidents. The position of state secretary, now confined to organization without scope for the policy pronouncements Hartley used to make, went to Jean Melzer, a former local branch secretary who had felt fettered and alienated by the rigid centralization and lack of consultation and information characteristic of the pre-intervention regime. Her predecessor, Hartley, showed that he was not a spent force by being chosen as a delegate to both federal executive and federal conference as well as being elected to the administrative committee.

Power sharing was also institutionalized in NSW. The investigation into NSW affairs authorized by the federal executive was conducted by Burns, and his findings were outlined in a scathing report. His indictment of the conduct of the NSW right-wing controllers covered 'contempt for proper procedures' in financial dealings and the pursuit of factional advantage in a variety of practices, including stacking of annual conferences, instances of bias by the conference chairman, 'rorted' preselections and exploitation of the party journal. 'Complete restructuring in New South Wales is the only way to overcome this very disturbing situation', Burns concluded in his report. Ducker realized the inevitability of reform and sensed that it would be less rigorous if he co-operated than if he emulated the Victorians' defiance. Accordingly, change was accomplished relatively smoothly in NSW while the fate of the Victorian branch was tending to monopolize the headlines. Proportional representation was introduced in NSW for the election of delegates to federal executive and federal conference, two assistant secretaries, members of the administrative committee (which, as in Victoria, was created to replace the old state executive), and other machinery and policy committees. Afterwards the New Right, as Ducker and his closest associates like assistant Labor Council secretary Barrie Unsworth and assistant state ALP secretary Geoff Cahill sometimes described themselves, remained the dominant faction although they had conceded some power to the left.

The Burns report to the federal executive contained some critical remarks about a preselection contest won by Keating in 1968. Since parting with the Ramrods, Keating had been striving to win preselection for Banks, a safe Labor seat about to be vacated by its retiring MHR. Still in his early twenties, Keating showed a keen understanding that the key to winning a rank-and-file preselection lay in painstakingly building local support. Like many aspiring Labor MPs before him, Keating was faced with tasks like persuading people to join the party, ensuring that they attended enough meetings to be eligible for a preselection vote, and checking that the branch secretary correctly recorded their attendance. His prominence at the Youth Council, where he was president (and Brereton was secretary), had also contributed to Keating's growing reputation in the NSW branch, but his ambitiousness was resented in some quarters. Keating was well placed to win Banks, but when it was significantly altered in a redistribution he opted to contest adjacent Blaxland, where his rivals included the vulnerable veteran sitting member Jim Harrison and a well-credentialled candidate with left-wing support, Bill Junor.

The Blaxland preselection votes were counted at a Bankstown scout hall on a Saturday evening in October 1968. After all other candidates had been eliminated and their supporters' preferences distributed, the position was Keating 108, Junor 124, with the validity of 49 uncounted votes under challenge. The local returning officer, a left-winger, refused to count the disputed votes. If the security and ultimate validity of these votes were left to him, the Keating camp feared the worst. There was no phone in the hall, so Keating's chief scrutineer Brereton roared away on his motor bike to see what could be done. Increasingly desperate, he eventually decided to contact Whitlam, who ordered the state branch's returning officer, Lindsay North, to get out of bed and collect the ballot box. Shortly afterwards Uren and other Junor supporters were incensed to learn that North had pronounced Keating the victor by 145 votes to 125. The reasons why the left cried foul over this questionable verdict were outlined in Burns's report to the federal executive, but there was no denying that Keating was well on his way, holding one of the safest ALP seats in the nation at the age of 25. Colbourne regarded Keating as a brash upstart, and his disapproval was reinforced by Keating's aspiration to have Colbourne's old enemy Lang readmitted to the party. At the 1971 NSW conference Keating's motion permitting Lang to rejoin was carried after Keating assured delegates spiritedly that Labor would be 'a party of great and unyielding spite' if it continued to ostracize the 94-year-old Big Fella.

Young and other ALP strategists hoping that intervention in NSW and Victoria would have a beneficial impact on Labor's fortunes nationally were buoyed by the defeat of anti-Labor state governments in WA and Tasmania. In WA the social problems left in the wake of accelerated development under the Liberals contributed significantly to the election result. Of the incoming Labor cabinet only Premier Tonkin and his deputy Herb Graham had been ministers before, although 69-year-old Tonkin was vastly experienced after 38 years in parliament and a decade administering various portfolios under three different premiers. Still in harness as state secretary and keen to keep Labor governments up to scratch was Chamberlain. His relationship with Tonkin over the years had been generally harmonious and, although they disagreed sharply in mid-1971 over the environmental implications of a proposed alumina refinery, there was no repetition of Chamberlain's spectacular and damaging clashes with other parliamentary leaders like Whitlam and Bert Hawke.

The 1972 Tasmanian election was a triumph for Reece. His own vote in Braddon was the highest ever recorded, and Labor obtained 21 of the 35 Assembly seats with a voting share approaching 55%. Allowed to choose his own ministers, a concession reflecting his dominance, Reece included three talented men first elected in 1969. Doug Lowe was a former state ALP secretary who had been appointed to that position in 1965 as a 22-year-old electrical fitter. Neil Batt was a teacher and history researcher who had headed the moratorium movement in

Tasmania. Michael Barnard, nephew of Lance, was yet another MP from the Barnard family stable. Reece concluded that he had a mandate to resume his 1960s governmental style based on hydro-powered development. However, it was clear that disgruntled Labor Youth activists and others disagreed, and Reece soon had uncomfortable internal dissension to deal with as well as the continuing discord in the state branch arising from the Harradine saga.

Developments in Queensland state politics were less encouraging for Labor's national strategists. At the 1972 Queensland election Labor continued the gradual improvement in voting share it had maintained since 1957, without really threatening the incumbent coalition government now headed by Premier Bjelke-Petersen, a wily hill-billy. The government looked vulnerable after allegations that the Premier and six other ministers had accepted donations of shares from a foreign-owned mining company which had received very advantageous treatment from the government. Bjelke-Petersen further illuminated his government's priorities by authorizing brutal police action against demonstrators. The coalition was also plagued by internal disunity. Yet Labor was unable to capitalize, and the gerrymander was not the sole reason – the same mining company had also compromised certain ALP identities.

The TLC group headed by Egerton still dominated the Queensland ALP. Egerton was widely regarded in Labour circles as a boorish bigoted boss renowned for his ruthlessness and also his distinctive dress, which often featured white shoes and garish wide tie. At the 1971 Queensland ALP conference Hayden advocated that homosexuality by consenting adults should be decriminalized, but the proposal was narrowly defeated after Egerton scorned the idea, belittled Hayden, and referred to supporters of the proposal as 'poofters'. The contrast between Labor under the Egerton regime and the ALP in SA could hardly have been starker. The Queensland controllers seemed primarily interested in entrenching their own power. Cloaking themselves in a spurious militant purity, they purged dissenters and labelled them 'Groupers'. Renewed tensions with the AWU led once again to its disaffiliation from the party. The Egerton clique seemed indifferent to the impact of its conduct on the party's electoral prospects, and showed no inclination to adopt sophisticated campaigning techniques to maximize Labor's attractiveness to voters. When Gair was Premier, Egerton and his Trades Hall associates had advocated more effective use of Labor's radio station 4KQ as a propaganda medium, but they were content now to run 4KQ on a purely commercial basis and reap the profits.

For Whitlam and the FPLP 1971 was a year of consolidation. Optimism, purposefulness and unity characterized a successful federal conference where Labor's programme received a final polish before the federal election due in 1972. Also successful was the trailblazing visit to China of an ALP delegation comprising Whitlam, Young, Burns, Patterson, Freudenberg and an expert on Chinese affairs, Dr Stephen Fitzgerald. It was not merely that Whitlam performed creditably in public talks with the Chinese Premier. The fact that the visit occurred just before President Nixon signalled a major thaw in Chinese-American relations by also visiting China confirmed that Labor was far more in touch with contemporary international developments than its embarrassed opponents, who had been loud in their criticism of Whitlam's visit. Later in 1971 Young inspired another unusual initiative by an opposition, a mid-term policy campaign.

Bob Hawke was now a household name. He had fulfilled his ambition to become ACTU president, and his energy, capability, eagerness to enlarge the activities of the organized union movement and, above all, his remarkable skill in utilizing the media were making him the best-known trade union leader in Australian history. He had initially subscribed to the orthodox views of the dominant Victorian ALP faction in the 1960s – favouring unity tickets, loathing the DLP, and hostile to the United States – and attained the ACTU presidency with left-wing support. But unionists and, through the media, the Australian people were realizing that Hawke was not the militant ogre simplistically portrayed by conservative detractors. His flair for resolving industrial conflict was becoming legendary, and television viewers saw a vibrant character who expressed himself with candour and clearly cared about his country. (Few viewers glimpsed first-hand the drunken larrikinism and other excesses of the 'wild colonial boy' of Australian public life.) By 1972 Hawke was recognized as a compelling spokesman for the labour movement and a formidable campaigner on the hustings. The left in Victoria, however, had become suspicious of Hawke because of his ultimate acceptance of intervention and his skill as an industrial fireman extinguishing disputes, a role which had a special political dimension since the coalition government in Canberra was scheming to maximize industrial unrest in order to pave the way for a 'law and order' campaign which would boost its re-election prospects. At the same time some right-wingers like Ducker, who had strenuously opposed Hawke's bid for the ACTU presidency, were beginning to warm to him. Other labour movement identities found Hawke a captivating companion. Combe was one who had established an immediate rapport with him, and the lead-up to the 1972 election provided yet another instance when Ducker assigned the task of driving Hawke around while he was campaigning in Sydney to 23-year-old organizer Graham Richardson, who was learning the political ropes under Ducker's tutelage. Richardson was struck by Hawke's outstanding talents, especially his brilliance in presenting Labor's message persuasively to diverse audiences in business boardrooms, universities and hotel bars; Richardson also liked the way Hawke treated him genuinely as an equal despite his inexperience and Hawke's celebrity status.

To many Labor supporters Whitlam was becoming an increasingly inspiring figure. Some of the uncommitted voters Labor needed were still unenthusiastic about him, but the ALP rank and file relished his supremacy over yet another Liberal Prime Minister – this time McMahon, who had succeeded Gorton in March 1971. Whitlam looked and sounded the part, with his imposing presence and confident speechmaking style. Freudenberg's skill ensured that on the big occasions Whitlam's message was likely to be memorably expressed. Whitlam frequently used wit effectively, and his tremendous intellectual capacity was obvious. He was inclined to be pompous, but there were times when he amusingly satirized this trait himself. At least, influenced by Young, he had restrained his tendency to be recklessly confrontational. Whitlam seemed not at all intimidated by the responsibility of leadership – he positively welcomed its burdens and challenges. Yet what was most refreshing and exhilarating to Whitlam admirers was the vision he projected of a reformed and revitalized Australia, and the hope he instilled that this objective was possible under a Whitlam Labor government; many gifted Australians had assumed that fundamental change was out of the question, and some had taken their talents elsewhere. When McMahon finally announced the 1972 election date Whitlam responded with a characteristically learned allusion and a gentle dig at his own temperament:

The second day of December is a memorable day; it is the anniversary of Austerlitz. Far be it from me to wish, or appear to wish, to assume the mantle of Napoleon, but I cannot forget that 2 December was a date on which a crushing defeat was administered to a coalition – a ramshackle, reactionary coalition. . .

At no previous Australian election had there been a better planned campaign than Labor's 1972 effort directed by Young. Prior to the previous election in October 1969 preparation had been minimal as late as August; by August 1972, however, the insights gleaned from the mid-term campaign had been put to good use, surveys had been commissioned and the results analysed, a slogan had been chosen, television advertisements had been produced, the itineraries of shadow ministers were being carefully monitored, and fund-raising was progressing well. An interesting participant in Labor's planning was Keith Murdoch's son Rupert, who was an ambitious newspaperman like his father. From the end of the Great War until his death Keith Murdoch was an increasingly bitter antagonist of Labor, but in 1972 Rupert Murdoch wholeheartedly backed the ALP campaign, providing lavish donations, useful tactical suggestions and firm support in his newspapers. Numerous well-known entertainers also associated themselves with the campaign, and were featured in television advertisements singing a catchy, contemporary 'It's time' jingle which promoted Labor's very successful campaign slogan. The phenomenal impact of the 'It's time' slogan was evident so early that New Zealand Labour Party figures asked Young if they could adopt it at their national election in November. Young agreed. In an uplifting precedent for the ALP, New Zealand voters decided that it was time to return Labour to government for the first time since 1960.

Whitlam delivered his policy speech to a jubilant live audience at the overcrowded Blacktown Civic Centre on 13 November 1972. Writing the speech had been primarily Freudenberg's task, but the final draft was a product of greater consultation than any previous ALP policy speech. It was the culmination of years of detailed policy research and formulation by Whitlam and many others. 'It's been a long road, comrade, but we're there', said Whitlam to Freudenberg before striding towards the electrifying reception awaiting him in the hall. 'Men and women of Australia', he began, echoing Curtin's wartime greeting, and the crowd fell silent.

> The decision we will make for our country on 2 December is a choice between the past and the future, between the habits and fears of the past, and the demands and opportunities of the future. There are moments in history when the whole fate and future of nations can be decided by a single decision. For Australia, this is such a time. It's time for a new team, a new programme, a new drive for equality of opportunities; it's time to create new opportunities for Australians, time for a new vision of what we can achieve in this generation for our nation and the region in which we live. It's time for a new government – a Labor Government.

The crowd roared its delight. The full policy speech was a remarkable document. In its printed form it encompassed 42 pages and about 140 specific promises, and was the most comprehensive reform blueprint ever unveiled at an Australian election. The Blacktown crowd and the television audience heard only a curtailed version, but the launch was still a memorable and emotional occasion. Young watched it on television to gauge how it appeared on that medium; it came over well, but he was too churned up to judge. Freudenberg felt that it 'was not so much a public meeting as an act of communion and a celebration of hope and love'.

The confidence of Labor supporters mounted as polling day drew nearer. Although there were avoidable mishaps and Young was critical of some instances of inept organization in Queensland, Labor's campaign was far superior to its opponents'. Labor Victorians under 40 had never voted at a state or federal election won by the ALP, and hopes were high that their state would provide some of the extra seats Labor needed to win government. 'The euphoria was extraordinary', recalled Melzer; the growing belief in an ALP victory was such that 'in that last week. . .it was like a great big party throughout Melbourne'. Thousands of Melbourne's Labor faithful crammed into St Kilda Town Hall to be part of the campaign climax. There were also singers, dancers, television celebrities, a band, and numerous joyful renditions of the 'It's time' song. In his speech Whitlam referred to the light on the hill, which had 'almost gone out'. 'Let us set it aflame again!' he urged. The tumultuous cheering and applause were still going even after Whitlam, covered in streamers, had made several curtain calls. It was surely the most ecstatic political meeting in Australian history.

Although the swing to Labor fell well short of the landslide anticipated by some analysts early on election night, it was enough to produce an ALP government. With an overall swing of 2·64% Labor finished with a comfortable majority in the Representatives after achieving a net gain of eight seats, capturing 12 and losing four – two in WA, and one each in SA and Victoria. That Victorian seat, Bendigo, was lost after the local Catholic bishop, not for the first time, misused his position in the community by persistently attacking the Labor candidate. The big ALP gains were in the two most populous states where intervention had occurred recently. Labor snared six seats in NSW. In Victoria Labor picked up four outer-suburban Liberal-held seats, and almost secured three others where the swing required was 7·8% or more. Hartley denied that intervention in Victoria was significant in Labor's improved performance there, but few observers agreed with him. In Tasmania Labor recorded a magnificent voting share of just under 59%, and was successful in all five Tasmanian seats for the first time. But it was a different story in WA, where Labor's vote slumped almost 4%, apparently owing to a degree of dissatisfaction with the Tonkin government which was blamed for an unemployment increase in the West. Surveys confirmed that a crucial element in the ALP resurgence under Whitlam was the transformation since 1966 in the level of support Labor was able to attract from younger voters. Fervent Whitlam admirers and campaign workers in their twenties – in the words of one of them, talented barrister Gareth Evans – 'had probably the most exuberant and totally joyous night of our lives on 2 December 1972'. For Labor supporters of all ages it was a night to remember.

14 'There won't Ever be Another One Like It': The Whitlam Government, 1972–1975

AUSTRALIA'S FIRST NATIONAL Labor government for 23 years made a stunning start. Right from the outset Whitlam made it clear that this government would be very different from its predecessors. Instead of waiting for the new caucus to choose his ministers, a procedure which could not occur for at least a fortnight until the results in marginal seats became known, Whitlam decided to form an interim two-man ministry with Barnard. Whitlam described it as the smallest ministry with jurisdiction over Australia since a temporary British administration under the Duke of Wellington in 1844. The Whitlam-Barnard duumvirate authorized a flood of decisions and announcements in consultation, where appropriate, with the MPs likely to hold the relevant portfolios when the full ministry was formed. The first, and very popular, decision was the abolition of conscription. Imprisoned draft resisters were released. Other early changes included the reopening of the equal pay case before the Arbitration Commission, the abolition of the imperial honours system, the inauguration of the Australian Schools Commission, the withdrawal of Australia's remaining soldiers in Vietnam, the removal of the excise on wine and the sales tax on contraceptives, and a halt to the granting of mining leases on Aboriginal reserves. Crean and others wondered whether acting early on wine and contraceptives gave the mistaken impression that these matters ranked with ending conscription and boosting education as the government's highest priorities. But Whitlam was deliberately signalling that Labor in power was committed to wide-ranging reform, and would pursue it vigorously and wholeheartedly.

This commitment was particularly evident in foreign affairs, reflecting Whitlam's special interest in the subject. Like Evatt, he had a broad international outlook and an attachment to global forums like the United Nations. He cherished the Foreign Affairs portfolio, and had earmarked it for himself in conjunction with the prime ministership. The duumvirate's early announcements included the belated formal recognition of the People's Republic of China, the cessation of wheat exports to Rhodesia and the exclusion of racially selected sporting teams from Australia. Early action was also taken to overhaul Australia's relationship with Papua New Guinea. No achievement of his government was to give Whitlam greater satisfaction than its success in expediting self-government and independence for Australia's northern neighbour.

The United Nations General Assembly was about to vote on a number of issues when the duumvirate came to power. In Canberra the Foreign Affairs departmental head advised Whitlam that Australia should abstain from voting, a course the newly elected New Zealand Labour government followed. Whitlam had other ideas. Gordon Bilney was in the Australian contingent at the United Nations:

> It was as heady an experience as I can remember to have been a member of that delegation in the two or three weeks which followed. Clear and definite instructions came, promptly, to support those votes giving real effect to Australia's new non-racial stance, to pledge those financial contributions to causes. . .formerly eschewed by timorous Australian Governments, to take the first steps to forging new relationships with countries [in] our region. . .

Shortly before the election Bilney had been offered a position on Whitlam's staff. He had been non-committal, but not any more:

> By the time the Duumvirate had been operating for a week all I wanted was to get back to Australia as soon as I could. There were thousands like me, accustomed to cringing culturally when as an Australian abroad one was either thought of as an Austrian or as a variety of South African, but who quickly found reason to take pride in what the new government was doing.

Caucus assembled in high spirits to elect the full ministry on 18 December. The old procedure of protracted exhaustive balloting for FPLP positions had been scrapped in the mid-1960s, and the selection of the 27 ministers occurred in stages. Whitlam, Barnard, Murphy and Willesee were re-elected unopposed as the leadership quartet and automatically included in the ministry. Then there were two separate ballots to elect another four Senators and 10 MHRs. In fact the FPLP executive in opposition had comprised the four leaders and 10 others, all MHRs, and these 10 – Cairns, Hayden, Crean, Patterson, Daly, Cameron, former boilermaker and Newcastle mayor Charlie Jones, Uren, Beazley and Stewart – were all elected. The successful four Senators were Doug McClelland, the SA pair Reg Bishop and Jim Cavanagh, and Tasmanian Ken Wriedt. In a final ballot for the remaining nine places, which were open to MPs from either chamber, all nine went to MHRs. Five were from NSW – Connor, Bowen, Les Johnson, former diplomat Bill Morrison and colourful Riverina MHR Al Grassby. Also among the nine was lawyer and ACT MHR Kep Enderby. The remaining trio, Capricornia MHR Doug Everingham and Victorians Gordon Bryant and Moss Cass, were all known for their radical views and forthrightness in expressing them. Although there were no major shocks, some observers had expected Wheeldon and natty dresser and former Grouper lawyer 'Diamond Jim' McClelland to become ministers; Whitlam was disappointed that caucus overlooked Queenslander Manfred Cross and one of the FPLP's many talented 1969 acquisitions, Perth MHR Joe Berinson.

Whitlam gave most of his senior ministers departmental responsibilities which had been theirs in opposition. He allocated Defence to Barnard, Trade and Secondary Industry to Cairns, Social Security to Hayden and Transport to Jones. Murphy became Attorney-General. Beazley was chosen to supervise the massive increases in education expenditure which were integral to Whitlam's fundamental objective of widening opportunities for Australians. Crean at last became Treasurer after waiting for over two decades to occupy the post which his background and training seemed to make naturally his. Profound fulfilment was felt particularly by Connor at Minerals and Energy, Cameron as minister for Labour, and Uren, who was given the new portfolio of Urban and Regional Development after being closely involved in the evolution of ALP policy in that sphere.

Other ministers were allocated responsibilities suiting their backgrounds and expertise. Doug McClelland's appointment as minister for the Media was no surprise. Bryant became minister for Aboriginal Affairs after having been a committed fighter for the cause of Aborigines for years. Morrison was eminently suited to External Territories, and Whitlam gave him Science as well. The new Works minister was Cavanagh, a militant and widely respected former Plasterers' Union secretary. Enderby was given ministerial responsibility for the Capital Territory and the Northern Territory, although there were warnings that making Canberra's local member its minister was asking for trouble. The nuts and bolts department of Services and Property went to Daly, whose talents and great experience superbly equipped him for his other important role as Leader of the House. Whitlam allocated Health to Everingham, one of two medical practitioners elected to cabinet. The other, Cass, was given his preferred portfolio, Environment.

One surprise was Whitlam's choice as Primary Industry minister, Senator Wriedt, a former merchant seaman who admitted that his knowledge of agriculture was negligible. According to Freudenberg, Whitlam was concerned that a minister 'representing a marginal seat would be too vulnerable to industry lobbying and parochial pressures', and the seats held by Labor's three rural MHRs in cabinet – Patterson, Grassby and Everingham – were all marginal. However, Wriedt applied himself to his portfolio with determination and became one of the government's most unlikely ministerial successes. Patterson was given a new department of Northern Development which included responsibility for the sugar industry. Grassby's solicitude for his electorate's Italian community, his hostility to racism and his flair for generating publicity fitted him well for Immigration. The remaining appointments were Johnson to Housing, Bowen to Postmaster-General, Stewart to Tourism and Recreation, Bishop to Repatriation, and Willesee to a new post of Special Minister of State with additional responsibilities including assisting Whitlam at Foreign Affairs.

Once the caucus ballots were completed the revelry was uninhibited. There were raucous renditions of 'Waltzing Matilda', 'Solidarity Forever' and 'The Road To Gundagai'. 'We felt we were going to change the course of history', recalled Johnson. Daly was not in the least fazed by the unglamorous title of his Services and Property ministry: 'I'm bigger than Hookers!' he beamed. The euphoria continued at the swearing-in ceremony, where Grassby was distinctive as usual in purple suit and sunglasses. Cameron, who had been presented by Whitlam with an inscribed photograph praising him as 'a principal architect of victory' for spearheading intervention in Victoria, joked at Government House that the ceremony guaranteed 27 more state funerals.

The advent of such a long-awaited Labor government was celebrated less exuberantly at a lunch Whitlam held for some notable ALP veterans. Forde, McKell, Dedman, Pollard and Chambers were all invited. The biggest conversation topic during this gathering was the double dissolution McKell granted as Governor-General to Menzies in 1951. At the time some Labor people had been very angry with McKell's decision, but the lunch guests all agreed that McKell had been correct, since it was axiomatic that in such matters the Governor-General must always comply with the wishes of the elected government.

The prospect of unwieldy decision-making by 27 ministers had led to suggestions that it might be prudent to exclude some of them from cabinet. In previous national Labor governments the entire ministry had formed the cabinet and the size of the ministry had gradually increased from eight ministers led by Watson to 19 under Curtin and Chifley. Since 1956 the coalition governments had divided their ministers into seniors with cabinet rank and juniors who only participated in cabinet talks when their departmental responsibilities were being discussed. However, in April 1972 caucus had decided by the narrowest possible margin to preserve the Labor tradition (qualified by the war cabinet in operation during the Second World War) that all ministers should have full cabinet status.

No national Labor government has come to office with less ministerial experience than Whitlam's cabinet. Indeed, only Daly, Beazley, Duthie and O'Byrne had been in the FPLP when Labor last formed a government in Canberra. The new ministers' inexperience did not inhibit them. Whitlam interpreted his government's mandate from the electors as an imprimatur to implement Labor's reform blueprint in its entirety, and the style of rapid and wide-ranging decision-making established by the duumvirate continued when the full ministry took over. After years of governmental drift the transformation was striking. About a year earlier a proposal to revalue the Australian currency had degenerated into prolonged unedifying haggling between the coalition parties with smart money operators speculating on the outcome. In complete contrast was the smoothly taken decision by Whitlam, Crean and Barnard to proceed with an overdue revaluation of the Australian dollar just before Christmas 1972. Crean was quietly proud that news of the decision remained secret until it was announced, and speculators were unable this time to harm Australia's interests.

The different attitudes and priorities of the new government were further underlined when President Nixon decided to resume American bombing raids on North Vietnam. Bilney, now back in Australia, joined other Whitlam advisers in recommending to the Prime Minister that a firm private protest to Washington was warranted. Whitlam sent one, but his message was overshadowed by the scathing public reactions from three of his ministers. Cairns described the resumption of the bombing as 'the most brutal, indiscriminate slaughter of defenceless men, women and children in living memory', Cameron remarked that maniacs seemed to be in charge of American policy, and Uren referred to 'a mentality of thuggery'. These outbursts captured headlines overseas. They stunned and infuriated American policy-makers who were accustomed to subservient Australian governments prepared to go 'all the way with LBJ'.

The adjustment to such a different government was not uniformly smooth in Canberra either. Many public servants welcomed the election of the Whitlam government. However, there were inevitably tensions between the incoming ministers and some of the senior public servants who were not used to such a cracking pace. Cameron was determined to replace the incumbent head of his department, and did so despite stern public service resistance. The use of ministerial staffers and consultants to provide alternative advice to Whitlam government ministers led to friction between some of the staffers and top bureaucrats, which was instrumental in the unexpected resignation of Barnard's press secretary, a respected identity in Labor circles, early in the government's

341

life. Some of the government's appointees from outside the public service managed to provide alternative policy advice. Mostly, however, the ministerial staffers were too busy on other tasks to formulate compelling detailed arguments to counter the departmental viewpoint. A few of the government's individual appointments became notorious. Cairns and Cavanagh placed their sons on the public payroll as their private secretaries, and these appointments were not the only instances in the government's early days of administrative laxity which left it vulnerable to criticism it could have done without.

The biggest talking point about the composition of the interim Whitlam-Barnard duumvirate had been Murphy's omission from it. Forming a temporary government comprising the leadership quartet would have been at least as logical as making it a duumvirate, and probably more prudent in order to avoid ruffling the sensitivities of Labor's Senators in general and Murphy's in particular. Whitlam's justification for his exclusion of the Senate leaders was his abhorrence of any Senate pretensions to equal status with the Representatives where governments are made and unmade. In opposition Murphy had galvanized the Senate from a sedate backwater into a more purposeful chamber which now possessed an influential committee system and a heightened awareness of its powers of review. Whitlam, Calwell, Daly and Crean were only some of the ALP figures critical of Murphy's efforts to boost the Senate's prestige when the party platform committed Labor to abolishing it. While Whitlam's desire to keep the Senate firmly in its place as the lesser chamber was genuine and deep, his relationship with Murphy was surely also a factor in the latter's exclusion from the temporary administration in December 1972. 'One of the minor tragedies of the Whitlam era was the deep-seated, though seldom overtly expressed, antipathy between its two ablest men', concluded Jim McClelland, who liked and admired them both. McClelland felt that the cause of this friction between Whitlam and Murphy 'was in reality not much more than a clash of mighty egos'. Observers noted a similar sense of wary, prickly rivalry between Whitlam and Hawke.

Once the full ministry was sworn in, Murphy sprang into action. Under his impetus the Attorney-General's department was soon involved in a wide range of initiatives including removal of some censorship restrictions, abolition of the death penalty, freedom of information, appointment of an ombudsman and protection of endangered species, as well as preparatory work concerning trade practices legislation, the establishment of the Australian Legal Aid Office, and Australia's unprecedented action in the International Court of Justice against French nuclear testing in the Pacific. No Australian national government has contained an Attorney-General more vigorous and imaginative in pursuing reform. Few, if any, public servants had a more testing adjustment to make after the 1972 election than senior officials in the Attorney-General's department. Murphy was a genuine threat to entrenched power, privilege and protocol. Accordingly, he was a special target for venom and vitriol.

Murphy's working habits continued to dazzle lesser mortals, especially in view of the rich life he led away from his office. In January 1973 Murphy, then in London, amazed officials by telephoning the British Foreign Secretary at 11 pm to inform him that he would call round immediately to discuss a joint statement about reducing the legal links between their countries. Having transacted that business at the Foreign Secretary's townhouse, Murphy breezed back to his hotel to begin preparing for the conference he was to attend later that morning. That episode was typical Murphy. One Canberra journalist who requested an interview with him was taken aback when given an appointment at 12.30 the following night. Arriving as arranged, the reporter found Murphy 'perfectly charming'; attired in electric blue suit with bell-bottomed trousers and a green and orange paisley tie, Murphy chatted amiably in his distinctive 'deep, nasally resonant voice' as if it was completely natural to schedule appointments at such a time.

Early in 1973 the Whitlam government was embarrassed by Murphy's impulsive attempt to introduce sweeping changes to Australia's divorce laws. A Senate inquiry was analysing Australia's divorce arrangements, but Murphy felt that the need for a more up-to-date and humanitarian system was too pressing to wait for that inquiry to finish; moreover, there was already a legislative bottleneck as eager new ministers inundated officials with 'a torrential outpouring of drafting instructions'. Murphy seized the expedient of regulations as a handy short cut, but his rushed Family Law Regulations produced a storm of criticism and he had to go back to the drawing board. Although divorce law reform was successfully accomplished by the Whitlam government in subsequent legislation, Murphy's haste in this initial attempt had led to faulty drafting as well as a failure to consult.

Shortly afterwards Murphy was responsible for the most controversial episode of the Whitlam government's early months. Murphy had ministerial responsibility for ASIO, which was widely regarded in Labor circles with suspicion and hostility, especially since the Petrov saga. On 15 March 1973 Murphy became concerned about security arrangements for the imminent visit of Prime Minister Bijedic of Yugoslavia. The conflicting advice Murphy received about the presence in Australia of Croatian terrorists known as the Ustasha led him to conclude that Bijedic might well be gravely at risk in Australia and also that ASIO was not being frank with him. Late that night Murphy met ASIO's chief Canberra officers. They told him he could not see ASIO's file on the Ustasha because the material was at ASIO's Melbourne headquarters. Murphy was staggered to discover that precautionary preparations for Bijedic's visit had been minimal. In the early hours of 16 March Murphy made further inquiries which increased his concern. He decided to travel to Melbourne on the first available plane. Arriving at Canberra airport, Murphy found that the tickets booked for himself and his small entourage had been mysteriously cancelled. Alternative arrangements overcame this problem, and Murphy proceeded to Melbourne. Also on his flight was an ASIO officer who, Murphy learned, was carrying in a briefcase a copy of the ASIO Ustasha file which Murphy had been told was only available in Melbourne. Murphy was driven to ASIO headquarters, where he found an array of journalists and cameras awaiting his arrival. Inside, Murphy was given access to the Ustasha file. He asked whether there was a file on himself, and was told that there probably was. After confirming his impression of ASIO's inadequate preparations for Bijedic, he departed. Bijedic's visit shortly afterwards proved uneventful.

Murphy's inspection became stigmatized as a sensational 'raid'. His admirers claimed that in the circumstances it was essentially a proper exercise of his ministerial authority, and some Labor adherents welcomed his willingness to act assertively against ASIO. The episode provided further confirmation that ASIO, like its surveillance ancestors during the Depression, significantly underestimated the threat to Australian security from right-wing sources just as it significantly overestimated the danger from left-wing groups. But many Labor supporters were disturbed that the melodramatic nature of Murphy's action and the whiff of some unexplained scandal had made it a public relations disaster for the government. The political fallout was aggravated by enmity between officers of the Commonwealth Police and ASIO, which resulted in the media being briefed about Murphy's travel plans before his arrival at ASIO headquarters. Accordingly, there was abundant graphic coverage of the 'raid' and the police force's enthusiastic participation in it.

The incident even had international ramifications. Shocked American decision-makers, who were still recovering from the Whitlam government's vehement response to the resumption of bombing raids over North Vietnam, were so alarmed by this other 'raid' on ASIO that they even considered severing ASIO's links with their powerful Central Intelligence Agency (CIA). Blinkered CIA chiefs had concluded that a wild revolutionary government had come to power in Australia, an impression presumably reinforced by Whitlam's hostile reaction when he received his first official briefing about the activities of the Australian Secret Intelligence Service (ASIS), which had been established by the Menzies government to conduct covert operations overseas. It seems that Menzies arranged for Calwell to be officially briefed about ASIS, but Whitlam never was until Labor won government (although he had picked up some information about ASIS unofficially). When Whitlam learned after becoming Prime Minister that ASIS agents were linked to the massive CIA operation to destabilize the Allende government in Chile, he took steps to see that this involvement ceased.

The Whitlam government's style was not conducive to a high level of cohesion. Strong-willed ministers, taking their cue from the duumvirate, sometimes gave the impression of busily charging ahead with reforms in their own spheres without much regard for how the government was faring as a whole. 'I don't care how many prima donnas there are', Whitlam declared, 'as long as I'm prima donna *assoluta*'. Indeed the pace of change was so hectic that only Whitlam, with his extraordinary ability to absorb masses of information swiftly, could keep abreast of it all, so that most of his ministers tended to concentrate on their areas of specialization.

Despite all his undoubted qualities Whitlam was not temperamentally equipped to exert much cohesive influence on his cabinet. When he declared on television in August 1973 that his government's 'greatest mistake' so far was 'to take the police into ASIO headquarters', Murphy observed that such a remark did not set a conspicuous example of cabinet solidarity. Whitlam 'was a leader who relied hardly at all on wooing, coaxing and negotiating, but rather, overwhelmingly, on his own fabulous skills of Cabinet and Party room advocacy and, when that failed, on crude intimidation'. Selective in his enthusiasms, Whitlam used his control of the cabinet agenda to postpone or prevent discussion of matters which did not appeal to him. He also antagonized his ministers by resorting to informal 'kitchen cabinet' gatherings of small groups at the Lodge. Among Australians unfamiliar with the inner workings of government Whitlam was more popular than ever before, owing to his panache, commitment to reform, stylish and erudite forays abroad, and commanding superiority over his fourth opponent as Liberal leader, B.M. Snedden. But these admirers did not see him literally grinding his teeth in frustration at colleagues during cabinet deliberations, or witness his recurrent eruptions. Whitlam lacked Chifley's affability and warmth with colleagues, and was not adept at inculcating a comradely team spirit in the government.

A higher priority for Whitlam was the fulfilment of his desire to become a dashing international figure. 'Whitlam revelled in striding the world stage; he was expansive and charming in treating with world leaders as equals, and at his vindictive best in putting some of them in their place'. He loved travelling abroad, and did so frequently as Prime Minister. These trips came to be ridiculed as junkets, although everyone accompanying him was invariably exhausted by the punishing schedule he maintained while overseas. His globetrotting placed himself and his country on the map internationally as he singlehandedly – he made foreign affairs exclusively his domain, and it was hardly ever discussed in cabinet – ensured that nations previously oblivious or contemptuous of Australia became aware that it was now led by a progressive government possessing enlightened attitudes.

The Whitlam government's difficulties in maintaining a cohesive image were not helped when caucus occasionally exercised its right to review or alter a cabinet decision. Whenever this occurred, or looked as if it might, the government's critics in parliament and the media pounced quickly, alleging that here was dramatic evidence that the government was 'in crisis'. This public image of instability was augmented by the practice of some ministers opposed to a particular cabinet decision to argue for its reversal in caucus. Backbenchers, being generally more sensitive to the electorate's moods, were aware that the helter-skelter approach to alleviating the neglect of decades not only led to some ill-considered decisions; it left no time for adequate consultation beforehand or explanation and promotion afterwards. Whitlam seemed not to grasp or care that while the dizzy pace of change excited and exhilarated some voters, more were alarmed and alienated by it. Dunstan was no less committed to reform in SA, but displayed a greater appreciation of the need to nurse the electorate with systematic explanation of the benefits being introduced. The low priority accorded by the Whitlam government to this important factor in maintaining the electoral appeal of a vigorously reformist government made it too easy for Labor's opponents to obscure and distort the truth. The great benefits arising from the government's vast expenditure increases in Education, Urban and Regional Development, Aboriginal Affairs and social welfare were not recognized or understood. In Queensland the Bjelke-Petersen government even brazenly stole the credit for many Whitlam government initiatives. For informed Labor advocates aware of the Whitlam government's achievements, it was annoying that the spotlight so often focused on comparatively minor hiccups and irritants like ministerial staff appointments, the ASIO 'raid' and the frequency of Whitlam's overseas travel.

More serious problems emerged in 1973. The 1972 election had been for the Representatives alone. In the Senate the FPLP still lacked a majority. By mid-1973 Labor's opponents had recovered from the shock of losing office for the first time in 23 years, and were impatient to return to what they regarded as their rightful place. The Australian parliament has known no more unprincipled opposition than the one that harassed the Whitlam government, and no more cynical party leader than the chief Liberal in the Senate, R.G. Withers. The opposition used every device at its disposal, and Murphy, Labor's Senate leader, endured a harrowing parliamentary ordeal after the ASIO 'raid'.

By September 1973 Senate recalcitrance was jeopardizing the Whitlam government's plans to overhaul funding for Australian schools. The Australian Schools Commission, one of many boards and inquiries established by the government in accordance with Labor's platform, had evaluated the requirements of Australian schools. Its report 'highlighted the legacy of decades of inequitable and inadequate funding'. The Commission's recommendations for systematic needs-based funding to raise educational standards were embodied in two bills which were amended in the Senate at the instigation of Liberal frontbencher Malcolm Fraser, who objected to the government's philosophy of directing aid away from the most advantaged schools. The government refused to accept the amendments. Whitlam threatened to call a double dissolution on the issue. After the health of Beazley, Whitlam's enthusiastic and effective Education minister, broke down and he had to rest in hospital, Beazley's temporary replacement, Bowen, used Whitlam's threat to persuade the Country Party to change its attitude, and the legislation was passed. The Whitlam government was responsible for a colossal boost to education expenditure, and Whitlam described the transformation of education in Australia as the 'most enduring single achievement of my Government'. Besides the needs-based funding for schools, there was the abolition of fees for tertiary students, vastly increased expenditure on technical colleges including the construction of residential accommodation for students, and special initiatives covering isolated children, Aborigines and the handicapped. In no other sphere did the government take such giant strides towards Whitlam's fundamental objective, equality of opportunity for all Australians.

When the Whitlam government began to encounter severe economic problems on top of its difficulties with the Senate, pessimistic observers with an eye to history began to consider in earnest the close parallels with the ill-fated Scullin government, which had also been jubilantly welcomed as the first Labor government for many years. Inflation became increasingly apparent in Australia during 1973. The last coalition budget had been expansionary, and aggravated strong inflationary pressures imported from abroad (derived largely from economic policies adopted by the United States to finance its involvement in Vietnam). The Whitlam government's expenditure on its numerous reforms further augmented Australia's inflation, but the government took countervailing action on several fronts to curb the inflationary surge. In addition to the early revaluation of the dollar and other steps to slacken capital inflow into Australia, the government implemented its election promise to introduce a Prices Justification Tribunal, which required larger organizations to justify proposed price increases at a public inquiry. In July the government made its most controversial economic decision, the sudden across-the-board 25% reduction in tariffs, with a view to making the overall economy more efficient as well as counteracting the inflationary spiral. In September, when a by-election in the Liberal-held seat of Parramatta resulted in an anti-Labor swing exceeding 6%, the government heeded advice from Treasury and the Reserve Bank and imposed a credit squeeze.

Late in 1973 the government tried another approach to tackle inflation. At a caucus meeting on 12 September a motion calling for a referendum to give the national government power over prices was narrowly carried. Whitlam had opposed the idea in caucus, but once it was forced upon him he persuaded caucus to approve a separate concurrent referendum seeking power over incomes despite opposition from the union movement, which was concerned that such power would enable a future anti-Labor government to introduce a wage freeze. The ACTU recommended a 'Yes' vote on the prices referendum but 'No' to power over incomes, the opposition advocated 'No' to both, and the government's prospects of dual success were slim. Whitlam told Australians that they had 'the only national government in the world which did not have power to regulate prices', but both referenda were convincingly rejected on 8 December.

During this period the ALP was scarred by damaging public discord between its two titans, Whitlam and Hawke. At an exuberant federal conference in July

Hawke was unanimously elected national ALP president. He believed that he would be able to bring Labor's industrial and political wings closer together. (Cameron's decades of experience in industrial affairs had instilled in him strongly held ideas and priorities for reform, and his swift moves as Labour minister to introduce a new era for workers had already caused some friction between the government and leading unionists when his views did not completely coincide with the ACTU's.) However, Hawke was not only increasing his already daunting workload by becoming ALP president as well as ACTU president; as well-meaning advisers told him, he would be in an invidious position whenever the unions disapproved of particular decisions by the Whitlam government. These warnings were quickly vindicated when the sweeping tariff cuts were announced. Hawke was appalled by the likelihood of increased unemployment, sceptical that inflation would be affected, and incensed that he was not consulted beforehand. He telephoned Whitlam, and had a blazing row with him over the decision. In public he awkwardly tried to stress its positive aspects, but was less inhibited in his reaction to the following month's budget. Hawke was again trenchantly critical when the chances of a pleasing result for Labor at the Parramatta by-election were dashed by the announcement during the campaign of a government decision to construct an airport adjacent to that electorate. Hawke described this 'act of imbecility' as 'political insanity', and his public reprimand went further:

the parliamentary party and the cabinet have got to be more finely attuned to the electorate. They are becoming removed from the realities of day to day politics. . .They are not keeping in touch with what is happening at the grass roots.

Hawke's forthright criticism of the budget was related to a discussion with Whitlam and others about Labor's tax policy before the 1972 election. Hawke (supported by Cameron) had emphatically opposed any idea that Labor should undertake not to raise taxation if elected. The upshot was that Labor's stance on future taxation was deliberately blurred during the 1972 campaign, but it was widely concluded that Labor had given an implicit assurance that direct taxation would not be raised. This influenced Whitlam, with his literal interpretation of the mandate, to rule out income tax rises in the 1973 budget. Instead, the government opted to boost its taxation revenue through additional levies on spirits, cigarettes and petrol. Hawke was critical: lifting direct taxation for the wealthy was a far better way to attack inflation than slugging the workers through indirect tax, which would only cause the prices of those items to rise further. Asked for a response to Hawke's comments, Whitlam delivered a stern rebuke:

The president of the federal executive of the Labor Party does not determine such matters; he is not consulted in such matters; he doesn't speak for the party on such matters. . .

Hawke retorted that the Prime Minister's remarks were petulant and gratuitous, and proceeded to campaign vigorously for a 'Yes, No' vote on the government's referenda on prices and incomes.

Whitlam and Hawke had different attitudes to economics as well as a measure of personal rivalry. It was no secret that economics was not a field that engaged Whitlam's interest. His political emergence had occurred during the 1950s and 1960s when Australians became accustomed to easy economic growth. Monitoring the economy and making adjustments to it were perceived by Whitlam as mundane and mechanical tasks for lesser minds. The real creative challenge in his view was to formulate imaginative ways to redistribute Australia's wealth. Whitlam's attitude to economics was challenged by Hawke, who had tutored in that subject at university, had a much better practical grasp of it than Whitlam, and regarded it as a fundamental component in the overall performance of a national Labor government. Before the 1972 election Hawke recommended to Whitlam that he should have some specialized private tuition, pointing out that it was 'no use having economic advisers if one could not determine the value of their advice'. Hawke felt that Whitlam was so 'extraordinarily intelligent. . .that he could acquaint himself with economics' very quickly if he put his mind to it, but the suggestion fell on deaf ears.

Early in 1974 relations between the ACTU and the government deteriorated further. The primary instrument for consultation at the highest level between the political and industrial wings of Labor was the liaison body now known as the Australian Labor Advisory Council (ALAC), which had functioned intermittently since its inception in the later 1930s. Hawke and other ACTU representatives had already found it annoying that their access to Whitlam through ALAC had been minimal, and they were furious when other business so detained Whitlam that he turned up 90 minutes late on 15 January 1974 for the ALAC meeting which had been arranged to resolve the differences between the government and the unions. Instead of reducing the friction, that abortive meeting led to the virtual abandonment of ALAC for the duration of the Whitlam government. Combe, who had been appointed national ALP secretary after Young vacated the position to pursue a parliamentary career, also found it disturbingly difficult to communicate meaningfully with the government:

> They just would not listen. After the Parramatta by-election I called on Gough. . .to voice my concerns about how we were performing politically, that we'd just had a disastrous by-election, it need not have been a disaster, we could have won the seat. . . Gough was lying full-length on his settee, reading papers and throwing them over his shoulder as he finished them while various senior public servants danced attendance. He heard me out, still prone. Then he sat bolt upright and stared at me. He said, 'David. You have often told me that this government has one thing going for it. You are wasting its time!' That was the end of our interview.

But Whitlam's actions late in 1973 showed that he did recognize the need for changes. In October he announced a cabinet reshuffle. Enderby, who was becoming unpopular among his Canberra constituents because of the decisions he was making as their minister, was transferred to a new portfolio of Secondary Industry. The new ACT minister was Bryant, whose stint at Aboriginal Affairs had been dogged by controversy. Some observers believed that Bryant had acted creditably in his clashes with senior bureaucrats, but he was succeeded by Cavanagh at Aboriginal Affairs, which became a less turbulent administrative arena. Whitlam also indicated that he would soon reluctantly surrender his cherished Foreign Affairs portfolio to Willesee. Another significant move was the appointment to Whitlam's staff of Young, who was set to become MHR for Port Adelaide at the next election; Young was seen as the type of all-purpose troubleshooter Whitlam badly needed.

After implementing these changes Whitlam was relaxed and confident as he ended his remarkable first year in office. His mastery of Snedden in parliament helped flagging FPLP morale to revive. He signalled that his government's momentum would not slacken, and economic difficulties and other problems would be no excuse for delaying reform while he was Prime Minister. On the first anniversary of Labor's election win he flourished a long list of his government's achievements. Snedden petulantly refused him permission to have it incorporated in Hansard unread, so Whitlam triumphantly recited it line by line. It took him two hours.

The progress of Whitlam's youngest minister, Hayden, was being followed with keen interest by many Queenslanders. Hayden was determinedly trying to overcome the shortcomings of his emotionally and materially deprived childhood. In his later twenties, while working as a policeman, he obtained his matriculation by correspondence and became a husband, parent and parliamentarian. After becoming MHR for Oxley he completed an Economics degree and read widely in the classics. Partial deafness hampered his social and educational development and contributed to his awkward speech, but he drove himself along his voyage of self-improvement with tremendous doggedness and application. Grizzled Queensland policemen swapped anecdotes about their serious-minded former colleague who used to wrestle with trigonometry as their police vehicle hurtled to the scene of the latest crime. Although Hayden acquired knowledge, experience and cultural understanding he still found it difficult to trust and form close friendships. Yet his dedication and refusal right from the outset to be intimidated by Menzies and other senior anti-Labor figures – despite his inner feelings of inadequacy – had established him as a politician of substance. His initial association with left-wingers Cairns and Uren continued, as did his passionate speeches against the Vietnam War, but he openly acknowledged that his studies had altered some of his economic views. His idealism and radical fervour were embodied in his 7500-word essay published by the Victorian Fabian Society, *The Implications of Democratic Socialism*, which influenced the political philosophy of many Labor activists including two WA Fabians, John Dawkins and Peter Walsh. Hayden had shown that his unexpected initial success in Oxley was no fluke when he gained a swing of almost 5% in 1963 although Labor's overall vote fell. The next election, however, was shattering. He retained Oxley but Labor was annihilated, and while he was out campaigning his daughter was hit by a car and fatally injured. The agony of 1966 for Hayden and his wife Dallas never abated.

Hayden had a difficult first year as a minister. He contributed to the government's early flurry of activity, introducing legislation to increase pensions and raise unemployment and sickness benefits on the first business day of the new parliament. In July 1973 Hayden initiated a benefit to provide single mothers with assistance which had formerly only been available to widows with children. But Hayden's biggest problem was the hostility to Labor's health and welfare reforms from the groups described by Whitlam as 'Australia's most militant trade union and its most self-serving bureaucracy, the medical profession and the health insurance industry'. Not only did doctors, through their organizations, display blatant avarice where their own incomes were concerned; some of them also circulated false rumours to undermine Hayden. He was supposed to be full of revenge after failing as a Medicine student; he was alleged to have had psychiatric treatment and used his ministerial authority to have the records destroyed; and a telephone caller told Dallas one night that her husband had gone berserk on a plane and been conveyed to a mental institution. Hayden persevered with his efforts to obtain acceptance of Labor's universal health insurance scheme, but it was not only doctors who made its introduction an uphill battle. By April 1974 anti-Labor Senators had rejected two health insurance bills twice.

During the Whitlam government's first year Rex Connor acquired a distinctive reputation. Connor was an arch-nationalist proud that he was born on 26 January (Australia Day) and passionate about Australian control of Australian resources. He dreamed about implementing gigantic projects like a pipeline grid to carry natural gas from one side of the Australian continent to the other. Connor imagined Australia leading the world in utilizing alternative sources of energy, especially after oil supplies in the Middle East suddenly became much more uncertain and expensive in 1973. He envisaged a large new government agency, the Petroleum and Minerals Authority, which would locate Australia's minerals and, instead of allowing overseas interests to transport the raw materials abroad, would undertake the lucrative processing and marketing of these resources in Australia. Having a business background himself, he was not, as his critics claimed, anti-business. Rather, he was hostile to inept business practices where Australia's national resources were concerned. There would be scope for private enterprise participation in Connor's colossal projects, but the national government would at all times be in control. Anyone who expressed doubts about his vision received the same brutally gruff treatment, whether they were corporation executives, journalists, opposition MPs or members of his own party. His intimidatory style was reinforced by his specialized technical knowledge and a certain secretiveness, as well as by his notorious temper and his burly frame. Customarily dressed in hat, braces and dark ill-fitting suits, he was a contrast in appearance to his more colourfully attired younger colleagues. His strength and demeanour were epitomized in his nickname, 'the Strangler'. Connor's stature in the party and the government was cemented by his close bond with Whitlam. This did not solely stem from Connor's strong support of Whitlam in his 1968 leadership contest with Cairns. The Prime Minister found Connor's sweeping vision immensely appealing when so many others seemed preoccupied with objections and obstacles to change.

By early 1974 farmers were as infuriated with the Whitlam government as the mining executives. 'For those of us in rural seats', recalled Duthie, 'the first 15 months under Labor were a nightmare'. Farmers accustomed to the special assistance they had enjoyed for so long, thanks to the Country Party's presence in coalition governments, reacted bitterly when some of these concessions were peremptorily withdrawn. Dairy farmers learned that they were to lose their subsidies. The petrol concession in rural areas was abolished. Most controversial of all, the superphosphate bounty was withdrawn. This decision, which almost resulted in Patterson's resignation, was described as electoral suicide by Duthie, who was annoyed that the decision had not been raised beforehand, as caucus rules stipulated, with the FPLP Primary Industry Committee he chaired. The bush was up in arms, but Whitlam was unrepentant. 'You've never had it so good', he told angry Gippsland farmers shortly after announcing the superphosphate decision. Rural sector statistics had convinced Whitlam that the concessions were inequitable and unjustifiable on two broad grounds. Farm incomes had soared recently, and had never been higher; in addition, the concessions (which also included special taxation allowances) tended to favour disproportionately the wealthier producers on bigger farms. Whitlam contended that the government's restructuring of its agriculture expenditure enabled assistance to be directed where it was most needed. He argued that farmers benefited from the tariff cuts and the additional markets created by his government's diplomatic and trade initiatives. They were also advantaged, he pointed out, by his government's increased expenditure on rural research, regional education and health, and by other upgraded country facilities. But aggrieved farmers only had eyes for what they had lost. Despite Wriedt's skilful damage control and the efforts of rurally based MHRs like Duthie, the government never overcame this early hostility. The damage to Labor's cause in some rural areas has been permanent.

It was also a crucial factor in the downfall of the Tonkin Labor government at the WA election on 30 March 1974. When Whitlam addressed a campaign meeting at Perth's Forrest Place he was besieged by enraged farmers: he was hit by various missiles including tomatoes and a full can of drink, and vigorous action by police and security officers was needed to protect him from serious injury. 'Supertonk', as the 72-year-old Premier was known, had wanted Whitlam to stay away during the election campaign. He felt that the timing and manner of some recent decisions like the cessation of the superphosphate bounty had shown little sensitivity to the state government's re-election prospects. Tonkin had lobbied strenuously in Canberra for the green light to a joint venture proposal for a 70% American-owned aluminium refinery near Bunbury, but 12 days before the election he learned that his efforts had been fruitless. The Whitlam cabinet endorsed Connor's refusal to compromise on the issue of majority Australian ownership and control, and indicated that it was also concerned about the environmental implications. One of the disappointed joint venturers with a financial interest in this Alwest project was Rupert Murdoch. On polling day there was a big swing against the Tonkin government in rural areas, although Labor's vote elsewhere held up satisfactorily. The statewide ALP vote declined only 0·81%, but the government could not survive the loss of three country seats.

In April 1974 a fresh controversy erupted. The sustained disruption of anti-Labor MPs had made it crucial for the Whitlam government to capture the numbers in the Senate. An election for half the Senate, with five vacancies to be filled in each state, was due in mid-1974. Combe calculated that to remove the Senate incubus Labor had to win two out of five seats at the election in Queensland and WA, the states where the party was then least popular, and three of the five vacancies in the other four states – a most unlikely eventuality, although not absolutely impossible. The government's objective became much more feasible when Whitlam and Murphy engineered a sixth vacancy in Queensland. As they knew, with six vacancies to be decided the proportional representation system would almost certainly deliver a result in Queensland of Labor three, anti-Labor three, thereby providing the FPLP with an extra Queensland seat. Early in April the sensational news broke that Gair, the hated Labor enemy who had been Queensland ALP Premier before the split and a DLP Senator since 1965, had agreed to become Australia's ambassador to Ireland. O'Byrne had learned that Gair was disenchanted with the DLP, and conveyed this intelligence to Murphy, who passed it on to Whitlam. The Prime Minister proceeded rapidly and secretly with the appointment despite the disapproval of Foreign Affairs minister Willesee, who was abroad. The appointment was, as Freudenberg conceded, 'audacious, opportunist and cynical', but the outrage of the opposition ignored the fact that its disruptive conduct had prompted Labor to resort to this manoeuvre. However, the ploy was stymied by Bjelke-Petersen, whose denunciations of the Whitlam government, skilfully publicized by his propaganda machine, were

351

cementing his previously shaky hold on the Queensland premiership. He rushed through the electoral formalities for a normal half-Senate election for five vacancies in Queensland before Gair actually resigned.

This setback to Labor's plans quickly became irrelevant when further momentous decisions were taken. The opposition resolved to use the Gair appointment as a pretext for rejecting a money bill in the Senate in order to force a government with a secure Representatives majority to hold an election. Obtaining ostensible justification for such unprecedented and unprincipled action had been the opposition's objective, as Withers admitted, ever since April 1973. There was a swift response from the government. Whitlam, who had been advised that the economic situation would get worse before it improved, retorted that his government would immediately initiate a double dissolution. There were plenty of grounds. The government had been in office for less than half the normal three-year term, yet in that time more bills had been rejected by the Senate than during any previous parliament (and, remarkably, more legislation had nonetheless been enacted than during any previous parliament). In addition to disallowing Hayden's health insurance bills, the Senate had rejected legislation to improve electoral fairness and to establish Connor's Petroleum and Minerals Authority. The double dissolution was accordingly granted, and on 18 May all 10 Senate vacancies in each state as well as every seat in the Representatives were to be decided.

Whitlam returned to Blacktown to launch Labor's campaign. Emphasizing how much the government had achieved despite being cut off in mid-stream, Whitlam claimed a number of firsts for his government. For the first time, he asserted, Australia's national government had pursued Australian ownership and control of Australian resources, had sought to achieve equality for all Australians with special attention to education and women, and had involved itself purposefully in urban issues, Aboriginal affairs, the national estate, and support for Australian culture and its creative artists. The sobering effect of the complexities of government, exacerbated by an unscrupulous opposition, had changed the mood of the Labor faithful. The audience at Blacktown 'was as enthusiastic as in 1972', observed Freudenberg, but 'the joyful exuberance of 1972 had given way to a kind of fierceness'. Snedden concentrated on economic issues, especially inflation, where the government was vulnerable. Among uncommitted voters the most compelling factor was Labor's appeal for a fair go. The result was so close that it took days to establish that Labor had won with a reduced majority in the Representatives. The final margin was 66 seats to 61. Labor's overall voting share had declined slightly since 1972. It gained the two newly created seats in ACT and WA, and its improvement in Melbourne's outer suburbs continued with the capture of Henty and Isaacs. But Labor's poor rural image proved costly. In NSW the ALP improved its statewide vote (as in Victoria), but lost three seats, two of them rural. One of them was Riverina, where the Country Party again mounted a campaign of racist slurs and scaremongering which Grassby was unable this time to overcome. The government lost another two seats, one of them rural, in Queensland, where the ALP voting share fell 3·17%.

Labor's win was distinctly creditable in the circumstances, but certain considerations robbed the victory of some of its lustre. The government had simultaneously submitted four referendum proposals seeking worthwhile constitutional amendments, but all four were defeated: each referendum was carried in NSW, but no other state voted in favour of any of them. Furthermore, the delay before the election result was known, coupled with Labor's narrow failure to obtain a Senate majority, created the impression that the government had suffered more of a setback than a victory. The opposition emerged unchastened after the failure of its grab for power. Country Party leader Doug Anthony, who was the driving force behind the opposition parties' decision to block supply, was unabashed about the adoption of this tactic and threatened to use it again. Clearly, the government faced renewed instability: every six months, whenever a money bill came before the Senate, the government might find itself forced to hold an election if the opposition could muster the numbers to block supply. But the opposition's ability to implement this threat was doubtful. The final result in the Senate, determined after five weeks of counting, was Labor 29, Liberal and Country parties 29, independents 2. One of the independents was a disaffected Liberal who formally rejoined his party not long after the election; the other was Hall, the former Liberal SA Premier, who was now representing a breakaway offshoot called the Liberal Movement and claimed a principled objection to blocking supply. Labor was tantalizingly close to a more secure Senate, but ALP supporters derived some consolation from the DLP's acceleration towards oblivion; that party entered the election with five Senators including McManus, but none were re-elected.

Whitlam had become the first FPLP leader to pilot Labor to victory at two successive elections. The Prime Minister was, as usual, inspiring, forceful and witty on the hustings. Only the most committed anti-Labor devotees would have disputed the correctness of Labor's campaign slogan 'Whitlam – he's so much better'. But he was affected by gloomy Treasury predictions about the economic outlook, and was not quite at his peak of 1969 and 1972. Hawke had good reason to seem somewhat preoccupied also. He had been experiencing more than his share of tribulations since his public clashes with the government late in 1973. His passionate commitment to the cause of Israel had distanced him from ALP activists like Hartley who supported Israel's foes in the Middle East conflict, and also resulted in death threats to his family. Nevertheless, Hawke plunged into a superb hardhitting campaign which greatly assisted the government. Other prominent Labor contributors at the 1974 election included Cairns, whose economic credentials and untheatrical sincerity made him a compelling ALP campaigner to swinging voters concerned about inflation, and Hayden, who was angry about Labor's poor effort in his home state. Outside Queensland Hayden and the government's health and welfare reforms were recognized as a vital component of Labor's pitch to the voters. However, at Labor's biggest campaign meeting in Brisbane the government's fourth-ranking minister found himself perched awkwardly on the same seat as Dallas in the audience while Egerton filled a central chair on the stage alongside Whitlam. After the election Egerton declared that the Whitlam government's decisions affecting rural regions were responsible for Labor's inadequate performance in his state. He defensively exonerated Queensland party officials from blame. Hayden was not alone in concluding that federal intervention into Queensland was warranted, but it did not eventuate.

A feature of the double dissolution was the election of three women Labor MPs. At the 1972 election Labor's total of 125 candidates for the Representatives included only four women and all were unsuccessful. In August 1973 Whitlam publicly admitted that the dearth of women in the ALP was embarrassing, and he was pleased that the 'sexist composition' of the FPLP was modified in 1974. Joan Child, one of the unsuccessful 1972 candidates, had broken through this time in Henty. A widow with five young sons, she had worked in a variety of jobs, most recently as a ministerial staffer for Cairns. Her win owed much to the efficient organization of a band of young enthusiasts who shared an Oakleigh residence and were known as the Henty House Mafia. The key figure in this group, Robert Ray, had contested Henty unsuccessfully in 1969 and had written a thesis for his Arts Honours degree on Frank Anstey. Another Victorian elected was Jean Melzer. As state ALP secretary she had been striving to have a woman included on the Senate ticket but had little success, and ended up reluctantly responding to a suggestion that she should nominate. She was allotted a virtually unwinnable spot on the ALP ticket. However, after the sudden double dissolution she emerged – to the chagrin of some male activists – in the highly prized fifth place on the amended ticket. Like Child, Melzer had considerable parental responsibilities; like Hayden on polling day 1961, she had private pangs of self-doubt and wondered if her candidature was a mistake. But the last thing she wanted was to be cited by smug opponents of women MPs as 'proof' that women could not cope, so she stifled her misgivings and in due course became a popular and respected Senator. Labor's third woman to be elected in 1974 was WA Senator Ruth Coleman, who had been a consumer activist and media publicist. The new Representatives seat in Coleman's home state had been named after the FPLP's pioneering woman Dorothy Tangney, a long-serving (1943–68) WA Senator; the inaugural MHR for Tangney was 27-year-old John Dawkins, a union secretary with a background in agricultural economics. The authors of a documentary collection entitled *The Australian Labor Party and Federal Politics* made a distinctive comment on the absence of any woman besides Tangney in the FPLP until 1974 when they included in their otherwise sober and serious textbook a chapter called 'Women in the Federal Labor Party' which consisted of two blank pages.

The success of these three women coincided with the Whitlam government's expansion of the horizons of Australian women. The 1972 platform and policy speech had contained few specific policies for women, but the early appointment of Elizabeth Reid as Whitlam's adviser on issues affecting the welfare of women helped to overcome this deficiency. In May 1974 the Arbitration Commission responded to the government's enthusiastic support for equal pay by extending the adult minimum wage to women. (Later that month the most dedicated battler for the cause of equal pay, Muriel Heagney, died aged 88.) Coalition governments from 1950 to 1972 had, despite pressure from the FPLP, repeatedly refrained from endorsing international conventions on discrimination, equal pay and political rights of women. The Whitlam government ratified them all, but it was hardly creditable to Australia that over 80 nations had already done so. Whitlam was proud of his government's achievements in advancing the cause of women:

> The Government initiated the most searching investigations into every kind of discrimination against women – in employment, in education, in social welfare, in the law. We established health centres and many women's refuges throughout Australia. We established a pre-school and child care program which catered for 100 000 children around Australia. We established the supporting mother's benefit. . .the most significant single innovation in social security for a generation.

In its appointments to boards, statutory authorities, courts and commissions the government broke new ground by choosing women whenever possible. Maternity leave was introduced for public servants. In 1974 a royal commission into human relationships was established, and the following year the government was acclaimed beyond Australia for its wholehearted participation in International Women's Year. Reid resigned in October 1975, and felt so scarred by the pressures of the job and media scrutiny that she left Australia. When she returned a decade later there was still much to be done in changing attitudes and removing discrimination, but the transformation since 1972 reinforced her conviction that Australian women had benefited greatly from the Whitlam government's initiatives:

> The Whitlam years gave women hope. They gave women and men new expectations. . .
> The Whitlam government made it clear to all women – rural, migrant, Aboriginal,
> women of all ages, levels of education and socio-economic class – that it was possible to
> take their lives into their own hands and change them.

Whitlam's cabinet was almost unchanged after the 1974 election. The only alteration in personnel was the inclusion of Wheeldon to fill the vacancy created by Grassby's failure to hold Riverina. There was one significant change, however: Cairns successfully challenged Barnard for the deputy leadership. With Uren and Hayden as his canvassers, Cairns won the ballot by 54 votes to 42. This victory reflected his high standing in caucus and a perception among many Labor MPs that Cairns would exert a stronger restraining influence on Whitlam.

The formulation of economic policy in the wake of the double dissolution caused the Whitlam government acute difficulty. Governments throughout the world were realizing that Keynesian economics was not the answer to everything. Economics students at Australian universities had recently been taught that inflation and unemployment were extremely unlikely to rise concurrently, yet this dual increase was exactly what the Whitlam government had to contend with in the perplexing third quarter of 1974. Its problems were aggravated by the large wage rises being won by some unionists and by the financial collapse of some brittle corporations. Treasury had recommended its traditional harsh medicine, 'a short sharp shock'. Hayden vigorously disagreed, and told his colleagues that Treasury had misjudged the state of the economy as well as callously disregarding the social consequences of increased unemployment. When convinced about a point of view Hayden could be very stubborn and dogmatic, no matter who disagreed with him. On this occasion a cabinet majority including Uren and Cameron concurred with Hayden, and the Treasury prescription was not implemented in the government's major economic statement in July. Whitlam, who had associated himself with the Treasury line, was annoyed by its rejection in cabinet and by Hayden's propensity to harangue him about the government's errors in economic policy. After one celebrated clash between them on 7 August Whitlam hardly spoke to Hayden for months.

Cairns was an influential minister in the anti-Treasury camp. After his election as deputy leader Whitlam had indicated that he could have the Treasury portfolio if he wanted it. But Cairns had declined, happy to stay at Overseas Trade provided he could take on a bigger role than formerly on broader economic issues. Cairns was in fact more suited to economic philosophy than day-to-day Treasury administration. In opposition days Cairns had advocated lower tariffs, but in government his willingness to provide financial aid for ailing enterprises in order to avoid unemployment earned him the nickname 'Dr Yes'. In September 1974 he flew to Sydney to discuss with Reserve Bank officials whether the money supply was being unduly contracted. He concluded, as Hayden had already, that monetary policy should be eased, and instructed the officials to end the credit squeeze. Whitlam was impressed with this intervention. Cairns was mistakenly hailed as the architect of the government's 1974 budget, which was in fact the product of something of a vacuum in economic policy. The Treasury medicine was again rejected, and cabinet framed the budget in a free-wheeling expansive mood, with most ministers providing enthusiastic mutual support for each others' expenditure proposals. Gross projected outlays rose over 32%, although the net increase in budgeted expenditure, allowing for inflation's impact on tax receipts, was around 10%.

Treasurer Crean found himself in an invidious position. Unlike Whitlam, he was not impressed by Cairns's sudden intervention in monetary policy. Crean was also appalled by the wild atmosphere prevalent during cabinet's budget deliberations, which he described in an uncharacteristically florid phrase as 'like a lunatic asylum'. He was dismayed by the approval of spending programmes he regarded as extravagant – particularly in Uren's Urban and Regional Development department, which increased its budget allocation by 173% – but he felt powerless to prevent it all by himself. Crean was almost invariably easy-going and unflappable, and it was simply not in his make-up to shout, rant and bombard colleagues with expletives to get his way; he regarded framing a budget as a collective process of give and take best handled in a reasonable and co-operative spirit without theatrics. He deplored the fierce hostility to Treasury officials displayed by ministers like Uren, Cameron and Murphy. Some detractors claimed that Crean was too 'weak' and 'low-key'; others admired his decency, sincerity and disinclination to grandstand about the budget, which he saw as an event grossly overrated by the media. As Crean knew, budgets often were significantly varied after being delivered, and in fact the 1974 budget strategy was soon amended as the government continued to grope for solutions to its daunting economic difficulties. While Crean was still upset about cabinet's budget decisions he indicated to Whitlam that he would have to consider his future.

The sequel was a prolonged fiasco which was unduly painful for Crean. Whitlam felt that if Cairns was making the running on economic policy it made sense for him to become Treasurer, and pressed him to agree. But Cairns was still ambivalent about Treasury, and Crean made it clear that his despondency had been fleeting and he wanted to stay where he was. For weeks Crean endured a distressing ordeal as rumours persistently circulated about his imminent demise as Treasurer, and the opposition had a field day. The impasse was further complicated by Cairns's absence overseas on government business early in November. A delegation of backbenchers urged Whitlam not to shift Crean, but after Cairns returned home Whitlam made the official announcement that Crean and Cairns would exchange portfolios. After the decision was taken Crean had a private word with Whitlam. 'Well Gough, you will be sorry. . .that you ever made Jimmy Treasurer', warned Crean, 'and. . .for goodness sake don't have anything to do with this loan business'.

Whitlam ignored Crean's warning. On 14 December Whitlam, Connor, Cairns and Murphy formally authorized Connor to borrow up to $4 billion. The 1973 oil crisis and the sudden big increase in the price of oil had endowed governments and individuals in the Middle East with fabulous riches. The investment potential of these billions of 'petrodollars' was undeniable, and the governments of Britain, Japan and France all negotiated large petrodollar loans. An Adelaide businessman who claimed he could obtain petrodollars at low interest rates was introduced by Cameron to Cairns and Connor in October 1974. After further discussions and inquiries, Connor met a Pakistani international commodities dealer, Tirath Khemlani, on 11 November. Khemlani was confident that petro-dollars were available at low interest rates, and he agreed to act as an intermediary between the Australian government and sources of wealth in the Middle East. The proposed loan was discussed and vetted at a number of top-level meetings involving senior ministers, lawyers, bankers and public servants. The possibility of acquiring development capital more cheaply than through more orthodox channels was worth exploring, and this unconventional avenue was all the more attractive to the senior ministers disenchanted with the advice the government had received during 1974 from the traditional repository of economic wisdom, the Treasury. For Connor, however, the massive loan was especially important. It would enable the government to finance his grand schemes so that Australians would be able to own, control and optimally benefit from Australia's resources. The minister 'who had refused to talk to mining moguls gave his instant trust to an uncredentialled small-timer from the back alleys of international finance'.

Having completed the formalities authorizing Connor to pursue the immense loan, Whitlam departed later that day for a lengthy overseas trip. Whitlam's international orientation and reformist zeal had greatly enhanced Australia's reputation abroad, but his penchant for extensive overseas travel was leaving him and the government vulnerable to damaging criticism, especially now that the economy was in strife. Circumstances conspired to make this European trip of five and a half weeks his most controversial. On Christmas Eve 1974 Australia suffered its worst natural disaster when Cyclone Tracy flattened Darwin. The death toll climbed to 66, and tens of thousands became homeless. Acting Prime Minister Cairns led the government's prompt and compassionate response. While Cairns was widely praised for his efforts, Whitlam's brief return to inspect the damage was seen as grudging and belated. When Whitlam resumed his overseas trip with a pre-arranged sightseeing visit to the Mediterranean, it was predictable that his detractors would assert that he preferred ancient ruins in Greece to present-day ruins in Australia. Twelve days later another disaster occurred when Hobart's Tasman Bridge collapsed after a ship crashed into one of the bridge pylons. Again there was loss of life and severe social dislocation (besides the numbers killed and injured, the accident ruptured the main traffic link between east and west Hobart). The last thing Whitlam wanted was pressure to break his journey again, and he was furious when informed of the Hobart tragedy: 'There's no possibility of a government guarding against mad or incompetent captains of ships or pilots of aircraft', he fumed on ABC radio.

Meanwhile some Labor MPs were concerned that one of the government's senior ministers was heading in the wrong direction. Late in 1974 two ALP Senators, Melzer and Gordon McIntosh, were startled to hear from a Labor staffer at Parliament House extraordinary allegations about Junie Morosi, a recently appointed assistant to Grassby, who had become a consultant to the government on community relations. These allegations were so disturbing that Melzer and McIntosh passed them on to Murphy, but he treated the accusations dismissively. Soon afterwards Morosi was a household name. Possessing an eye-catching presence and a strong personality, she rocketed into prominence in December 1974 when Cairns offered her a position on his staff. Their obvious rapport had been gossip fodder since September. Cairns was infuriated by the repeated advice he received not to proceed with the appointment because it was politically imprudent. He firmly believed that the frenzied media attention

357

endured by Morosi was derived from racist and sexist attitudes, which should therefore be resisted as stoutly as he had opposed irrational prejudice in earlier struggles.

Morosi was the catalyst for a transformation in Cairns. Two years at the pinnacle of government had not stilled his steadily growing inner doubts about the possibility of achieving real social change through parliamentary democracy in Australia. 'The Government is peripheral, its powers are not central' and it has 'limited scope to do things', he candidly admitted during a television interview in February 1975. For decades he had embodied controlled and rational resistance to economic and political suppression. Morosi convinced him that individual freedom could be restricted not just by these economic and political factors, but also by individuals' own self-repressive attitudes. Longstanding Cairns admirers were appalled by his fascination with Morosi and the possibilities of self-liberation. There was widespread resentment of his reduced accessibility after Morosi became his 'office co-ordinator'. She had no ALP background, and even Cairns admitted that she was not interested in economics. Cairns was of course entitled to personal growth and fulfilment, but Labor's rank and file understandably felt that while Cairns was Treasurer and deputy Prime Minister of a troubled national Labor government his preoccupation with such distractions was self-indulgent.

This intolerance was magnified by indiscreet remarks Cairns made to an anti-Labor journalist on the second last day of the ALP federal conference at Terrigal in February. Although this gathering had its exuberant and hedonistic moments, Combe and others recognized that it was an important opportunity for the government to gain some badly needed favourable publicity. But their strenuous efforts to achieve this were undermined by Cairns's comments about Morosi and his 'kind of love' for her. Labor enthusiasts winced when the down-market tabloids splashed these 'revelations' under lurid headlines.

Murphy's appointment to the High Court was announced two days after the Terrigal conference ended. A vacancy had arisen in November 1974, and Cairns had made the initial suggestion to Whitlam that Murphy could fill it. Murphy apparently approached the transition with some ambivalence – and it seems that his friendship with Morosi, and his consequent involvement in the extraordinary publicity she showed no talent for avoiding, contributed to the delay in filling the vacancy – but he accepted the appointment in February. Caucus elected Jim McClelland as Murphy's cabinet replacement. Whitlam gave him Manufacturing Industry, and Enderby succeeded Murphy as Attorney-General. After Murphy's controversial stint as Attorney-General his transfer to the High Court produced the greatest outcry about a judicial appointment since Evatt and McTiernan in 1930. It was the same old story. Choosing judges with Labor affiliations was scandalous, yet it was the acme of sound wisdom to elevate such notoriously anti-Labor identities as Latham and Barwick not merely to the High Court bench but directly to the post of Chief Justice, which gave them a casting vote in the event of deadlock and significant power over how the court functioned.

But the choice of Murphy's replacement as a NSW Senator resulted in even greater uproar. Ever since the introduction of proportional representation for Senate elections in 1949 a mid-term Senate vacancy had always been filled by a member of the same party as the departing Senator. On this occasion the convention was broken when NSW's Liberal Premier, Tom Lewis, decided to ignore

74. The Whitlam ministry with the Queen, 1973. Standing (from left): L. Bowen, L. Johnson, K. Enderby, G. Bryant, J. Cavanagh, K. Beazley, T. Uren, M. Cass, F. Daly, C. Cameron, K. Wriedt, C. Jones, R. Connor, F. Stewart, A. Grassby, W. Morrison, D. Everingham and D. Smith (the Governor-General's official secretary). Seated: D. McClelland, F. Crean, J. Cairns, G. Whitlam, the Queen, L. Barnard, W. Hayden, L. Murphy, R. Patterson. Absent: R. Bishop, D. Willesee. (*National Library*)

75. Don Dunstan, Rex Connor and Bob Hawke displaying contrasting dress styles as they lead a trade union march in Adelaide. (*Advertiser*)

76. Gough Whitlam on the Parliament House steps after the dismissal. (*Australian Consolidated Press*)

77. Tandberg's comment on the dismissal. (*Age*)

78. Neville Wran (centre) with Geoff Cahill (left) and John Ducker.

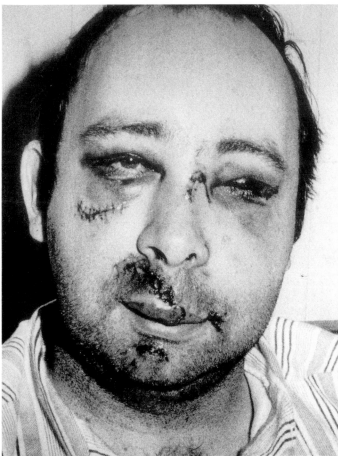

79. Peter Baldwin after he was bashed. (*John Fairfax*)

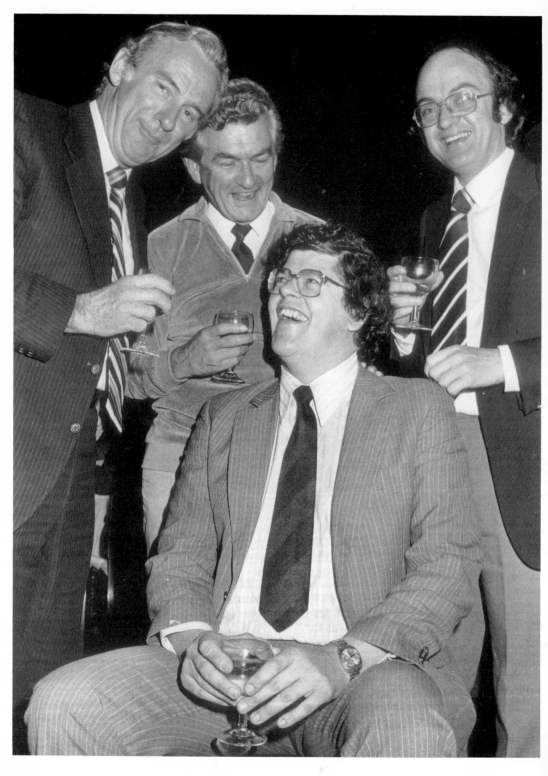

80. Bill Hayden and Bob Hawke with David Combe (seated) and Bob McMullan. (*Herald and Weekly Times*)

the voters' wishes expressed less than a year earlier. His selection was 'a political neuter', 77-year-old Albury mayor Cleaver Bunton. This outrageous manoeuvre was condemned by other premiers (Labor and anti-Labor), by a resolution carried unanimously in the Senate, and by numerous other senior Liberals including Snedden, who tried to have the decision reversed but suffered an embarrassing rebuff.

On 27 February there was a sensational incident in the Representatives, where the opposition's sustained disruption had created an explosive atmosphere. A clash between Cameron and the Speaker, Labor MHR Jim Cope, arising from opposition provocation escalated when Whitlam intervened to support Cameron. Cope resigned as Speaker, and was replaced by Scholes, who proved more adept at controlling unruly proceedings. Cope remained loyal to his party and publicly silent about the regrettable episode, but once again blaring headlines discredited the government. In adversity Whitlam characteristically counter-attacked. Snedden was so clearly outclassed that a second attempt by Fraser to topple him as Liberal leader was successful.

Meanwhile Connor was still yearning to hear that Khemlani had clinched delivery of the petrodollars. The upper limit of Connor's borrowing authority had been halved, in part because of the intervention of senior Treasury bureaucrats who strongly disapproved of the government's loan-raising attempts through unconventional sources. Although Khemlani had provided nothing more tangible than repeated optimistic assurances, Connor clung to the hope that the promised petrodollars would eventually materialize and turn his dreams into reality. Keating, who had interested himself in Minerals and Energy issues and befriended Connor,

> found him morning after morning, in March and April, asleep in his office, unshaven and dishevelled, waiting for the ring and rattle of the telex machine, which would herald Khemlani's message that he had at last delivered the goods. It never came. . . Keating pleaded with him, 'For God's sake, Rex, this is no way for a Minister to behave'. The strain was telling visibly. Connor's giant frame seemed to shrink. And still he held on, in pursuit of his dream.

The Whitlam government came under increasing pressure about its loan-raising activities. Opposition MPs had demonstrated by their actions since 1973 that they had never accepted the legitimacy of the government, and during 1975 it 'was subject to an unrelenting attack on its morality. There was a skilful and extraordinarily successful effort to portray it as shoddy, tainted, even corrupt'. The 'Morosi affair', Cope's resignation and Murphy's appointment to the High Court were three of many episodes elevated by the opposition to the status of 'scandal', but the biggest of all was the 'loans affair'. In its attacks on the Whitlam government the opposition enjoyed the support of powerful allies. Senior Treasury officials, who were resentful of the influence of Connor's Minerals and Energy department and appalled by the government's unorthodox borrowing procedures, leaked information and documents to destabilize the government they were supposed to be serving. The opposition was also greatly assisted by the media. The press had hounded previous national ALP governments – notably the Scullin government, and also the Chifley government from 1947 – but the media harassment of the Whitlam government in 1975 belongs in a special category. The government had denied Rupert Murdoch financial enrichment in the Alwest project as well as rejecting his request to be High Commissioner in London, and the Murdoch press was particularly virulent in 1975. 'Investigative journalism', which had recently been instrumental in the downfall of an American president, was all the rage, and Australian reporters (along with opposition staff) were sent overseas to probe the loans 'scandal'. Rumours flourished, and an atmosphere of crisis was created.

Connor's obsessive and secretive temperament contributed to the government's generally defensive attitude to the media emphasis on the loans affair. Publicizing its initiatives to the electorate was not one of the government's strengths, and it did not sufficiently emphasize the worthwhile aims of its attempted borrowing; nor did it make sufficient effort to dispel the damaging and unfounded innuendoes about ministerial venality, long-term repayment obligations and the non-involvement of government officials. There was in fact no loan. There was no financial commitment. The only payments in the loans affair were made by newspaper ferrets trying to persuade Khemlani and others to part with documents.

In autumn 1975 Barnard told Whitlam that he wanted to retire. With the integration of the Army, Navy and Air departments into a consolidated Defence department now completed, Barnard had achieved his significant portfolio objectives. Politics had lost some of its appeal after he was replaced as deputy leader. He was jaded after 21 years in parliament, he was increasingly troubled by a wartime ear injury, and his wife was ill. He accepted a posting to Stockholm as Australia's ambassador to Sweden, Finland and Norway. As Whitlam knew, mid-1975 was hardly the time for an avoidable by-election in a far from impregnable Labor seat, but his comradeship for a loyal and esteemed colleague (who was not as subservient to Whitlam as he was commonly portrayed) prevailed over political considerations. Whitlam was also aware that by acceding to Barnard's wishes he would gain extra flexibility in the cabinet reshuffle he was considering. Combe first heard of Barnard's resignation from a journalist and refused to believe it. He told the ALP federal executive (now renamed the national executive) that 'the creation of a by-election in Bass epitomized the total breakdown of meaningful consultation between the Government and the Party'. Hawke heard about it in Europe, and lashed out publicly against this 'act of Galstonian madness'. The ballot for the cabinet vacancy created by Barnard's resignation was won by NSW MHR Joe Riordan.

Whitlam attempted to arrest the government's slide by acting boldly. He decided to replace Cameron at Labor and Immigration with Jim McClelland. Cameron proudly claimed that during the 12 months from September 1973 he had presided over 'the greatest redistribution in the favour of wage earners ever to be recorded in any one year by any country in the world'. After Cameron's years of feuding with Dougherty and other AWU heavyweights, the reforms he introduced enshrining democracy in the internal administration of unions also gave him much satisfaction. But with a spreading awareness in the government that increases had to be curtailed if the inflationary spiral was to be checked, Cameron's undoing was his advocacy in cabinet of a wage rise sought by metalworkers in addition to their wage indexation entitlements. Cameron abhorred some of the wage differentials which had evolved in Australia, especially the relatively favoured position of clerical workers in the public service. To him it was outrageous that 'a 23 year old clerk can receive more than a highly skilled toolmaker with 23 years' experience at his trade'. Although wage indexation would hardly have been reintroduced for the first time since 1953 without Cameron's strenuous advocacy, it was adopted on a universal full percentage basis which preserved wage differentials instead of his preferred version which would have reduced them. This prompted him to back the metalworkers' claim: if they were denied it, he contended, indexation would not succeed. Vigorous opposition in cabinet came from Jim McClelland, who believed that a firm attitude to union demands had become essential; he deplored the notion of supporting the metalworkers' claim with its probable flow-on effects. Next day Whitlam offered him Cameron's portfolio. McClelland assented. Cameron, however, refused to accept the demotion from his cherished post as Labor minister to Science and Consumer Affairs. An uncomfortable visit by Whitlam to Cameron's office, where the Prime Minister found himself perched on the smallest chair Cameron's 32-year-old private secretary John Bannon could find after scouring Parliament House, brought no resolution. It was only after Uren and Daly intervened that Cameron agreed to co-operate. Smouldering with resentment, Cameron turned his prized photo of Whitlam to the wall, revealing the prime ministerial inscription on the back praising Cameron as 'a principal architect of victory' in 1972.

In another major switch Whitlam promoted Hayden to take over as Treasurer from Cairns. The economy had shown signs of responding to Cairns's humanitarian approach, but his stature had been eroded by the Morosi saga and by his erratic pronouncements about the direction of government economic policy. With the government reeling from the loans affair exposure, the last straw for Whitlam was the discovery that Cairns had encouraged additional unconventional borrowing ventures. This information was brought to Whitlam by the departmental head of Treasury unbeknown to Cairns. Hayden had overcome the fierce resistance to Medibank, which was about to begin operation. He threw himself into his new role, pushing himself to the limit as he burned the midnight oil poring over the files. He was determined to be a very different Treasurer from his predecessor. There was no more waffle about the economics of love, and Hayden also made it clear that there would be no more dabbling in funny-money deals with the shonky green-sunglasses brigade. Hayden was not fazed by occasional cabinet confrontations with even his most intimidating colleagues. His labours resulted in a budget which managed to attract widespread admiration at a time when the government was at its lowest ebb. Whitlam soon regretted that he had not made Hayden Treasurer earlier.

Cairns's swift descent continued. On 6 June he was sworn in as Environment minister, but less than a month later he became the centre of further dramatic developments. The Melbourne *Age* sensationally alleged that the involvement of Cairns's stepson Philip in a housing scheme had positioned him to profit from being on his stepfather's staff. The accusations were grossly exaggerated, but there was sufficient evidence that Philip Cairns had blurred the distinction between his public and private roles for his stepfather to be politically embarrassed. Even more damaging was the emergence of a document which indicated that Jim Cairns had misled parliament when he stated that he had never given anyone authority to negotiate a loan or agreed to a specific commission. The document was a letter from Cairns to a businessman authorizing the pursuit of loan-raising negotiations and stipulating a 2½% brokerage fee. Cairns fervently insisted that he had no recollection of ever signing that letter, and observers familiar with his administratively chaotic office accepted that he could easily have done so inadvertently, but Whitlam forced his removal from cabinet. When caucus met to fill the cabinet vacancy Cairns appealed to his colleagues to reinstate him. Berinson was ultimately successful, but the voting indicated that many FPLP members agreed with Cairns that he had been punished unduly harshly.

The ballot for a new deputy leader was won by Crean, who had always regarded the unconventional borrowing attempts as the height of folly. 'The chickens are coming home to roost in their own quiet way' was his wry comment about his comeback.

With the government under media siege, Whitlam made a desperate bid to regain the initiative by recalling parliament during the winter recess for a special sitting to debate the loans affair. He challenged the opposition to 'put up or shut up'. Masses of documents were assembled. When tabled by Whitlam in parliament, they filled 37 pages of Hansard. The Prime Minister upheld the propriety of his government's loan-raising objectives and methods in a powerful speech. He denounced the 'squalid intrigue', 'inquisition by innuendo', 'the orgy of trivia drummed up as investigative reporting' and 'the pseudo-events of the media'. He also spoke warmly about Cairns. That tragic figure made an emotional speech. 'Perhaps I do wear my heart too easily on my sleeve', he conceded. But the most memorable contribution came from Connor, who released at Whitlam's insistence a separate batch of documents which mostly comprised dozens of telex messages to and from Khemlani. 'I am an honest man', declared the Strangler.

> I deal with honest people. . .I have stood in the path of those who would have grabbed the mineral resources of Australia. I have no apologies whatever to make for what I have done. . .I fling in the face of the little men of the Opposition the words of an old Australian poem:
>
> > Give me men to match my mountains,
> > Give me men to match my plains,
> > Men with freedom in their vision,
> > And creation in their brains. . .
>
> I treat with contempt the allegations of the Opposition.

The verse was actually American and Connor, speaking from memory, slightly misquoted it, but it was a stirring conclusion to his speech.

The result of the Bass by-election confirmed that both the Whitlam government and the Tasmanian ALP were in desperate trouble. Bass had rural components and textile mills hard hit by the tariff cuts. The loss of Barnard's personal following was another crucial factor, and the inept and half-hearted campaign by senior Labor Tasmanians was also significant: 'To say that the local organization in Bass was atrocious would be to praise it', Combe asserted. However, even allowing for these special considerations in Bass, it was obvious that the catastrophic 17·34% anti-Labor swing which delivered the seat to the Liberals signified that the Whitlam government was, as Combe admitted, 'extraordinarily unpopular'. He was scathing about the tendency of leading Labor MPs 'to jump out into perk jobs without consultation with the Party' at a time when it was vulnerable: 'We look like a Party of junketeers who don't expect to be in Office often or long'.

The result in Bass also reflected Tasmanian Labor's internal strife. The heady developments in Canberra under Whitlam encouraged Tasmanian left-wingers, Labor Youth activists, conservationists and other radicals disaffected with their state government. For too long, they felt, Tasmanian Labor governments had been too conservative and too subservient to the HEC. Not for nothing was Premier Reece dubbed 'Electric Eric'. He insisted that the latest HEC project had to proceed irrespective of its ruinous environmental consequences. The

Whitlam government's repeated blandishments and pressure were not enough to prevent the flooding of beautiful Lake Pedder. The 1973 Tasmanian ALP conference 'provided a forum for an unprecedented outburst of anger and exasperation'. Afterwards there was persistent controversy and discord, featuring expulsions and allegations of corruption. Hostility to Reece and his authoritarian style resulted in a motion being carried at the 1975 state conference which introduced an age limit of 65 for ALP candidates, effectively ending the Premier's career. He resigned immediately. His successor, Neilson, took over at a very difficult time just after the Hobart bridge calamity. There was also the Harradine factor. Harradine still had plenty of sympathizers, and had been an influential member of the state ALP executive since early 1972. When he was again denied accreditation as a federal executive delegate he and his supporters boycotted the Bass preselection. As a result the party endorsed a left-wing candidate, who received from his factional adversaries during the by-election campaign lukewarm or non-existent support. According to Combe, the Tasmanian ALP 'was hopelessly divided by the preselection struggle' and its future prospects were 'disastrous'.

Labor's only other government was travelling much better than its counterparts in Canberra and Tasmania. The Dunstan government had been comfortably re-elected in 1973. The Premier was so impressed with Hudson's 'consumate skill' in handling the Education portfolio that, according to Dunstan, no other national or state minister for Education in Australian history 'could equal his record and achievements'. Attorney-General King was a busy reformer, especially in consumer protection, and Virgo was effective at Transport. Corcoran made an invaluable contribution as Dunstan's deputy, notably by maintaining governmental cohesion in his breezy extroverted manner. But it was the Premier who continued to dominate the government, the media and the state. Dunstan involved himself particularly in financial, industry, planning and cultural issues. He enhanced his celebrity status by participating in artistic events, and also by writing a book about the only hobby he had time for in his hectic schedule, cooking. This cookbook produced unexpected political benefits for its author and his party by boosting his support among SA women.

Yet even Dunstan found his tenure of office endangered in mid-1975 by the Whitlam government. Relations between Dunstan and Whitlam had been occasionally stormy. Whitlam believed that state governments were anachronistic and Australians would be much better served by a two-tiered system with a national government at the centre and regional administrative authorities. Often in his dealings with state governments he seemed to resent the fact that his preferred system, however desirable, was not in operation. At times he infuriated Dunstan, especially when he gave the impression that he would like to starve the states financially into handing over functions to the national government. Dunstan had other grievances with the Whitlam government. He 'couldn't fault' Connor's objectives – 'The Liberals' policy of making us a Japanese and American mine where we were once a British farm is hopelessly shortsighted', proclaimed the Premier – yet he found Connor's intransigence profoundly frustrating when it affected a development project in his state. But SA did accept when Whitlam offered the states conditional grants, whereas the anti-Labor states often refused to accept these payments. They also rejected the Whitlam government's offer to take over each state's railways, whereas the Labor governments of SA and Tasmania assented. These railways arrangements were particularly advantageous to SA, and, when its Legislative Council again flexed its muscles and rejected the Railways Transfer Agreement Bill, Dunstan immediately called an election. However, between the announcement and polling day on 12 July the Whitlam government attracted immensely unfavourable publicity arising from the loans affair, the Bass by-election and the downfall of Cairns. Denunciation of the Whitlam government was the SA Liberals' main campaign emphasis. Combe became increasingly concerned about the outcome. He estimated that in SA the Whitlam government's approval rating had plummeted to about 35%, and there were grave fears that this unpopularity was harming Labor's prospects on 12 July. In a late switch in Labor's advertising Dunstan disowned 'Canberra's mistakes', and urged voters not to be misled by the opposition's smear tactics which had placed his government in danger. This last-minute plea was widely credited with saving his government – on polling day he retained office very narrowly.

Bjelke-Petersen continued to be a thorn in Whitlam's side. The Queensland election in December 1974 was something of a personal duel between them. The Premier campaigned primarily on the alleged evils of centralism and communism emanating from Canberra. Whitlam answered the challenge, involving himself prominently and extensively in the campaign. Bjelke-Petersen had announced the election in parliament during a long and rambling tirade against the Whitlam government. The newly elected Queensland Labor leader, Percy Tucker, rose to reply, but the Premier demonstrated his regard for the political niceties by ruthlessly gagging debate. 'Democracy is dead in this State!' and 'You're gutless!' were two audible shouts from Tucker in the uproar that followed. 'Come out on the hustings Joh and I'll slaughter you!' he roared. However, this brave forecast proved spectacularly wrong. Tucker tried valiantly to stick to state issues, but was overshadowed by the Whitlam versus Bjelke-Petersen contest. On 7 December Tucker lost his seat and Labor was slaughtered. Its vote fell to 36%, which was still a higher voting share than any other party, but under the preferential system and the gerrymander Labor's parliamentary contingent was slashed from 33 to a mere 'cricket team' of 11.

Bjelke-Petersen compounded the FPLP's problems with an act of political infamy. The death of popular Queensland ALP Senator Bert Milliner occurred during those eventful mid-1975 weeks which were so traumatic for the Whitlam government. Flouting the convention on Senate replacements, Bjelke-Petersen rejected Labor's nominated representative to succeed Milliner and appointed instead little-known Pat Field, who, although ostensibly a Labor man, was determined to oppose the Whitlam government in the Senate. Whitlam was furious. Labor supporters were already nauseated by the cloak of pious homespun rectitude which accompanied Bjelke-Petersen's unscrupulous politics and narrow-minded hostility to enlightened reform. When Whitlam angrily described Bjelke-Petersen publicly as 'a Bible-bashing bastard' his remark was understandable, but it was not smart politics. It only further antagonized Bjelke-Petersen's admirers.

In October 1975 the loans affair returned to centre stage. Prior to the special parliamentary sitting on 9 July Whitlam had repeatedly asked Connor (whose borrowing authority had been revoked on 20 May) to furnish all relevant documents. When asked in parliament whether all loan-raising documents had been tabled, Whitlam replied that according to Connor 'all communications of substance between him and Mr Khemlani were tabled by him on 9 July'. However, the Melbourne *Herald*'s searches through piles of Khemlani's documents revealed abundant messages from Khemlani to Connor after 20 May, together with one from Connor to Khemlani on 23 May: 'I await further specific communication from your principals for consideration'. That telex caused Whitlam to seek Connor's resignation. Whitlam insisted that there was no impropriety in maintaining contact with Khemlani; Connor's fatal transgression was his failure to submit all documentation, thereby causing the Prime Minister to mislead the parliament. Connor protested that the messages in question were not 'communications of substance'. At the next day's caucus meeting he spiritedly defended his conduct, but added that his health was so poor that he would prefer to resign. Many FPLP members indicated that they wanted the Strangler to remain in the ministry, and his resignation was accepted 'with regret'. The ballot for the cabinet vacancy was held a week later and won, ironically, by Connor's friend Keating. It was less than three years since 27 elated ministers were sworn in on 19 December 1972, but only six of them now had the same ministerial responsibilities.

However, by the time Keating became a minister the situation had changed dramatically. On 15 October Fraser announced that the opposition would defer supply. Hall, the dissident Liberal Senator, had maintained his adherence to the basic principle that the lower house, the Representatives, was where governments are made and unmade, and it was alien to the traditions of parliamentary democracy for the Senate to block the passage of money bills. It was especially abhorrent when the Senate was only able to take this action because the convention-wrecking of anti-Labor premiers had distorted the Senate representation determined by the people in May 1974. As Hall so aptly thundered on 16 October, the opposition had 'marched on the sleazy road to power. . .over a dead man's corpse'. The opposition had opted for indefinite deferral of the budget bills in the Senate because a few anti-Labor Senators had sufficient scruples to baulk at outright rejection of the budget, which, after all, had been widely acclaimed when Hayden unveiled it two months earlier. In 1974, when the Senate blocked supply for the first time ever, an election had resulted, but on Whitlam's terms – a double dissolution, called with a view to removing the odious spectre of an overweening Senate. This time Whitlam had resolved not to accommodate the Senate in the slightest. In September he warned that if the Senate blocked supply again there would be 'no laws at all' covering the situation, and certainly 'no obligation by law, by rule, by precedent or convention' requiring the Prime Minister to call an election in such circumstances. On 15 October Whitlam assured caucus that he was determined not to submit to the Senate. He proposed to stand firm and intimidate the opposition Senators into an ignominious backdown. Wriedt and Wheeldon expressed misgivings, but there was strong FPLP support for Whitlam's tactical objective in the momentous struggle to uphold the fundamental primacy of the lower house.

Whitlam's profound attachment to the institution and traditions of parliament was evident in his stirring response to the denial of supply in October 1975. He characteristically placed the 'present crisis. . .in the grand line of the great constitutional struggles of the past – of 1640, 1688, 1832 and 1910'. The reference to 1910 underlined Australia's misfortune in having its inflexible Constitution determined, by a quirk of historical timing, a mere decade before the British House of Lords was humbled and stripped of its power to block supply. As Whitlam pointed out, in 1975 Australia was the only parliamentary democracy with an upper house able to take such action. The Prime Minister was at his inspirational best. Even Cameron, who still bitterly resented his demotion, was eulogistic:

How could any lover of democracy fail to admire the fighting qualities, the resilience and the intellectual qualities of the present Prime Minister? Why is it that the Federal Parliamentary Labor Party is now being seen at its magnificent best? Why is it that the Labor movement outside Parliament is now more solidly united than ever before? It is because of the inspiration given by the Prime Minister in this present crisis, the man who in this Parliament stands out like a giant against the intellectual and moral pygmies who sit opposite him. It is because the Prime Minister has thrown down the gauntlet in defence of parliamentary government that I stand proudly beside him. That is why I and my ministerial colleagues stand solidly behind the Prime Minister in this, the most important fight of his life, the most important fight that the Australian people have ever fought in their lives.

The government soon had the opposition on the defensive. As days and weeks passed with the deadlock unresolved, Whitlam and his ministers maximized the pressure on the anti-Labor Senators, pointing out the hardships that would ensue when the government ran out of money to pay wages, pensions and allowances. Hayden, in association with Crean, Whitlam and Enderby, began evaluating possible alternative methods of enabling the government to carry on its normal financial transactions without supply. Outside parliament there was a vast groundswell of support for Whitlam's defiance, while the opposition's stance attracted widespread condemnation and some violence. At no other time have Australians followed a political confrontation more attentively or more passionately. In a marvellous turnaround for Labor, opinion polling revealed that the government's approval rating had climbed back to 47%, and it was estimated that 70% of voters disagreed with the blocking of supply. Labor's pollster Rod Cameron cautioned that an imminent election would probably still be unwinnable, but there was optimism in ALP ranks that the government had turned the corner. After the turmoil of the preceding 15 months the government was beginning to demonstrate more competence in the crucial domain of economic policy. Jim McClelland had made himself unpopular with the unions by sternly resisting wage demands in order to curb inflation, and no minister in Whitlam's cabinet had advanced his reputation more than Hayden. Having barely spoken to Hayden for months, Whitlam was now promoting the excellence of 'the Hayden budget' and describing its architect as Australia's greatest Treasurer since Chifley. Whitlam himself was supremely confident. He and other Labor optimists believed that the government could use its forthcoming constitutional victory as the springboard for a sustained recovery which might see it returned to office at the election due in 18 months.

Meanwhile the Liberals were wilting. Newspapers which a month earlier had urged Whitlam to resign were now advocating the passage of the supply bills. So too were influential anti-Labor identities like ex-Premier Playford. Morale among opposition backbenchers was sagging. Anti-Labor interests again brought Khemlani and his copious documents to Australia, but the ploy backfired when Daly ridiculed it in one of his most hilarious parliamentary sallies. Withers was desperately trying to control several wavering Senators who were on the verge of buckling and allowing supply through. Some senior Liberals were privately trying to persuade Fraser to devise a compromise and back down, but he hung on doggedly.

Fraser and other conservatives made it increasingly clear that they were pinning their hopes on intervention by the Governor-General, Sir John Kerr. The son of a boilermaker, Kerr had risen through the law to become Chief Justice of NSW. He had an acute intellect, a fondness for alcohol and a prodigious white mane. On the morning after supply was first deferred Jim McClelland found himself briefly alone with opposition frontbencher R.J. Ellicott QC, who was a friend of Kerr's and had recently co-authored a legal textbook with him. 'You won't get away with this', said McClelland. 'Oh yes we will', replied Ellicott. 'In the end this will all depend on Old Silver and he'll do the right thing'. That very afternoon Ellicott, who was Barwick's cousin and Fraser's chief constitutional adviser, publicly claimed that if the Prime Minister could not obtain supply and refused to initiate an election the Governor-General should dismiss him.

The announcement in February 1974 that Kerr would become Governor-General was made almost six months after Whitlam first offered the post to him. At Kerr's request, Whitlam arranged to have the position's salary considerably increased and a Governor-General's pension introduced before Kerr was sworn in on 11 July 1974. Kerr and Jim McClelland had been very close during the 1950s when they represented the Groupers together in numerous bitter legal battles. They had since drifted apart as Kerr became drawn – in the phrase McClelland was fond of using – to 'the big end of town'. McClelland had always known Kerr to be fascinated by politics, power and the world of affairs beyond the law. According to Diamond Jim, Kerr saw himself as a potential prime minister, 'but he did not have the gritty perseverance to fight his way through the factional brawls and sheer political tedium which are inseparable from such a quest'. By becoming Governor-General Kerr could attain high office, salary and status the easy way and dabble in public affairs as well. It was a congenial position involving 'prestige without toil'. Whitlam had discussed Kerr and alternative choices beforehand with none of his ministers except Barnard. The appointment displeased some Labor people including Hawke, who while ACTU advocate had encountered and disliked Kerr, referring to him as 'Goldilocks' and 'the Liberace of the Law'. Other union leaders were also critical. But these few rumblings were nothing more than expressions of regret that an appointment to a post requiring little more than a ceremonial figurehead had not gone to a more worthy recipient.

Despite the pressure being placed on the Governor-General by anti-Labor interests, there was little concern in Labor's ranks about Kerr. Whitlam was adamant that the Governor-General was constitutionally obliged to follow the advice of the Prime Minister only, and his boundless confidence was infectious. Besides, Kerr's legal expertise and reputation, coupled with his humble social origins and earlier close links with ALP figures like Evatt and McClelland, surely precluded any possibility that he might blatantly assist the conservatives. Even Hawke and others inclined to disparage Kerr became convinced. During the crisis Kerr went out of his way to reassure Whitlam, McClelland and others about his intentions. To Whitlam he complained about intimidation from the Murdoch press, and said of Ellicott's appreciation of the constitutional situation, 'it's all bullshit isn't it?'.

Kerr received a number of visitors at Yarralumla on 6 November. Enderby called to deliver a legal opinion on behalf of the government. This document disputed Ellicott's memorandum, and stated that no government had been dismissed by the British monarch or a vice-regal representative since 1783. Enderby remarked to Kerr that his own personal view was that the Governor-General's reserve powers to intervene overtly no longer existed. He also told Kerr that the crisis would 'be over in a week' because some anti-Labor Senators were about to crack. Hayden gave Kerr an identical prediction when he called at Yarralumla that same afternoon to deliver a progress report on the government's alternative financial arrangements. Hayden was disturbed to find Kerr not very interested in that subject. The Governor-General's comments convinced Hayden that the government's faith in Kerr's reliability might be misplaced. Hayden had a plane to catch, but rushed back to Parliament House to warn Whitlam personally that his 'copper's instinct' told him that Kerr could be contemplating drastic action to break the deadlock. 'Comrade, he wouldn't have the guts', replied Whitlam scornfully.

The dramatic climax came on 11 November, a date already notable in Australian history. On that day Ned Kelly was hanged, and the Armistice ended the Great War; ever since 1918 Australia has commemorated 11 November as Remembrance Day. With Labor's approval rating in the polls continuing to rise, Whitlam had decided to hold a half-Senate election. On Tuesday 11 November 1975 (the anniversary of Connor's first meeting with Khemlani) Whitlam, Crean and Daly met Fraser, Anthony and Liberal deputy P.R. Lynch at 9 am to discuss a compromise proposed by Whitlam: if the coalition Senators persisted with their intransigence the half-Senate election would be held before Christmas, but if supply was allowed through Whitlam was prepared to postpone the half-Senate poll to mid-1976. The discussions proved predictably fruitless, but Crean was intrigued by the anti-Labor trio's confident air. 'They seem pretty cocky', he observed after they departed. Daly agreed. As Combe had done earlier that morning, Crean asked Whitlam if there was any doubt about the Governor-General, and Whitlam again brushed the query aside. Soon afterwards Whitlam briefed caucus about the latest developments, and announced that he was seeing the Governor-General at lunchtime to recommend a half-Senate election. Caucus exultantly endorsed this decision. The FPLP shared the Prime Minister's confidence that victory in the crisis seemed within sight.

At Yarralumla Whitlam experienced the biggest shock of his life. The conversation in the study was brief. Kerr pre-empted any discussion about a half-Senate election, and handed Whitlam a formal notice of dismissal and an explanatory statement. Kerr added that Barwick agreed with this course of action. Kerr had earlier asked Whitlam if he could obtain advice from Barwick; Whitlam had strong views about the impropriety of approaching the Chief Justice and vetoed the idea, but now learned that Kerr had proceeded to consult Barwick behind his back. 'We shall all have to live with this', observed Kerr. 'You certainly will', Whitlam retorted. As Whitlam departed, trying to adjust to the unthinkable, Fraser was summoned from a nearby waiting-room to be sworn in as Prime Minister.

From Yarralumla Whitlam proceeded not to Parliament House but to the Lodge, where he made preparations for a council of war with selected colleagues and advisers, including Crean, Daly, Enderby, Combe and Freudenberg. 'The bastard's sacked us' was his abrupt greeting to most of them as they arrived separately while he was devouring a steak. This numbing bombshell inhibited collective consideration, in the limited time available, of the FPLP's tactical options. 'All present were in a state of shock', recalled Daly. Whitlam's focus was instinctively and exclusively on how the FPLP could utilize its majority in the Representatives. He did not give the Senate a thought, and the others either did likewise or mistakenly assumed that Labor's Senate leaders had been informed of the dismissal. In the Representatives a censure motion was being debated, and Crean was scheduled to begin his speech at 2 pm, after the lunch break. The Lodge group, unaware that Fraser had been commissioned on condition that he could obtain the passage of supply, decided that Crean would make this speech as arranged and Whitlam would introduce a no-confidence motion later. Whitlam urged Crean not to mention the dismissal, in order to give Whitlam and his fellow tacticians the maximum possible time to refine their plans.

When the Senate resumed after lunch, Labor's Senators were still in the dark about Kerr's ambush. The FPLP had repeatedly resubmitted the deferred supply bills in order to maintain pressure on the opposition during the crisis, and they were due to be debated once again in the Senate just after lunch on 11 November. Withers, who had just emerged from a jubilant throng in Fraser's office, soon realized that there had been a communication breakdown in the FPLP when he indicated to Labor's Senate leaders that his anti-Labor Senators would now let the supply bills through. 'I always knew you'd give in at the end', Doug McClelland enthused. 'You've buckled at last, have you?' added Wriedt. When Withers told them that Fraser had become Prime Minister they thought he was joking. About 2.15 pm an aide rocked Wriedt by confirming that Withers had been deadly serious. With dumbfounded Labor Senators still in shock, supply was quickly whipped through the Senate, which then adjourned.

All eyes were then directed to the action in the Representatives. Crean had just completed one of the most extraordinary speeches ever heard in that chamber. He had been removed as a minister – indeed as deputy Prime Minister – because of the unscrupulous denial of supply, the very tactic which had also cut short his initial term in the Victorian Assembly almost exactly 28 years before. Yet, as Whitlam had requested, he managed to deliver a sturdy defence of the Whitlam government as if it still existed. He made only a few oblique references to the unprecedented situation:

> governments are made and unmade only in the House of Representatives. What should happen, for argument's sake, if someone else were to come here in a few minutes and say he was now the Prime Minister of this country? He would be voted out immediately in this House.

While he was speaking there was frenzied activity in ministerial offices where staffers, apprehensive that the new government might arrive any minute and take possession, frantically stuffed documents and files into cartons for immediate removal. Following Crean's speech Fraser, who was aware that the supply bills had now passed through the Senate, rose and announced that he had been commissioned to form an interim government pending a double dissolution. There was uproar. Shortly afterwards Whitlam played what Labor hoped was its trump card, a no-confidence motion against Fraser. Its wording requested Speaker Scholes to inform the Governor-General 'forthwith' that the Representatives had no confidence in Fraser, and Whitlam should therefore be commissioned to form another government. As Whitlam supported this motion with typical verve and style some of the stunned Labor supporters glued to the broadcast of parliamentary proceedings throughout the nation became fleetingly euphoric. Was it possible that Whitlam, with or without the connivance of Kerr, was about to turn the tables on the conservatives by regaining office with supply now through the Senate? Daly used Labor's numbers with ruthless efficiency, the motion was swiftly carried, and Scholes suspended parliament while he personally conveyed the motion to Yarralumla. However, no breathtaking reversal eventuated. Kerr again brushed convention aside by refusing to see Scholes. By the time he deigned to give Scholes an audience he knew that the Speaker's mission had been rendered futile by a proclamation dissolving parliament for the double dissolution.

Whitlam's response to the formal declaration of that proclamation generated the most memorable images of that unique day. A large crowd of curious on-lookers and furious Labor supporters had gathered at the front entrance of Parliament House before the Governor-General's secretary arrived to read the proclamation. The official ploughed through the proclamation to a cacophony of boos, jeers and shouts of 'We want Gough!'. The former Prime Minister was just behind him, towering and glowering. When the recital was completed Whitlam let fly:

> Well may we say 'God Save the Queen', because nothing will save the Governor-General. The proclamation which you have just heard. . .was countersigned 'Malcolm Fraser', who will undoubtedly go down in Australian history from Remembrance Day 1975 as Kerr's cur.

The crowd roared. 'Maintain your rage and your enthusiasm through the campaign for the election now to be held and until polling day', he urged. At a caucus meeting afterwards Whitlam gave his colleagues a rousing pep talk about the election campaign that lay ahead. Many caucus members, headed by Whitlam, sang 'Solidarity Forever' as they marched out of this meeting in single file back to the front steps, where there were further spirited speeches to the assembled onlookers.

The labour movement throughout Australia reacted with fury to the dismissal. There were angry scenes in all capital cities as workers walked off the job and joined spontaneous demonstrations. At the Liberal Party's Victorian headquarters there was wild brawling and windows were broken. The Liberals' Brisbane office also attracted an irate crowd. Among them was a 24-year-old lawyer with the Aboriginal Legal Service, Wayne Goss, who could see that inside the building beaming Liberals 'with slicked-down hair were drinking champagne out of long-stemmed glasses'. He resolved there and then to join the ALP, as did many other Australians who were appalled by Kerr's action. Hawke heard the news just after 1 pm and, with other union leaders, was on a Canberra-bound plane within an hour. A meeting of ALAC, which had recently seemed practically moribund, was hastily convened. At this meeting the labour movement leaders resolved – to the intense annoyance of militants throughout the nation – to hose down the flickering flames of unrest which threatened to erupt. Hawke's attitude was crucial. Alarmed by the prospect of blood in the streets if passions were further inflamed, he had already made an emotional public plea for calm, admitting that he had 'a terrible feeling of apprehension' because of the 'real possibility' that Australia could be 'on the edge of something terrible'. Furthermore, the only issue Labor had going for it was constitutional impropriety which Whitlam had been hammering for weeks. Endorsing and encouraging widespread industrial unrest risked dashing right at the outset whatever slim chance Labor had at the election. At the end of the ALAC meeting most of the participants adjourned to the Whitlam government wake at a Canberra restaurant which Labor MPs, staffers and sympathizers kept open until 5 am.

Kerr's conduct was unprecedented, premature and politically partisan. No Westminster-style government possessing a clear lower house majority had ever been dismissed because the upper house denied supply. The dismissal was premature because supply could still have lasted for weeks and, as subsequent revelations have confirmed, some opposition Senators would have cracked before then. Furthermore, the half-Senate election sought by Whitlam comprised a possible means of resolution despite Kerr's peremptory rejection of it. The dismissal was also a grossly partisan act. It deprived Labor of the advantages of governmental incumbency, and rewarded the opposition's intransigence by endowing it with a spurious legitimacy which inevitably influenced many politically unsophisticated voters. Kerr deliberately lulled Whitlam, his old friend Jim McClelland and other ministers into a false sense of security and then cut them down with a carefully planned ambush. This duplicity was necessary, Kerr later argued, because if Whitlam had gleaned any inkling of Kerr's intentions he would have approached the Queen to have Kerr sacked. Kerr professed high-minded concern about keeping the Queen above and beyond Australia's sordid political strife, yet by making such a precipitate and one-sided intervention – which she would not have made – he embroiled her in bitter controversy about the fundamental relationship between Australia and the monarchy. If his concern for the Queen had been genuine, he would surely have resigned after dismissing Whitlam, instead of continuing as her representative and guaranteeing that this controversy did not subside. Whitlam had no doubt that the fundamental motive for Kerr's deceit was self-centred: he liked the job, and wanted to keep it. Kerr had obtained from Whitlam and Snedden – but not Fraser – an assurance of a 10-year term; according to Whitlam, Kerr's insecurity about his future tenure if Fraser won office influenced him to gratify Fraser in the constitutional crisis. Certainly Kerr demonstrated a fascination with the perks, prestige and superficial glories of his office; he treated his relative status in the company of international dignitaries and his entitlement to imperial baubles as matters of the utmost gravity.

Kerr attempted to explain his conduct by a selective and fallacious analysis of constitutional conventions and principles. These distortions were defended by Ellicott's cousin, Chief Justice Barwick, whose abhorrence of the Whitlam government had prompted him to conceive and propagate untenable constitutional notions. Early in the supply crisis Barwick let it be known that in his opinion Kerr should act assertively to end the crisis but was too weak to do so. Kerr was almost certainly aware of this when he invited the Chief Justice's opinion on 10 November. Kerr used Barwick's views to fortify his conduct on 11 November and ostensibly to justify it afterwards.

Could the FPLP have somehow thwarted Kerr? Obviously he need not have been appointed in the first place. Perceptive assessments of individuals was not a Whitlam strength, but even McClelland, who knew Kerr much better than Whitlam, was unaware that Kerr was nurturing delusions of grandeur about the Governor-General's role well before 11 November. Once Kerr set events in train on that fateful day the FPLP's chances of frustrating his designs were significantly reduced by Whitlam's failure to notify Labor's Senators. This neglect was an undeniable oversight, but understandable in view of the very brief time Whitlam and the other tacticians had to plan, and the shock and bewilderment they were feeling. There has been speculation that Kerr deliberately chose lunchtime in order to make any resistance to his plans harder to organize in a hurry. When Whitlam was handed the formal notice of dismissal in the Governor-General's study he did not challenge Kerr directly as others later suggested he might have.

His wife Margaret said she would have torn up the document on the spot, and Hawke has also indicated that refusing to accept it was an option open to Whitlam. But Whitlam's instinctive response was to contest the dismissal in the arena where he was pre-eminent, the Representatives. His efforts were nullified by Kerr, who was determined to enforce his one-sided verdict. It seems that the FPLP could have delayed and possibly prevented the outcome Kerr sought by adopting alternative parliamentary manoeuvres in both chambers, although their conception and successful implementation required the sort of contemplative analysis that was practically impossible in the circumstances. As Speaker, Scholes was aware at the time that he could have adopted a more confrontational approach in his dealings with Kerr on that dramatic afternoon, but he did not consider that Kerr would simply refuse to see him. With the benefit of hindsight he would have acted differently to make Kerr's objective much harder to attain.

Sinister allegations have been made about the dismissal. Kerr's intricate planning and ruthless exercise of power convinced some Labor supporters that he would have had contingency arrangements ready to implement if events did not unfold as he desired. They concluded that Kerr's astonishing delusions about the Governor-General's proper role made it quite feasible that he would take seriously the archaic constitutional provision that he was commander-in-chief of Australia's defence forces. It was not far-fetched, they believed, to imagine Kerr calling in the army, with potentially catastrophic consequences, if Whitlam and the FPLP had defied Kerr or if the wider labour movement had reacted uncontrollably to the dismissal. Morrison, Whitlam's Defence minister since June 1975, was sufficiently perturbed about such rumours in the wake of the dismissal that he personally investigated them with senior defence force personnel. He satisfied himself that they were not involved in any contingency plans, but some of his cabinet and caucus colleagues and many rank-and-file ALP activists still hold a different view. There also remains widespread ALP scepticism about the denials by Labor's opponents that they were forewarned about Kerr's intentions.

There have also been repeated disturbing suggestions that international surveillance agencies were involved in the dismissal. This speculation has been fuelled by Kerr's own involvement in mysterious intelligence activities during the Second World War. It is clear that powerful nations like America, Russia and Britain have routinely and clandestinely interfered in the internal affairs of other countries including Australia. The CIA regarded the Whitlam government with distaste and intermittent alarm. Shortly before the dismissal Whitlam injected the CIA's role in Australia into the political arena. As controversy flared, some CIA agents were publicly identified and the CIA became increasingly agitated. Pressure to quell the furore was urgently applied by the Americans and also by Australia's experienced Defence department head, who described it as the most serious risk to Australia's security in its entire history. A cable was sent to ASIO expressing the CIA's acute concern about the implications for Australia's future relationship with the United States, especially the CIA's activities at Pine Gap. This installation in central Australia was regarded by the Americans as a crucial part of their global surveillance network, and they already held unwarranted fears that Whitlam might terminate the Pine Gap agreement when it came up for renewal in December 1975. They had also been jolted recently when Whitlam sacked the heads of ASIO and ASIS in quick succession. The CIA's November 1975 message to ASIO was not intended for Whitlam's eyes, underlining the reality that the international intelligence community operates in a world beyond the conventional doctrines of governmental loyalty and responsibility. CIA sources have confirmed that their alarm about developments in Australia was conveyed to Kerr, and it has been claimed that British intelligence services were used to relay the message to him. Although Kerr and his defenders have denied that his decision to remove the Whitlam government was influenced by intelligence agencies, Labor people who refuse to dismiss these allegations airily as unproven conspiracy theories have had ample nourishment for their suspicions.

The prospects for Labor were bleak and its financial position desperate. Its senior personnel had to make the sudden and painful adjustment to the removal of ministerial facilities and access to the public service. Their opponents launched a lavish offensive with heavy concentration on Labor's five Cs who had suffered humiliating demotions – Crean, Cope, Cameron, Cairns and Connor. Some journalists working for the Murdoch press went on strike in protest against the flagrant anti-Labor tone of their newspapers. Bjelke-Petersen chimed in with orchestrated mud-slinging about the loans affair. At public expense a Queensland detective was flown to Switzerland where he was supposed to be on the verge of locating sensationally incriminating 'documents'. The Premier foreshadowed spectacular 'revelations'. During the last week of the campaign he asserted that two Whitlam government ministers 'were due to receive staggering sums of money' in 'secret commissions and kick-backs'. There was never, then or later, even an attempt to substantiate this nonsense. Incensed ALP supporters in Brisbane responded with donations and vociferous support at huge Labor rallies. This intense enthusiasm was just as evident in the other states. Other portents were sobering. A feature of Tony Lamb's campaigning in Latrobe had been his use of a bus, which attracted local children like a magnet and, in Lamb's opinion, provided a useful barometer of their parents' political attitudes and voting intentions. In 1972, when Lamb captured Latrobe, the children were very friendly; during the 1974 campaign they seemed ambivalent; in 1975 they pelted stones at the bus. Hayden was in great demand all over Australia, but he curtailed his campaigning outside Oxley after the state ALP organizer, Bob Gibbs, warned him that the situation in Queensland was so grim that Hayden could only hold Oxley if he came home. The further the campaign proceeded, the further the dismissal and the constitutional issue receded. Whitlam was indomitable and Hawke campaigned with customary vigour, but opinion poll projections during the final week did not augur well for Labor.

Many Labor enthusiasts braced themselves for disappointing news on election night, but the result was worse than their most pessimistic expectations. Just like Lang in 1932, Whitlam had been dismissed by a viceroy, had seen his supporters respond with remarkable fervour during the ensuing election campaign, and had suffered a crushing defeat on polling day. On 13 December 1975 the ALP was devastated by the biggest landslide in the Representatives since federation. While Labor emerged with 36 seats (66 in 1974), the coalition won 91 and a very comfortable majority in the Senate. Labor's casualties included six ministers – Morrison, Patterson, Enderby, Everingham, Riordan and Berinson – and capable backbenchers like Cross, Dawkins, John Kerin, Lamb, Race Mathews, Child and Tasmanian MHR John Coates. Scholes just managed to retain Corio, the Geelong-based seat which had been such a significant by-election capture early in Whitlam's leadership. Labor won only one – Beazley's – of the 10 seats in WA, and only one of the 18 Queensland electorates. In Tasmania, where Labor had won all five seats in 1972 and 1974, it retained none at all, not even Duthie's,

373

in 1975. The crowning indignity in Tasmania was the success in the Senate of Harradine, who had broken with the ALP and stood in the election as an independent. Frustrated militants bitterly concluded that if there had been a general strike and other industrial action in response to the dismissal, as they desired, Labor could hardly have done worse at the election.

For Labor people that Saturday evening was dreadful. Hawke had consented to appear on television as a commentator. He privately doubted that Labor could win, but like most of the ALP faithful

> didn't have any perception of the magnitude of the defeat we were facing. That election night was one of the longest and loneliest nights in my life. I couldn't get up and walk away from the TV cameras, but had to sit there for the whole horrible performance.

At one point, reflecting on 'the shattered remains of all the hopes of 1972 and 1974', Hawke became overwhelmed. 'We've had the guts ripped out of us', he tearfully told television viewers. Hawke was there

> when Gough arrived in the tally room. . .a sense of tragedy spread through the hall. I felt terribly sorry for him as a person, a sorrow separate from what had happened to the Labor Party. There was this giant of a man, smashed to pieces. . .And he conducted himself admirably. . .

Labor supporters yearning for a crumb of solace consoled themselves that at least Hayden seemed to have prevented a whitewash in Queensland. 'He had introduced Medibank, increased pensions to their highest level for twenty-five years, introduced a whole range of new social service benefits, and brought down a responsible Budget'. Yet he had to scramble desperately to cling on to Oxley, which he had held in 1972 with a voting share of 68·9%. Not surprisingly, many Labor viewers found it all profoundly upsetting. One supporter (who recalled her reaction with amusement) burst into tears when she spotted a traffic sign ordering 'GIVE WAY TO THE RIGHT'.

Many of the Labor faithful venerated the Whitlam government, and the manner of its fall intensified their attachment to it. The dismissal was a staggering blow, but merely the culmination of escalating disruption by opponents of the government who had never accepted its legitimacy. When economic pressures largely derived from abroad began to threaten the reform programme and then the government's very existence, there were some wistful glances back to the near miss of 1969. If only Labor had won that election, some Whitlamites mused, the Whitlam government would have been blessed with propitious economic circumstances more conducive to reform. Calwell was responsible, argued Freudenberg, because he continued as leader until after the 1966 election and gave Whitlam an impossible leeway to make up between 1967 and 1969. However, Mathews maintained his rage against the controllers of the Victorian branch before intervention, blaming them for Labor's poor results in that state before 1972. Some ALP members were among the government's critics who subscribed to the 'too much too soon' school. But rapid reform, of itself, was not the main problem. What cost the government dearly was its failure to inform the voters sufficiently about the benefits they received from its activities. In fact the government's determination to press on with reforms, in the face of daunting economic and other difficulties, was one of its most attractive qualities to the many Australians who regarded it fondly despite its mistakes and exuberant excesses. 'There won't ever be another one like it', concluded Gareth Evans (who was a consultant adviser to Attorney-General Murphy, and occasionally had to cancel his constitutional law lectures at Melbourne University because he was suddenly required in Canberra). The people who turned out in droves during the 1975 campaign had not only been outraged by the removal of the Whitlam government; they had been inspired and liberated by its approach and achievements. These admirers would always regard the Whitlam government with an affectionate nostalgia tinged with sadness because of the hopes and dreams that were only partly fulfilled. For the rest of their lives their pulses would quicken whenever they saw or heard replays of the exhilarating St Kilda Town Hall meeting in 1972, Whitlam on the Parliament House steps on Remembrance Day 1975, and, especially, Whitlam at Blacktown beginning 'Men and women of Australia. . .'

15 Life wasn't Meant to be Easy for the ALP, 1976–1983

ON 14 DECEMBER 1975, the day after Labor's crushing electoral defeat, Whitlam was inclined to relinquish the FPLP leadership. It might be six years, when he would be 65, before Labor could hope to regain office. He phoned Hayden, who was still uncertain whether he had managed to retain Oxley. Whitlam asked if he was interested in becoming leader. Hayden declined. In opposition he did not even want to be on the front bench, let alone leader. He was tired, guiltily conscious that his dedication to his portfolio had caused him to neglect his wife and children, and planning to embark on a Law course. He also doubted whether he was temperamentally suited to leadership. Whitlam then contacted Hawke. Beside the Lodge swimming pool they discussed the future. Whitlam told Hawke that since Hayden had ruled himself out he was prepared to help Hawke become his successor. Hawke was surprised and delighted but, like Whitlam, he was aware that plenty of FPLP members would feel that the leadership was not Whitlam's to bestow and certainly not Hawke's to claim from outside parliament.

The unlikely possibility of a smooth transition from Whitlam to Hawke was soon out of the question. Predictably, some FPLP feathers were quickly ruffled by the idea. Hawke further antagonized his prospective caucus colleagues with public signals that he was willing to succeed Whitlam if it could be arranged. More significantly, Whitlam changed his mind. His depression on 'the morning of anguish' passed, and before long he became convinced that Labor could win the next election. There were also signs that finding a seat for Hawke might not be straightforward: Cairns, who had criticized Whitlam on election night, was pressured to vacate his seat, but firmly refused. In the wake of the election Whitlam's leadership was publicly attacked by other former ministers, including Cameron and Wriedt. Crean and Bowen made their disapproval of Whitlam clear by indicating that they would nominate against him for the leadership. Bowen's factional stable, the right-wing controllers in NSW, backed Whitlam in the contest and pressed Bowen to withdraw. Bowen, who had forged a reputation in government as one of Whitlam's more competent ministers, realized that he had no hope of beating Whitlam, but left his hat in the ring as a symbolic gesture signifying his dissatisfaction with Whitlam's leadership and the arrangement with Hawke.

The post-election review of FPLP office-bearers occurred on 27 January 1976. Whitlam showed signs of nervousness about the outcome but retained the leadership easily, obtaining 36 of the 63 votes with Bowen on 14 and Crean 13. Since Whitlam had been endorsed by both Hawke and Hartley – unlikely allies in internal party struggles – as well as by Ducker and the NSW machine, his success was not surprising. However, the other ballots gave him less cause for satisfaction. A large field entered the contest for deputy leader. After the elimination of Scholes, Cass, Bryant, Johnson and Beazley, three contenders remained – Uren, Keating and Young. Ultimately successful was Whitlam's least preferred deputy from this trio, Uren. Whitlam's vigorous support of Jim McClelland proved counterproductive when Wriedt easily won the ballot for the Senate leadership and Keeffe was elected Senate deputy. Disheartened, McClelland joined Crean, Cairns, Cameron and Hayden in declining nomination for the shadow cabinet. Daly and Willesee were also non-starters, having decided not to seek another parliamentary term at the recent double dissolution. However, one veteran, Connor, did pursue a position in the shadow ministry, and his success in this quest a few months after Whitlam had forced his removal from cabinet was widely interpreted as a reverse for the former Prime Minister. Half the new FPLP front bench were former ministers. The 10 shadow ministers who had not served in Whitlam's cabinet comprised, in order of their election, Keeffe, former ACTU advocate Ralph Willis (who had succeeded McIvor as MHR for Gellibrand in 1972), ex-accountant Chris Hurford (MHR for Adelaide since 1969), Tasmanian Senator and medical practitioner Don Grimes, Young, Scholes, Button, former Newcastle councillor Peter Morris, Mulvihill and Innes.

A month later a fresh scandal broke which rocked the ALP to its foundations. The furore implicated two of the party's most senior office-bearers, Combe and Whitlam, in a scheme instigated by Hartley to obtain funds for Labor's recent election campaign from Middle East sources. Hartley had first mentioned his idea to Combe and Whitlam on 16 November, when the ALP was still reeling from the dismissal and its leaders were appreciating that its financial resources for the unexpected double dissolution campaign were woefully inadequate. 'I could have scotched it at the outset', Whitlam was to concede later. Instead he and Combe, still shell-shocked and bitter that the convention-smashing by Labor's opponents had been rewarded by Kerr, endorsed Hartley's secret plan. The proposal ultimately involved a contribution of $500 000 from the Ba'ath Socialist Party of Iraq, but the promised donation did not arrive. The intermediary entrusted with the task of raising the money instead gave his story to Rupert Murdoch. Meanwhile Combe had authorized increased advertising and other campaign expenditure based on the supposedly forthcoming gift, and the party was accordingly about $350 000 in debt. Labor people still coming to terms with the dismissal and ensuing electoral débâcle found these revelations acutely demoralizing. Lessons had not been learned. Once again funds from the Middle East had proved embarrassingly elusive, and an untrustworthy go-between had led Labor luminaries a merry dance. Obtaining campaign funds from outside Australia was not traditional practice in the ALP (unlike the Liberal Party, which as long ago as 1949 was raising vast sums abroad to finance a propaganda offensive that paid electoral dividends). Furthermore, this proposed transaction – not a loan but a gift – left the ALP potentially vulnerable to pressure which might compromise the party's even-handed attitude to the hostilities in the Middle East.

There was fury and dismay in Labor ranks. 'I can't believe they could be so bloody stupid!' Young fumed after hearing the news. Jewish Labor MPs like Barry Cohen, MHR for Robertson since 1969, expressed their revulsion publicly. In caucus Beazley unleashed his outrage in a scathing anti-Whitlam tirade. He recalled the exacting standards Whitlam had imposed when he removed Cairns and Connor in mid-1975, and demanded Whitlam's immediate resignation. Hawke was especially livid, because of his own attachment to Israel and the involvement of Hartley, the ALP's most renowned pro-Arab advocate. Hawke had privately learned about the scandal on 12 February before it was public knowledge, and as ALP president immediately convened a special meeting of the senior national executive office-bearers. Combe was then enjoying a break on a Pacific cruise, but interrupted his holiday to attend. He frankly admitted that in the post-dismissal trauma he had made an appalling error of judgement. After hearing Combe's detailed account, the 'meeting just about broke up in tears', according to the off-the-record version of events which was recounted by Hawke to journalists and sensationalized in the Murdoch press; Hawke's remarks, including the comment that 'Gough's gone a million', were published under the headline 'Hawke to Axe Whitlam'. Hawke protested angrily about this breach of journalistic ethics, which had given the impression that he was pre-empting the imminent inquiry into the affair by the full national executive, and the labour movement's deep resentment of the Murdoch press was further reinforced. With Whitlam's position in the party obviously endangered by the episode, even some of his critics in the FPLP were hoping that he would not resign because of the victory this would represent for Murdoch. ALP activists disenchanted with Whitlam felt further motivated to rally to his support when the Fraser government sought to capitalize on Labor's plight by authorizing the Commonwealth Police to investigate the Iraqi funds affair. Fraser even ordered the highly secret dispatch of an ASIS agent to Iraq in an unsuccessful attempt to unearth information which might further harm the ALP.

There was a tremendous surge of support for Whitlam from the Labor faithful. Some of these expressions of warm admiration from ALP branches reflected the perennial rank-and-file irritation with publicly aired FPLP disharmony; some evinced a belief that the controversy was essentially a conspiracy engineered by the Murdoch press and other anti-Labor interests; and the messages which did concede the possibility of impropriety by Whitlam made it very clear that whatever Whitlam's role he should be retained as leader. A motion 'passed unanimously by a record 62 members' of the Narrabeen-Pittwater branch stated 'its unqualified confidence' in Whitlam, and went on to 'condemn in the strongest possible terms any move against him'. 'While noting outside pressures, we believe the Caucus. . .should close ranks solidly behind such a tireless leader as Gough Whitlam', urged 37 party supporters from 'The *Age* Classified Phone Room'. Individual Labor supporters also sent messages. Many repeated the 1975 campaign slogan 'We want Gough'. 'The five members of this household have voted Labor all their voting lives', wrote an enthusiast from Rosebery, 'but if Gough Whitlam is deposed. . .we will not be voting Labor in the foreseeable future'. Similar sentiments were expressed by a 65-year-old lifelong Labor voter from Tarragindi who recalled the Mungana controversy involving Theodore, noted that manufacturing scandal was a consistent anti-Labor tactic, and deplored the tendency of the ALP to react like 'sheep': 'every time the other mob comes out with some silly thing and hammers it, you all run around in circles and do what they want and sack your leader'. This deluge of support confirmed the veneration of Whitlam which was widespread among Labor people who had little or no personal contact with him. They were unaware of the animosity Whitlam had engendered within the FPLP. When the leader himself became vulnerable to attack, some MPs who had endured his too frequently insensitive treatment of them were not inclined to be sympathetic: 'all the anger at Whitlam's sackings, taunts, arrogance and occasional contempt of his colleagues was let loose'.

At a tense three-day meeting ending on 7 March the national executive resolved to 'condemn in the strongest terms' Combe, Whitlam and Hartley for their conduct in the Iraqi funds affair. Its lengthy resolution criticized the trio's 'grave errors of judgement', but stressed that only the ALP had advocated public funding of election campaigns and the disclosure of private donors, and the Whitlam government had embodied these objectives in legislation which had been rejected by Labor's opponents in the Senate. The national executive also denounced the 'totally unprincipled campaign by the Murdoch group', attacked the Fraser government's 'blatant attempts' to maximize its political capital from the episode, and urged all ALP members and constituent bodies to 'close ranks' and 'support the drive for financial support' to enable the party to discharge its financial obligations. Combe had insisted that there should be no deviation from equal culpability in the party's treatment of the three wrongdoers, and this principle eventually prevailed after some vacillation and tactical shuffling. There was intense media interest in the meeting, and it began in a highly charged atmosphere:

> everyone was as jumpy as hell. There was a buzzing noise. We were all so spook-conscious that we thought the room must be bugged. Bill Hartley clambered around trying to find bugs. After a while Arthur Gietzelt owned up. He had a new hearing-aid and he didn't quite know how to work the thing...

Combe wanted to have the proceedings taped so that he had an accurate record. The request was rejected. The tension was again eased by a characteristic Egerton quip that to solve the party's financial worries they 'should have bloody well sold the film rights'. Several resolutions were considered by the executive. Among those rejected were a motion from Batt and Wriedt calling for severe disciplinary action against all three participants, and another moved by Egerton which reflected Hawke's view that Hartley was more culpable than Combe or Whitlam and deserved to be expelled. Combe was full of praise for Hawke's constructive influence. After the initial manoeuvring there

> was a genuine endeavour on the part of everyone to face up to the problem and resolve it...Bob played a big role in preventing a faction-feud...He backed off very quickly from the idea that Hartley be expelled. He kept that executive under a tight rein for two days, determined to elicit all possible information about what had happened, determined to get a genuine, non-factional discussion. If only Whitlam had handled the Loans Affair in the same way that Hawke handled that executive – getting everything out in the open, admitting there had been an error – then the Loans Affair would never have damaged us the way it did...

The next FPLP meeting occurred on 17 March. After Uren briefed caucus about the national executive's inquiry, Whitlam had to endure antagonistic speeches from Wriedt, Beazley, Wheeldon, Keating and Senator George

Georges. Many MPs were disturbed about the revelations of their leader's involvement. However, as Whitlam knew, the effect of the Murdoch-Fraser over-kill and the overwhelming pro-Whitlam feeling in the branches had made his leadership secure. Beazley had announced that he could no longer serve in the shadow cabinet under Whitlam, and on 17 March Hayden signalled his readiness to end his period of self-imposed detachment by nominating for the vacancy. He won the ballot, but by a relatively unconvincing margin, which reflected the view widely held in and beyond caucus that his temporary withdrawal was to some extent self-indulgent. Two days later Wheeldon also resigned in protest against Whitlam's role in the Iraqi affair. The caucus ballot to determine his replacement in the shadow cabinet was narrowly won by Arthur Gietzelt; runner-up was Whitlam's preferred candidate, Senator Peter Walsh.

Continuing resentment about Remembrance Day 1975 was a feature of Australian politics in 1976. There were bitter and sometimes violent demonstrations at Kerr's public appearances. The FPLP maintained its rage in symbolic and unprecedented boycotts of parliamentary ceremonies attended by the Governor-General. Whitlam's public barbs against Kerr were caustic, frequent and remorseless, and there were recurrent attacks on the viceroy from Jim McClelland and other MPs. Combe strongly approved of this anti-Kerr campaign. After being notified by the Gap ALP branch in Brisbane that it supported 'non-violent demonstrations' against Kerr 'regardless of the political damage, if any, to the Party', since ALP 'members have a moral obligation to embarrass the Governor-General whenever possible. . .until he is forced to resign', Combe replied that 'I personally agree with the views of your branch in all respects'.

Hawke disagreed. He believed that the FPLP was demonstrating an excessive preoccupation with the past. The electors who were not committed ALP voters would not return Labor to office until they were convinced that the party had the correct policies for Australia's future, and Hawke felt that the development of this important forward-looking approach was being hindered by the party's fixation with Kerr. Hawke's view was not popular in the ALP, and some Labor people were also irked by his willingness to meet Fraser for talks about industrial and other issues. Another source of rank-and-file irritation was the promotion of Hawke in the Murdoch press as an alternative leader to Whitlam. FPLP members were further annoyed when Hawke publicly indicated that he disapproved of their anti-Kerr boycotts. Hayden responded that Hawke's 'impulsive, intemperate comments and his occasional emotional outbursts' were 'not always terribly helpful' to the Whitlam government. Hawke should decide, added Hayden, whether he was going to be a politician or a union leader, and should 'save politics for when he becomes a politician'.

The FPLP was a dispirited opposition in 1976. Whitlam was no longer the confident and formidable figure who had dominated Australian politics for a decade. He seemed more intent on vindicating himself and his government than reshaping Labor's policies to meet the challenges of the future. Many ALP activists condemned his acceptance of Indonesia's annexation of East Timor. His continued leadership was regarded with unveiled disenchantment by a large, diverse and influential group of MPs including Bowen, Cameron, Wriedt, Beazley, Connor, Keating, Wheeldon, Cass, Crean, Button, Cairns and Keeffe. Morale in caucus after the Iraqi funds affair hit rock-bottom. The Fraser government's vast majority in the Representatives was a depressingly visible reminder of Labor's plight, which was reinforced by the Victorian state election in March. The Victorian campaign was overshadowed by the sensational developments concerning the Iraqi funds; the resignations of Beazley and Wheeldon occurred just before polling day, when Labor's inroads into the large majority enjoyed by Victoria's Liberal government were minimal. In autumn 1976 there was pervasive pessimism about the prospects for enlightened reform in Australia, and despondency was widespread in the ALP.

But this despair was lifted in NSW by an exciting state election victory. On 1 May 1976, the eleventh anniversary of the 1965 election which had ended 24 years of Labor rule, the voters in the oldest and most populated state narrowly returned Labor to office. Ironically it was the Premier of the defeated ALP government in 1965, Jack Renshaw, who played a crucial role in Labor's success by one seat 11 years later. During a bout of ill-health Renshaw had relinquished the leadership in 1968, and had planned to retire at the 1976 election. But he was persuaded to stand again in Castlereagh – the rural seat he had held since 1941 – because no other Labor candidate could prevent its capture by the Country Party. As expected, Renshaw's candidature ensured Labor's continued tenure of Castlereagh, which was vital when the overall election result was so close that confirmation of Labor's victory did not come until after 10 tense days of vote-counting.

The new Labor Premier of NSW was Neville Wran. Born in Balmain in 1926, Wran rose from his working-class origins through the law. He was an exceptionally dedicated barrister, and his painstaking thoroughness and aggressive will to win were also apparent when he later devoted himself to politics. Other attributes served him particularly well in both law and politics. A renowned debater who expressed himself with outstanding fluency and style, Wran was in addition a natural performer, whose fondness for the stage prompted him to consider acting as a career. He joined the ALP in 1954, but was an inactive member for over a decade. By the mid-1960s he was a member of an untypical local branch, Double Bay, along with other wealthy lawyers – like his close friends Murphy and Jim McClelland – who resided in affluent Sydney suburbs. Wran and some other members arrived at branch meetings in Jaguars. McClelland recalled an influx of student radicals at Double Bay branch meetings during the Vietnam War: 'After making the wildest revolutionary statements, they would drive home in the old man's Mercedes'. For aspiring ALP politicians in branches like Double Bay, the price of living in affluent anti-Labor surroundings was the absence of available local seats; when Wran entered parliament he did so, like Murphy and McClelland, through the upper house. Wran was so circumspect about his political ambitions that even his closest friends did not suspect that he aspired to a parliamentary career until his meteoric ascent began.

The quartet most instrumental in Wran's rapid rise were Jim McClelland, Downing, Ducker and state Labor leader Pat Hills. McClelland facilitated Wran's entry to the Legislative Council in 1970. Labor's key man in the Council was still Downing, who had been a senior minister in all the ALP cabinets between 1941 and 1965, but by 1971 his health was dicey, and he was keen to retire. Wran's ability, verve and legal expertise quickly established him as Downing's successor. He had assisted Hills with legal advice on political issues, and with the powerful support of Hills and Downing became Labor's leader in the upper house less than two years after entering it. John Ducker MLC, the most influential machine figure in NSW, was the crucial identity in Wran's next step. After witnessing Wran's capacity at close quarters in the Legislative Council, Ducker decided that Wran should replace Hills as NSW leader. Not only did this notion flout the strong tradition in NSW Labor that patience and seniority were rewarded in leadership transitions, a tradition Hills had respected as Renshaw's heir apparent. In addition, Ducker was proposing from the pinnacle of Labor's right-wing machine that one of its favourite sons should be replaced by a silver-tail lawyer from a posh suburb who had neither factional support nor the normal background of longstanding committed party service. To achieve his goal Ducker had to convince senior left-wingers like the Gietzelts and Jack Ferguson MLA as well as powerbrokers from his own faction. His basic argument was that Wran could deliver the electoral success which had been customary in NSW but was now overdue. Ducker's advocacy and Wran's obvious talent proved a compelling combination. An Assembly seat had to be found for Wran, and the machine swung into action. The MLA for Bass Hill, a safe ALP seat in Keating's federal electorate, was encouraged to retire; Keating was placed in an awkward position when a friend of his possessing strong local support to become the next MLA for Bass Hill was elbowed aside to make way for Wran. A month later the 1973 state election was held, and Askin retained office with a 2% swing away from Labor. Wran immediately launched a leadership challenge. Aided by a lack of wholeheartedness in Hills's resistance and a controversial ruling by the caucus chairman when the voting was desperately close, Wran emerged a very narrow and fortunate victor.

NSW politics had not previously known a leader like Wran. He was meticulously attentive to the requirements of the media, especially television, in presenting himself favourably to the voters. Askin, together with his successors in the Liberal leadership after his retirement early in 1975, tended to be dismissive of the media generally and awkward on television. So did Hills. Wran was the opposite. He and his press secretary, Brian Dale, generated television coverage inventively, and Wran, the would-be actor, played his part with skill, thoroughness and flair. But there was more to Wran's success than unprecedentedly slick presentation. In opposition he worked harder than Hills, making frequent arduous tours of the NSW countryside to spread Labor's message. This concern for rural sensitivities was not the only way Wran distanced himself from Whitlam's leadership style. Unlike Whitlam, Wran placed a high priority on unthreatening communication with the electorate. Wran even declared on television that he did not want any participation by Whitlam in the 1976 state election campaign, and after becoming Premier announced that there would be 'no mad rush to introduce all of our policies overnight – this is government, not a sprint'.

An episode involving the ruthless NSW machine later in 1976 illuminated why it was described by some ALP insiders in other states as 'the Catholic mafia'. As Ducker rose to head the machine two of his close New Right associates, Geoff Cahill and Barrie Unsworth, ascended swiftly with him. Unsworth was an ex-electrician with authentic working-class values and a well-deserved reputation as a hardhitting debater. Cahill, now 40, was an affable and capable administrator who had the broad shoulders of a former swimming champion. During the three years since he had succeeded Westerway as state secretary Cahill had been campaign director at several elections, including the recent poll which had ushered in the Wran government. Cahill had an Irish Catholic background; Ducker and Unsworth had converted to Catholicism as adults, Unsworth after being rocked by his son's heroin-related death, which reinforced his abhorrence of drugs. Everything in the New Right garden should have been lovely with Ducker and his two mates in control of the machine and NSW Labor back in government, but friction had developed between Ducker and Cahill. As state secretary Cahill was a powerbroker in his own right, and it seems that Ducker became increasingly annoyed when his former protégé used the power levers in ways Ducker disliked. One instance concerned the vacant vice-presidency on the ALP national executive created when Egerton mistakenly presumed that he could retain his prestigious positions in the labour movement after agreeing to accept from the Fraser government a knighthood ceremonially bestowed by Kerr; Ducker aspired to the vice-presidency himself, and believed that scheming by Cahill had contributed to his narrow failure to win it. After the installation of the Wran government Cahill left for a 12-week overseas trip. He arrived back at 6.30 one morning to be met at the airport by Unsworth, who took Cahill and his family home and told Cahill that there was a meeting he should immediately attend even though he was tired. When they arrived at Labor's Sydney headquarters Unsworth ushered Cahill into a room where Ducker, flanked by other machine heavyweights, presented Cahill with a draft statement of resignation for him to sign. Cahill was assured that if he signed he would be 'looked after' and given a government job; if he refused to co-operate, the machine would oppose him at the next state conference, and when he lost he would not be looked after. Cahill signed. He and Ducker denied afterwards that he had been deposed, and 'the whole performance was played faultlessly in public by all those involved'. Richardson, now 27, was promoted from his position as assistant secretary to succeed Cahill.

In March 1977 Hayden decided to challenge Whitlam for the FPLP leadership. A mid-term challenge to an incumbent leader was a rare event in the FPLP's history, but Hayden's decision was rendered much less controversial by an innovative caucus ruling in January 1976 that all FPLP positions would be compulsorily vacated in mid-1977. Hayden had followed his return to the political mainstream with some incisive criticism of the Fraser government, and he was clearly one of the more competent performers in the generally ineffectual FPLP. 'During the 1976 budget session Hayden was chirpy and relaxed, belting out economic questions on his portable typewriter for colleagues to ask in Parliament.' Early in 1977 Hayden was considering whether to contest the deputy's position against Uren with Whitlam's blessing, and received encouragingly widespread caucus feedback urging him to aim for the top job. He remained ambivalent, influenced by nagging self-doubt and distaste for the manoeuvres that are part and parcel of a fiercely contested leadership battle. The turning point for Hayden was a meeting with Hawke at Combe's house on 8 March. Combe had brought them together to discuss the parlous state of the Queensland ALP, but Hawke insisted on pressing Hayden about his leadership intentions; Hawke had been drinking, and his own ambition was starkly apparent. Later that week Hayden announced his decision to nominate for the leadership, influenced partly by his misgivings about Hawke's suitability to lead the FPLP.

The FPLP conducted its mid-term ballots on 31 May 1977. Canvassing had been intense during preceding weeks, and a close result was expected in the main contest. Hayden was strongly backed by a group of ex-ministers now very hostile to Whitlam including Cameron, Beazley, Wriedt, Wheeldon, Bowen and Cass, and by a number of talented ministerial aspirants including Button, Grimes and Walsh as well as left-wingers like Uren, Gietzelt and Keeffe. Some former ministers like Connor and Stewart had no fondness for Whitlam but voted for him because they had a deeper loathing of Hayden, arising from his occasionally savage denunciation of them during the Whitlam government. Jim McClelland sensed that Whitlam was irretrievably tarnished to the uncommitted voters who would decide the next election, and that Hayden was the better rational option for the party's future; but he felt unable to deliver another blow to Whitlam after what Fraser and Kerr had done to him. Similar sentiments prevailed in a section of caucus and very widely in the ALP branches. He 'is truly an inspirational leader' and 'the only ray of hope for. . .the rank-and-file', wrote a Toorak admirer. From the Fairfield branch in Brisbane came a letter typical of many others in expressing a high regard for Hayden while stressing that 'Gough Must Stay' – he has 'become a folk-hero of the people'. Whitlam cultivated support with calculated affability, while Hayden refused to stoop to such transparent devices. Two very ill MPs in the Whitlam camp, Connor and Bryant, turned up to vote, but an ailing Hayden supporter did not. Whitlam won by 32 votes to 30.

In the wake of the leadership tussle there were further unsubtle signals from Hawke about his ambitions. At a dinner attended by FPLP members he was repeatedly critical of the leadership material in caucus, and asked some MPs directly how they would vote on the leadership if he entered parliament. When a backbencher replied non-committally that Hawke would have to prove himself, he became sarcastic:

> I see. I'd have to prove that I can put a case, would I? I would have to prove that I can debate, that I understand economics, that I can handle the media, that I poll well in public opinion surveys, and so on. Is that what I have to do?

He was similarly immodest about his own capabilities shortly afterwards when he addressed the Perth Press Club. He had travelled to the West for the ALP national conference. At the customary pre-conference national executive meeting he was devastated to learn that Uren claimed to have the numbers stitched up on the executive to replace Hawke as ALP president with Young. Ducker and Combe rallied to Hawke. With the vital ballot scheduled for the following morning, they had to move fast. Working in conjunction with ACT delegate Joan Taggart, they masterminded a spectacular reversal. It was not often that Hawke had lobbied on his own behalf in the past, but he made plenty of phone calls that night. Ducker was at his manipulative best – cajoling, persuading and, if necessary, threatening. The next morning Hawke was the only nomination for the presidency. 'The whole episode was one of the most exciting I've been involved in', recalled Combe. The quartet was ecstatic about the triumph, and celebrated accordingly. After much drinking and little or no sleep, Hawke was in euphoric mood when he turned up at the Press Club luncheon, where he made it clear that if he did transfer to the Representatives he would expect to become leader.

A big issue at the 1977 national conference was uranium. Australia's plentiful deposits were in demand overseas, and mining and processing them would greatly benefit Australia's economy by generating increased employment and lucrative exports. But there was passionate hostility to uranium mining in Australia on moral and environmental grounds. Anti-uranium activists demonstrated with an intense emotional commitment akin to the height of the anti-conscription fervour during the Vietnam War. They contended that Australia could not be certain that overseas consumers of its uranium would use it exclusively for peaceful energy purposes, and pointed to the grave consequences of any accident while the uranium was being treated, the unresolved problem of the disposal of radioactive wastes, and the threat to sacred Aboriginal sites. The Whitlam government initially approved uranium mining, but the labour movement's increasing concern about the environmental consequences was reflected in the government's establishment of a commission of inquiry in 1975. This inquiry's findings were selectively used by the Fraser government as ostensible justification for its authorization of uranium processing and export without the stipulation of Australian ownership and control which had been enforced by the Whitlam government. For the ALP, uranium was a complex and thorny question. Within the party there was plenty of heat, and also considerable uncertainty, which was heightened by the wide divergence of opinion among reputed expert authorities. There was, particularly within the left, abundant genuine revulsion about the horrors of nuclear war and the devastation of the environment by rapacious mining corporations. Some unionists, however, were attracted by the employment opportunities. The ALP also contained technological optimists who believed that the hazards were non-existent, exaggerated or would soon be scientifically overcome, and the party should therefore focus on the obvious economic benefits of mining and exporting uranium.

When the 1977 conference tackled the uranium issue the left emerged with a major victory. Conference endorsed 'a moratorium on uranium mining and treatment in Australia', and committed Labor in office to 'repudiate' any arrangements made by the Fraser government concerning 'the mining, processing or export of Australia's uranium'. This outcome was a triumph for Uren and the left. It also reflected a willingness to reconsider by influential former advocates of uranium development like Dunstan, who now accepted that more research was required into the disposal of radioactive wastes and other environmental problems before mining and processing could responsibly be authorized. It was a difficult question for Hawke. He decided that, on balance, because an isolationist attitude by Australia was futile, he was in favour of uranium mining provided that there were appropriate safeguards: 'My heart says no, but my head says yes'. His position was opposed by some of his closest political associates like Landeryou and Holding, was deplored by his older children who were active in the anti-uranium movement, and widened the growing gulf between him and the left.

Late in 1977 Fraser called an election, a year before it was due. He realized that his government's ordinary performance, the sharp recent increase in unemployment, the likelihood of further economic deterioration and his own unpopularity made it a prudent manoeuvre to seek a premature renewal of his mandate from the electors who had punished the Labor government in 1975. He believed that the uncommitted voters who had deserted the Labor government in droves in 1975 would not swing back while Whitlam was still leader, and he knew that anti-Whitlam forces in the FPLP were considering another leadership challenge (though Hayden publicly dismissed rumours that he would contest the leadership again before the next election). While Fraser was analysing his options he was aided by another unconventional and partisan intervention from Kerr. Responding to the speculation (which Fraser had engineered) about the unjustifiable early election, Kerr contacted a close friend, the federal president of the Liberal Party, and indicated that there would be no problems about approving an early election, and the date that would best suit Kerr's globetrotting arrangements was 10 December. The understandable confidence discernible in Liberal ranks that Kerr would oblige Fraser was rumoured to be related to the granting of a life peerage to Kerr. Combe privately warned the British Labour Party that any acquiescence by the British Labour government in the offer of a life peerage to Kerr would 'be viewed as an act of treachery by a close fraternal organisation'. No life peerage eventuated, but shortly after receiving Kerr's message Fraser decided to go to the polls on Kerr's preferred date, 10 December.

Early in the campaign there were some encouraging developments for Labor supporters. With a month to go Labor was ahead in some opinion polls. Contributing to this ascendancy was the discovery that Fraser's deputy, Lynch, had been implicated in the property development transactions which were undermining the Liberal government of Victoria. Lynch had been at the forefront of anti-Labor scandalmongering in 1975, and in ALP circles he was one of the most disliked Liberals: Cameron described him as 'a pompous attitudiniser'. There was more heartening news early in November when a by-election for the Liberal-held Victorian Assembly seat of Greensborough was won by Labor's hard-working and capable candidate Pauline Toner, an ex-schoolteacher who had become a lecturer and local councillor.

However, Labor lost its early advantage. Fraser dangled the bait of tax cuts, reinforced by strident 'fistful of dollars' advertisements. Instead of granting tax cuts, Labor proposed to abolish payroll tax in order to reduce unemployment. An economics journalist had persuaded Whitlam and some of his staffers that this proposal was seen by business and employer organizations as a way to solve the worsening unemployment problem, and Labor's chief pollster Rod Cameron was convinced that unemployment was the main issue in the electorate. Policy redevelopment had not been a feature of the FPLP's two years in opposition since 1975, and Whitlam committed Labor to this payroll tax idea after minimal consultation. Like other senior ALP figures including Hurford and Willis, Hawke felt that it was far too subtle to compete in the minds of politically unsophisticated voters with Fraser's fistful of dollars; he tried hard to persuade Whitlam that it was 'just lunacy, unbelievable lunacy', but did not succeed. The dramatic new initiative Whitlam was so keen to flourish did not help Labor's cause. It smacked of gimmickry, it failed to attract voters who were disenchanted with the Fraser government, and it contributed to the inconsistencies and confusion concerning economic policy which emanated from Whitlam, Hayden and Hurford during the campaign.

As polling day dawned there were few informed observers prepared to predict a Labor victory. Freudenberg, however, remained optimistic, and for him especially election night was desolate. It was not just that Labor had suffered another hammering; the extent of the loss meant that it was unquestionably the end of Whitlam's political career. In a dignified concession of defeat at the tally room, Whitlam indicated that he would not be recontesting the FPLP leadership which he had held longer than any of his predecessors. The final results revealed that the improvement in the FPLP's parliamentary strength since the 1975 disaster was minimal. Although the advent of a new party, the Democrats, caused the voting share of all other major parties to decline, it was a sobering fact that the FPLP had recorded its lowest proportion of the primary vote since 1934. Dismayed Labor activists were trenchantly critical of the payroll tax proposal. Action was taken by the national executive at its meeting in January 1978 to ensure that – as Combe replied to one of the many disgruntled communications he received from the rank and file – 'never again will policy speech preparation be left so late, and involve consultations with so few, as occurred in 1977'.

The new leader who gave these 'very clear undertakings' to the national executive was Hayden, who had, as expected, won the leadership after a contest against Bowen. In the ballot for deputy leader Bowen defeated Uren with the other contenders, Young and Willis, both well behind. Hayden, almost 45, was the youngest ever FPLP leader apart from the first, Watson. He had a very difficult task. With the benefit of hindsight it was most regrettable that in the May 1977 leadership ballot one or two waverers like Cohen had not stifled their sentimental regard for Whitlam and switched their support to Hayden (as Cohen and others shortly afterwards indicated they were prepared to do). With Hayden as FPLP leader there would have been no early election and, whenever Fraser did hold the election due in 1978, without the 'Whitlam factor' Labor could have hoped to make sufficient inroads into Fraser's majority to bring it within realistic sight of regaining office at the following election. Instead, Hayden took over a sadly dispirited and rudderless FPLP in the knowledge that the next Labor government was probably at least two elections away. However, Hayden began very impressively as leader. Even Clyde Cameron, who had supported Bowen in the December 1977 leadership ballot, was soon singing his praises:

> Bill has confounded his critics, including myself. He is very much like dear old Ben Chifley. He has the same humble dignity. There is no sign of arrogance or one-upmanship or of trying to pre-empt Party decisions. He is consulting his colleagues and showing all the qualities of leadership that will take him and the Party to Government.

Kerr's public appearances had continued to attract bitter abuse and disruption, and he had announced in July 1977 that he would resign at the end of that year. But the obloquy did not subside, especially after he made a spectacle of himself by appearing tipsy at the Melbourne Cup. At a farewell parliamentary luncheon in his honour – a function boycotted by FPLP members – with the election campaign under way, Kerr implicitly endorsed the Fraser government's policies by confidently predicting that the economy would make a strong recovery in the near future. These widely reported remarks infuriated Labor MPs, and Bowen lashed out against this 'most cynical and degrading exercise in attempted political point scoring'.

But this controversy was a molehill compared to the mountain of criticism which greeted the announcement in February 1978 that the Fraser government had found a remunerative sinecure, an ambassadorship to UNESCO, for Kerr in his retirement. 'On no public issue has there been such instant, spontaneous and unanimous outrage', observed Whitlam, who emphasized that the lucrative pension arrangements for the Governor-General introduced at Kerr's request had been designed precisely to prevent an unseemly appointment like this apparent reward for the services Kerr had rendered Fraser. Even newspapers unfriendly to Labor denounced it. 'Ripping the Scab off the Sore' was the headline of the condemnatory editorial in Murdoch's *Australian*. In parliament Hayden led the FPLP's attack, describing Kerr as 'Judas in a morning suit' and the appointment as 'an indecent exercise of the rankest cynicism' and 'an affront to this country'. Keating branded Fraser 'an insensitive totalitarian toff'. Jim McClelland, disillusioned with politics, was going through the motions in his last months in the Senate, but stirred himself for a rousing blast at Fraser and Kerr. Early in March Fraser announced that Kerr had decided not to accept the ambassadorship because of the tornado of criticism the appointment had received; McClelland was pleased to learn 'on good authority' that Kerr had made this decision after hearing a recording of his venomous speech in the Senate. For the next decade Kerr spent much of his time abroad, but whether he was in Australia or not he was always in exile.

After Labor's dual electoral disasters of 1975 and 1977 the national executive established a committee of inquiry into the party. The committee was asked to focus specifically on how the ALP could function more effectively in 'maximizing the involvement and satisfaction of Party members' and 'communicating the policies and ideals of the Party to the Australian community'. The committee was chaired by Hayden and Hawke, and also included Button, Ducker, Young, three union leaders, three university professors, a 20-year-old Queenslander representing Young Labor, and one of Hayden's most talented backbenchers, Dr Neal Blewett, who had been a politics professor in Adelaide before leaving academia to become MHR for Bonython at the 1977 election. Two committee members were women. The committee consulted widely, organized seminars and conferences, published discussion papers and considered hundreds of submissions from party units and individuals before delivering a detailed report to the national executive in March 1979. This report began by forthrightly declaring that reform was vital because the ALP had, in the national arena, 'one of the worst electoral records of any democratic socialist party in the western world'. The factors contributing to this included the comparatively small size of party membership, inadequate funds, 'the relative failure of the ALP to permeate the institutional framework of this society', and 'the parochial horizons of too many Labor chieftains'. Fundamentally, the party needed 'not the habit of occasionally falling into government, but a strategy and structure to make Federal Labor a continuously effective national entity and, hopefully, the dominant political force in this country'.

The committee made wide-ranging recommendations. It repeated the call made by Wyndham in the 1960s, and by others much earlier, for a radical change to the basis of national conference and national executive representation, which had always been founded on equal representation of each state. Acknowledging the difficulties posed by the generally hostile media, the committee concluded bleakly that there were 'no easy solutions'. The dream of Labor's own paper, a goal nurtured by many ALP adherents since the party's formation, was regarded by the committee as unfeasible. It suggested instead that the party should strongly support increased diversification of the media, and aim to get its message across systematically rather than in sudden bursts just before elections. On fund-raising, the committee considered that the party had to look beyond 'the traditional methods of having barbecues, raffles, dinners'. It urged special attention to the promotion of Labor's cause in ethnic communities, in white-collar trade unions, in rural regions, and in the states where the FPLP then had scant representation (Queensland, WA and Tasmania). Above all, there was an urgent need to make the party more welcoming and electorally attractive to women. Significantly fewer women voted Labor than men, the committee noted; while about 25% of party members were women, they were still exceedingly rare in its most senior positions. To overcome this situation the committee recommended 'a policy of affirmative action' to guarantee increased representation for women on all the ALP's constituent bodies.

While the committee of inquiry was scrutinizing the ALP nationally, some party activists had been impatiently agitating for reform in their state branch. Labor Queenslanders perturbed about party administration in their state had renewed cause for discontent when state and federal elections occurred in quick succession at the end of 1977. Although Queensland Labor managed to increase its meagre tally of seats in both elections, the results were once again unsatisfactory. Egerton had gone, but his henchmen remained firmly in control. His successor as the main pillar of strength on the executive was Neil Kane of the

Electrical Trades Union. Kane and company, who became known as the Old Guard, upset many ALP Queenslanders with their hostility to rank-and-file concerns. Party membership was declining, and morale at local branch level was dismal. The controlling clique manipulated the representative process to entrench themselves and their mates in power. They displayed inefficiency and secrecy in financial matters and management of 4KQ. They were unresponsive to modern campaigning techniques and contemporary political issues. They dismissed suggestions that the ALP would benefit by attracting into its ranks more middle-class professionals, academics and white-collar unionists as well as more women from every background: Kane even bluntly told the Toowong branch that 'professional people such as doctors, lawyers etc have no right to be in the ALP'. Most dispiriting of all was Queensland Labor's sheer political impotence. Confronting Bjelke-Petersen was no easy task, but many frustrated ALP supporters realized that Queensland Labor's ineffective opposition had made it easier for him to remain in office. Bjelke-Petersen's most recent act of repression had been to ban street marches. In some quarters it was believed that the real opposition to Bjelke-Petersen was not the Queensland ALP but purposeful groups like environmentalists, feminists, the anti-uranium movement and the Council for Civil Liberties.

The upshot was the formation of the ALP Reform Group. It was inaugurated on the day after the demoralizing 1977 federal election at a barbecue held in pouring rain at Indooroopilly. Soon afterwards a discussion paper entitled 'Can we improve the organisation of the Labor Party in Queensland?' was written and circulated by Dr Denis Murphy, one of the leading reform activists and an enthusiastic and prolific Labor historian. He had written a fine biography of one of Labor's legendary heroes, T.J. Ryan, and one of his next major projects was to be a biographical study of Hayden. As the Reform Group's agitation gathered momentum, over 400 ALP members including Senator Georges attended a meeting at Bardon in February 1978 chaired by 25-year-old clerk Peter Beattie. 'The future of the Queensland Branch is at stake', Beattie told the meeting. 'If changes are not made now. . .it will become nothing more than a small pressure group'. Before this Bardon meeting the controllers of the state branch warned the rank and file not to attend because the Reform Group's aims were 'malicious and destructive', but these threats proved counterproductive: they merely confirmed the Old Guard's oppression. The reformers were encouraged when Whitlam, the guest speaker at the inaugural T.J. Ryan Memorial Lecture, included in his remarks strong criticism of the Queensland branch. 'To win, the Australian Labor Party must have the best organisation and the best candidates', he said. 'In Queensland we have neither'. He likened the state of affairs in Queensland to the Victorian situation in the later 1960s, and predicted that 'if Queensland does not put its house in order then federal intervention is ultimately inevitable'. Three months later Queensland ALP officials retaliated by boycotting a testimonial dinner honouring Whitlam on his retirement from parliament. Whitlam's successor as MHR for Werriwa was Kerin, who defeated Riordan in the preselection and then won the by-election with a swing of 11% to Labor in a heartening result for Hayden and the ALP faithful.

There was no doubt where Hayden's sympathies lay in the struggle in his home state, but he was wary about plunging in precipitately. At internal party gatherings in March 1978 he aligned himself with the Reform Group, but refrained from attacking the state branch controllers publicly until Kane conveniently provided the excuse with a loose comment, gleefully publicized by the Reform Group, that Hayden should resign because he 'lacked worker support'. On television Hayden made a stinging reply, alluding to the 'serious health problem' troubling Kane, who was a renowned heavy drinker. Kane hit back at Hayden for 'hiding behind innuendoes' and supporting 'Groupers', but Hayden's jibes underlined a feature of the Egerton regime. Although teetotallers and even some temperance activists have been prominent in the ALP during its history, the reverse is also true: 'Drink afflicts the labour movement pretty badly in Australia', Henry Boote was lamenting as long ago as 1940. Egerton and his cronies certainly did not regard it as a disadvantage to have the Breakfast Creek Hotel located close to state ALP headquarters. In recalling his first impressions of Hayden at the 1973 federal conference, Walsh described his future leader as 'a misfit in the Queensland delegation; first he was sober, second he was younger, and third he spoke on policy issues'.

For some time anguished rank-and-file Queenslanders had been pleading for federal intervention, and Hayden was not exaggerating when he told the national executive that 'seething, festering unhappiness' was widespread in the state branch. Initially, however, he could only obtain from the national executive an investigation of the Queensland branch. The Reform Group welcomed the resultant changes while contending that they did not go far enough. Most reformers were disturbed that ballots under the new arrangements would be decided by first-past-the-post voting, rather than the proportional representation method introduced in Victoria and NSW in the early 1970s. About 30 Reform Group members issued a statement attacking the changes, describing them as 'so watered down by deals and compromise for political expediency as to render them ineffectual' in altering the 'autocratic, unrepresentative and incompetent' administration of the Queensland branch, which was 'a blot on the whole ALP'. The decision not to implement proportional representation owed much to a member of the investigative committee, Ducker, who feared that it could pave the way for the left to obtain national control of the party.

The Reform Group's concerns that the changes were insufficient proved correct, and the continuing turmoil in Queensland under the Old Guard's administration provoked the national executive to intervene more thoroughly. The Old Guard vindictively expelled or suspended some of its critics including Beattie and Georges, disbanded three pro-reform Toowoomba branches, and plotted secretly to sell a half-share of 4KQ to alleviate the consequences of its inept financial management. The secretary of a major union suggested that its affiliation fees might be more fruitfully donated to the Salvation Army, 'who are doing more for workers in this state than the ALP machine'. The saga of incompetence and dissension rolled on month after month, reducing the Queensland ALP to a laughing-stock. Not for the first time, correspondence which exacerbated upheaval within the party was disseminated on official ALP stationery proclaiming 'UNITY OF LABOR IS THE HOPE OF THE WORLD'. It was perhaps symbolic that the sturdy old Tree of Knowledge at Barcaldine, with its links to the stirring events of 1891, was in precarious health. Meanwhile Bjelke-Petersen continued on his way. Labor's ineffective state caucus was no impediment. The Premier arranged for one of Brisbane's finest buildings to be demolished without warning in the middle of the night, helped his wife become a Senator, and refused to allow Queensland children to receive sex education at school (even though schoolchildren benefited from it everywhere else in Australia, and Queensland had a relatively high incidence of both venereal disease and illegitimate teenage pregnancies). Eventually, despite the continued resistance of the right-wing

"NO THANKS! I DON'T WANT TO GAMBLE ON AN UNTRIED DRIVER."

81. During the 1983 election campaign Prime Minister Fraser unsuccessfully tried to boost his party's prospects by emphasizing Bob Hawke's inexperience as a party leader. (by Peter Nicholson; *Age*)

82. Prime Minister Hawke and Treasurer Keating.

83/84. Two Victorian Senators with contrasting physiques and a fervent commitment to their respective Australian Football League teams.

83. John Button resented that 'terribly boring' ERC meetings often kept him in Canberra at weekends when he would much rather have been following the fortunes of Geelong Football Club.

84. Collingwood's first premiership for 32 years inspired Robert Ray to demonstrate his skills. (*John Fairfax*)

85. The Creans. From left: Simon (ACTU president, then Hawke government minister), David (a Tasmanian MHA) and their father Frank (a minister in the Whitlam government). (*Frank Crean*)

NSW machine, the national executive on 1 March 1980 accepted by 11 votes to 7 Hayden's arguments that further surgery was necessary. This time proportional representation was instituted. An investigation into the branch's financial position disclosed what Combe described as 'mismanagement on a massive scale'. The Old Guard staged a protracted last-ditch stand, retaining physical possession of state headquarters and contesting the national executive's action in the courts. This litigation 'hung like a pall over the whole Labor movement in Queensland, producing disaffection among unions, branches and supporters'. Some insiders feared another spilt.

The climax came at the mid-1981 state conference. After Denis Murphy won the ballot for president ahead of Georges, Hayden – who had supported his biographer's bid for the presidency – lashed out at the Old Guard. The 'pig-headed attitude' of this 'narrow-minded, authoritarian group' was 'a travesty of our party's ideals and a debasement of its great traditions', asserted Hayden. Two days later conference delegates learned that the Supreme Court had just issued a judgement comprehensively rejecting the litigation launched by the Old Guard over a year earlier to block the transfer of power to the reformers. Overjoyed activists celebrated in emotional scenes. It was a special triumph for Hayden, and he was given a prolonged standing ovation at the conference. Murphy's eyes moistened when the delegates saluted his efforts with a similar tribute.

During the months following this conference Murphy lived up to the expectations of Labor people in and beyond Queensland who sensed that he had the makings of a parliamentary leader capable of spearheading a resurgence by Queensland Labor. He and the temporary state secretary, Manfred Cross, displayed a sufficiently conciliatory attitude to the vanquished Old Guard to avert any possibility of a split. When Cross vacated the secretary's position after regaining his former seat of Brisbane, the ballot to decide his successor was won by Beattie. Murphy and Beattie toiled with dedication and skill to nurse Queensland Labor back to political relevance. They made strenuous and much appreciated efforts to get in touch with local branches throughout the state, sometimes using a light plane to reach remote areas; they laboured to restore the state branch's financial position; and they tried to maximize harmony within the Queensland ALP as it climbed out of its trough of despair. It was likely that the introduction of proportional representation would, as in Victoria and NSW, lead to more intense factionalism in the state branch, but nearly all Labor Queenslanders accepted that an equitable system of power-sharing was far better than the winner-take-all structure abused by the Old Guard. After all, as Beattie correctly remarked following his election as state secretary, 'Labor is traditionally an umbrella political organisation'. Overriding all other considerations was the impact on rank-and-file morale. At last the Labor faithful in Queensland could look to the future with hope and confidence. Even the Tree of Knowledge at Barcaldine was recovering; expert care and attention had ensured its survival (although, ironically, the Old Guard apparently showed more interest in its preservation than the reformers).

In September 1977 Labor enthusiasts had no doubt about their party's rosy future in SA. The Dunstan government looked more impregnable than ever after being comfortably re-elected with 51·64% of the primary vote. SA now boasted the most equitable electoral system on the Australian mainland after possessing less than a decade earlier the nation's most flagrant gerrymander. The government's reform momentum had been somewhat slowed by a combination of the narrow election win of 1975 and the achievement of many of its highest priorities like electoral reform. But the government kept pursuing new avenues of change. Anti-discrimination legislation was enacted, a Constitutional Museum was founded, there was continued enhancement of the arts, shopping hours were extended, and a distinguished Aborigine, Sir Douglas Nicholls, became Governor of SA. Dunstan was particularly interested in upgrading worker participation in management; he familiarized himself with schemes elsewhere in the world, and in mid-1978 hosted in Adelaide an international conference on industrial democracy. An infusion of younger talented ministers had helped the government regenerate. Peter Duncan was only 30 when he became Attorney-General and minister for Prices and Consumer Affairs. Something of a protégé of Lionel Murphy's, Duncan had the same restless approach to reform as his mentor. His earliest achievements included the decriminalization of homosexuality and an overhaul of landlord and tenant law. Another capable newcomer, John Bannon, was added to cabinet only a year after entering the Assembly.

However, 1978 was a harrowing year for Dunstan. Until late 1977 his government had managed with marked success to insulate SA from the economic problems afflicting Australia, but a state government, particularly in one of the smaller states, has a limited capacity to counteract adverse national and international economic developments, and the financial stringency imposed by Fraser necessitated cutbacks to services in SA. Dunstan's difficulties were compounded by Fraser's refusal to provide financial support to the shipbuilding industry, which caused the closure of the Whyalla shipyard. The Dunstan government established a clothing factory in Whyalla to make uniforms needed in government activities, but unemployment rose sharply. Dunstan admitted that his state went 'from the best employment record to the worst'.

In addition to wrestling with intractable economic difficulties, the Dunstan government had to weather an extraordinary controversy concerning its dismissal of the SA Police Commissioner, H.H. Salisbury. As Salisbury admitted himself, and as both an inquiry by an acting judge and a subsequent royal commission confirmed, Salisbury deliberately deceived Dunstan about the SA Special Branch's surveillance activities and records. In fact, as the judicial inquiry revealed, the Special Branch had for decades engaged in outrageously extensive monitoring of individuals and groups (including civil liberties activists and Labor MPs) it regarded as tainted by radicalism. It was another glimpse of the traditional security force perspective, which regards all left-wingers as potential hazards while usually ignoring the wildest right-wing fanatics. Salisbury justified his deliberately misleading answers to Dunstan by claiming that he was not ultimately responsible to the SA government, because he had a higher moral obligation to the Queen and the wider intelligence community. This cut no ice with the Dunstan cabinet, and Salisbury was sacked. The outcry from anti-Labor interests was noisy and prolonged. Dunstan established a royal commission into the affair; he was convinced that his government's conduct would be vindicated, as it ultimately was.

On top of these political pressures Dunstan suffered agonizing private torment in 1978. For some time he had endured widespread scuttlebutt about his personal life. In April 1978 he and his second wife – they had been married little more than a year – learned that she had terminal cancer; she died in October. Under this accumulating stress his own health suffered acutely. Bannon's swift elevation to cabinet as an extra minister was arranged partly to lighten the Premier's immense workload. Meanwhile, the passionate debate in the party about uranium mining had been revived by the discovery of rich deposits at

Roxby Downs. The SA economy was desperately in need of profitable industrial development, and as Dunstan, tired and ill, departed for a hectic overseas trip to assess the latest technological progress there was widespread speculation that he would reverse his government's opposition to mining. On his return, however, he announced that his investigations had convinced him that there should be no change in government policy. Shortly afterwards he collapsed in parliament. After receiving medical advice that he had to rest for six months and severely prune his workload thereafter, the 52-year-old Premier called a press conference in hospital and stunned the labour movement throughout Australia by announcing his retirement from politics.

Dunstan was one of Labor's most outstanding leaders. Apart from T.J. Ryan, no other Premier could match Dunstan's success in spearheading the transformation of a previously conservative state. In his 1970 policy speech Dunstan claimed that his party had prepared 'the most comprehensive plan for change and growth any State has seen since Federation': 'We'll set a standard of social advancement that the whole of Australia will envy. We believe South Australia *can* set the pace'. Naturally there were shortcomings in the attempted realization of this grand design. The creation of a brand-new city at Monarto did not come to fruition, and diversified economic development also proved elusive. Nevertheless, after being renowned during the Playford era for its conservatism, SA became an enlightened pace-setter under Dunstan in many spheres, including electoral fairness, community welfare, consumer protection, planning and environment, education, equal opportunities, Aboriginal affairs, public administration and the arts. In the realm of housing SA home-buyers benefited from lower prices after the Dunstan government created a Land Commission which made 'the most radical intervention by the public sector in Australia into the private land and housing markets'. Of course Dunstan did not manage all this on his own. Talented advisers and administrators were naturally significant, but many of them were attracted to serve in the first place by the innovative flair of the Dunstan government. Important roles were also played by competent ministers like Hudson, Virgo, King and Corcoran. Dunstan and Corcoran formed a fine partnership: Corcoran, the gregarious beer-drinking ex-army officer, neatly complemented the visionary, flamboyant but rather shy Premier.

Labor soon had good reason to rue Dunstan's departure. Corcoran took over as Premier, with Hudson as his deputy, and moved quickly to assert his own style and sense of priorities. He made friendly overtures to the business sector, and quietly interred some incomplete Dunstan initiatives like industrial democracy and research into alternative co-operative lifestyles. Corcoran seemed to have made a promising start, but six months after becoming Premier he made a fateful decision to call an unexpected election. He was keen to obtain a personal mandate from the electors, the government was travelling well according to the opinion polls, and he was also apprehensive about the impact on his government of the forthcoming publication of a controversial book rumoured to contain scurrilous allegations about Dunstan. Although Corcoran obtained strong support from cabinet and caucus for his hasty decision, it was made without the customary pre-election preparation and private surveys which had benefited Labor during the Dunstan era. Astonishingly, there was no prior consultation with party officials before the election was called. Even the campaign director was in the dark. It was hardly surprising that Labor's campaign, by recent SA standards, was poor. Anti-Labor interests capitalized. The *News*, a Murdoch tabloid, launched one of the most vitriolic and sustained attacks ever made by a newspaper on a party during an Australian election campaign. A variety of employer and business groups gave their hostility to Labor an unusually high profile in the campaign, presumably influenced by the advanced industrial relations legislation the government had foreshadowed. Although SA industrial relations under Dunstan had been the most harmonious in Australia, the resentment caused by an untimely bus strike called in the week before the election played into the Liberals' hands. On polling day, 15 September, the government was annihilated. The state-wide swing was 10·78% but it reached 20% in some seats. In the metropolitan area, where Labor had not lost a single seat since the Second World War, the overall swing was 13% which cost the government no fewer than eight seats. One of the casualties was Hudson. This devastating result sank the SA ALP into deep gloom.

Hayden had continued to perform impressively as FPLP leader. His consultative leadership style was appreciated by senior colleagues including Young, Keating, Button, Wriedt, Willis, Hurford, Walsh and Grimes, and he was warmly supported by emerging talented backbenchers like Blewett, Dawkins and Kerin. His closest colleague was Button, Labor's deputy Senate leader. Button's knowledge of the intervention manoeuvres which overhauled the Victorian branch greatly assisted Hayden when the national executive authorized action against the Queensland ALP controllers. Hayden instructed his staff always to put Button's phone calls straight through to him irrespective of the circumstances. Although Hayden engendered a good team spirit on his front bench, he was wary of NSW machine powerbrokers like Ducker and Richardson. Sensing Hayden's reservations about them, they were unenthusiastic about him.

Hayden was contemptuous of suggestions that he should take steps to improve his presentation. With the electronic media increasingly important in shaping electors' perceptions of leading politicians, well-intentioned advisers urged Hayden to dress with more polish and expressed concern about his awkward speaking style. Its jerkiness and reedy timbre led Fraser to dub him 'belly-aching Bill' and 'whingeing Willy'. But Hayden challenged the necessity for what he described as 'artificial' and 'cosmetic' adjustments. 'The important thing is to be yourself', he insisted.

Establishing Labor's credibility in economic management was Hayden's top priority. He outlined this objective to delegates at the 1979 ALP national conference:

> First, and above all else, we must demonstrate beyond doubt that we are competent economic managers. That competence and the public's recognition of it is the absolute essential underpinning of everything we want to do. Without it. . .we might just as well pack our bags and give the game away.

Contemporary financial realities precluded a revival of the grand Whitlamesque programmes of the later 1960s, based on assumptions about continued economic growth. 'We will not find our future in the past', declared Hayden. Instead, he argued, Labor had to convince the electorate that it could manage scarce resources with more efficiency and compassion than the Fraser government.

The conservatives' boasts of superior administrative expertise were looking increasingly hollow. Unemployment kept climbing. The economic stagnation and the coalition government's failure to take effective preventative action against notorious tax evasion schemes were underlined by Whitlam's quip that during the Fraser years 'the Whitlam book industry was our largest growth industry after tax avoidance'. These taxation devices flourished unimpeded by

Barwick's High Court judgements, which defied social morality. Like Dunstan, Whitlam expanded Australians' horizons, but Fraser narrowed them with his austere and humourless personality and grim philosophy that 'life wasn't meant to be easy'.

The intense resentment of Fraser in Labor circles had not abated. Kerr had departed, but Fraser's continuation in office was a constant reminder of his path to power; Kerr had acted with deceit and impropriety in a supposedly impartial position, but he was only able to do so because of Fraser's ruthless convention-wrecking. The persistent bitterness towards Fraser was pronounced in the FPLP as well as among the rank and file. When Fraser informed Hayden and Bowen privately about some security matters in mid-1978, Hayden nodded intermittently during Fraser's briefing but there was no reaction from Bowen. Eventually Fraser asked Bowen what was wrong. 'I'm listening', retorted Bowen, 'it's just that I don't trust you, you bastard'. Afterwards Hayden complimented Bowen on his forthrightness.

Hawke's continued ambivalence about entering parliament was extremely frustrating for backers like Landeryou, who were trying to secure a safe seat for him despite the determined opposition of the Socialist Left. The hostility between that faction and Hawke was mutual. At the Victorian ALP conference in March he blasted the Socialist Left as 'a canker' and 'a telephone box minority' in a speech described by an observer as 'one of the most excoriating attacks heard within the Labor movement since the 1955 split'. It was little known in Australia that Hawke's overseas activities had made him an eminent figure in some other countries, but in mid-1979 another international foray became one of the most traumatic episodes in his turbulent life. Hawke had agreed to visit Moscow to plead for the long-sought release of detained Soviet Jews. His emotional commitment intensified after meeting the desperate families involved, and he was ecstatic to learn from a Russian official that the Jews would be released. But the euphoria turned terribly sour when the assurances Hawke had received were not honoured, and he felt so wretched about raising the families' hopes that he became fleetingly suicidal. On his return to Australia he was immediately embroiled in two substantial industrial disputes. Apprehensive about the decision he would soon have to make about contesting preselection, nervous about his related commitment to give up alcohol if he entered parliament, and with his marriage under some strain, Hawke was overstretched and frayed as he flew to Adelaide for the ALP national conference in July.

At that gathering the growing tension between Hawke and Hayden exploded. Hayden had a significant victory when he secured right-wing support to defeat left-wing attempts to commit the party to increased nationalization and public ownership, but it was a late switch by Hayden to support the left on a separate issue which triggered the eruption. Hawke and shadow Treasurer Willis were convinced that Labor in government should make another attempt to obtain the power over prices and incomes which the Whitlam government had failed to obtain at its unsuccessful 1973 referenda. (Ironically, that failure in 1973 was partly due to the ACTU's opposition, vigorously proclaimed by Hawke, to national government control over incomes.) Six years later some left-wing MPs and union leaders were no less hostile to the proposal. Hawke had been tied up in Melbourne dealing with a major strike, but made a special trip to Adelaide to contribute to the conference debate. On the morning of the debate Hayden met an influential group including Wran, Ducker and Richardson to stitch up support for the referendum proposal. However, by lunchtime Uren had persuaded Hayden that the left had the numbers on the issue. Hayden was keen to avoid a major personal defeat in his first conference as leader, and made a hasty last-minute deal with the left. Their compromise amendment, which was duly endorsed by conference, in effect dumped the referendum proposal. When Hayden was asked by journalists about Hawke's reaction, his response revealed his irritation at the constant media speculation about Hawke's parliamentary future and the implications for his leadership. 'Listen, I make up my own mind in these matters and I carried the conference', he snapped. The pro-referendum advocates had received little or no advance warning of Hayden's late switch. Ducker, Wran, Willis, Keating and Richardson were angry; Hawke, who was all set to bucket the left in the fiery speech he had made a special trip to Adelaide to deliver, was livid. To avoid a public confrontation with Hayden he remained silent, obviously fuming, during the conference debate, but his outburst afterwards in the bar, where he denounced Hayden in the strongest terms, became front-page news.

That tantrum was widely believed to have ruined Hawke's parliamentary aspirations, but his popularity among the Australian people remained phenomenal, even after one of the occasions when he shed tears in public, as Young witnessed:

> If I'd cried I wouldn't have had the nerve to return to my electorate. I would have been dead, politically. Soon afterwards I went with Hawkey to a public meeting. You would have thought that people would give him a roasting but they were trying to touch his hair, touch the sleeve of his jacket. There isn't another politician in this country who could arouse that response.

Hawke's agony of indecision about parliament mounted as the deadline for preselection nominations approached. His backers had earmarked Wills, the seat being vacated by Bryant, as the most suitable for their hesitant champion. For that seat the Socialist Left nominated Gerry Hand, who made clear his determination not to stand aside before the preselection ballot for anyone. Ultimately, influenced by his uncle's regret about rejecting an opportunity to enter the Representatives in 1945, Hawke opted to take the plunge. Landeryou organized the numbers, and Hawke won the preselection as expected. He turned his back on alcohol overnight. Parliament would be an unfamiliar forum for him, but his extraordinary popularity ensured that he would be a redoubtable newcomer. Months before he nervously announced that he would contest preselection for Wills, an opinion poll asked voters to choose their preferred prime minister. Nearly one-third picked Hawke, who finished well ahead of anyone else including Hayden and Fraser.

That survey confirmed that Labor had another ready-made alternative leader to Hayden outside the FPLP. In second place behind Hawke was Wran. He had confirmed his supremacy in NSW by leading Labor to a runaway win at the 1978 election, when his party gained an 8% swing after adopting the slogan 'Wran's Our Man' to capitalize on his approval rating in NSW of around 80%. The voters were clearly satisfied with his pragmatic approach. His government minimized mistakes, took care to avoid alienating sections of the electorate, and was noted for its sound economic management. Sprinkled in its cautious and moderate record were some very worthwhile reforms and achievements, notably in public transport and the transformation of the Legislative Council from an antiquated colonial relic into a chamber elected by the people. The distinctive features of Wran's leadership were his diligence, acumen, toughness and commanding stature as a performer in parliament, on the hustings and especially on the electronic media. His signals that he was contemplating a transfer to the bigger political stage in Canberra annoyed Hayden, who was particularly irritated by this graphic Wran utterance:

> If and when I decide to enter Federal politics, it will be the same way I entered State politics: by sitting down, studying the rules, finding out who has to be moved, who I've got to beat, then coming out smothered in blood and horror.

Wran's Canberra aspirations were stymied in 1980 by a throat complaint which required a series of operations, although while he was sidelined he did enhance his exposure outside his home state by using the redoubtable power of the NSW machine to secure the position of national ALP president after Batt, Hawke's successor in that post, decided on a complete break from politics.

Richardson delivered the presidency as Wran had requested, although he was then preoccupied with a very different matter. The NSW ALP secretary, who was nicknamed 'Jimmy Cagney' because he was 'short, very brash, toughtalking and superconfident', had unwisely formed connections with some very shady characters who operated in the murky municipal politics and Labor tribal warfare of Sydney's inner suburbs. Changing demographic trends in these suburbs had altered their political character. Traditional ALP strongholds like Balmain and Enmore became increasingly occupied by middle-class residents more concerned about environmental matters and other quality-of-life issues than the main preoccupations of the working class, jobs and wages. NSW left-wingers used this influx to contest the right-wing machine's dominance in these suburbs. A prominent figure in the left's challenge, 29-year-old Peter Baldwin MLC, was brutally bashed at his home in July 1980 by an unknown assailant, although Baldwin told police that he had recently been threatened by a self-confessed political thug associated with the machine. It was not the first violent incident during this inner-suburbs factional struggle, but the press photographs of Baldwin's battered and swollen face sparked an outcry. Dozens of protesters invaded state ALP headquarters. Wran was then recuperating after one of his throat operations, and Ducker had relinquished all his active political positions for a combination of health and family reasons. Well and truly in the hot seat was Richardson. He moved quickly. He instigated a special party inquiry into all the inner-city branches and the immediate deregistration of several of them, and recommended that the state government should overhaul three local councils straightaway and establish a Crime Control Commission. This response helped the state branch controllers to weather the crisis. So did the impending federal election, which encouraged the protagonists to close ranks. Although Richardson severed his links with associates of dubious repute, his former connection with them was occasionally raised by his detractors in subsequent years. The police investigation of the assault on Baldwin led to charges being laid concerning the falsification of the Enmore branch records; the Enmore controversy became a long-running saga, augmenting the damage the Baldwin incident had already done to the Wran government's prestige.

Labor's campaign for the 1980 federal election was much better than its muddled effort in 1977. Relations between Hayden and Hawke had been partially repaired thanks to Combe and Victorian state secretary Hogg. Hawke did not pretend that the legacy of distrust arising from Hayden's late switch on wages policy at the 1979 national conference had completely disappeared, but assured

Hayden that he was absolutely dedicated to maximizing Labor's chances at the 1980 election and would campaign 'to the last ounce of my energy' to make Hayden Prime Minister. Labor strategists decided to capitalize on the great popularity enjoyed by Hawke and national president Wran by featuring them prominently in the campaign alongside Hayden. All three worked with professional harmony for the cause, and the promotion of Labor's 'triumvirate' was a successful campaign tactic; Hayden performed better than anticipated on the campaign trail, and an unexpected ALP victory began to seem possible. During the last week, however, Labor's opponents launched a fear and smear campaign about the alleged dangers of inflation and a capital gains tax under Labor, and it apparently influenced enough voters, especially in NSW, to be decisive in the overall result.

Labor's creditable and well-organized campaign had brought victory at the following federal election well within reach. A swing of 5·5% had produced a harvest of 13 additional seats in the Representatives. None of them were in Tasmania, where Labor won no seats at all for the third election in a row. Wriedt made a gallant but unsuccessful bid to arrest this parlous situation by relinquishing the secure position he held in the Senate, where he was FPLP leader, to challenge one of the sitting Liberal MHRs. At the other extreme was Victorian Labor's best result in a federal election for more than half a century. Seven (over half) of Labor's nation-wide gains were captured in Victoria, where the outcome was a confirmation of the ALP's improved electoral performance at the May 1979 state election. Solicitor Michael Duffy captured Holt, and Henty was regained by Joan Child. Also boosting the proportion of women in the FPLP were two talented new MHRs, Elaine Darling (Lilley, Queensland) and Ros Kelly (Canberra). The solitary woman in the FPLP shadow cabinet continued to be Susan Ryan, a prominent activist in the women's movement who became Labor's inaugural Senator for the ACT in 1975.

ALP feminists were dismayed by the defeat of Senator Melzer after she was relegated to a vulnerable position on the ticket. A victim of increased factionalism in Victoria, she attributed her downfall partly to the intense number-crunching by both the supporters and opponents of Hawke's bid to enter the FPLP and take over the leadership. Popular and competent, Melzer was passionately hostile to uranium mining, and had adopted strong stances on other issues. She had distanced herself from the pro-Hawke Labor Unity faction without joining the Socialist Left. These factions secured one each of the two winnable positions on the ticket for themselves, and Melzer was allocated the number three spot. As she acknowledged, her chances from there were slim: the very likely outcome in Victoria was Labor two, National (previously Country) and Liberal two, with the Democrats snaring the other seat. Rank-and-file anger at Melzer's demotion fuelled a strong movement seeking a review of the placement of Labor's candidates on the ticket. Hogg remarked that Melzer's plight had sparked more animated correspondence from the grass roots than any issue since 1970. Fierce pressure was placed on the number two candidate, Labor Unity's Robert Ray – who was, unlike Melzer and the Socialist Left Senator heading the ticket, not a sitting member – to agree to swap places with Melzer. But Ray sat tight and waited for the storm to blow over. Eventually it did. Left-wingers inclined to support an exchange of positions by Melzer and Ray backed off when the right in NSW threatened to retaliate by enforcing a similar alteration on the NSW ALP how-to-vote card for the Senate, which would result in a left-wing candidate being switched from second to third place on the ticket.

Melzer believed that her predicament also stemmed partly from her involvement in a fiercely contested preselection for the Melbourne Ports seat vacated by Frank Crean in 1977. The rivals were Holding, who had decided to transfer to Canberra after a decade as Victorian Opposition Leader, and Crean's 28-year-old son Simon, a university graduate recruited by Landeryou into the Storemen and Packers' Union. Both Simon Crean and Holding belonged to Labor Unity and were strongly pro-Hawke. As a member of the preselection panel which had to decide between them, Melzer found herself in an awkward position. The numbers were very close, and she had been friendly with both Holding and Frank Crean. It was her eventual preference for Holding which settled the outcome. Two years later she sensed overtones of retribution when Simon Crean and others lobbied for Ray to be placed above her on the Senate ticket.

Melzer's fate convinced Labor women that the party needed affirmative action more than ever. Like other recommendations from the 1978–79 committee of inquiry, this proposal was evaluated by a special national conference in July 1981. This gathering ratified the most sweeping changes to the composition of national conference since its inception. The party's supreme policy-making body was enlarged to 100 delegates (subsequently amended to 99), and a certain proportion of the representatives had to be women. The 99 delegates included the four FPLP leaders, two delegates each from the ACT and the Northern Territory, and a Young Labor representative; the remaining 90 were allocated among the states in proportion to the number of federal electorates contained in each state. At last the system of equal representation for each of the states despite their varied populations had been abolished. The affirmative action provision stipulated that women had to comprise a minimum of 25% of each state delegation. While clearly raising the stature of women in the party, this innovation sat rather awkwardly with the increased factionalism guaranteed by another new requirement: henceforth, state delegations to national conference had to be determined by proportional representation in order to provide a voice for all minority groups in the party. The upshot was that women, like nearly everyone else, felt obliged to join a faction; accordingly, they frequently felt impelled to support a male representing their faction rather than a woman from another faction. No affirmative action formula had been devised to cover preselections for single-member constituencies, and Labor feminists were angered when left-winger Jan Burnswoods, who had pushed former Prime Minister McMahon uncomfortably close in Lowe at the 1980 election, was overlooked as Labor's candidate for the Lowe by-election in March 1982 created by McMahon's resignation. Her setback so soon after the party's endorsement of affirmative action amounted to a 'breach of faith', they claimed, and their bitterness was unleashed at the National Labor Women's Conference where Hayden was jeered and heckled. Burnswoods remarked that apparently the role of women in the party was 'still to be the cooks and the raffle ticket-sellers'.

The 1981 special national conference also debated proposals to amend the objective in Labor's platform. One of the main advocates of altering the objective was Gareth Evans, the former Rhodes Scholar and law lecturer who entered the Senate in mid-1978 and became shadow Attorney-General after the 1980 election. Clever, ambitious and hard-working with an engaging turn of phrase, Evans argued that change was needed because the objective was incomplete, misleading, lacked contemporary relevance, and had for decades given ammunition to Labor's opponents without doing the party 'any noticeably redeeming good'. He wanted to omit the reference to the 'democratic socialization of industry, production, distribution and exchange', which had been the cornerstone of the ALP objective for some 60 years. 'There comes a point when sentiment has to give way to reason', he asserted, aware that many left-wingers – Evans belonged to the Victorian Labor Unity faction – regarded the traditional wording he wanted to jettison as sacred. Evans proposed the adoption of a 'fundamental objective' affirming Labor's dedication to 'the realisation of a society founded upon the principles and values of democratic socialism – a society built upon liberty, equality and democracy'. He wanted this declaration to be followed by a list of specific goals, including social justice, constitutional reform, Australian ownership of Australian resources, anti-discrimination, the abolition of poverty, 'greater real equality' in wealth distribution, civil liberties guarantees, protection of the environment, and 'Control by democratic process, including where necessary social ownership, of the means of production, distribution and exchange'.

Labor emerged from its 1981 special national conference with a new objective comprising, as Evans had proposed, a fundamental statement followed by a number of specific goals. There was a clear resemblance to the old objective in the wording of the new fundamental statement:

> The Australian Labor Party is a democratic socialist party and has the objective of the democratic socialization of industry, production, distribution and exchange, to the extent necessary to eliminate exploitation and other anti-social features in these fields.

Moderates at the conference failed in a bid to remove the socialization component; also unsuccessful was an attempt by left-wingers to harden the objective by deleting the qualification 'to the extent necessary'. The list of 22 goals was longer than Evans wanted, but he was 'not unhappy' with the outcome: at least Labor's objective 'now offers more ammunition to the home side than it does to the enemy'.

Holding had resigned a year after his leadership was challenged in the wake of his third electoral defeat as Victorian Opposition Leader. One of his challengers in 1976 was Barry Jones, the MLA for Melbourne since 1972. Jones had been a schoolteacher, well-known quiz champion, solicitor, university lecturer in history, author, prominent anti-hanging activist and prime mover in the resurrection of the Australian film industry. His confidence about his chances of toppling Holding in March 1976 had induced him to predict victory before the contest, but he did not poll well. 'Quiz kids can't count', remarked Holding afterwards. When Holding did step down the following year and became MHR for Melbourne Ports, Jones accompanied him to Canberra after winning preselection for Lalor, the seat vacated by Cairns. Holding's successor as leader in Victoria was his deputy, Wilkes. Experienced, affable, principled and determined, Wilkes was methodical rather than imaginative, and the primary focus of his sense of social justice was the need to protect battling families struggling to pay the bills.

Some influential ALP Victorians increasingly doubted whether Wilkes could lead them back to government. They pointed to his shortcomings in charisma, acuity and media skills. Authority and stature were somehow lacking in his leadership, and the role of competent team-spirited lieutenant seemed to suit him better. His supporters emphasized that he had led Victorian Labor in 1979 to its best result at a state election for 27 years. Others countered that in the circumstances Labor should have done better still; instead of feeling pleased about finishing 10 seats adrift of an Assembly majority, they argued, Labor should be dejected about missing its best opportunity to win government for decades. After all, the Liberal government had been rocked by a series of scandals which had caused it to plummet in the opinion polls, and the state ALP looked in better shape than at any stage during its previous turbulent quarter-century. It was attracting MPs of generally better quality (although Labor's 58-year-old MHR for Batman, after losing preselection for his seat to 40-year-old sociology lecturer Brian Howe, lashed out angrily against the 'trendies, intellectual snobs and technocrats' who were, he alleged, invading the ALP and jeopardizing its future). The Victorian ALP was also benefiting from Hogg's astute administration at party headquarters. Formerly an organizer for the Socialist Left, Hogg was appointed state secretary in 1976. In that position he became widely respected for his political insight, general competence and concern for the welfare of the party as a whole. Under his administration Victorian Labor significantly boosted its campaigning expertise and effectiveness.

At the next state election the Victorians had a new leader. In May 1980 a challenge was stillborn when Landeryou and his co-plotters from Labor Unity realized that they did not have the numbers to replace Wilkes with Bundoora MLA John Cain, who was the son of Labor's last Victorian Premier. The crucial factor was the inability of Hogg, who preferred Cain, to persuade the Socialist Left to support the challenger. After this outcome was known the pro-Wilkes camp forced a spill of all caucus positions, and some of Cain's energetic supporters, including Steve Crabb and Tom Roper, lost their places on the executive. After losing to Wilkes in the Northcote preselection tussle which followed his father's death, Cain had concentrated on his legal practice and, although an active member of the Participants in the lead-up to intervention, had eschewed a parliamentary career until winning preselection for Bundoora. Cain was similar to Wilkes in his personal integrity, systematic approach and unpretentious tastes and interests, but had demonstrated a sharper intellect and a more effective combative style, especially in probing the scandalous land deals which had eroded the Liberal government's popularity. By the end of winter 1981 the possibility of an imminent election seemed to preclude any further leadership challenge, but early in September the Socialist Left agreed with Hogg that it should withdraw its support from Wilkes. Landeryou and deputy leader Robert Fordham visited Wilkes to inform him that his majority support in caucus had disappeared. After an initial outburst, Wilkes accepted the situation with commendable dignity. The only discordant note as the leadership change occurred came from Hartley. He underlined his declining support in the party by publicly attacking the 'disloyal' conduct and 'act of sabotage' by the anti-Wilkes forces, who included most of his own faction. Ironically, Wilkes had approved a 1979 move to expel Hartley from the party, which had been prevented by Hogg because of his concern that it would produce a severe schism in Victoria.

Seven months after becoming leader Cain led Victorian Labor into government for the first time since 1955. The Liberal government during its concluding months was scarred by internal discord in addition to the scandals which had plagued it since the mid-1970s, and Labor's election win was not unexpected. After 27 years in opposition any victory would have produced euphoria among Labor's rank and file, but to Labor enthusiasts with an eye to history the landslide of 3 April 1982 was breathtaking. In the state where Labor had been least successful and no party had secured an absolute majority of votes since 1917, Labor managed a voting share in 1982 of 50·01% (45·23% in 1979, and 42·43% in

1976) and captured no fewer than 17 seats from the Liberals. The key to this remarkable triumph was Labor's penetration of the south-eastern metropolitan area which had consistently been a happy hunting ground for the Liberals while Bolte enjoyed the valuable assistance of the DLP. Six of Labor's new MPs were women, and Pauline Toner became Victoria's first female minister. She and half her cabinet colleagues were from Labor Unity. There were two ministers each from the Independents faction (Premier Cain and architect Evan Walker MLC, the minister for Conservation and Planning) and the Socialist Left, with the rest factionally unaligned. The changing face of the party was exemplified by the presence in Cain's initial cabinet of only one minister who was indubitably working class. The new government began positively and impressively. It introduced sweeping structural changes to the public service and the management of government finance. Labor supporters were pleased by the early initiatives affecting Aborigines and teachers, and by the Premier's assertive – although ultimately unsuccessful – confrontation with Fraser over visits by nuclear-armed American ships. Cain also indicated a willingness to benefit from Don Dunstan's experience by abolishing the Victorian Police Special Branch and ordering the destruction of its thousands of files, and also by appointing the former SA Premier to head the Victorian Tourist Commission.

In 1982 Labor also regained the reins of government in SA. After the stunning reverse of 1979 the state branch had established a Committee of Assessment to review all facets of its structure and performance. Although the committee's findings concerning the 1979 defeat angered Corcoran, who felt unduly singled out for blame, the inquiry report recommended significant organizational reforms which were nearly all implemented swiftly. The debate within the party about these reforms reflected growing discontent with the decision-making style – based on informal consensus and the card vote – which had operated in SA for over three decades. The recent increase in factional turbulence in SA was reinforced by the national conference ruling that multiple delegations to conference had to be determined by proportional representation. A prominent figure in spreading dissatisfaction with SA's traditional consensus ethos was Duncan. He had successfully challenged the candidate anointed by the machine for the 1972 Elizabeth preselection in one of the few instances where the state branch controllers' choice was overturned. Duncan's involvement in this burgeoning factionalism had irked Dunstan; it induced Corcoran to move Duncan to the Health portfolio in an attempt to shift him away from the limelight; and it also led to a public clash between Duncan and Bannon, who had become state ALP leader after the 1979 election defeat discredited Corcoran's leadership and cost Hudson his seat. Before Dunstan's retirement Bannon was being groomed to succeed him, but when Dunstan suddenly resigned Bannon was judged too inexperienced at that stage to assume the mantle. In opposition Bannon refused to emulate Dunstan's flamboyant style, which, Bannon felt, was less appropriate in difficult economic times and did not suit his personality anyway. His low-key, cautious approach was vindicated at the election in November 1982, when Labor managed a narrow win after regaining half the voting share lost in 1979. The 1982 election resembled the close shave of 1975 rather than the clearcut victories of 1970, 1973 and 1977.

However, between those pleasing election victories in Victoria and SA there was another state election which resulted in the downfall of a Labor government. Tasmanian ALP governments had managed to survive in the past despite lacking cohesion, and to an extent the state elections of 1976 and 1979 continued this pattern. A copybook campaign led by Neilson produced victory in 1976 following a period of protracted wrangling about the introduction of organizational reforms, which had been recommended by the state branch rules committee headed by Coates. Neilson retired within a year, and was succeeded as Premier by 35-year-old Lowe, a decent and popular consensus-seeker who struggled to contain the internal friction despite his government's success at the July 1979 election. The most damaging issue for the labour movement – which divided unionists, Labor's rank and file, caucus and Lowe's cabinet – was the HEC proposal to dam the picturesque Franklin River and its archaeologically precious surroundings as part of further hydroelectric development. Lowe eventually sided with the environmentalists opposed to the project. On Remembrance Day 1981 the escalating discord culminated in Lowe's replacement as leader and Premier by ambitious right-winger Harry Holgate. Lowe resigned from the ALP and sat on the Assembly cross-benches, accompanied by Mary Willey who emulated Lowe's departure from caucus. The pro-dam Holgate government lost control of the Assembly and was forced to go to the people in May 1982. In addition to being plagued with disunity, Labor was handicapped by Holgate's unpopularity in the electorate after his scheming to supplant Lowe. At the election Labor was annihilated. Lowe retained his seat as an independent. Afterwards Wriedt, who had decided to settle for state politics after the failure of his bold attempt to become MHR for Denison, was elected Labor's new leader. In another sequel the national executive decided to intervene in the affairs of the troubled Tasmanian branch. Senator Grimes was appointed president, a 34-member interim administrative committee was installed, and affirmative action was later introduced (as it had been when the Queensland branch was reconstructed in 1980) to facilitate greater participation by women in the party. But discord continued as the Franklin dam issue not only remained a bone of contention in Tasmania, but began to have important ramifications on the national political scene as well.

During the later 1970s the WA ALP was in the doldrums. It was bedevilled by internal tensions and poor morale. There was considerable conflict about the relative emphasis on traditional concerns compared to more modern issues like the environment. Its performance at the 1977 state and federal elections was undistinguished. In February the state Liberal government was comfortably re-elected, and Labor's voting share fell nearly 4%. The result in December was even worse: WA Labor's primary vote in the Representatives slumped to 32·56%. Dawkins, who won preselection for Fremantle after Beazley retired, retained it for Labor in a close contest, but as in 1975 it was Labor's only WA seat in the Representatives. There was even some concern – later allayed – whether Labor could secure two of the five Senate seats contested. Restlessness about this unsatisfactory state of affairs resulted in the replacement of Colin Jamieson, who had become state leader in 1976 when Tonkin retired at the age of 74 after breaking Collier's record for parliamentary longevity. Jamieson was an ex-carpenter who had been a parliamentarian since 1953 and state president since 1959. He was, remarked a Liberal, as 'hard as flintstone and as rough as goat's knees'; his dedication to the ALP cause was unquestioned, but his unpolished style was not suited to the demands of television. No WA Labor leader had previously been unwillingly dethroned in mid-term. Jamieson's successor, experienced MP and former union official Ron Davies, met a similar fate in 1981 although WA Labor regained some ground at both the state and federal elections in 1980.

The departure from senior party positions of seasoned campaigners like Chamberlain, Tonkin and Jamieson had left something of a power vacuum in WA Labor which was being filled by a new wave of much younger activists. The path pioneered by Hawke in the 1950s – tertiary qualifications, followed by employment in the union movement – was becoming commonplace, as shown by the careers of talented individuals like Willis, Simon Crean and, in WA, Dawkins and state ALP secretary Bob McMullan. Capable and likeable, McMullan was only 25 when appointed the inaugural assistant secretary to Chamberlain in 1973, and succeeded Chamberlain when he retired. His contribution to the partial recovery WA Labor achieved in the 1980 elections was acknowledged when he became national secretary in mid-1981 after Combe resigned. McMullan's contemporaries included Dawkins and Labor's new MHR for Swan, Kim Beazley junior. Beazley the younger was a Rhodes Scholar and politics lecturer with a special interest in defence and foreign affairs. Like his father, he possessed a formidable intellect, but he had a more easy-going temperament.

This emerging group of younger activists also contained a number of state MPs. Among them were ex-schoolteacher Mal Bryce, lawyer Julian Grill, youthful dynamo David Parker, and brothers Terry and Brian Burke, whose father Tom had been MHR for Perth, protégé of Chifley, and expelled victim of Labor's 1950s split. These WA MPs were inspired by Cain's smoothly orchestrated ascent to the Victorian ALP leadership in September 1981, and 10 days later they successfully organized a similar operation (which was condemned by both Tonkin and Jamieson). Davies was deposed in what he ruefully described afterwards as an 'ambush', and WA Labor had a new leader, Brian Burke, with Bryce as his deputy. Like Cain, Brian Burke was profoundly influenced by his father's political experiences. He believed that his father's career had been painfully ruined by excessively ideological hardliners, Chamberlain in particular; Brian Burke was a populist with entrepreneurial instincts, and certainly no ideologue. While his contemporaries were protesting against the Vietnam War – McMullan made a successful appearance in court as one of Australia's first conscientious objectors to conscription on non-religious grounds – Burke was publishing a trotting magazine called *Punters' Guide*. It was Burke's outstanding communication skills which commended him to his colleagues; with a background in television reporting himself, he was superbly articulate on the electronic media. Under its aggressive new leadership team, WA Labor looked forward confidently to the state and federal elections due in 1983.

Hawke's inability to become a dazzling overnight success as a parliamentarian had not in the least dented his belief that he was destined to lead his party and his country. His strategy to supplant Hayden was devastatingly simple. He had to persuade his parliamentary colleagues that his extraordinary popularity among the Australian people would guarantee a Labor victory under his leadership at the next election, whereas that outcome was not certain if Hayden remained leader. Early in 1982 Hayden was convinced that he had the edge on both Fraser and Hawke, and consequently the prime ministership was within his grasp. However, in May Labor pollster Rod Cameron informed McMullan and Hayden of Australian National Opinion Polls (ANOP) research results which were very unflattering to Hayden. The ANOP report showed that uncommitted voters disliked Fraser, describing him as deceitful, arrogant and aloof, but they respected his leadership strength. In contrast, Cameron told Hayden,

you are seen as honest and modest, but also as weak, wishy-washy, a whinger, and people often just cannot understand what you are saying. They see you as carping, supercritical and. . .not. . .a strong leader.

This report and other survey findings very favourable to Hawke were circulated within the party by Hawke and his supporters. At a national executive meeting Richardson, who was unequivocally in the Hawke camp, asked McMullan to read aloud to the assembled delegates ANOP's damning conclusions about swinging voters' perceptions of Hayden. McMullan demurred, but Richardson, who knew the report's contents, forced the issue with a formal motion.

McMullan, intensely embarrassed, read the ANOP report, not lifting his head from the document. Hayden was even more embarrassed as his deficiencies as a leader were read out to his colleagues. The coming struggle would be a pitiless contest.

Speculation about a Hawke challenge mounted as the July 1982 ALP national conference approached. Hayden's fragile confidence was further shaken in June when he was forced by pressure from American officials and senior FPLP colleagues, notably Bowen, to make a humiliating backdown from his previous forthright declaration about changes to the Australian-American relationship under a Hayden government. On 26 June the *Age* published an influential article by its columnist Phillip Adams, who acknowledged the misgivings about Hawke held inside and outside the party but insisted that the FPLP would be foolish not to promote him to the leadership. 'Like it or not, he's a natural leader in a country crying out for leadership', wrote Adams, adding that Hawke 'towers over the political landscape' and was far better equipped than Hayden to tackle Fraser. Three days later Clyde Cameron, who had retired as a parliamentarian in 1980, announced that he had come to the conclusion – despite his personal regard for Hayden and his occasional differences with Hawke – that Hawke should become leader:

We've got to face facts. The public opinion polls show that Bob Hawke now commands more support than any other politician ever registered in these public surveys and Labor would romp home with Hawke as leader. There's no doubt about that.

That same morning Hawke received even better news when Uren telephoned. The FPLP's most senior left-winger told Hawke that he was so angry about Hayden's recent shift on uranium policy that he was prepared to add his influence to the momentum for a leadership change. Hawke was delighted by the turn of events. Asked by the media for a reaction to Cameron's comments, Hawke replied pointedly that 'the question of the leadership of the party and the electoral welfare of the party is a matter for the caucus'.

The conference at Canberra's Lakeside Hotel was dominated by the uranium issue and the leadership. Hayden had concluded that Labor's anti-uranium policy, which included the repudiation of commitments made by the Fraser government, was no longer sustainable. It had not deterred mining corporations from large-scale uranium projects, and Hayden feared that if a Labor government implemented its policy of repudiation the upshot would be a retaliatory capital strike by overseas investors, with crippling consequences for the Australian economy. He believed that the economic benefits for Australia of allowing uranium mining were undeniable and offset only by the unresolved problem of radioactive waste disposal; he was confident that effective disposal

405

technology would emerge before too long, and in the meantime the deadly wastes could be stored safely. Hawke and Richardson backed Hayden strongly on the uranium question while simultaneously plotting to force a leadership change. The atmosphere at the conference was a volatile combination of expectancy, tension and intrigue. Prominent Hawke supporters like Holding, Evans and Simon Crean were observed in 'the Lakeside bar, an assassination squad in leather and suede, studying the passing parade, refining their tactics'. Hogg was alarmed by developments. His growing stature within the party had established him as a potential successor to Combe, but when the vacancy for national secretary arose Hogg's main objective – guiding Victorian Labor to victory – remained unfulfilled, and he had decided to stay in Victoria. Hogg believed that Hayden's determination to change the uranium policy was potentially disastrous for the ALP. Hogg sensed that conference would probably rebuff Hayden, especially now that the vote had become inextricably interwoven with Hawke's leadership surge. If so, Hogg despaired of Labor's chances at the next election, which he regarded as an unusually important one for the ALP's future. Hogg feared that Fraser would be able to use Hayden's arguments (about the deleterious impact which Labor's anti-uranium policy would have on foreign investment and the Australian economy) as a potent scare tactic. But Hogg could not persuade Hayden to change his mind. Eventually, after considerable agonizing, Hogg decided to proceed with a compromise amendment which he knew would infuriate his left-wing colleagues, who were fanatically opposed to any moderation of the ALP's opposition to uranium mining. The complex Hogg amendment committed an incoming Labor government to uphold existing contracts, but not to authorize new mining without the most stringent safeguards. It also contained a provision which enabled the SA government to proceed with mining at Roxby Downs.

The ensuing wrangle over uranium was the most dramatic and traumatic debate at national conference for many years. Stressing the economic consequences of not altering the policy, Richardson contended that foreign investment in Australia 'will just dry up. . .and we will be faced with a balance-of-payments crisis', and Hayden warned that Australia 'would almost become a banana republic'. The left passionately denounced Hogg's amendment. Stewart West, the burly ex-waterside worker who had succeeded Connor as MHR for Cunningham, slated Hogg's amendment as 'irresponsible' and 'not even credible'. Uren described it as 'a tragedy' and a product of 'expediency' which 'will bring a lot of discredit to the movement'. Hogg's amendment was carried by 53 votes to 46, and anti-uranium demonstrators in the gallery voiced their disapproval as the ubiquitous television cameras hovered. For his contribution Hogg was ostracized by the left as a traitor, but he believed that his compromise was in the best interests of the party. He claimed that it provided the anti-uranium movement with scope to achieve its ends inside the ALP, while at the same time ensuring that Labor would be a credible contender at the next election irrespective of the identity of its leader.

Who would that leader be? During the conference further opinion poll research damaging to Hayden was published. These results, Hawke told the assembled media, had 'disturbed' him and should be 'closely considered' by the FPLP. Hayden decided to act. After the uranium debate he discussed his predicament with his closest senior colleagues Button, Dawkins and Walsh. Hayden also consulted Bowen, who had made his attitude clear when he told delegates that if Labor had to be led by 'a film star why not go the whole way and get Jane

Fonda?' The next day, as Hawke was about to make his major address to conference on industrial relations, Hayden upstaged him by releasing a defiant statement announcing that a special caucus meeting would be held on 16 July in order to resolve the leadership tensions generated by a 'deliberate campaign' of 'insidious destabilisation'. The battle was on. For the next eight days Labor was convulsed by one of the fiercest leadership duels in its history. Some of the most cohesive sections of the party were divided on the question. Although Uren had been castigated by some of his factional colleagues who believed that he had breached the left's collective ethos in his phone conversation with Hawke on 29 June, he was confident that the left's FPLP contingent could be persuaded to support Hawke. Uren's confidence was misplaced. The left's votes went to Hayden. The NSW right was also uncharacteristically divided. The key figure was Keating, who had accepted the presidency of the NSW branch and the role of titular head of the right-wing machine after Ducker's retirement. Keating was drawn to Hayden through a combination of personal regard and loyalty after their lengthy front-bench association, admiration for Hayden's recent contribution to platform changes congenial to the NSW right, and the fact that supporting Hayden suited Keating's own ambitions to lead the party in the future. Richardson strenuously exhorted Keating to support Hawke, but Keating remained ambivalent. It was only after a visit to Sydney on 14 July by a Victorian pro-Hawke delegation comprising Holding, Evans, Simon Crean and the challenger himself that Keating announced that the NSW machine would be throwing its influence behind Hawke. In Hayden's camp the chief lobbyists and supporters were Dawkins, Walsh, Button, Blewett and Kerin. On 16 July before the vital ballot Hawke and his Victorian backers were optimistic, Keating and Richardson less so. Button felt that Hayden needed a decisive victory to secure his leadership, and doubted whether he would get it. The final result was Hayden 42, Hawke 37.

Hayden had survived, but a poor by-election result later in 1982 made him more vulnerable than ever. The by-election was created in Flinders by Lynch's retirement. To capture Flinders Labor needed a 5·5% swing, which was realistically attainable at a by-election when the Fraser government was beset with so many problems including high unemployment and the generally ailing economy. Unfortunately for Hayden, the Labor campaign was not a success. He was not at his best, the ALP candidate was a go-getting estate agent who proved to have skeletons in his cupboard, and Hayden was also hampered by differences with the ACTU leaders. On 4 December Labor obtained from the Flinders voters less than half the swing necessary to capture the seat, and gloom spread quickly through all levels of the party. The rank and file, candidates in marginal seats, and senior strategists like McMullan, Hogg and Rod Cameron were all pessimistic in the wake of Flinders about Labor's chances at the next election, especially as Fraser was indicating that he was keen to call it sooner rather than later. Richardson, who had kept beavering away to undermine Hayden, redoubled his efforts:

> It was a nasty job, and that means you acquire a nasty reputation; that's one part I regret. With the benefit of hindsight, I'd have to say I'd do it all again. It needed to be done: I didn't think Bill would win, and I thought Hawke would be a better Prime Minister.

Richardson particularly concentrated on persuading Button to switch sides in the belief that Button's defection would have a devastating impact on Hayden's self-confidence.

Button's role became crucial. Just before Christmas Richardson extracted a commitment from him that he would talk to Hayden about the leadership. On 6 January Hayden and Button discussed the situation over lunch in Brisbane. Button told Hayden that there would soon be an election, Labor would not win it if Hayden remained leader, and he recommended that Hayden should resign. Hayden completely disagreed, but was acutely unsettled when such a close colleague and friend confirmed that he held that opinion. Shortly afterwards Hayden consulted Bowen who, like Button, advised him to stand down for the sake of the party. Hayden decided to shore up his leadership with an unexpected shadow cabinet reshuffle. Throughout the five years of Hayden's leadership Willis had held the Treasury portfolio and Keating had been very effective in the realm of energy and resources. Now, with an election possible very soon, Willis was abruptly demoted and Treasury was allocated to Keating. Both were shocked and angry. During January there were increasing signs that Hayden's judgement was being affected by the intense pressure. The indications that Fraser was planning an imminent election, partly because he wanted it with Hayden as Opposition Leader rather than Hawke, added to the tension and sense of urgency felt by the pro-Hawke powerbrokers who were desperate to arrange a leadership switch before it was too late. On 28 January Button tackled Hayden again, this time in a letter. He stressed that he had been 'consistently loyal' to Hayden personally ever since Hayden became leader, but his 'ultimate loyalty, however, must be to the ALP'. He stated that Hayden's performance since the July 1982 leadership ballot had declined considerably, morale amongst party members and supporters was 'very bad', and there was strong support for a switch at the top because the party was 'desperate to win the coming election'. Button's letter, which was later described by Hayden as 'brutal but fair', proved decisive. Following the funeral on 1 February of Frank Forde, who had held a temporary commission in July 1945 as Labor's sixth prime minister, Hayden and Button had an emotional private conversation lasting 2½ hours. Both wept during it. Ultimately Hayden agreed to step aside for Hawke, but wanted guarantees that his staff would not be left without jobs, his strongest supporters in the shadow ministry would retain senior positions, and he could have the Foreign Affairs portfolio. Button assured Hayden that all the conditions would be met.

Thursday 3 February 1983 was the most extraordinary day in Australian politics since Remembrance Day 1975. In Canberra Fraser advised the Governor-General to authorize a double dissolution on 5 March, and almost simultaneously Hayden resigned the FPLP leadership in Brisbane. 'Hayden's face was etched with strain and sorrow, his eyes red-rimmed but his voice was under concentrated control' as he addressed the media:

> I am not convinced that the Labor Party would not win under my leadership. I believe that a drover's dog could lead the Labor Party to victory the way the country is and the way the opinion polls are. . .As recently as Sunday I was still determined to fight the matter out, but it was increasingly clear to me that if I did I would be guaranteeing great damage to my own party and the return of the Fraser Government as the cost of my own personal hopes and aspirations.

In Labor ranks there was a mixed reaction to Hayden's sacrifice. There was amazement felt by Labor people who had no advance knowledge, and guilt felt by some high-placed individuals who did; there was admiration and sadness for Hayden; there was also relief and exhilaration arising from the realization that the party had managed to avoid the rancour and uproar which had been assumed by Fraser to be unavoidable in such a manoeuvre. Fraser's awareness of developments inside the ALP was a significant factor in his decision to hold a premature election, and in ALP circles there was immense pleasure that Labor's ruthless foe, who had in 1975 expressed his intention to catch Whitlam 'with his pants well and truly down', had himself been outsmarted this time. Fraser had dashed out to Yarralumla without an appointment to have his election decision rubber-stamped, but he was no longer dealing with Kerr. A different Governor-General with a greater sense of propriety politely told Fraser that he would not grant a double dissolution on the spot. Fraser had to return to Parliament House without the ratification he sought, and his prearranged press conference to announce the election had to be postponed. By the time Fraser was in a position to make his announcement Labor had clearly stolen the initiative.

At no stage before 5 March did Labor look like losing it. Hawke campaigned with masterly assurance. Confident and controlled, he utilized his unique rapport with the Australian electorate to the full, radiating harmony and promoting reconciliation as his central theme. Labor strategists chose 'Bob Hawke – Bringing Australia Together' as Labor's slogan, which neatly complemented Hawke's main campaign emphasis and recalled his reputation as 'the great conciliator' in his ACTU days. Hawke's message contrasted starkly with Fraser's abrasive confrontational style. Hayden's suspicions that the ACTU leadership had deliberately added to his difficulties – because they wanted the next Labor Prime Minister to be a former ACTU leader – were confirmed when Hawke received from the ACTU swift and complete co-operation which had been denied to Hayden. Midway through the campaign Labor adherents received a fillip from WA where a state election had been under way when Fraser called his double dissolution. Events on the national scene had overtaken the election slogan WA Labor had unveiled – 'Brian Burke, best new leader in Australia' – but the elevation of Hawke, with his WA background and popularity, nevertheless aided the ALP in the West. On 19 February WA Labor obtained its highest ever share of the primary vote in a state election, 53·16% (45·95% in 1980), in recording a resounding victory.

Labor's national triumph on 5 March was no less complete. The nation-wide increase in Labor's primary vote, 4·33%, brought a harvest of 23 additional seats which provided the Hawke government with a comfortable 25-seat majority. Only in Tasmania did the ALP lose ground, largely because of the continuing controversy over hydroelectric development. Delegates at the 1982 national conference had obliged Labor 'to oppose the construction of a hydroelectric power scheme on the Gordon or Franklin Rivers', a platform amendment inserted despite warnings from Tasmanian delegates that it would have dire consequences for Labor in the island state. Indeed it did, but Labor had not won any Tasmanian Representatives seat since 1974, so the decrease in Labor's voting share of almost 6% in that state did not reduce Labor's tally of seats. Moreover, the commitment to Australia's environmental heritage embodied in that policy change clearly assisted Labor's cause outside Tasmania. Labor captured seats in every other state, including five in Queensland where Hayden had tenaciously spearheaded intervention despite the Old Guard's retaliatory public endorsement of Hawke's leadership aspirations. The remarkable turnaround in Victoria continued. Of the 33 Victorian Representatives seats Labor had won only 10 in 1977, but won 23 in 1983, its highest proportion ever; one of the six new gains was Flinders, where the swing to Labor far exceeded the modest increase in the ALP vote recorded at the by-election only three months earlier. In the Senate Labor significantly improved its position without obtaining a majority, but with the balance of power held by the Democrats, who were unequivocally opposed to blocking supply, there was no likelihood of the chronic instability which had plagued the Whitlam government. Labor owed much to Hayden for leading his party to the edge of victory and selflessly making way for a superior communicator he had abundant cause to resent. But it was a dazzling triumph for Hawke, and exquisite vindication for his backers. As Fraser conceded defeat and millions of Australian television viewers saw his granite jaw quiver, few Labor supporters felt sympathetic – the wounds of 1975 were still too raw. But there was no better cure for those scars than the demise of Fraser and the advent of a new national Labor government. Very few of the Labor faithful were animated by the starry-eyed expectations of 1972, but most looked forward with keen anticipation to a competent government which would heed the difficult economic realities and learn from the mistakes of the past while maintaining a vigorous and purposeful commitment to reform.

16 'Some New and Alien Philosophy'? The Hawke-Keating Regime, 1983–1991

THE ELECTION OF four new Labor governments between April 1982 and March 1983 ushered in a victorious era for the ALP. Apart from the 1940s, there has been no equivalent period in the party's history when it enjoyed such electoral dominance. Between 1983 and 1990 Labor won four consecutive national elections under Hawke, who established himself as easily the most electorally successful FPLP leader. As the party approached its centenary the ALP governments elected during 1982–83 in Victoria, SA and WA were all still in office, and Labor had also recently come to power following electoral breakthroughs in Queensland and Tasmania; Labor was in opposition only in NSW, where the ALP lost the 1988 state election after almost 12 years in office.

A crucial factor in Labor's success during the 1980s was its clearcut superiority in campaigning. In previous decades ALP supporters had often been frustrated by their party's failure to win non-Tasmanian elections when it seemed poised to do so. But between 1982 and 1990 it was Labor who repeatedly won close elections when the conservatives seemed well placed to succeed. The key to these victories was the sophisticated electioneering techniques and expertise displayed by party officials and consultants like pollster Rod Cameron. Their efforts enabled Labor to do very well in the vital marginal seats which should have been vulnerable according to overall voting trends.

The corollary was that Labor's voting share tended to fall much more heavily in its safer seats than in the marginals. Many Labor traditionalists were disillusioned by the moderate unthreatening approach of 1980s Labor. The Hawke government attracted persistent criticism from activists for being insufficiently vigorous in implementing Labor's platform objectives and, at times, for contravening them. In the ALP the clash between sacred principles and practical politics is as old as the party itself. Every Labor government – even the most hallowed – has been bitterly attacked by ALP supporters during its existence. The Curtin government was assailed for modifying the party's traditional hostility to conscription for overseas service, the Chifley government was denounced for sending in the army during the miners' strike, and even the Whitlam government became more sanctified retrospectively than contemporaneously. However, the Hawke government generated more grass-roots dissatisfaction than any of the governments led by Curtin, Chifley and Whitlam.

This discontentment resulted from the Hawke government's Wran-like determination to differentiate itself from the style of the Whitlam government. The Labor faithful revered the Whitlam government's verve and wholehearted reformist drive, but most Labor MPs had concluded from the Whitlam experience that a crisis-prone 'crash through or crash' approach tended to alienate the vital uncommitted voters who determine the outcome of elections. '[W]e're so much wiser now – we know how hard it is. That's why we won't stuff it up', remarked an incoming minister on election night 1983. Hawke, in fact, aimed to entrench Labor as the natural party of government in Canberra, utilizing a blend of consensus, caution, nationalism and his own extraordinary popularity to position the party in the middle ground. The deep wariness of Hawke within the left before he became leader was evident in the suggestions that he had too many 'rich mates' to possess a real attachment to Labor principles, and it was likely that he would defect to the conservatives like Hughes and Lyons; during the later 1980s some left-wingers were lamenting that Hawke seemed to have hijacked the whole party and taken it in a conservative direction.

The differences in Hawke's approach were clear from the outset. Whitlam could not wait for his full ministry to be formed before embarking eagerly on overdue reforms; Hawke announced shortly after the March 1983 election that because Fraser had deliberately concealed the large blow-out in the deficit arising from his cynical pre-election budget the Hawke government would have to reconsider whether it could responsibly proceed with some of the reform initiatives highlighted during Labor's campaign. Whitlam treated his mandate from the electors literally, and insisted that economic difficulties were no excuse for avoiding reform; Hawke regarded economic management as paramount. Whitlam was eloquent and witty, and an outstanding performer in parliament; Hawke was more of an adroit fixer than a stylish orator, but his sledgehammer approach in the Representatives effectively removed any concerns about his parliamentary inexperience. Whitlam was not adept at presiding over cabinet meetings; Hawke, although not renowned as a fertile originator of ideas, was a brilliant cabinet chairman, who allowed his talented ministers plenty of autonomy (unlike Fraser, whose excessive interference with ministers was notorious). Under Hawke's leadership cabinet functioned with more efficiency and, Evans believed, with more cohesion than it had during the Whitlam government.

Perceived lessons from the Whitlam government's experience produced two significant innovations in March 1983. In all previous national ALP governments cabinet had comprised the whole ministry (apart from the period during the Second World War when there was a war cabinet), but caucus ratified Hawke's desire that only a proportion of his ministers (initially 13), who were to be chosen by him, should constitute the cabinet. Also, Hawke's ministers agreed to abide by cabinet solidarity whenever their decisions were being evaluated by caucus (a practice the Wran government had adopted). Clyde Cameron wished that they had made another change from the procedure adopted when he was a minister under Whitlam. Cameron felt that a Labor government's difficulties with uncompliant bureaucrats were likely to be aggravated if the public service was routinely present during cabinet deliberations, as it was during the Whitlam government but not in SA under Dunstan or NSW under Wran. But Cameron's advice that the Hawke cabinet should not follow this Whitlam government precedent was rejected.

Another significant difference since 1972–75 was the increased factionalism in the ALP. During the Whitlam government a small group of FPLP left-wingers had held their own separate meetings to determine the viewpoints which the left would collectively uphold in caucus, but these factional gatherings were not very regular, not very organized, and not at all typical of how caucus as a whole operated. Only a decade later, however, nearly all FPLP members belonged to a faction. The adoption of proportional representation to determine the composition of the party's most important decision-making bodies accelerated the development of factionalism, which was exemplified by the formation of the Centre Left in 1984. Its leading lights portrayed themselves as principled rationalists disaffected with the crude pragmatists of the right and the rigid ideologues of the left. At the Centre Left's inaugural meeting Hayden confirmed that its emergence was a reaction to the way 'the two heavy factions split heads and break arms in a most uncreative and unproductive manner'. Significantly, this meeting occurred in Adelaide; the more entrenched factionalism in NSW and Victoria meant that the Centre Left's most fertile recruiting ground was in the other states, which provided its most prominent initial personalities – Hayden, Young, Dawkins, Walsh, Blewett and able SA state secretary (and later Senator) Chris Schacht. Accordingly, the two more established factions, in order to retain their share of power and influence, intensified their organizational activities outside NSW and Victoria. Factionalism escalated. The Centre Left lacked a strong union base but managed to survive. Hayden underlined its vulnerability by describing it as a 'lonely hearts club squeezed between two super powers'.

Some Labor identities had misgivings about the increased factionalism. Each FPLP faction met regularly during parliamentary sittings to decide its collective policy attitudes and its candidate(s) for caucus or governmental office. The role played by some backbenchers as factional leaders – negotiating with their counterparts from other factions, or directly with Hawke when caucus support for particular government action was at issue – gave them more public prominence than even some ministers. Labor people who were relaxed about institutionalized factionalism argued that it enhanced the party's stability. In an umbrella party or coalition of varying interests like the ALP there are inevitable differences concerning the pace and priorities of reform, and defenders of entrenched factionalism argued that the presence of tightly organized factions helped define these differences sharply and therefore streamlined their resolution. Others disagreed. They deplored the tendency of some activists to be more concerned about outsmarting their factional adversaries as they carved up the spoils – ministerial representation, committee positions, even trips – than about framing party policy or defeating Labor's opponents. National secretary McMullan often aired his dissatisfaction with the extent of factionalism in the party. According to McMullan, it had produced excessive rigidity and conformity, which inhibited the quality of policy debate and also threatened to lower the quality of Labor ministries as vacancies went to factional warriors who were not necessarily the most able contenders. McMullan experienced this himself after he resigned as national secretary in 1988 and entered the Senate. Three successive elections had been won while he was campaign director, but his refusal to join a faction in the FPLP reduced his chance of promotion into the ministry after the 1990 election, and instead he became one of four backbenchers appointed to a newly created position, parliamentary secretary to a senior minister. Affiliation with a faction was less prevalent among the ALP's grass roots than among the party's high fliers or aspirants for preselection, who increasingly realized that without factional backing they had little hope of advancement.

Hawke handled the overwhelming demands and pressures of the prime

ministership very capably. Concern about his capacity to lead the party effectively had not been confined to the left. The letter Button wrote in February 1983
recommending to Hayden that he should vacate the leadership for Hawke
conceded that 'even some of Bob's closest supporters. . .do not share his own
estimate of his ability' and 'have doubts about his capacities to lead the party
successfully'. But Hawke's performance in the top job rapidly dispelled these
misgivings. The volatile, hard-drinking union leader had become more controlled and reflective, but his competitive instincts were undiminished. Hawke's
sustained popularity was an important ingredient in Labor's national election
victories in 1983, 1984, 1987 and 1990. His approval rating early in his prime
ministership was astoundingly high, and in the 1990 election campaign it was
still very satisfactory for someone whose long involvement in public life had
inevitably associated him with some unpopular decisions. Unlike Fraser, Hawke
sounded like an Australian, passionately enjoyed sport, and mixed readily with
all classes (too easily with wealthy capitalists, complained the left). Hawke's
nationalism was sincerely felt; his jubilation at the unprecedented America's
Cup victory in 1983 and his superb speech at Lone Pine in 1990 during the
commemoration of the 75th anniversary of the Gallipoli landing were two of
many occasions when he symbolized majority Australian sentiment.

Hawke's ministers were often claimed to be the most talented cabinet personnel in Australian history. 'We have a Cabinet which has a degree of economic
sophistication which puts the Whitlam government into the caveman class in
economic terms', claimed Keating. 'No other Labor government even gets within
cooee of it'. Besides Keating himself, the senior economic ministers included
Willis, Button, Dawkins and Walsh. Willis, who was widely liked, possessed
tertiary qualifications and acknowledged ability in economics, but he did not
relish the combative side of politics; he 'had all the expertise but no wham'.
Button had a long stint in the important Industry and Commerce portfolio. His
ability was widely recognized in business circles, but he regretted that Australia
had so few capable managers and he often felt frustrated by the inadequate
innovation and insufficient forward planning of Australia's manufacturing industry. Periodically Button's colleagues were acutely irritated by his propensity
for outspokenness. The WA pair, Walsh and Dawkins, were close friends,
Hayden loyalists and Centre Left luminaries; their prominence in cabinet confirmed that the guarantee given to Hayden about the political futures of his
closest supporters was honoured. Walsh brought to Hawke's cabinet the frugal
perspective of a tenacious and strong-willed wheat farmer who had left school
aged 13 in 1948. His parliamentary career resulted from his direct experience of
the inadequate results of the Country Party's agricultural policies, and from his
contact with the emerging new wave of younger WA Labor identities like
Dawkins, Beazley and McMullan when he became an external student in economics at WA university. Iconoclastic and fearless, Walsh abhorred inefficiency
and wasteful expenditure, and as Finance minister from 1984 to 1990 he was
able to do something about it. He was particularly offended by the distribution of
'middle class welfare' to recipients who were not in his view genuinely needy. His
sincerity in such matters was evident in his sparing use of the ministerial limou-
sine. He was no sanctimonious wowser, however; some of his uninhibited
late-night exploits became legendary. Like Walsh, Dawkins was renowned in
opposition for his uncompromising aggression, which was influenced by the
conservatives' conduct in 1975 when he and Walsh were inexperienced back-

benchers. After being Walsh's predecessor as Finance minister during 1983–84, he was allotted Trade following the 1984 election, and transferred to Employment, Education and Training in 1987. In each portfolio he demonstrated a commitment to structural change despite the controversy generated by his sweeping reforms. Friendly and unpretentious, Dawkins spoke with a polished enunciation which reflected his Establishment origins, but his rebellion against his background, along with his temporary beard and occasional penchant for unfashionable headgear, confirmed that 'Joe' Dawkins was his own man.

A number of other talented MPs had long stints in the Hawke ministry. From 1983 until his retirement from politics in 1990 Bowen was a fine deputy leader, content to adopt a low profile while nurturing the government's cohesion and stability. For seven years Blewett was a competent Health minister. He effectively established Medicare (descendant of Medibank, which was sabotaged by the Fraser government) and reacted to difficult problems like the spread of AIDS with enlightened and internationally acclaimed measures, despite being subjected to a campaign of defamatory innuendo by conservative medical interests. Another widely respected minister who sometimes had to contend with reactionary hostility was Kerin at Primary Industry. The product of an impoverished rural background, Kerin left school before turning 15 and laboured for five years as an axeman; later he obtained an Arts degree by correspondence, and worked at the Bureau of Agricultural Economics prior to his election to parliament. Even farmers who habitually voted anti-Labor expressed grudging admiration for Kerin's sound administration. Evans received a setback after the 1984 election when Hawke ended his brief (and somewhat ill-starred) term as Attorney-General, the position which he cherished and so eminently suited him, by transferring him to Resources and Energy. Evans was disarmingly frank about the steep learning curve confronting him in his new responsibility for 'pipes and holes', but he responded with characteristic resilience and zest before moving on to Transport and Communications and then to the more glamorous portfolio of Foreign Affairs. Duffy's ministerial career prospered despite his refusal to join one of the three main FPLP factions. Some of his colleagues from the small Victorian Independents faction aligned themselves with the Centre Left, but Duffy, after an initial flirtation, did not. Following stints at Communications and Trade, Duffy, a former solicitor, was delighted to take over as Attorney-General when Bowen retired. Like Duffy, Beazley did well to make the ministry after only a single term in parliament. Beazley's rise was not only due to his conspicuous ability – he had a powerful patron, the Prime Minister. Hawke's regard for Beazley was occasionally described as almost fatherly; when caucus chose the 1983 ministry Hawke privately exerted his influence in favour of apparently only two borderline aspirants, Beazley and Holding, and both were elected. In 1984 Hawke allocated Beazley the portfolio he most desired, Defence, which Beazley handled with great expertise and aplomb. By 1990, when he was transferred to Transport and Communications, Beazley had established himself as a potential future leader (although he repeatedly stressed Keating's superior claims). Another minister who ascended rapidly during the Hawke government was Howe. In 1983, as the most junior minister, he was allotted Defence Support, an incongruous portfolio for a left-winger who had been a sociologist, Methodist clergyman and urban environment activist. But he found that Defence Support offered unexpected scope, especially in industry policy, and his ability and commitment earned him promotion in 1984 to Social Security and a berth in cabinet where he became the left's most senior minister and won the respect of Hawke and Keating. Dogged and outwardly dour, Howe was dedicated to the administrative grind and persistently tried to prod the Hawke government in a more radical direction. Others who had stints in the Hawke ministry included left-wingers Uren (1983–87), West (1983–90) and Gietzelt (1983–87), seasoned MHRs Hurford (1983–87), Morris (1983–90) and Scholes (1983–87), and previously prominent state MPs Holding (1983–90) and Duncan (1987–90).

Three backbenchers who were the most prominent FPLP factional power-brokers during 1983–87 graduated to the ministry after the 1987 election. When Richardson entered the Senate in 1983 he immediately became the most significant government backbencher. Some FPLP colleagues resented his access to Hawke and his powerful role in the government; as a formidable persuader he matched such legendary ALP enforcers of the past as Chamberlain and pre-1910 Mat Reid. In cabinet the economic rationalists were intermittently irked by Richardson's tendency to focus on short-term political consequences, but his astuteness was important to the government's electoral success, especially in 1990. Not as close to Hawke personally but just as important in delivering right-wing support was Richardson's Victorian counterpart, Senator Robert Ray, the FPLP's heavily built, pipe-smoking, shambling bear. Ray's toughness, trustworthiness and sharp intellect were universally respected, but his strong preference for pragmatic gradualism over ideologically inspired idealism won him no friends on the left. Like Richardson, Ray was promoted to the ministry in 1987 and to cabinet in 1988. Prior to the July 1987 election the FPLP left's representative in negotiations between the factions was Gerry Hand, who succeeded Innes as member for the safe seat of Melbourne in 1983. Hand was initially allotted Aboriginal Affairs and, after the 1990 election, Immigration; both were areas of special interest to him. His gritty integrity and commitment to implementing policy changes were evident in the gruelling outback travel he undertook, rolling out his swag to sleep under the stars, as part of his extensive consultation with Aboriginal communities. A personal warmth developed between Hand and his 1980 preselection rival, Hawke, which was partly attributable to Hawke's keenness to establish amicable relations with people he had previously vanquished, a tendency apparent in his public rapprochement with Hayden in 1987 and his efforts (inexplicable to many Labor enthusiasts) to secure a prestigious international job for Fraser. After the Centre Left was established its inaugural convener was former WA TLC secretary Peter Cook, who was another of the FPLP's 1983 acquisitions. Senator Cook, son of a Melbourne wharf labourer and grandson of a Broken Hill miner, entered the ministry in January 1988, and was elevated to cabinet in 1990.

While no newcomers were promoted into the Hawke ministry in its first four years, which was a key factor in the government's cohesive image, there were a number of alterations to the ministry during the following 18 months. Senator Grimes stepped down because of ill-health; Susan Ryan resigned six months after being demoted in the 1987 post-election reshuffle; John Brown, who had been a prosperous meat wholesaler before becoming member for Parramatta in 1977, had exhibited entrepreneurial drive and a Hawke-like passion for sport in his high-profile administration of Tourism and Recreation, but his inattention to detail led to his downfall in December 1987 when he made an erroneous statement in parliament; and less than two months later Mick Young decided to end his political career at the age of 51. He had found some aspects of the transition from successful party official to senior parliamentarian exacting, notably the absorption of copious technical information, but his shrewdness and wit had made him an amusing and valuable figure within the government; however, his confidence had been eroded by a couple of highly publicized lapses, and when he was unjustly pilloried early in 1988 for another alleged mistake he suddenly decided that he had endured enough controversy. There was another celebrated departure from the ministry in Australia's bicentennial year when Hayden resigned after 27 years as member for Oxley. His Foreign Affairs perspectives had proved compatible with Hawke's, and they maintained an effective working relationship; Hawke readily acquiesced when Hayden disclosed an unexpected aspiration to become Governor-General.

In the aftermath of both the 1987 and 1990 elections there was a pronounced lapse in the government's collective discipline, in part because former ministers resented being demoted. Until the early 1980s FPLP office-bearers had been elected in caucus by ballot, but in the new era of all-pervasive factionalism caucus merely rubber-stamped an outcome already determined by a combination of internal faction ballots, high-powered negotiations by representatives of the factions, and carefully considered interventions by the Prime Minister. Hawke involved himself either to support talented individuals who were unlikely to make the ministry without his intercession on their behalf (Simon Crean and Northern Territory Senator Bob Collins were notable examples in 1990), or to achieve a more appropriate interstate and gender representation in it. As Prime Minister, he retained significant control over the shape of his government by virtue of his power to allocate portfolios and to choose which of his ministers would comprise the cabinet. In 1987 Barry Cohen was very irate about losing his ministerial place under the new factionally dominated process, especially when Richardson, the FPLP's most renowned factional powerbroker, was not only elevated into the ministry as Cohen was dumped, but also took over Cohen's former responsibilities for Environment and Arts. In 1990 West's anger at his removal from the ministry was also publicly vented, but the relegation of Barry Jones, who had been minister for Science since 1983, produced easily the biggest reaction.

Australian politics has known nobody like Barry Jones. His encyclopaedic knowledge, based on accurate recall of his phenomenally rapid reading, brought him fame in the 1960s as a quiz champion, and during the 1970s and 1980s he channelled his idealism, energy and extraordinary talents primarily into public life. In opposition before 1983 he singlehandedly mounted an educative crusade about the future impact of technology on employment, and his acclaimed book on the subject, *Sleepers Wake!*, was an international best-seller. In government he was a fine propagandist for science, continually urging Australians to honour cerebral achievers with the veneration accorded to sporting heroes. But his success in obtaining a higher profile for science and technology as he spread his gospel around Australia was not matched in the inner councils of government. Funding for science and research was repeatedly pruned during the 1980s, Jones's ministerial responsibilities were limited, and he was kept in the outer ministry without cabinet status. Apparently insensitive to his impact on others, he was criticized for being too discursive, but his intellectual ebullience was unflagging. Jones often expounded his ideas loudly and at length, but he had little facility for small talk and no interest in lowbrow enthusiasms like pub, footy and racetrack. 'If I could talk football, I'd have been in the Cabinet', concluded Jones, who once described his only exercise besides walking as 'jumping to conclusions'. It was ironical, as Jones realized, that he was omitted from the ministry immediately after an election when one of the main new Labor initiatives in Hawke's policy speech was an increased commitment to scientific research as part of an attempt to make Australia 'the clever country'. Concern about the Hawke government being too pragmatic was reinforced by the fate of Barry Jones, who, although not a consummate political operator, was undeniably a visionary and a thinker.

While Hawke made his mark clearly on the government right from the outset, Keating began in a much more subdued fashion. Initially Keating was acutely conscious of his limitations as Treasurer, and he maintained a relatively low profile for months. The inappropriate timing of Hayden's sudden portfolio re-shuffle in January 1983 had angered both Keating and his predecessor as shadow Treasurer, Willis. Keating was well aware that he had much to learn about specialized aspects of his new portfolio, and the calling of the election only three weeks later confirmed that he had very little time to become familiar with it. During 1983, however, Keating applied himself with characteristic diligence to mastering his portfolio, and once his first budget was behind him his customary confidence and assurance returned.

One of the Hawke government's most notable successes was its agreement with the ACTU, the Accord. Numerous commentators repeatedly predicted that it would break down (as overseas equivalents had); instead the Accord prospered, in its periodic renegotiated variations. It embodied the sort of close co-operation between the political and industrial wings of the labour movement envisaged late in the nineteenth century by Labor's founders. Such co-operation has not been conspicuous for most of the ALP's history, but the Accord was a product of the most constructive and harmonious relationship between the highest levels of the political and industrial wings that had ever been achieved since the ALP's for-mation. There was criticism of particular outcomes negotiated under the Accord, like the failure of wages to keep pace with price rises. But the success of the Accord mechanism was 'a remarkable achievement', wrote Whitlam, whose gov-ernment had been harmed by differences with the unions when he was Prime Minister and Hawke was ACTU president.

The key players in the implementation of the Accord were Hawke, Keating, Willis, Simon Crean and Bill Kelty. Crean was ACTU president from 1985 until he resigned to become member for Hotham at the March 1990 election. He and Hawke had been close associates for years. Hawke welcomed Crean's transfer to parliament, openly describing him as a potential prime minister, and with Hawke's firm support he went straight into the ministry without the normal backbench apprenticeship. Kelty, the shortish ACTU secretary with a shock of unruly white hair, was remarkably knowledgeable about the union movement, and passionately committed to the introduction of worthwhile reforms to pro-duce a better life for working-class Australians.

The Accord was cemented at the National Economic Summit in May 1983. This dazzling piece of theatre, conceived and directed by Hawke, reinforced his great popularity and was widely interpreted as a vindication of his emphasis on national reconciliation. Representatives from the union movement, state gov-ernments, business groups and other organizations assembled at Parliament House to discuss the nation's future economic direction. The government was frank in the information, projections and options for future policy it revealed at the summit. The upshot was a liberating circuit-breaker which banished the grinding confrontation of the Fraser era and ushered in Hawke's consensus-based approach.

However, some ALP enthusiasts became increasingly concerned that the

Hawke government was relying too much on a consensus approach. The summit showed that a Labor government led by Hawke would aim to occupy the political centre, negotiating agreements with the moderate left and the moderate right and leaving out in the cold the extreme right and the far left. This was a shrewd step towards the objective of making Labor the natural party of government in Canberra, but the shortcomings of the pursuit of consensus were illustrated at the 1985 summit on taxation reform, when some undistinguished contributions from business representatives ensured that agreement on the fundamental issues proved elusive. Some Labor activists had more fundamental objections to the consensus approach. They argued that Labor was supposed to be a dynamic radical party, and Labor governments in particular were expected to govern. Some developments in 1983–84 smacked too much to them of decision-making driven by opinion polls. They regretted that Hawke was persuaded to retreat from worthwhile reform initiatives like constitutional referenda and Aboriginal land rights, apparently because proceeding with them would jeopardize consensus, when in fact Hawke's staggeringly high popularity guaranteed that his government would never have a more advantageous time to introduce such reforms.

The Hawke government's emergence as an innovator in financial policy co-incided with Keating's transformation from an initially unconfident Treasurer into the most influential personality in the cabinet. Throughout the later 1980s Keating was a commanding figure, noted for finely honed political skills, unmatched prowess as a persuader and debater, and unswerving determination to achieve fundamental change. Colleagues and journalists testified to Keating's powerful advocacy when he outlined his enthusiasms. At his command was a distinctive racy vernacular which could be hilarious or savagely cruel, or sometimes both simultaneously. If caucus morale was flagging after a bad week for the government, there was nothing more likely to lift backbenchers' spirits than a vintage burst from Keating, whose withering attacks on the 'born-to-rule mob' were devastating:

> You were in office from 1949 to 1983, bar three years...And you left everything the way you found it. The place got old and tired and worn out, just like you are... You didn't bother with the detail, that was for the public servants...you never ran the policy. You never ran the place. Well, let me tell you this. We run the place. We run the departments, we run the policy. We comprehend. We know...Where you all come a gutser is, over here, we think we're born to rule you. And we're going to keep on doing it.

Keating's public image as a remorseless political adversary was at odds with his little-known devotion to his family, but that aspect of his life he took great care to keep out of the limelight. Beazley described Keating as 'the best family man in politics'. After Keating became Treasurer his wife and four young children shifted to Canberra to be with him on a permanent basis. No one queried the suitability of Hawke's move into the Lodge; however, although the Treasurer's workload was also immense, eyebrows were raised when the Keating family moved to Canberra. The criticism that Keating was deserting his origins and his constituency and becoming overly influenced by Treasury mandarins and high-flying entrepreneurs gained momentum when damaging allegations surfaced that he had omitted to submit his tax return on time and controversially claimed an allowance for living in Canberra. Keating brushed aside the suggestions that he was losing touch with the people he represented. In admitting he had wrongly neglected his tax return, he characteristically counterattacked:

> I did make a mistake but, unlike the leader of the opposition, my mistake did not cost half a million people their jobs. My mistake did not retard the economy for twenty years. My mistake did not induce a massive domestic recession, unlike his mistake which almost destroyed the fabric of the Australian economy.

Keating relished power and its trappings, but he was singleminded about using it to implement change. For 'the boy from Bankstown' who had left school early and acquired his extensive knowledge of history and culture – like some of Labor's heroes of the past – outside the formal education system, having his 'hands on the levers' of the economy was undeniably pleasing. But for him the important challenge was how to use the opportunity afforded by power. Conscious of what he described as the 'big picture', Keating was impatient to put 'the big changes into place' once he had mastered the intricacies of his portfolio. During 1983–84, while the economy was thriving, the Hawke–Keating partnership was warm and very effective politically. From 1985, when clouds began to darken the economic horizon, differences surfaced intermittently between them, partly because Keating remained eager to press on with change while Hawke, although not generally opposed to the Treasurer's policy objectives, was more mindful of the electoral implications. Their relationship was also impaired by Keating's keenness to become Prime Minister in 1988 when Hawke was not ready to relinquish the position, but his status as the acknowledged heir apparent was unaffected and he succeeded Bowen as deputy FPLP leader after the 1990 election.

Keating's overriding aim was to revitalize the Australian economy. He was contemptuous of 'the lazy days of postwar growth' based on Australia's traditional reliance on overseas demand for its primary products. Keating wanted to reshape the national economy so that it generated long-term growth for Australians. He insisted that his goal of a growth economy would consistently generate more employment, thereby benefiting Labor's traditional constituents in the most effective possible way. Late in 1987 Keating observed that the Hawke government by 1988 would have 'created a million new jobs' since 1983. 'That's what I think keeping the faith's all about', he asserted, 'that's looking after the people we're supposed to be looking after'.

In December 1983 the Hawke government signalled its novel orientation in economic policy with its decision to float the Australian dollar. The revolution in communications and international capital movements had reduced Australia's isolation from overseas financial markets and rendered governmental control of its exchange rate less effective. When large speculative movements of foreign capital threatened to destabilize the Australian economy for the second time in 1983, the government reacted by removing nearly all exchange rate controls and floating the currency. The government's deregulatory reforms continued in 1984. 'Government control. . .of the financial system has. . .given us a miserable growth rate', asserted Keating, who obtained cabinet approval for the removal of many of the controls restricting the activities of banks and other financial institutions. 'Policy can't stay static', declared the Treasurer. Foreign-owned banks were invited to operate in Australia. 'While it may have been OK for Mr Chifley to oppose foreign banks in the '40s', claimed Keating, 'we are entitled to review that'. The existing banking system had not given Australian commerce a competitive edge, he explained. In spring 1984, with the economy buoyant (inflation down, employment and growth both up), Keating flew to America to accept a prestigious international 'Finance Minister of the Year' award amid lavish praise for his 'bold, brilliant and, above all, brave' initiatives. In reply, Keating remarked that he had 'the privilege of serving with a very enlightened prime minister and a very enlightened cabinet'.

In 1985 the primary focus was on taxation reform. Keating achieved a significant injection of fairness into the tax system when he spearheaded the introduction of a capital gains tax and a fringe benefits tax. He held firm against predictable protests from individuals and groups with a vested interest in a continuation of the fringe benefits abuses which had been prevalent for years. Keating was also keen to introduce a consumption tax in 1985, but this was a struggle he did not win. Walsh and the Finance department were firmly opposed to it, and Hawke seemed ambivalent. Ultimately, to Keating's disappointment, Hawke sided with the opponents of the proposed tax. This setback did not inhibit Keating from forcefully attacking the conservatives for their subsequent advocacy of a consumption tax.

In 1986 the structural weaknesses in the Australian economy became starkly evident. Australia's serious foreign debt problem was exacerbated by a sharp decline in Australian exports (arising from adverse short-term fluctuations in demand and prices, coupled with a more critical deterioration in both the terms of trade and market share). The value of the Australian dollar fell rapidly and heavily. Even Keating, the great believer in the market, felt moved to comment reassuringly that getting the dollar up was not the be-all and end-all of economic policy, and should not be regarded as a sort of national virility test, but to many ALP members it seemed that by floating the dollar the Hawke government had placed Australia's economic destiny in the hands of money-market hustlers; the deregulatory course the government had taken might prove to be vindicated in the future, but numerous Labor adherents felt that some of these short-term results were hardly encouraging. This impression was reinforced when it became apparent that much of Australia's growing debt had arisen from the massive borrowing of tycoon cowboys, who seemed more interested in enriching themselves through takeovers and other paper-shuffling exploits than in applying their wealth to productive investment which would generate the increased exports so desperately needed by Australia. In the heady boom-time atmosphere then prevalent there was considerable imprudent lending by the deregulated banks, and a number of the tycoons ignominiously crashed during the next few years. There was also disquiet in Labor circles about the fact that these cowboys – whose irresponsible activities made it harder to raise overseas capital for worthwhile export-producing investment in Australia – could claim the interest on their colossal borrowing as a tax deduction.

By May 1986 Keating was convinced that the top priority in economic policy had to change from establishing a growth economy to remedying Australia's serious balance of payments problems. During a radio interview on 14 May he dramatically alerted Australians to the gravity of the situation with some sensational remarks which reverberated throughout Australia and beyond:

I get the very clear feeling that we must let Australians know truthfully, honestly, earnestly, just what sort of an international hole Australia is in. It's the price of our commodities – they [have never been] as bad in real terms since the Depression. That's a fact of Australian life now – it's got nothing to do with the government. It's the price

421

of commodities on world markets, but it means an internal economic adjustment. And if we don't make it this time we never will make it. . .We will just end up being a third-rate economy.

In other words, Keating added in a widely publicized phrase, Australia would be like 'a banana republic'. Community awareness of the situation was also increased by other actions of the Hawke government, including a publicity scheme promoting the need to buy Australian goods.

The Hawke government led by example in severely restricting its own expenditure. These unprecedented reductions were achieved by the Expenditure Review Committee (ERC), a group of senior ministers including Hawke, Keating, Walsh, Button, Dawkins and Willis. (Although not initially involved in ERC, Howe later became a significant participant.) There was some reward for this gruelling round of meetings, with their painstaking cutting and pruning, on budget night when Keating flourished the government's success in winding back the deficit. After inheriting a budget deficit of around $9 billion, the Hawke government turned this around with such dexterity that by 1990 there was a budget surplus of around $9 billion. Some Labor people, however, wondered whether all these cuts were necessary: some of the reductions affected worthwhile government initiatives, and the private sector had hardly distinguished itself in responding to its increased freedoms and opportunities under the policy settings of the Hawke government. A different criticism came during the 1990 election campaign from the Liberal shadow Treasurer (who became party leader after that election); he made the astonishing claim that the Hawke government had *not* cut government expenditure. He added that it should be doing more to alleviate the national debt problem, although the then Liberal Party president had been one of the most notorious contributors to Australia's ballooning debt, borrowing from abroad huge sums of Connor-Khemlani magnitude for transactions which entirely lacked the visionary national and social objectives of that ill-fated and heavily criticized 1974–75 venture.

The four years following Keating's arresting 'banana republic' comment proved to be a difficult period for national economic policy. To restrain consumption and increase savings, the Hawke government kept interest rates high for a long period, which was inevitably unpopular with new home-buyers and other Australians directly affected. The obvious political risks of such a course were partly offset by community recognition that the government's policies were designed to serve the nation's economic interest. This recognition contributed to the ALP's success at hard-fought elections in 1987 and 1990. As the party approached its centenary, however, there were signs that the electorate was growing in impatience, sensing that the short-term pain did not seem to be producing much of the longer-term gains foreshadowed by Hawke and Keating.

The biggest early controversy for the Hawke government arose from a security briefing only six weeks after the 1983 election. The ASIO Director-General informed Hawke (by-passing Attorney-General Evans, who had ministerial responsibility for ASIO) that Australia's national security interests were at risk because of the relationship between David Combe and a Russian diplomat, V. Ivanov, who was almost certainly a KGB agent. ASIO's focus was on Ivanov. From his expulsion ASIO would derive welcome kudos in the international intelligence community, as the Director-General admitted to Hawke. But the government was more concerned about Combe's involvement. Directly responsible for shaping the government's response was the ministerial security com-

86. Tandberg's comment on the findings of the Fitzgerald Royal Commission. (*Age*)

87. In the 1989 SA election the Bannon Labor government was almost defeated after the opposition campaigned vigorously on the high interest rates maintained by the Hawke government; with a national election imminent, it was a sobering result for Bob Hawke and Paul Keating. (by Peter Nicholson; *Age*)

88. The day after Brian Burke (left) and Mal Bryce resigned as Premier and deputy in WA they lost no time in adjusting to life after politics. (*West Australian*)

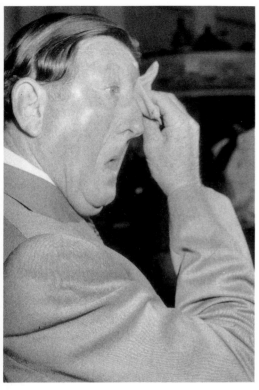

89. Jim Maher after being pelted with tomatoes by Victorian left-wingers incensed by the readmission to the party of four right-wing unions. (*Age*)

90. Carmen Lawrence.

91. Joan Kirner, another of the Victorian ALP's leading identities fanatical about a particular Australian Football League team.

mittee which comprised Hawke, Bowen, Evans, Hayden, Young and Scholes. The last thing they wanted was a scandal which could be used – just like the Petrov affair and Murphy's ASIO 'raid' – by anti-Labor interests to taint the newly elected government with the allegation that it was soft on national security.

The ministers' reaction was also coloured by their impressions of Combe's recent conduct. After his seven years as national party secretary Combe had sought preselection for a marginal Representatives seat (Barton, NSW), but despite Whitlam's backing his bid had foundered in the NSW branch's intense factionalism in the wake of the Baldwin bashing. The preselection was won by 24-year-old right-winger and Richardson protégé, Gary Punch, who won Barton at the 1983 election and served briefly in the Hawke ministry in the later 1980s. With a parliamentary career denied him, Combe decided to profit from his experience and contacts by becoming a lobbyist in Canberra. He did not hide the fact that he regarded the election of the Hawke government as a bonanza for him, an attitude which senior ministers regarded with distaste. As national secretary, Combe had displayed enterprise and skill in consolidating the party's financial position and establishing it in its own national headquarters, John Curtin House. While these achievements were immensely worthwhile for the party, some senior ALP figures found Combe's entrepreneurial characteristics not very attractive at a personal level. According to Hayden, Combe's attributes included intelligence, persistence, courage and toughness, but he was also 'brash, barging, a bit bumptious'. Senior Hawke government ministers concluded that the rumours on the Canberra gossip circuit about Combe's greedy intentions were consistent with what they regarded as his tactless and boorish conduct as a lobbyist during the government's first weeks in office.

This impression was reinforced by ASIO's extraordinary allegations against Combe. The ministers were stunned to learn that in ASIO's opinion Combe was on the verge of becoming gravely compromised by Ivanov. ASIO had reached this conclusion from its surveillance of Ivanov and information supplied to it by one of Combe's clients, L. Matheson, a devious and wealthy businessman who was hoping to use the election of the Hawke government to revive his previously very remunerative trade dealings with the Russians. Bowen's knowledge of Matheson equipped him to challenge ASIO's inferences and conclusions, which were sometimes based on dubious or glaringly mistaken analysis. However, the ministers' collective verdict was that Combe's conduct could have represented a potential risk to national security if his relationship with Ivanov had continued. Some ministers remarked that Combe's foolishness in this episode was equivalent to his involvement in the notorious Iraqi funds scandal late in 1975.

The government did not succeed in its attempts to contain the controversy. It acted quickly to expel Ivanov. ASIO delivered its initial briefing to Hawke alone on the afternoon of 20 April, and within 48 hours Hayden announced Ivanov's expulsion in a vaguely worded statement. How to handle Combe was not so straightforward. The ministers decided to refuse him access as a lobbyist. He had committed no offence, yet his livelihood was to be ruined, and he was not to be informed directly that this decision had been taken or why it had been made; nor was he to be given any opportunity to defend himself. To expect that this would be the end of the matter was optimistic. The rumour mill was soon linking Combe to Ivanov's departure, especially after Young confided the connection to a mate who had assisted him with the 1972 'It's time' campaign before becoming a Whitlam government staffer and later a wealthy lobbyist with an imposing list of clients also including Matheson. For this indiscretion on a national security matter Young had to resign from the ministry on 14 July. By then a royal commission was inquiring into the Ivanov-Combe affair. Hawke had moved swiftly to establish it on 12 May after adverse publicity from the government's viewpoint began to accumulate about Combe's plight. There was deeply felt unease within the ALP about the treatment Combe received. The victim himself was understandably bitter. He maintained that he had been merely trying to set up a trade deal, yet the upshot was that his livelihood had disappeared, a Labor government had approved ASIO's recommendation to place him under full surveillance, and his marriage had broken up. He was utterly devastated personally and professionally. The royal commissioner's findings, which were released late in 1983, managed to exonerate the government, Combe and even ASIO. Six weeks later Young was reinstated into the ministry. After intricate negotiations there was a public reconciliation between Hawke, acting on behalf of the government, and Combe at the 1984 ALP national conference. But Combe remained unable to secure fulfilling employment until mid-1985, when Dawkins's persistent efforts on his behalf led to his appointment as a trade commissioner. The nightmare over at last, Combe and his reunited family departed for Canada.

The government's initial reaction to the Combe-Ivanov affair was perhaps influenced by Hawke's keenness in his first weeks in office to send soothing signals to the Americans, who had overreacted in such alarmist fashion to the Whitlam government's heady initial months. During his first trip to the United States as Prime Minister Hawke fulsomely assured his hosts that Australia and America would be 'together forever'. Hayden was less effusive in dealing with the Americans, although he became more favourably disposed in office to their international influence than he had been in opposition. Hawke agreed to Hayden's proposal that Australia should appoint an ambassador for disarmament; the government was also a vital participant in the declaration of a nuclear-free zone in the South Pacific, and condemned the French nuclear tests at Mururoa Atoll. But some Labor activists regretted that the Hawke government did not extend its anti-nuclear stance in the region to encompass visiting United States warships. This acquiescence contrasted sharply with the refusal of the New Zealand Labour government – the remarkable similarity between the periods in office of the ALP and New Zealand Labour since the early 1940s continued in the 1980s – to allow nuclear-armed ships into its country, a policy maintained despite intimidating American pressure.

A measure of disillusionment among traditional ALP voters contributed to the unexpected jolt experienced by the Hawke government at the 1984 election. The thriving economy, the Prime Minister's extraordinary approval rating, and the government's generally competent performance since March 1983 all pointed to a runaway ALP victory. Instead the government was returned with a reduced majority. Some disaffected Labor traditionalists voted either informal or for the Nuclear Disarmament Party. Although it had only been formed just before the election, this fledgling party attracted considerable attention because its prominent leading identities, who included the former Labor Senator Jean Melzer, managed to evoke the idealism which had been customarily associated with the ALP. Other influences affected the 1984 result. Hawke was not at his best; the campaign was too long; and the general acceptance that Labor would easily win encouraged some electors who customarily voted ALP to register a protest vote on single issues like disarmament.

Shortly after the 1984 election the Hawke government's anti-nuclear credentials were again called into question when the MX missile controversy erupted. On 1 February 1985 it was reported that the government had decided to approve an American request for assistance in monitoring the performance of its new MX missile in tests to be conducted in the South Pacific. Hawke was about to travel overseas, where his engagements included talks with President Reagan. The accuracy of the MX report was uncomfortably confirmed by Beazley, who had succeeded Scholes as Defence minister only seven weeks earlier. There was an immediate outcry in the party. The agitation was spawned by the nature of the MX missile, the way the decision was made, and the difficulty of reconciling it with the Labor platform. All ALP members were pledged to strive for 'the elimination of nuclear weapons and the ultimate achievement of general and complete disarmament', and the government had trumpeted its disarmament credentials during the recent election campaign. The government's decision to assist the MX tests was made initially by Hawke, Hayden and Scholes, and approved by Bowen, Beazley, Young and Evans without ever being discussed by the full cabinet. Button acknowledged that he found it 'somewhat perturbing' to obtain his first knowledge of the decision by reading a newspaper, and Ryan also aired her disapproval publicly. FPLP backbenchers from various factions were outspoken in their condemnation, Premier Cain attacked the decision, and rank-and-file ALP members were appalled by it. Beazley, who was not privy to the initial decision, and Hayden, whose misgivings about it had prompted him to suggest that the full cabinet should consider it, both displayed ample loyalty to Hawke as the controversy escalated. On 5 February, however, Hawke, who was then in Brussels, decided after telephone talks with Richardson and Ray to reverse the government's decision. In the wake of this abrupt somersault there were earnest declarations that consultation mechanisms and decision-making processes needed improvement. There was also a blast from Keating, who bluntly told the FPLP's 'fourth-graders' that their inability to 'hold their tongues' in public was not helping the government.

Numerous Labor activists had also been dismayed by the Hawke government's attitude to uranium mining. In October 1983 cabinet announced that it would recommend to caucus that uranium should be mined at Roxby Downs. The only left-winger then in cabinet, West, dissociated himself from the decision, and was replaced in cabinet by Kerin. Hawke lobbied caucus so strenuously to have this pro-mining decision upheld that one of the left-wingers in the outer ministry, Howe, complained about his intimidatory tactics. After a vigorous caucus debate Hawke obtained the ratification he desired by 55 votes to 46. Considerable rank-and-file anger ensued, and there were critical responses from the Victorian and WA state ALP branches. In mid-1984 the uranium question was once again a stirring issue at an ALP national conference. With Centre Left support, Hawke and his right-wing supporters succeeded in having the government's 1983 decision accommodated by changes in the party platform. It was after this conference outcome that Melzer, a passionate anti-uranium activist, resolved to leave the ALP and join the newly formed Nuclear Disarmament Party.

There was another bitter pill for opponents of uranium mining to swallow in 1986. Shortly after Keating's 'banana republic' comment had dramatically highlighted Australia's balance-of-payments problems, Dawkins succeeded in persuading a number of his senior ministerial colleagues that Australia's plight necessitated the resumption of uranium exports to France. Hawke had assured

ALP left-wingers in 1983 that this would not occur while France continued its nuclear testing at Mururoa Atoll. Not only had France not ceased these tests; the specific ban on sales to France had been inserted in the ALP platform at the 1984 national conference and implicitly reaffirmed at the 1986 conference, only to be brazenly breached immediately afterwards. As uproar swept through the party, Hogg resigned in protest from the position he had held since 1983 as an adviser on Hawke's staff. But there was no repetition of the MX missile reversal. Disgruntled backbenchers were well aware that, as Young admitted in August 1986, the government 'faced an enormous hurdle to win the next election'; they grudgingly conceded that a fierce internal battle over uranium policy was the last thing the FPLP needed.

Labor supporters had much more cause for satisfaction with the Hawke government's record on environmental issues. After taking office in March 1983 Hawke explained that the poor state of the economy inherited by his government would preclude it from implementing the whole package of Labor's campaign initiatives, but the commitment to prevent the flooding of the Franklin River remained sacrosanct. 'The dam will not go ahead', Hawke affirmed in his first public statement after the election result became clear. Negotiations with Tasmania's obdurate Premier Gray proved fruitless, and the dispute was ultimately resolved by the High Court. Attorney-General Evans, who was keen to obtain evidence for the court case about the damaging construction work initiated by the Gray government, authorized RAAF jets to take aerial photographs of the site; when Gray vigorously protested, Hawke reprimanded Evans (unnecessarily, some Labor activists felt). A High Court majority including Murphy narrowly upheld the World Heritage Properties Conservation Act, which had been the first bill introduced to parliament by the Hawke government. The constitutional basis of the majority decision had not been available during the Whitlam government's equivalent controversy concerning Lake Pedder; but that government had paved the way for the Hawke government's Franklin success by ratifying the World Heritage Convention which, the High Court held in 1983, had brought Australia's areas of World Heritage significance within the ambit of the national government's external affairs power.

The Hawke government's election victory in March 1990 owed much to the adroit political skills Richardson displayed as Environment minister. Before the mid-1980s he had not been renowned for his dedication to particular policy issues, and his sudden emergence as a fervent conservationist was regarded cynically in some quarters. But his transformation was genuine, and mirrored the changed views of many other enlightened Australians as environmental awareness spread rapidly during the 1980s. The Hawke government's faith in the virtues of market forces and its generally pragmatic approach reduced the differences between the ALP and anti-Labor, but the conservatives' inadequate response to widespread concern about the environment did provide Labor with an issue where it could distinguish itself sharply and favourably from its main opponents. This process accelerated after Richardson became Environment minister in July 1987. Hawke was also well aware that by demonstrating sensitivity on this issue his government would be adopting a populist and visionary approach simultaneously. During the government's third term several major cabinet decisions gave far more satisfaction to the conservationists than the economic rationalists. Uren, the valiant left-winger who had been a dedicated battler for the environment over two decades earlier, well before it became fashionable, felt distinctly uncomfortable with some aspects of the Hawke government's performance, but he praised Richardson warmly: 'He's tough, he's deeply committed and he's in there fighting. When right-wingers like Richardson turn out to be great men, it gives you hope'. Richardson relished his different image: instead of 'people looking as though I'm something they've just stepped on in a paddock [they are] coming up in an airport telling me what a hero I am'. In September 1989 Richardson told an ALP branch meeting at Bungendore (ACT) that the next election would be held between March and May 1990, and at that poll independents would do well, preferences would be critical in the ultimate outcome, Labor would probably record its lowest share of the primary vote for some time, but he was nonetheless confident of a Labor victory. All these predictions proved correct. The success of Labor's innovative appeal to conservationists late in the election campaign – acknowledging that they might prefer to vote for 'Green' independents, but urging them to give their second preferences to ALP candidates – owed much to Richardson.

The emergence of the environment movement as a significant force in Australian politics was confirmed by a novel experiment in Tasmania following the 1989 state election. At that election the Gray government won 17 of the 35 Assembly seats (19 in 1986) to Labor's 13 (14 in 1986). The balance of power was secured by a group of five Green independents, whose success was attributable to Tasmania's proportional representation electoral system as well as the attractiveness of the environmental cause in a state which had experienced more than its share of the depredations of voracious development. One of the Greens claimed that their arrival paralleled the birth of the ALP, and the Greens did pursue an approach similar to the ALP's early 'support in return for concessions' phase. The Gray government was doomed when the ALP and the Greens negotiated an alliance, which was not a coalition along traditional Australian lines – there were no Greens in the ministry. Under the agreement the Greens were granted an inside role in the process of government while maintaining their independent status. The new Labor Premier was 41-year-old Michael Field, an amiable Arts graduate and schoolteacher whose sense of outrage at the Whitlam government's dismissal had propelled him into parliament in 1976.

The progress of the ALP-Greens experiment was keenly followed. Not only Australians were interested – Green activists in Europe closely monitored developments in Tasmania. Government under the alliance began auspiciously when a consultative process involving the government, unions, conservationists and the forestry industry culminated in the Salamanca agreement, which increased both the logs available for the timber industry and the areas of Tasmanian forest with World Heritage status. After years of so much confrontation, especially in Tasmania, arising from the frequently conflicting needs of environmental protection, resource generation and employment, Salamanca was hailed as the harbinger of a new era in which all interested groups would resolve their differences harmoniously and work towards their mutual objective, sustainable development. But a year later the optimism had vanished. Consensus on the essence of sustainable development proved elusive. In October 1990 the alliance was dissolved owing to differences between the Field government and the Greens, primarily concerning the appropriate strategy for Tasmania's forests.

One of the most divisive issues within the Hawke ministry was media ownership policy. Cabinet remained deadlocked for months with Hawke and Communications minister Duffy inflexibly at odds over the appropriate limits to be imposed on the ownership of television stations. Duffy, the factionally unaligned minister who had the determination and independence to stand up resolutely to the big battalions, was adamant that all existing and prospective owners should have equal entitlement under the government's proposed new arrangements. The Prime Minister was usually content to leave the formulation of cabinet proposals to the relevant minister(s), but on this question he was uncharacteristically interventionist, motivated by a concern to avoid antagonizing some of the powerful media barons whose influence could significantly affect voters' perceptions of his government. Keeping media magnates like Rupert Murdoch and Kerry Packer on side may have seemed to Hawke, Keating, Wran, Richardson and others a shrewd prudent approach to help Labor retain office so that it could (in Keating's words) fulfil 'its original and essential charter – to improve the lot of the common people', but this strategy required sensitive handling. Although Labor activists often resented the hostility of the media, they also disapproved of blatant attempts to curry favour with proprietors like Murdoch and Packer.

The Hawke-Duffy deadlock was broken by Keating with a decisive intervention which underlined his significance in the government. With his longstanding interest in the issue of media ownership, he proposed that the government should tackle newspapers simultaneously with television. Under his scheme the big players could essentially operate in television or the press, but not in both. They had to decide, as Keating put it, whether to become 'queen of the screen or prince of print'. His shrewd proposal embodied an element of increased diversity in line with the party platform, while suiting Murdoch and Packer in practice far more than other media conglomerates which the Hawke government regarded less favourably. Duffy was not convinced and many backbenchers were uneasy, but Keating's vigorous lobbying in cabinet and caucus proved successful. The upshot soon afterwards was upheaval in the media world, as the magnates scrambled to take advantage of the new arrangements. In the stampede some purchasers paid inflated prices, with ultimately costly consequences for themselves and the corporations they acquired. Keating and others explained that this unsatisfactory state of affairs was attributable not to the government's changes, but to the folly of greedy entrepreneurs.

The Hawke government's considerable achievements in education were somewhat obscured by the controversial reintroduction of tertiary fees which the Whitlam government had abolished. Walsh maintained that the cessation of fees had not, as intended, led to a significant increase in the proportion of students from working-class backgrounds continuing their education to tertiary level. Therefore, the increased proportion of workers' taxes devoted to government expenditure on tertiary education was benefiting the affluent much more than workers' families. Ryan, who was Education minister during 1983–87, opposed the imposition of tertiary fees, but Dawkins, who was allocated an enlarged portfolio of Employment, Education and Training in July 1987, agreed with his close friend Walsh on this issue. Dawkins moved quickly to introduce a scheme which required students to make a financial contribution towards the cost of their tuition; this amount became payable when the students began to earn a stipulated level of income after graduation. But that was only part of the major shake-up Dawkins imposed on tertiary education institutions. His wide-ranging structural changes included amalgamations of various institutions, the removal of the distinction between universities and colleges of advanced education, and the introduction of procedures to monitor the productivity of individual academics. Dawkins wanted to increase the number of tertiary places available and to make training and education more responsive to the needs of Australian industry, and the Hawke government made substantial progress in both. In secondary education the government significantly increased funding for schools, and provided financial assistance for students to help them stay at school longer. Jones and others had for years been lamenting that not enough Australians remained at school for long enough, and one of the most satisfying achievements of the Hawke government was the big increase after 1983 in the proportion of Australian students undertaking the final year of secondary school.

The Hawke government's achievements in welfare were also inadequately recognized. During the 1980s the political climate was dominated by the symbols and language of market forces – deregulation, the profit motive, developments on the stock exchange and fluctuations in the Australian dollar; there was comparatively little concern about issues such as pensions, benefits and services to assist the disadvantaged. The Hawke government's accomplishments in enhanced social services included increases in pensions and child care places, together with significant progress in directing assistance to the most disadvantaged recipients over the whole range of welfare benefits. Its primary welfare initiative was the family allowance supplement, which provided a sizeable and welcome boost to the incomes of genuinely needy Australians and was one of the most important reforms in Australian history. However, the government failed to get appropriate credit for it, mainly because of the rhetoric used in announcing it. 'By 1990 no Australian child will be living in poverty', Hawke proclaimed in the 1987 policy speech (a document apparently vetted by others before delivery). From 1987 to 1990 the ridicule inevitably generated by that imprudent pronouncement overshadowed the commendation the government received from welfare agencies for its pathfinding initiative.

Combe was not the only prominent Labor identity from the Whitlam government era to suffer from protracted stressful controversy during the Hawke government. In 1973 anti-Labor Senators had shown extreme animosity to Whitlam's Attorney-General, Murphy; 'you can see the venom drooling out of their mouths as they wait for the kill', observed an independent Senator. After the Whitlam government was dismissed there were persistent suggestions that Murphy 'will not survive on the High Court bench'. His judgments were innovative (and expressed in unusually plain language), and in his early years he frequently found himself in the minority in contentious cases; often he formed a minority of one. However, particularly after Barwick's retirement in 1981, Murphy began to find that his viewpoints and interpretations were increasingly endorsed by his fellow judges. This development naturally disturbed conservatives, who were also unsettled by Murphy's refusal to conform to the traditional expectation that High Court judges should be soberly aloof and remote from the pulse of society. Murphy's intellectual brilliance eminently qualified him for the judiciary, but he was a free spirit with an expansive temperament. He revelled in rollicking informality, ignoring the raised eyebrows of the conformists as he shared ideas, banter and food with students in university eateries. Craving the contact and stimulation of conversation about politics and public affairs generally, he saw neither need nor justification to cut himself off from old comrades and associates. But even such warm admirers of Murphy as Evans and Jim McClelland felt that his gregariousness was insufficiently discriminating. Nevertheless, some of his closest friends who talked with him frequently while he was a judge have emphasized that during their conversations he punctiliously avoided any discussion of cases pending or in progress.

For three years from November 1983 Murphy was repeatedly in the headlines because of allegations that he had improperly tried to influence the course of justice. During that period he had to endure investigations by two Senate committees, a committal hearing, a trial in the NSW Supreme Court, a review of the trial verdict in the NSW Court of Appeal, another Supreme Court trial, a royal commission and an additional commission of inquiry. All this originated from the publication of transcripts which purportedly verified telephone conversations which had been illegally taped; there were mistakes and distortions in the presentation of this material in the press, and the tapes themselves had nearly all disappeared so that authentication was highly problematic. To Wran and other Murphy sympathizers the sensationalized publication of this material and Murphy's subsequent treatment by certain newspapers seemed more like persecution than ethical investigative journalism, and equivalent to the worst excesses of 1975. Wran was fined $25 000 for contempt of court after his exasperated outburst in November 1985 that Murphy was 'innocent of any wrongdoing'. Murphy polarized people. His detractors claimed that he was unscrupulous and dangerous; ALP enthusiasts esteemed his warm humanity and substantial achievements. The animosity of the Establishment and the zealotry of sections of the press (perhaps motivated to 'prove' the validity of their decision to publish the transcripts in the first place) created a media-fuelled ordeal which has rarely been surpassed in Australia. 'I have never in all my life seen a man pursued with more relentlessness than Murphy', commented Hayden. Unsubstantiated rumours and innuendo flourished irrespective of the outcome of the various proceedings during his ordeal. This was profoundly ironic, since no Australian politician has had a more fundamental genuine commitment to human rights and civil liberties than Murphy. The intensity of the media pressure placed the Hawke government in an awkward position, especially Attorneys-General Evans, one of Murphy's staunchest admirers, and Bowen, who had known Murphy since kindergarten. After Murphy was exonerated by his second trial in April 1986, Chief Justice Gibbs indicated a lack of enthusiasm about Murphy's return to the High Court, and the Hawke government reluctantly authorized a further commission of inquiry to evaluate this issue. Bowen seemed so painfully nonplussed by this development, which was (he later revealed) in his opinion unnecessary, that Evans – although no longer Attorney-General – took over the role of explaining the government's decision to the media. Shortly afterwards came the stunning news that Murphy had terminal cancer, and he died in October. There were lavish tributes from ALP identities. Duncan spoke for many Labor people when he highlighted the link between stress and cancer, and directly accused Murphy's political foes and journalistic adversaries of hounding a fine Australian to his death.

The tenth anniversary of the Whitlam government's dismissal was a significant media event in Australia. There was a spate of newspaper articles, and also a number of television programmes which replayed old film footage showing Whitlam on the Parliament House steps after the dismissal and at Blacktown delivering policy speeches to exultant supporters. The centre of all this media attention was Whitlam himself. Now 69, he and his publishers had chosen the tenth anniversary of his government's demise to launch his huge book trumpeting its policy achievements. Whitlam was in scintillating form, handling an endless stream of engagements with wit, relish and aplomb. In this flurry of publicity Whitlam was tactfully taciturn when invited to contrast his government's reformist vigour with the Hawke government's more measured approach. During one interview he did admit that he would like the Hawke government to become 'more enthusiastic and inspiring'; the ALP 'is a party of reform or it is nothing', he added, and the government risked 'disappointing our supporters' by deferring reform initiatives, but he stressed that these remarks were not intended to be critical of the government.

On other occasions Whitlam's lack of reticence fuelled sharp exchanges about the relative merits of the Whitlam and Hawke governments. Whitlam was critical of the Hawke government's record concerning education, media ownership and aspects of its handling of the Murphy saga. He also contended that it had been too cautious in a number of spheres where the perceived need for expenditure restraint could not be used as an excuse – constitutional reform, a national compensation scheme, Aboriginal land rights and legislation to regulate the corporate sector. When the Hawke government came under fire for being insufficiently radical its principal defender was Keating. Late in 1985 Keating publicly saluted Whitlam's achievement in making the ALP more electorally credible, while delivering a mild rebuke to the Whitlam government for its 'belated recognition that the economic sands had shifted beneath it'. In May 1987 Keating was more forceful in rebutting assertions from Whitlam and others (including Jim McClelland) that the Hawke government had been too pragmatic. Keating insisted that the government had notable accomplishments in social reform to its credit (Medicare, environment, significant real increase in pensions, taxation reforms, child care), and critics who ignored its achievements in restructuring the economy 'just do not understand what the main game is all about'. During a major speech six months later Keating asserted that whereas the Hawke government had a responsible and productive relationship with the ACTU symbolized by the Accord, Whitlam's 'economic ministers spent much of their time attacking unions' in 'hostile press releases and petulant speeches'. Keating denied the 'lingering and mistaken view' that Labor under Hawke was being driven by 'some new and alien philosophy which has distorted its priorities', and scorned the historical perspective of 'the romantics who choose to regard the 1972 Whitlam program as a purist application of high-minded Labor principle'. Cairns and Jim McClelland responded to Keating's speech by casting aspersions on the willingness of Hawke and Keating to associate themselves with millionaire tycoons, and Whitlam's reaction was an angry outburst which included the assertion that 'I won't cop smart-arse comments about my Government'.

Most ALP supporters accepted that a degree of compromise was inevitable when a Labor government was in office during difficult economic times. Yet many of them felt frustrated that the Hawke government seemed inclined to use up most of its political capital in implementing change in financial spheres; these reforms demonstrated an attachment to market forces at odds with ALP traditions, and were often in line with the views of conservative economists. Getting the economy right was essential to the successful introduction of worthwhile reforms, argued the defenders of the Hawke government's performance, including some of its ministers who frequently praised its willingness to take the hard decisions necessary to restructure the economy. But some ALP adherents wished that the government had been prepared more often to take the hard decisions necessary to achieve Labor's objectives in other areas. As well as challenging the government's sense of priorities, some critics within the party queried the fundamental correctness of the economic reforms. In their opinion the deregulatory thrust seemed to have left Australia even more vulnerable to overseas economic fluctuations without providing significant compensating advantages. They were sceptical about Keating's enthusiastic portrayal in his more expansive moments of Australia's golden future under a mature internationally competitive economy. Some Labor people who felt the government could have tried harder to achieve a more equitable distribution of wealth in Australia regretted its reluctance to impose a wealth tax or an inheritance tax; they were also disappointed by its failure to curb the large and sometimes grotesque salary increases awarded to corporate executives and managers at a time when battling workers submitted to real wage reductions negotiated under the Accord.

There was also some puzzlement in Labor ranks about the dominance acquired by the economic rationalists, who seemed to exert a disproportionate influence in the senior levels of the Canberra bureaucracy, in general political discourse, in the media, and occasionally in the Hawke government. 'There has been in Australia a move towards the philosophy that whatever is spent on the poor adds to the deficit', observed Kim Beazley senior, whereas 'whatever is spent on the rich encourages investment'. However, this trend was not confined to Australia. Faith in collectivist solutions suffered a sharp and widespread decline during the 1980s. Australia had managed to avoid 'the worst excesses' of this development, wrote a progressive English observer, John Mortimer, who regretted the plight of the beleaguered British Labour Party during the Thatcher era and expressed his envy of Australia's 'achievement of a popular and successful Labor government'. Indeed, Dawkins claimed in mid-1988 that since 1983 the Hawke government had 'been probably the most successful left-of-centre government in the world'.

In this era which was not very conducive to reform the Hawke government certainly chalked up some commendable accomplishments. It developed and articulated a vision for the nation's economic future – although some of the Whitlamite Labor faithful regarded it as materialistic and sterile – and adhered to it despite short-term political difficulties. Under the grave pressure of adverse economic circumstances (of admittedly varying magnitude) the Scullin government had disintegrated and the Whitlam government had floundered for part of 1974, but the Hawke government tenaciously maintained its cohesion and kept winning elections. It displayed a proficiency in the art of government which had rarely been shown before by the ALP in Canberra. Combining employment growth with economic restructuring for the nation's long-term future was a notable achievement. This large increase in jobs was partly attributable to the successful Accord with the ACTU, which also improved Australia's economic performance through increased industrial harmony and wider acceptance of the concept of the social wage. The effective Keating-Kelty partnership was also responsible for innovative measures to extend the benefits and security of superannuation to the working class. Thanks to Button's efforts, the government had prevented the demise of the steel industry in Australia, and also involved itself closely in stabilizing other ailing industries like shipbuilding, textiles and motor vehicle manufacturing. A start had been made in overhauling the education system so that it provided Australian industry with a workforce possessing greater skills and better training. As Keating and others pointed out, there was a solid record of creditable social reforms including Medicare, the environment, welfare, taxation and the First Home Owners' Scheme. These achievements were substantial, even if the government at times seemed to some ALP enthusiasts deficient in dash and idealism.

The 1981 Supreme Court verdict which upheld the validity of federal intervention in Queensland had gladdened the overwhelming majority of the Labor faithful in that state, but their great expectations about the party's immediate future were not realized. Denis Murphy, who was seen by many ALP supporters as their big hope to lead Queensland Labor out of the wilderness, was, like his hero T.J. Ryan, cut down tragically and prematurely; he died of cancer in 1984 aged 47. Intense factionalism was also significant. Increased factionalism was inevitable in Queensland, owing to the introduction of proportional representation in the state branch together with the escalation of factionalism in the FPLP and the party's most important decision-making bodies. But too often during the 1980s the Queensland ALP seemed consumed by internecine warfare.

The most discouraging aspect for the rank and file was Queensland Labor's continued inability to make much electoral progress against Bjelke-Petersen and the Nationals. High hopes were held for the 1983 election, especially after Labor doubled its tally of Queensland seats at the national election earlier that year. With the endorsement of fresh faces including Murphy, Wayne Goss, former Test cricketer Tom Veivers and the Socialist Left's Anne Warner, Labor had boosted the calibre of its parliamentary candidates, and there was a more imaginative and professional direction in Labor's campaigning. On polling day Labor gained a pleasing increase in its share of the primary vote (up 2·5%) and its tally of seats (from 25 to 32). But the Nationals achieved a similar lift in their parliamentary strength, which enabled them to govern in their own right without the need for any coalition with the hapless Liberals. For Labor Queenslanders the prospect of an even more uninhibited Bjelke-Petersen was hardly encouraging. Such pessimistic reflections were vindicated by some characteristic exploits by the Premier, including his ruthless crushing of a major strike in February 1985 and his controversial acceptance of $400 000 from one of Australia's tycoons ostensibly in settlement of a defamation action. As the 1986 state election approached there was a widespread anticipation that this time the Premier seemed really vulnerable. State ALP leader Nev Warburton and secretary Beattie performed their roles competently, and during the last week of the campaign the National Party was sufficiently concerned to deluge the Queensland media with a huge advertising blitz. This saturation evidently paid dividends. To the consternation of Labor supporters, the ALP's voting share fell, the Nationals and the Liberals both increased theirs, and Bjelke-Petersen was returned to power with an enlarged parliamentary majority.

Shortly after his 1986 election victory the 76-year-old Premier embarked on a weird personal crusade which became known as the 'Joh for PM' campaign. He scornfully derided the leaders of the anti-Labor parties in Canberra, and claimed that he had a team of strong candidates and ample financial backing. There were suggestions that $25 million had been contributed by the 'white shoe brigade' (a popular label for the new breed of entrepreneurs who had flourished under the Bjelke-Petersen regime). Bjelke-Petersen did not realize, however, that certain characteristics of Queensland which had assisted his dominance there – the lower average educational attainments of its citizens, the more pronounced regionalism in its population distribution, and the greater attachment to rural life – were less prevalent outside the state. For over six months the ageing Premier aired his simplistic platitudes and bombastic ramblings, but when Hawke called the mid-1987 election Bjelke-Petersen was overseas – in Disneyland – crying foul because he had been caught unprepared. His much-vaunted candidates had proved as elusive as the $25 million, and the chief fundraiser from the white shoe brigade had been charged with tax evasion. After all the sabre-rattling bluster,

Bjelke-Petersen admitted on 3 June that he would not be a candidate. Outwardly unabashed after this humiliating withdrawal, he proceeded to undermine the anti-Labor campaign with occasional sniping from the sidelines. His important contribution to Labor's cause was reflected in the outcome. Labor won with an increased majority, capturing five seats, and four of these gains were in Queensland. 'We couldn't have done it without Joh', explained Beattie.

During Bjelke-Petersen's vainglorious crusade a nationally televised ABC documentary featured allegations about corruption flourishing in Queensland. With Bjelke-Petersen absent interstate, his deputy announced that an inquiry would be held, even though Bjelke-Petersen had just told a national television audience that there was no need for any investigation. The lawyer appointed to preside over the royal commission, Tony Fitzgerald QC, was little known outside legal circles at the time of his appointment, but he soon became a household name. With skill, courage and persistence Fitzgerald penetrated the pious folksy façade of the Bjelke-Petersen regime and exposed its evil underside. Many ALP supporters in and beyond Queensland had suspected that there was extensive corruption in that state, and the evidence was damning in the extreme. It was alleged that Bjelke-Petersen's handpicked and rapidly promoted head of the Queensland police force had been receiving large bribes for years. Also said to have been on the take were several other senior police officers. It had become understood in Queensland that a large donation to the National Party could procure a knighthood or a lucrative business deal with the government. Bjelke-Petersen had apparently ignored conventional practice concerning conflicts of interest between his public duties and private business and family dealings. One of his most notorious ministers, Russ Hinze, had allegedly received from various developers over $4 million in loans, gifts and other benefits. Five other ministers were charged with repeated abuses of the ministerial expenses system after being implicated in evidence tendered at the Fitzgerald Commission.

These sensational revelations guaranteed Bjelke-Petersen's downfall. After his ignominious and undignified departure the National Party remained in disarray, apprehensive of the voters' verdict on the Fitzgerald findings. The Liberals were confident that they would be the beneficiaries, but Wayne Goss had other ideas. His leadership challenge in October 1987 had been unsuccessful, but four months later Warburton accepted the inevitable and stood aside for Goss, whose elevation was unanimously endorsed by caucus. Born in 1951, Goss grew up in a disadvantaged Brisbane suburb – he described it as a 'wasteland' – which lacked basic community amenities. Goss displayed characteristic persistence and determination in becoming a lawyer despite this background; he worked for civil liberties groups, Aborigines and other reform activists. Intelligent and articulate with a quick dry wit, Goss was a marathon runner and had plenty of stamina. Although usually measured and controlled, he was also capable of rousing oratory:

> Will we, as Queenslanders, have to continue to accept the worst standards of integrity in government and public life? Will we build a community in which young people grow up and see that the way to go ahead is to follow the way of this Government – to lie, to bribe, and to take the dishonest short-cut? Or will we. . .show young people that the way to go ahead is to tell the truth, to earn their living and to earn it by hard work and by using their ability?

On 2 December 1989, the seventeenth anniversary of the election of the Whitlam government, Goss led Labor to its first election victory in Queensland for 32 years. It was a copybook Labor campaign, directed ably by Wayne Swan, a lecturer in public administration. Labor exuded competence and confidence as new policies were formulated, campaign techniques were honed and, above all, factional turbulence was stilled. Optimistic expectations had been dashed in 1983 and 1986. The main concern to ALP supporters this time was that even if Labor achieved well over 50% of the vote the gerrymander might prevent their party obtaining a clear parliamentary majority, which was essential to clean Queensland up properly. But these fears were put to rest by Labor's landslide victory. With the Nationals' vote falling 15·9%, Labor gained a swing of 9·7% and won 54 out of the 89 seats, giving the Goss government an absolute parliamentary majority of 19 seats. Considering the extent of the gerrymander obstacle, Labor's decades in the wilderness and the odium of the defeated government, few state election victories in the ALP's entire history have been more exhilarating. Labor Queenslanders were ecstatic. Goss received a tumultuous reception when he claimed victory, confirmed 'the end of the Bjelke-Petersen era', and expressed his 'special thanks to all those old timers who've hung in there for 32 years waiting for today'.

The new government disappointed some Labor enthusiasts who were hoping to see a sudden Whitlamesque flurry of overdue reforms. Such an approach was firmly rejected by Goss, who maintained a very high approval rating during 1990. 'I am not interested in magic wands or bolts of lightning', declared the Premier. 'I am interested in sustainable government, sustainable reforms, long-term Labor government.' However, the Queensland Police Special Branch, which Bjelke-Petersen had used to hound political opponents, was immediately abolished, and there were other important early initiatives, particularly in education. Furthermore, there was a significant public acknowledgement from Fitzgerald in July 1990 that he was satisfied with the government's progress in implementing the sweeping changes he had recommended in his royal commission report. In another development arising from the Fitzgerald Commission, Bjelke-Petersen was charged in October 1990 with corruption and perjury.

After almost six years of considerable success in NSW, Wran and his government began to experience some difficulties. At the 1981 state election, campaigning under the slogan 'It's Got To Be Wran', Labor had achieved a resounding victory, winning 69 of the 99 seats in the NSW Assembly, but the national recession of the early 1980s severely affected NSW. In this tougher economic climate the Wran government sharply increased state taxes and charges; it also embarked on rationalization initiatives affecting the State Rail Authority and the Health department, but these measures resulted in friction between the government and the union movement. Ducker had been adept at minimizing such tensions, but his successor in the key post of Labor Council secretary, Unsworth, was more inclined to be forceful in pursuing industrial objectives. The Wran government's image was also harmed by NSW's problems with electricity supplies during 1981–82.

The most troublesome issue for the Wran government was corruption. During the Askin regime organized crime became institutionalized. Drug trafficking and illegal gambling networks flourished, with the tentacles of corruption extending to the highest levels of the NSW police force and even to Premier Askin himself. Shortly after the Wran government was first elected to office in mid-1976 one of its talented younger ministers, left-winger Frank Walker, tried to convince his cabinet colleagues that firm action to clean up the police force should be one of the new government's most urgent priorities. Walker was not heeded. Wran, who

435

had ministerial responsibility for the police himself, felt that with Labor holding a one-seat Assembly majority and its opponents in control in the Council, his government initially had to tread warily. The lingering odium of the Baldwin bashing and the Enmore conspiracy charges was supplemented by several unsavoury episodes implicating the police and judicial system of NSW. Cropping up frequently in these controversies was Chief Stipendiary Magistrate Murray Farquhar. NSW Labor was indirectly tarnished by these occurrences, especially those concerning high-ranking police officers promoted since the Wran government came to power. But the government itself was unquestionably involved directly when Wran forced one of his ministers, Rex 'Buckets' Jackson, to resign over allegations of corruption (which later resulted in Jackson being charged, convicted and gaoled).

The biggest corruption controversy arose when a television documentary alleged that Wran himself was involved in an attempt to influence a judicial hearing. The Premier angrily denied any impropriety, but agreed with the opinion of his talented and ambitious Attorney-General, Paul Landa, that the seriousness of the accusation necessitated a royal commission. Wran stood down for 74 days during the inquiry while his deputy and friend, left-winger Jack Ferguson, took over the reins. The inquiry, which was conducted by the NSW Chief Justice, completely exonerated Wran and concluded that the culprit was Farquhar, who had spread the erroneous impression that Wran had contacted him. Throughout the inquiry Wran had expressed complete confidence in the outcome, and after its findings were announced he was understandably angry, blasting the documentary which had led to the 'destabilisation' of his government as 'a blot upon the history of so-called investigative reporting in Australia'. The controversy had inevitably affected his popularity in the electorate, and he immediately embarked on a determined campaign to repair the damage. He had achieved this objective with such success by February 1984 that he called an unexpectedly early election, and his government was re-elected with a very comfortable Assembly majority.

In mid-1986 Wran was in complete command of NSW politics and had just completed 10 years as Premier when he stunned the ALP by announcing his resignation to unsuspecting delegates at the NSW state conference. Wran had been at the top in NSW for a long time, and he was finding it more of a grind and less of a challenge. Although he did not hide his regret that his ambition to transfer to Canberra had been unfulfilled, his proud record in NSW established him as one of the ALP's most outstanding leaders. 'I've served under a lot of leaders', remarked Ferguson, 'but as a politician, tactician and innovator he was . . .just the best'. Ferguson described him as 'irreplaceable', with a brilliant capacity to 'master the brief' and 'an incredible ability to think on his feet'. One of Wran's ministers, Peter Anderson, remarked that 'whoever takes over from Neville will know what it is like to bat after Bradman'. Wran's reformist instincts were constrained by a pragmatic sensitivity to what the electorate would tolerate, but he was a visionary conservationist before the environment became paramount in deciding the outcome of elections. He was also noted for his commitment to the arts, and commended for his stylish impact on the cultural ambience of Sydney.

Steve Loosley, who had followed Richardson as state secretary, was not alone in concluding that if Wran had made his announcement in a caucus meeting the process of determining his successor might well have unfolded differently. At the conference the presence of numerous unionists was significant in generating a strong momentum of support for Unsworth rather than the most likely alternative, Brereton, who did not possess a solid union background. (Landa had been seen as a possible future leader, but in 1984 he suffered a fatal heart attack at the age of 43.) The numbers were locked in for Unsworth so quickly that Brereton withdrew from the contest, accepting the inevitable, the very next day. Anderson made a token bid, so that the parliamentarians rather than the machine could be seen to select the leader, but his candidature posed no threat to Unsworth's elevation. While Hawke praised Unsworth as an 'excellent choice' with 'an impeccable background', Hayden's reaction was rather different. Hayden was evidently settling some old scores arising from his 1982–83 leadership battle with Hawke when he bemused a Bangkok press conference with some droll remarks, likening the 'verve and style' of 'my mate Barrie' to 'a dreary confabulation of undertakers'. There was more: 'If you're the sort of person who gets your simple pleasure out of life tearing wings off dying butterflies, then Barrie's your man'. Unsworth did not possess Wran's charisma, and wisely did not pretend that he did. But his efforts to dispel the popular misconception that he was nothing more than a tough headkicker were hampered by the way the machine powerbrokers anointed him so swiftly that all other aspirants except Anderson were out of contention within about 30 hours of Wran's announcement.

As in SA after Dunstan's departure, developments in NSW after Wran resigned demonstrated how crucial he had been to Labor's recent success in his state. Unsworth was thrown onto the defensive very quickly by massive by-election swings against the government. Wran's seat of Bass Hill was captured by the Liberals with a swing of 16·5%, and Unsworth narrowly avoided great embarrassment for himself and the state branch when he survived an anti-Labor swing of 22% and scraped home by 54 votes at the by-election arranged to transfer him from the Legislative Council to a supposedly safe Labor seat in the Assembly. Unsworth valiantly tried to regain the ascendancy, but his government continued to look embattled. When pollster Rod Cameron's survey research indicated that Brereton's high profile was harming the government's image in the eyes of uncommitted voters, Unsworth responded by demoting Brereton, who then resigned from the ministry altogether. At the 1988 state election the Unsworth government was convincingly defeated. Unsworth was replaced as leader by Carr, who had distinguished himself in his three years as Planning and Environment minister. Carr was prevailed upon to forsake his longstanding plan to transfer to Canberra as Bowen's successor in Kingsford-Smith, which went instead to Brereton, who now saw a limited future for himself in state politics. These decisions signified the abandonment of ambitions nurtured ever since their Labor Youth Council days in the 1960s when Carr had dreamed of being minister for External Affairs in a Keating government and Brereton's goal was to become NSW Premier.

In WA the Burke Labor government which came to power in February 1983 moved swiftly to galvanize the flagging state economy. Aggressive entrepreneurs were encouraged to the hilt. The close association of the government (and Premier Burke in particular) with these thrusting wheeler-dealers gravely embarrassed WA Labor during the later 1980s, when it became apparent that some of them had not only failed to prosper but squandered large amounts of government funds in the process. In office Burke enhanced his reputation as a brilliant communicator. He also became known as a forceful pragmatist, who was prepared to confront Hawke or anyone else if he believed such action was necessary to protect his government's interests. This characteristic was most evident on the issue of Aboriginal land rights. Survey information commissioned by Burke from Rod Cameron persuaded the Premier that his government was threatened by the hostility of voters in a few marginal seats to the Hawke government's proposals for uniform land rights legislation. The Burke government's fierce opposition to these proposals was instrumental in the Hawke government's decision to abandon them. With the Premier maintaining a high personal popularity rating, the government retained its comfortable majority at the February 1986 state election. Burke had repeatedly stated that he was not inclined to remain Premier for longer than five years, and in December 1987 he and deputy Premier Bryce announced that they would both be resigning on 25 February 1988, the fifth anniversary of the Burke government's election to office.

Peter Dowding was Burke's successor. Dowding's father, like Burke's, had been prominent in the WA ALP; however, Keith Dowding – unlike Tom Burke – admired Evatt and was close to Chamberlain. After an unsettled upbringing Peter Dowding became renowned in Perth as an able lawyer with an assertive personality and his father's willingness to associate himself with radical causes. He defended many conscientious objectors to conscription, including McMullan, and became very involved in the Aboriginal movement. Dowding was a minister in Burke's cabinet from its formation, and Burke's active support was a crucial factor in Dowding's promotion to the leadership ahead of other contenders, particularly Parker, who had to be content with becoming Dowding's deputy. A difficult task faced Premier Dowding as the government he led became increasingly discredited by the Burke government's web of financial dealings with failed entrepreneurs, which was derogatorily labelled 'WA Inc'. In view of these adverse circumstances he achieved a notable success in leading WA Labor to victory at the February 1989 state election, but later in 1989 it became clear that 'WA Inc' transactions had continued under Dowding's leadership and further public funds had been lost.

At the end of 1989 opinion surveys confirmed that Labor's standing in the West had deteriorated alarmingly. The concern within the ranks of state Labor was augmented by anxious FPLP members who were worried that WA electors might express their dissatisfaction with the state government when voting at the imminent national election. One of them, Beazley, who felt vulnerable although a swing of 8·6% was required to unseat him, was particularly animated in urging that something had to be done. A majority of the state caucus eventually accepted that Dowding would have to be replaced. The Premier contributed to his downfall by his abrasive personality and confrontational approach. Nevertheless, the smoothly executed removal of the leader whose superb campaign had been an important factor in Labor's unlikely victory less than a year earlier was a startling manifestation of the ruthless professionalism which had become characteristic of the ALP during the 1980s. This reshuffle to remove the stigma of 'WA Inc' from the government also included the demotion of other ministers like Parker and Grill who had been active participants in the discredited deals between the government and the entrepreneurs. The new Premier was 41-year-old Dr Carmen Lawrence, who became the first woman to lead a state government anywhere in Australia. Her scholastic record, which included a PhD in psychology, was outstanding, and after entering parliament in 1986 she had acquitted herself capably as minister for Education and Aboriginal Affairs. 'Government involvement in business is over', she firmly declared after her election as leader on 12 February; she stressed her commitment to a new direction which would instil 'trust, openness and confidence in government'. The architects of the reshuffle felt vindicated not only by her sound start as Premier, but also by the results of the March national election when Labor avoided any erosion of its WA strength in the Representatives.

While Labor experienced fluctuating fortunes at state level during the 1980s the Bannon government continued to administer SA competently with a minimum of fuss and fireworks. SA Labor's uninterrupted tenure of office since 1982 confirmed its status as the ALP's most successful state branch during the fourth quarter-century of the party's history. Bannon's style remained low-key, but he consistently recorded a high level of popularity. The widespread respect in the party for his fine leadership was exemplified by the overtures, which he reluctantly accepted, to become national ALP president after Young resigned in March 1988. Although the SA economic climate restricted the Bannon government's capacity to introduce reform, it had accomplished some notable initiatives, especially in the Environment and Planning domain administered by the deputy Premier since 1985, Don Hopgood. These measures included urban renewal programmes to invigorate some of Adelaide's declining inner suburbs, and pioneering action to prevent vegetation destruction. Bannon concentrated on alleviating the state economy's difficulties, in particular by generating innovative sources of revenue for SA. The most celebrated instance was Adelaide's advent as a venue on the Formula One international car racing circuit. Immediately after Adelaide successfully hosted its inaugural Grand Prix in 1985, Bannon called an election and his government was returned with an increased majority. At the following election in November 1989 the SA Liberals conceded that the government was unbeatable on state issues, and spent much of the campaign attacking the high interest rates maintained by the Hawke government. This thrust proved very effective, and the Bannon government began to look vulnerable. On polling day Labor scraped home. Bannon's astute assessments of the electorate's moods was an important element in his success, and he acknowledged after this narrow escape that a new emphasis was required in SA. During the 1980s he had sensed that most SA voters wanted the government's top priority to be sound economic management rather than rapid and flamboyant reform, and he had 'very consciously tried to adjust' to that perception. But he now proposed to inject 'a bit of flair and light' and a distinct 'tinge of green' into his government to meet the challenges of the 1990s.

Like the Bannon government, Victoria's Cain government had performed impressively after coming to power in 1982. Cain was an earnest, hard-working Premier, who enforced the highest standards of probity, and insisted on paying for any stamps used in the Premier's office on his private correspondence. Landeryou soon fell foul of Cain's exacting requirements and was forced by him to resign from cabinet, but there were very few blots of this magnitude on the government's record. Cain's unimpeachable integrity and stern attitude to the expenditure of public funds won him widespread community respect as well as a dour wowserish image. The essential John Cain was a chirpy and amusing companion, but he seemed content to be portrayed as a sober unthreatening figure because he believed that it boosted Labor's prospects of staying in office. With his family background he was acutely aware that Labor had found it extremely difficult in Victoria to attain office and keep it. Indeed the weight of history overwhelmed him at the 1985 election. Poised to become the first Victorian Labor leader to win two consecutive elections – a feat not even his father had accomplished – Cain 'froze' and campaigned poorly; despite his lacklustre electioneering, however, his government's sound, clean, disciplined performance ensured a Labor victory. He campaigned much better at the 1988 election, when his government was re-elected once again. With that triumph Cain established himself – like Wran in NSW and Hawke in the national sphere – as a Labor leader immensely superior to all his predecessors as far as electoral success was concerned.

Factionalism in the Victorian ALP continued to be intense. An attempt was made to reduce the strong influence of the Socialist Left by readmitting to the ALP four right-wing unions who had been outside the party since the 1955 split. The Socialist Left bitterly resented this manoeuvre, but was forced by the national executive to accept it. Incensed left-wingers made their feelings clear at the April 1985 state conference when they hurled abuse and tomatoes at officials of these readmitted unions. At that time the Socialist Left was showing fragmentary tendencies, and eventually it splintered into a number of subdivisions. There was a hard-line old-guard section associated with identities like Crawford and Hartley (who was expelled from the ALP in 1986). More prepared to tolerate the compromises involved in attaining office was a moderate group headed by Gerry Hand. There were also other formations including the Socialist Forum and Democratic Left. In the state branch as a whole the Hand section was the most influential factional group, and was often able to muster the numbers with the aid of the other left groups and sometimes the Independents and unaligned individuals as well.

The Socialist Left gradually increased its influence in the Cain government. Whereas Cain's first cabinet contained only two Socialist Left ministers, there were eight in cabinet in 1990. The faction's senior ministers by 1990 included Dutch-born fitter Peter Spyker, English-born schoolteacher Caroline Hogg (whose husband Bob Hogg succeeded McMullan as national ALP secretary in mid-1988), and education activist Joan Kirner. Hard-working, competent and committed to a community-based approach to politics, Kirner became involved in education after discovering that her eldest child would begin kindergarten in a one-teacher class of over 50 pupils. Her wide-ranging activities during the ensuing years included a stint on the Australian Schools Commission after she was appointed its national parents' representative by the Whitlam government. The leading lights of Labor Unity continued to be Fordham, Crabb, Roper, Treasurer Rob Jolly and David White, who combined a sharp intellect with an insatiable appetite for work and a tough approach, which was typified by his quip that a minister had to be prepared to throw bureaucrats down liftwells in order to make clear who was in charge. Premier Cain had distanced himself from the Independents faction; its most prominent individuals in the government were Walker and barrister Jim Kennan, who had a swift ascent. Kennan was a stylish performer who admired Whitlam and was similarly wholehearted about pursuing reform.

Until the later 1980s the Cain government's determination to stimulate the Victorian economy seemed to be paying off handsomely. The government involved itself directly on a number of fronts, boosting the public sector enthusiastically and reviving a huge aluminium smelter project which had stalled under the previous government. Major government agencies and statutory authorities were instructed to invest their accumulated funds more creatively and profitably. Cain repeatedly talked about getting the state going again, and highlighted the increased number of cranes on the Melbourne skyline since April 1982.

When the activities of the Builders Labourers' Federation were perceived as a hindrance to Victoria's economic rejuvenation, Cain accused the union of 'disgraceful behaviour' and his government, with Crabb at the forefront, took unexpectedly vigorous and ruthless action against it. Government agencies like the Victorian Economic Development Corporation (VEDC) were authorized to provide venture capital for enterprises and projects judged to have merit and potential. The clear contrast between the Cain government's determinedly expansionary approach and the Hawke government's expenditure restraint generated some periodic friction between the two governments; occasionally Keating, in particular, was openly critical of the Victorians. But Cain and Jolly could – and often did – claim that Victoria was outperforming the other states. During the later 1970s national statistics had continually shown that Victoria's levels of unemployment and economic activity were both relatively poor, but after the Cain government came to office the picture changed dramatically. Victoria's proportion of national business investment rose sharply, and for seven years from mid-1983 no state had a lower unemployment rate than Victoria. Worthwhile social reforms were also initiated by the Cain government. The Premier was commendably prominent in enforcing changes to the practices of certain venerable Melbourne institutions which overtly discriminated against women. Other reforms included occupational health and safety legislation, equal opportunity initiatives and liberalized shop trading hours and liquor laws.

The Cain government was rocked by a series of disasters during its third term. While the VEDC had provided financial assistance to a number of successful enterprises, it became apparent that it was also associated with some costly failures and had accumulated losses of over $100 million. Defenders of the VEDC argued that some failures are inevitable whenever investment decisions are made concerning relatively high-risk ventures, and in fact the private banks had been demonstrably worse at 'picking winners'. But there were suggestions that some imprudent decisions had been made by the VEDC board, and the responsible minister, deputy Premier Fordham, eventually succumbed to mounting political pressure and resigned. Worse was to follow. One of Victoria's oldest institutions, the State Bank, had to admit that it had recorded huge lossses, over $2000 million, which were mainly attributable to the reckless lending activities of its merchant banking arm, Tricontinental. Although these activities were related only peripherally to the Cain government's interventionist economic strategy, the government's financial credentials were irretrievably tarnished by the grossly incompetent mismanagement of Tricontinental and the State Bank. It was ironic that such financial irresponsibility could occur while the government was headed by a person of Cain's undeniable frugality. In the hot seat now was Treasurer Jolly, who had already attracted considerable criticism for financial problems concerning WorkCare, the government's workers' compensation scheme. Like Fordham earlier, Jolly had Cain's support as he doggedly resisted calls for his resignation. The reeling Cain government was also troubled by a protracted industrial dispute arising from Kennan's attempts to introduce bitterly contested changes in public transport. With a national election imminent, there were renewed tensions between the state government and some Victorian FPLP members. Hand did not hide his angry criticism of Kennan's handling of the transport dispute. Certain other Canberra identities apparently regretted that the Victorian government had not emulated the deftly executed reconstruction of the WA ministry.

The Victorian ALP was thrown into turmoil by the results of the March 1990

441

national election. After a fine campaign by Hawke his government scraped back to power, capturing five Representatives seats and forfeiting 10. Remarkably, no fewer than nine of those losses occurred in Victoria. The problems in Victoria had singlehandedly brought the most electorally successful national Labor government and Prime Minister to the brink of defeat. For over a week after polling day the state government was in absolute chaos. After moves by some left-wingers for a leadership spill were comfortably defeated, Cain called on the factions to provide him with new faces in the ministry. To his regret, Walker unexpectedly decided to resign, and Jolly reluctantly did likewise. Cain made a sweeping cabinet reshuffle, which included the replacement of Kennan at Transport by Spyker. As the government began the long haul back to regain its former popularity it suffered another devastating blow with the financial collapse of the Pyramid Building Society. Thousands of Victorians had invested in Pyramid, whose proprietors had apparently used depositors' funds in high-risk speculative property development instead of managing it as a conventional building society. 'Deregulation and high interest rates are a pretty heady brew', remarked Cain, who admitted that in his view the Hawke government's deregulation reforms were 'a contributing factor of some consequence' in Pyramid's failure. The Cain government was placed under awesome pressure to reimburse agitated investors, especially since it had, on expert independent advice, publicly endorsed Pyramid's soundness only four months earlier. Although Cain was reluctant to announce a guarantee of reimbursement, which would represent another huge drain on Victoria's finances, a mutinous caucus forced him to do so.

Destabilizing speculation continued to spread about Cain's position as leader. Although Kirner, who had succeeded Fordham as deputy leader, showed unequivocal loyalty to Cain during this trying period, he no longer had the unconditional support of senior Labor Unity figures including Crabb and White. After Cain told stunned MPs at a caucus meeting on 7 August that he was resigning, he made it clear that his decision had resulted from the disappearance of the wholehearted loyalty he had previously enjoyed. Crabb and Kirner were nominated by their factions as leadership contenders. The factional composition of caucus made Kirner a hot favourite, and she won the ballot comfortably to become Australia's second female premier. Crabb did not contest the deputy leadership – 'I'm not the deputy type', he explained – and that position went to Kennan. The new Kirner-Kennan team made a satisfactory start, but as the ALP approached its centenary year every Labor Victorian sensed that the government faced an uphill battle to avoid defeat at the next election.

The turbulence evident in the ALP nationally after the Hawke government's electoral victories in 1987 and 1990 was attributable to the controversial issue of privatization as well as the aftermath of changes in the ministry. The unsettling effect of Cohen's disgruntled departure from the ministry in July 1987 followed by the resignations of three well-known ministers in quick succession (Brown, Ryan and Young) was compounded by the party's reluctance to endorse the sale of government-owned assets, including Australian Airlines, Qantas, Telecom and the Commonwealth Bank. Selling these entities was inconsistent with the commitment to public enterprise embodied in the ALP platform, but Hawke argued that the platform was not 'immutable'. Previous articles of faith like the White Australia policy had been properly deleted in the past, he asserted, and in 1987 there was no good reason why the Australian government should continue to own all of them, especially since they required hefty injections of funds at a time when the government was trying to reduce its expenditure. Labor parliamentarians who publicly aligned themselves with Hawke as the debate proceeded included Keating, Walsh, Evans, Button, Duffy and premiers Burke and Unsworth. Hawke was hoping that the 1988 national conference would recognize that selling some government assets was appropriate, but this did not occur. The strong opposition in Labor ranks to privatization encompassed criticism that its purported economic justification was flawed, but there was a deeper hostility which, as Hayden acknowledged, stemmed from its incompatibility with the 'history', 'traditions' and 'psyche of our party'. Some ALP stalwarts reacted bitterly to Hawke's proposal. Uren, who had just left the Hawke ministry, publicly attacked certain members of the cabinet for their 'blind faith in market forces'. Clyde Cameron blasted the proposal to hand public assets 'to the greedy profiteers of capitalism'. Frank Crean expressed his 'dismay' that an ALP government would consider dismantling successful public enterprises which were part of Labor's 'proud historic record'.

Following the March 1990 election Hawke returned to the privatization issue with redoubled vigour. This time the post-election ministerial reshuffle produced three ex-ministers (West, Duncan and Jones) who publicly vented their spleen at their demotion, but a fourth, Walsh, was the most destabilizing influence. For some time Walsh had been feeling the strain of his demanding role at the heart of the government, and it was no surprise when he opted to step down from the ministry. He was soon revelling in the new-found freedom to air his views unrestrained by cabinet solidarity, but his comments led to some angry exchanges with his former colleagues, Hawke in particular. Government cohesion was further disturbed by ructions involving Richardson and Willis, and also Richardson and Dawkins, but most of all by an extraordinary public rebuke from Keating to Button, who had made some frank remarks to the media once too often for Keating's liking. While all this was going on Hawke appointed Beazley to the Transport and Communications portfolio and encouraged him to get cracking on micro-economic reform and privatization. Beazley was equal to the challenge. He formulated proposals to reform Australian Airlines, Qantas and Telecom, and enthusiastically promoted them within the party. Keating countered with a more daring alternative proposal for Telecom. Many left-wingers refused to concede any need to restructure any of these enterprises, and the Centre Left, as so often, was the relatively indecisive meat in the sandwich. A special national conference was scheduled for 24 September, and debate raged through all levels of the party. 'What is going on', observed national secretary Hogg, who accepted the need for reform, 'is the most critical shift in party thinking. . .in the last 30 years'.

Late in August there was a dramatic new twist in the privatization debate. Keating and Kirner, who had been Victorian Premier for less than three weeks, jointly announced the sale of Victoria's troubled State Bank to the Commonwealth Bank for $2000 million. The Commonwealth Bank acquired the healthy operations of the State Bank, and the Kirner government obtained much-needed funds to reduce its debt. Kirner described her government's bold action as a regrettable but necessary decision to remove 'the Tricontinental albatross' which threatened to blight the state's finances for years. It was 'the toughest decision that I. . .will ever have to make', she said. 'It would have been economically irresponsible to do anything else.' The rapport quickly established by Keating and Kirner was underlined when he commended the Premier's 'forthright' and 'decisive' approach. For Keating it was a triumph. The beleaguered Victorian government was assisted, the Commonwealth Bank was enlarged and strengthened, and in the circumstances there was minimal party opposition to his plan to fund the purchase by a 30% partial privatization of the Commonwealth Bank.

But Keating was less successful in the battle over Telecom's future, since cabinet decided to support Beazley's proposal. After intense factional negotiations Beazley and the government carried the day at the special conference, where debate was spirited and at times – especially concerning Telecom – very technical. Grappling with the intricacies of telecommunications was, Beazley remarked, 'like amateurs preparing to deal with brain surgery'. Nevertheless, he added, 'we must confront these issues', which he described as crucial to Australia's future. At stake, he and Richardson insisted, were potential exports worth billions of dollars. The conference amended the ALP platform to allow the total privatization of Australian Airlines, the partial privatization of Qantas, and the introduction of 'an effective competitive framework' in telecommunications. Numerous rank-and-file activists felt dismayed and angry.

At the conference Barry Jones warned that if the party continued to treat its rank and file cavalierly it would do so at its peril. While praising the Hawke government's 'enormous achievements', he declared that the future of the ALP was 'under challenge':

> I would argue that a Party cannot survive simply on the basis of a commitment to economic efficiency, political pragmatism and a particular set of leaders. It must have an ideology too. I agree that that ideology has to be refined and updated. But it needs to be there.

Jones added that 'we cannot remake or reshape the party by bypassing its structures'. He called for 'a commitment by the Government that it will follow party processes in broad policy formulation', and recommended 'a membership drive' to make the ALP 'a large and growing party'. Branch membership had declined to around 50 000 nationally from about 75 000 in the mid-1970s.

ALTHOUGH THERE HAD been conflict between the actions of ALP politicians and the desires of the Labor faithful ever since the party's inception, in other respects the ALP had changed profoundly during its first 100 years. Labor's organization had become much tighter and more professional. Disciplined factions had become entrenched. National ALP conferences were conducted with such relative orderliness that onlooking journalists reminisced nostalgically about the blood-and-thunder gatherings of the past. Compared to the ALP's early years the party platform had become larger and more comprehensive, which reduced the scope for individual freedom on policy issues. Labor had also become much more of a national party with a national perspective. The capacity of the national executive to intervene in state branch affairs if the standing of the party as a whole was affected by preselection squabbles or other developments was firmly established.

Another change concerned the slick campaigning skills utilized by ALP officials and specialist consultants to maximize Labor's voting share, techniques which were substantially influenced by the media's coverage of Australian politics and unrecognizably different from the party's earliest electioneering methods. The days of spruiking on street corners while mounted on a soap-box were well in the past. Even the formal meeting, which was until relatively recently a standard item on the campaign trail, was, apart from the policy launch, no longer part of the leader's itinerary by 1987. By then Hawke's campaigning consisted of press conferences, a host of media interviews and 'photo opportunities' (staged stunts for the television news), and press-the-flesh promenades as he swept through suburban shopping centres surrounded by an entourage of minders and media personnel. From the mid-1960s politicians had to contend with intensive and intrusive media scrutiny, and the realization that the slightest slip could have momentous consequences when televised that evening. Electioneering for the rank and file had changed much less over the years. Still of vital importance were tasks like door-knocking and distributing propaganda, pro-Labor advocacy to work colleagues and social acquaintances, and handing out how-to-vote material on polling day. Another facet of campaigning was the escalating cost. With prime-time advertising rates high and media exposure regarded as crucial, the cost of national election campaigns soared during Labor's tenth decade.

Other changes in the ALP during its first 100 years mirrored changed social attitudes in Australia. For decades the ALP – unlike the British Labour Party – had been bedevilled by the prevalence of sectarianism in Australia manifest in the intense divisions over state aid. From this viewpoint the decline in committed religious affiliation in Australia since the 1960s was a blessing for the party. The attitude to Aborigines and White Australia had also become very different in both the ALP and the wider community. Developments in Australian society generally were also reflected in the changed composition of the ALP: the party's most recent candidates tended to be better educated and more middle-class and were more likely to be of ethnic origin.

They were also more likely to be women. As recently as 1978 only three FPLP members and 11 state Labor MPs were women, yet 12 years later the number of ALP women MPs in Canberra and the state parliaments had quadrupled to 56. The affirmative action programme had proved very successful. Not only had women become more prominent at senior levels of the ALP; their influence had contributed to the greater responsiveness to women's concerns by the party, which was in turn reflected in its electoral victories during 1982–83 and subsequently. Women and men at last voted Labor in similar proportions, ending the tradition that women were significantly less likely than men to vote ALP. In 1984 Hawke publicly acknowledged that the contribution of Labor women, enhanced by affirmative action, had been 'of central importance' to the party's recent electoral success. The Hawke government's commitment to women's interests was shown in its legislation on sex discrimination and affirmative action, and also in many other policy areas affecting women. More than 80 women were appointed by the government to senior administrative positions during its first 18 months in office; no woman had ever been appointed to the High Court bench until the Hawke government chose Mary Gaudron to fill the vacancy created by Murphy's death. During the 1987 post-election negotiations about the composition of the ministry, Hawke told FPLP faction leaders that he wanted three women ministers (there had previously been only one, Ryan). After his intervention Ryan was joined in the ministry by Ros Kelly and Senator Margaret Reynolds.

Two powerful constraints on the ALP's effectiveness had not changed. Most significant of all was the impact of developments beyond Australian shores. As a middle-sized player in the international arena, Australia was severely buffeted by disruptions originating overseas – continually by economic fluctuations, and periodically by other phenomena like major wars. Another major problem for the ALP was Australia's inflexible Constitution. By the 1980s its malign influence on the process of sound government in Australia was starkly apparent, yet changing it was fraught with difficulty owing to anti-Labor's negative attitude. Even the mild initiatives in the Hawke government's four referendum proposals in 1988 met with hostility from the conservatives. It was greatly to Hawke's credit that he was prepared in 1990 to embark on another bid to achieve bipartisan support for constitutional reform, even though precedent provided meagre grounds for optimism.

Some facets of the ALP had not altered during its first 100 years. 'The Trade Union Movement, with its strengths and its weaknesses, its insights and its myopia, its numbers and its financial support, its toughness and its tenacity, remains the core' of the ALP. That observation made in the early 1950s retained its validity almost 40 years later. The party was still a broad-based coalition of interest groups and individuals with varying perspectives on the desirable pace and priorities of reform. A proportion of its membership proclaimed or professed a commitment to socialism, as some ALP members always had; the collective attachment to socialism had fluctuated in the past, and it waned during the party's tenth decade. The differences within the ALP guaranteed internal tension, which was still manifested frequently in bitter discord derived from 'a peculiar amalgam of passion, principle and personality'. Preselections were as fiercely contested as ever; robust resilience continued to be a temperamental prerequisite for advancement. The activities of rank-and-file ALP members still centred around the local branch meeting and assistance with campaigning and fund-raising. Despite the prominence of the high fliers, these local branch activists remained the heart and soul of the party. At the end of the ALP's first 100 years, as at the start, these stalwarts were committed to uplifting the disadvantaged and downtrodden as Labor pressed on towards its goal of a more equal, just and tolerant society for all Australians, the noble objective described by Chifley as the light on the hill.

Endnotes

The range of sources relevant to a history of the ALP is massive, and this book is a product of very extensive research. The main areas of research were the party's own records, the substantial number of published volumes relating to the party, the Manuscripts collection at the National Library, the Oral History collection at the National Library, and articles in various politics and history journals: for example, I examined every issue of *Historical Studies*, *Labour History*, *Politics*, *Australian Journal of Politics and History* and *Flinders Journal of History and Politics*.

These endnotes are not exhaustive (although all sources of direct quotations are included) since complete documentation would have considerably lengthened an already long book and counteracted the most fundamental objective underlying this publication – to produce a comprehensive history which was not only accurate and very readable, but also as accessible and affordable as possible. However, I intend to deposit a lengthy bibliography in the National Library and, to assist non-Canberra residents who wish to use it, I will stipulate that it may be photocopied. Anyone interested should contact the Manuscripts section and ask for the collection numbered MS 8217.

At the start of each chapter's notes is a list of the sources which were particularly informative for that chapter. Some sources were very useful for many chapters – notably C. Hughes and B. Graham, *A Handbook of Australian Government and Politics 1890–1964* (and the sequels by Hughes covering the years 1965–1984), and the superb volumes of the *Australian Dictionary of Biography*. Abbreviations used in listing the sources are as follows:

A & R	Angus & Robertson
ADB	*Australian Dictionary of Biography*
AJPH	*Australian Journal of Politics and History*
ANUP	Australian National University Press
AWM	Australian War Memorial
CPD	*Commonwealth Parliamentary Debates*
H & I	Hale and Iremonger
MSS	Manuscripts collection
MUP	Melbourne University Press

NLA   National Library of Australia
OH   Oral History interview
OUP   Oxford University Press
UQP   University of Queensland Press
UWAP   University of Western Australia Press
VPD   *Victorian Parliamentary Debates*

1   'The Ballot is the Thing', 1891

MAIN SOURCES:
V. Burgmann, *In Our Time* (Allen & Unwin, Sydney, 1985).
R. Gollan, *Radical and Working Class Politics* (MUP, Melbourne, 1960).
P. Loveday, A.W. Martin & R.S. Parker (eds), *The Emergence of the Australian Party System* (H & I, Sydney, 1977).
D.J. Murphy (ed.), *Labor in Politics* (UQP, Brisbane, 1975).
D.J. Murphy, R.B. Joyce & C.A. Hughes (eds), *Prelude to Power* (Jacaranda, Brisbane, 1970).
B. Nairn, *Civilising Capitalism* (ANUP, Canberra, 1973).

page 1	Hinchcliffe's telegram: *Labor in Politics*, p. 145.
2	Hinchcliffe's angry reply: *Prelude to Power*, p. 268.
4	'Socialism is being mates': Burgmann, p. 24.
5	George's magnetic personality: L. Fitzhardinge, *William Morris Hughes Volume 1: That Fiery Particle 1862–1914* (A & R, Sydney, 1964), p. 26.
5	'Australia for the Australians': R. Ward, *A Nation for a Continent* (Heinemann, Melbourne, 1977), p. 24.
5	'Australians being degraded. . .': *Labor in Politics*, p. 137.
6	Lane's extravagant view of the ALF: R.N. Ebbels, *The Australian Labor Movement 1850–1907* (Lansdowne, Melbourne, 1965), p. 166.
6	The ALF's reasoning: W.G. Spence, *Australia's Awakening* (Worker Trustees, Sydney, 1909), p. 177.
6	'The Reorganization of Society. . .': *Labor in Politics*, p. 141.
7	Kidston's verse: *Prelude to Power*, pp. 271–3.
7	'Leave no stone unturned. . .': *Labor in Politics*, p. 146.
7	Bowman at the congress: *Labor in Politics*, p. 147.
7	Liberals' non-acknowledgement of UTLC: *Labor in Politics*, pp. 236–7.
8	Guthrie: *ADB* Volume 9.
8	*Advertiser* quoted in J. Scarfe, 'The Labour Wedge: The South Australian Council Elections of 1891', *Teaching History* 7, 2, 1973, p. 33.
9	'Fire low. . .': F. Crowley (ed.), *A Documentary History of Australia 1875–1900* (Nelson, Melbourne, 1980), pp. 304–5.
9	The ITUC resolution: Ebbels, p. 100.
9	Hancock on Australia's needs: J. Rickard, *Class and Politics* (ANUP, Canberra, 1976), pp. 27–8.
11	Spence-Brennan manifesto: Spence, p. 87.
11	Taylor's claim: Gollan, p. 135.
11	Platform planks: Nairn, pp. 44–5.
12	Bourke branch's platform variation: Nairn, p. 145.
12	Brennan jubilant: *Labor in Politics*, p. 25.
13	Edden: *ADB* Volume 8.
13	G.D. Clark: *ADB* Volume 8.
14	Murphy's view: Burgmann, p. 81.
14	Lane's summing-up: C.M.H. Clark (ed.), *Select Documents in Australian History 1851–1900* (A & R, Sydney, 1955), pp. 585–6.

14   Deakin on Labor's rise: J.A. La Nauze, *Alfred Deakin* (MUP, Melbourne, 1965), p. 144.

2   Support in Return for Concessions, 1891–1904

MAIN SOURCES:
V. Burgmann, *In Our Time* (Allen & Unwin, Sydney, 1985).
R. Gollan, *Radical and Working Class Politics* (MUP, Melbourne, 1960).
P. Loveday, A.W. Martin & R.S. Parker (eds), *The Emergence of the Australian Party System* (H & I, Sydney, 1977).
D.J. Murphy (ed.), *Labor in Politics* (UQP, Brisbane, 1975).
D.J. Murphy, R.B. Joyce & C.A. Hughes (eds), *Prelude to Power* (Jacaranda, Brisbane, 1970).
B. Nairn, *Civilising Capitalism* (ANUP, Canberra, 1973).

page 15   Black's forthright speech: C.M.H. Clark (ed.), *Select Documents in Australian History 1851–1900* (A & R, Sydney, 1955), p. 579.
16   McGowen: Nairn, p. 72.
16   *Australian Workman*: Burgmann, pp. 74–5.
16   Lane's reaction: Gollan, p. 146; Burgmann, p. 23.
17   Holman: *ADB* Volume 9.
17   Black disheartened: Nairn, p. 88.
18   Dodd's motion: Nairn, p. 95.
18   Black's suggestion and Clark's refusal: Nairn, p. 96.
18   Labor's 'wretched squabbling': H.V. Evatt, *William Holman* (A & R, Sydney, 1979), p. 45.
18   Griffith's sporting talents: Nairn, p. 118.
19   The reactionary MLC is quoted in J. Rickard, *Class and Politics* (ANUP, Canberra, 1976), p. 135.
19   No reward for past services: L. Fitzhardinge, *William Morris Hughes Volume 1: That Fiery Particle 1862–1914* (A & R, Sydney, 1964), p. 62.
19   Widening of opportunity: Nairn, p. 151.
19–20   Holman's grumble and Hughes's reply: Nairn, p. 151.
20   Hughes on 'what we prevent...': Nairn, p. 155.
20   Allegation that women were uninvolved: Nairn, p. 142.
20   Macdonell's views: P. Ford, *Cardinal Moran and the ALP* (MUP, Melbourne, 1966), p. 220.
20   Holman's retort: Ford, p. 216.
20   Black's criticism: Nairn, p. 164.
20–1   Ferguson's opinion: Nairn, p. 167.
21   Criticism of MPs' neglect: Burgmann, p. 86.
21   Labor's degeneration into a vote-catching machine: Burgmann, p. 88.
21   PLL as the people's watchdogs: Nairn, p. 188.
22   Labor's peculiar aura: Nairn, p. 186.
22   Henry Lawson wrote a poem about 'the hope of something better': C.M.H. Clark, *A History of Australia Volume 5* (MUP, Melbourne, 1981), p. 101.
22   Hughes on the Boer War: B. Penny, 'The Australian Debate on the Boer War', *Historical Studies* 56, 1971, p. 529.
23   Desperate Langwell supporter: R.N. Ebbels, *The Australian Labor Movement 1850–1907* (Lansdowne, Melbourne, 1965), p. 27.
24   Lane: *ADB* Volume 9.
24   Lane's lack of hope: G. Souter, *A Peculiar People* (Sydney University Press, Sydney, 1981), p. 186.
24   Labor candidates should be sober men: *Labor in Politics*, p. 153.

24   Ryan uncomplaining: W.G. Spence, *Australia's Awakening* (Worker Trustees, Sydney, 1909), p. 177.
25   Hoolan: *ADB* Volume 9.
26   Hoolan's cheerful acquiescence: Loveday & others, p. 126.
27   Hoolan: *ADB* Volume 9.
27   Reid cutting political throats and denouncing brainy democrats: *Prelude to Power*, p. 228.
28   Dawson's outspokenness: L.M. Field, *The Forgotten War* (MUP, Melbourne, 1979), p. 29.
28   'Bundaberg goes white': Gollan, p. 147.
29   McDonnell: *ADB* Volume 10.
29   Hooper: *ADB* Volume 9.
30   Archibald: *ADB* Volume 7.
30   Batchelor's 'unassuming manner': Fitzhardinge, p. 121.
31   *Southern Cross* hostile: *Labor in Politics*, p. 247.
32   Batchelor's lecture: E.L. Batchelor, *The Labor Party and Its Progress* (Webb & Son, Adelaide, 1895).
32   McPherson: *ADB* Volume 10.
32   Federation and the ULP platform: *Labor in Politics*, p. 247.
32   Archibald's attack: S. Bennett (ed.), *Federation* (Cassell, Melbourne, 1975), p. 125.
32   Guthrie's nautical metaphor: Bennett, p. 11.
32   Price's denunciation: L.F. Crisp, *Federation Prophets without Honour* (ANU Central Printery, Canberra, 1980), p. 49.
33   Roberts on feather-bed soldiers: Field, p. 25.
33   Roberts rebuked: Loveday & others, p. 260.
35   Conservatives' disclaimer: Clark, *A History of Australia Volume 5*, p. 113.
36   Turner: R. Bedford, *Naught to Thirty-three* (MUP, Melbourne, 1976), p. 264.
36   Tunnecliffe: N. Brennan, *John Wren Gambler* (Hill of Content, Melbourne, 1971), p. 203.
36   *Tocsin*'s attack: *Labor in Politics*, p. 303.
36   Hughes on Victorian Labor: Nairn, p. 163.
37   *Tocsin* on Trenwith: J. Rickard, *H.B. Higgins* (Allen & Unwin, Sydney, 1984), p. 107; *Labor in Politics*, p. 306.
38   Métin on Australasia: A. Métin, *Socialism without Doctrine* (Alternative Publishing Co-operative, Sydney, 1977), foreword.
38   Métin and the workers' paradise: Métin, p. 177.
38   Queensland Labor mocked: J. Tampke, 'Pace Setter or Quiet Backwater?: German Literature on Australia's Labour Movement and Social Policies 1890–1914', *Labour History* 36, 1979, p. 14.
38   Lux's impressions: Tampke, *Labour History*, p. 6.
38   SPD moderates: Tampke, *Labour History*, p. 7.
39   Kirk: *Labor in Politics*, p. 390.
39   North-south jealousy: *Labor in Politics*, p. 391.
39   MPs kicking away the ladder: *Labor in Politics*, p. 394.
40   Earle: *ADB* Volume 8.
40   Labor slow and unsatisfactory in Tasmania: Burgmann, p. 138.
40   Inter-village feuds: *Labor in Politics*, p. 344.
40   A 'stake in the country': Loveday & others, p. 302.
41   Vosper's streaming mane: Clark, *A History of Australia Volume 5*, p. 110.
42   *West Australian*'s displeasure: Loveday & others, p. 330.
42   *Westralian Worker*'s motto: Burgmann, p. 165.
43   *Westralian Worker* on Johnson: *Labor in Politics*, p. 356.
43   Labor's fundamental problems: *Labor in Politics*, pp. 354–5.

43   *Worker*'s Sydney office: I. Turner, *Industrial Labour and Politics* (ANUP, Canberra, 1965), p. 26.
44   Queenslanders' proposal: Turner, p. 26.
44   Mahon: *ADB* Volume 10.
44   Bamford: *ADB* Volume 7.
44   Parliamentary action as superior method of warfare: Nairn, p. 30.
45   O'Malley: G. Cockerill, *Scribblers and Statesmen* (Melbourne, 1944), pp. 113–14.
47   Watson's amendment: J.A. La Nauze, *Alfred Deakin* (MUP, Melbourne, 1965), p. 281.
47   Pearce's speech: *CPD*, 13 November 1901, p. 7160.
47   Watson's speech: *CPD*, 6 September 1901, p. 4633.
48   Maloney to Irvine: L. Benham & J. Rickard, 'Masters and Servants', in J. Iremonger, J. Merritt & G. Osborne (eds), *Strikes* (A & R, Sydney, 1973), p. 20.
48   Kalgoorlie branch's resolution: P. Weller (ed.), *Caucus Minutes 1901– 1949: Volume 1 1901–1917* (MUP, Melbourne, 1975), pp. 111–12.
48   Wellington TLC's congratulations: A. Cooper to J.C. Watson, 14 January 1904, Watson MSS, NLA.
48   Labor's organization praised: R. Norris, *The Emergent Commonwealth* (MUP, Melbourne, 1975), p. 175.
48   *Argus*'s wail: Burgmann, p. 112.

3   'To Lose Our Distinctness Would Mean Failure': Flirting with Alliances, 1904–1910

MAIN SOURCES:
L. Fitzhardinge, *William Morris Hughes Volume 1: That Fiery Particle 1862–1914* (A & R, Sydney, 1964).
P. Loveday, A.W. Martin & R.S. Parker, *The Emergence of the Australian Party System* (H & I, Sydney, 1977).
D.J. Murphy (ed.), *Labor in Politics* (UQP, Brisbane, 1975).
D.J. Murphy, R.B. Joyce & C.A. Hughes (eds), *Prelude to Power* (Jacaranda, Brisbane, 1970).
P. Weller (ed.), *Caucus Minutes 1901–1949: Volume 1 1901–1917* (MUP, Melbourne, 1975).

page 50   'To say we were astonished. . .': J. Groom (ed.), *Nation Building in Australia* (A & R, Sydney, 1941), p. 239.
50   Coalition ministry proposal: *Caucus Minutes*, pp. 125–6.
51   New Guinea massacre: W. Hughes to J.C. Watson, 3 May 1929, Watson MSS, NLA.
51   *Argus*: F. Crowley (ed.), *Modern Australia in Documents 1901–1939* (Wren, Melbourne, 1973), p. 63.
51   Forrest apoplectic: G. Cockerill, *Scribblers and Statesmen* (Melbourne, 1944), p. 165.
51   Deakin assuring fair play: J.A. La Nauze, *Alfred Deakin* (MUP, Melbourne, 1965), p. 368.
51   Deakin ruling out a coalition: *Caucus Minutes*, p. 131.
51   Watson exasperated: N. Palmer, *Henry Bournes Higgins* (Harrap, London, 1931), p. 177.
51   O'Malley feeling muzzled: H.S. Broadhead, The Australian Federal Labour Party 1900–1905, MA thesis, Melbourne University, 1959, p. 149.
51   Deakin on Hughes: La Nauze, p. 378.

51   Victorian executive's announcement: *Caucus Minutes*, p. 142.
52   Taylor's blast, then silence: *Labor in Politics*, p. 356.
52   *Geraldton Express*: *ADB* Volume 8 (J.M. Drew).
52   Daglish's mark time policy: *ADB* Volume 8.
52   Lynch: *ADB* Volume 10; L. Dumas, *The Story of a Full Life* (Sun, Melbourne, 1969), p. 19.
53   Inglorious episode: C.T. Stannage (ed.), *A New History of Western Australia* (UWAP, Perth, 1981), p. 350.
53   Bath's impeccable union background: *Labor in Politics*, p. 361.
53   Mann: *ADB* Volume 10.
54   Kidston 'a giant among pygmies': D. Murphy, R. Joyce & M. Cribb (eds), *The Premiers of Queensland* (UQP, Brisbane, 1990), p. 234.
54   Kerr resisting sectarianism: G. Kerr to A. Fisher, 7 May 1904, Fisher MSS, NLA.
55   Lesina: *ADB* Volume 10.
55   Boote's views: *Prelude to Power*, pp. 203–4, 65.
55   Reid's amendment: *Labor in Politics*, p. 171.
55   Kerr-Kidston statement: *Prelude to Power*, p. 280.
55   Dunstan's concern: T. Dunstan to A. Fisher, 9 November 1905, Fisher MSS, NLA.
56   The 1905 NSW conference and the objective: *Labor in Politics*, p. 67.
56   Demolishers of society: *Freeman's Journal*, 11 February 1905.
56   Moran's attack: *ADB* Volume 10.
56–7   Watson's rejoinder: unidentified newscutting in cuttings volume, C.E. Frazer MSS, NLA.
57   Proceedings at the 1905 federal conference are outlined in the printed conference report.
57   Locke abstaining: 1905 federal conference report, pp. 12–13.
57   Locke 'civil equality' motion: 1905 federal conference report, p. 22.
57   Watson's encouragement: La Nauze, pp. 390–1.
57   FPLP's stronger support for Deakin: La Nauze, p. 398.
57   Watson's caucus motion: *Caucus Minutes*, pp. 158–9.
57–8   Debate on the FPLP's policy on alliances is outlined on pp. 19–20 of the 1905 federal conference report.
58   Watson's letter to caucus members: Watson MSS (451/1/97), NLA.
58   Price's policy speech: *Labor in Politics*, p. 257.
59   *Weekly Herald*'s explanation: *Labor in Politics*, p. 258.
59   Labor's platform: Loveday & others, p. 279.
59   Price's acceptance of the compromise: J. Moss, *Sound of Trumpets* (Wakefield, Adelaide, 1985), p. 212.
59   The Reid-Holman debate: *ADB* Volume 9 (W.A. Holman).
59   Hughes's verbal pyrotechnics: Fitzhardinge, p. 171.
60   Watson on Queensland: J.C. Watson to A. Deakin, 17 December 1906, Watson MSS, NLA.
60   Reid's speech: *Prelude to Power*, p. 283.
61   Reid assessed: *Labor in Politics*, pp. 173, 176; *Prelude to Power*, p. 233.
61   VSP as a ginger-group: *Labor in Politics*, p. 313.
61   Foster recalling the debate: C. Larmour, *Labor Judge* (H & I, Sydney, 1985), p. 27.
62   Blue Mountains plea: E. O'Donoghue to J.C. Watson, 20 October 1907, Watson MSS, NLA.
62   Mrs Watson's disarming response: *Punch* (Melbourne), 24 October 1907.
62   Brunswick branch: W. Davis to J.C. Watson, 29 October 1907, Watson MSS, NLA.
62   Watson never the same: *Punch* (Melbourne), 24 October 1907.

63   Spence not at home in politics: Fitzhardinge, p. 120.
63   'Dashed off at top speed': Fitzhardinge, p. 206.
63   Fisher's speech: 1908 federal conference report, p. 13.
64   Hughes's scheme: Fitzhardinge, p. 138.
64   Fisher's 1903 opposition: *CPD*, 5 August 1903, pp. 3103–5.
64   Hughes clashing with British Labour critics: Fitzhardinge, p. 192.
64   Dwyer and O'Malley: 1908 federal conference report, p. 17.
65   Conference's extensive debate on New Protection is outlined in its report.
65   Frazer: *ADB* Volume 8.
66   Watson's concession: 1908 federal conference report, p. 27.
66   Watson's rearguard action: *Caucus Minutes*, p. 224.
66   Hutchison: *ADB* Volume 9.
66   'Pearce, old boy': G. Pearce, *Carpenter to Cabinet* (Hutchinson, London, 1951), pp. 68–9.
67   Fisher congratulated: British Labour Party to A. Fisher, 1 April 1909, Fisher MSS, NLA.
67   'Above all things...': W. Hughes to H. Mahon, 15 March 1909, Mahon MSS, NLA.
67   Spence's praise: W.G. Spence, *Australia's Awakening* (Worker Trustees, Sydney, 1909), p. 263.
67   With indecent haste: La Nauze, p. 535.
68   Holder: *ADB* Volume 9.
68   Hughes at high pressure: Fitzhardinge, pp. 218–19.
68   'On the one side...': Spence, p. 264.
68   'Monster meeting...': B. Watkins to A. Fisher, 30 May 1909, Fisher MSS, NLA.
68   *Mercury*'s woe: *Labor in Politics*, pp. 406.
69   SA Labor's triumph: *Labor in Politics*, p. 264.
69   Forrest's growl: J. Rickard, *Class and Politics* (ANUP, Canberra, 1976), p. 253.
69   Hutchison: *ADB* Volume 9.
70   The 'mystical element': E. Lyons, *So We Take Comfort* (Heinemann, Melbourne, 1965), p. 171.

4   'Our Unequalled Progress': Planks Made Law, 1910–1914

MAIN SOURCES:
H.V. Evatt, *William Holman* (A & R, Sydney, 1979).
L. Fitzhardinge, *William Morris Hughes Volume 1: That Fiery Particle 1862–1914* (A & R, Sydney, 1964).
D. Murphy (ed.), *Labor in Politics* (UQP, Brisbane, 1975).
P. Weller (ed.), *Caucus Minutes 1901–1949: Volume 1 1901–1917* (MUP, Melbourne, 1975).

page 71   Culmination of 20 years: biographical article on Fisher in Buchanan MSS, NLA.
71   O'Malley on Deakin: A.R. Hoyle, *King O'Malley* (Macmillan, Melbourne, 1981), p. 110.
72   McGowen's 'rock-like lack of brilliance': J.A. La Nauze, *Alfred Deakin* (MUP, Melbourne, 1965), p. 430.
73   'State Insects' and 'Big Australians': Evatt, p. 196.

73	Lamond attacking 'traitors': *Daily Telegraph*, 30 January 1911.
73	Kidston's claim: unidentified newscutting in Fisher MSS (2919/10/60), NLA.
73	Betrayal of the conference decision: Evatt, p. 204.
73	Rae's disapproval: G. Souter, *Lion and Kangaroo* (Collins, Sydney, 1976), p. 157.
73	Second plank of fighting platform: *Labor in Politics*, p. 78.
73	Holman utterly dumbfounded: Evatt, p. 208.
74	Batchelor on Aboriginal welfare: *ADB* Volume 7.
74	Fisher's relief: C.B. Fletcher, *The Great Wheel* (A & R, Sydney, 1940), p. 165.
74	Batchelor's commonsense and judgement: *ADB* Volume 7.
74	Watson on Batchelor: *Sun* (Sydney), 8 May 1927.
74	Gardiner-Rae motion: *Caucus Minutes*, p. 289.
76	O'Malley as 'jagged thorn. . .': R. Gollan, *The Commonwealth Bank of Australia* (ANUP, Canberra, 1968), p. 99.
76	Hughes complaining: W. Hughes to A. Fisher, 31 July 1911, Fisher MSS, NLA.
76	'This is not a damned circus': G. Pearce, *Carpenter to Cabinet* (Hutchinson, London, 1951), p. 109.
76–7	O'Malley on Canberra: Hoyle, pp. 107, 113, 117; L. Noye, *O'Malley MHR* (Neptune, Geelong, 1985), pp. 181–2.
77	O'Malley on the transcontinental railway: G. Souter, *Acts of Parliament* (MUP, Melbourne, 1988), p. 126.
77	'Fisher's Flimsies': A.N. Smith, *Thirty Years* (Brown, Prior & Co, Melbourne, 1933), p. 116.
77	Anstey's torrent of words: *CPD*, 19 August 1910, p. 1829.
78	Fisher and Hughes on the bank: Gollan, p. 103.
78	Verran: D. Dunstan, *Felicia* (Macmillan, Melbourne, 1981), p. 10.
78	Lundie: *ADB* Volume 10.
78	Verran's pronouncements during the strikes: J. Moss, *Sound of Trumpets* (Wakefield, Adelaide, 1985), pp. 221, 222.
78	The 'so called Labor government': Moss, p. 223.
79	The 'damned Wages Board system': Moss, p. 224.
79	More violence, police action, etc.: *Labor in Politics*, p. 265.
79	'Citizen defence force. . .': 1912 federal conference report, p. 52.
80	Fisher on unification: 1912 federal conference report, pp. 10–11.
80	Watson on state delegations to conference: 1912 federal conference report, p. 43.
80	Collings: *ADB* Volume 8.
81	Bowman's blast: D.J. Murphy, R.B. Joyce & C.A. Hughes (eds), *Prelude to Power* (Jacaranda, Brisbane, 1970), p. 139.
82	McDonald: *ADB* Volume 10.
84	Macdonnell: *ADB* Volume 10.
84	Carmichael: *ADB* Volume 7.
84	Holman out of sorts, then livid: Evatt, p. 235–7.
85	Fisher and McGregor embarrassing Hughes: Fitzhardinge, p. 273.
85	A 'mediocrity': G. Sawer, *Australian Federalism in the Courts* (MUP, Melbourne, 1967), p. 65.
85	Piddington's reply: Fitzhardinge, p. 277.
85	A 'blizzard of scandalized protest': *Bulletin*, 3 April 1913.
85	Constitutionally colourless: Sawer, p. 65.
86	Frazer's cable: M. Shepherd to A. Fisher, 23 May 1913, Fisher MSS, NLA.
86	No votes in yesterday's reforms: *Australian*, 26 March 1988.
88	Lowered expectations: P. Loveday, A.W. Martin & R.S. Parker, *The*

Emergence of the Australian Party System (H & I, Sydney, 1977), p. 115.

88   Falsehoods in Tasmania: *Labor in Politics*, p. 421.
88   Gladiators from across the Straits: *Labor in Politics*, p. 421.
88   Lyons: P.R. Hart, 'J.A. Lyons, Tasmanian Labour Leader', *Labour History* 9, 1965, pp. 34–5.
89   Hughes on constitutional butchery: C. Cunneen, *King's Men* (Allen & Unwin, Sydney, 1983), p. 114.
89   Mahon: newscutting labelled 'Punch Dec 1914', Mahon MSS (Series 13), NLA.
90   Labor MPs adjusting: B. Nairn, *Civilising Capitalism* (ANUP, Canberra, 1973), p. 18.
90   Lenin's criticism: R.N. Ebbels, *The Australian Labor Movement 1850–1907* (Lansdowne, Melbourne, 1965), p. 243.
90   Fisher on socialism: 1908 federal conference report, p. 14.

5 'Blowing the Labor Party to Shreds': The Great War and the Great Split, 1914–1919

MAIN SOURCES:
H.V. Evatt, *William Holman* (A & R, Sydney, 1979).
L. Fitzhardinge, *William Morris Hughes Volume 2: The Little Digger 1914–1952* (A & R, Sydney, 1979).
D.J. Murphy (ed.), *Labor in Politics* (UQP, Brisbane, 1975).
P. Weller (ed.), *Caucus Minutes 1901–1949 Volume 1 1901–1917* (MUP, Melbourne, 1975) & *Volume 2 1917–1931* (MUP, Melbourne 1975).

page 92   *Labor Call*: L. Robson, *Australia and the Great War* (Macmillan, Melbourne, 1970), p. 32.
92   Boote in the *Australian Worker*: I. Turner, *Industrial Labour and Politics* (ANUP, Canberra, 1965), pp. 69–70.
93   Fisher at Colac: Robson, p. 31.
93   Fisher 'absolutely in disagreement': Fitzhardinge, p. 6.
93   Fisher's understatement: A. Fisher to M. Fisher, 29 August 1914, Fisher MSS, NLA.
94–5   Anstey: Fitzhardinge, pp. 31–4.
95   O'Malley, Hughes, Brennan on the WPA: Fitzhardinge, pp. 34–5.
95   Anstey owing no allegiance: G. Sawer, *Australian Federal Politics and Law 1901–1929* (MUP, Melbourne, 1956), p. 141.
95   Australia wild with joy: G. Pearce to W. Bridges, 16 May 1915, Pearce MSS, AWM.
96   Inducement to Nevanas: *Labor in Politics*, p. 368.
96   Earle urging a truce: M. Lake, 'John Earle and the Concept of the "Labor Rat"', *Labour History* 33, 1977, p. 35.
96   Holman at state conference: Evatt, pp. 266–7.
96   O'Malley critical of Hughes: A.R. Hoyle, *King O'Malley* (Macmillan, Melbourne, 1981), p. 149.
97   Complaints about the black-coated brigade: *Labor in Politics*, p. 271.
97   'Probably at no other time. . .': D.J. Murphy, 'The Establishment of State Enterprises in Queensland, 1915–1918', *Labour History* 14, 1968, p. 15.
97   Adamson: *ADB* Volume 7.
98   Hamilton: A. Johnson, *Fly a Rebel Flag* (Penguin, Melbourne, 1986), pp. 30–1.

98 Fihelly: *ADB* Volume 8.
98 Resolution on the referenda: 1915 federal conference report, p. 10.
99 Boote's foreboding: *Australian Worker*, 28 October 1915.
99 Watt accusing Brennan: *ADB* Volume 7 (F. Brennan).
99 Barker's poster: I. Turner, *Sydney's Burning* (Alpha, Sydney, 1969), p. 15.
100 Murdoch letter: D. Zwar, *In Search of Keith Murdoch* (Macmillan, Melbourne, 1980), pp. 31–9.
100 Tribute to Fisher: *Caucus Minutes Volume 1*, p. 427.
101 Fisher's assurance: Turner, *Industrial Labour and Politics*, p. 78.
102 Hughes enthralled by the AIF: Fitzhardinge, p. 113.
102 Johnson's greeting: C.E.W. Bean, *Official History of Australia in the War of 1914–18: Volume III The AIF in France* (A & R, Sydney, 1935), p. 471, note 39.
102 Pearce greeting Hughes: P. Heydon, *Quiet Decision* (MUP, Melbourne, 1965), p. 236.
102 Pearce evaluating his colleagues: G. Pearce to A. Fisher, 26 July 1916, Fisher MSS, NLA.
103 Union congress against conscription: Fitzhardinge, p. 172.
103 Gardiner's rueful prediction: A. Gardiner to A. Fisher, 14 February 1916, Fisher MSS, NLA.
103 Boote's views: L.C. Jauncey, *The Story of Conscription in Australia* (Allen & Unwin, London, 1935), pp. 140, 143.
103 Pearce on the WPA option: G. Pearce to A. Fisher, 21 November 1916, Fisher MSS, NLA.
104 Higgs's observation: W. Higgs to A. Fisher, 23 August 1916, Fisher MSS, NLA.
104 Hughes's arguments in caucus: F. Anstey to H. Boote, 25 August 1916, Boote MSS, NLA.
104 Hughes addressing the Victorian excecutive: E.J. Holloway, From Labor Council to Privy Council, p. 29, Holloway MSS, NLA.
104 Lundie and militants on the effect of the resolutions: *Labor in Politics*, p. 274.
104 Fisher's caution: A. Fisher to G. Pearce, 11 August 1916, Pearce MSS, AWM.
105 'Richmond won't stand for it': G. Pearce, *Carpenter to Cabinet* (Hutchinson, London, 1951), p. 143.
105 Brennan's speech: *CPD*, 14 September 1916, pp. 8558–61.
106 Hughes describing the campaign: W. Hughes to A. Fisher, 26 October 1916, Fisher MSS, NLA.
106 Hughes's censorship direction: W. Hughes to G. Pearce, 8 September 1916, Pearce MSS, AWM.
106 Fihelly scathing about England: D.J. Murphy, *T.J. Ryan* (UQP, Brisbane, 1975), p. 195.
106 Curtin's zeal, Anstey's encouragement: L. Ross, *John Curtin* (Macmillan, Melbourne, 1977), pp. 50, 49.
106 'If Britain fell. . .': D. Horne, *In Search of Billy Hughes* (Macmillan, Melbourne, 1979), p. 79.
107 Somerville's rebuke: B. Latter, Dr William Somerville, MS, Battye Library.
107 Hughes meeting Munro Ferguson: Fitzhardinge, p. 212.
108 Declining faith in officialdom: R. Gregory to J. Latham, 2 August 1918, Latham MSS, NLA.
108 Hughes remorseful: Fitzhardinge, p. 214.
108 Pearce philosophical: G. Pearce to A. Fisher, 25 January 1917, Pearce MSS, AWM.

108   Russell poignant: E. Russell to A. Fisher, 14 October 1916, Fisher MSS, NLA.
108   'Enough of this': Fitzhardinge, p. 227.
108   Resolution to publish names: *Caucus Minutes, Volume 1*, p. 439.
108   Spence 'bludgeoned': C. Lansbury, 'William Guthrie Spence', *Labour History* 13, 1967, p. 10.
109   Holman relishing his freedom: Evatt, p. 319.
109   Guerin: *ADB* Volume 9.
110   Scaddan on Hughes's expulsion: J.R. Robertson, 'The Conscription Issue and the National Movement in Western Australia, June 1916–December 1917, *University Studies in Western Australian History* 3, 3, 1959, p.11.
111   Lynch: 1916 federal conference report, pp. 7, 16.
111   'Unless we can contrive. . .': W. Hughes to D. Lloyd George, 30 December 1916, Hughes MSS, NLA.
111   The strange epidemic: Fitzhardinge, p. 257.
111   Long's robust appearance: E. Scott, *Official History of Australia in the War of 1914–18: Volume XI Australia During the War* (A & R, Sydney, 1936), p. 382.
111   Belton feeling 'so sick': M. Lake, *A Divided Society* (MUP, Melbourne, 1975), p. 92.
111   McGrath upset: D.C. McGrath to A. Fisher, 9 March 1917, Fisher MSS, NLA.
112   Hughes's campaign: Fitzhardinge, p. 263.
113   Tudor's gloomy assessment: F. Tudor to A. Fisher, 15 August 1917, Fisher MSS, NLA; J. McCalman, *Struggletown* (MUP, Melbourne, 1985), p. 102.
113   Hughes and 'perpetual crisis': S. Macintyre, *The Oxford History of Australia Volume 4 1901–1942* (OUP, Melbourne, 1986), p. 168.
113   Motion endorsed by state Labor conferences: 1918 federal conference report, p. 11.
113   Chifley and the legacy of 1917: L.F. Crisp, *Ben Chifley* (Longmans Green & Co, Melbourne 1963), p. 11.
113–14 Fisher's ordeal: A. Fisher to G. Pearce, 9 October 1916, 1 December 1916, 5 September 1916, Pearce MSS, AWM.
114   Fisher at Western Front: Diary 60, pp. 29–35, C.E.W. Bean MSS, AWM.
114   1917 referendum campaign: Fitzhardinge, p. 286.
115   'We've had enough of your forgeries': Fitzhardinge, p. 308.
115   Hughes on 'pure piffle': M. Perks, 'Labor and the Governor-General's Recruiting Conference, Melbourne, April 1918', *Labour History* 34, 1978, p. 40.
115   ALP's attitude to recruiting: 1918 federal conference report, p. 28.
115   Scullin on Japan: 1918 federal conference report, p. 32.
116   Curtin on federal executive's performance: 1918 federal conference report, p. 48.
116   Naming the party: 1918 federal conference report, p. 47.
118   O'Loghlin: *ADB* Volume 11.
118   Boote praising the OBU: C. Larmour, *Labor Judge* (H & I, Sydney, 1985), p. 85.
119   Rae critical: Turner, *Industrial Labour and Politics*, p. 190.
119   Denunciations of AWU and OBU; Turner, *Industrial Labour and Politics*, p. 191; *Daily Telegraph*, 4 August 1919.
119   Proceedings of the 1919 federal conference are outlined in the printed conference report.
119   'I know that the position. . .': F. Tudor to A. Fisher, 27 November 1916, Fisher MSS, NLA.
120   Ryan's announcement: D.J. Murphy, *T.J. Ryan*, p. 452.

120   Ryan on the referenda: 1919 federal conference report, p. 110.
120   Anti-Labor posters: D.J. Murphy, *T.J. Ryan*, p. 472.
121   'I am afraid. . .': W. Demaine to A. Fisher, 26 December 1916, Fisher MSS, NLA.
121   Barnes: *ADB* Volume 7.

6 'There was Crookedness in New South Wales', 1920–1928

MAIN SOURCES:
B. Nairn, *The 'Big Fella'* (MUP, Melbourne, 1986).
J. Robertson, *J.H. Scullin* (UWAP, Perth, 1974).
P. Weller (ed.), *Caucus Minutes 1901–1949 Volume 2 1917–1931* (MUP, Melbourne, 1975).

page 123   Mahon's outburst: D.J. Murphy, *T.J. Ryan* (UQP, Brisbane, 1975), pp. 498–9; G. Souter, *Acts of Parliament* (MUP, Melbourne, 1988), pp. 182–3.
123   Anstey defending Mahon: Souter, p. 184.
123   Considine: *ADB* Volume 8.
124   Gardiner: G. Pearce to A. Fisher, 26 July 1916, Fisher MSS, NLA.
124   Catts's allegations: *CPD*, 6 July 1922, pp. 199, 205.
124   FPLP resolution: *Caucus Minutes*, p. 175.
124   'A bare-knuckles fighter. . .': I. Young, *Theodore* (Alpha, Sydney, 1971), p. 51.
125   Catts on the Goulburn preselection: *CPD*, 6 July 1922, p. 197.
125   Lambert: *ADB* Volume 9.
125   Storey offending the militants: I. Turner, *Industrial Labour and Politics* (ANUP, Canberra, 1965), p. 215.
125   Storey to Catts: *CPD*, 6 July 1922, p. 197.
126   The case against Grant, and Boote's comment: Turner, p. 127.
126   Brookfield: *ADB* Volume 7.
126   Congress recommendations: L.F. Crisp, *The Australian Federal Labour Party 1901–1951* (Longmans Green & Co, London, 1955), pp. 277–8.
126   R.S. Ross: *ADB* Volume 11.
126–7 Proceedings of the 1921 federal conference are outlined in the printed conference report.
127   Bailey on Garden: *ADB* Volume 8 (Garden).
128   Dooley's stinging attack: H. Radi & P. Spearritt (eds), *Jack Lang* (H & I, Sydney, 1977), p. 32.
128   Federal executive's tepid statement: P. Weller & B. Lloyd (eds), *Federal Executive Minutes* (MUP, Melbourne, 1978), p. 64.
128   Federal executive threatening intervention: Weller & Lloyd, p. 75.
129   Bailey expelled: *ADB* Volume 7.
129   Loughlin: *ADB* Volume 10.
129   Lang and 'sane finance': Nairn, p. 42.
129   Lang: *ADB* Volume 9.
130   Anstey on Bruce: D. Potts, A Study of Three Nationalists in the Bruce-Page Government of 1923–1929, MA thesis, Melbourne University, 1972, p. 49.
130   Bruce government's economic policy: K. Fry, 'Soldier Settlement and the

Agrarian Myth after the First World War', *Labour History* 48, 1985, p. 31.

130 Boyd's observation: H. McQueen, *Gallipoli to Petrov* (Allen & Unwin, Sydney, 1984), p. 7

130 Bruce trying to avoid political turmoil: S. Macintyre, *The Oxford History of Australia Volume 4 1901–1942* (OUP, Melbourne, 1986), p. 222.

130 Boote on Pearce: B. Walker, *Solidarity Forever* (National, Melbourne, 1972), p. 254.

130 de Largie: A. McDougall to A. Fisher, 11 December 1916, Fisher MSS, NLA.

132 Queensland Supreme Court decisions: D. Murphy, R. Joyce & M. Cribb (eds), *The Premiers of Queensland* (UQP, Brisbane, 1990), p. 320.

133 Chief Protector's powers: *ADB* Volume 7 (J.W. Blakeley).

133 McCormack on Aborigines: D.J. Murphy, R.B. Joyce & C.A. Hughes (eds), *Labor in Power* (UQP, Brisbane, 1980), p. 334.

133 Theodore's courageous statesmanship: 1921 federal conference report, p. 39.

133 Theodore critical of opposition's denial of pairs: K.H. Kennedy, 'Bribery and Political Crisis, Queensland 1922', *AJPH* 25, 1, 1979, p. 67.

134 'You cannot mix oil and water': 1924 federal conference report, p. 36.

134 Theodore on Queensland the best: *Catholic Press*, 6 August 1925.

134 Fihelly attacking Theodore: B. Schedvin, 'E.G. Theodore and the London Pastoral Lobby', *Politics* 6, 1, 1971, p. 39.

136 *Advocate* on Mungana: K. Kennedy, *The Mungana Affair* (UQP, Brisbane, 1978), p. 45.

136 'We absolutely don't know. . .': M. Denholm, 'The Lyons Tasmanian Labor Government 1923–1928', *Tasmanian Historical Research Association Papers and Proceedings* 24, 2, 1977, p. 46.

136 A.G. Ogilvie: R. Davis, *Eighty Years' Labor* (Sassafras, Hobart, 1983), p. 11.

136 Lyons on the Opposition Leader: *ADB* Volume 10 (Lyons).

136 'Deloraining': Davis, p. 20.

137 Ogilvie's appeal and the Trotsky label: M. Denholm, 'The Politics of the Push: An Examination of the Record of A.G. Ogilvie in the Lyons Tasmanian Labor Government, 1923–1928', *Tasmanian Historical Research Association Papers and Proceedings* 25, 2, 1978, pp. 39, 40.

137 Collier: G. Bolton, *A Fine Country to Starve in* (UWAP, Perth, 1972), p. 16.

139 Kirkpatrick: *ADB* Volume 9.

139 Gunn: *ADB* Volume 9.

140 Treasurer's neglect and underpaid police: L. Fitzhardinge, *William Morris Hughes Volume 2: The Little Digger 1914–1952* (A & R, Sydney, 1979), p. 526.

141 Prendergast's promise: 1924 federal conference report, p. 35.

141 The 'do-nothing' government: K. White, *John Cain and Victorian Labor 1917–1957* (H & I, Sydney, 1982), p. 53.

141 The four black crows: B.D. Graham, *The Formation of the Australian Country Parties* (ANUP, Canberra, 1966), p. 260.

143 Crookedness in NSW: 1924 federal conference report, p. 31.

143 Willis threatening Bailey: 1924 federal conference report, p. 64.

143 Theodore's frank response: 1924 federal conference report, p. 56.

144 *Sydney Morning Herald*'s objection: Radi & Spearritt, p. 75.

145 The 'seething mass of vendettas. . .': C.M.H. Clark, *A History of Australia Volume 6* (MUP, Melbourne, 1987), p. 148.

145 Constant insults and taunts: Nairn, p. 71.

145–6   Lang and Loughlin chalk and cheese: Nairn, p. 128.
146   Evatt on Lang: K. Tennant, *Evatt* (A & R, Sydney, 1972), p. 62.
146   Mutch on Lang: Nairn, p. 156.
148   McGrath furious: *Caucus Minutes*, pp. 304–5.
148   Anti-Labor newspapers: *Sydney Morning Herald*, 18 July 1928; *Argus*, 17 July 1928.
148–9   Anstey's counter-attack: *Argus*, 21 July 1928.
149   Multitude of footsloggers: L. Ross, *John Curtin* (Macmillan, Melbourne, 1977), p. 88.

7   'Spitting upon the Altar of Labour'? Floundering in the Great Depression, 1929–1932

MAIN SOURCES:
P. Cook, The Scullin Government, PhD thesis, ANU, 1971.
W. Denning, *Caucus Crisis* (H & I, Sydney, 1982).
B. Nairn, *The 'Big Fella'* (MUP, Melbourne, 1986).
J. Robertson, *J.H. Scullin* (UWAP, Perth, 1974).
G. Sawer, *Australian Federal Politics and Law 1929–1949* (MUP, Melbourne, 1963).
P. Weller (ed.), *Caucus Minutes 1901–1949 Volume 2 1917–1931* (MUP, Melbourne, 1975).

page 151   Scullin and Theodore on the election victory: Robertson, p. 167.
151   'Australia Is Ours!': D. Carboch, 'The Fall of the Bruce-Page Government', in A. Wildavsky & D. Carboch, *Studies in Australian Politics* (Cheshire, Melbourne, 1958), p. 249.
153   Moloney: *ADB* Volume 10.
153   'No body of men...': C.M.H. Clark, *A History of Australia Volume 6* (MUP, Melbourne, 1987), p. 321.
154   One Anstey is enough: A. Calwell, *Be Just and Fear Not* (Lloyd O'Neil, Melbourne, 1972), p. 47.
154   'Lend me a fiver...': L. Ross, *John Curtin* (Macmillan, Melbourne, 1977), p. 99.
154   Scullin staggered: Robertson, p. 185.
154   The bank board: Sawer, *Australian Federal Politics and Law 1901–1929* (MUP, Melbourne, 1956), p. 231.
154   Labour movement's defence of 'the people's bank': P. Love, *Labour and the Money Power* (MUP, Melbourne, 1984), p. 87.
155   Anstey accusing Gibson: P. Cook, 'Frank Anstey: Memoirs of the Scullin Labor Government, 1929–1932', *Historical Studies* 72, 1979, p. 368.
155   Anstey's verdict: Cook, *Historical Studies*, p. 368.
155–6   Brennan's statement: K. Ryan, Frank Brennan, MA thesis, La Trobe University, 1978, pp. 182–3.
156   James's speech: *CPD*, 3 December 1929, pp. 576–80.
156   'Never have we said...': *CPD*, 3 December 1929, p. 580.
156   James on starving constituents: Nairn, p. 186.
156   Theodore labelled: Nairn, p. 188.
156–7   Lang's assessment: J. Lang, *The Great Bust* (A & R, Sydney, 1962), p. 171.
157   NSW branch autonomy: H. Radi & P. Spearritt (eds), *Jack Lang* (H & I, Sydney, 1977), p. 220.
157   Eldridge on impending civil war: J. Iremonger, J. Merritt & G. Osborne (eds), *Strikes* (A & R, Sydney, 1973), p. 141.
157   Fear of a major uprising: Denning, p. 24.

157–8   Tariff touts: Denning, pp. 88–9.

158   Unemployment: S. Macintyre, *The Oxford History of Australia Volume 4 1901–1942* (OUP, Melbourne, 1986), p. 275.

158   'It was common. . .': Macintyre, pp. 277–8.

159   'There is no need for panic': Robertson, p. 228.

159   Scullin's appeal to wheatgrowers: Robertson, p. 229.

160   Collings's speech: 1930 federal conference report, pp. 23–4.

160   Unemployment a nightmare: 1930 federal conference report, p. 101.

160   Conference's well-intentioned statement: 1930 federal conference report, pp. 66–8.

160   LWIE subject to federal executive supervision: 1930 federal conference report, p. 10.

160   'Let them do their job. . .': 1930 federal conference report, p. 58.

161   Theodore 'guilty of the grossest impropriety': K. Kennedy, *The Mungana Affair* (UQP, Brisbane, 1978), p. 75.

161   Theodore's declaration of innocence: Kennedy, p. 78.

161   Hughes on Theodore's speech: L. Fitzhardinge, *William Morris Hughes Volume 2: The Little Digger 1914–1952* (A & R, Sydney, 1979), p. 602.

161   Theodore's speech: Kennedy, p. 80.

161   Theodore farewelling his secretary: Robertson, p. 250.

162   Niemeyer to Makin: J. Lonie, 'Good Labor Men: The Hill Government in South Australia, 1930–1933', *Labour History* 31, 1976, p. 20, note 36.

163   Niemeyer's verdict: W. Mandle, *Going It Alone* (Penguin, Melbourne, 1978), pp. 78–81.

163   'It made one hang one's head. . .': F. Crowley (ed.), *Modern Australia in Documents 1901–1939* (Wren, Melbourne, 1973), p. 477.

163   Scullin adamant: Cook PhD, p. 194.

163   Beasley's comment: Denning, p. 57.

163   Labor 'sets its face. . .': Nairn, p. 205.

164   'There is one man. . .': Nairn, p. 206.

164   Anstey on the cormorants and vultures: Mandle, p. 86.

164   Motions by Lazzarini and Beasley: *Caucus Minutes*, pp. 389, 390.

164   Fenton: C. Edwards, *The Editor Regrets* (Hill of Content, Melbourne, 1972), p. 50.

165   Theodore's proposal and the motion of appreciation: *Caucus Minutes*, pp. 391, 395.

166   Scullin critical: Cook PhD, p. 278.

166   Lyons furious: Cook PhD, p. 281.

166   Fenton to 'consider his position': *Caucus Minutes*, p. 397.

166   'For God's sake, Joe, don't do it!': Denning, p. 121.

166   Brennan's tension: R. Garran, *Prosper the Commonwealth* (A & R, Sydney, 1958), p. 159.

166   Brennan's speech at Geneva: Ryan, p. 218.

167   Scullin to Lyons: Cook PhD, p. 283.

167   Makin's motion: *Caucus Minutes*, p. 398.

167   Fenton on cabinet's view: *Caucus Minutes*, p. 398.

167   Scullin's message: Cook PhD, pp. 285–6; Robertson, p. 282.

167   *Labor Call*: C. Cunneen, *King's Men* (Allen & Unwin, Sydney, 1983), p. 420.

168   Strongly held views: Ryan, p. 225.

168   'Thank God Scullin has come back': Cook PhD, pp. 321–2.

169   Anstey, Yates and Lazzarini against Theodore: J. Fitzgerald, The Reinstatement of E.G. Theodore as Federal Treasurer, January 1931, BA Hons thesis, La Trobe University, 1971, p. 65.

169   Curtin supporting Theodore's return: Cook PhD, p. 327.

169   'At last this Government will fight...': *CPD*, 24 June 1931, p. 2956.
169   Gabb's departure: Cook PhD, pp. 329–30.
169   Yates on Scullin: Robertson, p. 300.
170   Lang plan's artful simplicity: Nairn, p. 226.
170   Scullin-Eldridge clash: Cook PhD, p. 344.
172   'If Australia were to surmount...': J. Coxsedge & others, *Rooted in Secrecy* (Committee for the Abolition of Political Police, Melbourne, 1982), p. 12.
173   Curtin's contention: Cook PhD, p. 358.
173   Curtin's motion: Cook PhD, p. 359.
173   Gibson encouraging the New Guard: E. Campbell, *The Rallying Point* (MUP, Melbourne, 1965), p. 138.
173   White Army out in force: Macintyre, p. 265.
174   Scullin always looking worried: Denning, p. 136.
174   Hill-Theodore exchange: Lonie, *Labour History*, p. 19.
174   The Premiers' Plan and 'equality of sacrifice': Macintyre, p. 271.
174   Scullin and premiers agreeing to 'bind themselves...': P. Cook, 'Labor and the Premiers' Plan', *Labour History* 17, 1979, p. 99.
174   An election 'would have been traitorous...': Robertson, p. 337.
175   Compromise formula: P. Weller & B. Lloyd (eds), *Federal Executive Minutes 1915–1955* (MUP, Melbourne, 1978), p. 166.
175   'This is the annihilation...': *CPD*, 8 July 1931, pp. 3563–5.
175   Curtin's speech: *CPD*, 24 June 1931, pp. 2956–7.
176   Holloway's career nearly ended: From Labor Council to Privy Council, p. 109, Holloway MSS, NLA.
176   FPLP 'beaten and broken': Denning, p. 138.
176   Anstey: Denning, p. 148.
176   Scullin and the interjector: Robertson, p. 363.
177   'Yes, We Have No Munganas': G. Souter, *Acts of Parliament* (MUP, Melbourne, 1988), p. 287.
177   Scullin's reaction to the defeat: Robertson, pp. 377, 381 & 379.
178   Watkins accusing Ogilvie: M. Roe, 'A.G. Ogilvie and the Blend of Van Diemen's Land with Tasmania', *Bulletin of the Centre for Tasmanian Historical Studies* 1, 2, 1986, p. 46.
178   The Attorney-General: *ADB* Volume 10 (Macgroarty); Kennedy, p. 113.
179   Niemeyer on Denny: P. Love, 'Niemeyer's Australian Diary', *Historical Studies* 79, 1982, p. 269.
179   Hogan dismissing state conference instruction: L.J. Louis, *Trade Unions and the Depression* (ANUP, Canberra, 1968), p. 125.
180   Lang resourceful, reckless and magnetic: Nairn, p. 253.
180   Langites cursing McTiernan: G. Sawer, *Australian Federalism in the Courts* (MUP, Melbourne, 1967), p. 67.
180   'Argentine gypsies': Nairn, p. 257.
180   SA Governor to Game: A. Moore, Send Lawyers, Guns and Money!, PhD thesis, La Trobe University, 1982, p. 184.
181   'The time is finished for talk': Moore, p. 317.
181   *Labor Daily*'s warnings: Moore, pp. 303, 304.
181   'Digger' Dunn's threat: Moore, p. 309.
181   Langites' posters: R.B. Walker, *Yesterday's News* (Sydney University Press, Sydney, 1980), p. 124.
182   Ross's lament: L.F. Crisp, *The Australian Federal Labour Party 1901–1951* (Longmans Green & Co, London, 1955), p. 87.
182   Brennan's defeat like a bereavement: Ryan, p. 247.
182   Moloney virtually destitute: *ADB* Volume 10.
182   Anstey disillusioned: F. Anstey to J. McDougall, 28 May 1932, Anstey MSS, NLA; Cook, *Historical Studies*, p. 391.
182   'It nearly killed me...': *Canberra Times*, 22 February 1966.

8 'There is a Huge Job to Do': Gradual Recovery, 1932–1941

MAIN SOURCES:
P. Hasluck, *Australia in the War of 1939–1945: The Government and the People 1939–1941* (AWM, Canberra, 1952).
L. Ross, *John Curtin* (Macmillan, Melbourne, 1977).
P. Weller (ed.), *Caucus Minutes 1901–1949 Volume 3 1932–1949* (MUP, Melbourne, 1975).

page 183 Government of the feeble for the greedy: *ADB* Volume 9 (C.A.S. Hawker).
183 Lang 'maintained popularity. . .': S. Macintyre, *The Oxford History of Australia Volume 4 1901–1942* (OUP, Melbourne, 1986), p. 264.
184 Coleman flaying the Langites: L.F. Crisp, *Ben Chifley* (Longmans Green & Co, Melbourne, 1963), p. 90.
184 Chifley's resolve: Crisp, p. 82.
184 *World*'s inaugural editorial: P. Cook, 'The End of the *World*', *Labour History* 16, 1969, p. 56.
184 'I feel utterly hopeless. . .': M. Grover to H. Boote, 2 December 1933, Boote MSS, NLA.
185 'What's the bloody good of being here?': Ross, p. 96.
185 Calwell-Curtin exchange: A. Calwell, *Be Just and Fear Not* (Lloyd O'Neil, Melbourne, 1972), p. 47.
185 Curtin-Theodore correspondence: Ross, pp. 131–5.
185 Curtin 'a genius with figures', and Collier's rejoinder: Ross, p. 137.
186 'It's the last thing I'll do: Ross, p. 148.
186 'Lang is greater than Lenin': B. Nairn, *The 'Big Fella'* (MUP, Melbourne, 1986), p. 269.
187 Calwell's claim: Calwell, p. 40.
188 'There is a huge job to do. . .': J. Curtin to H. Boote, 22 December 1935, Boote MSS, NLA.
188 Curtin's crusade: Ross, p. 151.
188 'Staying in second-rate pubs. . .': Ross, p. 152.
188 Curtin on the ALP rules: Crisp, p. 100.
188–9 ALP 'has been burdened. . .': H. Grattan in L.F. Crisp, *Australian National Government* (Longman, Melbourne, 1983), p. 178.
189 The 'zeal and sacrifice. . .': W. Denning MSS, NLA.
189 Workers 'getting tired. . .': C. Rasmussen, 'Challenging the Centre – the Coburg ALP Branch in the 1930s', *Labour History* 54, 1988, p. 49.
189 Daly: F. Daly, *From Curtin to Hawke* (Sun, Melbourne, 1984), pp. 4–5.
189 Duthie: G. Duthie, *I Had 50,000 Bosses* (A & R, Sydney, 1984), pp. 3, 11.
189 Cameron: C. Cameron, 'Labor Leaders Who Betrayed Their Trust', *Labour History* 53, 1987, p. 116.
190 Calwell on 'my constituents': C. Kiernan, *Calwell* (Nelson, Melbourne, 1978), p. 44.
190 'For two days. . .': F. McManus, *The Tumult and the Shouting* (Rigby, Adelaide, 1977), p. 20.
190 Calwell like a peacock: P. Moloney to P. Moloney, 25 September 1940, Moloney MSS, NLA.
190 'I wish there were. . .': W. Maloney to H. Boote, 9 July 1934, Boote MSS, NLA.
191 'If the Labor Movement. . .': D. Murphy, R. Joyce & M. Cribb (eds), *The Premiers of Queensland* (UQP, Brisbane, 1990), p. 410.
191 Forgan Smith's claim: *ADB* Volume 11.

192   Ogilvie's education record: R. Davis, *Eighty Years' Labor* (Sassafras, Hobart, 1983), p. 32.
193   'Ogilvie dominated cabinet. . .': *ADB* Volume 11.
193   Ogilvie's most significant achievement: M. Roe, 'A.G. Ogilvie and the Blend of Van Diemen's Land with Tasmania', *Bulletin of the Centre for Tasmanian Historical Studies* 2, 1986, p. 58.
193   Removing Tasmania's inferiority complex: Davis, p. 32.
193   Ogilvie's opponents: Davis, p. 37.
193   Morrow on Tasmanian workers: A. Johnson, *Fly a Rebel Flag* (Penguin, Melbourne, 1986), p. 104.
194   Collier and Mitchell 'went in and out of office. . .': V. Courtney, *All I May Tell* (Shakespeare Head, Sydney, 1956), p. 44.
194   *Westralian Worker*: R. Pervan & C. Sharman, *Essays on Western Australian Politics* (UWAP, Perth, 1979), p. 136.
196   'The Cabinet has one Leader. . .': Crisp, *Ben Chifley*, p. 70.
196   Curtin's frustration about NSW: Ross, p. 189.
196–7 Forde's speech: *Caucus Minutes*, p. 105.
197   Curtin's stance: *Caucus Minutes*, pp. 111–12.
197   Victorian executive's ruling: S. Blackburn, *Maurice Blackburn and the Australian Labor Party 1934–1943* (Australian Society for the Study of Labour History, Melbourne, 1969), p. 13.
198   Warning to 'look behind the Curtin': D. Carboch, 'The Fall of the Bruce-Page Government', in A. Wildavsky & D. Carboch, *Studies in Australian Politics* (Cheshire, Melbourne, 1958), p. 238.
198   Curtin on the deranged world: Ross, p. 145.
198   'Eyes are only to weep with now': H. McQueen, *Gallipoli to Petrov* (Allen & Unwin, Sydney, 1984), p. 49.
198   Australia 'should not be embroiled. . .': Ross, pp. 176–7.
199   Forgan Smith's resolution: 1939 federal conference report, p. 55.
199   Curtin refusing to defy the law: Ross, p. 180.
199   Brennan scathing about calculated panic: Hasluck, p. 87.
199   Holloway's optimism: *CPD*, 26 May 1939, p. 805.
199   Blackburn's reluctant concession: Blackburn, p. 19.
199   Calwell's isolationism: 1939 federal conference report, p. 56.
200   Menzies's announcement: F. Crowley (ed), *Modern Australia in Documents 1939–1970* (Wren, Melbourne, 1973), p. 1.
200   Curtin's manifesto: Ross, p. 183.
200   Embarrassing statements: *Caucus Minutes*, p. 212.
200   Anti-Labor disunity: L. Fitzhardinge, *William Morris Hughes Volume 2: The Little Digger 1914–1952* (A & R, Sydney, 1979), p. 650.
201   'Hitler's eyes are on Corio': Calwell, p. 79.
201   Dedman on 'social control': J. Dedman OH, NLA.
202   Curtin angry: Ross, p. 189.
202   Curtin's call for a special federal conference: *Caucus Minutes*, p. 222.
202–3 Labor's defence policy: 1940 federal conference report, p. 12.
203   Hanlon, Evans and Curtin: 1940 federal conference report, pp. 20–1.
203   Community demand for Labor to involve itself: 1940 federal conference report, pp. 20, 22.
204   Boote on Curtin's speech: H. Boote Diary, 8 August 1940, Boote MSS, NLA.
204   'Batting on a sticky wicket. . .': F. Green, *Servant of the House* (Heinemann, Melbourne, 1969), p. 126.
205   Chifley and the light on the hill: Crisp, *Ben Chifley*, p. 106.
205   'Then I'm done for': Calwell, p. 195.
206   Evatt's motion: *Caucus Minutes*, p. 238.
206   Evatt appalled: Boote Diary, 30 October 1940, Boote MSS, NLA.

206   Blackburn's conclusion: M. Blackburn to H. Boote, 14 December 1940, Boote MSS, NLA.
206   Evatt-Scullin motion: *Caucus Minutes*, p. 254.
207   'I find it very difficult...': *CPD*, 20 November 1940, p. 34.
207   Evatt at Kalgoorlie station: A. Fraser OH, NLA.
208   McKell's campaign: D. Clune, 'The New South Wales Election of 1941', *AJPH* 30, 3, 1984, p. 342.
208   McKell's horses for courses strategy: M. Easson (ed.), *McKell* (Allen & Unwin, Sydney, 1988), p. 104.
209   Curtin and the Advisory War Council's statement: Ross, p. 203.
209   'There are going to be...': Boote Diary, 8 October 1941, Boote MSS, NLA.
210   Federal executive's statement: P. Weller & B. Lloyd (eds), *Federal Executive Minutes* (MUP, Melbourne, 1978), p. 238.
210   Boote incensed: Boote Diary, 23 September 1941, Boote MSS, NLA.
210   Hughes on Menzies: D. Horne, *In Search of Billy Hughes* (Macmillan, Melbourne, 1979), p. 123.

9 'Dangers and Problems Unprecedented and Unpredictable': The Curtin Government, 1941–1945

MAIN SOURCES:
L.F. Crisp, *Ben Chifley* (Longmans Green & Co, Melbourne, 1963).
P. Hasluck, *Australia in the War of 1939–1945: The Government and the People 1942–1945* (AWM, Canberra, 1970).
L. Ross, *John Curtin* (Macmillan, Melbourne, 1977).
K. Tennant, *Evatt* (A & R, Sydney, 1972).
P. Weller (ed.), *Caucus Minutes 1901–1949 Volume 3 1932–1949* (MUP, Melbourne, 1975).

page 212   Scullin's motion: *Caucus Minutes*, p. 294.
213   Calwell on Curtin's 'slumbering resentment': A. Calwell, *Be Just and Fear Not* (Lloyd O'Neil, Melbourne, 1972), p. 51.
215   'Come over whenever you arrive...': Crisp, p. 214.
215   Curtin's broadcast: Ross, pp. 241–2.
216   Curtin on the cable traffic: Ross, p. 249.
216   Curtin's bluntness: Hasluck, p. 27; Ross, p. 245.
216   'Without any inhibitions of any kind...': *Herald* (Melbourne), 27 December 1941.
216   Reaction in Washington: W.J. Hudson, *Casey* (OUP, Melbourne, 1986), p. 134.
216   'The position Australia faces internally...': *Herald* (Melbourne), 27 December 1941.
217   'After all the assurances...': J.R. Robertson, *Australia Goes to War 1939–1945* (Doubleday, Sydney, 1984), p. 83.
217   'The Japs have bombed Darwin!': P. Spender, *Politics and a Man* (Collins, Sydney, 1972), pp. 148–9.
217   Brennan's hostility: *CPD*, 25 March 1942, p. 397.
217   Morgan's envy: S. Blackburn, *Maurice Blackburn and the Australian Labor Party 1934–1943* (Australian Society for the Study of Labour History, Melbourne, 1969), p. 37.
218   Curtin's insistence: Ross, p. 262.
218   'How can I sleep...': J. Thompson (ed.), *On Lips of Living Men* (Lansdowne, Melbourne, 1962), p. 71.

218   Boote to Curtin, and Curtin's reply: Ross, pp. 263–4.

219   'I came through. . .': W. Manchester, *American Caesar: Douglas Macarthur 1880–1964* (Arrow, London, 1979), p. 247.

219   Curtin's impromptu remarks: *CPD*, 8 May 1942, pp. 1060–1.

220   Curtin's exchange with Wren: Crisp, p. 158, note 4.

220   Beasley's admiration: Tennant, p. 139.

220   Evatt's nationalism and approach: Tennant, p. 141.

220   Bruce's tribute: D. Horner, *High Command* (AWM, Canberra, 1982), p. 203.

220   'I will not be a vassal. . .': Hasluck, p. 321.

221   'Like everyone else. . .': Hasluck, p. 324.

221   Curtin describing Ward as 'a bloody ratbag': Notes of Curtin's press conferences (MS 5675), NLA.

222   Harking back to 1916 conscription debate: Robertson, p. 146.

222   Proceedings of the 1942 federal conference are outlined in the conference report.

222   Thornton deriding Ward: J.J. Dedman, 'The Practical Application of Collective Responsibility', *Politics* 3, 2, 1968, p. 152.

223   Victorian executive's treatment of Curtin: Dedman, *Politics*, pp. 152–3.

223   'Rabaul is further. . .': K. Beazley, *John Curtin* (ANUP, Canberra, 1972), pp. 11–12.

223   Ward to Curtin: E. Spratt, *Eddie Ward* (Seal, Adelaide, 1978), p. 83.

224   Calwell's diatribe: H. Boote Diary, 5 January 1943, Boote MSS, NLA.

224   Boote acknowledging Curtin's sincerity: M. Blackburn & H. Boote, *Against Conscription*, pamphlet in Calwell MSS (Box 24), NLA.

224   Curtin-Calwell clash: Calwell, p. 55; *Caucus Minutes*, p. 313.

225   Ministers critical of Ward: J.J. Dedman, 'The "Brisbane" Line', *Australian Outlook* 22, 2, 1968, p. 145.

225   Ward enraging the opposition: Ross, p. 317.

225   Ward referring to the 'defeatist' plan: Spratt, p. 119.

225   Curtin's electioneering: Ross, pp. 327–8.

226   Murdoch's articles: C. Edwards, *The Editor Regrets* (Hill of Content, Melbourne, 1972), p. 108.

226   *Sydney Morning Herald*'s lavish praise: N.E. Lee, *John Curtin* (Longman Cheshire, Melbourne, 1983), p. 9.

227   Street's view: B. McKinlay (ed.), *A Documentary History of the Australian Labour Movement 1850–1975* (Drummond, Melbourne, 1979), p. 463.

228   'I've given Calwell Information. . .': D. Rodgers OH, NLA.

229   Evatt on constitutional reform: Hasluck, p. 456.

229   Forgan Smith's claim: *Courier Mail*, 31 October 1942.

229   Curtin's superb leadership: Dedman, *Politics*, p. 149.

230   Calwell on press owners and editors: R.B. Walker, *Yesterday's News* (Sydney University Press, Sydney, 1980), p. 217.

230–1   Calwell inflammatory: Hasluck, p. 409; C. Kiernan, *Calwell* (Nelson, Melbourne, 1978), p. 96.

231   McKell accusing Calwell: Hasluck, p. 413.

231   Forde's reproach: Kiernan, p. 103.

231   Calwell as 'Cocky': G. Souter, *Company of Heralds* (MUP, Melbourne, 1981), p. 249.

232   Hughes on referenda: Tennant, p. 98.

232   Evatt's strenuous campaign: Tennant, p. 162.

232   Extraordinary misrepresentation: G. Sawer, *Australian Federal Politics and Law 1929–1949* (MUP, Melbourne, 1963), p. 172.

232   O'Malley as death dodger: A.R. Hoyle, *King O'Malley* (Macmillan, Melbourne, 1981), p. 175.

233   The new social order: L. Black, 'Social Democracy and Full Employment: The Australian White Paper, 1945', *Labour History* 46, 1984, p. 45.
233   'I'm too tired to live': Ross, p. 390.
233   'Hasten thine hour. . .': Ross, p. 242.

10 'The Hope, the Inspiration and the Saviour of the Australian People': The Chifley Government, 1945–1949

MAIN SOURCES:
L.F. Crisp, *Ben Chifley* (Longmans Green & Co, Melbourne, 1963).
G. Sawer, *Australian Federal Politics and Law 1929–1949* (MUP, Melbourne, 1963).
K. Tennant, *Evatt* (A & R, Sydney, 1972).
P. Weller (ed.), *Caucus Minutes 1901–1949 Volume 3 1932–1949* (MUP, Melbourne, 1975).

page 234   Haylen's discussion with Forde: L. Haylen, *Twenty Years Hard Labor* (Macmillan, Melbourne, 1969), p. 67.
234   Chifley's 'slow hacksaw of a voice': Crisp, p. 149.
237   Duthie dismissed as 'chicken feed': G. Duthie, *I Had 50,000 Bosses* (A & R, Sydney, 1984), p. 31.
238   'Probing and harassing. . .': B. Nairn, *The 'Big Fella'* (MUP, Melbourne, 1986), p. 312.
239   'His small dark moustache. . .': Duthie, p. 38.
239   Haylen on Rosevear's diatribe: Haylen, p. 61.
239   Lang unmoved: Duthie, p. 38.
241   Kennelly and Crean: F. Crean OH, NLA.
241   Cain attacking Communist unionists: K. White, *John Cain and Victorian Labor 1917–1957* (H & I, Sydney, 1982), pp. 120–1.
241   Arbitration Court president's criticism: R. Pervan & C. Sharman (eds), *Essays on Western Australian Politics* (UWAP, Perth, 1979), p. 138.
243   Ward denouncing Bretton Woods: Crisp, p. 205, note 4.
243   Chifley supporting Bretton Woods: Crisp, p. 210.
244   McKell's decision not irrevocable: M. Easson (ed.), *McKell* (Allen & Unwin, Sydney, 1988), p. 155.
244   Chifley's requirements: V. Kelly, *A Man of the People* (Alpha, Sydney, 1971), p. 160.
244   Menzies's reaction: Easson, p. 163.
245   Attlee's view: *Caucus Minutes*, p. 28.
245   'One car and its occupant': L. Kramer & others (eds), *The Greats* (A & R, Sydney, 1986), p. 242.
246   Calwell on Evatt's motives: A. Calwell, *Be Just and Fear Not* (Lloyd O'Neil, Melbourne, 1972), p. 197.
247   Nationalization decision in cabinet: Crisp, p. 327; G. Souter, *Acts of Parliament* (MUP, Melbourne, 1988), p. 385.
247   Chifley's statement: D. Stephens, Political Theory, History and the Australian Labor Governments, 1941–49, MA thesis, Monash University, 1974, p. 185.
247   Dedman's disbelief: H.C. Coombs, *Trial Balance* (Sun, Melbourne, 1983), p. 116.
248   Duthie's observation: Duthie, p. 42.
248   Menzies's condemnation: P. Love, *Labour and the Money Power* (MUP, Melbourne, 1984), p. 175.

248–9   Cameron thrilled: *Financial Review,* 7 June 1972.
249   Chifley congratulated: Crisp, p. 342.
250   The 'national health and medical scheme. . .': Crisp, p. 315.
250   Chifley labelling the doctors: Sawer, p. 198.
250   Crean defending academics: *VPD,* 12 April 1949, p. 343.
250   Federal executive's congratulations: P. Weller & B. Lloyd (eds), *Federal Executive Minutes 1915–1955* (MUP, Melbourne, 1978), pp. 347–8.
251   Negation of democratic principles: Stephens, p. 343.
251   Chifley's strong opposition: Stephens, p. 342.
251   Hanlon's broadcast: D. Murphy, R. Joyce & M. Cribb (eds), *The Premiers of Queensland* (UQP, Brisbane, 1990), p. 453.
251   'If ever there was. . .': *The Premiers of Queensland,* p. 452.
252   'Within a fortnight. . .': P. Deery, The 1949 Coal Strike, PhD thesis, La Trobe University, 1976, p. vii.
252   Reactions of Ward and Holloway: Deery, p. 235.
253   Boote's salute: unidentified newscutting dated 15 August 1949, Boote MSS (2070/3/49), NLA.
254   Chifley's policy speech: Stephens, p. 382.
254   Federal executive's meagre funds: L.F. Crisp, *The Australian Federal Labour Party 1901–1951* (Longmans Green & Co, London, 1955), p. 78.

11   'Sad Days for the Party': Another Big Split, 1950–1960

MAIN SOURCES:
FPLP Minutes (held by ALP).
R. Manne, *The Petrov Affair* (Pergamon, Sydney, 1987).
R. Murray, *The Split* (Cheshire, Melbourne, 1970).
K. Tennant, *Evatt* (A & R, Sydney, 1972).

page 256   Mullens: Murray, p. 7.
257   Keon: Murray, p. 73.
257   Keon's attack on Wren: Murray, p. 93.
257   Chifley on the Dissolution Bill: L.F. Crisp, *Ben Chifley* (Longmans Green & Co, Melbourne, 1963), p. 386.
258   Chifley and the ACTU's views: FPLP Minutes, 3 May 1950.
258   'I do not want anybody to think. . .': Crisp, p. 388.
258   Menzies and inflation: Crisp, p. 394.
259   Chifley and Cameron reacting to Burke's decision: Crisp, p. 394; C. Cameron to R. McMullin (conversation), 4 April 1989.
259   'I honestly feel. . .': F. Daly, *From Curtin to Hawke* (Sun, Melbourne, 1984), p. 102.
259   Menzies on the ALP backdown: Daly, p. 103.
259   'Accept your humiliation. . .': Crisp, p. 396.
260   Ferguson at 1951 federal conference: see conference report, p. 5.
261   'Menzies or Moscow': A. Johnson, *Fly a Rebel Flag* (Penguin, Melbourne, 1986), p. 203.
261   Duthie on Chifley: G. Duthie, *I Had 50,000 Bosses* (A & R, Sydney, 1984), p. 107.
261–2   A copy of Chifley's speech at the NSW conference is in Calwell MSS (Box 75), NLA.
262   'Oh no. . .': Daly, p. 105.

262 Menzies announcing the news: Crisp, p. 413.
262 'I know Mr Chifley is in heaven. . .': H.V. Evatt, *William Holman* (A & R, Sydney, 1979), foreword by N. Wran.
262 'Chifley's Grave': Haylen MSS (Box 2), NLA.
262 'I never saw. . .': A. Calwell to E.G. Wright, 11 October 1951, Calwell MSS (Box 75), NLA.
262 'We've never had. . .': C. Cameron to R. McMullin, 4 April 1989 (conversation).
262 Daly's tribute: Daly, p. 106.
262 'Ben Chifley, I am sure. . .': A. Calwell to H.V. Evatt, 4 August 1951, Calwell MSS (Box 77), NLA.
263 Ferguson's motion: P. Weller & B. Lloyd (eds), *Federal Executive Minutes 1915–1955* (MUP, Melbourne, 1978), p. 467.
263 Evatt in caucus: FPLP Minutes, 6 July 1951.
263 Chambers's defiance: *Advertiser* (Adelaide), 14 December 1951.
263 Evatt's leadership saluted: FPLP Minutes, 26 September 1951.
263 Stern rebuke: Weller & Lloyd, p. 472.
264 Pollard-Mullens clash: Murray, pp. 74–5.
265 Scully's 'tireless organising. . .': Murray, p. 94.
265 'Kennelly's distress and rage. . .': Murray, p. 39.
266 Holt's walk-out and 'the sectarian spiral': Murray, p. 100.
267 'I'll never resign. . .': D. Murphy, R. Joyce & M. Cribb (eds), *The Premiers of Queensland* (UQP, Brisbane, 1990), p. 433.
268 Morrow 'didn't want to fire. . .': Johnson, p. 211.
269 Ward: P. Spender, *Politics and a Man* (Collins, Sydney, 1972), pp. 204, 211.
269 Ward on Menzies: E. Spratt, *Eddie Ward* (Seal, Adelaide, 1978), p. 176.
269 The 1951 pro-Grouper motion is on p. 27 of the federal conference report.
270 Evatt happy and relaxed: L. Haylen, *Twenty Years Hard Labor* (Macmillan, Melbourne, 1969), p. 76.
270 'I can't tell you more. . .': D. Whitington, *Strive to Be Fair* (ANUP, Canberra, 1978), p. 127.
270 Townley's tip-off: F. Chamberlain OH, NLA.
270 Evatt-FPLP pronouncement: Murray, p. 149.
271 Interception of Petrov's wife: Manne, p. 87.
271 The conservative quartet: D. Marr, *Barwick* (Allen & Unwin, Sydney, 1980), p. 108.
272 Evatt's counter-attack: Murray, p. 153.
272 Evatt's statement after the election: Murray, p. 155.
272 'His mind seethed. . .': Manne, p. 123.
272 Windeyer on Document J: Murray, p. 158.
273 Evatt's blistering telegram: Murray, p. 159.
273 'Terrible display of intrigue. . .': G. Duthie Diary, 3 August 1954, Duthie MSS, NLA.
273 Haylen-Ward clash: Murray, p. 163.
273 'All this tenseness. . .': Duthie Diary, 11 August 1954.
273 Mercilessness and bitterness in parliament: Manne, p. 138.
274 'Bad-tempered, dishevelled and flamboyant': Marr, p. 111.
274 Menzies worried: Manne, p. 147.
274 Evatt alleging 'one of the basest conspiracies. . .': Manne, p. 148.
274 Evatt's forceful statement: Manne, p. 150.
274 Ward chanting 'Santa, Santa': Spratt, p. 226.
275 Evatt's press conference: Manne, p. 154; Spratt, p. 226.
275 'There are some here. . .': Murray, p. 173.
275 Reid on Evatt's 'hydrogen bomb': Murray, p. 179.

275 Evatt's statement: Murray, pp. 179–80.
277 Mullens in caucus: Murray, pp. 192–3.
277 'Take down their names!': Duthie, p. 139.
277 Daly 'crossed over in rebellion...': Daly, p. 128.
277 Holt's allegation: Murray, pp. 195–6.
277 McManus 'no doubt the ablest...': Duthie, p. 150.
278 Chamberlain: G. Freudenberg, *A Certain Grandeur* (Sun, Melbourne, 1978), p. 27.
279 Chamberlain on the court action: Murray, p. 219.
280 Aftermath of Calwell's conference speech: Murray, p. 233.
280 Statements by Mullens, Evatt and Santamaria: Murray, pp. 230–1.
281 O'Byrne on Cole: Murray, p. 267.
281 'Those who took part...': Murray, pp. 252–3.
281 Barry on Lovegrove: Murray, p. 250.
282 Purposeful unity the keystone: *Traditions for Reform in New South Wales* (Pluto, Sydney, 1987), p. 136.
282 Federal executive's decision: Murray, p. 299.
282 Resentful victim's complaint: *Labor Forum* 2, 3, 1980, p. 27.
284 Egerton declaring 'the time for logic has passed': D.J. Murphy, R.B. Joyce & C.A. Hughes (eds), *Labor in Power* (UQP, Brisbane, 1980), p. 503.
284 Egerton's anti-Gair agitation: *Labor in Power*, p. 510.
284 'For two days...': Murray, p. 326.
285 WA executive's charges: C.T. Stannage (ed.), *A New History of Western Australia* (UWAP, Perth, 1981), p. 451.
286 Dunstan attacking Playford: D. Dunstan, *Felicia* (Macmillan, Melbourne, 1981), p. 47.
287 Mullens's quixotic gesture: Murray, p. 277.
287 Violence on 'bloody Saturday': P. Ormonde, *A Foolish Passionate Man* (Penguin, Melbourne, 1981), p. 50.
287 Cairns's speechmaking: Ormonde, p. 52.
288 Menzies and Australia's 'great and powerful friends': G. Souter, *Acts of Parliament* (MUP, Melbourne, 1988), p. 460.
288 Burke's protest: undated *West Australian* cutting in H.V. Johnson MSS, NLA.
289 Evatt's undertaking: Murray, p. 346.
289 Ward's fury: Spratt, p. 235.

12 'Doomed to Indefinite Opposition'? 1960–1966

MAIN SOURCES:
G. Freudenberg, *A Certain Grandeur* (Sun, Melbourne, 1978).
L. Oakes, *Whitlam PM* (A & R, Sydney, 1973).
L. Overacker, *Australian Parties in a Changing Society 1945–67* (Cheshire, Melbourne, 1968).

page 291 Ward 'sacrificed': E. Ward to C. Chambers, 22 April 1960, Ward MSS, NLA.
291 'I took a swing at Gough Whitlam...': E. Spratt, *Eddie Ward* (Seal, Adelaide, 1978), p. 249.
291 'There was something shocking...': G. Souter, *Acts of Parliament* (MUP, Melbourne, 1988), p. 449.
293 Early 1950s platform inclusion: 1955 federal conference report, p. 57.
293 Chamberlain's addition to the platform: 1963 federal conference report, p. 31.

293 Chamberlain's anti-NSW motion: Freudenberg, p. 29.
293 Barwick on North-west Cape: D. Marr, *Barwick* (Allen & Unwin, Sydney, 1980), p. 201.
295 Hawke's 'chest problem': B. d'Alpuget, *Robert J. Hawke* (Schwartz, Melbourne, 1982), p. 104.
295 Whitlam on Hawke: d'Alpuget, p. 105.
295 Australian electors clinging to Menzies: d'Alpuget, p. 103.
296 The DLP vote a wasting asset: B.A. Santamaria, *Against the Tide* (OUP, Melbourne, 1981), p. 258.
296 Santamaria on Kennelly: Santamaria, p. 260.
298 Mosman branch's criticisms: D. Clune, The Labor Government in New South Wales 1941–1965, PhD thesis, Sydney University, 1990, p. 165.
298 Sheahan's outburst: *Sydney Morning Herald*, 13 May 1965.
299 Mulvihill's reforms: *National Times*, 11–17 May 1984.
299 'I was concerned even then. . .': *Good Weekend*, 6 October 1984.
299 Murphy's 'outstanding grip of the law': J. Scutt (ed.), *Lionel Murphy* (McCulloch, Melbourne, 1987), p. 18.
299 Cameron-Holding exchange: *Good Weekend*, 6 October 1984.
300 'Labor Sheep': Haylen MSS (Box 3), NLA.
300 Duggan's angry comment: R. Fitzgerald & H. Thornton, *Labor in Queensland* (UQP, Brisbane, 1989), p. 185.
301 Chamberlain denounced by Hawke and in no-confidence motion: Overacker, p. 86.
302 MLCs' effrontery: D. Jaensch (ed.), *The Flinders History of South Australia: Political History* (Wakefield, Adelaide, 1986), p. 295.
302 Pioneering Aboriginal Affairs legislation: Jaensch, p. 294.
304 'Labor still lives in the past. . .': Clune, p. 165.
305 'In the Labor Party. . .': Overacker, p. 68.
305 Phyllis Benjamin on the kitchen angels: R. Davis, *Eighty Years' Labor* (Sassafras, Hobart, 1983), p. 65.
305 The Victorian 'feminine flying gang': *Australian*, 15 January 1966.
305 'I am absolutely sick. . .': Clune, p. 165.
306 Keating to the Ramrods: E. Carew, *Keating* (Allen & Unwin, Sydney, 1988), p. 18.
306 'If Sukarno rattles the sabre. . .': Freudenberg, p. 45.
307 FPLP executive's statement: P. King (ed.), *Australia's Vietnam* (Allen & Unwin, Sydney, 1983), p. 43.
307 'I offer you the probability. . .': Freudenberg, p. 52.
307–8 Whitlam's report: Calwell MSS (Series 5), NLA.
308 Calwell's earlier exuberance: *Bulletin*, 9 December 1963.
308 'Evatt had three goes and so will I': *National Times*, 3–8 January 1977.
308 'When you are faced. . .': Oakes, p. 122.
309 Whitlam on Calwell: Oakes, p. 117.
309 Calwell 'a prisoner of the left': C. Kiernan, *Calwell* (Nelson, Melbourne, 1978), p. 232.
310 The conference speeches by Whitlam and Calwell are in the conference report, pp. 249–60.
311 The 1965 state aid resolution: *ALP Federal Platform Constitution and Rules* (Canberra, 1965), p. 29.
311–12 Whitlam's statement: *Canberra Times*, 15 February 1966.
312 Whitlam's television interview: March 1966 federal conference report, pp. 60–8.
312 'We've got the numbers. . .': Oakes, p. 139.
312 Whitlam 'a tower of strength': Oakes, p. 139.
312 Keeffe and Whitby intending to 'knock him off': Oakes, p. 140.
313 'You can't defeat an ideal with a bullet': *Sun* (Sydney), 22 June 1966.

313   Kocan's motive: Kiernan, p. 255.
313   Holt going 'all the way with LBJ': F. Crowley (ed.), *Modern Australia in Documents 1939–1970* (Wren, Melbourne, 1973), p. 513.
313   Askin pleasing Johnson: Crowley, p. 517.
313   'I will not allow. . .': King, p. 49.
314   Wyndham's acknowledgement: C. Wyndham, 'The Future of the ALP', *Australian Quarterly* 38, 2, 1966, p. 33.
314   Wyndham gloomy: Overacker, p. 122.

13 'Whose Party is This – Ours or His?': Resurgence under Whitlam, 1967–1972

MAIN SOURCES:
G. Freudenberg, *A Certain Grandeur* (Sun, Melbourne, 1978).
L. Oakes, *Whitlam PM* (A & R, Sydney, 1973).

page 315   Calwell blasting the South Vietnam leader: 'Political Chronicle', *AJPH* 13, 2, 1967, p. 254.
315   Calwell's report to federal executive: Calwell MSS (Series 5), NLA.
315   'I have not had. . .': A. Calwell, *Be Just and Fear Not* (Lloyd O'Neil, Melbourne, 1972), p. 234.
315   'I believe the Labor Party. . .': Calwell's report to federal executive, Calwell MSS, NLA.
316   Whitlam's first statement as FPLP leader: Freudenberg, p. 88.
316   Chamberlain-Whitlam clash: Freudenberg, pp. 93–4.
317   'Let us have none of this nonsense. . .': Freudenberg, pp. 95–6.
317   Calwell to Freudenberg: Freudenberg, p. 96.
317   Bolte's comment: P. Blazey, *Bolte* (Jacaranda, Brisbane, 1972), p. 146.
318   Moral of Corio: 'Political Chronicle', *AJPH* 13, 3, 1967, p. 411.
318   Whitlam on organizational reforms: 1967 federal conference report, pp. 51, 53.
319   Dunstan: N. Blewett & D. Jaensch, *Playford to Dunstan* (Cheshire, Melbourne, 1971), p. 52.
320   Harradine's statement: Oakes, p. 172.
321   'Victoria has the smallest percentage. . .': G. Whitlam to W. Hartley, 26 February 1968, Calwell MSS (Box 79), NLA.
321   Calwell's complaint: A. Calwell to C. Wyndham, 2 April 1968, Calwell MSS (Box 79), NLA.
321   Whitlam's letter to caucus: G. Whitlam to A. Calwell, 23 April 1968, Calwell MSS (Box 79), NLA.
321–2 Cairns's letter: Freudenberg, pp. 134–5.
322   Connor: Freudenberg, pp. 133–4.
322   Calwell on Whitlam: Calwell MSS (Box 79), NLA.
322   Calwell's 'frightening malevolence: G. Duthie, *I Had 50,000 Bosses* (A & R, Sydney, 1984), p. 248.
323   'With all due modesty. . .': A. Calwell to H. Burton, 4 September 1968, Calwell MSS (Box 25), NLA.
323   'Who do you think. . .': P. Ormonde, *A Foolish Passionate Man* (Penguin, Melbourne, 1981), p. 111.
323–4 'There is no doubt. . .': J. McCalman, *Struggletown* (MUP, Melbourne, 1984), p. 275.
324   Young on Chamberlain: Fabian Papers, *The Whitlam Phenomenon* (McPhee Gribble, Melbourne, 1986), p. 96.
324   'After locking up. . .': *The Whitlam Phenomenon*, p. 96.

325   Chamberlain-Virgo amendment: 1969 federal conference report, p. 156.
325   Young's motion barring Harradine: A. Reid, *The Gorton Experiment* (Shakespeare Head, Sydney, 1971), p. 270.
326   Young on Labor's campaign: *The Whitlam Phenomenon*, p. 97.
326   Cairns on Whitlam: Ormonde, p. 114.
327   Cairns exultant: Ormonde, p. 128.
327   Victorian executive and 'phasing out': J. Fitzgerald, Federal Intervention in the Victorian Branch of the Australian Labor Party, 1970, MA thesis, La Trobe University, 1975, p. 88.
328   King accepting Dunstan's offer: D. Dunstan, *Felicia* (Macmillan, Melbourne, 1981), p. 169.
329   Ducker's electrifying speech: A. Parkin & J. Warhurst (eds), *Machine Politics in the Australian Labor Party* (Allen & Unwin, Sydney, 1983), p. 33.
330   Hartley suspicious: Fitzgerald, p. 175.
330   Murphy's motion: Fitzgerald, p. 176.
330   Crawford's provocative conduct: Fitzgerald, pp. 181–2.
331   Daron Anstey: Fitzgerald, p. 188, note 82.
331   Cameron's crucial motion: Fitzgerald, p. 218.
332   The Burns report: E. Carew, *Keating* (Allen & Unwin, Sydney, 1988), p. 25.
333   Keating on Lang's readmission: B. Nairn, *The 'Big Fella'* (MUP, Melbourne, 1986), p. 316.
334   Egerton at the 1971 conference: J. Stubbs, *Hayden* (Mandarin, Melbourne, 1990), p. 98.
336   'The second day of December...': L. Oakes & D. Solomon, *The Making of an Australian Prime Minister* (Cheshire, Melbourne, 1973), p. 89.
336   Whitlam to Freudenberg: Oakes & Solomon, p. 166.
336   'Men and women of Australia...': Oakes & Solomon, p. 167.
337   Freudenberg on the Blacktown launch: Freudenberg, p. 228.
337   Extraordinary euphoria: J. Melzer OH, NLA.
337   Whitlam and the light on the hill: *Age*, 1 December 1972.
337   Evans on election night: *The Whitlam Phenomenon*, p. 157.

14 'There won't Ever be Another One Like It': The Whitlam Government, 1972–1975

MAIN SOURCES:
Fabian Papers, *The Whitlam Phenomenon* (McPhee Gribble, Melbourne, 1986).
G. Freudenberg, *A Certain Grandeur* (Sun, Melbourne, 1978).
L. Oakes, *Crash Through or Crash* (Drummond, Melbourne, 1976).
M. Sexton, *Illusions of Power* (Allen & Unwin, Sydney, 1979).
G. Whitlam, *The Whitlam Government* (Viking, Melbourne, 1985).

page 339   Bilney's reaction: *The Whitlam Phenomenon*, p. 28.
340   Whitlam's concern: Freudenberg, p. 255.
340   Changing the course of history: *Sydney Morning Herald*, 19 December 1987.
340   'I'm bigger than Hookers!': F. Daly, *From Curtin to Hawke* (Sun, Melbourne, 1984), p. 195.
340   Whitlam on Cameron: *Herald* (Melbourne), 4 February 1990.
341   Cairns, Cameron and Uren: 'Political Chronicle', *AJPH* 19, 2, 1973, p. 241.

342   'One of the minor tragedies. . .': J. McClelland, *Stirring the Possum* (Penguin, Melbourne, 1989), p. 125.

343   The 12.30 am appointment: *National Times on Sunday*, 2 November 1986.

343   Murphy's voice: G. Souter, *Acts of Parliament* (MUP, Melbourne, 1988), p. 471.

343   Torrential outpouring of drafting instructions: J. Scutt (ed.), *Lionel Murphy* (McCulloch, Melbourne, 1987), p. 40.

344   'I don't care. . .': *The Whitlam Phenomenon*, p. 176.

344   Greatest mistake: *Whitlam and Frost* (Sundial, London, 1974), p. 147.

344   Whitlam's leadership style: *The Whitlam Phenomenon*, p. 176.

344–5 'Whitlam revelled. . .': J. Walter, *The Leader* (UQP, Brisbane, 1980), p. 68.

345   Australian Schools Commission report: Whitlam, p. 316.

346   The most enduring single achievement: Whitlam, p. 315.

346   Australian government uniquely powerless: C. Lloyd & G.S. Reid, *Out of the Wilderness* (Cassell, Melbourne, 1974), p. 300.

347   Hawke's trenchant criticism: J. Hurst, *Hawke* (A & R, Sydney, 1979), p. 141.

347   Whitlam's stern rebuke: Lloyd & Reid, p. 234.

348   Hawke's recommendation: B. d'Alpuget, *Robert J. Hawke* (Schwartz, Melbourne, 1982), p. 212.

348   'They just would not listen. . .': d'Alpuget, p. 244.

349   'Australia's most militant. . .': Whitlam, p. 329.

350   'For those of us in rural seats. . .': G. Duthie, *I Had 50,000 Bosses* (A & R, Sydney, 1984), p. 284.

350   'You've never had it so good': Whitlam, p. 272.

351   Freudenberg on the Gair appointment: Freudenberg, p. 290.

352   The 1974 Blacktown audience: Freudenberg, p. 298.

353   Labor's campaign slogan: P. Ormonde, *A Foolish Passionate Man* (Penguin, Melbourne, 1981), p. 171.

353   FPLP's 'sexist composition': Whitlam, p. 515.

354   'The government initiated the most searching investigations. . .': Whitlam, p. 518.

355   'The Whitlam years gave women hope. . .': *The Whitlam Phenomenon*, pp. 154–5.

355   Treasury's harsh medicine: B. Hughes, *Exit Full Employment* (A & R, Sydney, 1980), p. 86.

356   Like a lunatic asylum: F. Crean OH, NLA.

356   'Well Gough, you will be sorry. . .': F. Crean OH, NLA.

357   The minister 'who had refused to talk. . .': McClelland, p. 168.

357   'There's no possibility. . .': F. Crowley, *Tough Times* (Heinemann, Melbourne, 1986), p. 156.

358   'The Government is peripheral. . .': Sexton, p. 61.

358   Cairns's 'kind of love': Ormonde, p. 201.

359   Bunton 'a political neuter': Souter, p. 529.

359   Connor clinging to his faith in Khemlani: Freudenberg, pp. 353–4.

359   The government 'was subject to an unrelenting attack. . .': Freudenberg, p. 317.

360   Combe on 'the total breakdown of meaningful consultation. . .': Combe's report on the Bass by-election July 1975, ALP MSS (Box 39), NLA.

360   This 'act of Galstonian madness': d'Alpuget, p. 280.

360   Cameron on 'the greatest redistribution. . .': G. Evans, J. Reeves & J. Malbon (eds), *Labor Essays 1981* (Drummond, Melbourne, 1981), p. 18.

360 Cameron on outrageous wage differentials: Hughes, p. 113.
361 The inscription revealed: Whitlam, p. 289; *Herald* (Melbourne), 4 February 1990.
362 'The chickens are coming home to roost. . .': *Australian*, 8 July 1975.
362 Whitlam's speech: Freudenberg, pp. 357–8; Souter, p. 533.
362 'Perhaps I do. . .': Souter, p. 534.
362 Connor's speech: *CPD*, 9 July 1975, p. 3625.
362 Combe's assessment: Combe's by-election report, ALP MSS, NLA.
363 The 1973 Tasmanian conference: R. Davis, *Eighty Years' Labor* (Sassafras, Hobart, 1983), p. 80.
363 Tasmanian ALP hopelessly divided: Combe's by-election report, ALP MSS, NLA.
363 Hudson: D. Dunstan, *Felicia* (Macmillan, Melbourne, 1981), p. 172.
363 Dunstan on Connor's objectives: Dunstan, p. 231.
364 Labor's late switch in advertising: Dunstan, p. 259.
364 Tucker enraged: H. Lunn, *Johannes Bjelke-Petersen* (UQP, Brisbane, 1984), p. 202.
364 Whitlam on Bjelke-Petersen: Oakes, p. 147.
364 Whitlam's reply in parliament: Freudenberg, p. 362.
365 Connor's telex to Khemlani: Freudenberg, p. 362.
365 Connor's view and the reaction in caucus: C. Cameron, 'Rex Connor Memorial Lecture', University of Wollongong, forthcoming (1991).
365 Hall's remark: Freudenberg, p. 373.
365 Whitlam's resolve: Freudenberg, p. 375.
365 Whitlam on the constitutional struggles of the past: Sexton, p. 216.
366 Cameron eulogistic: Freudenberg, p. 381.
366 Whitlam on 'the Hayden budget': D.J. Murphy, *Hayden* (A & R, Sydney, 1980), p. 141.
367 McClelland-Ellicott exchange: McClelland, pp. 169–70.
367 McClelland on Kerr: McClelland, pp. 184, 173.
367 Hawke on Kerr: d'Alpuget, p. 120.
367 Kerr on Ellicott's memorandum: G. Whitlam, *The Truth of the Matter* (Penguin, Melbourne 1979), p. 83.
367 Enderby to Kerr: Freudenberg, p. 380.
368 Hayden's warning and Whitlam's reaction: Oakes, p. 197.
368 'They seem pretty cocky': Whitlam, *The Truth of the Matter*, p. 105.
368 Kerr-Whitlam exchange: Whitlam, *The Truth of the Matter*, p. 110.
368 'The bastard's sacked us': P. Kelly, *The Unmaking of Gough* (A & R, Sydney, 1976), p. 295.
368 'All present were in a state of shock': Daly, p. 231.
369 McClelland and Wriedt disbelieving: C. Lloyd & A. Clark, *Kerr's King Hit* (Cassell, Sydney, 1976), p. 229.
369 Crean's speech: *CPD*, 11 November 1975, p. 2925.
370 'Well may we say. . .': Lloyd & Clark, p. 232.
370 'Maintain your rage. . .': Whitlam, *The Truth of the Matter*, p. 119.
370 Liberals 'with slicked-down hair. . .': *Sydney Morning Herald*, 28 May 1988.
370 Hawke appealing for calm: *Age*, 12 November 1975.
373 Bjelke-Petersen's mud-slinging: Lunn, p. 231.
374 Hawke on election night: d'Alpuget, p. 291.
374 'He had introduced Medibank. . .': J. Stubbs, *Hayden* (Mandarin, Melbourne, 1990), p. 148.
374 The 'too much too soon' school: *The Whitlam Phenomenon*, p. 143.
375 'There won't ever be another one like it': *The Whitlam Phenomenon*, p. 177.

15 Life wasn't Meant to be Easy for the ALP, 1976–1983

MAIN SOURCES:
B. d'Alpuget, *Robert J. Hawke* (Schwartz, Melbourne, 1982).
P. Kelly, *The Hawke Ascendancy* (A & R, Sydney, 1984).
A. Parkin & J. Warhurst (eds), *Machine Politics in the Australian Labor Party* (Allen & Unwin, Sydney, 1983).
J. Stubbs, *Hayden* (Mandarin, Melbourne, 1990).

page 376   The 'morning of anguish': Stubbs, p. 150.
377   'I could have scotched it. . .': A. Reid, *The Whitlam Venture* (Hill of Content, Melbourne, 1976), p. 445.
377–8   Young fuming: C. Cameron, *The Cameron Diaries* (Allen & Unwin, Sydney, 1990), p. 26.
378   Hawke's off-the-record version: Cameron, p. 42; d'Alpuget, p. 297.
378   All these expressions of rank-and-file support for Whitlam: Folder 36 (1976 files), ALP MSS, NLA.
379   Many FPLP members unsympathetic: P. Kelly, *The Unmaking of Gough* (A & R, Sydney, 1976), p. 320.
379   National executive resolution: Kelly, *The Unmaking of Gough*, pp. 342–3.
379   Delegates 'as jumpy as hell. . .': d'Alpuget, p. 298.
379   Egerton's quip: d'Alpuget, p. 299.
379   Combe's praise: d'Alpuget, p. 300.
380   Gap branch correspondence with Combe: Folder 25 (1977 files), ALP MSS, NLA.
380   Hayden on Hawke: Kelly, *The Hawke Ascendancy*, pp. 21–2.
381   'After making the wildest. . .': M. Steketee & M. Cockburn, *Wran* (Allen & Unwin, Sydney, 1986), p. 57.
382   No mad rush: Steketee & Cockburn, p. 130.
383   Whole performance played faultlessly: Parkin & Warhurst, p. 43.
383   'During the 1976 budget session. . .': Kelly, *The Hawke Ascendancy*, pp. 30–1.
384   Toorak admirer: P. Richards to D. Combe, 16 March 1977, Folder 81 (1977 files), ALP MSS, NLA.
384   'Gough Must Stay': Fairfield branch to D. Combe, 9 April 1977, Folder 25 (1977 files), ALP MSS, NLA.
384   Hawke sarcastic: Cameron, p. 566.
384   'The whole episode was one of the most exciting. . .': d'Alpuget, p. 323.
385   New uranium policy: *ALP Platform, Constitution and Rules* (Canberra, 1977), pp. 25–6.
385   'My heart says no. . .': F. Crowley, *Tough Times* (Heinemann, Melbourne, 1986), p. 348.
385   Combe's warning: D. Combe to R. Hayward, 23 October 1977, Folder 1 (1977 files), ALP MSS, NLA.
386   Cameron on Lynch: Cameron, p. 749.
386   Hawke trying to persuade Whitlam: d'Alpuget, p. 333.
386   Combe's assurance: D. Combe to G. Jones, 2 May 1978, Folder 50 (1978 files), ALP MSS, NLA.
386   These 'very clear undertakings': D. Combe to C. Fay, 30 May 1978, Folder 15 (1978 files), ALP MSS, NLA.
387   'Bill has confounded his critics. . .': Cameron, p. 863.
387   Bowen lashing out: *Age*, 8 November 1977.

387   'On no public issue. . .': G. Whitlam, *The Truth of the Matter* (Penguin, Melbourne, 1979), p. 170.

387   *Australian* headline: Whitlam, p. 170.

387   Hayden leading the FPLP's attack: *Age*, 1 March 1978; J. Kerr, *Matters for Judgment* (Macmillan, Melbourne, 1978), p. 428.

387   Keating on Fraser: *Age*, 1 March 1978.

387   McClelland pleased: J. McClelland, *Stirring the Possum* (Penguin, Melbourne, 1989), p. 194.

388   The inquiry: ALP National Committee of Inquiry: Report and Recommendations, 1979, pp. 1–2, 7, 38, 11.

389   Kane to Toowong branch: Parkin & Warhurst, p. 118.

389   Murphy's discussion paper: R. Fitzgerald & H. Thornton, *Labor in Queensland* (UQP, Brisbane, 1989), p. 212.

389   Beattie at the Bardon meeting: Parkin & Warhurst, p. 117.

389   Controllers' warning: Fitzgerald & Thornton, p. 214.

389   Whitlam's criticism: Fitzgerald & Thornton, pp. 222–3.

390   Kane on Hayden and Hayden's reply: Stubbs, p. 204.

390   Kane's retort: Fitzgerald & Thornton, p. 226.

390   'Drink afflicts the labour movement. . .': H. Boote Diary, 17 May 1940, Boote MSS, NLA.

390   Walsh on Hayden: Stubbs, p. 190.

390   Hayden on seething, festering unhappiness: Fitzgerald & Thornton, p. 229.

390   Reform Group's statement: Fitzgerald & Thornton, p. 234.

390   Salvation Army better for workers than Queensland ALP: Fitzgerald & Thornton, p. 262.

391   Massive mismanagement: Fitzgerald & Thornton, p. 296.

391   Litigation 'hung like a pall. . .': Parkin & Warhurst, p. 124.

391   Hayden on the Old Guard: *Courier Mail*, 1 July 1981.

391   'Labor is traditionally. . .': Fitzgerald & Thornton, p. 301.

392   Dunstan on SA employment: D. Dunstan, *Felicia* (Macmillan, Melbourne, 1981), p. 310.

393   Dunstan's 1970 policy speech: A. Parkin & A. Patience (eds), *The Dunstan Decade* (Longman Cheshire, Melbourne, 1981), pp. 6–7.

393   Land Commission: Parkin & Patience, p. 105.

394   Fraser on Hayden: Stubbs, p. 183.

394   Hayden's resistance: Stubbs, pp. 185, 188; Kelly, *The Hawke Ascendancy*, p. 76.

394   Hayden at 1979 conference: Kelly, *The Hawke Ascendancy*, p. 71.

394   Whitlam's quip: Fabian Papers, *The Whitlam Phenomenon* (McPhee Gribble, Melbourne, 1986), p. 9.

395   Fraser's philosophy: J. Edwards, *Life Wasn't Meant to Be Easy* (Mayhem, Sydney, 1977).

395   Bowen's retort: Stubbs, p. 186.

395   Hawke's attack on the Socialist Left: d'Alpuget, pp. 356–7.

396   'Listen, I make up my own mind. . .': d'Alpuget, p. 375.

396   'If I'd cried. . .': d'Alpuget, p. 378.

396   'Wran's Our Man': Steketee & Cockburn, p. 135.

397   'If and when. . .': Steketee & Cockburn, p. 256.

397   Richardson: *National Times*, 21–27 October 1983.

398   Hawke's assurance to Hayden: Kelly, *The Hawke Ascendancy*, p. 84.

398   Labor's triumvirate: H. Penniman (ed.), *Australia at the Polls* (Allen & Unwin, Sydney, 1983), p. 72.

399   A 'breach of faith': Parkin & Warhurst, p. 262.

399   Burnswoods's remark: *Canberra Times*, 31 January 1982.

399   Evans outlined his views in G. Evans & J. Reeves (eds), *Labor Essays 1980* (Drummond, Melbourne, 1980).
400   The new fundamental statement: B. O'Meagher (ed.), *The Socialist Objective* (H & I, Sydney, 1983), p. 64.
400   Unsuccessful attempt by left-wingers: Parkin & Warhurst, p. 244.
400   Evans on the outcome: O'Meagher, pp. 63, 64.
400   'Quiz kids can't count': *Australian*, 31 March 1976.
401   Trendies, intellectual snobs and technocrats: Parkin & Warhurst, p. 85.
401   Hartley's public attack: *Age*, 9 September 1981.
403   Jamieson: *Australian*, 27 March 1976.
404   Davies ambushed: 'Political Chronicle', *AJPH* 28, 1, 1982, p. 116.
404–5 ANOP research on Hayden: Kelly, *The Hawke Ascendancy*, p. 173.
405   'McMullan, intensely embarrassed...': Kelly, *The Hawke Ascendancy*, p. 202.
405   Adams on Hawke: *Age*, 26 June 1982.
405   Cameron on Hawke: Kelly, *The Hawke Ascendancy*, pp. 196–7.
405   Hawke's reply: Kelly, *The Hawke Ascendancy*, pp. 198–9.
406   The assassination squad: Kelly, *The Hawke Ascendancy*, p. 203.
406   Richardson, Hayden, West and Uren in the uranium debate: Kelly, *The Hawke Ascendancy*, pp. 207–9.
406   Hawke on the opinion poll research: Kelly, *The Hawke Ascendancy*, p. 206.
406–7 Bowen's attitude: Kelly, *The Hawke Ascendancy*, p. 210.
407   Hayden's statement: Stubbs, p. 224.
407   'It was a nasty job...': Stubbs, p. 237.
408   Button's letter to Hayden: Kelly, *The Hawke Ascendancy*, pp. 2–4.
408   Hayden on Button's letter: Kelly, *The Hawke Ascendancy*, p. 387.
408   'Hayden's face was etched...': Stubbs, p. 253.
408   'I am not convinced...': Stubbs, p. 253; Kelly, *The Hawke Ascendancy*, pp. 388–9; A. Summers, *Gamble for Power* (Nelson, Melbourne, 1983), p. 41–2.
409   Fraser's 1975 intention: P. Ayres, *Malcolm Fraser* (Heinemann, Melbourne, 1987), p. 428.
409   Labor's slogans: Kelly, *The Hawke Ascendancy*, p. 398; 'Political Chronicle', *AJPH* 29, 3, 1983, p. 519.
409   1982 platform amendment: R. Davis, *Eighty Years' Labor* (Sassafras, Hobart, 1983), p. 114.

16 'Some New and Alien Philosophy'? The Hawke-Keating Regime, 1983–1991

MAIN SOURCES:
Print and electronic media.
E. Carew, *Keating* (Allen & Unwin, Sydney, 1988).

page 412   Incoming minister on election night 1983: *Age*, 7 March 1983.
413   Hayden on the Centre Left's emergence: C. Lloyd & W. Swan, 'National Factions and the ALP', *Politics* 22, 1, 1987, p. 100.
413   Hayden on the 'lonely hearts club...': Lloyd & Swan, p. 108.
414   Button's letter: Kelly, *The Hawke Ascendancy* (A & R, Sydney, 1984), p. 3.
414   Keating on economic sophistication: Carew, pp. 146–7.
414   Expertise without wham: Kelly, p. 352.

417 Jones on talking football: *Sydney Morning Herald*, 8 October 1988.
418 Jones on jumping to conclusions: *Mercury*, 21 June 1984.
418 Whitlam praising the Accord: Fabian Papers, *The Whitlam Phenomenon* (McPhee Gribble, Melbourne, 1986), p. 82.
419 'You were in office. . .': Carew, p. 227.
419 Beazley on Keating the family man: Carew, p. 194.
420 'I did make a mistake. . .': Carew, p. 167.
420 Keating putting the big changes into place: *Four Corners* (ABC television), 18 August 1986.
420 Keating on 'the lazy days of postwar growth': *Four Corners*, 18 August 1986.
420 Keating on keeping the faith: Carew, p. 223.
420 Keating on the deregulation reforms: Carew, pp. 105–6.
421 Keating's award: Carew, p. 112.
421–2 Keating and the 'banana republic': Carew, p. 157.
423 Hayden on Combe: D. Marr, *The Ivanov Trail* (Nelson, Melbourne, 1984), p. 97.
424 Australia and America 'together forever': M. McKinley, 'Problems in Australian Foreign Policy January–June 1983', *AJPH* 29, 3, 1983, p. 423.
425 Labor's platform on disarmament: *Australian Labor Party Platform, Constitution and Rules* (Canberra, 1984), p. 91.
425 Button perturbed: *Sydney Morning Herald*, 7 February 1985.
425 Keating's blast: *Sydney Morning Herald*, 9 February 1985.
426 Young's admission: 'Political Chronicle', *AJPH* 33, 2, 1987, p. 101.
426 Hawke's Franklin comment: *Age*, 7 March 1983.
427 Uren's praise: *Age*, 20 February 1990.
427 Richardson on his different image: *Good Weekend*, 10 March 1990.
428 Keating on Labor's charter: *Traditions for Reform in New South Wales* (Pluto, Sydney, 1987), p. 186.
428 Keating and 'queen of the screen or prince of print': Carew, p. 179.
429 Venom drooling: M. Sexton, *Illusions of Power* (Allen & Unwin, Sydney, 1979), p. 79.
429 Murphy 'will not survive. . .': Kelly, *The Unmaking of Gough* (A & R, Sydney, 1976), p. 97.
430 Wran fined: *Age*, 13 March 1987.
430 Hayden on the pursuit of Murphy: *CPD*, 22 October 1986, p. 2495.
430–1 Whitlam's interview: *Age*, 12 November 1985.
431 Keating on the shifting sands: *Traditions for Reform*, p. 178.
431 Keating on the main game: *Age*, 9 May 1987.
431 Keating's major speech in November 1987: *Fabian Newsletter*, December 1987, pp. 12–15.
431 Whitlam's reaction: *Age*, 7 December 1987.
432 Beazley's observation: K. Beazley OH, NLA.
432 Mortimer's assessment: *Age*, 21 January 1988.
432 Dawkins's claim: *Bulletin*, 31 May 1988.
434 Beattie's conclusion: D. Murphy, R. Joyce & M. Cribb (eds), *The Premiers of Queensland* (UQP, Brisbane, 1990), p. 509.
434 Goss on the 'wasteland': *Sydney Morning Herald*, 29 April 1989.
434 'Will we, as Queenslanders,. . .': *Good Weekend*, 18 November 1989.
435 Goss claiming victory on election night: *Sunday Age*, 3 December 1989.
435 'I am not interested. . .': *Age*, 2 June 1990.
436 Wran's blast: M. Steketee & M. Cockburn, *Wran* (Allen & Unwin, Sydney, 1986), p. 304.
436 Tributes to Wran from Ferguson and Anderson: *Sydney Morning Herald*, 9 June 1986.
437 Contrasting reactions from Hawke and Hayden: *Age*, 10 June 1986.

438–9 Lawrence's comments after becoming Premier: *Age*, 13 February 1990.

439 Bannon foreshadowing a new emphasis: *Advertiser*, 27 November 1989.

441 Cain attacking 'disgraceful behaviour': B. Galligan (ed.), *Australian State Politics* (Longman Cheshire, Melbourne, 1986), p. 44.

442 Cain linking deregulation to Pyramid's collapse: *Age*, 3 July 1990.

442 Crabb not the deputy type: *Age*, 10 August 1990.

442 Hawke affirming the platform not 'immutable': *Age*, 24 August 1987.

443 Hayden on ALP tradition: *Age*, 7 March 1988.

443 Uren, Cameron and Crean on privatization: *Age*, 31 August 1987, 8 April 1988, 25 August 1987.

443 Hogg's observation: *Age*, 8 September 1990.

443 Kirner and Keating announcing the sale of the State Bank: *Age*, 27 August 1990.

444 Beazley's remarks are reproduced on p. 12 of the conference transcript.

444 Jones's speech is reproduced on pp. 49–53 of the conference transcript.

444 These party membership figures have been supplied by the ALP National Secretariat; insufficient records seem to have survived to enable definite comparisons with party membership nationally in earlier years.

445 Women 'of central importance': M. Sawer (ed.), *Program for Change* (Allen & Unwin, Sydney, 1985), p. 46.

446 Unions the core: L.F. Crisp, *The Australian Federal Labour Party 1901–1951* (Longmans Green & Co, London, 1955), p. 204.

446 A 'peculiar amalgam': D. Aitkin, 'Political Review', *Australian Quarterly* 38, 2, 1966, p. 101.

Index